A GAY DIARY

Volume Four

1967-1975

Also by Donald Vining

A GAY DIARY 1933-1946

A GAY DIARY 1946-1954

A GAY DIARY 1954-1967

AMERICAN DIARIES OF WORLD WAR II
(Editor)

A GAY DIARY

Volume Four

1967-1975

DONALD VINING

THE PEPYS PRESS
1270 Fifth Avenue
New York, N.Y. 10029

Copyright © 1983 by Donald Vining

All rights reserved. Except for brief quotations in a review, the text or parts thereof must not be reproduced in any form without permission in writing from the publisher, The Pepys Press, 1270 Fifth Avenue, New York, N.Y. 10029

First Edition

Library of Congress Catalog Card No. 78-71282

ISBN 0-9602270-8-3 hard cover

ISBN 0-9602270-9-1 paperback

To

THE ACTIVISTS

who fought for gay civil rights before, during, and since the Stonewall Rebellion.

TABLE OF CONTENTS

PREFACE............... IX
1967.................. 1
1968.................. 26
1969.................. 70
1970.................. 117
1971.................. 168
1972.................. 218
1973.................. 298
1974.................. 371
1975.................. 427
INDEX................. 486

PREFACE

Editing one's own diary for publication grows much more difficult as one approaches present time. Dealing with years long gone, one has perspective as to what was and was not important; dealing with people now changed past recognition in age and circumstance, perhaps even dead, one has few worries about needing to protect their identities beyond assigning them a pseudonym. Neither, since so many have ceased to be a factor in one's life, need one worry overmuch about their reaction to one's comments about them in the privacy of a diary. With current friends and acquaintances it is quite different and one finds onself feeling a need to censor to a degree that tends to distort the diary.

I had always supposed that life contracted in one's later years; I never dreamed it could expand as mine has and grow richer in texture each year due to the accretion of friends, experiences, and interests. This makes the cutting an increasing chore. With each year's diary running in the original to more than 200 pages of 8½ x 11 looseleaf notebook paper, cutting 8 years down to fit a 500 page book means paring away between 900 and 1000 close-packed pages. My hope had been that the fourth volume might come up to 1992, rounding out fifty years of diary and coming up to present time. This objective proved unrealistic when dealing with a period when the Sexual Revolution in general and its subdivision Gay Liberation in particular were in full flower. It was, at any rate, a rather pointless goal.

This probably final volume goes, I hope, far enough into my later years to help dispel the myth that haunts so many young gays, that there is little happiness and only paid-for sex ahead for them once they have left youth behind them. While I do not pretend that mine is a typical gay life (we are so various that I doubt if such a thing as a typical gay life exists) neither is it exceptional. I hope this record of my own and contiguous lives will help allay the largely unjustified fears many gays have of growing old. Gay life can be gay in both the old and the new senses of the word for more decades than we dreamed were possible in our youth.

    To those readers who have written me to say they found the diary historically informative or simply entertaining, I want to express my gratitude. The pleas for further volumes have kept me going when the cutting seemed to be becoming an impossible task. A number have written that I influenced them to start keeping a diary themselves and this I'm always happy to hear as I firmly believe that examination of one's own life and of those touching on it almost inevitably leads to lives more richly lived.

A GAY DIARY

Volume Four
1967-1975

ALCAZAR GARDENS, SEVILLE 1968

As this fourth volume of A GAY DIARY begins, my long-time partner Ken and I were working in the Development Office (a voguish euphemism for all those charged with institutional fund-raising) of Teachers College, Columbia University. We were at the beginning of a dizzying, and often quite dizzy, series of changes in our work that involved repeated relocations of the office, an increasingly rapid turnover of bosses, and a floundering entrance into the world of automation with no steady or competent hand at the helm. The student world in general, and Columbia University in particular, was poised at the brink of an academic and political revolt soon to erupt into headlines. The gay world was also shortly to have its own smaller act of revolution in what is now known as the Stonewall Riots, more important, perhaps, in gay mythology than in fact in view of the fact that many of the changes now attributed to it were already in evolutionary process.

Ken and I lived, with our cat Lavinius, in a jointly owned co-operative apartment on upper Fifth Avenue. To the address-snobs of the world this may sound fancier than it is, just as the fact that it is located in Harlem may raise visions of a sordid ghetto equally removed from actuality. Situated across from that uppermost part of Central Park which contains the lovely little lake, Harlem Meer, behind which are wooded hills, the building has a view those living down on the more fashionable blocks of Fifth Avenue might well envy. It also has a resident group of cooperators, almost equally divided between blacks and whites, who live in an inter-racial amity that those downtown <u>should</u> envy, though I know many don't.

A vacation on the West Coast was imminent.

A GAY DIARY

THURSDAY, JUNE 29, 1967

The Buildings and Grounds man said they would move our office next Wednesday so we are no longer in suspense that it might happen when we were there. Forkner asked if we had left a list of places where we could be contacted while we were away and I almost laughed. It certainly aggrandizes our work unduly to think of him calling across the continent to ask some business question.

SATURDAY, JULY 1, 1967

We gave the house a more thoro cleaning than is customary with us, hoping to set an example for Sandy. (*The live-in cat-sitter who was to look after Lavinius in our absence*) We got an early start for Roslyn Heights. As when she was at Alice's, Pearl was laughing and gay despite her exertions as hostess. (A *victim of kidney failure, Pearl was undergoing dialysis several times a week.*) In the course of the conversation with Pearl I mentioned that in 1954 I was not able to get a pass to Paramount Pictures even tho I had worked there. (*See Volume One*) She immediately called to Ben and asked if he couldn't get us passes. He said he could and took our Los Angeles address and dates. I have never used friends like this before and never would have hinted.

SUNDAY, JULY 2, 1967

We arrived in superb weather and when we found our very nice hotel we found a letter waiting from the Leonards. They had so much fog here that they never saw the Golden Gate Bridge. I changed to slightly less casual clothes and we headed for the Top of the Mark by cable car, an experience I didn't have when I worked here. It proved to be a very nice cocktail room with an excellent view, tho fog was creeping up the bay. Dinner at the Old Zurich, which we had seen when making the car reservations. We had cheese fondue and it was delicious. The atmosphere was thoroly Swiss and we ended the day in a euphoric glow about everything.

MONDAY, JULY 3, 1967

After leaving our purchases at the hotel we headed for Union Square and our Gray Line city tour, for which we had booked early in the morning. On the tour were a pair of sailors who distracted me greatly from what I was supposed to be seeing. The blond was attractive enuf but completely overshadowed by his companion, a dark youth of incomparable beauty. I had already noted a high degree of male and female pulchritude out here but this boy was nonpareil and it was nice to think he also had the good sense to come on this

tour instead of throwing his money away in honky-tonks. By
the time the tour crossed Golden Gate Bridge to Vista
Point, the fog had all cleared away and we had superb visibility.

WEDNESDAY, JULY 5, 1967
   We went to the Visitors Information Center and found
out how to get to Golden Gate Park. Once there we visited
the aquarium (free and ten times better than the one Prince
Rainier gets a dollar for in Monaco) and the De Young Museum (minor as museums go but not without some lovely
things). We then paid a return visit to the Japanese Tea
Garden, had tea and cookies for a laughable 30 cents, and
found out how I missed it before--it didn't come into being
until 1952. We discussed how hard it is to see a policeman
here. It's all right to say there are fewer negroes here
than in New York and that Chinese police themselves but
there remains the question of traffic. I've seen just one
cop giving a ticket and the woman I thought was a policewoman turned out to be a letter carrier. I've also noted
that many of the male bohemians wear beads. I haven't noticed this in Greenwich Village but it's quite common here.
They don't resemble women's beads but are generally long
primitive strings. We followed the advice of our Frommer
book on California and ate at the Kuo Wah on Grant St. It
had the darkness of an opium den but was quite a lush place
with delicious food. They gave one souvenir chopsticks in
an envelope which had printed instructions for use so I accepted the challenge and ate my meal with them very successfully. We intended to go see the drag show at Finocchio's but when we got to Broadway the whole street was so
sleazy with 'topless' shows that we decided to save our
money and spend our time browsing in the shops of Chinatown. They proved very disappointing as quality goods were
nowhere on display and the junk grew repetitious and depressing.

FRIDAY, JULY 7, 1967
   Carried our bags the two blocks to the Avis garage.
When we got in the dashboard seemed covered with a million
gadgets compared with the European cars Ken is used to. He
expressed confusion and I told him to go get some instruction but he said he'd find out. He started out with his
brakes on, however, and an Avis man drove up beside us to
tell us. That got straightened out but the problem of making all the right turns to get onto the Bay Bridge and out
of town kept me in a state of nerves for a long time. (*As
I don't drive, I can only read maps and watch for signs.*)

Eventually I found the road so well marked and the traffic so light that I quite calmed down. The California landscape and the burning sun were not appealing but as we got near Yosemite and saw the wild white water of the Merced River beneath the hills, I enjoyed it. The cabin was conveniently located near restrooms, the amphitheatre and the cafeteria and beautifully situated by huge boulders and under huge trees. Chipmunks and purple grosbeaks begged in the area and were very cute about it. The piney air is marvelous. Neither the ranger's talk nor the vaudeville show of semi-professional talent was very good but the firefall was as lovely as ever. Coming back from the latrine I noticed that the light in our tent profiled the occupants so decided we'd better undress in the dark, tho Ken scoffed.

SATURDAY, JULY 8, 1967
    We drove to the Big Trees, where I got out and took Ken's picture as he drove thru the tunnel tree, as everybody else was doing. We also got pictures by the huge roots of a fallen sequoia, another common gambit. On our way back to Camp Curry we stopped at the foot of Bridal Veil Falls and I was surprised one could walk to the foot of it. The wind played tricks with the mist and we got soaked but I loved it. For supper I thought trout was appropriate and at $1.50 cheap, but I was astounded when they put TWO on my plate for that price. We went up and sat in the chairs by our cabin as a large and loud group of sports car enthusiasts was making the central area clamorous. Their women seemed vulgar and as loud as the men, perhaps from shouting over the roar of motors. Some neighboring people seemed anxious to talk to us--at least the grandfather was. Finally he could stand it no longer and came over and introduced himself. When he had told us a lot about himself, he started asking what business we were in. He was a nice enuf man but I prefer British reticence. If I want to tell something about myself, I'll tell it. I don't want to be asked.

SUNDAY, JULY 9, 1967
    I find the many children here a rather pleasant addition--at least those up to five and some even older. I also relish the strong part many of the fathers play in family life. It makes me quite envious--of the children, not the fathers. After breakfast we drove to Mirror Lake, which the ranger had said was a shadow of its former self because of silting. He said they tried to halt nature's course for a while then decided to let it evolve into a meadow as such lakes do. It's still attractive but not really a major sight any more. Since the sign said Vernal Falls Bridge

was only .8 of a mile, we started up the trail. They said
nothing about the elevation, however, and the climb almost
killed us. We rested but still the climb knotted the muscles of our calves and made us puff. Ken kept claiming he
was too old for this but I've heard that refrain ever since
I met him and I thought if older people and children could
do it, we could. I know how quickly the body recovers from
exhaustion. It was a lovely sight and we sat taking it in
for some time before turning around. Ken recovered his high
spirits, especially after I suggested after lunch that he
rest while I got a haircut.

TUESDAY, JULY 11, 1967
    Our impressions of Monterey improved still further as
we drove out today and saw further historical buildings,
plus nice modern ones. The rewards of doing my homework
were made clear when we found the Carmel Mission poorly
marked on the road. Only because I'd read about it and had
told Ken to slow down so I could look for signs did we see
the single sign. The mission not only had lovely flowers
both in the outer garden and the cloister but was historically fascinating since it contained the library and death
cell of Fra Junipero Serra, founder of the 21 California
missions. I had intended to see the Santa Barbara mission
but until I did my reading last nite I didn't know that
this was historically the most important. The road down the
coast was as lovely as everyone has said in spite of the
nasty masses of kelp that fringed the coast. At least we
couldn't smell it as we could yesterday on the 17 Mile
Drive. It looks like a great sewage backup and yesterday it
smelled like it too. Much of the time we were high enuf
above it to concentrate on the blueness of the Pacific on
either side of the kelp mass. Part of the journey there was
heavy fog, which was dramatic but obscured the scenery. This
was a small part of the lovely winding journey, however.
When we finally reached the area where the San Simeon motels were clustered, we found ours was possibly the least
attractive but still nice enuf outside and very fine indeed
inside. We watched a little television then turned in to be
ready for the tour of the Hearst Castle tomorrow. We can
hear the surf tonite and by day it was visible from our big
picture window.

WEDNESDAY, JULY 12, 1967
    Our first tour, the standard one of the downstairs and
grounds, was guided by a nice blonde girl and was fascinating. I don't even complain of Hearst's taste except that he
did mix styles a good deal. I was surprised that they

transported us back to the gate after the tour to start the second one. The upstairs tour was just as great as the downstairs and the numbers were limited to a quarter the number included in the downstairs tour, where the rooms are larger. Neither on the tours or in the booklet was one word said about Marion Davies but since the family gave the estate I guess they can control what is said. I thought of her a lot on the tour, however, for she is the grand mistress of our era (and I liked her movies to boot-the implications of some people that she had no talent is nonsense). When we got back to the gate we had a little dificulty finding our car in the sea of autos but eventually we came on it. We drove down to Santa Barbara without incident. As we wandered, I stepped on a penny scale and tipped it at 198! I don't believe it, tho I could hardly fail to have gained, considering all we've been eating, for that would be a gain of over a pound a day since we left and I sincerely hope that is impossible. August is certainly going to be an austerity month. I will not let myself weigh more than 180 and I shouldn't even weigh that, really.

FRIDAY, JULY 14, 1967

We ate breakfast at Clifton's on our way to the bus terminal, where we soon caught a bus to Disneyland. The ugliness of the route made me think better of some of New York's outlying districts. Disneyland itself, however, was a marvel of wonderful landscaping, from the flower bed at the entrance, which depicted Mickey Mouse, to the many varieties of tropical trees on the banks of the Jungle Cruise. We were constantly reminded of Freedomland, which was, after all, designed by one of the staff which designed this, but Disneyland has several advantages. The name is less stultifying, its theme less binding, and its layout is more compact. From a central plaza at the end of the turn-of-the-century street one can quickly get to the start of almost all the rides. The rides themselves may go far afield but one's legs are spared. Our first ride was on the bobsleds which go thru and around the replica of the Matterhorn which dominates the grounds with its height. My palms were so sweaty as we took the dips and turns that I could scarcely hold on. By going on most of the more desirable rides early in the day we avoided much waiting, which at any rate never seemed to reach the formidable proportions it did at Freedomland *(which had failed after two or three seasons, at least partly because Northeastern weather does not permit the year-round operation possible in Florida and California--it was quickly replaced by a huge housing complex called Co-op City.)* By mistaking it for the Jungle

Cruise we got on the best ride of the day, one new this
year and therefore less well-known--Pirates of the Caribbean. It was a very long ride and elaborately worked out--
with our boat going between the shots of shore cannons and
the boat's cannons, going thru the sacking and burning of a
city and off to the treasure islands. All the details of
animated movement were excellent and we kept calling each
other's attention to things like the quaking knees of a
grandee about to be dunked in a well by the pirates or to
the fact that following a scene showing three pirates chas-
ing three girls, there was a scene of a fat servant woman
pursuing a pirate, etc. We left exhausted after about nine
hours, but with very happy memories of such things as the
ingenious Swiss Family Robinson's tree house (probably
lifted bodily from the Disney movie made from that book),
the Peter Pan flight which Peter and Tinkerbell led right
out of the Darling's nursery window and over London to
Never-Never-Land,the Jungle Cruise with its bathing elephants, hippos, rhinos charging hunters, etc. Keying most
things to a literary motif is the great secret, I think,of
Disneyland's peculiar charm. I called my Paramount contact
from Disneyland and found arrangements made for us to go on
a tour Tuesday at 10:30 and have luncheon there. Ken feels
I have left much out and I have but when one has gone on
16 paid attractions and three free ones, one would get
writer's cramp from just listing them all, let alone describing them. Too tired to say more.

MONDAY, JULY 17, 1967
     To the bus terminal for the bus to San Pedro. The ride
to the harbor was just as ugly as when one went by trolley.
The boat ride was also dull and when we got there I didn't
think much better of Santa Catalina. We walked over to the
museum of Catalina history, housed in the Casino. The museum proved more interesting than I expected, showing the
many famous bands that played the casino in the island's
heyday, showing the Chicago Cubs team who for 26 years
trained here, and giving much lore about the settlers. I
would say that the island's glamorous days are behind it
(they have cases of sheet music of songs about Avalon or
Catalina) but on the other hand the store frontage and
beach seem much improved since I was there and the effect
is less junky. It being late when we got home, I thought I
was safe washing my drip-dry shirt in the shower across
the hall. *(We were staying at the rather run-down YMCA)*
For the first time in all my showers I acquired company.
The shirt didn't bother him and I think he meant to make
himself available but as attractive as he was (and he was

the first decent-looking fellow I've seen in this place) I didn't know what to do about it. Ken was waiting so I took my shirt and left.

TUESDAY, JULY 18, 1967
Some pleasant fantasies about my attractive, conversation-making shower companion. One doesn't realize how much one misses the pleasures of the flesh until one gets a chance at them. Today we started late but still got to the studio ahead of time. On the dot of 10:30 a nice young girl appeared and handed us our pass for lunch in the commissary and took us on a tour. Right at the outset she admitted that few movies were made there any more but that tv plays were. When I was there they had a short "western street" which now stands abandoned and replaced by a whole complex of western streets used for BONANZA and other big tv successes I never watch. She showed us scene docks, dubbing rooms, and finally we saw two tv shows being made. The second involved eight little boys on a camping trip and it was interesting watching the 8 year old pros at work, their mothers hanging about the set. Our guide left us to conduct another tour. As we were unguided I was able to show Ken the building where I cleaned (*when a janitor there in the 40's, work that had been done by Japanese-Americans until they had all been sent to concentration camps during World War II*) and the row of dressing rooms, which the guide had failed to point out. Perhaps she was afraid we'd ask "Who is she? or he?" for the names on the doors today are of very minor magnitude compared with my day. Elvis Presley and Jack Lemmon were the only really major stars. There is, in fact, something very sad and quiet about the lot today.

WEDNESDAY, JULY 19, 1967
Took an earlier bus than planned for Laguna Beach. The ride was as ugly as all rides in this area and for the first time the smog was so heavy it had my eyes streaming but it didn't seem to bother others. When we got to Laguna Beach it was clearer and I was okay. We wandered the street to pick out a restaurant when we'd be ready for it then sat on the beach and watched the beautiful figures. When we decided to eat we bypassed two seemingly popular places for the French restaurant we had originally chosen, also busy. It was a great choice from many angles. In addition to all the boons of food and service there was a feast for the eyes in a golden youth who served as busboy. Not at all the busboy type, he looked like a college boy and surfer and they none of them dressed in the usual busboy

way but as young collegians in slacks, summer shirts, and
ties. The menu was a bit campy and I think the proprietor
is gay but I don't think for a moment this lovely gold
creature was. The owner must, like me, prefer just to stare
at the fabulously beautiful rather than have lesser creatures around just because they're available. The way this
boy moved was magnificent and he was moving constantly. He
also stood and waited with beautiful posture. When his arm
was before me as he refilled my glass it was smooth and
lovely enuf to eat right up to the shoulder and one looked
up into a smile full of lovely teeth. I think he knew I
admired him but he neither played up to this nor frowned
on it; he just accepted it easily and went about his work,
meanwhile filling the surroundings with the radiance of his
beauty. It's a wonder I was able to pay any attention to
the food. As for the Pageant of the Masters, it was great
and Ken shared my enthusiasm. (*In a special amphitheatre
the townspeople posed in a series of tableaux simulating
great works of art, accompanied by classical music.*) One
good aspect of the pageant is that it called attention to
many forms of art. They did the Cellini saltcellar, three
American coins with models as three forms of Liberty, a
Roman sarcophagus, a Pompeiian mural, Steuben glass, the
Cimabue crucifix as it appeared before the Florence flood
and afterward, plus paintings, sepia drawings, statues,
etc. We got plenty cold and shivery before the performance
was over but that was enjoyable.

THURSDAY, JULY 20, 1967
    Our last day in Los Angeles was our first really bru-
tal one for smog and my eyes streamed terribly. We had a
long wait for the bus to San Marino but there were other
people going to the Huntington Gallery so we were well alerted as to when to get off. The houses and lawns out that
way are lovely. Ken was more impressed with the house and
grounds than with the art but we enjoyed the very specialized and unbalanced collection too. Ken loved the Japanese
garden but found the cactus garden not to his taste. Ken
was getting preoccupied with being hot by then anyway and
when he gets concerned with his discomfort no pleasures of
the mind or senses are likely to distract him. He wants you
to keep looking at his wet armpits as tho a medal were being given for quantity of sweat production and as tho one
weren't perspiring on his own account. After our final dinner at Clifton's we sat for a while in Pershing Square.
There was a little of the old activity but not so much as
formerly. The new landscaping since they put a garage under
it all doesn't lend itself so much to cruising. We were

surprised to find that the Biltmore still sells colored postcards showing the park as it used to be tho this present form existed at least by 1954, when I was last here. Probably they wanted to make it as unsuitable for sexual rendezvous as possible and nowadays it surely is. Home to pack, a chore quickly over with.

SUNDAY, JULY 23, 1967
(We were completing our vacation at VALERIA, a former estate endowed as a vacation resort for white-collar workers. Located just North of New York City, it lost its tax-exempt status following a suit by the local government and has been converted into condominiums.)
   I had a restless night as the air-conditioners made so much noise. I enjoy the adjusted temperature but felt as tho I were sleeping in a factory. Ken got up in energetic mood and right after breakfast we paid our fee and signed up for use of the golf course and swimming pool. We walked down to the cute 9 hole pitch-putt course and were able to tee right off. The couple ahead of us asked if we wouldn't like to play around with them and we did--twice. They were more or less in our league so it went well. In spite of all the shade on the course, we were soaking wet when we got thru and had to go shower and change before going to a marvelous Sunday dinner. After lunch we signed up for our locker at the pool then checked out paddles and cushions for a canoe from the very attractive lifeguard (the only attractive man around except Ken). We did a complete circuit of the quite sizable lake in which there are many swans and, as we discovered, many turtles also. Hovering over it were also lots of bugs. After supper, at which I began to be bored by the hearty geniality of my tablemates, I finished reading the Times then we went to the clubhouse to see if we'd meet some bridge players. There were some game players there but no bridge people. We watched the clumsy dancing for a while and I thought, as I had at the pool, how unnecessary it was for some of the men to let themselves look so awful. They don't even try to hold their stomachs in or make a chest and they seem to fully accept their unsightliness. I cannot stand people who are gratuitously ugly and I want to shake some of them and order them to stand straight, pull that pod up, and try to move with some grace. As Ken and I walked home from the clubhouse we realized that the athletic day had made us lame.

FRIDAY, AUGUST 4, 1967
   I thought a good deal about the way Anais Nin keeps

her diary and how opposed I am to it. She apparently carries the book with her at almost all times and writes, writes, writes at all odd moments. One may get some immediacy this way but also lose a lot of perspective. Sometimes I plan to include a morning event, a quarrel with Ken, for instance, but by evening it has shown itself to be insignificant in the day's overall account and I leave it out. By writing when one had a moment one might easily distort terribly and carrying the book and writing constantly one would certainly overwrite. I do that even writing at nite when I'm tired and God knows she must have written far more than I. Her habit of showing the diary to all and sundry almost immediately is too self-conscious for me.

SUNDAY, AUGUST 12, 1967
    To John's. As usual, the martinis flowed freely and were strong. Mostly we heard about their two weeks at Expo 67 and their evaluation of the pavilions we should give priority on our short stay, which was useful.

SUNDAY, AUGUST 13, 1967
    Up fairly early and got the Times read. The temperature was a mere 66 and I got a sudden rush of ambition so that after all that reading I felt like washing the livingroom rug. I had planned to do it as a mere act of will but today I actually felt like it and I never believe in ignoring such whims. The rest of the day went into the quick reading of DRAWN FROM LIFE, the memoirs of the youth of illustrator Ernest Shepard. Even after I bought the complete Pepys I couldn't bear to part with my copy of EVERYMAN'S PEPYS because of the wonderful Shepard illustrations. Looking at the generous illustrations he did for this volume of autobiography, I felt once more how unfortunate it is that illustration of books for adults has gone out. As I read his book I thought what a wonderful life he had had, living in possession of such a talent, and living to use it till a ripe old age. I never envy the moneyed but I do envy those golden souls with a real talent, a real vocation and a lifelong pursuit of it.

MONDAY, AUGUST 21, 1967
    Ken left early to get to his class in automatic typewriter. Of course all sorts of people quizzed me as to where Ken was. This was Jean's last day so my nice summer crew is now down to just Phyllis and likely to stay at that level for a while. Ken arrived fairly early in the afternoon and his head was aching from the complications of the machine.

WEDNESDAY, AUGUST 23, 1967

Half asleep this morning, I heard Ken heaving deep despairing sighs and I woke completely, knowing he was in a bad way. He had been in and out of bed since five, sick with dread of going to the typewriter class and failing again. He alarmed me when he said, "I don't know if I'm having a heart attack or a nervous breakdown or what." On being pressed for details of what made him think he was having a heart attack, he admitted he wasn't. What he was having was a plain old attack of nerves and I fully sympathized with him. I said I'd go to Frank and explain how it was disturbing him. "If only you would," he said, "the most wonderful thing that could happen would be for me to walk in and have you tell me Frank said I could drop the class." I sent Ken off with a kiss of encouragement but he needed more than that and more than I could give him. When I went to work I myself was a bit sick with concern for him and the necessity of confronting Frank. I got it over with at once and as I expected, Frank was understanding, tho he thinks Ken could master it if he had more confidence in himself. I thought Ken might have had a better day today and feel differently but when he came back he said he'd rather commit suicide than go back to that class again. I told him he needn't go any more and his relief was tremendous.

FRIDAY, AUGUST 25, 1967

Our new office space is really being worked on, with the plaster of the wall having been patched and the floor half torn up for replacement. In the evening I finished reading A QUEER KIND OF DEATH, absolutely the worst murder mystery I ever read. Even the gay atmosphere was not used in any witty way as I had hoped it might be.

THURSDAY, SEPT. 14, 1967 — Montreal

Our bus and subway connections were excellent and we were at Expo 67 before it opened. As a starter, to get our bearings, we took the minirail ride. It was so good that we agreed to repeat it Sunday as a farewell survey of the fair. The architectural imagination shown here far surpasses what we had at our fair. I cannot think of any way in which Expo is not infinitely superior. They provide all kinds of free transportation from island to island, have lots of food places far neater than those in New York, and have a late Twentieth Century mood about so many things whereas our fair was barely au courant. After the minirail we went to Cité du Havre, the first section of the fair, which was our goal for the day. We saw the Art Museum,

A GAY DIARY   13
where my favorite was a colossal head of Aphrodite and
Ken's was as usual Van Gogh (but I don't care for that
field scene because it's all horizontal lines). After that
to the Man and Community pavilion, a wonderfully imaginative building made of the wood so plentiful here and with
a series of interesting shows in its main supports and a
swan and duck-filled lagoon in the middle. That was my favorite pavilion of the day. We staggered home completely
out of energy after 13 hours of Expo. We both agreed that
we had seen today an absolutely fabulous number of good-
looking young men. Many had really ravishing complexions
with a touch of pink in the cheeks. We saw a lot of pretty
girls too but while they're easy on the eyes, they don't
ring bells like the boys and men do.

FRIDAY, SEPT. 15, 1967
    Off a bit later than yesterday but still a long, long
tiring day. We headed for the Czechoslovakian pavilion
right away but when we got there the guard was telling
people on the end of the line that it would be noon before
they got in. We joined those who refused such a wait. We
next went to the Canadian Pacific Pavilion where we first
saw a superb movie made by the people whose TO BE ALIVE was
such a hit at our fair. We then went to the superbly planned exhibit which exploited all the five senses, having
sections on touch (These two cubes are different--feel the
difference--one hot, one cold--These two spheres are dif-
ferent--feel the difference--one stationary, one moving--
feel this but not with the hand--and smell--all kinds of
scents to be sniffed in pipes, from strawberries to pine,
etc.) It was all beautifully done and thought-provoking
and Canadian Pacific immediately became one of my favorite
pavilions, particularly since I couldn't see what all this
had to do with their business and suspected nothing. We
then visited India, perhaps even more exquisite than at our
fair because they had more space and left it as space. I
got the brilliant idea that since one could get a pass to
get in the Czech pavilion if one ate in their restaurant
we should splurge for lunch and go. Ken was agreeable. We
had a wait of over an hour and a half even for the restaurant and our feet and legs killed us but the meal was only
$5 and extremely tasty. When we got in the Czech pavilion
we found it deserving of its reputation but so crowded we
could scarcely enjoy its display of Bohemian glass and lace
and the technically very advanced films. We visited a whole
block of Arab nations, all modest but lovely, then a bunch
of African nations which I could have done without but from
which Ken wanted to get the stamp in our guidebook.

Apparently some of the African nations can't afford personnel to sit and stamp people's books to show they've been there so Canadian Boy Scouts do it for them. Toward supper time we noticed there was hardly any line for the normally crowded Russian pavilion so we went tho we had intended to bypass it. It was a crashing bore for the non-technically-minded. The only really worthwhile thing in there was Yuri Gagarin's original space capsule. I thought that if Russia was unbusy maybe Italy would be at supper time so we worked our way down there with a stop for a Planters Punch at the Barbados-Guyana pavilion, where they had a parrot that danced to the music. Sure enuf, there was only a short line for Italy and when we got in we found it one of the most imaginative and impressive pavilions at Expo. Built like a fortress, it had sections on history, films, religion, fashions, and avoided confusion at all turns. We both raved over it and decided to let that close our cultural day. From there we went to La Ronde to have a cheese fondue at the Swiss Fondue Pot. Once more we staggered home at ten tho hoards were just arriving. Ken was too tired to take a bath but I needed it to take the ache out of my muscles.

SATURDAY, SEPTEMBER 16, 1967

As the crowded busses passed us by it was clear today was going to be mobbed at Expo. Even small pavilions often had lines. In spite of this we had visited ten national and state pavilions on Ile Ste. Helene by afternoon. Iran, which we had admired for its lovely flowered blue tiles from the outside, also proved to be much to our taste inside. Nobody had the Iranian pavilion on the list they gave us but we were both enchanted by it. Perhaps because it isn't much of an industrial nation we were spared pistons and crankshafts and television, which can get wearing to our non-mechanical nerves, and were given instead Persian carpets, silverwork and color pictures of such gorgeous detail of ruins that I wanted to take off for Iran at once even tho I never before had any hankerings to visit the country. In the Belgian pavilion pool there were enuf coins to pay for the pavilion. Every little bit of water leads a large number of fools to toss coins but in the Belgian pavilion it reached the most absurd heights I have yet seen, unless it was the way coins defaced the beauty of Australia's coral reef. I still say I'm going to get myself a pool of water, set it up at some busy corner, and live on the proceeds fished out at night. Scandinavia, which had been on nobody's best list either, ranked high on ours because when they did want to push their industry they did it in an artistic fashion by making abstract sculpture out of pipes

and joints and railroad rails. Dutifully we looked into the
Maine pavilion then considered Ile Ste. Helene cleaned up
and returned to Ile Notre Dame. We had an afternoon rum
drink at the Jamaica Pavilion, right on the canal, and had
interesting conversation with a nice young Ottawa couple--
he homely, she pretty, both intelligent--who shared our
trestle table. It made a nice change from just talking with
each other.

FRIDAY, OCTOBER 6, 1967
     We went home from work and napped a bit before setting
out for Alice's. We were the only guests and she stuck to
her objective of devoting the evening to showing us her
slides and snapshots on Portugal. She also had news of a
remarriage. Sam Gruber is marrying a woman who's just as
forceful as Lil but a millionaire sweater manufacturer.
Alice was pretty disgusted at him for letting Lil castrate
him so much (she had everything put in her name and didn't
even leave it all to him because she hated the thought of
another woman's getting what she thought of as 'her' money
but the new wife needs her pittance like she needs a hole
in the head)but the new wife is going to make every decision as the old one did. As a matter of fact, I'm sure that
despite his occasional complaints about my having to have
my own way, if something happened to me Ken would take up
with someone else who'd make his decisions for him. At work
he sometimes drives me crazy by asking me to decide every
little thing because he hates to be responsible for the
consequences of his decisions. And of course he really
doesn't want to decide anything much about vacation. I have
tried to force him to a decision about next year's vacation
and whether we should hire a car or take one of the tours
but tho he gave in and looked thru the brochures, he just
said, "They're lovely" and made no decision at all nor any
part of a decision. This doesn't bother me terribly because
decision-making comes easily to me and having decisions
made for him doesn't at all bother Ken except on very rare
occasions.

SUNDAY, OCTOBER 15, 1967
     We had dinner early since we wanted to go to the His-
torical Society before the circus and see their exhibit of
theatre posters for the years 1880-1920. The exhibit was
even more extensive and more interesting than I expected. I
thought I wouldn't have heard of the stars but in most
cases I had. We also saw a manuscript exhibit which contained several volumes of Hone's diary. The entries I read
were dull as hell. If he did a two-sentence entry he wasted

one sentence to say the weather was fine, or otherwise.
I've never been able to cotton to Hone's Diary much. They
had it open to his entry about Jenny Lind Fever but it
really didn't say anything. We had a nice walk down to Madison Square Garden. The tacky old Garden, in its last season this year, was by no means full for this last performance of the Moscow Circus. Only the aerial act was repeated
from the previous visit. There was only one bear this time,
but what a bear and what an act! It turned somersaults,
rode scooters and motorbike, twirled torches on its feet,
walked parallel bars forward and backward, and God knows
what else. There were no gymnasts this year but some attractive acrobats. The whole pace was wonderfully fast and
this always appeals to both of us. I'm sure that one reason
neither of us can bear Harold Pinter's plays is that they
drag along slowly with constant pauses. I can't bear people
who have hesitant, slow speech either and never could. I
want plays, operas, conversations, to move along briskly.
Chekhov dawdled and no doubt reflected his time but the
modern Russians seem to have a very good sense of pace. It
was my father's inability to move or talk fast that drove
Mother mad but I would never have entangled myself with a
slow mover in the first place. I just hate a moderate pace
too much to have ever been engaged to somebody slow for two
years as she was without becoming aware of a temperamental
incompatibility. Not that I want hyperthyroid activity all
the time, either. In living I like alternation of speed and
excitement with spells of passivity but in a theatrical
performance I think there's nothing like a good crisp pace.

TUESDAY, OCTOBER 17, 1967
When we got to the office we found that Buildings and
Grounds had left boxes for us to pack and at 9:30 they sent
a maid to help us but by that time we were virtually all
ready. *(This was the second move of the office for the
year.)* The move was effected with a minimum loss of work
time and since we had packed in an organized way, I was
able to get Elsbeth started typing labels as soon as her
desk and chair arrived. People poured in all day to look
us over and we had a mighty sociable time. We have infinitely more room than before, the sun pours in our two huge
windows, the light is so good that we got rid of some of
the desk lamps, and by a rearrangement of desks we get
still another freshening of our so-long-stale situation.

THURSDAY, OCTOBER 19, 1967
The lounge at the Yale Club was crowded already when
we got there at what we thought was an early hour and

before the lecture started there were standees all around
the edges. A greater proportion than I expected were young
recent graduates and I realized why when I heard them telling each other that in their day almost everybody agreed
that Scully, Trumbull Professor of the History of Art, was
the greatest professor they'd had. On the basis of tonite's
lecture, I can see that he might well be. The lecture series was introduced by Kingman Brewster, the President, who
got one of the currently fashionable standing ovations and
then Scully got under way with many slides. There were
complications with the slides for a while and much hilarity.
The generous amount of laughter thruout the lecture took
me back to the wonderful educational atmosphere of Yale. At
West Chester so many of the professors were such prosaic
sobersides, and when I gave a report and got laughter out
of what seemed like serious subjects, people were surprised
and delighted. But learning is fun and tonite perfectly ex-
emplified it. As when I was at Yale I felt I would almost
sell my soul to be a regular Yale college student (*as opposed to a playwriting major in the Drama School*), my mind
nearly bursting with all the stimulus on so many subjects.
However, there were graduates very near us who showed that
even a privileged life and the finest education doesn't
always turn out poised young men for there were some very
nervous, self-conscious types. Nevertheless, on the average
it was a damned nice group to be with, as it was when I was
there. I must consider myself lucky to have had my two
years at Yale, tho what I was getting there was training
and not what I call education. It was an emotional experience to go there and tonite had its overtones of emotion,
too. Ken, I was happy to note, enjoyed it too.

FRIDAY, OCTOBER 20, 1967
    After supper we went downstairs to be picked up by
Peggy and transported to Pat's. There were few spectacular
hands all night except one small slam which I bid (but in
Ken's suit so that playing it was his problem). We won by
just about the margin of the slam. There was discussion of
both their failed marriages tonite and I lost respect for
Peggy when I found she was getting alimony even tho she is
a nurse well able to support herself and even tho the reason the marriage broke up was that her husband wanted children and she didn't. She said she was sure he'd always be
faithful to his wife, said he was a nice witty man from
whom her separation was amicable, but how unfair that he
should have to pay when the fault, if any, was hers. He re-
married and now has the two children he wanted. I said nothing against alimony but I sure thought a good deal. Pat, on

the other hand, tho her husband drank and was cruel, got
nothing but a freedom she relishes. She, more than Peg,
would like to marry again but says men worth having aren't
easy to find in New York. I think both are sensible enuf to
know they have not found any prospects in us for there is
nothing of the hint in their talk. Pat said infidelity
would leave any marriage broken as it could never be forgotten and she thought infidelity was rife but Peg said
she thought lots of men were less highly sexed than some
people believe and felt satisfied and fulfilled if they
had sex once a month. I gather that her own husband was not
highly sexed. Their two viewpoints were interesting. Pat's
views on infidelity seem immature to me for a woman in her
forties. Perhaps a marriage is never the same after infidelity but perhaps it is just as good or even better. I certainly know my infidelities did not in any way reflect a
lesser interest in Ken and while I am never likely to forget his infidelities, particularly with my friends, I can
certainly forgive them. Our relationship could not be more
solid than it is right now--which I grant is partly due to
the fact that temptation doesn't come the way of either of
us very frequently these days, not available temptation at
any rate. There are numerous people at school with whom I
would gladly be unfaithful if I were given responsive interest and had the time and the place but this still would
not alter my love for Ken nor my intention to stick with
him till death do us part.

SATURDAY, OCTOBER 21, 1967
    To the Alvin to see ROSENKRANTZ AND GUILDENSTERN ARE
DEAD. It's a wonderful production and the play is very provocative in its tale of two unimportant ninnies who get
caught up in the affairs of larger people and go to their
doom without understanding what has happened to them. The
scenes from Shakespeare were neatly dovetailed into the
newly written scenes and the playing was superb. A boy among the players played the queen in the mime and one could
perfectly see how boys played the female roles and proved
convincing. I didn't pretend to understand it all but preferred having some of it over my head instead of beneath
my contempt, like a mechanical farce.

WEDNESDAY, NOVEMBER 1, 1967
    On the way home I picked up Ned Rorem's NEW YORK DIARY
at the library, having had notice that they were reserving
it for me. We hadn't time to have a nap but since Lavinius
went on in to bed as we did the dishes, I went in and lay
down with him a few minutes so he wouldn't be too awfully

disappointed. He looks forward to that nap together so
much. When he hears pans being put away he heads in there
but tonite he didn't even wait for the pans. I always look
forward to going to the George Abbott Theatre as it is perhaps my favorite of all theatres in town, tho it is known
as a hard-luck theatre which seldom has hits. I don't know
why. *(Soon after, it was demolished. It stood just East of
Seventh Avenue on 54th St.)* There was a sparse but responsive audience and the actors played just as well as if they
had a hit. Tho the totality is undoubtedly less important
than ROSENKRANTZ AND GUILDENSTERN, I think the play is more
amusing and more generally applicable to life as most people live it. ROSENKRANTZ is full of the currently fashionable existentialist despair, which could only be in fashion
in a society where people had so little to despair about
actually, and THE UNKNOWN SOLDIER AND HIS WIFE is more in
the mainstream of anti-war plays but it has enormously
clever bits. Those who say American actors can't play unrealistic drama or suggest period are just talking about
the wrong American actors. Those tonite were convincing as
Romans, Crusaders, Moslems, Barbarians, Germans from the
Thirty Years' War, Revolutionists, First World War soldiers
etc. The men wore all-purpose tights which revealed lots
of handsome legs and this did nothing to reduce my pleasure
in the evening.

FRIDAY, NOVEMBER 3, 1967
    The evening was devoted to reading Rorem's diary,
which I like much less than the first. In trying to be
philosophic he gets all tied up in mixed metaphors and
various kinds of pretentiousness that make for murky and
sometimes rather silly writing. As for his love affairs,
they seem so unintelligent altogether. As a masochist, however, he has special problems that I probably shouldn't
judge. Sadists and masochists by their nature cannot appreciate tenderness in a lover, which to me is chiefly what
matters.

SATURDAY, NOVEMBER 4, 1967
    Ken and I went downtown together but separated so I
could shop for his birthday. Headed for 42nd St. to buy him
one of the European nudist magazines which censors have
recently passed despite their frontal views of male nudes.
I feel sleazy going into such a store but after all we've
been reading about them, was determined to have this as a
gimmicky present. Tho in the window little pieces of tape
have been pasted over the genitals to protect the sensibilities of the young, inside the store all is on view. The

magazines are wrapped in plastic, however, so that one cannot browse in the contents. I quickly picked one out and presented it to the cashier but he wasn't about to have me leave so precipitously and said "Those are 3 for $5" so I went back and got two more. Then as I paid he said, "Would you like to look through our latest?" and he put three thick ones on the counter. I said, "No, this will do," and he said, "Oh, go ahead. Just look at them." I did and was amazed to find them less sexy than the old type physique magazine where one could imagine more attractive genitals than these boys seemed to possess. In my fairly considerable experience I only rarely encountered people with such unattractive genitals as these exhibitionistic types possessed. I was glad to get out of the store. I then proceeded to the new Korvette store, just opened this week in the site of the old Saks-34th St., and mobbed, where I got him an Instamatic camera to use for color shots. After that to the household department of Macy's. I felt myself being pushed and there was Ken. I had just about completed my shopping so I joined him and we headed for the theatre. He went to AFTER THE RAIN without high expectations but despite the fantastic form of it, he seemed to derive enjoyment from it. At intermission we discovered John and Dave, who had turned in tickets to something else to see this in case it closed. We chatted with them afterward and were a bit pressed for time when it came to getting home, having soup and running down to be picked up by Peg. We had a good evening of bridge with Ken and I winning by a large margin. He and I were made extra amiable by our short separation. He said he had seen a jacket he liked but didn't want to buy it without me along to see how it looked. We need only be apart a short time to rush at each other with a hoarding of items we want to share. When he has retired and gone to work elsewhere I shall miss him but I think our evenings will be veritable love feasts.

TUESDAY, NOVEMBER 7, 1967
    It was one of those fine evenings at the ballet. For one thing, all the ballets were new to us and one, MONUMENT TO A DEAD BOY was an excellent thing done to electronic music. The fact that the ballet had a homosexual element in it made it no less interesting. Aside from depicting a sentimental friendship, it had what looked like a gang rape by four school toughs, tho it was so nicely stylized that it wasn't absolutely explicit. Intermissions were almost as pleasant as the ballets because a handsome audience was in attendance. Ken and I stood on the lounge mezzanine and kept pointing out beauties to one another.

FRIDAY, NOVEMBER 24, 1967

Started the addressing of my Christmas cards. I got a superbly appropriate card for Lavinius to send Ken. It shows a lion and a lamb and is meant to emphasize peace, of course, but it fits Lavinius because when he fights with me Ken goes over to him and says, "Now you be a lambykin with Ken" and Lavinius calms down immediately then goes right back to fighting with me. Since Ken seldom fights with him, Lavinius is never rough with him tho they do have nightly boxing matches after supper, come to think of it. Anyway, the lion and the lamb rolled into one suit him well. Got the customary three kings card for Ken but much less lovely than sometimes. I don't know why I ever started with the three kings to Ken so many years ago except that this theme lends itself to sumptuous cards and I like his to be more sumptuous than my routine cards. After supper I let my food settle so I could face contact with food and then I went out and made the salmon casserole, following none of the recipes in any of the books but taking a bit from this and a bit from that and adding olives, which were in none. We watched a rather good British television play about Harold of Wessex and William the Bastard and how the latter extracted from Harold the oath about succession. After it was over I suddenly realized I was to have made snow pudding for tomorrow. Too little time remained for me to let gelatine half set before adding egg whites and there seems not enuf time to do it tomorrow, what with our going out to a travelog, so I changed the menu.

SATURDAY, NOVEMBER 25, 1967

After dinner David made what was to me an astoundingly naive remark. Speaking of the homosexuals who sit hopefully on the fence, "The Meat Rack", in Washington Square Park, he said, "Why don't they just go home and go to bed with each other?" I was so astonished I could scarcely gasp, "But they aren't each other's type!" How simple life would be if any two homosexuals who met and had hot pants could just agree to satisfy each other. How simple it would also be if any man and woman with lusty feelings could pair off with the first person they met who was also feeling sexy. Why should homosexuality be simpler than heterosexuality?

WEDNESDAY, NOVEMBER 29, 1967

Read another New Yorker and the paper, which had a front page story to the effect that a symposium of Episcopal clergymen has decided that homosexuality is "morally neutral". Homosexual acts between consenting adults were approved as long as they stemmed from love and weren't just a matter of using each other for selfish purposes. It was at St. John the Divine that the symposium was held and Morningside Heights will soon be the intellectual capitol of the homosexual world for Columbia was the first college to grant a charter to a "homophile league", which happened last year. This would be more interesting if Columbia students were more interesting. If one sees an attractive Columbia boy every second month it's a bonanza.

MONDAY, DECEMBER 4, 1967
At noon Ken and I went together to the barber shop. As we sat waiting for chairs I saw Ken's reflection in the mirror and thought how much he looked like a handsome major executive. This started me on a chain of reflection as to why he wasn't and why I wasn't more than I am. In Ken's case it's not hard to figure--he never had the slightest ambition except to come by money without working for it. He is interested only in legacies and big alimony settlements, never in earned money, which pains him with the thought of the work involved. He could never have been an executive even if luck had tossed the opportunity his way, which it does with some people, because he dreads decision-making. He fusses over trifles and needs somebody to take responsibility for every decision he has to act on. He is incapable of aggressive action. My case is somewhat different. I did have ambition but was a lot more interested in fame than in money. Even now that I have lost all hope of success as a writer I cannot get interested in business success, which leads only to affluence. But I too, tho small decisions come as naturally to me as breathing, lack aggressiveness. Reprimanding or firing people used to upset me considerably and I still don't think I could ask for a raise. Fortunately, I am not seriously disturbed either by Ken's lack of success or my own. Saturday nite Pat was saying that in her twenty years on two jobs she had always had to work a lot of overtime and I was saying I never had and never would. My private enjoyments are just too important to me, trivial as they are. I remember Jim Boothe's saying that even tho there was no work to be done, it was not the thing to rush out of the J. Walter Thompson office at five. One hung around to convey the impression that one wasn't eager to be elsewhere. I thought that was nonsense then and I think it's nonsense now. I work hard and willingly but when work hours are over I have a lot of other things to do. There are other ways in which I am not cut out to advance. Jim early understood that he had to invest much of his income in clothes, even if it meant doing without other things, but men's clothes bore the hell out of me, business

clothes in particular, and even if I hadn't preferred to
spend my money on travel, I probably never could have faced
the excruciating boredom of picking out suits, conventional
shoes, hats, etc. All in all, Ken and I are well met for if
either of us had been too successful we would have left the
other behind. I don't think it's possible for men of widely
disparate incomes to make a success of living together and
like the traveling I've done, I wouldn't give my life with
Ken up for any amount of power or success. Now offer me
fame and I'd have to rethink the matter. I mean, of course,
lasting fame and not just the momentary notoriety of my
face on the cover of LIFE.

SATURDAY, DECEMBER 9, 1967
    To the gift shop of the Museum of Modern Art for a re-
production of Ken's favorite painting, Van Gogh's STARRY
NIGHT (why has it taken me so many years to act upon this?).
With two things for him in hand I felt very good and everything else was gravy. Got home just in time to hear NOZZE
DI FIGARO in a good but not compelling performance. Marjorie was first to arrive, followed by the others in a group,
Alice having ridden in with the Rockmores. Pearl looked
like hell and in addition to her kidney troubles was tonite
in agony from a bad hip. She put up a brave front socially,
however, and the evening went well. Everybody but me said
they felt more a sense of impending doom now than at any
time in their life. I could not agree, having felt far more
oppressed and depressed in the late thirties than I have
ever felt since. The increase in crime is what is chiefly
bothering them for tho they hate the war and President
Johnson (I oppose the war but do not hate Johnson, as fashionable as that is) their misgivings seem to keep coming
back to violence in the streets. I'm not sure why I feel
less depressed than they, tho at least equally nervous about
muggings and robberies. I said that the fact that I was in
the house as a child when a burglar came in the back of the
apartment may help me feel that bad times didn't just start
yesterday but I wonder if the fact that I am a homosexual
does not have a little something to do with it. We, after
all, have always been prey to violence and my brushes with
the threat of it go back twenty-five years. I was throttled
in the Village in '42, robbed in Hollywood in '43 and the
danger was always there with any casual pickup. At any rate,
I definitely do not feel that we are now living in the
worst of all possible times. I still think the thirties
were the worst.

FRIDAY, DECEMBER 15, 1967

Working on a change of address for someone named "Donald", I realized how I have come to terms with my name. I used to dislike it because it was so common but since the war there have been few Donalds--mostly Michaels, Stephens, Peters, Geoffreys, etc. and so I feel better about it. I have even resigned myself to the nickname Don tho I still can't say I like it. The sound is all right but I have never fully recovered from my revulsion to the idea that I was given my name because Mother played the lead in a play called MISTER DON. It was a transvestite role, in which she specialized, and I hated the idea even before I knew what I was hating. I intensely disliked the picture of Mother in men's clothes for the role, a picture long since disappeared (and good riddance). But in addition to this potent psychological reason there was an almost equally strong one that simply had its base in aesthetics. I don't like a short nickname with a longer last name. We have an alumnus whose legal name is Dr. Joe Apple and the Joe just seems so unsuitable. We also have an alumnus whose legal name was Dr. Bobby Rothschild. He changed it first to Bob and that too seemed wrong to him as well as to me so he eventually ended up as Robert, which his parents should have had the foresight to dub him in the first place. But I no longer get strong waves of aversion when called Don and actually like my full name. With most of my workers now much younger than I, I am generally called "Mr. Vining" now and that eliminates a lot of "Don"s. We sent cards to those who were not on our original list. When I opened mine from Ken I let out a delighted howl for he had sent me exactly the same card I sent him. For two days since mine arrived he has held his tongue waiting for the moment I opened mine and when I did we rushed laughing into each other's arms, overcome by the coincidence that of all the cards in New York we should pick the same for each other. Every time we saw the two cards standing on the credenza we broke up again.

THURSDAY, DECEMBER 21, 1967

Miriam included on her card an invitation to dinner on the 6th so we had to call and tell her we were previously engaged. Actually, since we're to see them at Alice's a week earlier and the guest list would be virtually the same, it's perhaps best we can't go. It would be like parties in small towns where you see the same people all the time before they've had a chance to build up a new supply of small talk. The nice thing about city parties is that there are always people you haven't seen for a while and usually some you've never seen so that conversation of some decent substance is always possible.

SATURDAY, DECEMBER 23, 1967
    Downtown and in for a look at F.A.O. Schwarz, where I have been only once before in my life. That was in the days when electric trains were the big thing but changes in transportation are reflected on their sales floor and while they still have a train set up, it is a much smaller thing than formerly and now racing cars get equal prominence. I was impressed by the many wonderful educational games and toys and for half a minute I wished for a child to give something like that to (half a minute is as long as I have ever wished for a child at any one time). Fifth Avenue was lined with an absurd number of policemen, put there in case the peace demonstration to be staged at Radio City was attacked by toughs from the longshoremen's union (who naturally love the overtime they get shipping goods to Viet Nam and whose vociferous patriotism by no means includes loading this material free).

TUESDAY, DECEMBER 26, 1967
    Lavinius, having had success yesterday in getting us up by means of flying runs under the tree to tinkle the bell before leaping on us, tried it again today. We ignored him at first but he knew he was registering so he'd simply go back out and run in more vigorously, giving the bell a harder ring and eventually bringing down some of the plastic decorations from the tree. Finally he began to bat the fallen decorations about as he made his journey to our beds and we got laughing so hard that we gave in and got up. We had to pick up four balls off the tree and rehang them. We subwayed down to 42nd St. to see if there were any movies there we wanted to see but there weren't so we decided on CLOSELY WATCHED TRAINS, a Czech film at the 34th East, where we had never been. A fine film that made one wonder why the Czechs are now so strong in film-making whereas the Germans have probably not made a good film in forty years.

THURSDAY, DECEMBER 28, 1967
    Ken and I agreed that HAIR was an experience which left us shaken up as good theatre should do, re-examining our values. *(This was neither the original production at Joseph Papp's PUBLIC THEATRE nor the later Broadway production but an interim production at CHEETAH, a fairly short-lived discotheque on Broadway.)* One wonders whether the use of four-letter words in such profusion is necessary to the revolt of the young and ponders also the scene in

which a negro boy nibbled the bottom of a girl as she sang, the scene in which a boy put his friend on top of his girl friend, grabbed his belt and pumped him up and down on her, and the scene in which a cute blond boy is given a poster of a pop singer and exclaims, "I love this man. He turns me on. I'm not a homosexual, really I'm not, but I'd love to go to bed with this man and make love." Etc., etc. Men freely hugged each other at many points and love was the message but I was interested to see that one of the main plot points was that despite the waves of love for all races and both sexes, all sorts of people were frustratedly in love with people who did not respond but loved someone else. Love among the hippies was just as unhappy as in LA BOHEME.

SUNDAY, DECEMBER 31, 1967
     Snow began to fall about noon, dictating boots for the trip to the parties. When we walked in to the Christenson's my heart sank. Such a layout of food I never saw. It was so beautiful that we thought it should be photographed so guests who lived also in Butler Hall went and got their camera. When I'd talked to Alice she had enjoined us not to eat anything much at the prior party as she was having more elaborate hors d'oeuvres than usual but after all the work Ellen went to (she had baked bread as well as cakes and cookies) I couldn't refuse to eat nor was I inclined to in the face of such gorgeous food. It was noticeable that two-thirds of the men present were gay and I guess Ellen likes that type because they're chatty and gallant. The straight men there, mostly husbands brought by invited wives, sat silent and uncontributing most of the time. I hated to tear myself away after an hour and three quarters, much as I looked forward to the other party. We fretted a bit about getting to Alice's late but had good connections. There was champagne and despite all the cliché scenes in plays and movies I defy anybody to get tiddly on champagne.

1968

MONDAY, JANUARY 1, 1968
     I untrimmed the tree and took it to the basement, went thru the Christmas cards with Ken and made sure we had our books marked correctly. Ken's day was almost ruined by the discovery that the chowder had curdled. He forgot to put it in the refrigerator yesterday. More disappointing than that were news bulletins that the President planned to clamp

down on travel to Europe to help stem the dollar drain.

SATURDAY, JANUARY 13, 1968
We went over to Marjorie's at seven and it turned out to be a largish party for twelve. As the room was full of emigrees, I had a good time. In addition to the Scot, the German, and the English hostess, we had Wies, the Dutch girl, and Ruth's argumentative Bulgarian, Tasso. Concern was expressed about possible travel restrictions as most of the emigrees have parents back there whom they must see at intervals. Tasso, who hasn't and doesn't care to go to Europe, was all for the defense of the American dollar and we must all sacrifice. I told him he was very broad-minded in being so willing to sacrifice what meant nothing to him in the first place and that I in my turn was perfectly willing to have automobiles taxed to the hilt since they meant nothing to me. Ruth said that under Hitler they were not allowed to leave the country and she had felt frustrated because her school had always had an exchange arrangement with schools in Paris and London which she felt done out of.

WEDNESDAY, JANUARY 17, 1968
We were only half way down the block when we saw the number 4 bus start to pass the end of the street. Then it halted and the driver's hand waved to us to come and he pulled over at the far curb. It was our friend who's done this before but never when we were still so far away. "I'd wait for you guys anytime," he said. Some of the grouchy old ladies who are always full of complaints about the bus service would never believe this happens in New York but three different drivers have done it for us at different times. Went on with Bernice Fitzgibbon's MACY'S, GIMBEL'S AND ME. Last night I had been very impressed with the first chapters but the disorganized rambling and repetitiveness of the book began to annoy me tonite. She may be the world's best writer of retail advertising but a book she can't write.

MONDAY, JANUARY 22, 1968
Ken got a haircut at noon and for some reason a haircut always makes him look older, just as a hat does (not that he's worn one of those in eighteen years except for his awful knitted cap, which puts ten years on him in cold weather). I like his hair when there's more of it, nice white waves, but he hates it. In the evening we went down to see STAIRCASE, the English play about two homosexual barbers. Much of the bitchy talk was funny but I thought it

was unnecessarily cruel. The very mixed audience was very tolerant of the homosexuality but only because they were miserable, perhaps. I have yet to see depicted on stage or screen a homosexual couple of reasonable attractiveness that sticks together even tho each has reasonably acceptable alternatives. The trouble with this is, where's the drama? Home fairly early (plays run short this year).

FRIDAY, JANUARY 26, 1968

On one of my jaunts down the hall I ran into Al and got one of his lovely blushing smiles that made me realize how I miss him now that he's changed jobs and no longer checks things in our files. I realized that part of his appeal is that he wears cotton shirts. I have always found crisp cotton shirts sexually appealing and love the mingled odor of a warm clean body and nicely laundered shirts. Shirt sleeves rolled just half way up the forearm are for some unfathomable reason very sexy to me but only if they are cotton. The new fabrics lack the right textures and the right odor. The origins of this little bit of erotica I couldn't fathom but it's a definite thing with me.

FEBRUARY 3, 1968

Among my purchases downtown was a can of men's hairspray. My hair was being very unruly and Ken thought it might help. I tried it and it keeps it in place but at what a price. If one touches one's hair with that gook on it feels just terrible. I hate to keep brushing my hair back when it's unruly but if I do I like it to feel silky and this stuff offends my fingers. I don't see how women stand it. They must have no sense of touch at all if they are not absolutely repelled by the feel of this. I don't even like the look of rigid hairdos because they don't look as tho you'd want to touch them. The other day at the post-office there was a not-very-good-looking boy with long, lovely, clean, taffy-colored hair that I would love to have run my fingers thru.

TUESDAY, FEBRUARY 6, 1968

Ken had a recurrence of indigestion and after his morning toast got really distended. Mary and I said it was probably due to working on taxes and kidded him that it was because he had to draw money out of the bank this noon. "I always thought 'withdrawal symptoms' referred to dope," I said.

SATURDAY, FEBRUARY 10, 1968

Over to the Museum of Natural History, where we nearly

had the pants bored off us by a lecturer whose topic was
WILDLIFE ANNALS. He had no idea of when to cut the film
short and showed too much of everything. The opera was well
under way when we got home but I didn't mind because it was
LOHENGRIN and I paid little attention to the remainder,
letting myself drift off to sleep, tho one foul note by the
tenor woke me. His attack on the next high note redeemed
him but that clinker was a lulu. When I went in for my bath
I summoned Lavinius, thinking I could spare Ken the trouble
of getting up and letting him in. He wouldn't come but the
minute the water started running, he started screaming to
come in. He used to come in and wait for me on the hopper
occasionally but lately he does it very consistently, sitting there with his toes tucked in, and asking nothing but
a kiss when I come out. His call to come in is different
from his food cry. In fact this morning he screamed and I
knew from the tone that his water dish was empty. I went
sleepily out, stuck my finger in the dry bowl, filled it,
and staggered back to bed. I couldn't describe how his water cry differs from his food cry or his orders for us to
get up, but it does.

SUNDAY, FEBRUARY 18, 1968
    We set out to see Albert Finney in JOE EGG, by all
odds the best play we have seen this year. The subject matter, parents with a spastic "vegetable" child, didn't keep
people away and the full house was wonderfully responsive
to the many hilarious lines. I liked the audience and really enjoyed the play, laughing far more than I did at SPOFFORD, whose only object was to amuse the audience. If I
ever write another serious play, may I spice it with as
much laughter as this. I have thought much of the reported
last words of playwright Howard Lindsay, who died this week.
He said to his wife,"It's been a wonderful journey. I've
had a fine companion. I've enjoyed every minute of it." I
could echo that and hope I feel the same when the end comes
and am not put off by a final illness, illness having such
a way of giving one a jaundiced view of life (O'Neill, for
example).

TUESDAY, FEBRUARY 20, 1968
    Patty checked with us on dates as she and Amanda are
trying to put together the cancelled party. Michael is to
come and as far as I can see all the men present will be
gay. I have never made up my mind as to whether Patty is a
lesbian. I have always hated very butch lesbians but don't
know much about that world because Mother never really
travelled in it. She was a bit like me, living her life in

a heterosexual world, but whether she drifted into that (as I suspect) or did it as a matter of policy as I do, I don't know. It may be that Patty and her set simply prefer the chatty, unaggressive kind of gay man as a party companion. Anyway, I certainly don't object to lesbians if they're the type about whom one can't be sure. What I hate is Mother's type, out to prove they're more everything than men are, as I hate all other forms of aggressive women.

FRIDAY, FEBRUARY 23, 1968
At break we were astounded to be joined by Frank, bearing a tray full of drinks for the people in the office, which he let the ice melt in as he talked to us. When we talked of dieting, Frank said, "Please! You embarrass us 24-year-olds who've already developed paunches." I think both Frank and his wife will be quite heavy when they get older. They're a bit bulky already but very nice. Frank, like so many young men today, is quite frank about his desire to escape the draft. He reported the coming baby to his draft board and after his wife's miscarriage he didn't report it till they sent a questionnaire but he said,"We're working hard to get another in the hopper."

WEDNESDAY, MARCH 6, 1968
Bob R. came in to pick up Ken's monthly list of large gifts from individuals (there were none this week) and when Ken asked how the summer place was coming, he suggested we have coffee with him. When we got seated he shocked us with the news that he and Jorge had decided to separate while they could salvage something of their former friendship. Jorge has moved in with his brother, who left Spain to settle here, leaving the apartment to Bob, since he works near there. He also has custody of the dog. Ken and I were both saddened at the news and the subject kept coming ruefully to our lips all day. If ever I had thought there was a loving couple who could make it over the shoals of homosexual stormy weather, Bob and Jorge were it. When Darrell and Jerry split I regretted it because I like to see two attractive people together but there was no denying their extreme incompatibility. Darrell not only didn't share Jerry's interest in theatre, museums, art, and books but resented every moment of attention he gave them. Jorge and Bob seemed to feel alike about everything. Well, an outsider can do nothing, particularly if no closer to the parties involved than we are. Both will find other loves for Jorge is bright and personable and Bob is cute and cuddly. I was enjoying a broadcast of BLUEBEARD'S CASTLE and thinking the Met should put it on when a TV program on Monaco came on

that Ken wanted to watch. We then watched the first of
three parts of THE RISE AND FALL OF THE THIRD REICH and I
wondered how I could have been so self-concerned while all
that was going on. The young people today are so politic-
ally concerned and I guess some people were then too but
while so much of that horror was accumulating I was concerned with getting to college, with Goshen Theatre, with getting my love life in order.

SUNDAY, MARCH 10, 1968
    Up about nine and read the paper, including a reassur-
ing article that says the travel tax the President asked
for is a dead issue with Congress. At 5:30 we took our lemon dessert and our salad and went down to the Anniversary
Supper. It was a roaring success and much pleasanter this
year than in some previous years because the children have
grown to a less troublesome age. There was an excellent
racial mixture, perhaps 50-50, and it really made me very
happy about this building. (*There was a pot luck supper
every year to celebrate the life of our building, with its
still regrettably rare inter-racial makeup.*)

FRIDAY, MARCH 15, 1968
    We stopped at Columbia Travel and booked our three-day
tour in the environs of Madrid. While we were there a representative of Portuguese Airlines came in to call on Carlson and if there are many men in Portugal as suave and
handsome as he, I'm going to have a feast for the eyes
there. When I started home at night I meant only to go to
the bank and then buy some green carnations for Sunday but
I enjoyed walking so much that I walked all the way home
and got there just as Ken got off the bus. I'd love to do
that walk more often and perhaps in this interim season between the nights that are too dark to be safe and the days
that are too hot to be safe in explosive Harlem, I could
do it.

THURSDAY, MARCH 21, 1968
    In the evening, after another of the diet dinners, we
napped and then went to the opening of the City Opera's new
MANON. It was a sumptuous production, superbly staged, acted, and sung. Around me people were saying they thought the
Puccini version superior but I will never give in to that
theory. It is all very well to say this music is pallid by
comparison but I think the period and subject call for
depiction by a Boucher or Fragonard and not by a Carvaggio.
Beverly Sills was the best Manon I have ever seen and has
a genuine trill, so rare today. She's a gifted, graceful

actress and the director helped her at every turn. Her
temptation in the inn scene was made beautifully clear and
in the Ste. Sulpice scene there was an iron gate thru which
she tempted Des Grieux effectively. I was often moved and
I don't care what anybody says about the opera. It is still
one of my half-dozen favorites. It offers such wonderful
acting opportunities and Sills took full advantage of them.
Ken too enjoyed it thoroly so that he has finally had a
good time at the opera this year, after suffering thru the
others I took him to.

FRIDAY, MARCH 22, 1968
    The review of MANON in the Times was all I could wish
and for once I didn't have to be defensive about Massenet.
In the evening I finished, after my fashion, NO LAUGHING
MATTER. As usual, I lack patience to read thru a long novel
word for word or even page for page. I began to follow only
the story of the homosexual son, not a very appealing or
even a very convincing character. Originally a "renter", he
was picked up by a rich jew and installed in luxury, where
he lived for many years till the jew died and left him his
fortune. To me this is mere fantasy. It's what many homosexuals dream but it seldom if ever comes to pass for the
male ego interferes with such rosy little sagas. The kept
man rebels, the keeping man grows irritated at supporting
the other, and in no time it is on the rocks. Only women
can be kept without restiveness. I don't know of any instance where a man was kept for any length of time by another man, especially not in amity.

WEDNESDAY, MARCH 27, 1968
    We heard a fine broadcast of the Nilsson recording of
TOSCA but Ken irritated me somewhat by constant fiddling
with the volume dial. He completely ironed out the composer's dynamics by turning it down when the volume went up
momentarily and then, finding the music had softened into
inaudibility, turning it up again. Mother and Nana both
used to drive me nuts doing this when I lived at home and
neither ever seemed to learn that loud passages in music
are followed by quiet ones and that if you will set the
dial at some medium volume and keep your fingers off it
thereafter, all will be well. I used to reach a high pitch
of annoyance with them but Ken wasn't as bad as that and
enjoyed the opera himself, especially Corelli as Mario.

THURSDAY, MARCH 28, 1968
    Deciding it would be fun to go to the theatre more
spontaneously than we usually do, I called the Biltmore to

see if there were cheap seats for LOOT, which I wasn't sure would last long. The house was nearly full and roared all night long at the perfectly outrageous doings the late Joe Orton cooked up. No reverence was shown for corpses, the Catholic Church, the police, or anything much else. Lots of satires make fun of things all middle-class people agree are foolish and take no risks but this play must stomp on a lot of toes. The dialogue and the pace were crisp and made it seem a great shame that the playwright's lover saw fit to murder him and then commit suicide because he feared that Orton, in his success, was growing away from him. There is quite a play in the author's life but I wouldn't try to write it because the public already thinks of the homosexual life as more violent and wretched than it is.

THURSDAY, APRIL 4, 1968
    I think the Spring weather is getting to our nerves. Ken, always somewhat crabby in recent years, is a bit more so lately or maybe he just gets on my nerves more. He said he didn't think Mrs. Stewart did much today and wanted me to name what she'd done. I later discovered she'd had the books out of the bookcase and got the accumulation of dust behind them but at the time I could only say I thought the house looked nice and if he didn't, then we should for God's sake let her go and do it ourself, thus saving money. This quieted him. If she straightens the linen closet he says she shouldn't have wasted time that way, and if she washes and irons the kitchen café curtains and our dresser scarfs, he thinks she's wasting time there too but when I say he should then leave a list of what he DOES want her to do, he can name nothing. The trouble with letting her go and doing it ourself is that we DON'T do it. On the off week I do vacuum because I can't stand the dust but Ken doesn't do his cleaning of bathroom and kitchen till the nite before Mrs. Stewart comes. I'm also getting fed up with Ken's turning the alarm off after our nap and sleeping on till nine but I've just been getting up and letting him sleep on. I refuse to nag but Lavinius took over about eight tonite and screamed his head off for Ken to get up. Ken mumbled something at him and went on sleeping while I did the Portuguese and Spanish lessons. When he did get up we were amiable for I recognize the symptoms of Springtime nerves in myself. We really used to fall out in the Spring but that doesn't happen so much any more. We had the second news bombshell of the week when, after President Johnson's decision not to run we tonite heard that Martin Luther King had been assassinated in Memphis, probably by white men, alas.

FRIDAY, APRIL 5, 1968

We were not at all surprised when we were roused from our nap by a call from Florence to see if we were being beseiged by angry negroes in the civil disorders that have broken out in most major cities following the assassination of Martin Luther King. Today there was a feeling as the negroes with whom we work and live greeted one, that they were making it plain that they were not among those about to take up arms against "Whitey". The midtown area was plagued with roving groups of disorderly negroes at nite and I guess it's well that our theatre tickets are for a matineé. We'll have to be cautious for a while and the white community will have to enact reforms quickly but it isn't as bad as it sounds to outsiders yet. A small number of hoodlums and thieves is setting back the progress of the good negroes terribly.

SUNDAY, APRIL 7, 1968

Got some of the paper read before we took off for Staten Island. Taking no risks with trouble on Lenox Avenue we went down in the East Side subway but in this area all seems calm and as a matter of fact New York is one of the least riot-torn cities in the nation. When Eddie met us, a little late, he explained that the delay was due to Mother's early arrival. Mother at first looked very old to me but later I got used to her appearance. She has one old lady's mannerism that bothers me and that is sticking her tongue out after saying something or laughing. I'm sure she doesn't know she does it but it looks awful and may I be spared these marks of old age when my time comes. For dinner we had fresh ham and almost the best part of it was the rind, nice and crackling, of which I ate enough to give me indigestion but I never suffered. When Mother was speeded on her way and they took us to the ferry I got a bit depressed. I think it was because I felt so detached from Mother. The hero in yesterday's play was always complaining that he felt he <u>ought</u> to love his father but hadn't ever been able to and <u>my</u> problem was analogous. I feel sorry for Mother in her old age not having more familial love but I just don't feel any noticeable amount. I cheered myself up with the reminder that she's in good health, earning her own living, and that there is nothing sad or self-pitying about her. After all, my father had no love of hers or mine to see him thru and if I live to be old, I'll have nobody either.

THURSDAY, APRIL 11, 1968

The Columbia Spectator had a long, excellent article on THE ANGUISH OF THE HOMOSEXUAL STUDENT by that Stephen

Donaldson, who has founded the Student Homophile League. The boy can write rings around me and thoroly discouraged me from tackling the subject if he can write so well of it when still a college junior. That was my first reaction, at least, and I was also discouraged by the discovery that there is new gay jargon I hadn't known about and so what I might say might be laughably old-fashioned. I'd heard the term "fag-hag" once but hadn't known it was common parlance for a girl who goes around with gay boys. I had never once heard the term "CT" for "cock-tease", a man who consciously or unconsciously excites a homosexual, and while in my day we spoke of "coming out", I never heard the term "in the closet" for one who is a latent homosexual nor heard the whole term "coming out of the closet" for becoming an open homosexual. As to the student problems mentioned, such as common temptation in the dormitories, they were very well dealt with but when I looked at some Columbia students after work the whole article lost a lot of its poignance for, naked in the shower or not, I cannot see how they would tempt anybody much. As a matter of fact, even in my day I was spared a lot of this sexual tension by the fact that by and large my classmates at Carnegie Tech, at West Chester, and at Yale, were just not all that attractive. I mooned over half a dozen all told at the three colleges but the rest left me cold. My room-mate at West Chester was an attractive boy but on the heavy side and I don't recall having one moment's sexual thoughts of him. This must have been quite clear to him as there was never any tension in the air even tho he knew about me. I have more or less decided that I was a special case all along the line and that my experiences have little applicability to the general run of homosexuals so why write them up. I certainly never quivered with the sensibility of Donaldson but then I didn't really come out till after college days. I knew what I was but not just what to do about it and so really did nothing except long romantically for those I loved without graphic sexual desires.

SUNDAY, APRIL 14, 1968
In the afternoon we went down to the East Village to see YOUR OWN THING, which proved to be as good as everybody said it was. A modernization of the basic plot of TWELFTH NIGHT, it was built around the fact that young girls and boys dress alike these days and are hard to tell apart. When Orson (Orsino) fell in love with the disguised Viola he took to the psychology books for understanding about latent homosexuality. This was all handled tastefully on the thesis that any kind of love which doesn't hurt anybody

is okay. The production was crisply paced, the rock music very good, and it didn't have a spare word anywhere. On the proscenium there were projections of prominent figures from time to time and recorded dialogue supposedly spoken by them was used. This came to a climax at the end when the God figure in the Sistine Chapel ceiling was projected with the blurb "Son?" and then a Christ head with long hair said "Yes, Father?", to which the God figure said, "When are you going to get a haircut?" I admire enormously the young people who created this snappy, irreverent show but it made me feel old and I wondered if I wasn't misguided in growing sideburns and letting my hair grow long. (*At no time was I attempting shoulder-length hair like the young.*) I hate women who try to be young and while that wasn't my impossible objective, I more or less decided to give up on the long hair and settle for the sideburns, which all ages are taking up, tho the young more than the elderly.

WEDNESDAY, APRIL 17, 1968
   Ken and I decided to leave work early so we could get tickets to THE BOYS IN THE BAND before we met the Leonards. There was a line but not a long one so we were ahead of time at the rendezvous. Dinner was good as usual (I had boneless shad, which I haven't had in years). Then to the Biltmore, to see the proscenium theatre version of HAIR. We expected that the proscenium would dictate a few changes in the staging but we didn't expect the wholesale changes in the material that were made. We could see early in the evening that we had made a grave mistake in bringing the Leonards to see it. Two of the scenes that were a bit tasteless before are gone but in their place is a scene in which the boys emerge from under a big blanket stark naked. The lights were dim and I didn't realize what was happening till almost too late. When we got home Lavinius was so eager for love that he couldn't pay attention to his late dinner and had to have hugs and kisses at intervals and then go back to his dish.

SATURDAY, APRIL 20, 1968
   We washed the living room and dining room windows to cut down on what we have to do next week in getting ready for Patty and Amanda. Lavinius had orgies all day with the lilacs and we had to keep watch to save the vase from being tipped over. The crowd gathering for THE BOYS IN THE BAND was far more sexually mixed than it was for FORTUNE AND MEN'S EYES and by searching one could actually find some attractive male couples. As in so many recent plays the language was untrammeled but unlike HAIR it was amusing

and not just dirty words said to shock. In the first act we
screamed with laughter as the gay party got under way but
the second act, as they got drunker and nastier, was much
more sober. Fortunately, only one of the characters was
terribly campy, one was mildly so, and the rest were allowed some dignity and masculinity despite their sexual proclivities. The scene where they played a game in which each
man phones the one person he loved best to tell him so was
a bit unbelievable but very well done and touching. At
least one couple was allowed some happiness together and
despite jealous scenes, chose to call each other during the
game and eventually retired to the bedroom to make love.
When we came out we walked down Broadway to get a Times and
then bussed up Madison, recalling the funnier lines to each
other. Ken rather acted as tho we had never been part of
that world, which amused me, since he fitted into it better
than I did tho we were both somewhat outside it even when
we were in it.

THURSDAY, APRIL 25, 1968
    In the evening we went to IPHIGENIA IN AULIS at Circle
in the Square, which is no longer on Sheridan Square and
isn't circle shaped either, if it ever was. The original
Achilles had been criticized but now they have a young man
named Gastone Rossilli who is excellent and a beauty to
boot. I wanted to wrap him up and take him right home over
my shoulder. It was an arena stage and some of the audience
was embarrassed by the intensity of the emotion at such
close range so looked away at climactic scenes. The arena
staging brought the gorgeous Gastone close to me at times
and the sight of those long lovely bare legs and the smell
of bees wax that seemed to emanate from all their costumes
was maddening. The men all had attractive feet but some of
the girls in the chorus had horrible feet with corns and
twisted toes and prominent veins.

FRIDAY, APRIL 26, 1968
    The turmoil on the Columbia campus is well reported in
the Spectator but tho the university is completely disrupt-
ed, with students sitting in various buildings, we see and
hear very little of it. I heard girls chanting, "Hell, no,
we won't go", which seemed very silly. That makes a good
motto for boys of draft age who are opposed to the war in
Vietnam but since nobody is asking the girls to go, it
strikes an absurd note. Many police are surrounding the
campus, which is sealed off, and I guess there is plenty
of action as the "huskies", who think they'll beat up protesters for interrupting their education, are kept apart

from the left-wing protestors by cordons of faculty. I'm on both sides. I agree with the students protesting the building of the gym in Morningside Park for I don't think Columbia or any private institution has a right to park land even if they throw the public a small bone of letting them use a corner of it. But when the students demand total amnesty for all agitators regardless of whether they were among the ones who rifled the files of the President of the University or held faculty hostages, I am with the administration in feeling this is intolerable. As we didn't hear from Peg we supposed we were to get to Pat's on our own so bussed down to 8th and walked over. As we were looking at a window full of Nehru and other mod jackets for men with chains and pendants around the neck, we met Frank Ellsworth and his wife. They adore the Village, and go there a lot. Poor Frank, absolutely born to be the stuffy salt of the earth, has such hankerings to be a freer soul. He's letting his hair grow and he was wearing an Ascot, which may change the outer image but will never change the inner man hovering on the edge of pomposity. Still, he's trying and must get credit for that. Peg drove up just as we arrived at Pat's. We were all out of practice for bridge and a lot of silly errors were made.

MONDAY, APRIL 29, 1968

After work I took some library books back but found the library in Butler closed, I suppose because Columbia was shut down today as dissident students continued their sit-in occupation of several buildings. On my way down Amsterdam Avenue I had seen a girl taking food orders thru a grill from one of the beseiged students, whom conservative students are now trying to starve out by interfering with those students who bring them food. I must say that I felt exhilarated by all this excitement on the campus and for perhaps the first time warmed to Columbia as a whole. Those students will remember this all their lives. I caught the same bus Ken was on and some grande dame was giving her opinion as to how to put these rebels in their place. She claimed she had intended to make a substantial legacy to Columbia but no longer intends to. I don't believe for a moment that the woman ever intended to leave so much as one cent. Bob R. is possibly right when he said that this is going to put Columbia on the map with young people and increase applications from those who want to be where the action is, a statement that horrified Grace Mason. Bob looked very mod today and told us that tho he already has a necklace he has to get a Nehru jacket as he's invited to a party at which all guests have been ordered to wear them.

TUESDAY, APRIL 30, 1968

In the night the police were called in and arrested over six hundred students who were occupying the Columbia buildings. This released such hostility as you wouldn't believe in those opposed to the students. Marjorie Ellis was ranting and raving this morning on the bus. Mary Rowe came in the office in an absolute froth because one of the students had bitten a policeman in the stomach. She said it with such tones of outrage and horror that one would suppose a student had slapped the face of God. I couldn't help speculating on the problems of biting a policeman's stomach thru all those layers of belts and uniform. She claimed the students had been released and were back in the Columbia buildings but like so many of the stories retailed by this born Irish gossip, there was no foundation to the story whatsoever. I think Mary Rafferty shares her indignation but has better control and that her continued silence in the office stems from her feeling that she is in the minority there. I think Catholics, bred to accept authority no matter how misguided, are more upset by revolt than are Protestants and jews. When we went to the bank with our checks there was some kind of mass meeting going on by the Columbia gates. It was exciting but by no means threatening and we watched as we ate our lunch across the street at Chock Full O Nuts but when the two Marys talk about it, it's as tho the neighborhood were about to be razed. We completely circled the campus at noon since I needed stamps from the postoffice and there was nothing alarming going on at all. Lots of policemen but the students are good-humored. I heard chanting outside and ran upstairs to see and found protesters circling the Columbia buildings with posters and beckoning those of us on the TC steps to join them. Again, they were good-humored. It was very seductive when all the marchers were going by trying to lure TC into the line with their "Come join us" and their beckonings. I'm suddenly crazy about Columbia and it's certainly taken a long time to get me to that pitch.

THURSDAY, MAY 2, 1968

We left the office fifteen minutes early in order to go home and bathe and dress for Bill's cocktail party. As we walked along 57th St. looking for the number, a woman stepped out and asked, "Are you friends of Mr. Washburn?" then led us in to the elevator of a building which is basically galleries, like most of the buildings along there. His apartment on the fifth floor was a very nice one, however. One of the people we talked to at the party said Bill's only regret is that it has no view but their previous three apartments had no view either. Bill, skinnier than ever if that is possible, was wearing a light grey suit in a sea of dark ones but perhaps it made him stand out more. Warren was as affable as ever. We have always clicked more with him than with the more snobbish Bill. Warren is up here (*from Florida*) for a month of refueling and may come up in the fall but otherwise I guess they have separated. I was very happy over Ken at the party for he was the most attractive person there. Warren and Bill, ill-favored by nature, don't assemble company that will give them much competition.

WEDNESDAY, MAY 8, 1968

To Lincoln Center to see the Royal Ballet. SYLVIA was so old-fashioned I couldn't keep my mind on it and tho the lead ballerina, Svetlana Beriosova, has a reputation, both Ken and I thought she was heavy as lead. If she got nine inches off the ground on her leaps she was doing well. A fairly nice abstract ballet followed and then Fonteyn and Nureyev in MARGUERITE AND ARMAND. They mimed nicely but I'm afraid this attempt to make a ballet out of Lady of the Camellias fails just as previous efforts have. The scene with the father just won't choreograph and since he can't sing his arguments as he does in TRAVIATA, he has to stand there and mime an argument, which struck me funny, tho the audience as a whole accepted it. We met Ken Weaver at intermission and he said, "Isn't it exciting?" I could only envy him if he really felt that way. I enjoyed seeing the two star personalities, whose curtain calls are real milking jobs, but the dance at no time excited me. I look forward to the Graham company, to the Joffrey, to the Harkness and others whose subject matter is adult. With this company I almost always feel I've wandered into story-telling hour for the kiddies.

THURSDAY, MAY 9, 1968

At noon the student rabble-rouser Mark Rudd spoke to the strike meeting in Russell Hall Court. Those meetings have been very poorly attended and while this drew more, one could see the strike movement was petering out. Of those who were there briefly, many were people like me who were merely curious about the young man. As a matter of fact he didn't come across like a firebrand but spoke quite well and seemed not altogether without a sense of humor. We spent the evening reading. I devoted my attention to COCKERELL, which I am reading only because the man kept a diary for 77 years. He didn't keep it well, tho, wasting time and precious space on weather and a list of the people he'd written to that day. He also kept it in a printed diary, which kept him from expanding when the occasion might have called for it.

FRIDAY, MAY 10, 1968

In the evening I finished COCKERELL and was impressed at the number of friends he had and the durability of his friendships. I'm afraid I have little talent for friendship, tho I once thought I had. People must behave in a convenient way if I am to continue friendships with them. They must not make love to my lovers as George and Jim and Bob Lockwood did, they must not be too wildly extravagant and given to indebtedness as Bob and Jerry were, they must not arrive unannounced at inconvenient times as Merle did, they must not be too temperamental and given to tantrums as Joe Heil was, etc., etc. In my youth I was ready to give and receive confidences but now I am ready for neither. I confine my intimate counsel to Ken and can think of nobody else with whom I would discuss my problems. Probably if I didn't have him I would rely much more on friends for just before I met him I was at my most outgoing. Ken, too, had many friends when he was young but he has, if anything, even more strictures than I have about what impositions are allowed friends.

MONDAY, MAY 13, 1968

John S. called. The conversation was as hilarious as ever and when he uses strong language he says, "Oh, David told me I must never use such words with you and Ken." "We've heard them before," I said. "That's what I told David. After all, you're not the two little match girls." John could not explain the references to Monopoly and Atlantic City in BOYS IN THE BAND and indeed asked me if I could explain the term "closet queen", which was new to him and would have been new to me but for that article in the Columbia Spectator. I'm glad to find others besides me are falling behind on the jargon. Said he, "I thought they did it in a closet and that seemed so confining."

SATURDAY, MAY 18, 1968

As we took our nap Alice called and arranged to meet us at Union Turnpike to get the bus for the Englanders'.We were the first to arrive, followed in time by the Kleins and a nice couple new to us, he a lawyer much involved in civil rights, and she an artist and author of a freezer cookbook. They, it turned out, had a son involved in the Columbia strike and they were behind him almost every foot of the way. The Kleins told of taking LSD while on a trip to Japan with Zen author Alan Watts. They claimed mind-expanding experiences but as described they sounded very much like any dream and a lot less interesting than many I have without drugs.

WEDNESDAY, MAY 22, 1968

Home to change our clothes before going on to Bill Washburn's. It was a perfectly marvelous party. Since everybody was gay the talk turned much on BOYS IN THE BAND and I got an interesting new viewpoint from, ironically, an interior decorator named Matthew something. He won't go see it because he wishes these things weren't so much in the open now. He fears that the general public will suspect all men who live together or like each other's company tho he didn't disagree when we said that the line in the play which says when men live together after the age of thirty they're lovers, not room-mates, is true. Women can live together without causing talk but men can't and in most cases I imagine the talk is justified. Heterosexual men who aren't married generally live alone. Maybe he would like a little mystery, a little sense of forbidden fruit, put back into the gay life to lend it pungency, tho he didn't express it that way. After dinner there was much talk of opera and all in all I thought that if gay parties were always like this how nice it would be. Mat and his lover were both attractive, especially the older lover Bruce (probably my age) but there was no flirtation or silliness because the three couples are all so long-established with each other. We didn't leave till one o'clock and I was dehydrated by gin. Knew I had a sleepless nite ahead.

THURSDAY, MAY 23, 1968

As we had our coffee Ken and I exchanged tid-bits from conversations the other hadn't heard. We also reminded each other of things we both had heard such as somebody's joke about the graffiti-of-the-week. Someone had written on a washroom wall, "I'm 9½ inches" and below this there was a scribbled reply "That's all right, but how long is your cock?"

FRIDAY, MAY 31, 1968

We met Peggy at the door and headed down for our session of bridge. Peg had brought a chocolate cake and, knowing I don't like chocolate, a banana cake for me. I thought it a shame to cut into two cakes and said I didn't mind chocolate all that much but it was the most chocolate cake I ever had in my life and Pat finally had to stop eating it, saying "It's so rich it gives me a headache".

Ken later said it almost turned his stomach and I seemed to suffer less from it than anybody.

SUNDAY, JUNE 2, 1968

Our corner news dealer lacked two sections of the Times so I walked to Lenox Avenue, enjoying the sumptuous greenery of the park, refreshed by further rains in the night. Ken and I were terribly congenial all day and I thought that really we are most of the time. In public we are sometimes contentious as he distorts facts and I correct him but at home we can be as gentle as doves with each other. Today we were in agreement about absolutely everything. Lavinius is so placid about the giant firecrackers constantly exploding on 108th St. that we speculate as to whether he is growing deaf or just sophisticated.

MONDAY, JUNE 3, 1968

Browsing in early diary I was startled to come on passages in which I showed self-consciousness about my looks and I thought how things have changed for I am now almost vain about my looks and certainly don't lack confidence. But in truth I still don't think I was very good-looking in my early twenties and I think the lack of confidence was justified then. In my late twenties, however, my face and figure came into their own and I stopped feeling apologetic. Then friends began to lose their petals and I luckily remained on a sort of plateau which left me feeling positively cocky. Also, the world around me began to get much uglier and that helped me shine. I can't quite explain how it could be that people as a whole got uglier but they have--permissiveness about sloppy clothes explains only a part of it, permissiveness toward being almost deliberately ugly explains more for people don't seem to care as much as they used to if they're too fat, too thin, or walk and talk badly. Actors aren't even attractive as they used to be--there was an article to that effect in the Times a week ago which contrasted the stars of the era when beauty was one of the requisites for the actor and the stars of today, called "the uglies". The theory is that the uglies are more "real" than the beautiful, which I beg leave to doubt. At any rate, no young person would need to worry as I did if he is not beautiful or handsome. Only a few of us old codgers would even notice.

TUESDAY, JUNE 4, 1968

We napped briefly after supper and had a terribly logy feeling when we set out for the Martha Graham performance. We were scarcely in our seats when we saw Dave and John coming up the stairs. We spent intermissions with them and met two of their friends who were there. One inclined to be flirtatious when we were talking alone but cooled it when my repeated references to Ken made the closeness of the relationship plain. He was a bald young man but pleasant. The audience was as usual for Martha Graham, marvelous, the absolutely best audience in New York--all ages, all variations of sexes, but united in enthusiasm. And rightly so, for the program was superb. Afterward, in a daze, we went to the Continental Bar of the Barbizon-Plaza hotel and had drinks. I talked mostly to John and Earl, who were playing the game of "With whom do you identify in THE BOYS IN THE BAND?" John identified with the bitchy host, Earl with the colorless guest Donald (we all said "But he hardly exists as a character!") and I identified sometimes with the jealous teacher, sometimes with his boy friend. Ken and Dave were having their own conversation and when Ken reported on it later I was shocked for David had gone into his early love life quite specifically. I think of him as more prudish than I am and it seems so out of character for him to talk about sexual affairs, tho it rather amuses me that he did. He told of one lover who now has three children but has an arrangement with his wife which permits him to have one nite out a week to have sex with men. I remember Dick Bennett told me he felt sure he could be happily married if only he could have sex with a man about every two weeks. I find bisexuality very hard to understand.

THURSDAY, JUNE 6, 1968
    Ken wanted to watch the television about the bringing of Robert Kennedy's body to New York so I retired to the bedroom to finish another New Yorker. He stayed up last nite till after one watching the news special which repeated things we had already seen three, four, and five times. I had heard the President address the nation over and over, had seen the pandemonium following the shooting numerous times, and had heard major figures comment on the tragedy until I could repeat what they said word for word so I went to bed. I am sorry he was killed, tho he never interested me, but I am not going to wallow in his funeral as we did over his brother's. The shooting is a dreadful thing but whether Kennedy is a real loss politically I don't know. Like his brother he has not been notable for introducing any legislation and indeed has been campaigning around the country so much that I doubt he even has a very good attendance record in the Senate. He may have been for the right

things but neither Kennedy was very good at actually getting things done. John had a certain urbane style but Robert didn't even have that. But my grudge is not against the Kennedys per se--I momentarily hate whoever is getting the excessively heavy treatment in the news because it all grows so boring.

THURSDAY, JUNE 27, 1968
  Florence called to wish us goodbye and joined the legion of people who cannot tell us apart on the phone. She was talking to Ken and was certain she was talking to me. Mother also called and one of her first questions was "What part of Spain is Valeria in?" She didn't connect it with the place we went last year.

SUNDAY, JUNE 30, 1968
  Ken and I signed up for weekly golf and swimming tickets right after breakfast and headed for the golf course. We played our first nine holes with an old jewish lady who was a duffer but pleasant. She grew exhausted so dropped out when we went round again. That practice isn't everything was shown when we did worse the second time around. We were soaked with perspiration and the showers felt great but we had a hard time getting our pores to close, even with cold water. I washed the sweaty clothes then we had a drink before the marvelous dinner of chicken divan. The afternoon we spent at the pool but well out of the sun, of which we had had enuf on the golf course. As I did last year, I didn't go in till the last half hour, by which time the pool was deserted enuf to let me get in many undisturbed laps. The young lifeguard, who was the only easy-on-the-eyes male last year, is still here, looking nice with longer hair. When one has had an afternoon of fat-pocketed, varicose-veined female legs, it is nice to see the women come to dinner in crisp summer dresses.

TUESDAY, JULY 2, 1968
  First on the golf course again and with Stella and Andy once more. They settled for nine when they saw the wait to tee off a second time but we had time to spare so we waited and went round with a man named Marty. We were behind some women who had never heard of the 7 stroke limit and putted from the middle of the fairway up the hill but I could have stood this better if they had moved a little faster in taking their 64 strokes and had shown a little joy in the game but they were glum and persistent. We didn't stay so long at the pool today. I was studying Portuguese when Frances picked up my Spanish phrase book and

began to drill me. I found I knew more than I thought but
she came to the section on a visit to the doctor's and lit
on the sentence for "Take off your clothes", "Lie down",
etc. and she and Marie, a common man-hungry baggage, got
quite vulgar about them and wouldn't drop the joke. I went
in the pool early then we left an hour before we usually
do and rested in our rooms , where it is pleasanter anyway.
I got a bit depressed at the difficulty of being minority
members surrounded by people whose lifestyle is necessarily
different from one's own. I suppose negroes who were too
long in the company of whites would feel the same weariness
eventually and long to relax among their own. Yet when we
once told of the golfing and swimming we planned to do up
here someone of our own set said, "My God, it sounds like
summer camp", so we don't entirely fit there either. The
evening altered my outlook for the first winner of the
bingo this year was not me but Ken. He forgot we were going
on to Portugal and picked a bulky ceramic pigeon-bank as
his prize. After the bingo prizes were exhausted we were
joined by Betty II (the place is full of Bettys) and her
very ladylike friend Mildred for bridge. Ken and I had phenomenal cards and seldom gave each other less than a jump
raise. I also played rather better than I usually do. They
took the taste of those forever talking about the shortage
of men out of my mouth. I really don't think men are worth
so much fuss and I've always hated women who talk about the
lack of available men as Marie has done from the first day.
It makes me self-conscious, of course, but I don't think it
would make much difference to Marie how many men or what
kind were here.

WEDNESDAY, JULY 3, 1968
    The greyness of the day somewhat changed our routine.
We still played eighteen holes of golf in the morning but
as the cloudy skies kept it cooler, Stella and Andy stayed
with us for the two rounds. The bugs were terrible and I
killed three mosquitoes on myself while dressing the ball
to tee off the first hole. Despite all our good resolutions
to be quiet at table, we laughed till we hurt, set off by
Gertrude's announcement that she had received a letter from
her table companions of last week. I feel convinced we'll
never be allowed back but the hilarity tonite was almost
worth the blacklisting. Ken and I played gin in the main
lobby while waiting for the amateur talent show to start.
They use the game room as a dressing room so we knew we
couldn't go over there. Betty I and a woman we didn't know
kibitzed, adding nothing whatever to the fun. The woman
said she was very good at spotting the bachelors but she

hadn't supposed we were bachelors. Ken and I had some private amusement later over our apparently married look. Marie and Frances were sitting right by the entrance door saving two seats for us and we couldn't ignore their proprietariness. The talent show was very good, not to be compared to last year's fiasco. Two couples who have a dance studio did very good ballroom dancing. Marie said, "Don't you fellows dance?" and we declined as we had when Mary, at the table, said we had to dance with all the girls at the table on Friday nite. The pressure is mounting and is very tiresome. Gertrude told me tonite at the table that I was "gorgeous" then insisted upon it and soon all were calling attention to my blushes. I am beginning to get more than enuf of this atmosphere and to look forward to Europe. I could never be a resort or cruise person for I don't truly like the kind of person who likes that and I quickly get sated with the good aspects of it.

TUESDAY, JULY 9, 1968
    The leg room on our plane was the best I ever had, the meal was the worst ever aloft. But we got there not terribly late and passed quickly thru customs. We taxied to the Metropole and found Lisbon the only city we know of in the world where the drive from airport to city center is really lovely. Our room, filled with charming old-fashioned furniture, has a balcony looking right out on the Rossio. We were a bit confused by money at first but nobody gypped us outrageously and by night, with practice in checking store window prices against our conversion table, we were getting accustomed to it. I loved Lisbon instantly, for its urban beauty and its human beauty. The Portuguese are a handsome people, male and female, young and middle-aged. Much lighter than one supposes and with a complexion thru which roses peek. After we settled in we had a good long intense nap to make up for the sleep lost in flight. I had planned that from the beginning of itinerary-making and will always do it again. When we got up we did some wandering, learned about tours and about dry-cleaning. We went to a cafe on Avenida Libertade and sat a long time in a state of great euphoria. I became a complete vegetable but Ken eventually got restless and eager to get back to the hotel to eat. I thought we might as well get in training for Spain and eat as late as possible, tho the hotel dining room is open from 7-9. Ken shied away from tonite's specialty, veal tongue, and they offered steak and chips for him but I had the tongue and enjoyed it thoroly. After we topped the meal with fruit we went to Avenida Libertade again, buying some postcards on the way, and I wrote some cards

while we sat on a bench. Two good-looking, well-dressed men went by and were obviously taken with one or both of us (I was looking my absolute best because of my general euphoria) and back-tracked to take the bench next to us. I was just as interested in the tall one as he was in me but in fairly short order I guess they came to the same conclusion I did, that nothing could be done under the circumstances, and off they went with backward looks. Ken got eager to return to the hotel room so I let him go and I stayed. Further interest was shown in me but while it's flattering, it's also frustrating. Wouldn't make any difference if I were alone for the battery of concierges would prevent one from taking even the most presentable back to the room. Ken had done a laundry but had not had his bath when I got there. When he finished, he drew a bath for me. Vacation now seems to have really started and my love affair with Europe is at high peak. How have I put off Portugal so long? It's a fabulous country.

THURSDAY, JULY 11, 1968

Up in good time and to Praca da Restauradores to join our tour bus for the day's trip to Queluz-Mafra-Sintra-Estoril. Queluz looked seedy and quite unimpressive on the outside but the rooms and the gardens were lovely. Ken didn't take to Sintra but I found many rooms fascinating. The trouble was that by that time hardly anybody but us was listening to the guide. His English was harder to follow than that of yesterday's guide and we had so many people who chattered instead of listening. This time it was not the Americans, who were few, but Germans, Brazilians, etc. The Brazilian couple was totally obnoxious in the gorgeous restaurant at Ericeiro. Scarcely a course was served that either the husband or wife didn't wave away or send back. I entered without much appetite but the room was so lovely with its tiles and its bouquets of flowers and the many serving men were so universally attractive that I downed my dinner very well. Apparently women are not used as waitresses here in Portugal but as long as the men and boys are so attractive and so well-trained I won't complain. The one real disappointment was Estoril, which had none of the glamor I expected and was so glaring with hot sun that our flesh crawled in revulsion. I had thought we could spend a relaxed Sunday at Estoril and Cascais going thru shops and watching lovely people on the beach but there _were_ no lovely people on the beach and I couldn't stand unshaded in that sun to watch them if there were. By mutual and immediate agreement our plans were cancelled. We were very tired when we got back and wondered how young or old survive the

coach tours of Europe which keep you going day after day.
They're a good way to see things on occasion but I do hate
them. There's no time to linger over anything, no real time
for photography, not enuf time to pick out postcards, and
the other people can be very nerve-wracking with their
chatter. We both have misgivings about our three-day tour
out of Madrid but I guess we'll survive. We forced down
our dinner then went out to people-watch. I decided to go
home with Ken tonite as nothing of promise had passed our
bench. Suddenly I became aware that we were being cruised
by a handsome, well-dressed young man. I was rather startled as he kept stopping every time we looked in a store
window, etc. for I couldn't figure out what he thought the
three of us could do tho I know some couples pick people
up and share them. Eventually he turned back without Ken
ever having been aware of him.

FRIDAY, JULY 12, 1968
   Up late after intolerably boring dreams. Off on foot
to the Alfama quarter, taking the little guide pamphlet
Alice gave us. We decided to have our nap right after
lunch and we slept solidly, drugged by food. When we got
up we went to pick up our dry-cleaning. In the store was a
striking mature woman, a radiantly beautiful boy about
twelve, and a ravishingly handsome man in his late twenties
and I feasted my eyes on all of them. I have always supposed the Italians were the handsomest people in Europe
but I don't remember being so consistently attracted by
one individual after another the way I am here. Aside from
the fact that they aren't super large in height or super-
broad in beam and thigh, like so many strains of Americans,
their formality of dress helps them look attractive. The
drawback about a melting pot is that you may cross-breed
the worst features of various national types. Here there
is great consistency of fine complexion, lovely teeth,
soft clean hair, moderate build, etc. We walked out to the
Ritz to have a drink in the bar. Nothing but Americans
there and they bored hell out of me with what I could over-
hear of their conversation. "Wasn't it a mess?" "I paid___"
"I bought___" etc.

SUNDAY, JULY 14, 1968
   At Alcobaca we had fun in the refectory when the guide
showed us a narrow door thru which the monks must be able
to come or not be allowed to eat. From a distance I would
have said I couldn't make it but standing next to it I
found I could, tho many in the party were too fat. Lots of
people were in the water and on the beach at Nazaré but

the cabanas shut them from view so I saw only a few cute
little figures on display. After lunch we went on to Fatima, which of course set my teeth on edge with anti-Catholicism. The little shrine on the spot where the Virgin
chose to celebrate the year of my birth by appearing to
the three children had in front of it two stinking piles
of candles which were absurdly long and melted in all directions in an unsightly mess. The wax drippings appeared
to be collected under the grill and are no doubt re-used.
The church is rather simple and not unattractive but as
the priest went thru the last mumbo-jumbo of a mass I kept
looking for voodoo. On the sides people were confessing
and I wondered what such religious people would have to
confess. What would I have confessed--that I have lusted
after 5000 young Portuguese men in a week and am totally
unrepentant and still would be even if I had acted upon my
lust? I'd like to shake the priests up by confessing that
the sight of a whole market of stalls selling religious
articles turns my stomach. The funny thing is that I am not
unduly skeptical about the fact that the children had a
vision but hate the way it has been exploited and cannot
help wondering why it is never Christ who appears but always his mother, for whom the Bible claims no special powers. I was glad to get away from there and on to Batalha,
a truly lovely monastery where I was surprised to see the
tomb of Prince Henry the Navigator. The long hot tedious
ride back to Lisbon was broken by a stop for tea. I began
to tire of the Portuguese landscape, which had pleased me
on the way. I'm never long in the country before I'm anxious for city life again. Only a waiter at the tea stop
and a bather or two at Nazaré had been easy on the eyes all
day. Everybody else was burned and aged by the sun and hard
work. Everybody was working today, Sunday or no, at threshing, laundry, tilling of the fields, baling straw or whatnot. Because various people had not got back to the bus
when told, we got back to Lisbon late and just made it to
the dining room. After our last meal at the hotel, a lovely
Tournedos Rossini, we paid our bill. For six nights' hotel,
fresh flowers in our room at all times and ten or twelve
towels of all sizes in the bathroom, breakfast and dinner
every day, wine, service, and taxes, it cost us less than
$45 apiece. It's been a wonderful stay and I hate to leave
tho at the same time I don't quite know what I'd do if I
stayed (which means it's time to move on). We didn't go
out tonite but instead did our packing and our reckoning
of money, which seems to be holding up nicely.

MONDAY, JULY 15, 1968

I put my Portuguese phrase book away and got out my Spanish. I have only one complaint and that is on the pronunciation. They didn't give the proper s sound, at least not for Lisbon. It may be regional, like Southern dialect, but in Lisbon they don't use a simple s such as the book gave but pronounce "dois" as "doiszh" and say "Liszhboah", "Ineszh de Castro", "Vaszhco da Gama", etc. Later in the day I fancied I heard traces of this kind of s in Madrid, tho less pronounced. On the plane to Madrid with us were the people we overheard complaining in the bar at the Ritz. They were still at it today, sitting in the Madrid airport bus loudly saying that our perfectly smooth landing was the worst landing they'd ever had and booing the pilot when he came off. We taxied to the hotel, which proved to be very nice and very central. Went to the Prado Museum. I cannot say that I took to it any more this time than ever. The Goya drawings were good but the amateurish way he renders clothes puts me off the portraits. I liked the Moros but somehow wasn't in the mood for the ill-lit museum. We went to a cafe at the juncture of Gran Via and Alcala and were forced to the conclusion that our feast for the eyes is over. One or the other of us kept saying, "The people certainly aren't beautiful". Most are far more coarse-grained than the Portuguese and the sleek are very slicked down whereas the Portuguese seemed to have clean, unoiled hair and very naturally glowing skin. We also noticed that long hair and mod clothes are common here whereas they were not in Portugal.

TUESDAY, JULY 16, 1968

Ken was hit by Madrid stomach this morning but it didn't get me till later in the day. We went to the Royal Palace and signed up for the complete tour. They've opened many more sections of the palace to the public since I was here and the whole tour is rather too much. They warned us that tho we would have English-speaking guides for the first two hours, the last half hour would be only in Spanish. In our groups we had a large number of very upper-class Japanese ladies who were accompanied by a male guide who repeated as much as he could remember of what the Spanish guide said. This was usually about half of what she said but what fascinated me was the words he carried over intact from English, such as "green". Because our complete ticket entitled us to see the private apartments of the last royal family (which I would advise anybody to skip) our party got reduced to six. When the Spanish man took over for the tapestry collection and the religious objects

he did very well with gestures and by speaking slowly. I
understood far more than I expected to but Ken as usual
wandered away and didn't give the man a chance and seemed a
bit impatient if I passed any information on. People who
won't pay attention if the guide speaks another language
miss so much for a well-aimed finger can call attention to
some marvelous things. The guide told us we could use our
tickets for the armory, library, and pharmacy "esta tarde,
manana, la proxima semana" or any time we wished so I suggested
to Ken we take advantage of postponing it. I was
footsore, headsore, eyesore, dry as a bone, and Ken had the
additional problem of not having smoked for almost three
hours. We went over to the Plaza Oriente and he lit up in
the nice cool shade. I studied the map and found a short
cut back tothe hotel which worked beautifully. I no sooner
got there than I was hit by the runs. I didn't quite make
it so had to wash underwear.

FRIDAY, JULY 19, 1968
      Taxied the short distance to ATESA, where we found
our whole tour group was to be just nine people. The first
crushing disappointment was the girl guide who was to be
with us for three days. Her English was inadequate, especially
when combined with a small, piping voice projection
and a suggestion that this might be her first trip. As tho
she weren't hard enuf to follow, the three Dutch passengers
(an arrogant priest and two companions) seemed determined
to talk whenever she did and in loud voices. Fortunately it
turned out that we are to have local guides at the various
sights and at both Escorial and Segovia they were excellent.
Our second disappointment came at La Granja, where the palace
turned out to be closed because it had not been put to
rights after special ceremonies for yesterday's holiday (*a
celebration of the coming to power of the dictator Francisco
Franco, I believe*). TV cables were all over the gardens,
which we <u>could</u> see. Because La Granja was reduced to gardens,
we got to Segovia early and met our guide at the Alcazar.
For reasons that are totally incomprehensible to
me now I didn't go in before and I can only say I was out
of my mind. I was fascinated by the room where Isabella
was crowned, by the chapel where Philip II married his
fourth wife and by the other rooms so well described by our
guide. He took us to the cathedral, which I love, and from
there to the hotel. Ken and I took a nap then a paseo thru
the nice busy street to the Roman aquaduct, which looked
marvelous in the twilight. As the dining room didn't open
till 9:30 we talked to the two teaching couples who are our
traveling companions. We had earlier discovered how nice

they were and we joined them at table. The waiter, in
tails, was one of the handsomest men God ever created, and
all by himself helped balance the score with Portugal. I
got too involved in table conversation to pay him the attention he deserved but when I did I was often flattered
to find his eye as full on me as mine on him. He had gobs
of charm and no arrogance whatever and I'd love to find him
in my Christmas stocking. I finally had the suckling pig,
served without the head since I was the only one having it.
It has as little meat on it as I expected but was tasty and
after all I had had was sufficient. Suddenly the lovely
waiter passed out Segovia matches and when I was the first
to exclaim at how beautiful they were he looked pleased as
a boy. After dinner we went out for a paseo but the streets
were relatively deserted by then, Segovians not keeping the
late hours that Madrilenos do.

SUNDAY, JULY 21, 1968
    Our guide Fred rejoined us at ten and we had our tour
of Toledo. Fred gave us a wonderful talk on THE BURIAL OF
THE COUNT OF ORGAZ, which I always thought an impossibly
busy picture before. He was also wonderful in the cathedral, where I could have sat for hours having him point out
the beauties of the choir, the organs, the altar, etc. He
led us back to the hotel for lunch and tour parties poured
in, one led by a grotesque Spanish aunty. In the afternoon
we rode back to Madrid, thru uninteresting landscape. When
we went up in the elevator and gave our floor in English
the boy, without freshness, asked if I knew how to count
in Spanish so I had to accept the challenge and give him
our room number in his language, which seemed to please
him. I certainly don't find the Spanish dour.

MONDAY, JULY 22, 1968
    The flight to Seville was very smooth and I noted one
Madrid suburb in which you could see one pale blue swimming
pool after another. When we got to Seville, about which
Madrilenos had said "Mucho calor", we said, "Why, it's no
hotter than Madrid" but we learned better later. We set out
to see the cathedral, found it closed for siesta, and decided that when in Seville one should do as the Sevillians
do. Our gorgeous big room is air-conditioned so we slept
like logs. Up at four and over to the cathedral, remarkable
mostly for its size, its choir screens, and its retable.
The Alcazar far surpassed my expectations. It was cool in
there (comparatively) and the gardens with their running
water were heavenly.

54   A GAY DIARY
WEDNESDAY, JULY 24, 1968
         When we got to Algeciras it proved to be a larger,
noisier, more confusing place than I had expected. Ken began to lament that he had ever suggested the Tangier trip,
feeling the confusion and heat made it not worthwhile. I
said it was just about an hour of confusion and would turn
out all right. The boat ride was nice and when we got to
Tangier and were threatened with more confusion we were
approached by hotel guides who directed us to the one for
Hotel Rif. He got us registered and signed us up for a tour
tomorrow. Our nice room was heavenly cool and has a good
view of the street and (at a distance) the beach. The arab
costumes lend color. When we went out somebody asked us if
we wanted to go to the Turkish baths and fondled us in a
way that made Ken think they were picking his pocket, made
me think they were trying to get us aroused. Then I admired
a kitten and the older boy grabbed it, thrust it at me, and
said, "It's mine. Just give me one dirhan for it." I asked
what I could possibly do with it and later I saw its owner
take it inside the café where it belonged. Ken was so upset
by all this street activity that he wanted to retreat to
the hotel, to my regret. Approached by two people, one
selling night club tours and the other shoeshines, Ken
wanted to retreat again. I didn't think the merchants were
unduly high pressure but they bothered Ken. I find them
part of the atmospheric charm and find, "No, thank you"
very easy to say.

THURSDAY, JULY 25, 1968
         At 9:30 to meet the guide for our tour. The moment I
saw that we were the only ones and that he had a car and
driver waiting for us, I knew that we had made our faux pas
for this tour. We had thought we were signing up for a
group thing and salt was rubbed in our wounds at every stop
as busses pulled up and disgorged their passengers. I decided, however, that since there was no getting out of it
I might as well enjoy it. We drove out to the remarkable
Cave of Hercules and eventually to the Casbah, where we
left the car and walked. We saw a private house, which was
sumptuous and in process of being cleaned, then a museum
on top of which was a restaurant where we had mint tea. The
guide had a lordly way of saying "Give a tip", to the man
who lighted the steps into the cave, a little girl in the
private house, etc. but we weren't prepared with small
coins for this largesse and got cleaned out. Children begged in the Casbah but otherwise we weren't bothered. When
we got back to the hotel at noon the moment of reckoning
came. Ken, in his naivete, thought it might cost us $10 but

I was prepared for $10 apiece and thought we were lucky to
get out of it for $18. We decided to do a turn down the
beach walk as the beach was more crowded at noon than afternoon. Some of the boys are passably attractive but Arabs
don't do for me what Spanish and Portuguese do. They wear
bathing suits with loose (or no) support and their genitals
make a frank bunch that doesn't look at all lewd since that
is how men are built.

MONDAY, JULY 29, 1968
     On the plane with us were a lot of people who had been
on an American Express tour together and I could barely
stand them thru   seven hours of the flight, let alone however many days they had been together. Our seatmate was a
woman who had been with them and said never again a tour.
39 out of 40 on the trip (and the driver and the guide)had
come down with dysentery in Morocco and several were still
suffering from it. Kennedy Airport surprised us with a new
customs system (they inspected a lot of the little bags
and handbags and bypassed the big luggage) and a new baggage system (a moving belt such as other airports have long
had) and as a result we got thru without any impatience or
frayed tempers. The house, unfortunately, was filthy and
there were rings on top of the credenza, which distressed
me, but Lavinius was fine. The girls left a note saying
looking after him had been a pleasure, that he was the most
affectionate cat either one had ever known and that if he
ever needed a place to stay they would be glad to take him
in. Perhaps embarrassed by these flattering comments, Lavinius had chewed the bottom of the note to bits. We changed
into work clothes and before we unpacked we cleaned. I took
the living room, Ken the bath and kitchen. All of a sudden
my energy evaporated and I realized I had had a 21 hour day
so we went to bed and Lavinius curled up beside me, happy
as a lark and singing like one.

WEDNESDAY, JULY 31, 1968
     One of Ken's favorite anecdotes of the trip is one I
don't think I even recorded herein. We were sitting at the
Seville airport writing postcards when an old lady next to
Ken leaned over and said, "Are you travelling with your
son? I just thought that might be a good idea for my husband. I can't get him to come with me." This is a story
I'll leave it to Ken to tell as it wouldn't sound good coming from me but he really tells it quite gleefully.

WEDNESDAY, AUGUST 7, 1968
     We got our second Christmas invitation today, from

Florence. Neither of us would dream of leaving New York at Christmas but will counter with an invitation to her, which she is most unlikely to accept. Suddenly we heard mass screaming on 108th St. and thought there was another fight, there having been a couple lately among the kids. Looking out, we saw them pointing up to our building and when we thrust our heads out the window, we saw smoke and flame coming from OUR floor. I rushed to the door and found the halls also filled with smoke and in the elevator, with the alarm bell pushed and the elevator going nowhere, was the man at the end of the hall who drinks and that little boy who lives there, both standing stunned. I rushed to call the fire department but as I got them I heard the trucks coming and they told me they knew about it. It was quite a while before the flames and smoke subsided and the apartment must have been a mess. Then the firemen started heaving the burned furniture out the window, doing our hedges no good at all. I feel sorry for the woman who has that apartment as her husband died soon after she moved in and she has had a succession of roomers (which she's not supposed to have) to keep her head above water and more than one has been a drinker. We were glad we had fire insurance but still didn't relish the thought of putting Lavinius in his carrier, grabbing my diaries, and taking to the streets. Lavinius worried me by sniffing at the door for I was afraid his little lungs would fill too easily with smoke but he came away when ordered.

MONDAY, AUGUST 12, 1968
   After our naps Ken and I exchanged books, he reading THE GENTLE BONAPARTE and I, NICHOLAS AND ALEXANDRA, but he finished the whole book this evening and I got only 62 pages read. I meant to skip as he did but found most of it too interesting and besides I had a long hilarious call from John S., which shoots a hole in any evening. He had me rolling on the bed tonite with his quotes from THE BOYS IN THE BAND, which he has seen three times. He says the audiences are now heterosexual, all the gay boys having seen it way back there.

SATURDAY, AUGUST 17, 1968
   The morning slipped away from us as we talked about our various favorite spots and happy times on our travels. When we went out to the cleaners and the liquor store we fell out. I took my new pants to be cuffed and before I could ask the tailor to use the excess material to make belt loops, Ken jumped in and asked, as tho I were either shy or incompetent. I was outraged, as there is nothing I

A GAY DIARY

hate like not being in charge of my own life, but I swallowed my anger, which was out of all proportion to the provocation. In the liquor store Ken priced Smirnoff's vodka and the man said, "But I have a cheaper one." "No,no, I want the best," Ken said. "Why, no, you don't either," I said aghast. "You can't drink that cheap stuff,' he insisted and I withdrew because the sudden flaring difference of opinion was embarrassing both me and the proprietor but when we got outside I flared. I hate this silly pride that makes Ken grovel before people of money and I pointed out that we served Macy liquor to all our best friends and it was ridiculous to put on airs suddenly for Warren and Bill, who weren't above boasting that their drinks were made with an aperitif "just like Dubonnet but a fraction of the price". He said he'd pay the difference, knowing full well I wouldn't subject him to this traumatic experience. I fumed all afternoon about it while Ken, who had gotten his way, was conciliatory. The last has not been heard of it, however. If he were consistent in elegance, dressing elegantly and keeping an elegant house, I could respect this nonsense about the liquor. But for a person who keeps out-of-fashion clothes to get "one more wear out of them", who resists all nagging about changing socks and underwear more often, not to mention nagging about not constantly calling attention to how wet his armpits are as tho a medal were being given for the most moisture, this sudden demand for the best liquor is farcical. I remember now we have had trouble before when he wanted to save good brand bottles and put the cheap stuff in it. On the one hand he claims the cheap stuff isn't fit to drink and on the other hand assumes people aren't going to be able to detect the difference. If there is anything I hate it's the gay type (Ken, Howard L., Gerry F.) who are always talking elegance and going around looking like bums. I'm no fashionplate either but neither have I ever uttered a word about elegance. All three of those fellows talked it all the time and saved their good clothes for "special occasions" which hardly ever came. Ken CAN look wonderful but I'm after him all the time to polish his shoes or wear a fresh shirt or take a bath and I get nowhere. No doubt he resents it as much as I resented his jumping into the conversation with the tailor. By the time we got up from our naps I, tho still very angry, decided to let him get away with all his conciliatory chit-chat and we had a pleasant enuf evening. Now if Ken kept a diary, I wonder what faults of mine would be irritating him equally? I finished NICHOLAS AND ALEXANDRA, very put out at both of them for being so stupid.

SUNDAY, AUGUST 18, 1968

Tho Ken definitely did not read my diary for yesterday and tho I said nothing to him of the irritation I expressed herein about his old shorts, he knocked on the wall before entering the living room and asked if I were ready for the fashion show. He then came in wearing the khaki shorts he'd long owned but wouldn't wear when I suggested a change. What was even more of a surprise was that without a further word from me, he threw out the old shorts tho he wondered if perhaps they shouldn't be offered to the Smithsonian. My relief was intense and Ken looked so much nicer in clean, pressed shorts. We then proceeded to have a very congenial day. When Warren and Bill got here, Ken's party manner bothered me as it so often does--the excessive ingenuousness which even the young today eschew and which 60-year-olds should certainly abandon, the repetition of worn anecdotes, the wildly excessive statements. I tried to stop some of the old anecdotes but said nothing about anything else because I had the bad example of Bill and Warren's picking at each other before me. I have to remember, anyway, that Ken's social style has always been far more of a success than mine, however much I may deplore it, so other people may actually like it. He does seem such a child at times but there's another side to his childlike view of life which I myself like so I guess if you like one side of the coin you have to take the other. Bill looked thinner than ever but was charming as usual while Warren concentrated on being sincere, something of the same combination Ken and I have. I don't suppose two people competing in the charm arena or two in the sincerity ring could make a go of living together.

MONDAY, AUGUST 26, 1968

We had the conference on list maintenance today and Forkner was satisfied with the progress report I gave, was reasonable in his expectations, and it all went off very well. Forkner has a sense of humor and it helps a lot. Frank, who really hasn't, got a bit stuffy with me over some of my remarks and I only realized later why they would be offensive to someone with such a sober outlook. He had offered me as potential employees his rejects from interviews with people who had answered his notice for "researchers". I said they weren't apt to view kindly a file clerk's job if they had come seeking a job with the prestigious title "researcher" and that anyway I had found that people who gravitated to such jobs often did so because they couldn't really do anything, such as type or file. I expressed satisfaction with the screening done by the

A GAY DIARY

Personnel Office, which he likes to circumvent. Forkner smiled as I said it and accepted my judgement. We had a visit from Judy Berry Griffin (*an employee in my office during the days when she was studying for her Master's degree, subsequently married to a graduate of Columbia Law School*) who brought her baby with her. She's just as sensible and charming as ever and is going back to teaching this year because she can't stand sitting around the house and has perfectly adequate care for her child. Her mother worked when she was young (tho her father was a doctor) but her mother-in-law thinks it's terrible. I'm all for it as I can't see how a woman with a brain can sit home either and I respect Judy for being a twentieth century girl. Her brother is apparently no longer barred from being a pilot in the United States for he's now chief pilot for a helicopter in San Francisco. (*When first demobilized after being a military pilot, he found American airlines did not hire even well-qualified blacks so he moved to Canada to pursue a flying career.*) So negroes do make some progress after all.

THURSDAY, AUGUST 29, 1968

Ken had no money to take in for the school at all so worked all day sorting the returned questionnaires. At first this seemed not to be much help for Ken doesn't much like decision-making even on the most minor level and would like someone else to confirm his decision or even make it for him so he asks me about almost every one until I go mad trying to do my work and still make all the decisions he should be making. I am a visually-oriented person and could make a very snap decision if I had the paper before me as he does but I don't take things in aurally so well and have to make a great effort to pay attention and get all the facts straight, while still trying to do my own work. I finally snapped and said that sorting should go "boom, boom, boom" without so much agonizing over every petty decision as to what category the change of address fell in--major, minor, zone change, or name change. Ken subsided without sulkiness and proved he could make decisions if forced to focus his perfectly good mind. I felt a little guilty about jumping on him but it is like wading thru huge snow drifts to try to make forward progress on my work and still have to consider every piece of paper that is before him.

FRIDAY, AUGUST 30, 1968

Ken decided on our way back from the bank that he didn't feel bad but also didn't feel well. He couldn't decide whether or not to go home so I decided for him and insisted on it. The quiet, lonely afternoon I had was a sample of what it will be when Ken retires. For all the irritations I feel with him from time to time, I miss him when he's gone. I've thought all along that we will be very tender with each other when we see no more of each other than most mates but I've been very lucky to have him working with me all these years.

SATURDAY, AUGUST 31, 1968
    Having seen that my lion-maned South African beauty was playing on the Stadium Court at Forest Hills, I suggested we go. Ken leapt at the idea and the impulsiveness of our decision was part of the pleasure, where we are accustomed to planning everything so long in advance. The turnout was poor, which was too bad because the tennis was superb. After broiling to a fine red in the sun I was shivering thru most of the Moore-Lutz match. We stayed to the bitter end. We staggered home and when we got there decided we didn't feel at all well. Our backs hurt after 7 and a half hours on the backless benches, but besides that we were sunstruck and as I wiped the supper dishes (both of us had felt hungry but turned out to have no appetite) I really felt ill and dizzy. We decided to go to bed tho it was only nine-thirty and there was much groaning as we eased our lame bodies into bed. Still, it was worth it for one could hardly see closer tennis matches than we saw and the beauty of Smith and Moore was a joy to the eyes.

TUESDAY, SEPTEMBER 17, 1968
    After supper I called the Alvin and found they had cheap tickets for the preview of THE GREAT WHITE HOPE so we went down and got some. It has been a long time since such an elaborate production has been given a straight play--60 actors in 120 roles, and it was quite a pleasant change from the two and three-character plays. The subject matter wasn't to Ken's taste--it was about how the white community ganged up to have the heavyweight boxing championship taken away from the first negro champion by a white hope and how the champion deteriorated under persecution. (*In 1942, the year I moved to New York, this champion, Jack Johnson, was making personal appearances in an amusement arcade on 42nd St., which I visited to see one of the other attractions, a flea circus.*) The central performance by James Earl Jones was a tour de force which got him a standing ovation from much of the audience, tho I found myself able to show my appreciation sitting down, the new vogue for standing ovations being much overdone.

SATURDAY, SEPTEMBER 28, 1968
    Downtown to see the new General Motors Building at
Grand Army Plaza. They have a nice plaza of their own with
a flower border and below will eventually be restaurants
and shops. The only car in their display room that interested me was a historical model in an excellent state of
preservation. In those days one sat high with plenty of
leg room and one's body expanded at the sight of it whereas it contracts uncomfortably at the sight of their current
models. The engine and the luggage have all the room and
the people squeeze in as best they can. They give about six
inches of leg room in the back and when one man moved the
front seat forward to give his friend more room in the back
it pushed him up against the steering wheel in a ridiculous
posture in which it would be impossible to drive safely. As
Americans get grossly larger, the spaces designed to contain them (apartments as well as cars) get smaller. We
walked down by a few airline offices to pick up brochures.
The upshot was that we discovered a better deal for Italy
at Alitalia than the Lufthansa trip we were sold on. We
napped then got ready to go to the opera. In front of us
was Ken W. with his snitty little friend that I can't stand,
a good-looking boy who spoils it all by acting like a bad-
tempered spoiled little girl, always tossing his head in
impatience and always seeming to be on the verge of stamp-
ing his feet. He must had staged a tantrum between the
third and fourth acts because Ken came back alone, looked
rather embarrassed that his friend never returned. ADRIANA
LECOUVREUR isn't a very good or exciting opera but it was-
n't that bad and was very well done. 20 minutes before curtain time Corelli decided he was unable to sing so Placido
Domingo, from City Opera, who was to make his debut in the
role next week, made an unscheduled and highly successful
debut tonite. He's heavy but moves well and uses his excellent voice superbly. Tebaldi was also in good voice and
gave a far more representative account of herself both vocally and dramatically than she did in last year's GIOCONDA.

TUESDAY, OCTOBER 8, 1968
    We left work a little early and it was good we did
because the Leonards arrived early and we were barely ready.
I hadn't made salad yet nor the dessert so I did it
while they had their drinks. I turned off the radio, which
Ken always has on, and proved my theory that if he'd leave
it off during parties he could follow the conversation in
the living room and not always be coming in to tell what I
just finished telling or to ask what I just asked. Later in
the evening he turned it on again and I didn't notice till

I realized that at the table we were all having to raise our voices to talk over the damned thing. I went out and turned it off again, whereupon we were all able to lower our decibel level and the feeling of irritation that comes with a raised voice disappeared. They have located a house which they intend to buy, not far from Albany, but they are now putting off leaving till March.

MONDAY, OCTOBER 14, 1968

After supper we went downtown to see two of the Albee short plays which are playing in repertory on Broadway. THE DEATH OF BESSIE SMITH has its awkwardnesses but shows a mastery of the stage and Rosemary Murphy played the hysterical central character very well. AMERICAN DREAM, however, was well-nigh perfect in both writing and playing. How I envied Albee's accomplishment. Ken was a bit disturbed by the surrealistic elements, but of course I lap these up and I went home in a glow. I thought some today of a rather pathetic moment yesterday when Mother and I went thru our age-old routine, she trying to get me to say I loved her and I evading with all the devices I have perfected over about forty years. She still, as she always did, says, "Donnie, I love you" then immediately follows this with "Do you love me?". Because I know the first statement is calculated to oblige an affirmative answer to the question I have been contrary about answering the way she wants me to answer since my early teens. If she would ever say she loves me and let it go at that, perhaps I could find it in my heart to be more responsive but I always know the direct question is coming immediately and I have never been able to convince myself that I could sincerely say "Yes". It's no trouble to tell Ken I love him (not that I often do in so many words) and no trouble for me to demonstrate it with spontaneous hugs and kisses, as I often do, but I haven't for a long time known if there was any love in me for Mother or not. I don't really think so. Unable to get me to be serious about it, she took another tack. "Well," she said, "it doesn't really matter if you love me or not, as long as you admire me, as long as you think I've done well in life." "Now what has that got to do with it?" I said, aghast, for while there may be some doubt as to whether I love her, there is no doubt at all that I distinctly do not admire her or think she has done well in life. I suppose the day may come when I'm sorry I didn't give her some satisfaction but she never gave her mother any either. I've always hated being badgered by her to say I loved her. I don't know what value a statement wrung out of a person can be. Well, on the other hand, I once wrung a reluctant statement out of Ken and I guess I did get some small satisfaction out of it. I have never asked in the twenty years since, however, contenting myself with what tokens of affection are freely offered and feeling no loss. What I really do hate, and always have, however, is that when I do give in and admit I love her even tho I have reservations in mind, it is never enough for her. She wants the statement expanded, repeated at intervals, and demonstrated and soon she is at it all over again. It would be tiresome, I'm sure, even if I really did care. She has always needed so much assurance that she is smart, clever, etc. and she asks for this kind of praise repeatedly tho nothing about her suggests a lack of self-confidence. In contrast, my exterior (and my personality) doesn't suggest such optimistic extraversion at all and yet I can survive on little or no praise, little or no love, and may even be embarrassed by both. If I don't think something I did was wise or good or clever, it would take a heap of outside praise to reverse my opinion and I doubt if it could be done.

THURSDAY, OCTOBER 17, 1968

I ate supper here at home and then set out for the New Haven train. (*As I had done some telephone solicitation for the Yale Alumni Fund, I had been invited to a weekend at Yale designed to encourage further such solicitation.*) Even on the express trains it's a two-hour trip and I don't see how my grandfather could commute every day as he did when he had his livery stable here in New York after his ship was rammed and sunk and he promised Nana he'd stay away from the sea. He may have been glad when his partner absconded and gave him an excuse to go back to sea as a captain on somebody else's boat. Four hours a day on trains is too much. When I got to New Haven I decided to walk from the station and see the new centre of town which has made New Haven so famous for urban renewal. It was wonderful but it was a bit of a relief to reach the green and see something that had not changed. I reported to the Campus Police at Phelps Gateway and a young man who wasn't even born when I was here last took me in a station wagon to Ezra Stiles, one of the new and excitingly modern colleges. A guard appeared and took me to my rooms, the guest suite of Ezra Stiles, consisting of a lovely living room, bedroom with twin beds, and kitchen and bath. Heard the sounds of music and student voices and must confess I melted with love of the place. Saw several students pass and it was clear that Columbia has no corner on the ugly and informally dressed, but, oh, what a difference in the beauty of this campus and that. What a supreme experience it must be to go thru here

as an undergrad (with sufficient money) but how glad I am
I went here at all.

FRIDAY, OCTOBER 18, 1968
      The dreaded day has been survived and without too
much social discomfort. Coffee was served outside Connecticut Hall and here an architecture grad, at least as lost
and lonely as I, joined me, asked if he might sit with me
and eventually asked if he might sit with me at lunch. The
morning session was very interesting and inspiring and I
was ready to forget God and country and live just for Yale.
The lunch was light enuf not to disturb my diet and conversation with Damico on the subject of architecture was very
pleasant. I found that my tablemate to the right was also
my room-mate for the night. A somewhat earlier vintage of
Drama School student than I am, he is now manager of the
Philadelphia Orchestra. Much of the afternoon was devoted
to the presentation of three students--one editor of the
Yale Daily News, one paid president of the political union,
one head of the student committee on teaching and all very,
very impressive. By and large I was also impressed with
the old grads, not as reactionary in their questioning of
the students as I had expected. The only one who was was
a Drama grad, of all things, really upset about Yale having
forsaken its former mission to educate the elite in favor
of coddling liberals. During the reception I had only one
weak drink. Damico came up to me and asked if he could sit
with me but we both got otherwise involved and it didn't
work out that way. It might have been better if it had for
the reactionary Drama student held forth on his views until
even the woman who had declared herself a staunch Republican thought he was seeing Communists where none existed. One
strong impression of the day is that there is less long
hair among the students here than at Columbia and suddenly
I identify with Columbia. It was a name much mentioned today as a horrible example and the cumulative effect of that
on me was to make me think the student riots there had been
very salubrious for the academic community from coast to
coast and for all the difficulties they present in fund-
raising, I'm glad they happened. This whole day till dinner was soul food and I knew again that Yale, New York,
Europe, and Ken are the great loves of my life.

SATURDAY, OCTOBER 19, 1968
      Another gray New Haven morning and I remembered how
depressing they could be, particularly if I had financial
worries about staying at Yale. Our meetings this morning
were in the Hall of Graduate Studies. It became clear that

except for medicine and law, we all have just as hard a time raising money as TC does. When I first applied at the Drama School boxoffice for my ticket there was none there but by the time I came back from the Art Gallery they had straightened this out. There was a good crowd but, oh, my God, the play was rotten. I rushed from the theatre back to Ezra Stiles for my bag and realized en route that New Haven, Yale, and my years there were real to me at last and that New Haven was much too small a city for me now and I couldn't wait to get out of it. I thought of calling Ken from the station but bussed home. As I went in I saw Lavinius on Ken's lap, where he never goes, but he flew off when he saw me. I reported to Ken as I unpacked. He told me he was glad I was home, having been even nervous here alone. He'd saved the papers for me so after diary I read.

TUESDAY, OCTOBER 22, 1968
    It feels very healthy to be rid of my sentimentality about Yale but what took place and what triggered it? Was it being at Yale under the lush circumstances I had always longed for when living there from hand to mouth? Was it encountering that reactionary boor of a Herschel Williams and realizing that under no circumstances of financial ease could I have been really upper class because in my very core I identify with the working classes and liberal causes (tho I did discover that liberals exist at Yale in considerable numbers)? Was it the discovery that Yale had no magic in fund-raising and therefore was a more ordinary institution than I supposed? Was it the wearing out of both Yale and New Haven after only a two-day acquaintance? This may be getting closer for I have had twenty-five years of a rich and varied city that makes almost any place in the provinces really intolerable.

TUESDAY, NOVEMBER 5, 1968
    Out early to vote. As usual, Ken and I just cancelled each other out as all my ranting about how the Republicans fought Medicare and all other social programs didn't convert Ken from his habitual Republicanism. Downtown to see THE FIREMAN'S BALL, a Czech movie. Most of the best gags had been mentioned in the reviews and there wasn't much beyond that to laugh at. The returns up to the time we went to bed were inconclusive as to the Presidency but a lot of the Senators who were supposed to be in tourble got in handily and I felt relieved to think that even if we must have that plastic mediocrity as President (*Richard Nixon*), he won't have Congressional backing to retract the social legislation the Democrats put thru.

FRIDAY, NOVEMBER 15, 1968

As we had supper the radio announced that Mark Rudd, leader of the student riots at Columbia, was being reclassified by his draft board. Ken said "Good!" and I blew up. Usually I keep my cool when people are being reactionary but I was simply infuriated that he should support these miserable old farts who are using their position on the draft boards to try to suppress dissenting young men. If the army is to be a punitive organization then they ought to send the prisoners to war and be done with it.

SATURDAY, NOVEMBER 16, 1968

Downtown to the Music Hall to see BULLITT, co-authored by Harry Kleiner, who at Yale fomented against writers who sold their souls to Hollywood. From the Music Hall to the Morgan Library. The Morgan had a wonderful exhibit of Persian miniatures and we reveled in the delicate brushwork, the lovely color, and the quite wonderful way they had of depicting animals and birds. Bought some sherry to take John. It was the usual rather drunk, chatty, pleasant evening with John and Dave. I discovered that Dave dislikes the company of women and hates mixed parties, which surprised me. I might have expected that from John but he doesn't mind women at all. Mild Dave, however, simply cannot stand them. David is more of the homosexual world currently than I supposed. He talks of being withdrawn from it but he knows more wild, practicing homosexuals than we do and goes to more of their parties than we do, however unsatisfactory he may find them. Never have we talked so unguardedly about it as we did tonite. When we were at the table I heard Ken say, "Sweetie, go get my pills." Astounded, I said, "Are you talking to me?" "Yes, darling, go get them and I'll give you a big smooch." So I did and he did, which floored me for I am scarcely used to being talked to by him in this way when we're alone, let alone in front of others. Drink usually brings out Ken's various resentments against me instead of his affection. After dinner there were the usual show records from John's huge collection and we stayed much too late.

TUESDAY, NOVEMBER 19, 1968

As I read the Strachey biography, I came on frequent references to this or that person who was "badly educated" which meant usually that they were poorly acquainted with English, French, and German literature and must be set on a course of education by Strachey. I have always been aware that I, too, am badly educated but I feel that it takes more than mere literature to constitute a good education.

There are other branches of knowledge. What is worst, I have never since my teens made any real effort to fill the gaps. I might better, for instance, forego this ridiculously long and detailed biography of a minor literary figure and get at some of the real classics, but of course I never will.

WEDNESDAY, NOVEMBER 20, 1968
   We spent the evening reading, I trying to finish STRACHEY by Friday since I got a card that one of my other reserve books is ready. The sex and love lives of the Bloomsbury set are so tangled and bizarre as to be funny. Despite the pages of other detail, it is seldom clear whether or not these affairs are consummated. The homosexual affairs sometimes seem to reach their sexual climax with a tweaking of ears.

FRIDAY, NOVEMBER 22, 1968
   Lavinius had one of those nites when he wakes up in the living room in the middle of the nite and feels abandoned. His banshee wails must have waked everybody in the house except Ken. I called to him not to be so silly and to come to bed. He kept on screaming for the longest time so that by the time he jumped on the bed I was thoroly provoked with him and pretended not to notice him. The first thing I knew he put his paw gently to my lips. I ignored him and he did it again, then the third time to my eyelids. Getting nowhere with that, he resorted to his old ace in the hole, standing on my bladder, which he knows will usually get me. I ignored that too and he began to howl in frustration. I gave him a bat on the backside and, contented that he had been noticed at last, he went and curled up at the foot of the bed.

SATURDAY, NOVEMBER 30, 1968
   Because Ken didn't set the alarm we got up late and I rushed to be dressed and downtown before the crowds made the stores uncomfortable. Ken was laggard so I left him. Today was my day for the Bloomingdale's area and I did very well there. Bloomingdale's, I'm glad to see, is hiring some very elegant negroes. The one who sold me the belt was surpassingly handsome and I wondered why, tho I find negroes of beauty so gratifying to the eye, I can never work up any sexuality over them. I dropped in at the Hallmark Gallery to see the collection of antique toys. It was well presented and interesting but stirred little nostalgia in me as I was not a great one for toys in my childhood. The few I had--toy airplane, train, chemical set, stereoptican--were

played with very little. Further down the street I went in KLM to look at this year's section of the Madurodam, better than those of previous years, I think, since it contained the cheese market at Alkmaar.

TUESDAY, DECEMBER 10, 1968

Somewhere Ken found an old address book with his list of 1946 Christmas cards. As he read off the names I found myself seething with anger and jealousy over some of the people who in those days tried (and succeeded) to cut in on Ken. Then a wave of shock came over me as I realized that I was in several cases expending this fury on people who have been dead for several years. Furthermore, I don't think there was a single name on that 1946 list except Mother and myself who still get cards. How glad I am that those fierce emotional days are behind me. I'm not one to run down middle age at all. Of course one has to have lived a little like that to make the peace of safe harbor appreciated.

SUNDAY, DECEMBER 15, 1968

I got out my boots for the first time this year when I went for the paper for a blizzard was in progress. Got two copies of the Times as Mimie, who has flu, had asked me to get hers. In the evening we had to sally forth to see THE HOUSE OF ATREUS as done by the Minnesota Theatre Company with men in masks playing the women's parts. HOUSE OF ATREUS drew a wonderful young crowd, long of hair and very mod of clothes. Now and then I wish I were young now but on second thought I know that if I were my money would not be going into these very expensive, high-fashion-of-the-season clothes for I would be saving it for my first trip abroad, or would be building up a library or collecting records or seeing every show in town--in other words devoting my money to the same things I did devote it to when young. There were some beautiful young men there, as well as some who merely hoped they were. The production was magnificent, one of the most impressive things I ever saw in the theatre. By use of boots, stilts, and padded costumes, everything was outsized. The vocal work was fine with a small quibble about the man who played Electra and used perhaps too much high voice. The chorus sometimes spoke, sometimes sang, but at all times their words were intelligible. The setting, too, was timeless and powerful, especially the great gate to Agamemnon's palace. When this play opened in Minneapolis and I read the reviews it was the first time I ever envied people who lived in the Middle West; now I don't have to envy them even that for it

has come to New York. Anyway, I don't think there would be
such wonderful young people anywhere but New York, at
least in such numbers, for those to whom theatre is meat
and drink must inevitably come here.

WEDNESDAY, DECEMBER 18, 1968
     In the middle of the night one of Bill Snell's drunk-
en phone calls, from which we have been free for four or
five years. (*He was one of the 1940's interlopers of whom
I wrote a few entries back. Long ago drawn back to living
with his mother in Florida, he periodically, when in his
cups, got a wave of nostalgia for the affair he never quite
had with Ken.*) By the time Ken persuaded him coyly to hang
up I was seething and even after I finally put it out of
my mind, my system was so full of adrenalin that I didn't
get to sleep until morning was virtually here. Ken claimed
in the morning that Bill wasn't drunk but my reply was that
I didn't believe it but if so it gave Bill less excuse than
ever, since he should know that phone rates are just the
same at 7 in the evening as at two or three in the morning. (*The almost invariable hour for his calls.*) He had a
cold and I can't think of anybody I'd rather see get in-
fluenza (or pneumonia or tb). I guess I shouldn't say that
as I'm a little superstitious about what happened to
George Worrell and Jim Boothe in the wake of my ill will.
(*Two other interlopers, both of whom contracted tuberculosis, the first subsequently a cancer victim.*) I may be a
warlock unawares.

SUNDAY, DECEMBER 22, 1968
     Up early and out to get the paper, mercifully thin. I
made a wild effort to get it read before we buckled down
to work as I knew that once Florence arrived one couldn't
read. We bussed over to Broadway and took advantage of the
supermarket's Sunday hours, which we've never done before.
Among our other purchases was more rug shampoo, as we had
run out last nite before completing the living room rug.
Ken finished it up and we had the place in good shape before we set out to meet Florence. The minute we got home
Florence unpacked all sorts of goodies, candy, etc., which
is going to ruin our diets but to hell with it. Florence
made lobster stew with a container of wonderful lobster
meat she brought. There are many more plebeian dishes
which I enjoy equally well but still it was nice, tho I
nearly foundered when I got up from the table. I went in
to lie down after the dishes were done, leaving Ken and
Florence to talk but I had to fill in so much of Ken's
conversation when he forgot names or dates that I

eventually got up and joined the company.

MONDAY, DECEMBER 23, 1968
    Up early because Ken intended to get an early start downtown with Florence. He wasn't reckoning with her passion for the kitchen for first she had to make a crabmeat casserole with crabmeat she had also brought in a thermal bag. At the same time I was making the plum puddings. Finally the puddings were on the boil, the dishes from the casserole were washed up, and Ken and Florence took off. I caught up diary and then began wrapping presents. I was at it for over five hours, with short breaks to have visits from Lavinius, who wanted to cuddle. I always think I hate wrapping but it couldn't have been too distressing for I kept finding myself singing. At about the time we had planned to start for the Old Garden Restaurant, Florence decided to change clothes so we were a bit late in starting. Traffic was terrible and Ken began to fuss that we'd never make it. We walked to the theatre and showed Florence the changes in Times Square, so relatively drab now that the Paramount Theatre and Astor Hotel are gone. ZORBA entertained Ken more than had been expected but entertained me less. I didn't find that the music added that much to it and kept remembering how much more effective the various scenes had been in the movie. Florence liked it, however, and that was the important thing.

1969

FRIDAY, JANUARY 10, 1969
    We left a little early to be sure to get tickets for the showing of RASPUTIN AND THE EMPRESS at the New School. Dave arrived about half an hour before the movie but they were meeting a friend who likes to sit in the first row and we balked at that so they took turns coming back to talk to us. The friend is the one who saw Garbo in QUEEN CHRISTINA 153 times and boasts he has the largest collection of Garbo pictures in the world and was to buy 75 more tomorrow. How John could go to see this movie a second time I don't know for I found it tedious in the extreme the first time. The liberties taken with history were terrible and one couldn't really believe a single scene, between the crudities of the writing and the acting. But when we met the others afterward, they had loved it. They have seen none of the things I liked this season----

MISANTHROPE, AMERICAN DREAM, HOUSE OF ATREUS---and I finally figured out why. They don't go to see theatre but to see stars.

FRIDAY, JANUARY 17, 1969

After supper we lay down for a nap and but for Lavinius might have missed the ballet. Ken apparently turned off the alarm so fast that I didn't hear it and we slept on. Lavinius, however, has a habit of reinforcing the alarm if we ignore it and he's not so easily turned off, being both loud and persistent. I was rather annoyed at Ken but grateful to Lavinius. We would have missed a wonderful evening of ballet had we overslept. The Music Box is a wonderfully intimate theatre for ballet and one hardly needed opera glasses, tho I used mine anyway for a closer look at the beautiful dark boy from Iceland, Helgi Tomasson, whose attractions are in no way lessened by his apparent lack of concern with them. It's as nice to be here in New York while it's the dance capital of the world as it must have been to be in Vienna when it was the symphonic capital or the operetta capital. We have seen three different companies this week alone, all with packed houses. (*This particular company was the Harkness Ballet, critically frowned upon but one which I liked throughout its brief life.*)

MONDAY, FEBRUARY 3, 1969

When we got on the scale this morning, the news was bad. Ken was up two pounds and I was up FOUR in a week, which shows the overindulgence of the weekend. We at once planned our attack on this and I told Ken to cut back on the hors d'oeuvres he gives me with my wine, which have been creeping up and up until they become a meal instead of an appetizer. After supper took off for the Morosco Theatre to see FORTY CARATS. The improbable matinee story of a 40-year-old woman wooed and won by a 22-year-old boy was made credible by having the woman played by Julie Harris, who always seems immature, and the boy well characterized as an unusually mature young man with a heritage of robber-baron characteristics. Ken and I were saying that whereas the theatre of the thirties was filled with strong star actresses--Hayes, Cornell, Anderson, Fontanne, Cowl, Bankhead, etc.--we currently lack strong and glamorous female stars. Julie Harris and Maureen Stapleton, tho competent and fine actresses respectively, have no glamour about them and lack both the rich voices and the capacity for grandeur that would let them play great roles.

TUESDAY, FEBRUARY 4, 1969

We set aside the evening to do taxes. Ken struggled on with his after I finished and came in from the dining room once saying, "I've got to ask you another question. Now don't lose patience with me, please." I guess perhaps I had once or twice but that so disarmed me that I had to put my arm around him in his mathematical distress. This made me reflect on the difference in our ages, compared to those of the characters in the play last nite. With both Dick Bennett and Bob Lockwood I was somewhat paternal (and they liked it, without caring much for any other aspect of my personality) but with Ken I am paternalistic too, despite being much the younger. This was not how we started but it is how things developed and it laughably reversed chronology. I could never for long lean on anybody for it isn't in my nature. I just couldn't bear to have somebody plan my vacation itinerary and be completely passive about it as Ken is when I set up our trips, nor could I let somebody control my social life and theatrical activity as I do Ken's but I think he was just waiting for somebody to take him over and the irony of fate is that it was a younger man, not an older. I was born to take care of somebody and Ken was born to be taken care of so we are very well met. We may look like a classic case of older man-younger man but we in no way illustrate it (nor do I know of any such classic case among the homosexual couples of my acquaintance--I just run across it in casebooks, not life.)

SUNDAY, FEBRUARY 9, 1969

Looking out our dining room window, I thought I was looking at a Japanese print for the soft snow was clinging to every little twig and all the outlines of the park were blurred. I did a laundry before Ken got up. We cancelled our plans to go to a movie and stayed in cozily all day. In the middle of the afternoon we had tea with honey in it and I enjoyed it thoroly, loving the pot, the teacups, and all the appurtenances as much as the tea. I looked at Lavinius with especial favor today because he was so different from Marjorie's wild Blaise, who spit and struck at those who tried to pet him last nite.

FRIDAY, FEBRUARY 14, 1969

At supper I had one of my spells of being extremely irritated by Ken's affected English way of eating. To him it suggests Buckingham Palace, to me it suggests a cockney queer. Even the English don't hold their knives in that dainty way and they have a lot more skill in keeping their food on their downturned tines than he does. I can go for

weeks without noticing it much or going into a flap, but
then comes an evening when I could just scream to see him
eat that way, putter, putter, putter, sliding all that
much onto his fork at once in what strikes me as an unutterably common way, and using his knife to cut all kinds
of soft things that would yield to a fork. I don't object
to the fork in the left hand as if I am cutting and eating meat I keep it there myself and don't do all this putting down and picking up and shifting of forks and knives
that Americans do so much, but I loathe shoving vegetables
onto the upside down fork, especially several vegetables
and a piece of meat at the same time. I can tell when Ken
is feeling English for his puttering with the food gets
daintier and daintier until the effeminacy of it all makes
me want to throw up. Ken mentioned at the party Saturday
how much he liked the English way of eating and how much
it bothered me when he did it and of course I said nothing
with so many British there, but I watched them and, believe me, the way the people to whom it is native do it
bears no resemblance whatever to Ken's performance. Even
the British girls eat with more masculinity than he does.

SATURDAY, FEBRUARY 15, 1969
    Took clothes out and then down to the Music Hall to
see MAYERLING. The settings were authentic and the story
made passes at being, if you can take a romantic view of
the to-me squalid Mayerling business, but they undermined
the authenticity by using too many females of a too-modern
thinness. God knows the real Vetsera was chubby, to put it
charitably. I would love to see her played sometime as
what she probably was, a royalty-bedazzled youngster delighted with the notoriety she knew would come to her
above all Rudolf's other mistresses. The Music Hall stage
show wasn't bad and I hoped the rumors of closing were
false. They're having a hard time getting films to book
nowadays because the producers who once would have been
happy to quote records broken by the films at the prestigious Music Hall now prefer to roadshow their attractions
on a two-a-day basis. We walked down Fifth to eat at a
Chock Full of Nuts and then went over to 42nd St. as I was
determined to buy one of the pornographic novels sold
there. I got over my nervousness about going in when I saw
the studied impassivity of the clerks and the casualness
of the many customers. The several stores were both appalling and funny. They had racks of books and pictures for
homosexuals as well as heterosexuals and the two groups
did their browsing with no concern for the others. This
kind of permissiveness is great but really some of the

nude pictures are enough to turn one against sex forever. I never knew there were so many ugly genitals in the world, it never having been my misfortune to come across many. Quite attractive young men were displaying fantastically ugly private parts. On these I spent little time as it was the novels I wanted to investigate and I finally bought one called THE FAMILY JEWELS. While Ken napped, I read THE FAMILY JEWELS, which surely provided one with every possible combination and form of sex. I don't understand why so much heterosexuality was in it for that would probably put off the reader who was interested in the homosexual encounters that make up the bulk of the book and those would most certainly put off the people interested in the heterosexual encounters. Well, maybe there are more bisexuals in the world than I suppose. Ken amused me by rising above it (but still reading it as soon as I got thru with it). When I first discussed buying one he said he thought he was getting too old for pornography, which amused me at the time since he was always more reliant on it than I with my vivid imagination ever was.

TUESDAY, FEBRUARY 18, 1969

After supper and a nap we were off to the Theatre de Lys in the Village to see SPITTING IMAGE, a play about two homosexuals who have a baby. The audience was just about what you would expect except that there were more women there than I might suppose. There was no intermission so we couldn't chat with John and Dave, who spoke to us briefly beforehand and said they'd meet us afterward. When I had seen the pictures of the two men who played the lovers I was disgusted that they picked such a homely boy to play the one who gave birth but to my surprise, as the play proceeded, I found that homely and skinny Sam Waterston did a superb job of acting and what is rarer, radiated gentleness and loveability. I can never tell if an actor is really good in a villainous part for they are so easy to play but if he or she can portray goodness interestingly, I'm impressed and I was tonite. The play was very inventive and hilarious and the audience roared constantly, never more than when the doctor who was trying to stop the spread of motherhood among homosexuals ran out thru the audience crying, "I'm surrounded", which he certainly was. After the show John invited us back to his place for a drink, apologizing for the state we'd find it in. Actually I was pleased to see that his normal way of keeping it makes our normally disordered household look positively neat. We had a drink and some chatter and then subwayed home with Dave. John asked us to drop in for drinks before and after seeing GEESE next week, that play being just around the corner from him.

THURSDAY, FEBRUARY 20, 1969
   At coffee break Bob told us that it was Spain where Jim D. and his friend have gone to buy a house. The friend, three or four years older, retires this year and wants Jim to live with him there as he has done for so many years here but Jim would have to retire early and take the lower pension and Social Security this involves. His friend is willing to compensate him for his company by turning over some of his stocks to him but masculine pride makes Jim hesitate, as it would make most men but few women hesitate. Hazards of homosexual affairs and marriage. Mrs. Mendelson, still working in our files for them, said they get very busy upstairs about five o'clock and sometimes don't go home till seven but we weren't impressed for we have long noted that it's useless to go upstairs and hope to transact any business before 10:30. The American business world impresses itself mightily with its late afternoon industry and overlooks its morning tardiness but I have never been able to fit into this pattern--the evenings belong to me. There is nothing much you can do with mornings but lots to be done with evenings.

SATURDAY, FEBRUARY 22, 1969
   Downtown early and kept our appointment with Macy's optical department. While another man fitted me for frames Ken had his exam. I could hear him chatting away with the examiner, telling him where he worked and what he did, and I thought how typical this was. I had kept strictly to business, as I generally do, and the man knew no more about me when I left than when I arrived. Ken has the same openness that Mother has, telling all his business to everybody and chatting away. I tell it all in here but am close-mouthed with casual contacts. Home in time to hear DAS RHEINGOLD, which I used to find easiest to take of the Ring Cycle because the shortest but today it never caught me up at all. Peg was waiting for us when we went downstairs and looks much better with her hair, formerly piled on her head like Marie Antoinette's, cut off until, as I said, "My hair is longer than yours". We were happy to hear, when we got to Pat's, that the Leonards would be coming. *(They had been in a bad automobile accident, which left Ginny with many health problems and curtailed their social life.)* When they arrived they weren't sure how long Ginny could stay but as it turned out, they stayed the full course. Pat's cats were very sociable, particularly Pinkie,

who sat for two extended periods on Ginny's lap, but I don't imagine the Leonards relished the sight of Pinkie jumping up on the table after dinner and eating daffodils from the centerpiece, about which Pat was quite permissive, nor the sight of Whiskers on the other table with his tail flicking over the butter. Fortunately nobody has ever had to put up with this from our cats but I take no bows for firm training as our cats never had any impulse to get up on tables or sideboard or kitchen work space.

TUESDAY, FEBRUARY 25, 1969

After supper we went to the Village to see GEESE. When we approached the theatre we saw an awful lot of policemen on MacDougal Street and wondered if the theatre were going to be raided. Reviews had warned us that the plays were not very good but David had said they were not without qualities. I'm sorry to disagree with him but I think they were totally without virtues. I haven't seen such awful plays in ages and I was not compensated by seeing bare-breasted lesbians making love in the first play nor totally nude young men making love in the second. When we came out at intermission so Ken could smoke two policemen came up to us and one said with what I thought was deceptive sweetness, "Pardon me, sirs, but what is this play about? I'm not familiar with it." I thought the second was just waiting for us to admit it before he trotted us off to jail and I was nearly speechless. Ken stammered something vapid and I confined myself to saying they were terrible and amateurish. A third policeman then came over and said, "What's the trouble here?" whereupon Ken said, "Nothing. It's just intermission," and they went away. When they had gone I suddenly got the most awful lower back pains from sheer tension and then I began to shake. Though Ken too thought they were going to arrest us, he claimed not to be as frightened as I was, but then, he has less experience with the arbitrariness of the police than I have. The time is certainly coming when this full frontal nudity on the stage is going to be clamped down on. As soon as the really dreadful plays were over we rushed around to John's and found that he expected us this time and had straightened the house up beautifully. We had one drink with him and he gave me the schedule of the Royal Ballet so I could copy off the programs I wanted to see. He also presented us with a copy of SCREW, THE SEX REVIEW, which is sold right on the newsstands and in text and pictures is absolutely filthy. I really am ready for tonite to have been the zenith and for this to recede from this high point back to where sex is depicted with some innuendo instead of being thrown

naked in your face. This direct presentation really isn't
sexy at all and the funniest line tonite was when the
lights went out just as the boys took off their clothes
and got in bed and one member of the audience said
"Damn!". He thought that was all he was going to see but
in subsequent scenes there was a great kissing of lips and
body plus a quick indication of anal intercourse and it
was really much too much. As for total nakedness, it was
very disillusioning for whether because they were cold or
for other reasons, the boys were very lightly hung. One
began to wonder how they controlled themselves thru all
the sexual byplay, whether they were jaded as I used to be
when I lived at the Club and used the steamroom daily,
whether they were straight boys whom other men could not
possibly arouse, or whether the cold and stage fright kept
them preoccupied.

WEDNESDAY, FEBRUARY 26, 1969
       My developing interest in writing a play about homo-
sexuality was smashed last nite by a feeling that before I
got it written, let alone produced, this wave of permissiveness will be over and the public will be sated. I want
to emphasize the love and the friendships but whatever the
emphasis I think I was ahead of my time with THE UNABASHED
and would be behind it by the time I got a play constructed. Love was a much misused word last night--the coarse
dike claimed she loved the young girl but she was so tough
and gratuitously used such foul language that I never believed either she or the author knew what love was all
about. The misuse of the term by the boys I could better
accept as the innocent thought it must be love if he had
a good time in bed with somebody and God knows I used to
get confused that way for a long time.

THURSDAY, FEBRUARY 27, 1969
       We left work early and went to Town Hall for the
travelog on France. The lecturer's French was absolutely
atrocious but even his English pronunciations were sometimes accented on the wrong syllable. What mattered was
that his films were very good, with some especially good
shots of Mt. St. Michel and Annecy. We grabbed a bite at
Nathan's and then subwayed to the State Theatre to see the
premiere of the new production of PRINCE IGOR. It's a
patchy opera but they gave it a production of very cleverly simulated sumptuousness and the scene in the Polovetsian Camp was full of lovely melody. I hadn't heard that
Edward Vilella was going to dance the Polovetsian Chief
and so this was a nice bonus for he brought down the house

with his fierce leaps. The house was packed with an alert
crowd and the variety of male hair styles was very interesting. I don't generally like men as well as women but
tonite I was thinking how men seize an enthusiasm and pursue it with passion, which women seldom do. Without the intensity men bring to things, the world wouldn't get very
far. Tho it is wearing to me, I like the intense interest
that young men can bring to artistic events and the devoted
young standees were very much in my mind tonite. In my
feelings of love for all young aesthetic people who rush
from the provinces to feast at the banquet of New York, I
was also aglow with love for the city and its activities
myself.

SATURDAY, MARCH 15, 1969
    We did some errands on our way to the Eugene O'Neill
to see CANTERBURY TALES. Despite mixed notices, more bad
than good, the show drew a full house. I liked the rock
music, tho it was so loud I heard the words of only one
song (I HAVE A NOBLE COCK) but the four bawdy tales from
Chaucer struck me as rather simple-minded and dull. Four
of the chorus men looked marvelous in their tights and
codpieces and as they had long hair of various lengths and
thicknesses, I was in heaven. It was roughly ten times as
sexually arousing to see those men in their tights as it
was to see the totally nude men making love in GEESE.

MONDAY, MARCH 17, 1969
    N sooner had we reached the bus stop than we realized
we had committed the unforgiveable sin and forgotten to
wear green on St. Patrick's Day. We knew it would be remarked upon when the Irish at TC saw us. I told Mae, when
we went for coffee break, "You just think I don't have any
green on, but I'm wearing green underwear." "Well, then,
take off your pants." Robert and Jim joined us for coffee.
Jim said their new house in Spain is small. Again Jim said
something about our coming out to Long Beach to visit him
and his friend but tho I'm willing no date is ever set. We
decided to wear green tomorrow as a gag.

TUESDAY, MARCH 26, 1969
    In mid-morning Alice called and said he had bad news.
My mind at once leaped to Pearl Rockmore and she knew it
would so said, "Not Pearl, not Pearl, not Pearl. It's Henry." Seems he woke, reached out to turn his electric blanket on or off, gave a deep sigh, and died. Miriam is taking
it with her customary calm but both Alice and I felt it
might be better later if she released a little emotion. I

guess she has too much to do at the moment as their boys are traveling in Africa and they're not sure where to locate them. It's ironic that Lil Gruber died when we were going to a party with her and Henry dies just before he's due here for a party.

SUNDAY, MARCH 30, 1969
    The chapel was lovely and Miriam was receiving in the side room. Eddie had been located in Florence and was there but Teddy had not been located in time to get home and will arrive tomorrow for the cremation ceremony. A man we've met at one of the Englander parties did a very nice job of recollecting fine aspects of Henry's life. I must say that today's non-religious ceremony did show me the value of certain rituals such as marriage and funerals for it must have been consoling to Miriam to see that she and Henry had so many friends, tho it can't have been news. I'm going to be very alone when I bury Mother but as I don't know any of her current friends and as I wouldn't expect any of mine to go over to Trenton, there is no point in a funeral and I won't have one. I do so like the de-emphasis of grief at these two non-religious jewish ceremonies I've attended. Today they specifically quoted some Latin author who said, "Death plucks at my ear and whispers, 'Live, for I come'" or something like that, and explained this did not just mean "Live it up". Henry did have a rich life founding a fine family, maintaining fine friendships, and helping good causes. I felt my life very shallow in comparison but consoled myself that he made his money from a liquor store, which contributes joy to many lives but a great deal less than joy to others. One would hope that education contributed only joy or constructiveness, but who knows?

SUNDAY, APRIL 13, 1969
    Called John to see if he'd seen WAR GAMES, which was previewing for only $3. He hadn't but Dave had and said it had some quality so we decided to try for tickets to today's matinee. It had the subject of draft dodgers all mixed up with homosexuality, which seemed unfortunate for both subjects, but it had many well-written scenes. Among these were some fairly affecting homosexual love and sex scenes. There was none of the total nudity they had in GEESE and the boys were thoroly characterized. LAUGH OF THE DAY: When the girl climbs into bed with the boy who has been having a homosexual affair, she says,"You have no idea how erotic a scratchy beard can be," and he smiles and replies, "Oh, yes, I do!" Blackout.

SATURDAY, APRIL 19, 1969

Both Peggy and Pat arrived on time and we had a very nice evening. Peggy had seen BOYS IN THE BAND last nite and was dying to talk about it but Pat was silently avoiding the subject and while we didn't dismiss it out of hand we didn't encourage Peggy to go on as long as she might have. It would be a rare woman indeed with whom I would discuss any aspect of homosexuality. We didn't act embarrassed, just casual about it. We all tried to get out of eating at Peggy's next time, saying it took too much time from bridge, etc. but Peggy was insistent that we have dinner there. "I'm cooking strictly gourmet these days," she said, and my misgivings were increased. The minute anybody announces that they're a gourmet cook these days, it means they are scarcely a cook at all.

SATURDAY, MAY 3, 1969

23 years ago today Ken and I met, naked as jaybirds, in the steamroom of the club. We went down to the Music Hall to see IF IT'S TUESDAY, THIS MUST BE BELGIUM, a movie whose title comes from a New Yorker cartoon about American tourists on a whirlwind tour such as Mother took. We went just because we wanted to see the backgrounds but the picture wasn't without its amusing moments. It contained cliches but it did occasionally have something fresh, such as a visit to Bastogne in Belgium and a visit to Gruyere in Switzerland rather than some of the triter spots. As Ken said, the backgrounds made one homesick, for in many ways I do feel more at home in Europe than I do here, tho at bottom I suppose I am a thorogoing American. I read almost half of Helen Hayes' autobiography, not nearly as sickeningly sweet as I expected from one who simpered in public for so much of her career.

WEDNESDAY, MAY 7, 1969

From work to South Ferry, where for a change we waited for the Leonards rather than the other way around. About 70 in Eddie's firm are attending a farewell dinner for him. Their apartment wasn't as dismantled as I expected. They had saved six of everything to serve dinner on. We had much laughter all thru the evening, tho I'm damned if I can remember now what it was about. As we came back on the ferry and saw the lovely view of lower Manhattan we realized that next week's trip will be the last of that sort we make, so we drank in the scenery. I'm not sure Ginny and Eddie are going to be happy in Nassau. The neighbors seem terribly friendly but quite intrusive. Two men, of course, could not live together in such a small town but

even if I were half of a heterosexual couple I couldn't
stand it for there would be nights when I wanted to read
or watch television and would turn down bridge dates,
which would make me seem unfriendly. I had a jolly, sociable time tonite but tomorrow I look forward to reading
magazines.

WEDNESDAY, MAY 14, 1969
    From work to Seamen's Church Institute's new build-
ing. The Leonards were waiting out front and we went up
for dinner in their lovely cafeteria. Since we had time to
spare before reporting to the Thatchers' house, Ginny and
Eddie gave us a tour of some of the new construction on
the lower end of the island, including the new World Trade
Center. Their life is a real round of farewell parties
this week, business and social. We weren't the last guests
to arrive at the Thatchers'. Most had large families, presumably being Catholic like the Thatchers, but they seem
sensible about their children as George and Rita are. The
Thatcher kids, all seven of them, were trooping in and out
and up and down stairs until one got dizzy trying to keep
track of them but they said almost nothing and are very
nice kids to whom their parents never have to raise their
voice in public. I was very aggressive in my bidding all
evening and tho I never know what I'm doing in duplicate,
I came out the winner for the evening by a wide margin.
Lavinius had so many things to do in the short time between
our getting home and going to bed that he was rushing
around, greeting us, eating a little supper, going to the
bathroom, greeting us some more. How he controls his bow-
els the way he does, I don't know. Nothing senile about
his control of his body. Well, no more 18 hour absences
after this. I imagine this was our last trip to Staten
Island, last time we'll see the Leonards for a while.

MONDAY, MAY 19, 1969
    Just after we got home Lavinius, full of beans, start-
ed to play with my garters. He usually gets an old, cold
garter to play with to save wear and tear on those we wear
but he whisked these out of my hand before I could put
them away. Suddenly he shot into the living room and this
alerted me to the fact that in his excitement he had probably peed on the bed, as the smell of my clothes or of
laundry will from time to time make him do. As the plastic
cover was on the bed it was a simple matter of blotting it
up with newspapers and wiping if off but the first thing I
knew Ken was saying, "Sometimes I wonder if it's worthwhile having a cat." It was probably a more casual remark

than my extreme reaction would indicate but I gave him a blast, saying I didn't wonder and that if he wanted to live a childless, petless, dustless existence like the Christensons, he'd have to become a damned sight better housekeeper. He made no response but didn't sulk either but my fury continued right till suppertime. I was probably angry as much on my own account as Lavinius', for I full well know that it behooves me to stay well to the end or I'll be set adrift on an ice floe like an aging eskimo. Animals or people that get to be too much trouble have no place in Ken's life. Only yesterday he was running on far more than I wanted him to about what an extraordinarily good and untroublesome cat Lavinius was and today, one minor mishap and he thinks we'd be well rid of him. I would fare no better. I can only feel sorry for Ken that he has never felt for anybody the passionate commitment I have to both him and Lavinius. I had a call from George Hope, the boy from Guyana who worked for me many years ago. He thought he had seen me in church yesterday where he was singing in THE CREATION. I assured him he was unlikely ever to see me in a church and that I must be a common type as people frequently tell me they saw me in this place or that where I haven't been. It was nice talking to him and the nicest thing was the compliment he paid. "You know, that office is very dear to some of us. It's the most democratic place I've ever worked and I've been in this country 17 years and worked on both coasts." I was glad to hear that George is doing well as an engineer and his daughter is doing well in the High School of Music and Art.

TUESDAY, JUNE 3, 1969
    Wonderful day for the graduation ceremonies. Bill brought his father in and introduced him. I was terribly pleased by their relationship and envious of it. So many fathers are either overbearing or pitiably mousy, but Mr. Olewiler struck a very happy medium, joshing his son and praising him in just the right measure. He told us that his was the last class for many years to take a graduation trip to Washington from West Philadelphia Boys High School because of the pranks and vandalism they perpetrated. So this sort of thing which is supposed to be showing the decadence of our day did after all go on 52 years ago. Father and son seem actually to be very friendly, a wonderful sight for anyone father-deprived to see and Bill took his father to dinner and a baseball game after the graduation.

THURSDAY, JUNE 5, 1969
    Since reviews had been so phenomenal for the new Off-Broadway musical, PROMENADE, I suggested that I leave the office early to go get tickets. I found a long line and had quite a wait. Two or three behind me was an old queer, nattily groomed but with old liver-spotted skin, and he turned my stomach in his attempt to show a young ugly gay fellow in front of him that he was very "with it". He was using all the young jargon such as "I hear that Berlin is also Insville" and I prayed to God that I grew old with more grace. He was touching base on all the gay shibboleths and I thought to myself that if an older man really wants to be seductive he should be as mature as possible for he could live up to whatever appeal this has whereas he could by no stretch of the imagination be really convincing as a youth.

SATURDAY, JUNE 14, 1969
    As L. still wanted nothing to eat, no matter how many different things we trotted out, we decided we would have the doctor come and look him over and while he's at it, clean his teeth. It was mostly Ken's idea, he who used to worry about the vet bill, and he felt relieved the minute the decision had been arrived at. Actually Lavinius is a mass of the usual affection, is lively, and does all his tricks, if perhaps a little listlessly in the heat, but the food strikes and the limp bother us and at his age (17) a checkup is certainly in order. After naps and showers we set out by bus for John's. We had the usual pleasant evening and the dinner was capped with a CHOCOLATE birthday cake for me. John said,"After I bought it I thought 'Suppose somebody doesn't like chocolate!'" I didn't lie and say I did but I raved about how pretty it was and how thoughtful it was of them, etc., but Ken was not in a mood to let me be diplomatic. He seldom is. He said "I like it" with heavy emphasis on the pronoun, and in case they didn't get the implication the first time, he repeated this about six more times until I nearly ran out of distracting ploys. He was having one of those competitive evenings anyway, during which, if I chose to draw a veil of silence over my opinions to avoid a contentious evening, he must announce what my opinions are and word it in the most offensive (and inaccurate) way. I don't really understand his compulsion to try to take over friends originally mine then ours, and try to make them his alone. Last nite during the bridge game it came out that he has been writing to the Leonards. He hasn't asked me if I want to add a few words or say anything. He hasn't even told me he was

writing, but has written on the sly. One reason may be his gossip's compulsion to be first with all news, another may be aversion to my corrections of facts or quotes in what he has embellished or interpreted, but there is more to it than that. I never feel competitive with him but indeed what field would I possibly compete in? He also has a compulsion to compete with Mother, which I find particularly unappealing, and when he serves a meal he'll say "I'll bet your mother serves it just like that" or, when he's washed up dishes he'll say, "Just like your mother", as tho she lived in a mass of dirty dishes. I've pointed out to him several times that whatever her faults, a tendency to leave a sinkful of dirty dishes was never one of them. But the idea of his competing at all I find repulsive. It matters to him but it has never mattered to me that she doesn't like to cook or clean house. Despite Ken's attempts to inject a few discordant notes, the evening went very well. I do find David's tendency to label all kinds of celebrities as homosexuals, lesbians, or latents a bit sick. He's really too old to go in for that game. We are numerous but not omnipresent.

MONDAY, JUNE 16, 1969
I had expected that Lavinius might day by day begin to eat a little more but when he didn't I got an attack of galloping blues. When the radio played WOULD I MAKE THE SAME MISTAKES IF HE WALKED INTO MY LIFE TODAY, a song I always find poignant, I burst into tears. Fortunately Ken was out of the room and when he started to come in the hall I quickly went out thru the dining room. But tears welled up all day at the thought that my life with Lavinius is nearing its end. I have told myself often that he cannot last more than two or three years more at the outside, but he was well then and I thought we might make it to the outer limits. We had no less than three calls in the afternoon in answer to the ad about looking after the cat. When we went home L. was so lively that it greatly helped my spirits for he gives no indication of being sick. He still doesn't eat much so after dinner I called Dr. Johnson, who said he would try to come by Wednesday evening. He didn't remember L. nor had I expected him to, but when I mentioned Octavia's death while we were away, he said, "Oh, yes, you live with your---associate."

WEDNESDAY, JUNE 18, 1969
We rushed home thinking Dr. Johnson would call or drop by but he never did. As it happened, Lavinius had greeted us with his old-time impatience for food, his mouth

spreading back to his ears as he screamed his orders to
us. I had to restrain Ken so he wouldn't overfeed him and
lead to a falling-off of appetite tomorrow, which has often
happened. We want Dr. Johnson to check him anyway. To the
Met to see the Stuttgart Ballet do their premiere of ROMEO
AND JULIET. The full house was one of those alert and responsive audiences that appreciates dance and actually roars
its approval. Their reactions were as electric as the performance, which had authentic magic to it tonite. The last
act, with a lot of story to tell that doesn't lend itself
to crowd scenes or to dance at all, rather induced the
longueurs. Earlier, tho, in the ballroom scene and the
street brawls, it had been magnificent with costumes which
I'm sure were created just for this American visit and with
dueling that was the best I ever saw on stage or screen.

FRIDAY, JUNE 20, 1969
      A perfectly lovely birthday, beginning with a pile of
presents on the dining room table when I came out of the
shower. Home at five to find a lot of birthday cards (I had
said nothing at work so there was no nonsense there) and a
sentimental note from Mother. She said that many years ago
I had written her a letter saying I was glad she was my
mother and now she just had to say that she was glad and
proud that I was her son. She said I had accepted trying
situations gracefully when I was growing up and that she
often thought about this and appreciated it. She called
and I let her run on rather than reminding her what a bill
she's running up, as I often do. Again on the phone she got
a bit weepy about the things she would like to have done
for me when times were hard but I cut her short with,"Well,
I got everything I wanted out of life as an adult and I
think it's better to have it at the latter end of your life
and earn it for yourself than to have it handed to you when
young." Since as a child I showed the same characteristics
I have now, of not wanting much, I really didn't suffer as
much as some thru the lean years. I had imagination to fill
in the gaps. The one scar the Depression left on me was
that I had to avoid contact with my contemporaries and
avoid having them in my home lest there be a financial
crisis involving repossession of something, eviction, lack
of food, or whatnot. Even this may not have been the hardship for me that it would have been for others since I have
demonstrated thruout my life that I do not have a particular talent for friendship anyway.

SATURDAY, JUNE 21, 1969
      When we got home I had a birthday card from the

Leonards, which only partially relieved Ken's frustration at not hearing from them. He said this morning that he had written FIVE times. We got what we thought was a late start for Alice's but because all three of our subway connections came along just as we got out of the previous subway we were the first guests to arrive. We had been talking before we went out about Miriam's reserve but she rather fooled us tonite. When she arrived and came over to shake hands with me she started raving, "You look BEAUTIFUL. I mean it, you look ab-so-lutely BEAUTIFUL!" This I took to be mostly a tribute to my white linen jacket which, despite its flukish $5 cost, is terribly enhancing. She was in very good spirits tonite and we really laughed a lot, never more than when Miriam told how Henry persuaded her to help herself break the smoking habit by recording in a low voice, "I do not need cigarettes. I will stop smoking. I don't need to smoke" which was to play into her ears in her sleep so that she was subliminally persuaded by her own voice. This idea was funny enuf but was capped when she told us that the mechanism went wrong and instead of getting a low persistent whisper in her slumbering ear, the loudspeakers blared it all over the house at tremendous volume. She needed a cigarette immediately to quiet her nerves.

SATURDAY, JUNE 28, 1969

Mother called early and after three minutes of conversation about her diet, asked "Is Donald awake yet?" "Well, who do you think you're talking to?" I'm resigned to people mixing us up on the phone but when our own families can have considerable conversation and still not know, we must sound more alike than we do to each other. Dr. Johnson arrived half an hour early to check Lavinius and I hadn't finished straightening up for him. He said his eyes, ears, heart and kidneys were in good condition and that he was in very good shape for his age. He surprised me by saying 17 was quite a remarkable age, 12 being more normal, for I know so many old cats. For his arthritis he recommended a quarter pill of bufferin twice a day but only when he limps badly and he recommended concentrated cod liver oil for him. I wrote it all down so I'd have it straight. In the lake across from us a fishing contest was going on and the edges were lined with young fishermen trying to get some of the fish with which the lake was recently stocked. That kept the kids away from the hydrants for a while. In the evening they caused an accident at our corner as a car that was being given the full force of the hydrant water put on its brakes as the driver was blinded and the car behind it slammed into him.

A GAY DIARY

TUESDAY, JULY 1, 1969

In the evening, sad about Lavinius' refusal to eat, we went to see OH, CALCUTTA. The reviewers were right about how anti-erotic this erotic review is. The skits were all terrible. No proper editing was done for two of the skits had a quite good and natural blackout point at mid-point but insisted on continuing to ever diminishing returns to weak endings. The bodies were beautiful, however, and in particular I was smitten with Mark Dempsey, a tall, lithe, bearded young man with lovely balls. His dignity was terribly appealing but none of them leered when nude, thank God. The audience was almost more interesting than the show. I had expected that Clive Barnes was right when he said it was for the "sexually and socially deprived" for the homosexual shows have sometimes drawn dreary audiences of old aunties who, if they ever had it, had it long ago. But tonite there were lots of young couples in their sexual prime and even the middle-aged people were often still quite juicy. Tho the skits failed, the nude dances seemed to me a great success and the ripple of muscles and the lovely flesh tones, tho not erotic, were beautiful. During the many dull parts of the show I kept trying to resign myself to the loss of Lavinius, telling myself on the one hand that Mary Rafferty's cat wasn't eating in the heat either, then trying to make myself face the loss. Why couldn't this happen in winter, when we weren't going away? If this is his terminal illness I loathe the thought of being away. He did eat a little when we got home and raised our spirits a bit but he's really not well.

WEDNESDAY, JULY 2, 1969

A cool nite and Lavinius spent it all with me. When he wanted to get under the sheet and cuddle next to me it revived unfortunate memories of the last nite I spent with Octavia. She too wanted to be close to me and sing. He was perky as hell this morning with the cooler weather but still had no appetite. I had a lump of grief in my stomach all day over him. Probably under the influence of pre-dinner wine, I began to cry at the supper table. This irritated Ken, who started to harangue me about how silly I was, that Lavinius might linger for six months and if I acted that way all the time I'd get sick. "Wait till he dies and then get it out of your system. I love him too but he has to go." This did nothing to stem the tears but when they stopped I felt relieved of much of the inner pressure I had felt all day. He still didn't eat enuf to keep a bird alive and is a bit wobbly on his pins but maintains his routine and seems in no great distress,

SUNDAY, JULY 6, 1969
   I suggested we might ride up to the Cloisters even though I remembered it as a rather boring place if you've seen medieval buildings intact in Europe. Ken agreed and off we went on the long ugly ride. Unfortunately I was carrying a heavy weight of sadness in my stomach. My grief over Lavinius led me to be subject to other anxieties such as a sudden realization that Ken is nearly 64 and that the obituary pages are full of people only slightly older than that. It is not totally bad to be poignantly aware of such things and to love people in full consciousness as a result but one doesn't want that terrible lump. The return journey was calculated to minimize my troubles for the bus seemed full of cripples, dwarfs, lonely widows, and a spastic child, all of them calculated to shame my melancholy. In my prayers at nite I thank God that Ken is well and also that he comes from a long-lived family for that is a great consolation considering that he's older than I. Never a nite that I fail to mention this in running over my blessings.

MONDAY, JULY 7, 1969
   When we had our morning weighing we found that grief-stricken non-appetite has led to a three-pound loss for each of us this week. Whereas on Thursday I grew depressed and afraid to go home lest Lavinius not eat, today I was anxious to be home with him, and resigned to his going but determined to enjoy every bit of love we can cram into these days before our departure. As we had our pre-dinner drinks I couldn't help crying again but this time Ken was not indignant. We discussed whether, on our last day, we should not call Dr. Johnson and authorize him to put Lavinius to sleep if Sandy called and said he seemed to be suffering or was unable to walk. I think we will but, as I told Ken, he'll have to do it as I'd make a blubbering fool of myself on the phone. Later we decided we might better order it done before we go if he doesn't start eating. This led to a lot more tears but seems probably best.

TUESDAY, JULY 8, 1969
   Lavinius was so quiet that I began to hope he had slipped away quietly in his sleep but then I heard him in the pan and knew I wasn't going to get off the hook of decision that easily. While Ken was in the bathroom I blubbered and thought I got it out of my system but I soon found that it doesn't stay out of my system long and that the wells soon fill up again. A difficult day at the office kept me reasonably distracted. All sorts of people

wished us well and it would have been a nice day if hanging over me hadn't been the decision that tonite we call the doctor and ask him to put Lavinius to sleep. I felt almost strong enuf to call him myself until I saw Lavinius and burst into tears. A look at the food we'd left this morning, however, showed that he had eaten a dish of Ideal and a saucer of milk and furthermore he came out to have some supper. At once all plans to call the vet were off and we both had a glorious evening. Suddenly our normal perspective on life returned.

THURSDAY, JULY 10, 1969

Lavinius ate more in the night and woke me at six to give him breakfast. That sent me off to the movies feeling good. We went to the Music Hall to see TRUE GRIT, an absolutely marvelous western with good story, good characterization, and good dialogue, not to mention lovely scenery. The stage show was also one of the Music Hall's best, including of all things a Loie Fuller act. When we came out they were setting up a life-size model of the lunar landing vehicle over at the Time-Life Building so we studied it. While Ken rested I did a laundry. I wrote the authorization for Mimie to have Lavinius put to sleep, wondering if I should even bother to leave it since he is improving so rapidly. I cautioned her not to take any panic action if he backslid and didn't eat for a few days. I have had such a scare by his recovering like this when I had made up my mind to have him put to sleep that I am simply horrified at the thought it might have been the next day before he recovered and then it would have been too late. Mimie called to say she was coming down (*it was her nephew and his wife who were to stay in our apartment and look after Lavinius but their arrival from Peru had been delayed so she was getting the instructions*). Her visit was eminently reassuring. Before she had gone L. had jumped on the coffee table, begged me to pick him up, then went over to the couch and lay down beside Mimie. At 10:30 he woke from a nap, marched to the kitchen and ate five helpings of fish which Ken had just cooked. He couldn't give us a better sendoff than he has today. Among the Bon Voyage cards was one from Ginny and Eddie, who started work yesterday at Albany Medical Center, he in accounting and she in the architect's office. They had to go to work to save their sanity for her mother is failing fast. They had to change her bed three times one nite, she fell down the stairs backwards and put her feet thru the wall, and she almost burned the house down so they now disconnect all the burners when they leave her alone.

JULY 11-12, 1969

Leavetaking was not so horrendously emotional as I had recently feared. Lavinius got up to see us to the door and I was pretty much in control of my tearducts. On our way to the bus stop I picked up my fourth penny of recent days and put it in my shoes. In these days of inflation apparently nobody stoops to pick up a penny if they drop it. When we reached the lounge of Alitalia we noted a certain inelegance of passengers and well-wishers which extended somehow to the flight itself. I decided to concentrate on solving the problems of this trip as it proceeds then solve the problem of Lavinius when we get home, then the problem of automation when I return to the office, and the problem of mother's dependency when it comes. I didn't completely stick to this view, however, for I found myself <u>willing</u> Lavinius to go to the kitchen and eat. If such willing didn't work when I was home with him I don't know how I thought it would at such a distance. I got sleepy and slept a fair amount fitfully (and guiltily because Ken could not and it seemed like a withdrawal from him, which is the last thing I'm in the mood for these days). When we arrived we found customs inspection meaningless. The staff in Milan's lovely terminal was beautifully trained. Some people were complaining loudly that they couldn't get all their luggage in the trunk of their car (they had brought an absurd amount) but we got along fine with the people and without our asking for it they gave us a larger car than we had paid for. The route was as simple as the men claimed and we were soon installed in a lovely room in a very modern skyscraper motel.

SUNDAY, JULY 13, 1969

Going north toward the lakes we got caught in slow-moving traffic and Ken began again to say we might have made a mistake in having a car. I agreed that we would not do it again, especially as when we got to Bergamo we could not for the life of us find our way to the old upper city. We'd follow a sign that said "Centro Citta Alta" then get lost and find ourselves going the wrong way on a one-way street. Eventually we decided to get on to Lake Iseo for our nerves' sake. Traffic got thin up there and the mountain scenery pleasant. We stopped at the little resort town of Lovere for gelati, lemonade, and a rest stop then started down the other side of the lake. Here adventure in its starkest form awaited us. We entered the first of several tunnels and discovered Ken didn't know how to turn the headlights on. We were proceeding in pitch dark, discovered by the dim light of the man behind us that we were on the wrong side of the road and cars were coming at us. Ken found the proper button just in time but it was several minutes before my heart stopped pounding and then my back ached fiercely in reaction.

MONDAY, JULY 14, 1969
    Not one wink of sleep all nite. Once insomnia starts it induces a panic which one spends a lot of energy trying to suppress. We stopped at the first farmacia we passed and tho I wasn't sure where the accent fell on "sonnifero" the girl understood me at once and sold me something called <u>Fadormir</u>. Tho doubtful of their efficacy, I felt better for having them to try. The trip up the western side of Lake Garda was dramatically lovely and Riva, at the other end, was a lovely little resort scented by magnolia or camellia trees. It was filled with Germans and caters especially to them. We got into Verona easily, had luck in finding a parking spot, and set out to have lunch, tho neither of us had any appetite. Neither of us could figure out why this trip is going wrong--whether we left home in too nervous a state, or were repeating Italy too soon, or had the wrong itinerary, or were getting too old, or what.

WEDNESDAY, JULY 16, 1969
    Again fell asleep on my own but when I woke at 12 I took the pill to be assured of a good nite's rest and I may continue to do so since this trip is so much more nerve-wracking than most we've had. Ken still gets very nervous driving in cities and parking is nearly impossible. I wonder if I'll get him in to Rome at all or if we'll spend a week in the motel. At any rate today we achieved a third objective, Ravenna. We did succeed in getting a public parking place by the hour, only because a woman drove out and we did see all the major sites in the Michelin except S. Apollinaire in Classe, which was closed until two and didn't seem worth waiting an hour for after so many other mosaics. Ken was being affected by mid-day heat, lack of food and liquid, and a feeling that all mosaics look alike. Even with my health restored I can see that this vacation is not a success, tho it may become one in retrospect. In the future I must plan so they are very easy for Ken. As he says, if he drove daily at home he wouldn't be so nervous but he got quite touchy today for a while on several subjects. Food helped, as it so often does, when we found a café that served "toasts", our discovery of yesterday. For myself I thought S. Vitale and the tomb of Galla Placida lovely, S. Apollinare Nuovo very attractive and tho I have never been able to stomach Dante I was glad

to see his tomb and the nearby cloisters. Perhaps once we hit Rome and if we find a bus goes by to the city as it has at all the other motels, we will both feel more secure. We don't know why we were so intrepid in 1955 and are so cowardly now. Of course auto traffic has greatly increased in Europe and on that trip we were in northern Europe where streets are not narrowed to keep out the sun.

SATURDAY, JULY 19, 1969

We caught the tour bus right out front and it transported us to the Borghese Gardens, where everybody was sorted out according to which of the several tours they wanted. We got on a bus beside which a guide stood bearing a sign saying "English-Spanish". Fortunately there were no Spanish-speaking on the bus so we got the full attention of the guide. Basically our tour today was of the Vatican Museum and the guide said 10,000 people would go thru it today. Our guide was excellent and I learned some things I didn't know but it was a horrible way to see it. The crush was absolutely absurd, a great contrast to what we encountered in '63 when we beat the tourists by coming in May. I sweated buckets and my hair was dripping. When we arrived home we collapsed and had naps. We got up in time to have a good lunch, knowing we wouldn't have time for a big evening meal between 7, when the dining room opens, and 8, when we leave for Sound and Light. Sooner or later every fragment in the Forum was lighted up in the course of the narration of the history of Rome. Sound and light is a limited dramatic medium but such things as the entrance of Caesar's triumph into Rome, with the sound and light starting at the Arch of Titus and proceeding slowly over to the Arch of Septimus Severus were effective.

SUNDAY, JULY 20, 1969

It was amusing the way we formed a cordon around the boy and girl who had ill-advisedly worn shorts so they could get in St. Peter's. The Vatican still frowns on bare arms and shorts tho they recently lifted a ban on slacks and apparently long ago gave up insisting on head covering for women and jackets for men, such as I had to wear in 1949. We had another nap when we got home, then a shower, then dinner. The waiters were all listening to a transistor some man had, excited by the landing on the moon. We tried to watch in the jammed tv room but in Italian it meant nothing to us. I left Ken watching and went up to pack. We heard by word of mouth that the strike situation in Naples is particularly violent, that cars are overturned, and someone advised putting an American flag on the car but where could one obtain one? This increases our fear of going there.

MONDAY, JULY 21, 1969
     A few inquiries located the AGIP Motel in a rather grim quarter of Naples but when we took in our bags we were informed by the lone staff member in attendance that the motel was closed because the staff was on strike. We decided to retreat to Rome and maybe take their 3 day tour of the Naples area. *(Our tour was a package deal offered by the AGIP chain of motels and gas stations.)*

WEDNESDAY, JULY 23, 1969
     Even when all candidates for all Bay area tours were gathered up at the Rome office we had only nine, the same pitiful number we had last year on our Spanish tour. The ride down the autostrada to Naples was a repeat of our ill-fated dash the other day but under what immeasurably more relaxed circumstances. A short tour of Naples and we liked the city even less than we remembered and were rather glad the Naples motel was closed when we got there. It was a hot, dirty, clamorous city--clamorous without the compensating beauty of Rome. To Pompeii for lunch--adequate--and we knew we were in Naples from the dreadful serenading we got from three over-age musicians. Tho they must have sung and played <u>Santa Lucia</u> and <u>Funiculi Funicula</u> thousands of times they haven't learned to do it right. But this didn't stop their passing a plate lined with highly optimistic thousand lire notes. Our guide for the excavations of Pompeii seemed adequate but I kept hearing other guides tell their people things ours never mentioned. It was hot as hell and we walked and stopped in the shade as much as possible.

THURSDAY, JULY 24, 1969
     Before our Capri bus started a monk came thru begging and Ken gave him something, for which he got a multi-language blessing for him and his. He said that was for Lavinius. Later, at Villa San Michele, there was a Sphinx one was supposed to touch with the left hand and wish. I wished more years of life for Lavinius so we tried religion and superstition on his behalf today. Not for the first time, as I have been wishing on stars and praying in churches too. Our boat went right to the Blue Grotto, where masses of tourists were bobbing around in boats outside. We transferred to the small boat and eventually got in. Many expressed disappointment that it wasn't larger but I found it quite a sight still. I would rather see something

worth seeing, like Capri, with masses of tourists than see something like Brescia and have it all to myself. Tho Capri is clamorous with tourists now, it also has really nice shops whereas all I remember from '49 tended to be junky.

WEDNESDAY, JULY 30, 1969

We got up early and with some trepidation started out for Ostia Antica. As tho to show we had unjustly neglected it, the car started like a dream after 10 days and in hardly any time we found the old city. It turned out to be one of our great travel experiences of all time. Unlike Pompeii it has lots of greenery including many lovely pines which make shady areas in which to rest or read guidebooks and thru which lovely breezes blow, making sounds like waves. The ruins were more extensive than we realized and our enthusiasm kept mounting. In the theatre Euripides' HELEN is currently being presented and the Egyptian scenery set up there made it a perfect score for us as there was Egyptian scenery also set up in Verona and at Caracalla (*for AIDA in both cases*). Behind the theatre was a marvelous square of seventy shops with excellent mosaics in front of each showing what the shop dealt in. These excavations started only in 1909 and they've done a marvelous job, posting at intervals an architect's rendering of what this apartment house or that wine shop may have looked like prior to 400 A.D. A few unguided groups were wandering around but there wasn't one herd of tourists following in the wake of a guide. After about three delicious hours (during which we saw one lightning-quick cat stalk and successfully pursue one of the many lizards) we drove on to the Lido. The sand was not very attractive and neither were any of the bathers so tho we had brought our suits we decided not to bother renting a cabana. As we near time to go home our thoughts are turning to Lavinius, about whom I have dreamed several times.

FRIDAY, AUGUST 1, 1969

We left for the airport about ten, worrying in our usual fashion, this time about the possible difficulty of turning the car in. When we got there a man waved to us and said, "We've been waiting for you". While one man inspected and then drove the car away, another went in the airport with us and settled accounts. We were late taking off and spent an extra hour or so in the air at the other end, which made the journey tedious but it was helped by a better meal than we had coming over, by much talk with our acquaintances, and by two good-looking stewards. As we made our way home Ken got a bit apprehensive about what we would find, but I was strangely numb, perhaps because I had persuaded myself that Lavinius would make it. The minute I opened the apartment door I knew he had not. There was no plastic on the furniture, the room looked dead and uninhabited and when we got to the kitchen his dishes were gone. A note had been left but I didn't have to read it and the dam burst. Both superstition and prayer had been all for naught. The note said they made four telephone contacts with Dr. Johnson and finally had him make a call, on which occasion he gave Lavinius anti-biotics for an abscessed tooth but the next day (last Monday) he died in his sleep. I felt guilty for once again being away from a loved one when they died. I know it's easier for me this way but I'm sure Lavinius would rather have had us here when he died than the most attentive of strangers. I would get hold of myself and then something would remind me poignantly of Lavinius and I'd be off again. Sandy and his wife had set the table for us and left a nice salad and roast chicken but neither of us had the slightest appetite. We unpacked to keep busy and took baths. It was terrible not to see my little bathroom boy sitting on the hopper waiting for me when I came out of the shower. We will get two new cats shortly but neither of us has any expectation that we will ever have as human, good, and loving a cat as Lavinius.

SATURDAY, AUGUST 2, 1969

Slept off and on till almost four but never thereafter. I thought that was too late to take a pill and kept hoping I'd go back to sleep but I was in too anxious a state. The demise of Lavinius made me fearful of losing Ken and the thoughts of that made me think how few friends we have to lean on in case of trouble. With the Leonards gone I wonder if we have any at all, or just acquaintances. I made my usual vow to enlarge our circle as I'm sure it's friends and relatives who have helped Miriam bear up so well. I was glad when Ken woke about six and I had someone to talk to to keep my mind a bit off my anxieties. I just hated going in the living room because somehow I kept hoping to find Lavinius there and instead it is so empty. From the time I first had an apartment there has been at least one cat living in it, something living to greet you, and I don't know how people stand an apartment without that living element of pet or child. We called Mimie and invited them all down for a drink since we didn't feel up to joining them for a drink last nite. Ken had asked Sandy last nite not to discuss Lavinius when we did see him. When Sandy and Michele arri.ed with Mimie they proved to be

absolutely charming people. Ken took him in the bedroom
and paid him the $5 it cost to have Lavinius' body picked
up by the SPCA and cremated. One thing the visit proved is
that Lavinius couldn't possibly have been in better hands
at the end.

MONDAY, AUGUST 4, 1969
        Without Lavinius to reinforce the alarm clock, we had
to heed it. As I walked toward TC from the bus I felt
heavy as lead but it turned out to be a marvelous day. The
minute I walked in the office I spotted the air condition-
er which had been installed with no previous hint that we
were to get one. Then everybody's greetings were so effus-
ive and continued to be all day. I decided I would not let
Ed Grefe's personality drive me out of there. Ed told them
all August vacations were cancelled and everybody must pre-
pare to work 10-15 hours a day converting to automation.
Mary says he's ominously quiet and she'd rather he yelled
but I wouldn't. He can be as ominous as he likes as long
as he keeps his voice low. In the afternoon Ken and I, used
to recent siestas, sagged terribly and wondered if we could
get thru the day. We looked forward to our after-dinner
naps but just as we were lying down Pat called to say somebody she knew had two adorable grey kittens we could have
(but I balked at their both being female) and we talked a
long time.

TUESDAY, AUGUST 5, 1969
        The long spell of daily rain is leading people to say
that the moon landings have affected nature, tho they don't
seem very clear as to how. As I worked during the morning
I tried to think of names for cats that would be acceptable
to Ken. When I named the last two I didn't have to consult
him. He suggested "Tom", which is too ordinary for me but
he didn't like any of my ideas either. We are agreed only
on "Victoria". Called Dr. Johnson about cats and he says
he hasn't located any yet, but doesn't want us to take cats
from the SPCA shelter as they have so much virus and other
diseases. I told Dr. Johnson that all the long-lived cats
I'd known were male and was there any basis for thinking
males lived longer? He said he didn't know but thought not
and gave me a sales talk about how females were smarter,
gentler, etc. This doesn't jibe with my experience at all.
I told Dr. Johnson I found it hard to believe any female
could be either smarter or gentler than Lavinius. I almost
feel it's disloyal to him not to have one male. I don't
mind one female but grow more determined not to have two.

MONDAY, AUGUST 11, 1969

I left work early to go to Pat's office and get the kitten. She was immediately adorable, a good singer, a pretty Maltese color, and very sociable. I got home just a minute or two before Ken, who also fell at once in love with Victoria. Our hearts were lightened by having something to love, but not for long. Within an hour Victoria had disappeared. We looked in all closets, under all furniture, not once but six times. We then concluded she must have snuck out when Ken came back from emptying the garbage so I looked up and down the fire stairs, took the elevator to all floors and looked, asked the guard if anyone had reported finding a kitten, put up notices in the elevators and laundry room and then went home to search for the umpteenth time. We both lost our appetite and put the supper in the refrigerator. We lay down to calm our nerves, knowing we couldn't sleep, and then Ken got up to look behind the books in the foyer. Sure enuf, there she was, fast asleep. Ken had been feeling so guilty that his appetite didn't come back immediately but eventually we ate. I called Dr. Johnson but he hasn't located a male. I called Pat to tell her how we both adored Victoria and how she had already given us grey hair.

SATURDAY, AUGUST 23, 1969

John arrived a bit early but we were ready. I never knew before that Dave is terrified of cats. He never showed it or mentioned it when here with Lavinius who, of course, gave him the same wide berth he gave all guests. He said again that he disliked women because they could be bitchy and that seems so stupid for one of his intelligence, for gay boys didn't get the name of "bitch" for nothing either. He said married people treated each other terribly, which is another incomprehensible opinion in view of the way gay lovers can act with each other. Of course we all know nagging wives but if he doesn't also know some devoted couples whose quarrels are in reasonable proportion to the time they are together, I can only say he is unfortunate.

SATURDAY, AUGUST 30, 1969

The Leonards were waiting and showed us around Albany before taking us to their new house in Nassau. The city is in a great state of reconstruction but is and still will be, rather unattractive and uninteresting. Nassau is nothing of beauty either. Ginny's mother was waiting to see us arrive and seemed to be quite pulled together, tho we later heard horrifying tales of her lapses of memory and her demands for dinner when they would like to relax with

drinks after a day's work. In the evening we went to the
Chatham Fair, which is supposed to be the oldest county
fair in the state. I know enough about fairs to have realized that we should have put off visiting the midway until
we had gone in the exhibition barns, since the latter close
earlier, but I didn't press the point and so we missed
barns devoted to preserves, etc. We did see the poultry
barns and the varieties of chickens were amazing. When the
barns began to close up, we went home. Their street was
pitch black and quiet and I'd go mad there. I was surprised
to learn that in this year of grace they get only three tv
channels up there and very erratic radio, which is also
very local. They feel that they are close to New York and
they are but at the same time they are worlds away.

SUNDAY, AUGUST 31, 1969
    Two couples from the neighborhood had been invited
over for bridge and tho we changed partners every two hands
I didn't seem to get nervous no matter who I played with.
When we were having cake and coffee afterwards the conversation got very small town and I could see the Leonards
suffering more than we were. One woman complained that she
couldn't sleep mornings because the street sounded like a
factory and I was overcome with hilarity for one cricket or
two was all we could hear at the moment. They said there
were 18 dogs on the street, all of whom fertilized their
lawns and barked in the morning, and they complained about
such petty noises that it was just funny to us, with all
the street serenades, transistor radios, fire engines and
whatnot of 108th St. They were all content with living
there, which is nice, and Ginny says one couple hasn't used
the husband's vacation in 15 years because the wife won't
go away from home more than two or three days.

MONDAY, SEPTEMBER 1, 1969
    Ginny said she was disappointed at all the gossip and
cattiness that went on last nite but I realized we were being just as gossipy in talking about the guests in a post-
mortem sort of way. In the cities one doesn't do this so
much because your friends don't know your other friends,
so neutral ground must be found (and celebrity gossip sometimes takes its place and seems less catty but perhaps it
isn't). Ken and I decided to take an earlier bus than we
had originally planned. Victoria was delighted to see us.

FRIDAY, SEPTEMBER 6, 1969
    I called the friend of Vi's who had the kitten and
arranged to go down there with the carrier after work. She

said if we didn't take it she'd have to give it to the
shelter as she and her husband were allergic. When we
got there we found it a pitiful thing, harassed by child
and dog (which had to be shut up because it barked at us
so) and tho we felt its age and sex had been misrepresented
(suddenly, when we got there,there was hedging as to both
its age and sex) we took it. We were also dubious about the
state of its physical and mental health for there was never
a peep out of it on the noisy way home. Victoria found it
a wonderful new toy and leapt at it playfully but is larger and older. The kitten defended itself with spirit, which
gave us some hope but it looks so bedraggled and badgered
that we are torn about keeping it. Victoria had an immediately winning personality but this one needs much love to
bring it out and perhaps it may never improve but we're
looking for every sign of spirit. Right now it backs away
from me when I approach it, which is not the kind of cat I
care for. Ken says five years from now we may remark on how
close we came to giving a wonderful cat to the shelter but
we will see what Dr. Johnson says when he comes Sunday to
give Victoria her shots. Tho I would like a male I will not
turn her out if she turns out to be female (tho I hate to
waste the name Titus) but if he thinks the cat is too neurotic or too sick I will turn her in and wait for the kind
of home-grown cat we should have waited for in the first
place. Eventually the somewhat jealous Victoria settled
down and gave the new kitten some peace.

SATURDAY, SEPTEMBER 6, 1969
    We heard no fights between the cats in the night but
Victoria has the poor thing so browbeaten that it huddles
next to the garbage can, the only place where she will
leave it alone. As soon as it ventures forth, which it soon
ceased to do, she goes at it with great jealousy, badly
disguised as a desire for rough house. There were few signs
of animation from the frightened thing and Ken kept saying,
"I feel sorry for it but there's no use penalizing ourselves by having a cat which is going to spend its life
quavering by the garbage can". I think it may be sick or
retarded as well as bullied but am torn between keeping it
and seeing what love may do and giving it to the shelter
and getting a cat which can give Victoria her comeuppance.
She is more actively jealous than Lavinius ever was and
his jealousy was fairly plain. Rain killed our plans of
going to the tennis matches at Forest Hills so we stayed
housebound. I got a bit depressed in the afternoon by the
cat situation and my reading didn't help for so many people
were being killed in the First World War in the Asquith

diaries. The little cat came to life a bit in the evening and under strict surveillance Victoria was a little nicer to it, tho she got one hard whack when her roughness brought screams from the little one. She was adorable all evening, the greatest possible contrast to the baby, which is easy to pity but hard to love.

SUNDAY, SEPTEMBER 7, 1969

Slow getting to sleep as I debated sending poor Titus to the shelter. This morning I tried a new system to keep Victoria from bullying Titus--I shut her in the bedroom whenever she did and being a good learner, she got the message. While she was in there Titus got bold enuf to chase the tennis ball back and forth across the room and he did the exploring she would not allow till now, so we decided he was not necessarily a retarded cat nor permanently neurotic. When Dr. Johnson came he said we had a gem in Victoria and said Titus wasn't as bad as he expected, since he had neither fleas nor ear mites. He said that Victoria would probably be jealous of any cat we brought in at first but that he thought they would adjust to each other in time. He gave them both shots. Titus was declared definitely male and we resumed use of his name after calling him "The Little One" and "The Baby" all morning. Dr. Johnson thought he might have worms since he has a distended belly and he left some pills which I must administer tomorrow.

FRIDAY, SEPTEMBER 12, 1969

Titus had a good evening. While Ken and I went thru our ties and discarded those too worn or unfashionably narrow, he played in the closets and with Victoria but later she got rough with him and had him screaming. Ken really lost his temper with her and I think Titus was as much alarmed at Ken's charging and shouting at Victoria as he was at what his sister did to him. Titus no longer cringes by the garbage pail but roams freely about the house and would willingly play if only Victoria wouldn't get so carried away. To our amusement, later in the evening Titus leaned over and bit her twice and you never saw anybody so injured. She ran first to Ken and then to me for sympathy. Still later they had a roaring romp and Titus chased Victoria all over the place and twice she leapt about two feet into the air as he attacked her. Our laughter injured her pride and eventually she got furious and set upon him but he did very well for his size.

WEDNESDAY, SEPTEMBER 17, 1969

Spent the morning reading the rest of the proposals

from computer companies. At noon I walked over to the Men's Faculty Club with Gene Landriau, the purchasing agent, who was one of twelve on the panel to choose a computer company. Gary Pomerantz, the new alumni man, had virtually instructed me to say nothing, saying we would let Elaine and Bill Griffin do the talking since they had interviewed most of the computer people. I must say I find it just farcical that Bill Griffin, an admittedly poor student at a jerkwater college,who just started work on an hourly basis this summer, should be delegated to make such an important choice for the college, having no background in alumni work or in computers either. As it turned out, he said not one word. In the end a Boston firm was chosen but I took no part in the decision so if things go wrong I don't want any fingers pointed at me.

THURSDAY, SEPTEMBER 18, 1969
   In the afternoon I had the confrontation with Ed that I have been expecting, wherein he asked me to go to Boston to supervise the key-punching (*for three months*). I refused and he nicely said "Well, maybe for two or three days." "Two, possibly," I said. He didn't push too hard, which is not to say he might not in the future. After supper we went to the gay play AND PUPPY DOGS' TAILS. The title was the best part of it (as with some of my works). What plot there was meandered, the dialogue was generally witless, and I was not compensated for this by the fact that three of the four characters appeared frontally nude at some point or other nor even by the fact that for a change two homosexuals living together were shown to be kind and loving to each other and genuinely smitten.

FRIDAY, SEPTEMBER 19, 1969
   I thought a lot about last nite's play and saw again how I don't fit in to the gay picture in so many ways. There was, as in BOYS IN THE BAND, much talk of the more mannered movie actresses that gay boys, for some reason I don't understand, all idolize. I never like mannered actors or actresses (but they never seem to concern themselves with actors) nor am I an addict of old movies, which seems to be another **gay trait**. The **wifely boy in the play** had a mania for cleaning and decorating and I missed out on this too (here I have some regrets as this could be a useful aspect of personality). There were also references to Monopoly, which is supposed to be big with gay boys, tho I don't know any with whom it is. The nice living and loving relationship was pleasant to contemplate but I am very happy with what I have. I used to think that as long as I could

love it didn't matter much whether or not I was loved but I have lately been quite touched by Ken's concern for my insomnia and my general emotional state about the job. He says he loves to hear me breathe deeply in sleep and he worries about my reaction if Ed blows up, and I must say I like this. What never came up in the play is the way your friends try to cut in on any really choice romance you get going. When David says homosexuals are kinder to each other than married couples, he's nuts. He must never have had a really attractive love or else he didn't have a really attractive friend who had any chance to take the lover away. Both my beloveds and my friends were extremely attractive and when this is so you have real trouble on your hands.

SUNDAY, SEPTEMBER 21, 1969
Ken called to me to come quickly and I went to find Victoria and Titus side by side in the pan, each having a bowel movement. After supper we set out for the City Opera to see the first performance of MEFISTOFELE given in this city since the Met did it in 1926. It was an exciting nite in the opera house, with the audience responding to the superb work of chorus and orchestra and lighting designer. The libretto goes by fits and starts so it didn't entertain me as MANON did but still it was a nite of a certain magic and not the least magical was the way Carol Neblett did Margharita's big aria. Muzio's wonderful recording of that has been one of my favorites for years and I didn't think it likely that any modern soprano would even approximate her but she did a marvelous job. Treigle moved well as the devil but he turned me off with his absurd curtain call, coming out with a deliberate show of exhaustion as tho he had just sung all three Wotans. Neither vocally nor dramatically is the part that strenuous.

WEDNESDAY, SEPTEMBER 24, 1969
We ate dinner in the college cafeteria then went on to Lincoln Center so we'd have time to look over Alice Tully Hall, the newest public hall in the complex, set in Juilliard but completely separate. THE MERRY WIDOW was a long and rather tedious silent film but had interesting aspects. It struck me funny that every closeup of Mae Murray was in soft focus with back lighting to make her a blonde blur and then when the camera swung to the men it was clear, sharp focus. The way Roy D'Arcy played the villain was so absurd that you realized how far movies had come. We met Dave and John outside and walked them down to 57th St., which we were crossing to get the Madison Ave. bus. Dave

accompanied us. He insisted we must have a copy of AFTER
DARK, a new magazine which he insists is a CUE slanted to
the homosexual, and he dashed from newsdealer to newsdealer
till he bought us one. When I read it later I couldn't see
what on earth he was talking about. David said, "I'm going
to bring a little erotica in to your life" and later, "I'm
living in an erotic era and I'm going to make the most of
it." Well, I'm certainly not unresponsive to erotica and
have had dreams of one of the boys who played in PUPPY DOG
TAILS but I can't keep in a constant froth about this handsome performer or that, especially when I don't find most
of them nearly as attractive as Dave does. I think David
must have been shocked when I told him I threw out our
joint collection of young male physique pictures for he
said, "If you ever have the impulse to throw this out, give
it to Ken. HE won't throw it out." But, Good God, in this
era pictures of men in briefs or sexy clothes are so easy
to come by that you don't need to hoard them as one had to
in my youth. The supply could inundate you.

SATURDAY, SEPTEMBER 27, 1969
    Downtown to buy some tickets for Joffrey Ballet and
A FLEA IN HER EAR before proceeding to the Film Festival.
HE WHO GETS SLAPPED was rather a travesty on the original
play and a pretty tedious movie to boot. I found myself
falling alseep as I used to do in silent movies at the Museum of Modern Art. John and David like it, however. We met
them outside, stood watching the Leonard Bernstein-Adolph
Green-Betty Comden-Stephen Sondheim group kissing each other (and Bernstein and Green kissed too) then subway to the
Village. John brought out a score or so copies of Theatre
Magazine from the early Twenties which he bought three
years ago at the Flea Market and to my considerable surprise has not looked at yet. I looked thru them all, tho
it was rather saddening on several accounts. One wondered
what went wrong with the careers of several people pictured
who faded into obscurity, one missed in today's theatre the
type of glamour theatre had then, but one also realized
when one saw the list of plays recommended by their critics
that most plays then were worthless trivia, little if any
better than today's tv plays.

SUNDAY, SEPTEMBER 28, 1969
    No sleep all nite but I was very calm about it and
never even considered a sleeping tablet nor even reading
the book I had beside the bed. For one thing, the ginny evenings with John and David are invariably followed by a
restless nite, even if not a totally sleepless one. When

Ken awoke we talked a lot and agreed that we had more than just the physical hangover. The intensity of interest John and David show in the two subjects of theatre and sex gets to be too rich a diet. I would like to switch to something else but one subject or the other or a combination of the two is all we ever talk about. David, for instance, went to every showing but two during the run of COME OF AGE at the City Center. The very thought of seeing 14 straight performances of that really dreadful play makes me ache with boredom. We cleaned and after dinner we bussed down to the Metropolitan to see the new European painting galleries. Beautifully lighted and carpeted with red carpeting which is making fluff as people walk on it, the galleries go in for the old-fashioned way of hanging pictures above each other as they do at the Royal Academy. Since the lighting is geared for that, I don't mind it and for their centennial celebration they have brought out things like Bonheur's HORSE FAIR, featured at the top of the grand staircase when I came to New York but hidden away in storage for years.

WEDNESDAY, OCTOBER 1, 1969
    In the evening we watched a program called IN SEARCH OF REMBRANDT, which had a wonderful commentary and superb closeups of details in Rembrandt's paintings and drawings. It made us realize how poignantly we miss the old weekly art program from Boston. I was a little startled today to see Rena wearing pants in the office but I said nothing and was even more startled when Ed asked how I felt about it, as tho he rather disapproved. I shrugged and said, "Well, I guess it's no worse than mini-skirts and it isn't as tho she had any contact with the public." He apparently decided that that settled the matter.

MONDAY, OCTOBER 6, 1969
    A nice nite's sleep for the sixth nite and then we got to the office and had a 9:15 staff meeting that is likely to shatter my sleep for some time to come. Ed was in an absolutely vile mood, said things were going wrong because the people he'd asked to plan the automation had not thought things thru, etc. (*He had been touted when he was hired as an expert on automation but turned out to know nothing about it and to not claim he did*). He then announced that this Spring we were going to work nite and day for three months and that anybody who couldn't or wouldn't do it had better say so now, tho privately to him. I went to coffee with the shakes and was some time getting over them. I couldn't decide which was wiser, to let the matter ride and see if things collapse before then or tell

A GAY DIARY   105

him we weren't going to work such long hours so that he
couldn't say we didn't speak up when he said to. I decided
to bide my time for a while.

TUESDAY, OCTOBER 7, 1969
     Despite my disturbance over the scene Ed made and des-
pite knowing I had to get up early to go to Boston, I slept
well so insomnia must be really fading. The ISI (*the computer firm chosen to convert the records of our 80,000
alumni*) said they had no luck in getting temporary help to
work on marking the books so it was suggested that one of
the Babson College boys who works for them recruit some
students. When he arrived with the two who were to work for
us I nearly swooned for they were two terribly attractive
and charming boys. One, with his left leg in a cast, had
beard and moustache; the other, a real doll baby, wore
little love beads around his neck under his shirt and had
hair I would love to run my fingers thru. As they worked
with us they also proved to be nice fellows and good workers. I grew so enamored of them that I didn't even mind
working till 7:30. Warner, the doll, was so succulent that
I wanted to kiss him from top to toe if I could ever tear
my lips away from his moist kissable mouth. I thought that
if men are to wear beads I hope they go beyond these little
wampum things they now find permissible but even the little beads peeking out thru the neck of his shirt were seductive, tho Warner was by no means trying to be with either Elaine or me. Just working with them was a better sexual experience than sleeping with lots of other people would
be, tho going to bed with them would be nice, too. The boy
who had recruited them very nicely took Elaine and me to
the Wellesley Inn, where rooms had been engaged for us. I
needn't have brought my sleeping tablets for I could barely
finish the Times before I wrapped my arms around the pillow, pretended it was Warner (tho I would have been as happy pretending it was Greg, leg cast and all) and went to
sleep quickly.

FRIDAY, OCTOBER 10, 1969
     It turned out the school was going to permit those
who wanted to participate in the Moratorium against the
Viet Nam War to do so without penalty. I had rather scoffed
at Rena's desire to participate without losing pay as I am
rather contemptuous of those of the younger generation who
want to revolt at no cost to themselves tho they want muni-
tions manufacturers and others to cut off their profits.
In my day the young pacifists like David and Bob Scott
were willing to pay a high price for their opposition to

the system and this is how it should be. This has some element of heroism in it but Rena's way does not. However, as long as it is official policy I don't object.

WEDNESDAY, OCTOBER 15, 1969
      This was Moratorium Day for Peace Now in Vietnam and the school had all sorts of activities. Mike and Rena took the day off to participate and Bill left early to do so but tho I agreed with the objectives I didn't even wear the black armband as I perhaps should. Those who manned the table with armbands and buttons coerced nobody into joining them and the spirit of things, at least around Columbia, seemed truly peacable. I hope it is also effective. What a change from the days of the First World War when women (including Mother) were contemptuous of their men if they didn't go. (*I had trouble as a child figuring out why she sneered at his claiming me, newly born, as a reason for exemption from the draft. Only later, realizing her lesbian nature, did I grasp that, having served his purpose by engendering the child she wanted, he was disposable to her.*) In the Second World War there was no passing out of white feathers but there was mighty little pacifist talk except for the misguided America First business for which I fell. Now, however, mothers like Miriam Englander frankly admit their sons are back in college to escape the draft and girls are right beside the men in protesting the war. The power of youthful protest was shown when Lyndon Johnson was prevented from running for another term (I think we'd be better off with him than with Nixon) and I think a lot more can be accomplished.

TUESDAY, OCTOBER 21, 1969
      We were scarcely settled at work today when Ed sailed in and started lacing into Ken, saying, " I TOLD you when I gave you that check, etc." Ken was flabbergasted but I spoke up immediately and said, "You didn't tell him anything because he wasn't in the room when you brought that check around. You gave it to me and you didn't tell me that either." The wind went out of his sails at once and he apologized, saying it must have been Elaine to whom he gave the instructions. Even tho he was thereafter as calm as could be and had said he was sorry two or three times, I continued to fume that Ken at his age should be talked to that way. He's too damned conscientious and too damned obliging and the result is that at 64 the kids call him Ken except for the colored girls, who call him "Mr. Ken". Tho we are spoken of as "Don and Ken", I am addressed by all as "Mr. Vining" and I consider it highly appropriate

that this should be so. Tho I shall miss Ken there will be
one good thing when he changes jobs and that is that I will
not feel the need to defend and protect him (tho I shall
wonder how much he is being taken advantage of on the new
job). In the Columbia Newsletter circulated today I learned
that Eric Kocher has been appointed Associate Dean for International Affairs. *(Probably my closest friend while I
was at Yale Drama School, he had been overseas for many
years with the State Department and I had seen him not more
than a dozen times, if that.)*

THURSDAY, OCTOBER 23, 1969
     From work we went to the Yangtze River Restaurant on
57th St., where John soon joined us. I liked everything
Dave and I picked out (John and Ken talked thru the ordering). A PATRIOT FOR ME was attended by a sparse house and
we were able to move down. I agree with the play's detract-
ors, who say you never really get to know or care about
Alfred Redl, the Austrian Counter Intelligence agent, who
was blackmailed for his homosexuality and became a double
agent before the First World War. There were so many dull
and unecessary scenes and on the other hand obligatory
scenes were skipped and things took place between scenes
that were far more potentially interesting than what was
shown. Even the notorious drag ball scene disappointed me
as I thought it lacked campy wit (or any other kind) and
added nothing to the show. The play had no suspense, as it
should have had, and nothing fresh to say about homosexuality either then or now. But I didn't mind the evening because the company was pleasant.

SATURDAY, NOVEMBER 1, 1969
     To 79th St. to do some gallery-hopping and as always
I took a vow to do it more often because I enjoyed it so.
When we saw that the line outside Cartier's was not long we
got in the queue to see the diamond for which Richard Burton recently paid over a million when Elizabeth Taylor's
agent fell out of the bidding at $1,000,000. I have never
cared much for diamonds and this was no exception, tho
beautifully displayed, but I liked jewelry involving emer-
alds and rubies that I saw en route and I certainly enjoyed
the two handsome guards who stood either side of the diamond and for me quite outshone it. Ken and I lunched together and then he set off to get tickets for BUTTERFLIES ARE
FREE, which Florence had mentioned wanting to see when she
visits Christmas. I set out to shop for his birthday and
did very well indeed. I got home feeling wonderful about
Ken's birthday, especially since I already had the tickets

to COCO for him. At once my joy was crushed for Ken had not been able to get the tickets he was sent for so had gone up and bought three for COCO for the 29th. That had been my best gift for Ken has been dying to go and I have been just as determined not to go since I think it presumptuous of an actress to undertake seven songs in a musical at the age of 60 plus, when opera singers have to retire at 50. For at least two hours I was upset and depressed by this turn of events, tho I shall of course go ahead and present Ken with the tickets to show that I made the gesture. When I was the one presenting the tickets I had vowed to keep mum during the show no matter how much I hated it and the star but now it is going to be real work for me. I never liked Katharine Hepburn (nor any other mannered actress so beloved of the gay set). I don't believe for one moment that she will make the slightest effort to seem French, to behave like a couturier, or to be anything but a Bryn Mawr girl approaching Senior Citizenship.

SATURDAY, NOVEMBER 15, 1969
John and Dave called to say they would be later than they expected so I turned off the pepper steak only to have them arrive sooner than they predicted. Their overall impression of COCO, which they had seen this afternoon, was good but I don't know why because as the evening went on they said, "Hepburn can't sing AT ALL" "There's only one dance number, if you could call it that." "The songs really aren't a bit memorable", "There's no story AT ALL", etc. They brought me the first copy of GAY, an offshoot of SCREW but done in much better taste. SCREW turns me right off sex but this magazine has on the one hand a dignified approach to the homosexual world and on the other hand a sense of humor about it. It is the first erotic publication they have tried on me to which they won me over.

SUNDAY, NOVEMBER 16, 1969
Ginny called to say they would be delighted to accept the tickets to COCO and then we could meet downtown for dinner and afterward see the city lights. I thought with amusement of two aspects of David's sexuality as revealed last nite. He brings me all these gay erotic magazines but when I said Mother was a lesbian he reacted just as any burgher would, "Oh, she wasn't!""Yes, she was." "But she didn't realize it." "Yes, she did." Apparently mothers aren't supposed to be lesbians or lesbians aren't supposed to be mothers, tho he knows full well that many men who have fathered children are homosexuals. Another funny thing

was when he was trying to persuade me to lower my standards of beauty. "After all, the lights are out,"he said. "Oh, no," I said, "they certainly are not." "They're NOT?" he said, as tho he had never heard of sex with the lights on. I figure that if a person is attractive enuf to be slept with, they are attractive enuf to be looked at in the process. In fact, if I wanted the lights out I would know that I had compromised my standards and that light or dark it probably was no go. I don't mind sex in the dark but if I have it at all I would have to be willing to have it with lights on. David's shock at this tickled me for it shows there are numerous cracks in his sexual sophistication after all.

SATURDAY, NOVEMBER 22, 1969
    Titus, who would have no part of me yesterday, allowed me all kinds of petting today. He rather likes us all to be together on Ken's bed and here he will let us play games with him as well as pet him. I can put my hands under the covers and tickle his belly from below and he will attack my arm and have a great good time. My bed isn't the same kind of magic place but then we don't gather there. Bob called us when he was ready to leave his house and said he'd be here in ten minutes but it was well over an hour, which I suppose one must get used to when dealing with Latins. His room-mate was not with him and on the way out we learned that they are breaking up. When we arrived at Jim and Dick's house in Long Beach Jim was staring out the door pixyishly and Bob said "You don't see him at the office like that." Well, thank God I don't for pixyishness just doesn't seem becoming to someone who's sixty and looking more worn than Ken looks at sixty-four. There was another gay couple of mature years there and I liked Leo, with whom I agreed on a number of points. The first part of the evening went well but after dinner Jim and Dick kept on drinking and soon the dancing started. Dick first asked Robert, who declined, then Ken, who a little bit to my surprise, declined, then me. But they persisted. They seemed to accept Leo's refusal but they kept after Ken and me till the embarrassment mounted sky high. Bob eventually gave in and Dick got what he wanted, which was an excuse to paw a good-looking boy. Bob is one of those who can let himself be kissed by horny old goats without minding it but I just kept hating myself more and more for not being able to relent and be a good guest but in the first place it is no lie that I don't dance, tho I could have done as well as they did, and in the second I found all the dancers save Robert repulsive and I wouldn't dream of inflicting

myself on Robert. Jim said, "We expect our guests to participate" and Bob said, "Maybe on the second invitation." "There won't be any second invitation if they don't dance." That will be all right with us. When Bob got us back to the city he wanted us to see a gay restaurant run by some friends. With tomorrow's entertaining chores ahead of us, we preferred to go home. When we got there Ken said,"Well, what did you think?" and we had a post-mortem. He had felt just as stuffy as I had but less guilt-ridden about it. I was some time getting to sleep because I was so disturbed by it all.

SUNDAY, NOVEMBER 23, 1969
Up early and found the weather had turned warm so I had no excuse for not doing windows. The party was a great success. We played charades and at last learned the symbols for plays, tv, movies, song, etc. and how to give clues. We were not surprised to learn that Len had been out to Jim and Dick's for indications last nite were that the whole gay personnel of Teachers College, which is numerous, knows each other socially, knows the names of each other's cats, etc. We have been the holdouts, apparently, for last nite Bob said, to Ken, "To think that we have known each other for four years and never came out in the open with each other." This party took away the taste of last nite. These girls all hang around with gay boys almost exclusively but tho I think they hear confessions from some, we still keep our hair up.

TUESDAY, DECEMBER 2, 1969
After supper we headed right for City Center as this was opening night of the Alwin Nikolais Dancers and the curtain was therefore at 7:30. The ushers at City Center said right at the outset that they didn't expect many people in the Second Balcony so we were allowed to take seats in the forward part. It is just such nonsense when people complain that prices are too high for the theatre these days for the cheap seats go begging. All the music for the Nikolais company is electronic and I loved it as I did the fantastic use of lights and costumes. From a purely dancing standpoint they don't do many athletic feats but their use of multi-media is wonderful and a sense of humor crops up delightfully often.

WEDNESDAY, DECEMBER 3, 1969
At noon my browsing in the library led me to an interesting copy of PSYCHOLOGY TODAY devoted to sex. The article on homosexuality was by the author of THE GAY WORLD,

who again propounded his theory that homosexuals who feel unsure of their masculinity like to have a penis inserted in their mouth or anus with the subconscious thought that they will draw the masculinity into themselves. It sounds very logical if you don't know how much more complex homosexuality can be than any theory. I, for instance, like to suck AND fuck, but do not care much for being fucked and am so indifferent to being sucked that I frequently cannot reach orgasm that way. Now one of the things I like involves having a penis in me and one involves inserting my penis in someone else, and the things I don't like are equally mixed. Furthermore, I know many people who have these mixed tastes. My sexual preferences are both aggressive acts and the passive acts don't interest me much, tho on occasion they can if performed by masters. We're a varied lot and I've seen few theories that fit many of the people I know.

THURSDAY, DECEMBER 4, 1969
    Ed came in the office this afternoon in the company of the new young man from Buildings and Grounds. Ed hemmed and hawed then admitted they were going to move us. First he said it would be down the hall and the office would be nice, then eventually he got courage enuf to admit that we were going in next door with Mary. Later we were very interested that he showed such trepidation about telling us the truth but at the time our only reaction was profound shock. That room wouldn't even comfortably hold the employees and appurtenances of our office, let alone Mary's too. The contrast between the great waste space of Ed's new office and the cramped quarters in which we will have to work is fantastic. We each went out on a late break and had dinner separately in the cafeteria so we could leave right at five and get to 96th St. for the 5:15 start of a double bill. THE GAY DECEIVERS was a trivial but funny movie about two boys who pretend to be gay to get out of the draft.

TUESDAY, DECEMBER 9, 1969
    Topped yesterday's proofing record. After work I dropped off at the library to pick up MY FATHER AND MYSELF, a frankly homosexual memoir by Ackerley. After supper we left at once for City Center to see the Paul Taylor Dancers. Taylor is a large man as dancers go, looking as tho he might weigh 190, but what a sense of humor he has. Not only his stage effects (a chandelier that was lowered and kept on being lowered till it touched the ground and collapsed in a heap, then was drawn up and away) but in his

movement. I think the programming was bad as the first
number, PIECE PERIOD, was the kind of light thing that
ballet companies wisely send their audiences away remembering by scheduling it last on the bill.

WEDNESDAY, DECEMBER 10, 1969
Ken tried to have a nap when we got home but I decided to stay up and write more Christmas cards so the kittens also decided to stay up and get into mischief. Ken finally gave up and joined me, signing the cards I had left for his signature. Settled down to MY FATHER AND MYSELF, a very explicit book about an unhappy homosexual life. He seemed somewhat put off by intelligence whereas while I don't find it sexy in itself, I never found a mind put me off sex with anyone as long as it didn't make them precious. I was at least spared a definite attraction to the lower classes. That must really make for a totally hopeless situation and explains why he never found anybody he wanted to live with. Ken has only a year at an accounting school and a year at an architectural school but has a good mind and an interest in books which has greatly contributed to making our life together extremely pleasant.

SATURDAY, DECEMBER 13, 1969
We got an early start and separated at once. The Altman windows are not animated this year but are breathtakingly lovely and again I wished colored cards were sold of them. Each of the six windows was a regional building made out of cookies and candies--a mosque, a Victorian house, an English castle, a pagoda, a Swiss chalet, and a Russian church. The details were marvelous and seldom repeated from window to window. The roof tiles of the Chinese pagoda, for instance, were made of fortune cookies. Popcorn was used for snow surrounding some of the buildings and I want to have several more looks at those windows to study the fascinating use of gumdrops, peppermint sticks, glazed fruit, candy orange slices, etc. What a shame that such marvelous work should be so ephemeral. I listened to COSI FAN TUTTE, which was broadcast via recordings to fill the time scheduled for the Metropolitan broadcast. As the contractual difficulties have not been settled nor the season opened, they are using recordings as tho they were the real performances and giving the usual live intermission features. It was nice to hear the distinctive voice of Eleanor Steber in her prime once more. Ken ran into the Swedish sculptor who lived next door to me when Ken and I were first beginning our affair. He always seemed so tolerant of the noises he must have heard thru our connecting door that I had

wondered about him and it seems he has for many years been living with a man. At first they lived in Queens but as development squeezed it in they moved to Madison, Connectcut (which is where my grandfather is buried and where, I think, my great-grandfather's ship-building yard was). He now hates the city, feeling it dirty, filled with negroes and Puerto Ricans, and crowded. All that may be but he also implied to Ken that it wasn't easy for two men to live together in a small New England town and I can certainly believe that. I wouldn't want to try. Crowds or no crowds, negroes or no negroes, I love the city at Christmas and Altman's enchanted windows alone could keep me here.

MONDAY, DECEMBER 15, 1969

Poor Titus suffered a setback this morning. When Ken was cleaning out their pan, Titus stood up on the toilet bowl to watch the coming flush as both he and Victoria love to do. Suddenly the toilet seat fell down and cracked him on his head and after a day like yesterday when he allowed us to pet him endlessly, he is right back to harboring his worst suspicions of human beings. He wants no part of our apologies. By the time we got home at nite this regrettable development had worse consequences for his left eye was kept mostly closed. Eventually he reached the point of trusting us to pet him and he played and ate but the closed eye worried us. After supper I wrote the remaining letters to European hotels. All the Christmas cards that came today were from people I had hopefully dropped so I had some additional cards to write.

WEDNESDAY, DECEMBER 17, 1969

Titus' eye is now almost completely recovered. This morning he proved himself a retriever as when I was shaving he kept bringing me the catnip mouse and chased it when I threw it from the bathroom thru the kitchen and into the dining room. He must have brought it back a dozen times and put it at my feet.

THURSDAY, DECEMBER 18, 1969

Finished the proofing today but when I told Ed he didn't seem impressed and asked if I had a count of their errors. Mary called us to come up to a party they were having. It was just wine and cookies but that was pleasant and we had much joking about our crowded new quarters. I said we would have a housewarming but that the guests would have to come one at a time as there wasn't room for more. Mary seems actually to look forward to being back with us as she was telling Kathy all our cracks and pranks. Wish I could say I'm as happy to be sharing an office with her but I'm not. When we left there we went to Amsterdam Avenue to buy our Christmas tree. Ken was perhaps a little high on sherry and rushed thru the purchase faster than I wanted and I wasn't too happy with the tree we got but it will do. I decorated it as soon as we got home.

FRIDAY, DECEMBER 19, 1969

So many dreams are said to have sexual symbolism so if one has an outright sexual dream, does it have a nonsexual meaning underneath? I had a frankly sexual dream that was very enjoyable and I wish one could arrange to have more of them. I was groping an attractive young man who resembled nobody I can think of and we went on from there very pleasantly. Today was a wearyingly social day of a type I wouldn't want too many of, tho lots of New Yorkers have them all the time. At twelve we had the office luncheon. Then to the cafeteria party. Our office party was well under way when we got back. Ed was eventually very drunk. We ate in the cafeteria then went to Vi's party at the Women's Faculty Club. We talked to the woman from whom we got Titus. Home to whip the house into shape. Ken was feeling tired when we started out again but I felt that the tiresome part of the day was over and that with our meeting the Leonards the fun part of the day began. Jim and Dick sent us a Christmas card that says on the front, "On the Twelfth Day of Christmas, my true love sent to me" and then you open it to a picture of a naked youth and the legend "You were expecting perhaps a partridge?" Somehow I don't mind lewd cards on birthdays and minor holidays but I really don't like them on Christmas, irreligious as I am. Ken said, "They really are a pair of dirty old men, aren't they?" Perhaps I wouldn't have minded so much if the youth in the picture hadn't had such ugly genitalia, with such prominent veins and excessive foreskin, but as it was I found my sense of humor failed me completely.

SATURDAY, DECEMBER 20, 1969

The logistics of four people using the bathroom worked out okay and we got the Leonards off on their shopping expedition nice and early after a hearty breakfast. We were very happy that Titus had proved himself so sociable, not at all nervous about strangers (he had made off with Eddie's socks). We met Ginny and Eddie at Larré's and they said COCO had been wonderful (I will be surprised if I agree). Went home, where we had drinks and much talk.

WEDNESDAY, DECEMBER 24, 1969
     As the cats scampered about playing I thought how nice it is to have two again. I think we did the right thing by Lavinius by not plaguing him with a younger cat in his old age but the interplay between the two is fun. From a little misbegotten-looking thing, Titus is turning into a raving beauty. We went downtown in time to do a little more shopping before meeting Florence at four. We taxied home thru the park, which was pretty with a dusting of snow. Florence brought lobster and made a stew for supper.

THURSDAY, DECEMBER 25, 1969
     Up early and at the presents, which for all the moaning Ken and I had done about having no ideas, seemed unusually numerous. Just after dinner Florence noticed that it had started to snow and suggested that Mother start home. To my surprise she immediately agreed and it was a good thing she got under way because the snow continued and the forecasts got more and more threatening. We were napping when she called that she was safely home and was going to settle down and look over her gifts. With three heavy smokers going full blast all day, the house smelled terrible. Florence and Ken started talking family and Maine friends and I retreated first to a book and then to bed. One can certainly see the cause of Ken's lifelong preoccupation with unearned (oh, definitely not earned) money. If a marriage is mentioned, the first question is "Do they have money?", if a house is mentioned it is always in terms of what it cost or what it would now fetch on the market and people are discussed almost exclusively in terms of what they inherited, stand to inherit, stand to leave, or ought to have inherited. Eventually I begin to grow a little nauseated at the obsession. Almost never is there discussion of anybody who by virtue of his or her talent or hard work has made their money; it is always money come by thru marriage, divorce, or inheritance. But money as an unending topic of conversation bores me anyway. When I retreated to bed I realized that at some point of every visit by or to Ken's family I react violently to the way they bring out his less appealing characteristics and then when over the hump I adjust. Ken and Florence also share a preoccupation with weather which while not as deplorable as the preoccupation with money can be just as boring. They like to hear a radio weather report every half hour and fuss with the weather like a doctor constantly taking the pulse of a mortally sick patient. I really don't give a damn about what kind of weather they have in Ohio or Virginia or even the Long Island suburbs. My only interest in weather is to

know how to dress when I go out and I can look out and see what kind of clothes or equipment is called for. I don't have any faith in weather prediction and when I don't plan to go out for a matter of hours I certainly am not going to stop my conversation dead to catch the latest prediction or statement of weather for all states East of the Mississippi.

SUNDAY, DECEMBER 28, 1969

As we ate English muffins with coffee Ken broke off a front tooth. He announced he couldn't go to Ellen's party and at first I tried to persuade him that if he'd talk normally and not make such revealing grimaces, it would go unnoticed. He wouldn't believe it but hated to call Ellen, knowing what work she had gone to preparing her party and when I said I wasn't going either, there was a big scene. Florence, who has no idea how inseparable we are and no stomach for facing the thought, blew up the most and said there was no reason for me not to go. Knowing my New Yorkers a little better, I expected that Ellen would really expect me to cancel too but when we went in the bedroom so Ken could get the call over with instead of fretting so much, the first thing Ellen said was "Don't tell me you're sick, too!" I knew then that she had had other cancellations and I couldn't do it to her. When I took over the phone she said, quite acceptingly, "Would you want to come without him?" and I agreed, which made everybody happy but me. As it turned out, I enjoyed myself very much, partly because I now know the core of people and partly because illness reduced the numbers so that we had a little more flexibility in moving about. As the evening wore on, I realized that the 4 busses cease running about then and that I would either have to find a taxi or walk home. I took the latter course, not unaware of the danger of assault nor pleased with the icy footing but I made it safely and the brisk air had been very enjoyable.

MONDAY, DECEMBER 29, 1969

We went to COCO and I hated it even more than I expected to. Katharine Hepburn must have the ugliest voice and accent in the world. Sometimes it made me wince and at other times she gabbled so as to get thru the interminable exposition that I could hardly understand her and even Florence, determined to like it, said, "I think she's going a bit fast." Lines didn't get the laughs they might and it was a horribly boring nite in the theatre for me. The characters were half-dimensional. Chanel was a witch whose feminism began to sound uncomfortably like lesbianism before the evening was over. Her lovers were shown on film since the story, if one can call it that, started when she was 71 but one couldn't believe she had ever really had lovers because she had contempt for every male character in the show. I think I laughed exactly once, and it certainly wasn't at the swish designer, grossly overwritten and overplayed, just as if there hadn't been all kinds of developments in the depiction of gay men. This was just a fag act from 1921. I restrained my comments since Florence was trying so hard to persuade herself that she had liked it, but Ken, who had been equally determined to like it, sighed and said, "It really isn't very good."

1970

THURSDAY, JANUARY 1, 1970
    Downtown, the transit strike having been temporarily settled, and to the movies on 42nd St. BUTCH CASSIDY AND THE SUNDANCE KID was a wonderfully humorous rerun of the old theme of Western outlaws who find that the time for that sort of thing is past. Based on fact, it had some hilarious sequences after the outlaws transfer operations to Bolivia and forget their hard-learned Spanish phrases when trying to rob a bank. The beauty of the landscapes and of the two leading men, Paul Newman and Robert Redford, did nothing to lessen my pleasure. We had baths and then ate a sandwich to fortify us for June Metcalfe's cocktail party. The people I talked to were mostly those who had been at Ellen's party.

FRIDAY, JANUARY 2, 1970
    John's Christmas decors was stunning, as one might expect from a gay artist with a flair for that sort of thing. It is inconceivable that Ken and I would ever go to the trouble. They had lots of gay magazines for us and a record on which somebody named Zebedy Colt sang songs usually reserved for women singers, such as THE MAN I LOVE. He didn't leer and sang them very well. David had trouble cooking rice and made more martinis to fill the time gap. These did me in and with champagne on top of them at dinner I became ill. I had to go lie down. John played nurse and unfortunately also made love to me at this unpropitious moment. He said,"It's so nice to have someone to take care of" and then he'd start soul kissing for which, to say the least, I was not in the mood. After I fled to the bathroom and threw up he was very good, however, supplying me with mouthwash

and Pepto-Bismol. For a long time I thought I'd never make it home but eventually I felt able to attempt the trip. Ken wasn't in too good shape himself as he put on David's coat and then left his glasses and tobacco pouch there. We found the Christmas tree knocked over and decorations all over the room. Ken picked them up but made no attempt to redecorate as it all comes down tomorrow anyway. I don't understand why the cats were so good when the tree was fresh but have been attacking it and chewing off bits since it dried out.

SATURDAY, JANUARY 3, 1970

Woke with the worst hangover, perhaps the only real hangover, I've had since George Worrell's party 24 years ago. This one will do for the next 24 years too. I thought later of another parallel for that time when I was feeling so sick, Bob Lockwood picked that time to go in for sexual jiggery-pokery and last nite John. He even insisted on taking my socks off last nite (has he a thing about feet?) and he took a fleeting pass my basket that made me bridle, sick as I was. I ate some cereal, hoping this would settle my stomach but eventually it came up. Making my bed was quite a slow process as I had to lie down after every operation. I couldn't face the prospect of going to Peggy's tonite as I knew I'd never make that huge flight of stairs up to Park Terrace so Ken called and cancelled. We had talked some of turning in our tickets to PRIVATE LIVES for another date but after a little exposure to the cold moist air and a bowl of chicken soup I felt I could get thru it, and I did. Tammy Grimes has a very idiosyncratic voice, to say the least, but I liked her in spite of that. The whole thing was quite stylish and certainly amusing. John was waiting for us after the play with Ken's glasses and tobacco pouch.

THURSDAY, JANUARY 20, 1970

At 12:30 went to Butler Hall Penthouse to meet Eric. His first remark was, "Well, you still have your hair, which is more than I can say," but actually he is just a little bald on top and since he towers so above me, I wouldn't have noticed it if he hadn't called my attention to it. I had been a little nervous before meeting him, awed by his position as Associate Dean of International Affairs but he was the same old Eric and we had a very pleasant lunch. He said he found it hard to think of me not turning out two or three plays a year but he too has stopped writing, his novel having gotten nowhere. It will be awfully nice if we see each other with some frequency. Got the

announcement of the Spring Season of New York City Opera
and counted 69 performances, which is about what they do
in the fall season. This means they do as many performances
as the Met did when I first came to New York (*1942, before
City Opera had been born*) and the Met itself normally does
a much longer season than it did. In every way that matters
to me, New York is greater than it was when I came here--
more opera, more dance, more theatre (if you count Off-
Broadway, which I certainly do).

THURSDAY, JANUARY 22, 1970
      Ken was off again to the dentist's so I ate alone and
the cafeteria had the most marvelous beef hash, with few if
any potatoes in it, but lots of onions. I savored the memory of it the rest of the day. I reminded myself of Doris
Landman, who used to come back from the cafeteria tea and
sit daydreaming about how good the cookies had been. (*She
was a former employee who had been smuggled over the German border to France by French Boy Scouts, had been hidden
by French families in the South, and when the Gestapo came
by looking for jews, had been sent into hiding in the woods
till the danger passed. Bereft of all her family by the ho-
locaust, she honored those who saved her by enjoying all
the homely details of life.*) If I hadn't known how to savor
life before, she would have taught me (but I think I did
know). Last nite as I read I thought, as I so often do, of
how pleasant it was to sit there with Ken reading, with one
cat on laps and another at our feet. I lose a lot of time
savoring life instead of getting on with it, but I don't
think I regret it. We devoted this evening to reading, too,
after watching Julia Child prove that all French cooking
doesn't take a long time by getting a whole dinner in half
an hour.

WEDNESDAY, JANUARY 28, 1970
      Both of us woke early and decided we might as well
get up because we were upset over sending the cats to the
hospital (*for neutering*). Titus made it harder for us by
being more loving than we have ever seen him and generally
broke my heart at the thought he might think I was betray-
ing his trust. Dr. Johnson was waiting in his little office and said he'd give them a booster shot for virus. Ken
started to flee from the room rather than witness it and I
said I was willing to hold her but that he was likely to
lacerate me within an inch of my life. Dr. Johnson thought
not and it turned out that poor Titus was so scared that he
gave me no trouble at all. In the end I was glad I was comforting them when they got the needle. Ken turned out to

be even more upset about the cats than I was and on the
way down got one of those nervous backaches such as we got
when driving in the tunnel in Italy and unable to find the
way to turn on the lights. Dr. Johnson called to say the
cats were still dopey from the anesthetic but had come thru
fine and were good healthy cats.

THURSDAY, JANUARY 29, 1970
    When I went into the ward where all the cats were,
Titus huddled silently against the back of the cage but
Victoria began jawing at me immediately. Titus had not
turned against me for subjecting him to that. We had a nice
evening with the cats, reading quietly while they licked
their wounds. Titus had a hard time jumping up on things
but otherwise seemed fine.

TUESDAY, FEBRUARY 3, 1970
    The men from Buildings and Grounds came early to move
us and it went smoothly. Our only real trouble was that the
room was hellish hot from the pipes and the Buildings and
Grounds men were in and out trying to adjust the air con-
ditioner.

WEDNESDAY, FEBRUARY 4, 1970
    Ed summoned us to a ten o'clock conference and as we
went down the hall I said, "He's probably going to announce
his resignation", which was exactly what he did. I was not
as shocked as some since he had said to us once that he
never stayed more than one good year in a job and it seemed
unlikely that he could make this fund-raising year equal
last.

SATURDAY, FEBRUARY 7, 1970
    The phone rang and it was the Nadelmans being apolo-
getic about inviting us at the last minute but asking if
we could come to a party this afternoon and evening. They
claimed they had thought of us originally but simply hadn't
room with the 20 they were having but now some had cancelled and if we didn't think it was too terrible of them, etc.
We didn't but it meant I had to rush out for clean shirts.
Ken and I got along famously with the other guests, at
least with the wives. The men were somewhat dull, as men
seem too often to be, but one woman named Mildred immediately took my fancy with the way she got right into the act
when Ken and I started one of our silly fantasies about
having met her before in Paris and Ken starting an apache
act with her as his partner. "I can still show the bruises,"
she said, and we were off and running. Gabe Nadelman, tho

of course not believing the apache part, really began to
think we had met her in Paris. Another woman who is a real
estate agent (every last wife worked) took a shine to us
and kept saying, "I don't want to dominate your whole evening but I like you so much," and would follow me when I
moved chairs in an attempt to circulate. Whenever I mentioned Ken, who helped a lot with the serving, as usual, she
would say, "Such a lovely man. Marvelous man." And he is.
As I looked at the other men there I thought Ken looked
mighty handsome as well as much more socially bright. We
were going to leave when the general exodus took place but
Mimie said Lenore wanted us to stay a while since we didn't
have a journey so we did, while they relaxed. It was funny
when it came out that we knew Mildred was blind in one eye
because she cut the cornea with a pair of scissors she was
using to do something to her eyelashes. "That's funny,"
said Gabe. "She's my cousin and I never knew that."

TUESDAY, FEBRUARY 17, 1970
    Ken got up after a sleepless nite and said he didn't
feel well. By noon it was clear he had some sort of virus
and he went home without needing any particular persuasion.
I did the shopping by myself. Had supper at school and Ken
just had some cereal before we set out to see the preview
of NORMAN, IS THAT YOU? John and David were there so we
talked to them at the single intermission. The play was
undeniably funny but I couldn't share Dave and John's enthusiasm nor join in their predictions of success because
to me it harked back to George Abbott's heyday in the 30's
when character was distorted for the sake of a gag. A
"farce" about a Mid-Western drycleaner who comes to New
York and discovers his son is a homosexual, it showed that
the authors were either unobservant or of no mind to deal
with the subject in any terms but those of cliches. The
apartment was furnished in purple and lavender, the Mid-
Western father considered possession of a pet cat in itself
effeminate (whereas I doubt that even Mid-Westerners think
of cats as sissy and dogs as masculine and surely the authors know how many gay people dote on their dogs) and the
gay room-mate wore very mod clothes and beads, a garb I
have never seen a homosexual wear tho lots of male men
are doing so. I laughed a great deal, however, even as I
deplored so much of the play.

FRIDAY, FEBRUARY 20, 1970
    We kept lying down then getting up and doing something
else for the party. We persuaded ourselves that the distraction would be good for us. The party didn't go too

well as John dominated the conversation with dictums on
actors and plays that were at complete variance with what
most of the rest of us felt and his machine-gun delivery
was too fast for Bob's comprehension so he just fell out
of the conversation. Again there was much of what I call
silly talk about people at TC being gay when I'm certain
they're what they seem, straight people with children. I
kept my doubts to myself instead of scoffing this time but
again I felt I don't like gay parties as well as mixed
parties. We went to bed overwhelmed by the amount of food
left, disappointed that the party hadn't gone better, but
relieved that we now had a clear calendar and could be as
sick as we wished, tho I think party-giving pulled us together.

SATURDAY, FEBRUARY 21, 1970
    Simply couldn't get out of bed this morning at all. I
hadn't had as bad a nite as the previous one but when I
coughed it was as tho my lungs were being ripped and the
pain would continue for twenty minutes. Ken felt better and
went out for the paper, then read me all about the flu ep-
idemic which is supposedly subsiding. There have been a lot
of fatalities and when I coughed I thought I was about to
be one of them. I hope our guests didn't catch anything.
At noon I got up, made my bed up fresh, shaved, had some
cereal, and then ran out of steam and had to lie on the
couch. I brought books over beside me but somehow being
miserable proved a full-time occupation. My eyes hurt, for
one thing. I listened to the broadcast of TURANDOT and with
Nilsson in the title role one was assured of as solid a
performance as one got when one tuned in TRISTAN in the
thirties and heard Flagstad and Melchior. Domingo was a
fine Calaf.

TUESDAY, FEBRUARY 24, 1970
    Felt like work after all and got thru the day without
particular sag even tho the office was so hellish hot that
I would have thought my fever had come back if everyone
else had not been complaining equally. I returned the mystery book to the library. Walking felt so good that I walked the rest of the way home and thoroly enjoyed it. And
only yesterday just getting up out of a chair took such effort that I had to think about it for five minutes and I
groaned at the thought of crossing the room to get something. Remembered the German lesson for a change, tho not
until it was well under way. I was glad I did as they had
pictures of the Kurfurstendam, on which we will be living,
and some usable sentences were taught about the U-bahn.

When we turned the television on, Titus went over to watch, as he often does. A spark jumped out at him from the metal stand and he was so outraged that he repeatedly hit back at the table.

THURSDAY, MARCH 5, 1970
Dave sent me pictures of Mark Frechette, the supremely handsome new actor. What a gorgeous nite one could have with him but my first choices would be Mark Dempsey, the bearded one of OH, CALCUTTA and Jean-Louis Trintignant, both men I would like to be married to, not just sleep with. I always prefer the kind of man I would like to shop for socks with as well as sleep with, which I suppose is why I am in effect married instead of bed-hopping.

SATURDAY, MARCH 7, 1970
Went to 42nd St. to see OH, WHAT A LOVELY WAR. It wasn't a good movie but it had effective scenes and I cried all thru the scene of that remarkable Christmas when the Germans met the British in No Man's Land. I have seen it better done but it is a moment of history that always moves me. We saw the newspaper GAY POWER on the stand so I bought a copy and while Ken napped I read it from cover to cover. The militancy of some of the gays astounds and delights me. It has a centerfold picture of a nude man much as Playboy Magazine has a centerfold of nude women but these are frontally nude. As we passed thru Times Square there was a total eclipse of the sun, the first visible in a thickly populated area since the one in 1925. I remember in 1925 that we had smoked glass to look at it but they issued dire warnings about looking at it this time and didn't seem to think smoked glass was enuf. I kept sneaking quick glances out the side of my eye but mostly contented myself with seeing how dark it got.

SUNDAY, MARCH 8, 1970
We bussed to the Village to see LA FEMME INFIDELE, a movie that was good enuf but did not, I thought, live up to the praise some reviewers had given it. On the corners people were passing out handbills which, when we read them, turned out to be a summons to a rally for gay people to protest the raiding of The Snake Pit last nite and the arrest of 165 people. The Mafia must not have paid the police their protection money. I can't think of any other reason why dozens of gay bars should be allowed to function while others are raided. My hat is off to those who have the courage to declare themselves publicly as gay and stage protests against discrimination.

TUESDAY, MARCH 24, 1970

Tedious day. I walked home with a stop at the library to see if any of my reserve books were being held till the end of the mail strike allowed them to send notices. None were. I so enjoyed my walk along the park and found myself singing happily under my breath, all the numbers from MAME that were played at Patty and Amanda's the other nite. Got home feeling very exhilarated and liberated after that confining day at the desk. What a daily five miles would do for me!

WEDNESDAY, MARCH 25, 1970

Downtown to City Center to see the Joffrey Ballet. THREE-CORNERED HAT had a fresh new production based on the original Picasso designs but it certainly shows its age with all that pantomime to tell the story. The group numbers offered a pleasing amount of dancing but I don't need to see that ballet again for it convinced me that dance moves on. As a matter of fact I think it disappointed me some twenty years ago when I saw Massine dance it. The second ballet, CONFETTI, was a new trifle but what a circusy, spectacular trifle, to the SEMIRAMIDE overture. I loved it and could see it again because the dancers all looked as tho they were having a perfectly wonderful time.

THURSDAY, MARCH 26, 1970

We went right from work to the Village to see THE DAMNED at the Art Theatre. We bought the first issue of GAY PARTY and the latest issue of GAY, then ate a light supper at Zum Zum. Barbara had predicted that I would be depressed by the movie, which is a fictional account of the Krupp family and their part in the rise of Nazi Germany. I was not, however, because I detest the Krupps so much that I didn't care how much the woes were piled onto them. My only regret is that in real life the Krupps came off very well during and after the war while little, relatively innocent people suffered. The casting director had rounded up an astonishing number of terribly good-looking males and in the scenes in which the Gestapo surprised Roehm's homosexual storm troopers in their vacation revels there were a lot of lovely bodies strewn about, tho the esthetic effect was somewhat spoiled by all the fake blood spattered over them after they'd been machine-gunned. We read the two gay magazines and from the wantads got a partial education. Several invited others to join them in internal water sports and one specifically mentioned an enema. My God, do people really get sexual pleasure out of this? Several others wanted to meet heavy men, one

specifying that partner must be over 260 pounds. I find
this absolutely repulsive. I must be a hopeless romantic
for almost nobody was advertising for tenderness and affection and companionship.

SUNDAY, MARCH 29, 1970
    It was more like White Christmas than Happy Easter. I
ran out for the paper but had no time to look at it before
our departure for Trenton. There was snow on the way but
only sleet when we got there. Later, after this had coated
the trees with ice, the snow came and added up to two or
three inches by the time we left. When I first caught sight
of Mother I was shocked at how old she looked but I got
used to it. When we got to her apartment and she took her
damned wig off, she looked ten years younger. As we drove
up to the wonderful building she now lives in, I almost
broke out in laughter for I saw Brothers of Israel Trent
Center over the door. "Well," I said, "You've finally got
some advantage out of looking jewish." When I think of our
battles over her anti-semitism in the forties but she's
all right on that subject now and very grateful to the jewish girl who pulled strings and got her in there. The public rooms on the first floor include a sort of lobby where
people can entertain, a game room with several card or
checker tables, a large sort of dining room with kitchen
where special suppers can be served, a little library, etc.
The apartment is just ideal, with lots of closets, nice
kitchen facilities, and a very nice view from her several
windows. I tried to persuade her to give some of her books
to the little library so others could enjoy them but she
couldn't be induced to part with them. I moved a pillow in
my chair and saw a small burn in the upholstery then a huge
burn two inches in diameter and very deep, then when we set
the table I saw about thirty burns on the table and she
said that was when she used it as a desk, which may seem
like an explanation to her but not to me. She has also had
another auto accident, minor, was ticketed for careless
driving and had to pay a lawyer $125 to get the case dis-
missed. When it came time to go we found the car windows
coated with snow and ice so insisted on walking.

FRIDAY, APRIL 3, 1970
    We went to Radio City to get photos taken for the
Czechoslovakian visa. Down to the German Tourist Office
for pamphlets and hotel information on Regensburg, Bamberg,
and Bad Godesberg. To the Little Carnegie to see FELLINI
SATYRICON. There was much frank homosexuality. Downtown
was so crowded today and uncomfortable to make one's way

about in. I see why some people turn against New York for they don't see it in the serene mood we usually see on our Saturday morning forays downtown.

MONDAY, APRIL 6, 1970
Ken had to leave before me this morning, as jurors have to check in, but after this he can leave later. All sorts of people asked me where Ken was. "Where's your friend?" "Where's your buddy?" was the refrain all day. Since the census form came and I found that a person living with someone else unrelated is officially to be called "Partner" I have felt I had a good approved word for him. I had got the marvelous idea yesterday that I would surprise Ken by renting a television set so he could see the blasted Academy Awards tomorrow nite. I was a little set back by the $9 cost but it was worth it and I also arranged for a repairman to come look at our set Saturday. Walked home after work enjoying the nippy dampness and very pleased with myself for what I had done but when I got there I found the reception was very poor on the channel that will carry the Award ceremonies.

MONDAY, APRIL 13, 1970
My task for the evening was lining the kitchen cabinet shelves with new paper. After the kitchen chore I read the other pornographic novel, BATH BOY, set in Ancient Rome but giving the merest brushoff to history. As is so often the case there was much about the terrible pain of penetration. This may be aimed at the masochistic set but it sure isn't the whole story of penetration for five or six people in my limited sex life have penetrated me without pain and I have penetrated others, big as I am, without all that moaning and groaning, screaming or any other sign of intense discomfort. If the penetrator is of sensible proportions and the penetrated is in a properly receptive psychological state, it can be managed without all that agony.

WEDNESDAY, APRIL 15, 1970
I clung to the thought that the boring day would end by our going to the first preview of the musical COMPANY and that for dinner before that we were going to have steak. Fortunately both the steak and the show were good. There was by no means a full house and I rather think that the Alvin is too large a house for COMPANY for at intermission many people were complaining that they were missing the lyrics. We were way up at the back and I heard almost all of them and enjoyed them, as I did the music. One thing I would like removed is the scatological humor, but that

gets more and more common this year. Soon no show will be complete without at least one "shit" and one "asshole". Nudity in the theatre is great but I dislike the scatology.

THURSDAY, APRIL 16, 1970
When Ken sewed the Venetian blind tapes the other day he also sewed Titus' green mouse, which Victoria had disemboweled. When we throw it for him to retrieve she also goes after it and while Titus stands staring in horror, she starts to tear it limb from limb again but we always interfere. Now we have found the little blue ball which is the only thing Victoria will retrieve so we throw his mouse one direction and her ball another but every now and then both will go off together after his mouse or her ball. This morning a chubby jewish boy and a little colored boy came in and asked if they might have some of my spare time. Asking that was the duty of the colored boy and when I agreed the other boy told me they would like to interview me about my opinion on legalizing drugs. They asked very pertinent questions and without any physical assets at all were very cute and impressive. At lunch I was approached by a team of three, all with cute long hair, and I said I had already been interviewed, at which they looked crushed. Then it turned out it was not about drugs but about yesterday's Peace Moratorium that they were assigned to interview me. They were not quite as thoro but still very impressive. My God, the wonderful things they do in school now. I won't hear a word against the teaching today nor, for that matter, about how awful children are today. I'm glad I have work that keeps me a little in touch with youth since I have no children. What a wonderful teacher those kids must have to give them real burning issues to consider even at their age.

SATURDAY, APRIL 19, 1970
All day long we got ready for the party but without rush or pressure so that I didn't feel exhausted and even if I had, it would have been worth it for the party was one of our best in years. Ken took instantly to Peg Kocher. I had met her 21 years ago and remembered her favorably but was impressed anew. Everything I had hoped for in a meeting of the minds took place--Miriam plied Eric with questions on foreign affairs, Mimie and the Kochers compared notes on people they mutually knew in the foreign service, and Eric and Alice and I discussed travel in Greece and Turkey. Ken's pie was a great success and Mimie took the recipe to xerox and give to Miriam. The evening just flew by. Eric has a new play nearly finished. He says he can no longer

stand the well-made plays like CHILD'S PLAY (I have not turned against them when they're as good as that).

THURSDAY, APRIL 23, 1970
Good German lesson before work, the book I am using now being the best yet and one I bought more years ago than I remember. After supper took off for Carnegie Hall to hear the London Philharmonic. I had not realized that this was their first appearance in America. The crowd was interesting but in particular a tall, thin blond boy with long, immaculately clean hair who got into the elevator in front of us with his girl friend, also nice-looking and with equally lovely hair. He seemed very nice and sensitive without losing manliness and I was quite smitten. They sat about a dozen rows ahead of us and his eyelashes were so long that I could see them batting in profile when he turned sideways to talk. The music was lovely. Arrau played a Liszt Concerto (2nd?) and the Bruckner Second Symphony was not familiar music but I loved it. Home and right to bed without the nightly ginger ale, which meant that Titus couldn't sit and watch the bubbles in my glass as he does nightly. He never takes his eyes off those bubbles, which mean absolutely nothing to Victoria.

SATURDAY, MAY 2, 1970
Downtown with a longish shopping list and also looked at television sets. Home after a lovely time on uncrowded streets and in gorgeous weather. I saw so many tourists and was glad they were having such a lovely day in our city. We had a very light supper then Ken started to make the custard for the marmalade pudding. He was interrupted by the arrival of Pat and Peg and as a result it burned on a bit but he rescued it and while it didn't taste normal, it tasted good. The evening started well with our catching up on what we'd all been doing, then as we started bridge Ken got on one of those spells where he tried to demonstrate to guests how hard I am to live with and hopes to elicit agreement with him in all the domestic disputes we may have had in the previous six months or six years. I finally said, "You're having a hard time tonite, aren't you?" after he made a scene because I thought he had misdealt the cards when dealing for Pat and was proved to be wrong. He had been similarly exasperated when I suggested the custar was burning, altho in fact it was. I consider it beneath my dignity to enter into the discussion when Ken goes on this way before guests--squabbling couples are bores enuf, and two squabbling men are an embarrassment. Peg asked me to go down to the car with them and Ken didn't hear her so

when I stepped into the elevator he said, "Where are you
going?" and I said, "I'm leaving you." At that moment I
thought back to the dear old days of the Men's Residence
Club when I could say that in earnest and stomp out and
slam the door on him for a week or two when I was that angry. When we went to bed I was a long time getting to sleep
because of my accumulating anger. I was fully aware that I
was just as busy feeling sorry for myself as he had earlier
been. It was the first time in a long time that I had con-
templated separation but in reality I wasn't actually contemplating separation but just a THREAT of separation,
which is quite a different thing. And I really knew it
would blow over tomorrow.

TUESDAY, MAY 5, 1970
    At noon I went down to Columbia Travel and ordered our
train tickets. The university was on strike against the war
in Cambodia and was seething with activity--card tables at
which one made donations for telegrams to the President and
various Senators, petitions being signed, etc. Before Bob
R. came in with a petition to Senator McGovern for us to
sign I had already sent off my own postcards to the two New
York Senators, plus Nixon and Fulbright. Ken keeps saying
protest is futile, which infuriates me. He knows absolutely
nothing of political action and is strictly a sidelines
case. It was warm and anyway I wanted to ride on down with
Ken to the Conservatory Gardens, so I bussed home. Last
nite I had walked on down to see what state the blossoms
were in and found them just in their prime so I wanted him
to see them. The pinkish-white ones were at their breath-
taking peak. Those gardens are so underpublicized and under-
appreciated.

WEDNESDAY, MAY 6, 1970
    We went to our coffee break early because we figured
the general emergency meeting called by the President would
run on. It did and was eventually carried over to tomorrow.
It had started quite calmly with everybody standing for a
moment of silence in memory of the four Kent State University students who had been killed by National Guards when
innocent bystanders at a campus revolt. It continued to the
passing of a well-worded resolution deploring the War in
Cambodia and the repression of dissent on the campuses but
then some of the students got silly. They tried to add to
the resolution instructions for the trustees of TC to refuse to withhold taxes from the employees lest this help
the war effort, they tried to get TC to use its assets as
bail money for the Black Panthers, etc. All this nonsense

was decisively voted down but took a lot of time and my
bladder began to complain. I did no voting on such questions as to whether students who took the rest of the year
for revolutionary work should be graded, whether classes
should be reconstituted to deal with questions of peace and
academic freedom, as I figured that was between students
and teachers and no concern of staff. Some of the lazier
and sillier staff raised the point that if students were
going to get credit for anti-war and anti-repression activities, the staff should be paid for any time they took for
such activities. These young are contemptuous of business
men because they take war profits and don't give them up
but they want to be paid for their idealistic activity.
Went to the Village to see CIRCLE IN THE WATER. Only two
women in the audience as the near-nude photographs outside
were a warning that it wasn't a play for mixed audiences.
As far as I'm concerned it isn't a play for homosexual audiences either. There was frontal nudity all right and the
bodies were very well-chosen, but the play is about cadets
in a military academy and entirely too sado-masochistic. We
have outgrown this old tale of the latent homosexual awakening to the real nature of his desires in the end. We want
less latency and more blatancy.

SATURDAY, MAY 9, 1970
    BORSTAL BOY was not Ken's dish and for the first act
I didn't think much of it either. When we came out there
were young girls getting signatures on petitions and as we
passed the Palace Theatre a nice girl asked us to sign one
to McGovern. I told her we had already signed one to him
at Teachers College and she was charming. I heard some
people behind us whom she had asked saying," I don't know
what it was, but I sure as hell wouldn't sign it," to which
the wife replied, "I wouldn't even be sure that's where it
would end up." I wanted to turn and spit in the face of
such stupid asses, so damned smug. By no means was the girl
a hippy. I almost think the students had gone to pains to
select girls whose hair and dress would not offend even the
most reactionary people and certainly her manner was soft-
sell and charming yet these assholes act as if she's a
flaming revolutionary. Yesterday construction workers attacked the peace marchers and marched to City Hall to insist that the flag, at half mast in memory of the slain
students at Kent State, be raised to full staff. I may get
mad at Mike's opportunism but when the chips are down I am
with pacifist youth all the way. There are times when it's
nice to realize that soon educated youth will outnumber the
old fools. Some will grow conservative but in general I

think our nation will improve as they come into positions of power.

SATURDAY, MAY 16, 1970

    We had one of the old trains going to Long Beach and the windows were so dirty that they made the gray day look even grayer. We got there before the other guests. They turned out to be all "gay marrieds", including the two lesbians from Babylon. All, that is, except the very late-arriving Bob and his new lover Tom, very attractive in an off-beat way tho conversationally dull. At first I thought it was a very cozy atmosphere, all us stable old gay people, but eventually it palled and I decided again that I much prefer a mixed party. I cannot see homosexuality as a full-time occupation or even a full-time preoccupation as they seem to. I liked almost everybody and had a good time till I decided I should circulate and went over to sit by Robert. Suddenly, over the babble, Jim called out loudly to stop talking TC with Bob and break it up. Robert and I protested we hadn't been talking TC but were silenced and so was everybody else for about ten minutes while Jim pumped and pumped and pumped to get some life back into the party. I was furious and stopped drinking thereafter. I'm not sure whether jealousy played a part in Jim's reaction or not but Bob had been fussing with my hair to show me how I should wear it down over my forehead in the current fashion and both Jim and Dick like to fondle Bob in a way I find a little revolting. I thought we were going to escape the dancing but eventually they started. Ken gave in quite quickly this time and eventually even I did, agreeing to dance with a nice man named Mac just to prove I didn't dance. I think I convinced him but soon I was trying some of the more modern steps under tutelage from Robert. The older men don't like modern dances where there is no contact between partners as the contact is the whole point of it for them but if I have to dance with a lot of people I find a little physically repulsive, that kind of dancing is more tolerable. When Ken surprised me by saying we should practice some time I suggested right then. He was agreeable but the first thing I knew Jim was at our side saying, "Don't you think it would be better if you danced with somebody besides your regular partner?" Having had just about enuf directives from the host as to what I should do and whom I should do it with, I retired from the floor shortly thereafter. Ruth asked us if we were free Memorial Day weekend and when I said we were she asked us to dinner. We also made a hit with Leo, whom I liked last time, and who got our address from Ken so that we could all play bridge some day. He got going for a long time on how much he respected my opinions on plays and how much he liked the way I expressed myself in general but later he got incoherent. Not so much as Jim, who could hardly get his words out. One of the funniest things was when Leo was holding forth on modern dance on one side of the room and Jim picked a quarrel with him (after thinking he said I know not what) by saying, "Leo, we've had a war every 25 years and it's never going to be any different." I never heard two people argue before when each was talking about a totally different subject. When Ken and I got in and had our post-mortems we agreed that we hadn't hated it as much as the previous party but that we didn't care for gay parties and that Jim's stopping the party dead was appalling. I am not cut out for these things as I am too unforgiving.

WEDNESDAY, MAY 20, 1970

Worked on Ken a little more to accept the Babylon invitation. He says he doesn't like either woman very much and I guess I don't either but the number of people we like very much is limited and I think we may have to settle for people we find just "all right". I felt rather depressed by the news that 150,000 people turned out at the City Hall Pro-War Rally sponsored by the building trades unions and that a lot of people around the country are saying things like "Hurray for the National Guard" and "They should have killed all those students".

SATURDAY, MAY 30, 1970

At three we left to catch the 4 o'clock train to Babylon. Lee rushed right up and kissed us and hospitality reigned from then on. We drove to their lovely house, found Jim and Dick waiting there, and were given a tour of house and grounds by Ruth. Like Gene and Mac and Dick and Jim they apparently like working on a house but Ken and I hate all that. There are just so many other things we'd rather do, starting with reading. Before we left Mac said he wanted our address and phone number as they'd like us to come up for a weekend at their place. Jim wasn't a bit hostile tonite and when something was said about Ken and me having been together 24 years this month, he said, "Congratulations," in some sincere awe tho I think he and Dick have been together longer than that. Mac and Gene have put in 21 years together.

TUESDAY, JUNE 2, 1970

After supper a nap and then to the Met to see CAVALLERIA RUSTICANA and PAGLIACCI. Ken had not seen them since he was in Naples during the war and I hadn't seen the pair since San Francisco in '43 tho I saw PAGLIACCI in Rome in '49. I never expect to see either better done. Franco Zeffirelli did sets, costumes, and direction and if he hadn't tried to extend his talents to the writing of a libretto for ANTONY AND CLEOPATRA I would be less grudging in my admiration for him. Both operas were given very busy productions with life in a Sicilian village minutely depicted in the first and lots of detail in the second, too. Corelli may be the imperfect musician many claim he is but what a glorious natural voice he has and in addition to that he is handsome and a gifted actor. His performance as Turiddu would have done credit to an actor unable to sing a note. Since these June performances are non-subscription, the audience was not the impassive one the Met usually draws and screamed bravos for all their favorites.

THURSDAY, JUNE 11, 1970
Miss Gelinas joined us for coffee again and we are certainly going to miss her when she stops Sarah Bernhardting about her retirement and moves to Boston. Today she told us again about working in the operating room with the great Dr. Harvey Cushing. An interesting and in many cases attractive audience gathered for THE DIRTIEST SHOW IN TOWN, which certainly lived up to its name. Ken and I had singles on opposite sides of the theatre and I just knew he was hating the unstructured form of the play. The boys and girls were attractive, they stripped utterly, and there was no kind of sex I know of which was not simulated sooner or later. I was much smitten by one boy who had low-swinging balls and a handsome head. Ken was grim when I rejoined him and I made no attempt to win him over to the play but all the way home I kept laughing at the memory of certain scenes. I am amazed at myself for not being uptight about the nudity and the simulated sex but again it is because everybody was beautifully built and of an age when sex should be natural and joyous. When Ken and I got to bed we talked at length about the play and Ken seemed most disturbed by the foul-mouthed lesbians fighting in a bar, and of course bull dyke lesbians disturb me too. Mother was definitely the butch type of lesbian but at least her language was never foul any more than my speech is campy just because I'm a homosexual. Lesbians haven't been given as fair a show on stage as homosexuals have. Ken expressed a degree of distaste with the homosexual world and homosexual parties that surprised me a little bit for I used to think he fitted in better with all that than I did. I think he did, too, and that the reactions of his more

mature years are not really what his reactions were at the time. Certainly he could always bear flirtation and more with men of less looks and greater effeminacy than I could ever stand.

TUESDAY, JUNE 16, 1970
We did some extra cleaning this morning in anticipation of the visit of Miss Dockery to see about cat-sitting. Our impression of her improved still further as we talked with her and heard her sensible questions. Both cats were so nervous about her that they wouldn't eat their supper but after she left they settled down.

SATURDAY, JUNE 20, 1970
An absolutely lovely birthday in every way. We had actually been chilly in bed even under a blanket. Ken piled the presents on the breakfast table. To Alice's. The other guests were Pearl and Anton, Allan and Florence Perl, and Rosalind Alpert, the woman Alice met at the Sterling Forest Bach weekend. She seems a rather silly sort (flunked out of the Peace Corps) and the cat Hector, who usually stays timidly on a shelf in the bedroom or under the bed, hates her. He had already attacked her twice and in the course of the evening cornered her again. Seems that a year ago she stepped on Ajax, his brother, and Hector has apparently never forgiven her. This was such unaccustomed fierceness for Hector, the frightened, that we couldn't believe it. He stayed right in the living room all evening and has never tolerated so much of my petting but for Rosalind he had no time. After a marvelous dinner Alice showed her slides of the Seychelles, and then at the request of the Perls, of the Galapagos Islands. I would pay money not to go to either place. Rosalind, who usually stays over nite rather than go home late, apparently thought it better to be mugged than to be attacked by a cat, and went in on the subway with the rest of us.

FRIDAY, JUNE 26, 1970
Dan personally delivered our new contracts. There was a $700 raise for me and $1000 for Ken, who is still $300 behind me. It won't affect his pension as much as it will affect mine but it was a nice gesture for his final year and I was very happy for him. Read more of GAY magazine and speculated as to why I rather bristle at all things lesbian. I guess it's because I went thru all that a bit too much in Mother's heyday--the possessiveness, the jealousy where men were concerned, the pipes, the pants, the swagger, the constant downgrading of men, the wooings

and the breakings up. Even as a child I saw something terribly sad in her pursuit of women who just didn't care as much for her as she cared for them or who still wanted men in their life, as Mildred did, to Mother's disgust. Mother could have forgotten my birthday (my 13th) just as well while in a flutter over a man as she could have while wooing the teachers of Moorestown High but it happened to be women of whom I was jealous on that occasion. She could likewise have run away from home just as well over a man who betrayed her, but she did it because she was upset at the interest Mildred was taking in Jim (*and I, taking seriously her announcement that she was leaving and never coming back, ran screaming after her begging her not to leave me, pleas which in her upset she ignored, so that I returned to the house in tears, feeling abandoned*). I could have been caught in the cross-fire between her and an interested male admirer but it happened that I was caught in the cross-fire between her and Claire II and between her and Ethel. It was also upsetting that Claire I was involved in the lesbian charges brought by her dike pupil and lost her job over it, which rather embarrassed me since Mother was known to be her close friend and I was known to be Mother's son. Of course I don't disapprove of lesbianism but still the dike type gets my back up. Mother's trouble was chiefly that she was constantly attracted to women who were only passingly lesbian. Both she and I might have been happier had she found someone thoroly committed to that life. I would also have been happier had she not got involved with teachers in the school systems I was attending. No sooner did we get away from Moorestown, where we had had the scandal of her being asked to resign as head of the Business and Professional Women's Club she founded (for reasons vaguely stated at the time but which I then and now suspected to be of a lesbian nature) than we went to Bloomsburg so Mother could be near Claire I and then that scandal broke. Well, anyway, despite my proclivities I prefer the company of heterosexual women to that of lesbians.

SUNDAY, JUNE 28, 1970

We decided to go down to Christopher St. and Sheridan Square, where Gay Pride Week was to be celebrated by assembling for the march north to the park. As we walked to Sheridan Square we saw handbills posted which said the march to the park was to have started at 2 so we were not surprised to find no activity on Christopher St. Ken bought bananas, which are supposed to put potassium in his system when the pills take it out, and we subwayed toward

home. As we approached 72nd St. I began to toy with the
idea of getting out and walking thru the park, just to see
what was going on. "I want to be authoritative when I report to John," I said. "I'll take your jacket home," said
Ken,"I want to know, too." The first thing I saw in the
park was busloads of policemen but as it turned out they
were not there to round up the homosexuals but to protect
them. I never thought I'd live to see that. If they had
expected resentment from the heterosexuals, none was in
evidence. Some went on with their sunning and games, ignoring the large assemblage on the South of the Sheep
Meadow, and others went down to mingle with the crowd and
see what was going on. I saw only two outlandish outfits,
jeans being the order of the day. I did see a lot of long
hair, which up to now I have thought of as being confined
to heterosexuals, but I didn't see much pulchritude. A
priest from the American Church, which welcomes homosexuals if their affairs are sincere and of long standing, was
answering questions. A homophile group from Philadelphia
had a big banner around which they rallied and one girl
had a big poster which said "I am a Lesbian and I am Beautiful". An endurance kissing contest was going on but from
as much as I could see looking over the crowd it appeared
to be a boy and a girl, tho with today's long hair one
can't be sure from the quick glance I got. I didn't stay
too long as I merely wanted to see what was going on and
to be counted, but the count doesn't mean much since there
were so many sightseers with cameras in the crowd. I don't
think the camera bugs got anything spectacular for there
was very little freakishness or campiness. On the Mall a
British West Indies group was entertaining a group with
some very interesting native music, blissfully unconcerned
with the gay-in a few hundred yards away. Central Park is
just a wonderful place.

WEDNESDAY, JULY 1, 1970
     As Ken made room for Miss Dockery by clearing out a
couple of drawers, he unearthed all kinds of lost and/or
forgotten things including unused Christmas presents. We
waited in vain for Miss Dockery and finally had to leave.
I called from the East Side Terminal, however, and she was
there. She said Victoria was being friendly but Titus had-
n't made up his mind. When we checked in at the airport
they said our nine o'clock flight had been delayed till
10. This seemed a boring prospect but was as nothing to
what really lay ahead of us. Hours wore on and nothing was
said about our flight. The terminal was filled with jewish teenagers in red jackets and red hats, all en route to

a teen-age camp in Israel. At last one plane-load got off but we lingered and after about two hours we saw the long-departed passengers returning to the lounge. One of their engines had conked out. Finally we were told to board busses which would take us to our plane and at quarter of five our nine o'clock flight took off. We were famished by then as we had repeatedly put off buying a sandwich in the arrivals building because we thought we'd be leaving any minute.

THURSDAY, JULY 2, 1970
    We caught the bus to the Central Station, which I knew was at the beginning of the Damrak and before we walked to Hotel De Roode Leeuw I inquired about the times for tomorrow's train to the Alkmaar cheese market and for Sunday's trip to Berlin. We both felt very euphoric about Amsterdam. From our window we can see the hippies gathered in the square in front of the palace and we have lots of street life to observe, as we did in Lisbon, and as in Lisbon there are plenty of handsome youths.

FRIDAY, JULY 3, 1970
    In company of many other readers of EUROPE ON $5 A DAY, we saved ourselves 12 guilders by going to Alkmaar by train instead of by guided tour. Our train was the Cheese Express, which meant that girls in costume came thru with samples of cheese and a man passed out maps of Alkmaar and an announcement of an hour's organ concert in the Great Church. We followed the crowd to the Weighing House and eventually edged close enuf in the crowd to see the porters carrying the sleighs loaded with cheese. There was quite a crush and when we fought our way back out of the crowd to go to the organ recital I realized my back hurt a bit from the shoving (not confined to Americans). The rest I got during the organ recital cured me and was good for tired feet, too.

SATURDAY, JULY 4, 1970
    We had an excellent woman guide for the Marken trip and a nice crowd except for three extraverted boys from Israel, whose distracting chatter had to be shushed several times. Much has changed since I went to Marken 18 years ago. For one thing it is no longer an island as land has been filled in and for a second thing the young people no longer dress in traditional costume. Some older people do but when they die I wonder if the Marken-Volendam trip will not have to be discontinued. The amusing lady who showed us the inside of her house also showed the costumes once

worn by the children, little boys and girls both in skirts, but now they all look like little modern children anywhere. At the cheese farm where we stopped for a demonstration (tho the guide said all cheese sold at home and abroad is now factory-made) we bought a cheese. As soon as we got back to town we deposited the cheese in our room and set out to visit the attic where Anne Frank and family hid out from the Nazis for so long until finally discovered and sent to concentration camps. One wonders if Anne Frank's fame won't fade like Edith Cavell's when other heroines star in other wars.

SUNDAY, JULY 5, 1970

We had to change at Amersfoort, about half an hour out of Amsterdam, and from then on it was ride, ride, ride thru not terribly fascinating scenery. When we got to East Germany all sorts of officials piled on board and we had to buy a sort of transit visa. As we progressed we saw soldiers with machine guns and even tanks in the woods. This seemed to affect Ken more than was called for. When we passed out of East Germany into Berlin there were more soldiers, guns, and police dogs. The Zoo Station proved to be three minutes walk from our hotel on the Kurfurstendam. We were both famished after a day of nothing but snacks so we went right out to Haus Wien, one of the recommended cafés. There a gay waiter was prone to keep catching my eye as he served us and those around us. He was nice enuf but paled beside the many beauties strolling the Ku-dam in their Sunday best. The blonds tend to emphasize their blondness by wearing white and look really stunning. The older people dress quite formally and I noticed more ladies wearing hats here than I've seen in a long time.

MONDAY, JULY 6, 1970

We signed up for a combined West and East Berlin tour. We had a nice girl as guide in West Berlin, a wonderful young man in East Berlin. The wait at Checkpoint Charlie was tedious and the sun beat thru the glass roof but it was interesting. We saw the guards slide mirrors under cars passing thru, to see that no East Germans were trying to escape that way. We were astonished at the building going on in East Berlin. Historic buildings have been rebuilt and they have even contrived to make them look old. Because the plans have been lost, they work from photographs. The new architecture, which I thought might be dowdy under Russian influence, is wonderfully modern. We stopped at the Soviet War Memorial, where 5000 of the 20,000 men they lost in the Seige of Berlin are buried and while taking pictures there

I found my camera jammed. When I got to a camera shop, the girl told me it was not my fault, that the camera needed repair. We are not here long enuf to have it repaired, however. We have both become very enamoured of Berlin, with its many parks and open places. It must have been exciting and lovely in pre-war days and now it's exciting because so new and full of interesting architecture and current history. We saw a wonderful sight this morning, of which I would love to have had a picture. The streets were being repaired by a number of workmen, three of whom were working naked to the waist and with shoulder-length blond hair. One was standing stroking his hair like a woman and then decided to comb it so jumped over the trench in the sidewalk and combed as he looked at his reflection in a bank window. The youths are lovely to look at here. Once the cut of European pants was apt to seem dowdy but not now. Trousers are tailored to display firm little buttocks and firm little baskets and long, slim legs. Looks disappear in maturity, tho, for Germans almost seem to embrace old age. Certainly they don't fight it as Americans do, dressing in youthful garb and doing their hair in coy youthful ways. The right way must lie somewhere between the two national approaches. After a nap we went out to dinner at the Schultheiss opposit the Kaiser Wilhelm Memorial Church, an ugly ruin which like Coventry on the other side of the fence in the war has been left standing but is flanked by beautiful modern structures made of many little panes of blue glass which glow beautifully.

TUESDAY, JULY 7, 1970

We found that the Dahlem Museum was open today and how to get there by U-bahn. Next to us on the train for much of the way was a tall, gorgeous blond, dressed in white as so many are. I wanted to kiss up the insides of his thighs right to Mecca. Dahlem was a lovely suburb and the museum, tho still being constructed and with installations incomplete, had more than enuf to weary us. We concentrated on paintings and I loved the Holbeins, the Bellinis, and the Botticellis except for a St. Sebastian whose facial expression was ridiculously casual as tho to say, "So I'm full of arrows. What else is new?" The floors were newly polished and they had warning signs, which were necessary for I nearly slipped several times anyway. The afternoon we spent at the zoo. We ate at another Schultheiss tonite and for the first time the portions were so large as to kill my appetite. My appetite wasn't improved by the number of people around me who were having steak tartare. When we saw people eating that in France it was very lean

meat but here it was half fat. Not that I'd want it even
if lean. At least we saw our first and so far only policeman, a traffic cop on very casual duty. We have heretofore
been amazed at the absence of police.

WEDNESDAY, JULY 8, 1970
        Breakfast early and caught a 54 bus to Charlottenburg
Palace. The bus driver was very nice and told us to sit behind him and he'd tell us when to get off. The guards at
Charlottenburg were also very genial and nice and guided
us from the historic rooms to museums in other wings. We
had cold meat and fruit for lunch in the room and then set
out for our Potsdam bus. Much work was going on at Sans
Souci and Ken found the place disappointing. I don't think
this was so much due to the shabbiness of the exterior as
to the fact that it had only 12 rooms. When we later visited the Cecilianhof, where the Potsdam Conference took
place, and were told that it had 74 rooms, Ken felt more
impressed even tho the rooms date only to 1916 and are
heavy and dark and architecturally undistinguished and even
tho we saw fewer than 12 rooms, the bulk of the Hohenzol-
lern castle now being a hotel. For myself I'll take Sans
Souci for I prefer small castles and except for worn up-
holsteries and damask walls, the interior is in a fine
state with fresh gilt and such highly polished floors that
only those of us with rubber soles could walk on them without donning big felt slippers that went over shoes. After
seeing the two castles we were bussed to the Interhotel
Potsdam, a big showplace I had seen from the train, and
there we had tea and a banana pastry. I nearly went out of
my mind at the conversation at the table next to me between
two sets of people staying at the Berlin Hilton. They wanted iced tea, ice water, and they compared hotels in the
various cities rather than experiences. Home with less delay at the border checkpoint than we had had going out. It
had been hot and we were sticky so had our showers before
lying down. Neither of us was as tired as usual so we talked instead of sleeping. Out for a return visit to Haus Wien
again waited on by the gay waiter who was just as appreciative of us as ever. We ordered a Berliner Weiss and loved
it. The raspberry flavor did wonders for the beer and it
was inexpensive so that I wished I had discovered it earlier. We had a table just inside the glass and street construction forced all the beauties right up against the
glass. We took to speculating as to which might be US GI's.
If their clothes were form-fitting and they moved briskly
with good posture, we knew that they were Berliners. If
their clothes were sloppy and their gait shambling so that

they looked as tho moving their body was a chore, we were
sure they were Americans. One thing we've noted is how happy Berliners seem. The whole city seems a happy one despite
their political problems. We don't ever expect to return
but we have liked it very much. I didn't really anticipate
that I would.

THURSDAY, JULY 9, 1970
   We caught a train at the Zoo Station which took us to
the East Station in East Berlin and there, after purchase
of an East German visa, we got our train to Prague. All
the passport control people were very nice and the landscape we passed thru was much more interesting than what we
came thru on the way from the Netherlands. As we approached
Czechoslovakia, a nice river with excursion steamers and
hills that rose sharply and dramatically appeared. Joining
us from time to time was a charming Yugoslav who works in
Sweden. His compartment was next door but he came over and
talked two or three times then eventually went forward in
the train in search of girls. At the border we were required to purchase $3 worth of Czech currency for each day
of our stay. A statue of a woman offering bread and salt
was set among lovely flowers at the first station in the
country. Joining us in our compartment after the departure
of our Yugoslav friend were two Czechs in their thirties,
of the intellectual class. One read a book, leaving his
friend nothing to do but look handsome, which he certainly
did. When our taxi deposited us at the Flora the desk man
said we had paid for a room without bath but he would give
us one with bath because he didn't think we could possibly
spend all the money we had paid in four days. Seems there
has been devaluation or something and for four days we are
very rich.

FRIDAY, JULY 10, 1970
   On the lovely way to Carlsbad we saw a "motorest" at
which the little cabins were shaped like beer barrels. When
we arrived in Carlsbad we at once had lunch at the Grand
Hotel Moskva Pupp. It was a good lunch and we enjoyed conversation with the Canadian ladies. Our guide Helen walked
us down the main street afterward, showing us several houses where Goethe stayed on his numerous visits, taking out
a silver cup at the old colonnade and letting us taste the
water, and pointing us toward a Russian Orthodox church
built by and for the Russian nobility that favored the spa
in its glorious days. We had till 3:30 to wander and were
amazed to see fish in great numbers in the warm river that
flowed from the many hot springs. Carlsbad looked just as

we thought a spa in Mittel-Europa should look, with great
six-story houses rising up the hills on either side of the
central river, crossed often by bridges and bordered with
trees and flowers.

SATURDAY, JULY 11, 1970
    We decided that if we weren't to be late at Cedok for
the city tour we had better taxi there. Our guide was wonderful, with far more fluent English than Helen had. We
went first to see the not very remarkable performance of
an astronomical clock then up in the tower of the city hall
(where a gypsy wedding with two brides was taking place on
a lower level). There proved to be some advantage in being
older as we were allowed to go to the tower in an elevator
whereas the young were required to walk up. I asked the
guide if we would see on this tour the theatre where DON
GIOVANNI had its premiere and she said we would not but she
pointed it out to me from the tower. My interest in this
and in Kafka's birthplace caught her fancy and she told me
a lot of interesting extra things. She was violently anti-
Communist but chose her moments to make her remarks. A
6'6" American youth who didn't yet know how to handle his
height and walked like a newborn giraffe asked a couple of
political questions, which I would never do lest it endanger the person. I let them take the initiative for they
can choose the safe moment. For instance, in the Senate
room of the Town Hall the woman said,"Many historic events
have occurred here and are recorded in the windows--but
not the latest one." By which she meant the Communist takeover and her tone of voice told what she thought of it but
nothing could be done to her as a result of that remark.
Later, in quiet asides, she told us much of the true situation, which she of course deplores. We saw gorgeous old
libraries in a former monastery, Hradcany Castle, the
cathedral (where another wedding was taking place and the
organ booming impressively) with the grave of St. Wenceslas
and then the Golden Lane where Kafka had lived. We never
got a chance to buy postcards and when we came back across
the river we saw the shutters down and knew the town was
going to be shut up for the rest of our stay. Went to a
restaurant recommended by our guide and found her eating
there with some of the French from our tour. Considering
the low standard of living, I wondered how two handsome,
well-dressed young men (one dark and a blond with his girl)
could afford that restaurant. We had a lovely meal and
then went in search of the station to get our seat reservations for Monday. It was a bustling, confusing place and
nobody spoke English but my German seemed adequate to the

occasion. Hearing it and seeing it so much, I am improving greatly. I had used it in the restaurant, too, with great success. I am much less self-conscious about it here than I would be in Germany. At home I fight German, which I don't like as well as French, Italian, or Spanish but over here I don't seem to feel the antipathy to the language that I feel at home, probably because I like the people so much. One thing we've noticed is how nicely groomed the Czechs are. I had also been impressed by the attractiveness of the couples. At home so often a pretty girl will go with a homely boy or a handsome boy with a dog of a girl but here I have seen so many couples where both are attractive and slim and neatly dressed so that one loves seeing them together. For instance when we went to dinner there was a couple at a corner table who were living dolls--blond, apple-cheeked, very much in love. He was large and loving, she a little timid and they may have been honeymooning, but at any rate I could hardly take my eyes off them and their wonderful complexions. We were so stuffed at dinner that we went for a short walk. There were people on the street but again so few lights visible in the houses that we wondered if electricity was so expensive that they felt they must grope around in the dark. We had some nice radio music, much of it American records, but the best of it symphonic. We also had some interesting political talk--in English to our surprise, about countries behind the iron curtain. It turned out to be from Berlin and I don't understand at whom this quick-flowing English is aimed but we found it fascinating to hear it here. We then heard more English from Warsaw and the propaganda level increased. I found it interesting to hear America excorciated and as far as Vietnam is concerned, I agree, but the Soviets are in no position to talk after their suppression of freedom here in Czechoslovakia.

MONDAY, JULY 13, 1970

We went down specifically to see the old synagogue, which our tour had pointed out without visiting. The 1270 Gothic synagogue, the later baroque one, the cemetery and the museum in memory of the Czech jews who died at the Terezin concentration camp were all fascinating and the woman who explained the gravestones was particularly thoro in explaining the symbolism of the names and of the many little stones on the grave of the great Rabbi Low. We walked down to the river and regretted that we had forgotten the camera for we could have gotten excellent shots not only of Hradcany Castle but also of the empty pedestal where, before de-Stalinization, the largest statue of

Stalin in Europe once stood. We waited in our room for the dining room to open and I got diary up to date. Again we stuffed ourselves but when we went to settle our bill we still had 70 crowns unspent. The nice woman said she wasn't supposed to give us the surplus but would arrange something and we wouldn't say anything, would we? We said we wouldn't but we were hardly on the train before Ken started to tell a fellow passenger and I had to cut him short. The woman hoped we would come again and shook hands in a charming manner. We taxied to the station, got on the right train without too much trouble, and had a pleasant trip. I was not as bothered as Ken by such things as the search of the train by Czech soldiers, who looked under the cars and up in the roof compartments for fellow citizens who might be trying to escape to the free world, but even I felt a little relieved after I knew we were in Austria. Looking out the window I saw four little boys in bits of Indian garb pretending to attack the train. On reaching Vienna's Franz Josef station, a rather ratty place, we changed money then taxied to the hotel, which proved admirably central. Waiting for us was a letter from David asking us to call him. As soon as we washed up, we did, and he said he'd be right in from his hotel, which is out near Schonbrunn. While waiting, we signed up for the tour to Mayerling, the Vienna Woods, and operetta at Baden. David soon appeared and we went out walking. He is full of enthusiasm for the many historic sights and this I share but he is also full of enthusiasm for tacky little souvenirs and was astounded that we had bought nothing so far and weren't thinking much along those lines. We stopped in for banana splits and wandered some more then went back to our hotel lobby and planned our day together tomorrow, building it around things David has not seen and things close together.

TUESDAY, JULY 14, 1970

To the Maria Theresa statue, our appointed meeting place with Dave. When David met us we found we couldn't get started right away on museums because they didn't open that early and in the case of the musical instrument museum, it proved not open at all. What we finally saw, in the course of a tiring day, was a wonderful royal collection of silver and china which I think Ken and I must have missed before, the warehouse full of abandoned Hapsburg furniture, which was new to David, and the Wagenburg of Schonbrunn. In between David had us running in and out of souvenir shops, most of them dealing in shockingly cheap souvenirs. We ended up at David's sumptuous hotel out by Schonbrunn, supposedly the emperor's former guest house.

There a cute bellboy proved the first really attractive Austrian I have so far seen. David showed us all his many purchases and while we were impressed with his ability to see more in Prague in one day than we had seen in 2½ and still make all his purchases, we were horrified at the quality of the stuff he bought. When the rain stopped we all trammed down to the Ring and walked to the Rathskeller for dinner. To the memory of my raspberry in aspic pastry at Demel's was added the Salzburger Nockerl with which we finished our dinner. We had two in fact and the handsome waiter was charmingly amused as we struggled to consume it. We walked David to his tram and then walked home. Both David and Ken were all turned around and would have gone in exactly the wrong direction but I got obdurate about direction of movement as I am seldom wrong about that. Just about five minutes before we reached the hotel fatigue hit me suddenly. Writing diary was a tremendous exertion and I have to plan our sightseeing for the rest of our stay. I simply didn't allow enuf time for so marvelous a city as Vienna. I'm sorry there aren't more pretty people for we have had legions of them up to now but at least the city is gorgeous. We keep telling each other how much we love it every two minutes.

TUESDAY, JULY 15, 1970

To the military museum. We saw not only the car in which Franz Ferdinand was riding when shot but also the bloody uniform he was wearing at the time. The other highlights of the military museum were a death mask of Maximilian, tents captured from the Turks in 1683, lots of things belonging to Radetzky, uniforms from various periods from 1683 on and a little uniform belonging to Franz Josef at the age of 13. We decided to eat at the restaurant we had seen down in the Opernpassage. On the menu was tea with rum for only one more shilling than tea with lemon so I tried it and found it so delicious that I'm going to have it that way at home. One thing we've noted is that waitresses here all wear a special type of shoe with the heels out but with sides that lace up above the ankle to give them support. The waitresses in America might be glad of such support but might reject them as dowdy, tho I don't think they really are. Before going to supper Ken had missed one jacket and had fretted that he would be so stupid as to leave it in Prague. When we got home I looked and saw all my jackets in the wardrobe then realized I had sent his jacket out to be cleaned by mistake. I got a laughing jag as Ken got silly about it.

FRIDAY, JULY 17, 1970

We had a very full final day in Vienna despite steady downpour. After breakfast we set out for Schonbrunn, taking the trolley out Mariahilferstrasse. As we got on we asked a woman if this trolley went to Schonbrunn, just to be sure we weren't heading in the wrong direction again, and then we forgot about her. Lo and behold, just before she got out she came well back in the car to tell us we should get out at the next stop. People have been so nice in Vienna, as in Prague. By great good luck we got mixed up with an American Express tour at Schonbrunn and their fat, humorous male guide proved to be marvelous. He was even rich in American parallels to events in Austria, such as the anarchist who assassinated McKinley and the anarchist who killed Elizabeth. I also never knew that Crown Prince Rudolph knew all 11 languages of the Austro-Hungarian empire. Schonbrunn again impressed me as being the loveliest and most interesting palace I have ever seen. Back in town and to the clock museum, which proved to be very near the hotel. When we finished there we went shopping for soap and toothpaste as the only hotels to provide us with soap were, ironically, those of Communist Czechoslovakia.

SUNDAY, JULY 19, 1970

We got up to discouraging weather. We set out for the Kaiservilla, thinking that would keep us out of the rain for a while and there we had a wonderful guide, an older woman who must have conducted the tour hundreds of times but who made it sound like no more than the sixth or seventh time she had done it. We saw the desk at which Franz Josef signed the declaration of war (I never knew he did it at Bad Ischl) and the woman said, "You never saw or heard such rejoicing. I'm sure the war would have been declared even if it had been put to a vote." He never returned to Bad Ischl once the war started but everything is as he left it. When we finished the tour the sun began to break thru and we walked in the Kaiserpark, discovering the little summer houses and pavilions on the hill, hidden from the villa by the magnificent trees. We sat and watched large parties come to go thru the villa and were glad we had been so early as we had only six or seven in our group. We set out to walk to the Katrin Seilbahn, the chairlift to the top of a nearby mountain. Ken was afraid we would get chairlift No. 13 and we just missed it by one. There was a cafe at the top and we had some tea with rum. There was a father there with hair just graying (we had seen him at the gondola loading place and were to see him later in town) who attracted me enormously. Men his age often

attract me visually but leave me cold sexually when I come
to imagine sleeping with them but I would leap into bed
with this one without second thoughts. He was so admirably
proportioned, so good with his boys, and so handsome. We
walked back to town, played two rounds of mini-golf, at
which I was terrible, then went home to take baths.

MONDAY, JULY 20, 1970
    Up to lovely clear skies. After breakfast we walked
down and signed up for the trip to Hallstatt and the Gosausee then went over to the Lehar Villa. It was really quite
interesting, even to Ken, who really prefers mediocre roy-
alty to top-drawer creative artists. (*The villa had belonged to Franz Lehar, composer of THE MERRY WIDOW and many
other operettas less well-known in America.*) After we came
out we had tea with rum at a café along the river. We then
walked further along the river to have lunch at Zauner's.
Here the day began to fall apart. We had gone there, I
thought, because they had a good menu for $1. Suddenly it
turns out that Ken didn't want the menu, wanted an omelette
(which they didn't have) and we began to quarrel. I said
that if he'd said so before we could have gone where they
had them, he began to sigh, whine, feel put upon, and go
out of focus. Fortunately (or unfortunately as it later
proved) we agreed on a salad plate. The poor over-worked
waitress was so long bringing it that we grew afraid we'd
miss our tour. When we got to the tour place we found there
were only five of us for the tour and we were going by
taxi. The Gosausee was gorgeous and cars by the score were
parked there but the people were mostly dispersed, walking
around the lake, I imagine. We did the best part of one
side, marveling at the views of mountains and glaciers at
every turn. I was tempted to send Ken back and try the
circuit but I was afraid it would take longer than the allotted time and I didn't want to keep people waiting. Good
thing I went back with Ken for as I was picking out postcards he began to feel sick. The tour went on to Hallstatt,
as charming a lakeside village as one could find and Austrian to the teeth. I adored Hallstatt, from the waterfall
plunging down the mountain in the middle of town to the
chalet-type houses and the wonderful market place but I was
sorry Ken was not in condition to appreciate it. I barely
got him back to the hotel as he got uncontrollable shakes
and no sooner did he get there than he had to go to the
bathroom and soon after that he threw up. He went to bed
and I wrote diary.

WEDNESDAY, JULY 21, 1970

    We had to change three times to get to Berchtesgaden but it wasn't difficult. On the last leg of the journey I sat next to a young blond dream who was inclined to flirt and flaunt his conspicuous basket. Both Ken and I were delighted and I had to use all the restraint at my disposal to keep from running my hand along his leg. When we all got out of the train he said, "Now your holidays begin," and we were glad we hadn't made any remarks about him, not that we would, for I always expected educated youths here to be bilingual. We taxied to the hotel, found that we had a balcony looking out on the panorama of the valley and were ecstatic. When we changed our money we found that the miniature golf course was in the park right next door so we went. It proved a far more ingenious course than the one in Bad Ischl and on three or four holes I had to give up and take my limit of strokes. A man playing around in front of us badly split his pants when bending over to pick up a ball and there was much hilarity over it. When we turned in our clubs we found another raving blond beauty, also full of charm, and also wishing us good holidays. Much as I love Austria, the men are not handsome and in six days I doubt if I saw six attractive males. No sooner do I hit Germany than the world is lit by beauties and charming ones too. I wish I had been charming when I was young and attractive. Instead I was always braced against attracting those who didn't attract me and therefore probably repelled some I liked. It would be beneath my dignity now to pursue a youth so much younger than I and at the age of the blond in the train I wouldn't have thought of teasing or enticing men so much older but it was delightful to have this boy offer matches when Ken got out his pipe and slide down in his seat so that I could see his basket as he read. After our round of golf we set out for a walk but got no further than the hotel when it began to rain and we retreated to our balcony, where we watched the rain recede. The dining room proved lovely with a view over the valley and a waiter who was homely but who sold everything he brought. Of my venison steak he said, "This is a specialty of the house. Our boss is a hunter," and of something he brought to an adjacent table he said, "Das ist mit liebe gemacht". People arrived to dance and it was all very lively. When the people were dancing I said to Ken, "We must practice this winter in case we go to any more parties at Jim's." "I'd dance with him," Ken said, nodding toward a handsome Englishman at the next table. "You wouldn't dance with me," I said, rather loudly because of the noise the orchestra was making but just then it stopped dead and I clapped my hand over my mouth. If anybody noticed, they gave no sign. We went out and played another round of golf, being greeted as old familiars by the blond. I had three holes in one to balance the holes I had to take the limit on and I beat Ken.

FRIDAY, JULY 24, 1970
After breakfast we wandered down the street and bought some more souvenirs. As we walked I was smiled at by a handsome blond in the uniform of the Hotel Watzmann. When we belatedly realized that it was the boy from the train we greeted him and he came forward to shake hands. He works in the hotel mornings. We left our purchases in the hotel then went out to play one last round of minia-ture golf. That blond was not on duty at that hour of the day but in the foursome just ahead of us was one just as good and maybe better. Every time he bent over to pick up a ball it tightened his pants so that the outline of his underpants showed sexily. In THE SAND FORTRESS (*a gay novel we had found on sale among paperbacks in an ordinary Vienna bookstore*) a character rants about jockey shorts because they don't show the basket but while I am not averse to seeing a man's basket down one leg of his pants, I have the invention of jockey shorts to thank for the tight pants that so nicely display bottoms. I am not a size queen and I don't need to see a great bunch on a man. Except for less than half a dozen freaks, I have seldom encountered a man whose genitals weren't of adequate size. Enuf is enuf and indeed too much is too much. We returned to the hotel at eleven, settled our bill for a mere 14 marks over our de-posit, and took a taxi to the bahnhof. As we left the high mountains behind I was a bit sad but as we pulled into Munich we found it rather nice to be back in a city. Until we saw the city, that is. Our hotel room in the Bundesbahn Hotel was fine but when we went out we found the whole city torn up to build a subway. I thought the English Gardens would be a welcome change from the dusty main street so we set out. By the time we reached the gardens we were hot and fatigued and Ken was of a mind to be pleased with nothing. I fear we are reaching that point of the trip when tempers shorten. I loved the rush of water thru the gardens but could see that the only thing to do with Ken was get some food and drink into him for we had had little. We walked back to the Ratskeller but this didn't work well either. By this time God himself couldn't have pleased Ken and we proceeded to get a bad waiter who put him in even more of a pet. The shuffling man first forgot our soup and jumped right to bringing me my cordon bleu. Then he came back to

say there was no more Hungarian goulash and would Ken settle for fillet goulash. With very bad grace he did and it came ten minutes after I started my meal. When his came I made the mistake of asking if it was good and he snapped, "It's just a piece of fried meat with sauce on it." "Sorry I asked." From then on I held my peace, waiting for food and a bath to have a soothing effect on Ken, which they eventually did. I can't myself say that Munich in its present state is a very nice place to visit but we'll go to Nymphenburg Sunday for a palace ought to help Ken.

SATURDAY, JULY 25, 1970
    Just as I was going off to sleep all our windows started banging. It was a wind storm that preceded drenching rain but by morning it was all over. The storms within us had abated too and Ken got up in a good mood. Clouds coming and going in the sky kept the sun from raising the temperature much and there were wonderful breezes so when we walked toward the Rathaus today we were in quite a different mood from yesterday. Set out to see the Cuvillies Theatre but we found it didn't open till two so we went instead to the Residenz Museum and the Schatzkammer, one of the luckiest decisions we ever made. I can't imagine why we didn't do it before except that I doubt if the restoration had been completed 15 years ago. The gilt looks as if it had been finished yesterday. I have been in many treasuries but Ken and I agreed we had never seen the like of Munich's. More secular than clerical, I liked it all the better for that. Marie Louise's gold traveling set was fantastic but the two prizes were a bejeweled St. George and the Dragon with St. George decorated in rubies, diamonds and pearls and the dragon done largely with emeralds, and a necklace from 1570 or thereabouts with gorgeous jewels. We went to eat at Spatenhaus, right on the same square and Ken was enchanted. To illustrate perfectly that mood is all, I came back from the washroom to find that the waitress we'd said made such a contrast with last nite's dodderer had brought me a hot soup instead of the cold fruit soup I'd ordered. I let that pass but then she brought us Schweinebraten with semmelknodl instead of our madras curry and since we are off dumplings I flatly refused this. Yet Ken accepted it all calmly today and we so adored the bananas cooked in with our curry that we decided to cook some this winter. With dinner over, we decided to try the Cuvillies Theatre again. It proved breathtaking in its beauty. I believe it too is reconstructed after the war damage and what a gorgeous job they have made of it. I really adore baroque. For some reason not clear to us all

the church bells started ringing at three and the sound
was just magnificent.

MONDAY, JULY 27, 1970
        Into the adjacent station to catch our train to Regensburg. We liked the little city at once and our hotel turned out to have been, for 100 years, literally the Bishop's House. We checked in and set out at once to find the old stone bridge over the Danube, dating from about 1135. It turned out to be just a stone's throw away, which is how Ken would like all cities arranged, and just next to it was the little wurst kitchen at which some book advised one to have sausages, kraut, and beer. We decided to do it at once and it was heaven.

TUESDAY, JULY 28, 1970
        Even tho English was not spoken at the Bischofshof, we managed to get the desk clerk to call us a taxi and we were off to the station in blazing sunshine. We caught our little train to Nuremberg and had a very charming ride. First the conductior, without being asked, look up our connection to Bamberg in his book and showed me that it was 11:02 on track 2. Then two teen-age girls got on and asked if we were American. Her father is American and her mother German and she has come home every summer since they moved to New Orleans 8 years ago and spends the summer with her grandmother. Father has a night club and mother a beauty parlor. Talking with her about the difference between the two countries was very illuminating. She said, "Older people put a lot of pressure on young people here. My grandmother doesn't allow me to do a lot of things I'm allowed to do at home." We got our connection to Bamberg with no trouble at all and arrived at the hotel before the room was ready. We left our bags there and went out sightseeing. The unique town hall in the middle of the river was just around the corner but to get to the cathedral we had bit of a climb and to get to the Michaelerkirche more of a one. The ceiling was painted with flowers and herbs, as tho for a nature study class, and it was lovely but I couldn't figure why a church should be so botanical.

MONDAY, AUGUST 3, 1970
        We discovered a Museum of Amsterdam History right off the Kalverstraat but somehow neither of us was in the mood for a museum and since checkout hour was 11 at our hotel, we decided to go on our way to the airport. It turned out to be by far the most comfortable and best-organized airport I ever encountered. One could actually understand the

public announcements whereas in New York the amplification system always has a buzz and anyway would be drowned out by the babble of visiting relatives. Ken had one of his togetherness days. When I suggested that I watch the luggage while he investigated the free port, he said he wanted us to do it together, and when we went for lunch and there were two seats with just one or two people in between he didn't want to take them because he wanted us to be together. Our plane took off on time and the flight was smooth but the food rather poor again. We taxied from the terminal and walked into a very tidy apartment, where we were greeted by two slim and lovely cats. Christine had meticulously listed all her phone calls and the tax and had left money to cover it. Some things weren't as clean as Ken keeps them and other things were better. Each housekeeper has his own virtues and failings.

TUESDAY, AUGUST 4, 1970
    Dreamed of Lavinius and woke deeply sad. Neither cat was with me and I thought how Lavinius would be cuddled up beside me, thus growing sadder. Just then Titus jumped up and threw himself down beside me. He started to sing, something he doesn't do often or well, and before I knew it he was cuddling as close as Lavinius would have. Obviously Christine wasn't on to Victoria's trick of hiding whatever she steals under the foyer rug for when I investigated the lump I felt, I found two pens, a stirrer, a hair curler piece, a stone, and a couple of other things. We bustled around in the morning, taking all our vacation clothes to the cleaners. We weren't long home when Mac called from Connecticut to invite us up for the weekend of the 15th and 16th. I accepted and was delighted when Ken seemed amenable and said we really couldn't refuse.

FRIDAY, AUGUST 7, 1970
    Alice called to welcome us home and I asked about Pearl R., getting the bad news that she is failing badly and could die any day. The kidney transplant just isn't working out.

SATURDAY, AUGUST 15, 1970
    Off to Meriden in good time and as we looked out the train window, we kept pointing out eyesores to each other and saying "America the Beautiful?" It was really a very ugly hour and three-quarter ride. When Gene and Mack picked us up (with their air-conditioned car) we found the small Connecticut towns not very beautiful either but their house in Yalesville was very nice. We could see from the house

and the carefully tended grounds that they would make embarrassing guests in our Spartan, ill-tended home. When one of their friends came for cocktails and dinner and reported on all the work he had done on his home in the course of the day, even with the help of three men, it tired me out to hear about it. We had cocktails on the lawn and it was very pleasant then we went in for dinner. I went upstairs to wash up and was a little startled when I came downstairs and Larry, the guest, came over to hug and kiss me, saying, "I couldn't do that outdoors." At that point I wondered how old I was going to have to be before this kind of nonsense stopped, but as dinner counteracted his drinks he simmered down. The evening, however, was a great trial. They started on endless, not-very-interesting anecdotes about this friend and that, all people we don't know. There was no talk of books, movies, public events, or anything like that but just Steve and Ken, Chuck and Cliff, John and Edmund, etc. etc. Except for a few lesbians, women play no part in their lives and it does seem terribly unbalanced and boring that way. My boredom reached such a point that I felt I was hanging on a cliff by my fingernails and just couldn't last till bedtime. When Larry finally kissed me goodbye and we went to bed, I was really exhausted from trying to stay attentive for hours to stories which interested me not one whit. I didn't get to sleep fast but just lying quietly beside Ken was a relief. He said, "I'd rather have been home reading this evening."

SUNDAY, AUGUST 16, 1970

Up a little after eight and Mac had prepared more breakfast than we could comfortably eat. After that we went with Gene for the paper and he gave us a tour that included Choate School and the otherwise not excessively beautiful Wallingford. Back to the house, where we were soon joined in the yard by Hal and Brud, two quite nice fellows from their extensive collection of lover friends. We had been told Hal was swishy and a hairdresser but I didn't find him objectionably swish at all and Brud, 47, was very masculine and attractive without being afraid to use a campy word now and then. Again the only women who seem to play any part in their world are their mothers. I certainly found out this weekend that the provinces are more tolerant of homosexual couples than I had supposed they would be. None of these boys seem to have any trouble with backyard parties, some of which I gather get fairly wild. Dinner was marvelous and then we sat in the yard a while till train time approached. Titus and Victoria were delighted to have us back and Titus was at and on my feet all the time I did

diary. I thought much of all the various things I learned
this weekend, not all of them news to me. For instance, how
prejudiced very nice people like Mac and Gene can be (they
hate 'niggers' and use that term even tho they aren't
Southern, and they can't stand long-haired young men and
don't like the younger generation anyway), and for another
instance, that one is not safe from crime in the country
either, for Brud's house has been twice burglarized and
he goes home in just as much fear of another robbery as any
city-dweller. When I defended negroes and the younger generation, they had at least the politeness and good sense
to stop their rantings and so there was no rancour on either side, but it's a measure of the problem that in combat-
ting prejudice one doesn't just have to deal with the obvious villains but with people who are very nice except for
the little pockets of hate in them. I don't think they
could be won over to any other view and I didn't really
try. They live in isolation from the two groups they hate
(they don't like Latins either). I think the only thing
that really breaks down prejudice is personal acquaintance
with members of the despised group. Argument certainly never changes feelings.

WEDNESDAY, AUGUST 19, 1970
    One thing I was really revolted by in Connecticut was
how mother-ridden or mother-attached everybody was. Until
his mother died, Gene went up every weekend to be with his
parents and this went on until he was chronologically a
terribly mature man, 54, I think. He did eventually make
that long and expensive trip only every other week but I
think even that is ridiculous. One is entitled to a life
of one's own. I admit that I overdo it with what is close
to neglect of my mother but I could hardly believe that
a man as masculine-seeming as Brud, for instance, had an
apartment downstairs while his parents lived upstairs.

SATURDAY, AUGUST 22, 1970
    Ginny and Eddie arrived at ten as they had said they
would and we took off. North Jersey proved as attractive
as people have always said it was, if without much distinctive flavor. Pennsylvania was immediately attractive
and the highway marvelous, with no billboards, but as it
went on for miles it grew monotonous and Ken went to sleep.
Ginny suggested that since we had left the traffic behind
and had plenty of time we should get off the highway and
get on some secondary roads. This was a good excuse to
cut off to Benton. On the way we went over to see the Twin
Bridges, supposedly the only twin covered bridges in the

nation. When I stayed with the Chapins in the 30's those
bridges were in use but now a new bridge takes the traffic
and the wooden bridges have been shut off and picnic tables have been installed in the bridges, which according to
a plaque are 120 years old. Another bridge, also withdrawn
from use, is at Stillwater but the ones I knew at Light
Street and on the road to Asbury are gone. As for Benton,
it turned out to be larger than Ken had supposed from my
description but the house in which I was born seemed smaller than I remembered it and the house on Third Street where
I lived till 5 has either been torn down and replaced by a
modern one or has been remodeled out of all recognition.
The houses on either side, however, look just as they did.
After a look at Benton Park and the happy discovery that
the creek which was almost completely dried up in the 30's
is now flowing nicely and makes a swimming hole at the dam
again, we drove down to Bloomsburg. (*Lumber and tanning
mills had so denuded the forested hillsides that until the
Civilian Conservation Corps reforested them in the Franklin Roosevelt era the creekbed was mostly a mass of dry
stones under which a trickle flowed.*)

SUNDAY, AUGUST 23, 1970
   The Leonards being early risers, there was none of the
lying in bed that Ken might have liked. Tho it was misty
much of the lovely way to Hershey, it was not unpleasant.
The mountains in mist were attractive. When we got to Hershey we went first to see the gardens, where the roses were
passé but where many other flowers were lovely. They sell
Ko Ko Mulch, made from the hulls of cocoa beans and as the
day progressed Eddie said, "Hershey sells every part of
the pig but **the** squeal." There is Hershey candy and Hershey
baked good and Hershey permeates every part of the town
with banks and department stores and schools. We located
our motel and checked in then went back to the amusement
park. As we noted all the colored people there, I said,"I
think it's carrying 'Chocolatetown,U.S.A.' too far to have
even the people chocolate."

MONDAY, AUGUST 24, 1970
   A heavy breakfast at a nearby restaurant and then off
to the Hershey factory for the plant tour. Supposedly
790,000 people took the tour last year and there were plenty today. There were no guides, nor could there have been,
for the factory was impossibly noisy. The route for visitors was marked by a yellow line and the machines were
mostly self-explanatory--wrappers, chocolate mixers, etc.
All of us decided that we would not last one day as workers

what with the monotony, the pervasive smell of chocolate, and the noise. Even Ken, who loves chocolate, was turned against it and bought nothing in the salesroom where the tour ended. We made a quick trip to Gettysburg and immediately signed up for the 11:15 tour of the battlefield. This was a 1 3/4 hour bus tour with tape-recorded commentary and went thru perfectly lovely country (we even saw a deer). I began to understand the outline of the battle and I understood it even better when, after signing in at our motel and having a light lunch, we went to see the Electric Map, on which the troop movements were shown clearly by blue lights for the Union and orange for the Confederates. We walked to a miniature golf course which was one of the most ingenious any of us had ever played. Eddie beat me this time but I was at least second. We bought rum on the way home and the Leonards came in for a drink with us. Ken had to try the massage device attached to our bed. Eddie and Ginny said they had once been embarrassed by one because it made the bed thump against the wall and they got self-conscious.

TUESDAY, AUGUST 25, 1970

Off to Penna. Dutch country. We found York and a number of smaller places very lovely. Usually when I have given glancing thought to getting out of New York to live, I have thought of New England but after last week's unaesthetic visit to Conn. and this week's aesthetically satisfying tour of lovely Penna. towns I would be inclined to skip New England and think in terms of Pa.. Of course I never really seriously consider leaving New York for the provinces. I am only a Pennsylvanian by birth, as neither parent came from there but on this trip I've discovered a certain pride in it. One thing I noted which may account for my hatred of sun and love of shade. In explaining my loathing for sunbathing I have often said, "I come from the country, where one gets out of the sun if possible," but I didn't remember quite how deliberately Pennsylvanians wrap verandas around their houses and shade their living rooms, then surround the house with shade trees so that sun seldom breaks in. Obviously I grew up in the shade and I still love it. Here it is everywhere, cooling one house after another and making them look fresh and inviting. We stopped at the country store in Bird in Hand and we all made some purchases then we cut thru back roads and saw a lot of Amish in their horse-drawn vehicles or doing hand work in the corn and tobacco fields. I had thought there might be a few running around, as in Marken, but there are lots of them all over the place, not just being colorful

A GAY DIARY

to lure tourists, but working their huge and lovely farms the hard way, out of religious conviction. The Leonards suggested we look up the miniature golf course in New Holland, which I had read about. We found it and had a new challenge in the longest holes I have ever played in miniature golf. They also had two holes over long fairways of grass and those always stymied me. Instead of coming in first, as I did in Hershey, I was last despite my conquering in three strokes a hole that the others all had to give up on after taking their limit of strokes. Since we were the only men with jackets on at the Lamp Post last nite, we decided not to dress formally to go eat at Plain and Fancy Barn. Good thing we didn't for few in the huge crowd wore jackets. When our number was called we were seated at a big table, introduced to the six people sharing it (that is, told where they were from), were told what all the relishes on the table were, and then plunged in on those. Soon the waitress delivered a huge mound of roast beef, a heaping platter of sausages, vegetable dishes of mashed potatoes, noodles, stewed tomatoes, corn, and mountains of bread. I was a real trencherman and had seconds on tomatoes and potatoes and no less than <u>four</u> desserts. I don't know how they serve so much for $3.25. I had to stagger out of there. I was glad Ken and I had separate beds tonite as I expect nightmares.

WEDNESDAY, AUGUST 26, 1970

We had a foggy morning and we wondered why some of the Amish wagons out on the ghostly roads didn't get hit by cars. Every foot of the New Jersey Turnpike was an eyesore and as we got North the odor was not to be believed and scarcely to be tolerated. I tried to make each breath last as long as possible so that I wouldn't have to breathe again too soon. The Leonards wanted to be on their way to Albany so wouldn't even come up. The cats were delighted to see us.

TUESDAY, SEPTEMBER 1, 1970

I have been noticing with amusement that Ken, who years ago was reluctant to make any real commitment to me or at least to verbalize it, is now constantly telling people we have been together 25 years. It is typical of him that he has to make it 25 years rather than 24, which it really is. He can never quite let a statistic alone to speak of itself but must always stretch it a bit in the direction of whatever effect he wants to make. He knows perfectly well that I am exactly six feet tall but today he was speaking of me as 6'1". One would think six feet

was enuf, and that 24 years was enuf, but the truth is
never quite good enuf for Ken and must always be improved
upon.

FRIDAY, SEPTEMBER 4, 1970
    Having seen a United Parcel man in the lobby, I ran
down. I found he had delivered the vacuum cleaner. The new
machine makes a terrific racket and the cats were terrified. Titus was infuriated and the first thing I knew he
was striking viciously at the cord. After supper I went on
with ZELDA. Both the Fitzgeralds had a way with words that
I envy terrifically. Aside from his drunkenness, I also
like his character, whereas I simply cannot abide that pos-
eur Hemingway. I do think, however, that I have gone thru
the life of Fitzgerald often enuf now in books. This will
be the last.

FRIDAY, SEPTEMBER 18, 1970
    A gloomy rainy day and I was blue all day, mostly be-
cause this was Ken's last year working beside me. I told
myself that no other couple I knew had had the privilege
of working together at all (except that Eddie and Ginny
now work for the same institution, tho not in the same office) but that didn't help.

SATURDAY, SEPTEMBER 19, 1970
    When Ken woke me he announced it was quarter of nine
and I got out of bed in a towering fury. He saw no reason
to get an early start on Saturday tho we have been all
thru this before and he knows I hate to get downtown late
when the crowds have become bothersome. Considering how
sentimental I was being about him only yesterday, I was a
raging harpy this morning, grumbling that we had beds to
make up fresh, baths to take, clothes to take out to the
cleaners, etc. When I came out of the bath he had cut his
coffee short and was already putting the clean sheets on
the bed. I calmed down and amity was the order of the day.
We went first to Alexander's, which was having a sale of
Harris Tweed jackets for $19. Then walked to Carnegie Hall
to get tickets for Stokowski's first concert, which cost
us all of $1 apiece. We went to Air India and Scandinav-
ian Air Line to see about their tours to Moscow and Leningrad. When we got home Ken suggested we might take that
tour next year instead of the one we have planned.

WEDNESDAY, OCTOBER 7, 1970
    All day we anticipated the start of the new tv series
CIVILIZATION and I wished that there were more things on

tv that I looked forward to, as I used to do a number of educational programs. I guess I should be glad for this 13 week series, plus the return of Julia Child in a new series on French cooking, and the fact that Carol Burnett seems to have rounded up new writers who have freshened her series. Both Julia on Bouillabaise and Kenneth Clark on Civilization were all that I hoped.

FRIDAY, OCTOBER 9, 1970

We were scarcely home and into house clothes when Mimie called and said she had a voucher for free tickets to COLETTE which she couldn't use. I knew Ken would grumble and I myself am not too adapted to sudden impulsive changes in plan but I accepted the tickets. We did indeed have grumbling and sulking and not entirely without reason for the Ellen Stewart Theatre, where COLETTE is playing, is way over between Aves. B and C on Third St., not at all an easy location to get to. It being Friday night, the streets of the East Village were full of young people with long hair and outlandish garb, who make Ken nervous. They don't at all bother me because I know that most of them are not "hippies" even tho America would dub them that, but middle-class children out for a night on the town. To me a real hippy has separated from his family, is quite possibly on drugs, and really may be as dirty as middle America claims all the long-hairs are (which is a ridiculous libel, as anyone can see by really looking at the long hair and seeing how most of it gleams with shampooing and attention). The play was good and superbly acted. There were two cats in the play, tho no dialogue ever referred to them, and Colette let a black and white one go, which I have never seen done on the stage before. He got down from the chaise longue and had a long bath, which was very distracting to us catlovers, which is why actors wouldn't normally let a cat have the stage. He wandered off on his own and later back again in a very poised manner. The stage was greatly raked, which I haven't seen to that degree except in historic theatres, and it was huge, with no curtain and of course no footlights. Both are becoming obsolete.

SUNDAY, OCTOBER 11, 1970

We went to the Whitney, where we saw both the Georgia O'Keeffe show, which didn't please me as much as anticipated, and the Thomas Eakins show, which pleased me more. We had a nice stroll on Madison Avenue, saw some of the Spanish-American parade, which had some nice floats (every ethnic group is steadily improving their parade with floats except the damned Irish, who still think policemen, firemen, and Catholic school bands are all you need to make a parade), and then bought some fancy pastry to have with tea. We are quite hung up now on having rum in our tea as we did in Austria.

THURSDAY, OCTOBER 15, 1970
    Ken suggested that since the curtain for the opening performance of ROBERTO DEVEREUX was at 7:15 we not go home. This meant I couldn't have opera glasses, couldn't change my jacket as I had intended, and also meant a hassle about where to eat. To insure that we wouldn't go anywhere really nice, which might cost money, Ken ate a brownie at teatime so he could immediately pull his old line,"I'm not really hungry now so it's a waste to go anywhere fancy." Ken has relaxed wonderfully about expenditure as far as improving the house but he still has not been converted to the pleasures of eating out in a nice place where the food rises above hot dogs, hamburgs, and such junk food. There was a very gala and alert audience present and the house crackled with electricity as the Met seldom does, thanks to its stodgy old audience. At first we didn't think we were going to care for the opera. A light high coloratura didn't seem appropriate to a woman of such command as Elizabeth of England. A dramatic soprano seemed more fitting. From the second act on, however, the action and the music got more dramatic. Beverly Wolff wasn't entirely equal to Donizetti as the Duchess of Nottingham but of course Beverly Sills was as Elizabeth and Placido Domingo was plump and a bit awkward but sang well as Essex. The ovations were terrific but nobody who hasn't got a ticket already is going to be able to get in this season for all performances were sold out before opening. The cats were beside themselves with joy at our return and romped wildly as we watched the Dick Cavett Show.

MONDAY, OCTOBER 19, 1970
    Ken devoted his evening to the unusual pursuit of letter-writing, starting a note to Ginny and Eddie which I finished, and a letter to Florence turning down her invitation up there for Christmas and countering with one to come here. When we were discussing it with Kathi today and I said I wouldn't consider leaving Mother alone on Christmas, she said, "But I thought you didn't like your mother." I was aghast. So many people get that idea because I joke about her being accident-prone, and mock her ineptitude in the kitchen, etc. but they seem to think this constitutes hostility, which is ridiculous. Even if I hated

Mother I'm damned if I would ever be one of those who complains in public in full seriousness about their parents. It's the most boring and futile thing in the world. Anyway, as I said to Kathi,"I don't dislike my mother at all but even if I hated her, I still wouldn't dream of leaving her alone at Christmas at this time of her life." People so totally misread my character. Pat had a little story she told Saturday night and then asked which of the characters each of us liked best, as that was supposed to reveal our character. She was completely flabbergasted at the character I chose, as he was supposed to represent "Hearth and Home" and she didn't expect that from me, she expected it from Ken. She should know how long it took me to get Ken to settle down to hearth and home. She expected me to select the character who represented philosophy and wisdom. Hah!

TUESDAY, OCTOBER 20, 1970
When I walked into the Martinique and found it was a theatre in the round I felt sure there could not be total nudity that close to the audience and how wrong I was. All five characters stripped at least once, most twice, and there was simulated sex in a bed right in front of one row. The play was not purely a peep show, however, for it had both construction and amusing dialogue, tho in the end no real quality. The bisexuality of one man was overt, in the other latent, so in most ways, tho a better play, SCORE was not as advanced as PUPPY DOG TAILS, which went all the way and showed men thoroly in love with each other and committed to living together as lovers. For myself, if I ever get around to writing that kind of play about homosexuality, I shall not use total nudity, I think. It really isn't all that sexy. It would be all right to reduce my lovers to jockey shorts but the baring of the genitals in a shriveled and impotent state negates any sexy effect one is striving for. If the actors are partially clothed, one can imagine them to be in a state of sexual excitement. One thing these plays are doing is give me quite different notions about the female body. So often in pornography great bulbous or pendulous breasts are shown, just as men with grotesquely large genitals are sought for, and all this kind of exaggeration is repulsive to me. On the other hand flat-chested women don't appeal to me either. In THE DIRTIEST SHOW IN TOWN and SCORE the breasts were of a decent but not exaggerated size and were quite an acceptable part of the body. A lovely body is a lovely body, male or female.

SATURDAY, OCTOBER 24, 1970

We picked Mimie up at quarter of six and made good time. Ben Rockmore was already on hand when we got to Miriam's and soon a couple I never met before arrived and I liked them both enormously. The wife, Lillian, is somewhat crippled but they go abroad anyway and she travels in a wheel chair, seeing what she can see, and waiting while her husband sees the rest. They like to enroll in a foreign university and get to know people that way, and their last enrollment was in the University of Ghana. Conversation held to the usual intelligent level, with Mimie not contributing much till the subject turned to China. Ben looked very well *(he was newly a widower)* tho I understand he is still not sleeping well and he was quite jolly.

MONDAY, OCTOBER 26, 1970

Bothered all day by a fear that my urethritis had returned. I have been fighting these fears off and on, trying to convince myself that it was just nerves and excessive awareness of that part of my body because Titus' trouble focussed my mind on the urinary tract. True to my principles of not going to the doctor till something has plagued me at least three days, because so many things go away of their own accord, I got my reward in the evening when I suddenly became comfortable in that area, quite possibly because I was more distracted by my pleasures than I had been by my work.

THURSDAY, NOVEMBER 12, 1970

Went to work with Ken and started Aggie on filling out computer forms for people who had sent in their own changes of address, leaving Mike to further instruct and advise her when it came time for me to keep my appointment with Dr. Fretz. He said it sounded to him like chronic prostatitis and gave me a pamphlet about it, a prescription for antibiotics which he said I might save money by having filled at the St. Luke's pharmacy, and then suggested that some patients felt better after prostatic massage. This time I had no doubt that that was what hurt. Had I not been so accepting of pain when the first doctor was prodding, this might have been diagnosed sooner. I was relieved that there was no mention of going in a hospital but not so happy when I read in the book that prostatitis is never really cured but just goes away for a time. In general the book was reassuring. Ken was delighted that I had at last had a diagnosis and got some medicine. I guess he thought I'd be less of a pill to live with but the booklet describes the nervous tensions as being very common to the trouble, particularly when it persists.

SATURDAY, NOVEMBER 14, 1970
We were relieved when we saw women at the party in addition to Lee and Ruth for we thought this would make for a more decorous party. To a certain extent it did but there was plenty of frank talk just the same. One of the toughest women at the party was a woman who read our handwriting. She asked us to write our name, address, the date, and a sentence full of i's and t's and then she would say, "I don't know whose this is and I don't want to know", with the name right before her. When she read Ken's she said he was introspective and didn't need or care about people, was stubborn, and then said she'd tell him what was wrong with his sex life. Everybody looked at me and somebody asked why I was blushing. She said he liked sex but could turn it off and do without it easily. When she read mine, she said,"Oh, you're such a conventional person. You have imagination and a streak of deviltry which, when you let it out, can maybe go too far. But you're such a conventional person that I can't see anything else." I was surprised to learn that so many of them are churchgoers, four of them attending St. Bartholomew's on Park Avenue, and one has been an usher for years. Ken made a terrific hit with male and female, Lida saying, "Look at that profile. Apollo," and Dick saying at one smoochy point,"You're charming. I love you." As always, he doesn't want to go and then he shines.

SATURDAY, NOVEMBER 28, 1970
We made no haste to go downtown and made our first stop at the new Mid-Manhattan Library, which has been lushly set up on the upper stories of the Arnold Constable store.It's an absolutely fabulous place, with lots of tables and chairs and study cubicles, and rugs on the floor plus sound-proof ceilings and lots of windows. The seats in the Morosco Theatre were firm and I had not the slightest twinge in my back. HOME was not a play to our taste as it had no plot and too little characterization besides. I thought John Gielgud's role was dreadfully underwritten and very unrewarding, with Ralph Richardson's a little bit showier but still sketchy.

SUNDAY, NOVEMBER 29, 1970
Another good nite's sleep but today it was Ken's turn to be sick. He had diarrhoea, loss of appetite, and stayed in bed till evening. I would have been happy to wait on him but he didn't want anything. He has been sympathetic

to me since my trouble was officially diagnosed, however impatient he may have been before that. I still have not gone into my bad moments in any detail with him but his attitude is quite different since Dr. Fretz gave my trouble a label and prescribed for it. Ken reminds me of my pills and of my sitz baths and is supportive after all. I have meant to correct the record on this score in view of my earlier complaints about him but I have repeatedly forgotten to. I started addressing Christmas cards while Ken wrote Florence.

WEDNESDAY, DECEMBER 2, 1970

I left Ken listening to tv and went to bed, being asleep by the time he came to the bedroom. This made a full week of sleep and glad I was of it. This was the last day for my supply of pills and I had hoped to be cured by the time they ran out but instead I had a rather bad day. I tried not to get depressed but to face the fact that I had to live with this until it cures itself. I will certainly be a restricted tourist and this will put Ken and me more on a par so that I will not be walking the legs off him any more. I was anxious to get into my sitz bath in hope that it would relax the nerves in my buttocks as it usually does, and it did. We had a wonderful CIVILIZATION on THE PURSUIT OF HAPPINESS, which dealt with baroque and rococo and showed so many wonderful places we've been to, like the Residenz in Wurzburg and the Amalienburg in Munich, not to mention the Wieskirche and all accompanied by wonderful music of Bach, Handel, Haydn, and Mozart. I'm going to look at it again Sunday as it was one of my favorites. What a privilege to have this series and somehow his talk of how the people of that age thought pleasure something worth taking seriously reinforced my growing freedom from the Protestant ethic. I have always wanted to work and felt guilty at the thought of not working, but suddenly, envious of the retirement of Mother, Ken, Ellen, Miriam, and others, I see how I could fill my days pleasurably and have no qualms of conscience whatever. This may drive me back to writing, one of my original motivations for writing being hope of escape from workaday labor. With the office so busy these days, however, I don't even get time to daydream about things to write.

SUNDAY, DECEMBER 13, 1970

No traffic trouble with the bathroom this morning. I went out for the paper while Ginny and Eddie were in there (they always go in together, which is a bit much). We had a light breakfast since dinner had to be early enuf to let the Leonards catch the five o'clock bus to Albany. We had lots of pleasant talk. Ken's cheese souffle came out just beautifully so I rushed to take a picture of it. We heard the cats rustling in the living room and went in to find that they had ferreted out a catnip Santa Claus which was in the bag of presents the Leonards were planning to leave for us. Both cats were drunk as lords on the catnip.

TUESDAY, DECEMBER 15, 1970

Ken and I got haircuts. He hates his curls and waves and is always spanking them down with water, to my distress since this makes his hair look greasy and matted and brings out oils so that the nice white hair turns yellow. Unfortunately the barber gave him a new way to comb it with water and he was delighted to have professional backing. I fumed but just as I have told him he has said his piece against boys with long hair and I don't need to hear it any more, so I have made my point about his wetting his hair and I should desist. We bought tickets to THE GINGERBREAD LADY for next week and to LOVELY LADIES, KIND GENTLEMEN for the following week then went to tonite's theatre. The audience was not sleazy tonite, the word apparently having got around that the one nude scene was brief and not too revealing. I liked the play (FOREPLAY), however, tho it has no claim to literary distinction. The campy dialogue was in places very funny and the observation rather good at points. I liked particularly the long scene where the husband who has discovered he is gay and the boy he has picked up in the park overcome their mutual shyness and try to get around to going to bed together, each of them wanting more than just the physical act and gradually discovering that they feel alike about this and therefore like each other, maybe even love each other. Being a romantic at heart I liked this extra dimension. I was also amused that the husband, the older, said he needed somebody strong and the young man ended the play by saying, "Wouldn't it be funny if I turned out to be the strong one?" People so often think of young men leaning on a strong older one but I am sure Ken and I are not the only instance of where the reverse is true. I don't really think people are strong by virtue of age anyway. I think a strong person is strong in their teens and a weak person is a weak person all their lives.

THURSDAY, DECEMBER 17, 1970

Mary returned to work and Ken asked if it was flu. "No, just nerves," she said. That they are all scared of the new boss was revealed when Kathi frankly confessed that

she didn't like change any better than anybody else and
had had four bosses in a year and four months. Ken, having
so little time left on the job, is not worried, and neither am I, perhaps because I have not so many delinquencies
to be discovered. I was surprised when Kathi and I were
talking about last nite's CIVILIZATION and she confessed
she and her husband had never heard of either Turner or
Constable and had not been to the Tate on either of her
trips to London. She was excited to learn about him and I
have to respect her frankness about her previous ignorance.
Elaine would not only have tried to fake long knowledge
about him but would claim to have delivered a lecture on
him once in the Middle West.

FRIDAY, DECEMBER 18, 1981
    After work we went to the Columbia market to buy our
Christmas tree. As we worked together to put it in the
stand, a sudden storm blew up. Ken said,"Let's get it
straight. Last year it was crooked." I said that the main
trunk looked straight and that tho the top curved, that
couldn't be helped as trees just didn't always grow
straight. Suddenly Ken said, "Let's not quarrel about a
Christmas tree", and stomped off to the kitchen to get
supper. I trimmed till dinner was ready and made half a
dozen attempts at conversation but Ken wouldn't reply.
When I went into the dining room I asked,"Are we going to
have sulks all evening?" and he said, "I guess so." "What
did I say that was so terrible? That all trees are not
straight?" "I don't know." "Well, I'm having nothing more
to do with the tree, I'll tell you that." While I waited
for him to get dishes ready to wipe I put the rest of the
decorations back in the closet. I would have gone on to
wrap presents but I was just as determined not to wrap
presents in the mood I was in as I was not to decorate the
tree. Those things should be done with love and good feeling and they were hard to muster tonite.

SATURDAY, DECEMBER 19, 1970
    Getting our relationship going again this morning
gave Ken and me a bit of a problem. I gave lacklustre answers to his first overtures and he retreated but I told
myself a second day of that would be silly so when Titus
came in to the pan while I was shaving I announced he'd
had a good bowel movement and immediately Ken had the excuse he needed to be his normal chittery-chattery self.
As always when we haven't been speaking (that doesn't happen as often as it used to) we have an accumulation of
things to say and we rattled away today. After supper I

suggested to Ken that we finish trimming the tree together
and we did, in total compatibility and that extra measure
of amity one has after a quarrel has been patched up. I
decided that I had better treasure him for I had a very
sad card from Dave, much upset because six friends have
died in the last sixteen months.

SUNDAY, DECEMBER 20, 1970
    Decided to have a wrapping session. I got everything
wrapped except the four large things. At one point I realized I had been awfully quiet for some time and came to
the realization that for the last twenty minutes I had not
wrapped a thing but had been working out in my mind a play
on a homosexual theme. Now it has been quite a long time
since I have devoted twenty minutes to writing problems
and I was delighted. May I do more of this in the coming
year and also follow thru on it.

TUESDAY, DECEMBER 22, 1970
    When we walked into the party we met the new boss and
I was crushingly disappointed. He seems very pleasant but
again not the sort of man who can take command. Why is the
fund-raising field so full of inadequate men when the pay
is so wonderful? Went to Dr. Fretz this morning. We had a
chat about non-medical subjects that I suppose was designed
to make me feel I was getting my $15 worth of his time and
then he quickly gave me prostatic massage, which hurt more
this time because he put more pressure on. He said he had
so many intellectuals around the University who had prostatitis and they got very neurotic about it. This remark came
after I said I had learned to live with it. Supper at home
then downtown to see THE GINGERBREAD LADY. Neil Simon writes
a lot of funny lines. Perhaps my favorite came when a friend
asked the singer why she didn't move out of that awful
neighborhood and she said,"Where else can I get three rooms
for $130? I have this place on sub-lease from Mary Todd
Lincoln." The friend was a homosexual and when he made his
first exit there was a round of applause that seemed to be
not only for the actor but in support of homosexuals who
were such kind friends. I remember that happening in A TASTE
OF HONEY, too, as tho the audience were showing its tolerance. Of course, just as in that play, the homosexual was a
homely misfit without a visible love-life and that could
make a whale of a difference in public attitude.

THURSDAY, DECEMBER 24, 1970
    We went to the passport photographer's and got the
pictures taken for the Russian visa then while they were

being developed we went to the Museum of Modern Art. We saw the exhibit of paintings and drawings collected by the Steins (*Gertrude and brother*) and then we had lunch in the cafeteria. The food was ordinary and expensive but the view into the sculpture garden with its dusting of snow was lovely and inside we had also a lovely view of a young boy with long blond hair, a marvelous profile, and alabaster complexion. Almost the only time I feel I was born too soon is when I see these youths with the lovely long hair and wish that those I once made love to had lived in a time of long hair so that I could have run my hands thru it. I am also curious as hell to know what it would be like to make love to someone wearing a beard and moustache but even today the gay ones don't wear them.

|97|

FRIDAY, JANUARY 1, 1971

Washed the Venetian blinds in the dining room and kitchen but postponed those in the bedroom. Lay down on the sofa and read some of the Barrie biography. When Ken announced it was time for us to start so we could have a leisurely dinner before the ballet, I got up and found myself queasy. I thought the crisp air (it had been snowing all day) would surely cure this and since Ken had been the one to suggest, some time ago, that we eat out on New Year's Day, I was damned if I was going to be the one to conk out on the idea. The crisp air was nice but did not revive me and I grew increasingly nauseous. I realized when I ordered the sweetbreads that they would probably be too rich for me but since we were at Larré's I thought I should take advantage of the rarities. I could eat only a quarter of the serving and as I knew would be the case, Ken began to mourn the $5 we had spent eating out. Ken suggested skipping the ballet and as I struggled to keep from throwing up or making return trips to the bathroom, he kept suggesting we leave, but I stuck it out and enjoyed the ballet in spite of my illness. The dancing distracted me but the intermissions were hard to get thru and seemed interminable. Makarova, the Soviet ballerina who defected, made her first appearance in the modern type of ballet she defected in order to appear in and grasped the novel style very well. It was a relief to get out in the air where I felt I could go to the curb and throw up if I had to but I never had to. Worried that I wouldn't recover in time for the party.

A GAY DIARY

SUNDAY, JANUARY 3, 1971

A better nite's sleep and yet the diarrhoea persisted. Paregoric just didn't seem to catch hold. Since in every other way I felt better I was able to keep working on the party. Mac called from Yalesville and said they didn't plan to come to town in the next two months and since we had included the 30th in our possible dates for them to come to dinner, could we come up there? We had no time to discuss it right then so I said we'd call him back tho I gave a tentative affirmative. Mac understood my hesitation when I said we had twenty people coming and insisted we call back collect as Gene is retired from the phone company and doesn't get bills, or something. Mac is a person I feel warmly about even on short acquaintance. He's warm and he's funny. He started off by saying, "Am I talking to the pretty one, or to the pretty one?" We were ready well before our guests came and sat for about half an hour in anticipation. My cheese ball made a sensation, with three women asking me for a copy of the recipe. Unfortunately I can only remember who two of them were.

WEDNESDAY, JANUARY 6, 1971

From work we went to the Village to have another go at eating out and this one was a great success. We went to the Fedora Restaurant on West 4th St., recommended as inexpensive by our book PLACES AND PLEASURES OF NEW YORK. The book said the restaurant was patronized by "fruity Villagers" and this was true as one homosexual couple after another came in, but all very decorous. The waiters were also gay and good-looking, one blond ravishingly so. For $2.75 we had an excellent meal. It was a nice intimate place and of course the Anspacher Theatre is also nice and intimate so we had a lovely evening even tho I did wonder in the end if TRELAWNY OF THE "WELLS" was worth reviving. After seeing the blond waiter's cute little buns neatly encased in corduroy jeans passing up and down the aisles of Fedora, I could have wished for a leading man with looks or personality or both. We had instead one that the eye just passed right over. As all theatre now has a 7:30 curtain, we were home nice and early. I hope that this time the early curtain is a success because we think it's just great. Before they tried it only one nite a week, the worst nite at that, and it flopped but this year all theatres, on Broadway and off, are trying it at all performances and I think it will be a much fairer test.

WEDNESDAY, JANUARY 13, 1971

We watched Julia Child cook an apple tart that didn't

quite come out right and this made it all the funnier later when as a segment of THE GREAT AMERICAN DREAM MACHINE there was a takeoff of cooking shows. Tears rolled down my cheeks as the inept hands of an unseen cook followed the utterly disgusting and silly instructions, such as "Remove the pits from half a dozen cherries and half a dozen black olives. Now put the pits of the olives in the cherries and the pits of the cherries in the olives," and "Take a handfull of mashed potato and put an onion in the middle of it. Now close your hand and squeeze." The casserole got messier and messier until it was really revolting, but hilarious.

MONDAY, JANUARY 18, 1971

Ran into Jim in the hall this morning and he gave me the crushing news that the doctors diagnosed Gene's trouble not as hepatitis, which would have been bad enuf, but as cancer of the pancreas. They had phoned Mac, who cried all thru the phone call as I would have done in his place. I would be bothered no matter what acquaintance this happened to, but somehow my affection for those two is out of all proportion to the length of our acquaintance, as I told them in a note we wrote in the evening. Gene was to be operated on today but the doctors gave little hope. My thoughts ran on Gene and Mac all day and their troubles made my little bother with prostatitis seem not of much account.

WEDNESDAY, JANUARY 20, 1971

After a little time at home, playing with the cats, we went down to Carnegie Hall to see the female impersonator Lynne Carter. I expected the usual takeoffs of easy people like Bette Davis and Phyllis Diller but he went beyond that and had really funny material. His takeoff of Dietrich trying to trade on a beauty long gone was hilarious. I was often doubled up with laughter. Instead of a straight rendition of Falling in Love Again for Dietrich, he had altered the song to Having It Done Again--It's Falling, in reference to face-lifting and at one point pulled his chin strap down and snapped it. Carter is just incomparably better than the only other female impersonators I have seen. Francis Renault may have been good in his time but when we saw him he was too old and passé to pay for new material, too tired to really play it if he'd had it, and apparently not capable of writing it as Carter does with some numbers. T.C. Jones didn't have very clever material either and wasn't very accurate in mimicry. Carter really showed me the possibilities. Florence pressed a step further in her letter tonite on her plan to get Ken to retire to Maine.

I rather thought that her gift of the weekly paper Maine Times was supposed to be a lure and tonite she went back some years to telling what a nice town for retirement South Freeport was and how many people from Mass. and Conn. were buying Cape Cod cottages there for $25,000. Even tho I know Ken hates small town life and the responsibility for a house it disturbs me to have Florence play this game. It's bad enuf that Ken says he wants to go to the old soldiers' home in Augusta when he gets old and helpless for I want him here to the end, but to have her trying to get him up there to share her retirement is worse.

WEDNESDAY, JANUARY 27, 1971

For the first time in over five weeks, a totally sleepless night. For no reason that I can think of except that when I found myself slow in going to sleep I tried too hard. To the bus in a brief blizzard, with dry snow flying every which way and umbrellas impossible to use. Amazing how soon after suffering from the biting cold we were complaining about the excessive heat of the office. Home a short while with the cats and then off to City Center to see Nureyev's production of DON QUIXOTE with the Australian Ballet. When you see Nureyev you see an authentic star, which I don't always feel with some other equally advertised personalities.

FRIDAY, FEBRUARY 5, 1971

Excellent sleep. Utterly wonderful day as to prostate. I was going down the hall this morning and said to myself, "See how wonderfully unneurotic you can be when feeling well." Within an hour all had gone awry and my dizzy spells returned. A venture out of the overheated office into cooler territory sometimes cleared my head but that could be either the cooler air or escape from the job, which I frankly hate these days. I noticed that when a few mysteries came up in the office work and I got engrossed in them, I felt better. But, alas, when we left the office behind and went home I had an attack of something that can only be emotional disturbance. I didn't intend to say anything to Ken but when I went to supper I found he had piled my plate high with food and I just couldn't face it. I went for a container to put some away in and he asked if I didn't feel well. At first I just said I couldn't eat that much but he smelled a rat and asked me in what way I felt ill and I said, "I feel alarmingly like the way I did in 1966 and I don't even want to think about it." Amanda called to ask us up next Saturday for dinner and bridge.

SATURDAY, FEBRUARY 6, 1971

To the 46th St. Theatre, where an audience almost devoid of young or even middling young people was gathered for the revival of NO, NO, NANETTE. Ken had higher expectations than I did and pretty soon he looked at me and said,"It IS old-fashioned, isn't it?" It is indeed and disspelled once and for all the longings I have sometimes had to have been of theatre-going age in the 20's so that I could have seen all the plays and musicals that played New York at that high-water-mark (of quantity) of the theatre. This was an abridged version of the inane book and yet it hardly seemed succinct enuf for none of the characters had any reality or dimension at all. What bothered me was that the costumes weren't really accurate. But I had read that they took the book from the 20's, the costumes from the thirties (but not really, for there were many twenties touches) and the orchestra style from the fifties. I didn't mind that Ruby Keeler had been dressed in timeless and flattering chiffon things for I wouldn't expect her to capture period style (she can barely deliver lines) and her contribution was to be very endearing, which she certainly was even to me, never a fan of hers. Helen Gallagher was the one who really captured the period, or seemed to (for I wasn't really going to theatre then). I wasn't enraptured as so many people have been but I certainly did have a pleasant afternoon and this in spite of a neck that tightened up painfully as the afternoon progressed.

SUNDAY, FEBRUARY 7, 1971

After breakfast we set out for Brooklyn Academy and again were delighted to find it just exactly a 30 minute ride, which is less time than we often spend on the bus going to mid-town. The audience was in great contrast to yesterday's, loaded with young people in all kinds of interesting garb. The dance critics of the Times have found that tho the Bejart Ballet is considered avant-garde in Europe they are old-fashioned compared to American troupes. The public has ignored the poor reviews and flocked to the performances, however, and in this case I am on the side of the public. While the company wasn't as loaded with beautiful males as I had been told it was, Jorge Donn was absolutely godlike in both face and figure. Danced superbly, too, as they all did. Last week there were 45 performances of dance in New York, drawing audiences of over 100,000, and I have seen three of the companies so why grieve for the missed days when 10 tacky Shubert musicals were playing in New York. I might not have gone anyway. Ken lived in New York from 1928-1931, the zenith of theatrical activity but seldom went to the theatre because he lived out in Jackson Heights with his adored Randy, who cared nothing for the theatre.

MONDAY, FEBRUARY 8, 1971

The day was a horror. When I got to the office I had the most terrific aversion to it and my neck began to tighten up. I began to fear that I might develop hysterical blindness the way Mother did, and how awful that would be. *(On the first occasion my mother was advised to give up the smoking of cigars and when that didn't cure her sight, my father was sent for to take over family responsibility. He was not long back before she recovered her sight and sent him into exile again. A few years later, when her financial and emotional affairs got tangled, she once again had an attack of blindness, of mercifully short duration.)* By the time I went to tea I was in a terrible state of anxiety and nausea, almost exactly like the dreadful days of 1966. Vianne joined us for tea as she has been doing lately and I could hardly pay any attention to a word she said. I said nothing to Ken and was glad I hadn't for when I got back to the office the awful feeling passed. I still hated the office and the job but in a rational way rather than in the emotionally sick way. Unfortunately I didn't keep my silence but mentioned later in the day that I had had that spell and the result from Ken was just what I expected. "I certainly hope you're not going to be sick on our trip. It isn't much fun. Maybe we'd better not spend all that money to go if you're going to be sick. I think you think yourself into a lot of these things." I MUST, I really MUST keep this kind of thing to myself, just as tho I were living alone.

THURSDAY, FEBRUARY 11, 1971

I had a night of the holy horrors, not quite suicidal but not far from it. I was sure I needed a psychiatrist and sure I couldn't afford it, sure I couldn't manage the Russian trip, etc. When morning came and I faced reality, it wasn't quite so bad. Ken asked me if the fact that he was leaving TC was bothering me and thus put his finger right on one of the sore spots. I think he was rather pleased by the affirmative answer for when we went to tea with Mary in the afternoon to celebrate her 14th anniversary at TC he told her and said he'd told me it was childish. "That may be," Mary said, "but it's understandable that he feels that way." This sudden understanding almost brought a flood of tears on the spot and I caught them just in time. As Mary said, however, it is not the whole story for I really have an aversion to the lack of diversification in the job as it is presently constituted.

SATURDAY, FEBRUARY 13, 1971

Ken and I lay down to take a nap but tho I get sleepy when he is talking to me or the radio playing, when all is quiet and I am supposed to sleep, I just get anxious. Life seems much less formidable when I getup. When we set out for Patty and Amanda's we found the lake shrouded in fog and the whole atmosphere very Londonish. We had lots of talk over drinks and Ken again took an obvious delight in telling them that I had been upset because he was leaving TC. His pleasure pleases me. Dinner was delicious and my fears of not having an appetite for it were all unfounded when the time came. We then played bridge and had a nip-and-tuck evening.

TUESDAY, FEBRUARY 23, 1971

Maggie came late as she had been to the doctor's about her headaches, which he said were eyestrain. Later in the day Mary came in and described dizziness and lightness of head much like that I have been experiencing. If the school heating plant didn't run on oil I would suspect coal gas was affecting us all. Certainly the intense heat in that basement, so close to the steam pipes, does nothing good for us. There is something about the nature of our work that is getting to us all. At least the variety I am trying to work into it for everybody is helping a bit.

WEDNESDAY, FEBRUARY 24, 1971

In Time there was an article telling how upsetting too much change can be to people and of course that is what is wrong with some of us, notably me. We have had five bosses in five years, plus many sub-bosses, three changes of office, a change in the system (many changes, for that matter, besides automation, which is now to change again but for the better), and now Ken, after 17 years, will be going. I let myself think too much of what it would be like at work without Ken and got quite upset.

SATURDAY, FEBRUARY 27, 1971

To the Village. It was a typical evening with John and Dave. John had five different albums of NO, NO, NAN-NETTE--English, French, American--and they were played over and over again. Dave tried to get John to turn them down so we could talk better but if he obliged for a moment, it was soon going again. After dinner they began to talk about the several friends who died recently and it became somewhat depressing. Most of their friends are strange, strange people far gone in the homosexual department and I have yet to hear of any halfway normal friends or acquaintances. David goes to great lengths for his friends, I must say, and some take a lot of toleration but his utter lack of interest in heterosexual people of either sex strikes me as unfortunate. John and Dave are so intense they're tiring. Cesar killed himself lugging 120 pounds of Garbo pictures all the way from Louisville, Kentucky, where he'd bought them from a collector and Dave took them over after his death, being also an avid collector. I just don't have that kind of intensity about anything. They are also intense about vicarious sex and have all the homophile magazines, tho they say they have given up GAY, GAY PARTY, etc. just as we have.

SATURDAY, MARCH 6, 1971

We bought our lottery tickets and hurried to the Lyceum to see SCHOOL FOR WIVES. I wish they'd refurbish that marvelous old theatre, which Ken hates, because it has wonderful period flavor and tho the balcony is steeply raked, the balcony is close to the stage. I will accept a good deal of the old-fashioned elevation for the privilege of being near the stage instead of half a block away as in modern theatre construction. The set for the Moliere play was charming and the acting very stylish. It was amazing to hear such an old play getting so many laughs from the audience without director or actors corning it up.

SUNDAY, MARCH 8, 1971

Ken suggested we go to the Brooklyn Museum to see the Van Gogh exhibit and while I wasn't enthusiastic I wasn't going to do anything to dampen his quite unusual willingness to go on an expedition. Actually it took just 35 minutes by subway and our bus trips downtown sometimes take longer. We were shocked when we came up from underground and saw a line going way down the block and around the corner. If I had given the matter any thought at all, I would of course have expected that. Not only is Van Gogh extremely popular but the museum has been advertising this exhibit very cleverly with ads that say "Next time you see these pictures, it will cost you $413" (the fare to Amsterdam). I was being so patronizing in condescending to go to the Brooklyn Museum that I forgot other people aren't so provincial and go over all the time. We must go back this summer and see some of their regular exhibits for today was a madhouse. One could hardly see the pictures. Having seen so many just last summer in Europe I was not as thrilled as some but I was still pleased that Ken had suggested going and I did like the room that showed 100 prints which had served as inspiration to Van Gogh. Our evening was passed in reading the Times and watching THE EARLY CHURCHILLS. Reception grew poor, which we attributed to the aerial being disturbed by the high winds, tho some stations were okay.

THURSDAY, MARCH 11, 1971

Cramps woke me this morning. I felt terrible and decided that I too would stay home. Ken said that if I did he'd better go to work. I couldn't see the logic of that since he soon isn't going to be around to understudy me. I couldn't let him go out in the rain so decided to go but then would get further cramps. Every time I decided to stay he talked of going and I got annoyed. "Now stop that. You're giving me no option but to go to work no matter how sick I feel." In the end, in order to keep him at home I went and in the long run I guess I was none the worse for it, tho at the end of the day I felt achy and for the first time in many days was lacking an appetite. Had coffee break with Jim and Bob, who were at first rather inhibited till I started the gay talk. These days without Ken are really good for me for they are laying to rest all my fears that I will have a difficult adjustment. I really have gotten along quite well and enjoy Ken's daily phone calls as I used to before he worked there. At one point today, as yesterday, I found myself alone in the office and burst into song. I am so seldom alone nowadays and never feel like singing unless I am and as always it was a great pleasure. I was forced to keep my voice low but I was having a lovely time with DEPUIS LE JOUR, Massenet's ELEGIE, the MISERERE from PEARL FISHERS and all my old French favorites.

WEDNESDAY, MARCH 17, 1971

Today I actually thought of a certain advantage when Ken leaves the office. On our way back from the dentist I saw green-iced cupcakes in the Party Cake window and suggested we take some back to the office. When we got there, however, Ken dispensed them as tho he had both thought of it and paid for them all and I was damned if I was going to be so petty as to reinsert myself in the picture. This kind of thing happens a lot and people may be surprised to find, when he goes, that I have these impulses occasionally.

SATURDAY, MARCH 20, 1971

When I looked at the program for ALL OVER and saw that the characters were given such handles as WIFE, MISTRESS,

DAUGHTER, SON, DOCTOR, NURSE, I said, "I hate it even before the curtain has gone up. This means that there isn't going to be any real characterization." And there wasn't. Tho Tandy as the wife had reams of dialogue, one never got to know her as anything but an abstraction. The BEST FRIEND was never convincing as that since he never spoke of anything he had pleasurably shared with the man dying in the next room, not good games of chess, or delectable chamber-music playing, or hunting trips, or anything. I don't think Albee had even thought thru his abstract relationships. At intermission of this depressing play (which would have been far more depressing if any of the characters had seemed real) we met Leo and Larry, who told us that Gene had gone back into the hospital, was never expected to emerge. Home to feed the cats and pick up liquor and dessert to take to Pat's. When Peg arrived she was drunk, having had half a bottle of Scotch to kill her pain resulting from dental surgery. She was unable to continue the bridge game so lay down on the sofa and Pat got out a new game of Monopoly, which she had bought to entertain a niece who would have none of it. I cleaned out both Pat and Ken and ended up fabulously rich. We were a little leery of driving home with Peggy but it turned out that she was not much wilder a driver drunk than she is sober.

SUNDAY, MARCH 21, 1971
Larry called to inform us that Gene had died in the nite. I tried to decide what I wanted to do that I had not done, in case death struck us, but I could think of nothing. I certainly don't want to go roaring out on a round of parties, having seen Peggy last nite. I would like to publish the diary, of course, but that can't be done and beyond wanting to publish (that or a creative work that currently seems unlikely) I can't really think of much. I wish Ken would get a proper will made up but my affairs are in good order to take care of Ken and Mother if I should go.

WEDNESDAY, MARCH 24, 1971
When we got home we had a notice from the Cancer Society that a memorial notice had been sent to Mac, which is very fast work. We also had a brochure for the Majorca-Costa Del Sol vacation I read about in Sunday's Times. By the time I had read it over to Ken he was sold on it. We had to leave the dishes after dinner (this is the second time lately) and rush to the Winter Garden for the first preview of FOLLIES. This proved even more of an exercise in nostalgia than NO, NO, NANETTE for it was loaded with

well-known performers (mostly known from movies, however, and making their Broadway debut) and it ended with a mock Follies which resolved the plot. The framework was a reunion of people associated with the Follies, held on the stage of a theatre that was being torn down. Girls in costumes much like those worn in the old Follies drifted like ghosts thru the action and were a wonderful touch. Their costumes were all in black and white to emphasize the ghostliness. If there were not tunes as memorable as those in COMPANY, Sondheim nevertheless provided very usable music. All the old stars were given one socko specialty and the audience loved it. It was a terribly gay audience, with every ugly gay boy in town in attendance, but a very alert audience and the theatre cracked with electricity as everybody felt as I did, that it was wonderful to be in at the absolute beginning of a smash hit. Ken and I both want to see it again and I don't doubt that John and David will go monthly for the next two years at least. Yvonne De Carlo, few of whose movies I ever saw because they were almost all trash, was fine in a bit part but her body mike failed in the middle of her very good song and it was cruelly revealed that in actuality she had no voice at all. In the old days one wouldn't have been allowed on a stage to sing unless one could project one's voice to fill bigger houses than that but De Carlo couldn't get a note over the footlights without electronic help and the same may very well be true of the others. Mikes now line the stage where footlights used to be and body mikes are worn as well. I imagine Ethel Merman is the sole survivor of the singers who can belt songs out without amplification. We went home in a glow.

WEDNESDAY, MARCH 31, 1971

To the office for the morning and despite the calls of all the well-wishers, we really did some work. I wrote out instructions for everybody. With the cats so young and healthy, I don't get such poignant feelings as I got when leaving Lavinius and Octavia in their later years. Probably because it is earlier in the season there was no wait for the plane to take off once we were aboard. I was a bit nervous when I saw police scuffling with a young Indian who said, "I don't have to go aboard that plane." I didn't want to be on any plane he didn't care to go on if his luggage was on. All of us had to have our hand luggage inspected for bombs or weapons as they are trying to prevent further hijacking. I don't know what happened to the young man but we weren't hijacked or blown up.

THURSDAY, APRIL 1, 1971
    It was drizzling when we arrived in London and we decided we were too tired to rush around and book an afternoon trip to Chartwell. Our room at the President looked right across at the Ashleigh Hotel, from which we last time looked over here toward the President. I immediately wrote diary and then we rested. Ken slept but I couldn't and got a bit upset for fear that 1966 was going to be repeated. Finally I routed Ken out because we were to pick up our free tickets between 3 and 5. (*Ours was a package tour called THE BARD AND THE BOLSHOI, offering tickets to theatre in three countries.*) We had already bought a paper to look over the theatre list and had decided that there wasn't much London theatre that really attracted us. We decided to see the silly little comedies they gave us tickets for but would discard our tickets for THE WINSLOW BOY and try to buy some for VIVAT! VIVAT REGINA. Upstairs to take baths and I decided to try the bidet for my sitz bath. First I turned on the spray and got it full in the face but when our laughter died down and I mastered the knobs, it still wasn't very satisfactory and I ended up in the regular tub. Decided to try the Carvery in the Regent Palace, about which I had notes. We had a drink before being called to our table. A waitress brings the first course and then one goes to the great table and carves as much beef and/or lamb and/or pork as one wants and helps oneself to wonderful vegetables. Everybody makes absolute pigs of themselves and more roasts are constantly brought out. The amount I ate made nonsense of my afternoon fears that I was going to suffer the same loss of sleep and loss of appetite that I underwent in '66. We walked down to Trafalgar Square feeling very much in love with London. On our walk we visited a store called <u>Lovecraft</u>, which sold such products as penis-shaped massagers, contraceptives, and something called <u>Extendamour</u>, all with bright lights and no sleazy atmosphere. So much for the cold British, who seem anyway to have as many sexy movies as we do.

FRIDAY, APRIL 2, 1971
    We went and got tickets for DANNY LA RUE AT THE PALACE to replace those for Priestley's mild WHEN WE ARE MARRIED which we were given. They were hard to come by and we got them only because some were turned in, which may speak well for the show or only mean that the British like drag shows. We were neither of us able to even think about a meal as big as yesterday's so I found a modest place on my list that was just a couple of blocks away. For a modest $1.10 we had soup, plaice and chips very nicely fried and

apple turnover with custard. We asked the man in the Underground what station we should go to for the Palace and he didn't know so I guessed at Holborn, which turned out to be very wrong. Ken suggested a cab and for 30 new pence including tip we got there. The driver was befuddled by the new currency (Britain had just adjusted its currency to the decimal system Americans are used to, making a pound consist of 100 pence as the dollar does.) or pretended to be, but it was easy for me and I straightened him out. The theatre was packed and the old ladies laughed at the succession of dirty jokes as much as any performer could hope. I found them rather distasteful and they went on and on till I found I just couldn't respond. Costumes were nice and an act by the Black Theatre of Prague made a welcome unsmutty interlude.

SATURDAY, APRIL 3, 1971

To the Cheshire Cheese, not at all busy on a Saturday with so many nearby businesses closed. A middle-aged gay man traveling with his mother was seated with us but we both played it the British way and never spoke tho he frequently took off his glasses so I could admire his fading beauty and once he winked at me when Americans at an adjacent table ordered coke. The meal was expensive but I was glad to have finally done this tourist thing that I have heretofore omitted. From there we went to Dr. Johnson's house. We saw the garret in which Johnson's six Scottish clerks worked on the dictionary. In each room the objects were described on things like hand fans which one could carry around with one as one looked at pieces of furniture or pictures. After that we took off for Lincoln's Inn Fields and the John Soane Museum. I never saw so many art works crowded into one place as in the Soane Museum. When the guards opened the walls on which the Hogarths hung and showed us more pictures on the backs of the panels, it was laughable. The guard said there were over 100 pictures in that small 12 x 14 (or thereabouts) room. That completed our scheduled day and I thought it wise to get Ken back to the hotel. We had tea in the lobby at length, settled up our accounts, and then went up. We talked then napped and I came closer to sleeping than I yet have. VIVAT! VIVAT REGINA has an awkward title but is an excellent play. Eileen Atkins was excellent as Elizabeth but I thought Sarah Miles as Mary Stuart absolutely abominable. Her vocal mannerisms never gave her lines the ring of reality and in addition made her sound common. I had to keep imagining the role as it might be played by Vanessa Redgrave but since Miles is the playwright's wife I don't imagine she's ever going to relinquish the role to a better actress. Much of the time her line-readings verged on the amateur. Nevertheless I enjoyed the play a great deal and can say the same for the whole day. Until now I have been seeing London thru a veil of exhaustion and neurosis but today I had my strength and my health and enjoyed my vacation as one should.

SUNDAY, APRIL 4, 1971

Good nite's sleep without a pill, over which Ken rejoiced as much as I did. On our way to the Wallace Collection we stopped in the Gloriette, a nice little Viennese pastry shop, where I renewed my acquaintance with Florentiners, which I discovered last year in Munich. Nobody need any longer complain about British food for one can get anything from any land now and in very nicely decorated places. Among the ads that line the escalators of the Underground seem to be an inordinate number advertising underwear and swim suits, all featuring live models (there are not as many different styles of ads here as there are at home and all seem to be produced by the same ad agency and the same art director). One ad for blue jockey shorts shows the spread hairy legs of a man whose upper body is encased in astronaut's garb. Ken and I have been having a running gag about it, I saying the man is too short of thigh for my taste, Ken saying he'd give it a whirl. On one trip up the escalator when we were alone, Ken reached out and stroked the basket.

WEDNESDAY, APRIL 7, 1971

Good nite's sleep, again on my own. After breakfast I insisted that Ken take the London book and pick out something he wanted to see. He was reluctant but I was insistent and he picked Camden Passage for its antique shops. Tho I'm not much interested in such things I was happy Ken had made a choice and off we went. We saw a lovely cat inside one shop and I went in to pet it, followed by Ken. A rather homely but coy proprietor emerged from the back and said, "Nobody does that to me!" With more than my usual diplomacy I said, "I don't believe that" and with less than his usual diplomacy Ken said, "You're not as pretty as he is," which nearly sent me thru the floor. HELOISE AND ABELARD was very good and the new leads were thoroly acceptable so that I never missed the original stars who have gone to New York. I went prejudiced against Daniel Massey because he looks and sounds so much like his father Raymond whose homely looks and inability to play anything except in a measured way always bothered me. The son has the dynamic quality his father always lacked and can play in several gears, altering both speed and intensity of delivery.

THURSDAY, APRIL 8, 1971

To the Manuscript Room of the British Museum. It was a great thrill all over again. I don't remember seeing Scott's diary before and tho it dates from only about 1910 it's nearly faded past legibility whereas letters 400 years older are remarkably well-preserved. I think Scott wrote in pencil because ink would have frozen in the Antarctic and the other people wrote in good ink. Ken found several whose script was smaller than mine at its worst. George came into the room and recommended, just before he went back to pack, that we go upstairs to see the Mildenhall Treasure. After we looked at Elizabeth's warrant for the death of Essex, found in the back of a disused safe as late as 1946, we went up and found the silver plates dating from 400 A.D. really were spectacular. Back to the hotel to rest in the lobby before going on to the Dickens House. George decided to go with me but Ken, tho 8 years younger than George, decided not to. It contained the desk at which Dickens worked as a clerk, a sideboard from Gad's Hill, and the lectern he took on all his reading tours. I don't know that Ken would have cared about it because in the B.M. he had said he liked the historical figures more than the authors and I had said that the autographs of Shakespeare, Leonardo, Michelangelo and several others meant more to me than any monarch who ever lived. When we got back to the hotel we decided to catch a cab to the BOAC Air Terminal and from there we quickly got a double-decker bus to the airport. When we got our boarding cards we discovered we weren't seated together and Ken began to fret. Since I have adjusted to the fact that we aren't going to be working together I can certainly stand not sitting together for three hours but it bothers Ken. George traded with some boys for the seat across the aisle from me and when dinner was about to be ordered, he traded with Ken so we could be together. The flight was a little rough and I thought I might join the several sick but I never did. Moscow Airport was a huge, dead-looking place with few signs of life. The apartment houses on the way in looked nice but few cars were on the road and the trolley cars were almost empty. The only time we saw many people on the great wide streets was when a shift seemed to be leaving a factory. The Metropole, our hotel, has faded grandeur and the upper floors have an odor uncomfortably like sewage but the rooms are nice, with hard beds that are a nice contrast to the excessively soft ones of London. I had no doubts I was going to sleep.

FRIDAY, APRIL 10, 1971

After Vi's tales of pickles for breakfast I was prepared for anything but we got lovely bread and butter, a plate of cheese, fried eggs, and coffee. Our guide Giulia met us at 10 and gave us our program for our stay here. Many were disappointed because we weren't seeing Bolshoi Opera but the Congress is still on and some performances are reserved for them. What most impressed me is that 85 per cent of the doctors and 45 per cent of the representatives in the Soviet are women. Why is America so far behind? We saw the University, lots of very modern housing and the exotic New Convent of the Maidens and got a nice view of the Kremlin in glorious sunlight which gleamed on the golden domes. Back to the hotel for lunch. Afterwards Giulia took us for about an hour's ride on the Metro with the fantastically beautiful stations done in marble, mosaic, and crystal. I had already noticed how attractive and well-dressed the people were and in the subways we saw how polite they are too. So often they are painted as barbarians at home whereas I would say we are more barbaric. Little girls and young men stood up to give Ken and the ladies their seat. Haunting the subway were young boys, one superlatively handsome, who asked for chewing gum and if one gave it to them, gave one a cheap little pin in return. Giulia counseled us not to give them anything because then they would trade for cigarettes and eventually become black marketeers. We are all getting chummy now since we can't disperse as we did in London and many of the people are very nice indeed, way above the level of people on more orthodox tours. An exception must be made for the blonde bitch who, from the first time I spotted her, has found something to complain about and who runs her blind-in-one-eye husband around like a bulldozer. She was at the head of our table for supper, complaining about the lunch the rest of us had found interesting and saying, "I'm a meat and potatoes girl myself", running down the Soviet system loudly, then saying, "I don't want to talk politics. I get too heated," tho nobody had ventured a word on politics, and then, as two well-dressed but long-haired youths in our group entered the dining room, ranting about how that made her sick, that in their high school in Michigan there wasn't one long-haired boy, and when the rest of us said it was here to stay a while, she said, "Oh, I wish we had a table for two. I can see nobody agrees with us." Such a ghastly reactionary to come on this trip and she wears a pin in the shape of the American flag. Since tickets were distributed at the table I was afraid Mrs. America would be seated near us but she wasn't. We were bussed to a hall said to be owned by Pravda and here we had a wonderful show much like the Moiseyev Dancers from some province whose name I couldn't catch. They were talented, beautifully rehearsed, gorgeously costumed, and the girls were beautiful. So was one balalaika player and one of the male dancers. I'm very taken with Russian looks.

SUNDAY, APRIL 11, 1971

Our afternoon was free so we took our cameras and walked to the Kremlin to get the pictures we hadn't time for the other day. The doctor who has been here so often went by subway to the Russian Orthodox Church and said 5000 people were there, so religion is certainly practiced here. For supper stroganoff and some new table companions then bus to the Kremlin Gate and to the new Palace of Congresses (6000) seats) for the Bolshoi in DON QUIXOTE. This is not, of course, my type of ballet but it was sumptuously produced and beautifully danced. All our people (mostly from the mid-West and naive about theatre and dance) exclaimed that it was the highlight of their trip, that they could die happy now, that the final scenes were the most beautiful they had ever seen, and yet 6000 people could hardly produce enuf applause to get the artists out for curtain calls. I spotted more gorgeous Russian youths and even a couple of attractive mature men. The young often have those gorgeous pink and white complexions and I must have seen dozens of men to swoon over.

MONDAY, APRIL 12, 1971

Our tour today was to the Exhibition of Economic Achievement, a sort of permanent fair with about 70 exhibition buildings. Julia turned over the reins to a local guide, Sophia, and we piled into little train-busses such as they had at our '39 Fair. Sophia was a good guide but our bleached blonde bitch obscured much that was said by her constant instructions to her husband. "Get a picture of that. NOT on the slide camera. On the other camera." We stopped in the Space Pavilion, where Sophia gave a wonderful explanation of the wonderfully displayed Soviet space vehicles. I've never been much interested in that kind of thing but she got me fascinated. When we came out it was raining. To the hotel for lunch and Ken invited George up for a swig of our paregoric, he being the latest victim of turista. Almost everybody was glad of the rain as an excuse for an afternoon to stay in and do cards. Bussed to the Circus, an unimpressive building which is to be abandoned soon in favor of a newly completed one which we have seen but which is not quite ready. Unfortunately we were seated next to the blonde bitch, who was infuriated because the red flag was featured in the opening and who hates circuses anyway. Several of the performers and a few of the roustabouts were wildly attractive and most wore sexy white tights with little underpants that covered the top of the thigh in a way not usual with tights in our country.

TUESDAY, APRIL 13, 1971

The morning tour was to the Tretyakov Gallery of Russian Art. Except for the icons, for which I developed a little appreciation at last, most of the paintings in the gallery would not be displayed by major galleries of the western world but I enjoyed them enormously anyway. I liked the Russian historical paintings for their subject matter as well as for their often breathtaking use of color and characterization. Back to the hotel to get our hand luggage out of the rooms as soon after twelve as possible. We had a nice hour's flight to Leningrad, sharing seats with the only two other men who are traveling together. One would never suspect them of being gay but the younger, of Armenian extraction, has been cultivating us and told us today that he and the man he has lived with for 17 years have a shop in Provincetown but can't take their vacation together as one must mind the store and the St. Bernard. We had light snow when we arrived in Leningrad. We were driven thru the grand streets of Leningrad to the Miami-modern Hotel Leningrad where Ken and I drew a room with a magnificent view of the Neva and a river that runs into it, which contains a World War I battleship, the Aurora. Most of the group got put in the back of the hotel with no view but ours is spectacular and the window runs all across the room. We have a radio here but there seems to be only one channel and mostly talk. Of course Ken must have it on even tho he understands not a word. Dinner was good but a party was going on in the huge dining room and there was much amplified music and some community singing that made the place too clamorous. Many of us were startled out of our skins to hear the orchestra play <u>Ave Maria</u>. Peter and Jack asked if they might tag along as we explored the vast hotel but the shops were closed and we didn't feel like utilizing the beautiful bar so Ken proposed going to the room for baths tho it was quite early.

WEDNESDAY, APRIL 14, 1971

When our tour started out after breakfast and the blonde bitch got on our bus we had a chorus of "Wrong bus! Wrong bus!" but it turned out she had arranged to change busses. She said the kids were driving her nuts but we later heard that she expressed her distaste to them and they thereafter mocked and laughed at her, which the adults have done only covertly. Only once did she out-talk the guide, tho she shook her head in disgust when our wonderful guide Eugenia told of Lenin's taking over and redistribution of land. Eugenia has more sense of humor than Julia, (as Leningraders in general seem gayer than Muscovites) and she lets us out of the bus to take pictures. I loved the many colors of the palaces and official buildings, from the yellow of the classical Russian style to the green of the Winter Palace and many other buildings, with cream, red and other colors in between. The river and canals add so much to the city too. Since the afternoon was free a lot of us decided to have an extra dose of the Hermitage and set off in various ways. We took the minibus which for 10 kopeks takes one from the hotel to Nevsky Prospect. When we looked at our watches when we got there, tho, and realized that we still had to find the entrance, still had to check our coats, etc., we decided we didn't feel up to rushing around before an opera like KHOVANSCHINA so we went in a couple of stores, including the big department store, where goods are adequate but not exceptional and very erratically priced. Back to the minibus but we got in one going the wrong direction and the driver smilingly told us then got out of his bus to show us where to wait. As we waited a boy who turned out to be a chemistry student came up to practice his English on us. He wanted to buy Ken's lighter but of course Ken wouldn't sell. Supper then off to KHOVANSCHINA at the Kirov, which I was delighted to find is the former Maryinsky. A sumptuous theatre it is, too, with the gold leaf as fresh as if applied yesterday. The orchestra was in white tie but there were no long dresses in the audience. The music and the spectacle were wonderful and I really enjoyed myself. Blondie had led a revolt that culminated in one busload going home at intermission. I really don't know why she came on this trip. At intermission we found a lovely foyer with a six foot wide rug around the edges and on this one promenaded, leaving the whole center of the room unoccupied. We found it so fascinating that we took Mrs. Sterling up at one intermission and the Hurleys another. After the opera we also took the Hurleys up to our room to see the view as they are on the back.

THURSDAY, APRIL 15, 1971
    Another gorgeous nite's sleep. The Hurleys say the early dawn wakes them up but I haven't been awake early

A GAY DIARY

enuf to notice it. After breakfast we were off to Csarkoe Selo. I had not known that there were two palaces there-- the one belonging to Nicholas and Alexandra, which we did not go in, and the Catharine Palace, almost totally destroyed by the Nazis but now being wonderfully restored by craftsmen from a specially created school. I find it fascinating that the Russians spend money and labor to restore these artistic treasures from the Czarist days and that even in the heat of Revolution they did not tear down the statues of the Czars (*as New Yorkers tore down the statue of George III that stood on Bowling Green*). Perhaps they did the lesser Czars but Peter, Catherine, and others seem to have their respect. Home in time for lunch and then off on our afternoon tour of St. Isaac's. Eugenia said it had once been an anti-religion museum but now it is just a museum of the history of its construction. It is probably the most sumptuous church I have seen.

FRIDAY, APRIL 16, 1971

Ken got up at 5 with stomach cramps and I saw the night-time daylight which has been giving many insomnia. I went back to sleep after he'd taken paregoric and seemed to be resting comfortably. The Hurleys went independently to the Hermitage again but we were content to let Eugenia lead us on a tour of the greatest masterpieces. The decoration of the museum interested me rather more than the art. There were some great paintings there but not better, I think, than in any of the world's leading museums. For quantity they may take some prize but as to quality I have my doubts. Certainly their Botticellis are pitiful, their Raphael minor and their Rubenses far from the greatest. Tho Eugenia passed them by, I saw a case of portrait miniatures and a case of decorative keys so I was happy. I also saw some Ter Borchs and Metsus which she hurried past. After lunch we set out to walk to Peter and Paul Fortress. It was gorgeous sunny weather and the rivers were full of ice floes from Lake Ladoga. We peeked in at Peter the Great's original wooden house, now protected within another building. I knew the Romanoff tombs were in the church on the island but I didn't know these included Catherine the Great and Elizabeth. The golden baroque thing rising way up into the dome was gorgeous. We walked back another way, past Tchessinskaya's palace, saw people buying eggs loose, and also saw a gorgeous black and white cat in a window. We had just about time for baths before supper and the opera. After supper we rushed into an elevator to go get our coats, went a couple of floors and suddenly the power went dead. A lot of us were crowded in there and one girl kept saying she had claustrophobia, which I knew would make Ken worse and did me no good either. There are phones in the elevator and the man called but the only help this brought was one girl with a screwdriver who tried to pry the outer door open as we had pulled the inner door apart. Finally power came on again after about twenty minutes but by that time Ken, George, and I had decided to go to the opera without our coats. The bus had gone, however, so we decided to take a taxi but all of us had disposed of our last rubles. George dashed up and got somebody to give him two rubles for two dollars and we grabbed a taxi with a woman driver and I showed her our tickets. Ken went to tell some of the others of our adventure in the elevator and suddenly a man behind me leaned over and said, "Who is that gentleman you're with and why do I know him?" He turned out to be a TC professor of psychology who's serving with the TC team in Afghanistan. When the orchestra pit rose I figured it was going to be a long overture as they didn't do that the other night. It was and I was sure from the sound of it that we were going to hear an operetta. What followed, however, was an opera that took itself very seriously and was melodic but old-fashioned and to me bad enuf to be funny. Most hated it and decided to go home on the early bus but George, Dave, and a man whose name I don't know decided to stay and so did I but Ken left with the majority. It was apparently a premiere so all sorts of men in civilian clothes were brought out for hilariously disorganized curtain calls. Even the hero got a bouquet of flowers with, of course, the cellophane wrapping left on as always.

SATURDAY, APRIL 17, 1971

There was more exchanging of addresses as we knew we would be going to three different hotels in Paris and going our own ways. As a matter of fact, we were probably not alone in feeling we had had enuf for the time being of even the nicest people. I wouldn't want a world cruise or any extended tour. Ken and I got separated at the Leningrad Airport, getting into two different lines somehow. When I joined those who had passed thru--Leota, George, Frances and others told me Ken had been held up and not allowed to proceed but I thought they were kidding. It turned out to be true, however, and we never knew why unless it's because Ken's passport picture doesn't look like him. Eventually a higher-up was summoned and okayed Ken's boarding the plane. As soon as we got to Paris we got French money. Since we were last here English seems to

have spread and the taxi driver, hotel personnel, and
waiters all seem able to cope in English. This is the real
French Revolution. We set out for a walk down the Champs
Elysees. Both of us felt Paris was really our city, even
more so than London despite the language. Paris is just
beginning to leaf and bloom and is lovely. I'm sure Leningrad will be soon for it's full of trees and as we left
today hordes of people were contributing a day's work in
the parks in honor of the recent Congress. I never did say
how startled I was to find all store clerks in Russia reckoning with an abacus.

SUNDAY, APRIL 18, 1971
    Slept okay but the minute I got up I realized I had
what Ken had last nite, plus diarrhoea. The evil-tasting
paregoric cured the diarrhoea for the day but I still felt
miserable. Edith was such an unconscionable time coming
that I began to have difficulty holding up my head. Finally she arrived, wearing a lovely green African dress. The
drive to her apartment took us to areas of Paris that we
don't know. The first secretary of the Liberian Embassy
was there, his mouth gleaming with gold (but our two North
Dakota couples also have a lot of gold teeth). Apparently
he comes around a lot to sponge a meal and some drinks.
Philippe was again a bundle of energy, firing cap pistols
in Ken's ear, insisting that we read to him, etc. and
eventually he got soundly spanked for being a nuisance. We
hadn't time to go back to the hotel so they took us right
to the Ambassadeurs Theatre. The Shadow Theatre of Malaysia was even duller than I expected it to be and none of
us stayed long. I pulled into the hotel room feeling really horrible but aspirin, rest, and a little groaning therapy helped a bit. I'm not alone in this illness.

MONDAY, APRIL 19, 1971
    Complete recovery, thank God! After breakfast I call-
ed and booked the morning tour for which we had the voucher. We had an excellent guide and a gorgeous blond driver.
I at last saw Rue de Fleurus, where Stein and Toklas lived.
We couldn't believe Notre Dame, so light in color since
its cleaning. We'd have taken a picture but couldn't back
up enuf because there, too, the square is being torn up to
make underground parking. When the tour ended we got out
at the Opera, where *more* construction is going on and several people who heard us say we were going to a Self-Service asked if they could follow us. We went to Le Rallye
and there I got a wonderful slab of pork, mashed potatoes,
and strawberry yoghurt for about $1.20, which shows that

eating in Paris can still be kept within bounds. Peter and Jacques sat with us and Peter, who has been dying to let his hair down with us, finally did. He said he couldn't keep his eye off the bus driver and nudged me. We had decided to see HAIR tonite, so subwayed to the Theatre St. Martin. Tho I did almost no reviewing of French for this trip, it seems to be coming to me more easily than ever. I got the theatre tickets easily, tho I went blank for a moment on the word for "twenty", of all things, one of the first things one learns. There were quite a few changes from the New York version but I agree with Ken that we have now seen it enuf. I still like the first version we saw far and away the best but tonite's lead was the best. There certainly isn't the nudity in the subway ads here that there was in London.

WEDNESDAY, APRIL 21, 1971
    The ride home on Olympic Airways, Ken and I agreed, was the best flight we ever had. As our seat companion we had a man we hadn't come to know before because he went in the other sight-seeing bus. I don't generally care much for adult men but he was not only pleasant but very interesting. He lives in an integrated neighborhood in Washington, teaches reading to boys in a reformatory, five of whom proved to be in for murder, and seems like a very good man. His oldest boy is the bearded hippy who was refused entrance to Lenin's tomb because his dress suggested a lack of respect and this son is as homely as hell with dreadfully pitted complexion and not one good feature but his younger son has gorgeous eyes, creamy complexion and is a dream boy at 11. Both boys played chess with Russian boys while there. I was most entertained by the man and thought how many men I had liked on this trip, Frank Hurley and George also being nice. George had spent his Paris days in bed in the hotel with a marvelous French doctor coming and going. His illness made him look his 74 years today, which he usually doesn't. (*An inveterate traveler since youth, he was married to a woman who preferred to stay home and did.*) He had whiled away his illness by making sketches of Paris landmarks, mostly from memory, and he gave us our choice as a memento. How I envy his sketching ability. What a glorious way to travel, making sketches like that. The apartment and the cats were in fine condition and the cats full of love.

SATURDAY, APRIL 24, 1971
    We went to the Park-Miller to see the male nude films. It was an experience that is topped for excruciating

boredom only by the Malaysian Shadow Plays we saw in Paris. The photography is excellent, the sex explicit and in close-up, but it's amazing how quickly one gets bored by it. One needs a tease, a story, not these immediate plunges into sexual activity. Finally there was a film·GAY GUIDE TO CRUISING (which the Times ad converts to GUY GUIDE TO CRUISING, tho how this strikes them as less sexy I don't see) and this had some writing and a modicum of wit, but Ken and I agreed that we wouldn't go see that kind of film again even at $1 admission fee, let alone $5. We have been curious since hearing Dave, John, and Bob R. talk about them, but our curiosity is satisfied. They had oral, anal, and masturbatory sex and it all looked equally unappealing in closeup and color. After supper I called Alice to find out what time we were to come tomorrow and she told me she is moving to Roslyn at Mike's request as he feels Queens, like Manhattan, is a jungle. I reminded her that the Rockmores once told us that every house on their block had been robbed and thieves had come in their house while they were watching tv. As Ken says, it didn't seem like any jungle as we ambled in sunshine down an uncrowded Fifth Avenue today, delighted at the plantings in the Channel Gardens of Radio City, watching men install a display of orchids in the Manufacturers Trust windows, and giving several stores favorable marks in comparison with Paris. Mother called and seems to be having an active social life.

FRIDAY, APRIL 30, 1971
    Bill Olewiler came by saying that if we still planned to go see the movie at the Harry Langdon Festival, he would tag along. Once again I notice that tho the young film buffs claim to find these old film comedies awfully funny, little or no laughter is to be heard in the theatre. I was a long time laughing myself, but I expected them to be more audibly amused, since they say they are. I find old movies pretty tedious on the whole. The styles in clothes, motor cars and in movie-making interested me, however. I forgot to say that yesterday it was announced in the Spectator that the Undergraduate Dormitory Council has voted to set aside a lounge for the gay. They had been agitating for one, saying they were as much a minority as the blacks and the Asians, each of whom now have separate lounges. The leader of the gays said that eventually people will get used to seeing gays holding hands on College Walk. Now this is not something I have ever had a burning desire to do but I do remember that in the days when Ken spent his vacations in Maine and I went to see him off on

the train, I used to be consumed with desire to kiss him goodbye, no matter how passionate a leavetaking we had had in advance at the club. Sometimes I wonder how it would have been for me to be young in this permissive time. Would I have become sexually active sooner? I do wonder. In the first place I wasn't all that attractive in youth and in the second I wanted beauties only. I couldn't then and I couldn't now settle for some of the unappetizing types who are leading the Gay Liberation Movement. I would rather die celibate if I couldn't sleep with something better than that. Anyway, I wasn't born in this time and I did quite well enuf.

WEDNESDAY, MAY 12, 1971

I got a haircut. The boss was alone in his shop and said business was so bad he gave his assistant the day off. He says barbers are going out of business right and left because of the long hair and the trend to let wives do the trimming. Darryl H. started work today and training him kept me busy. He seems very bright. My haircut today reminded me of a dialogue with Mother on Sunday. After all kinds of fussing about my long hair, she came out in the kitchen and said, "Are you losing your hair?" "Well, for God's sake, does it look it?" "No," she said, "but I meant are you losing it around your what-you-may-call-it." Without batting an eye I said, "No, I'm not losing it around my what-you-may-call-it, either," and she dissolved in lewd giggles. What she meant to say I don't know but perhaps she was hoping that if I didn't have thin spots like she does, I had a receding forehead. Unfortunately for her hopes, my forehead is no higher than it has ever been.

SATURDAY, MAY 15, 1971

Ken had another sickly Saturday. Since my main errand downtown was to go have my eyes examined at Macy's there was no real need for Ken to go and he went back to bed while I went on my way alone. He has lost five pounds this week from diarrhoea and loss of appetite. As the time approached for John and Dave to arrive I noticed more consecutive expenditure of energy and Ken said he thought he was feeling a little better. We had a good time with Dave and John. One thing I did learn while downtown today is that I don't mind being alone; however, as Dave and John speak with horror of the very idea of sharing their apartments with man, dog, or cat, I realize that I also do this rather easily so I have the best of two worlds. I would hate to fear sharing and also hate to fear being alone.

SATURDAY, MAY 22, 1971
    Lazy morning and then off to catch the Babylon train, picking up a bottle of liquor as a gift en route. Also on our train was a Dick O., a sixtyish Swede who recently lost his lover after 32 years. About five Dick and Jim arrived, Jim looking simply dreadful. I think he had already had a lot to drink and he seems to just disintegrate under the influence of liquor. The last time we were at Ruth and Lee's he said he and Dick had reached the point of blacking out from liquor and were finding it alarming but it doesn't seem to inspire him with any caution. I think Jim is very unhappy over this forced retirement so that they can move to Spain. At the dinner table, higher than ever, he mentioned that he and Dick had been together 33 years but that there had been four or five divorces, some of which he had been quite hysterical about. I never get in on these true confessionals, nor does Ken. We had our separation, too, but it was long ago and I'm not inclined to go into it. I'm afraid none of that set represents what people mean when they talk about witty homosexuals. Not one memorable remark was passed all afternoon or evening.

MONDAY, MAY 24, 1971
    Patty met me in the hall and said she and Amanda want to give a cocktail party in honor of Ken's retirement and asked me about guests. I said none should be from the Development Office and she said she had never planned that they would be. Just as Ken started his nap after supper, Rita called. She said she wanted the Leonards and us to come to dinner Sunday. I think myself that if we see them on Saturday that might very well be enuf but Ginny had more or less agreed when she talked to her so there wasn't much we could do.

FRIDAY, MAY 28, 1971
    Left ahead of Ken since he was going to the Health Clinic. He didn't know why Dr. Goldstone wanted him to go since he wouldn't be there anyway, but it turned out Dr. Reifsnyder, specialist in tropical medicine, is on duty then and this Leningrad diarrhoea is rather a specialty with him. He says it has been recurring in visitors ever since the city was called St. Petersburg. He prescribed a medicine which he said might turn Ken's urine red and give him a fungus in the mouth. After Ken was back some time he called to say he had forgotten to caution him against liquor. Too bad with this big social weekend coming up but better he should regain his health for Spain. We don't know what the score is with Darryl. Yesterday he

talked about a party at which the boys danced with the boys and the girls danced with the girls and Gay Liberation came around because they thought it was a good place to recruit. We let the subject lie but today he brought up a news item about homosexuals who had a church marriage and he wished them well. He may be making a bid as Terry F. made years ago, for a confidant.

SATURDAY, MAY 29, 1971

When we subwayed to the theatre, it occurred to us that the Leonards might not know that matinee curtains are now at 2 and began to worry that they might not make it. As a matter of fact they didn't know and sauntered into sight with just about three minutes to spare. We enjoyed FOLLIES just as much the second time as we did the first. Afterward we went to the Americana and found Rita and George waiting in the lobby. We went down to the bar, which was very nice and drinks were only $1.50, with marvelous mixed nuts on the table, on which I made a pig of myself.

SUNDAY, MAY 30, 1971

We had breakfast and talked a while then got ready to go to Rita and George's. It was a lovely day and as we walked along the park I saw four black boys turn in the park ahead of us and was relieved because otherwise I was going to suggest we cross the street to the other side. We walked on but suddenly the boys were beside us. I thought they were going to pass us but they each grabbed one of us and the one who had me said,"You're going to get shot. Come on over and sit down." I didn't believe he really had a gun and said, "I will not," pulling toward the curb. The sequence of events was then confused. My man kept pulling toward the wall and telling me I'd get shot, Eddie jumped the fellow who'd taken Ginny's handbag while Ginny yelled, "Eddie, let him have it, for God's sake." Eddie yelled, "Help! Police!" and a colored man leaned out of the window across the street and said, "I see what you're doing and I I'm calling the police." Then there was a shot and the men started to run. I didn't know who had fired but knew I was alive and well and then wondered about Ken. It turned out that the fellow got his wallet. As we went on our way to Staten Island Eddie and Ginny kept thinking of things that had been in her handbag (which did not include her wallet as she had left that at home). We tried to look on the positive said, saying we were all unhurt and none of us had lost our watches, tho only Ginny's was valuable. Ken's first remark after they left was, "I'm so sorry. You'll never come again." Another positive aspect was that

people came to our aid, the man yelling out the window,
the man who fired the gun (we don't know who he was but
Eddie and Ken saw him fire a blank about twenty-five feet
from us) and a lady who was behind us on the street came
along saying, "I've been praying for you," plus two men
washing a car, who didn't come over to help but yelled.
Ken, whose medicine doesn't make him feel too good anyway
(his urine is now red and his tongue coated as predicted)
felt so queasy of stomach that he wanted to go home and I
was willing to go with him but we all went on and arrived
shaky at the Thatchers'. Here our nerves had to cope with
seven children (very mannerly and charming but still numerous) and a huge new dog, a cross between an English setter
and a Saint Bernard, which jumps up on one with wet paws
and chews one's shoes while they're still on the feet. I
called the police and got very polite treatment but a referral from one precinct to another. Finally we got detectives who wanted to speak to the man who had suffered
the loss and I put Ken on. Apparently the man filled out a
form and then decided that still wasn't the right precinct
and gave Ken another number. When we called that number
after getting home, we got more runaround and gave up. As
we came out of their house I suddenly had a terrible case
of panic and began to shake. Fortunately this passed in
about ten minutes without my mentioning it to anybody. Eddie asked Ginny if she would mind driving home tonite so
they came to our house and got their bag then left. To
tell the truth we were relieved. I could hold Ken in my
arms and express my appreciation that he wasn't hurt.

THURSDAY, JUNE 3, 1971
    Ken still didn't feel good this morning. His illness
gets me right in the pit of the stomach. I get depressed,
just as I do when the cats are seriously sick. All morning
long Ken debated as to whether he would go home or not. He
stuck it out and at noon I was able to persuade him to eat
some roast beef and mashed potatoes. To my great joy, he
ate a very good plateful and naturally felt stronger as a
result. Kathi approached me and said they wanted to take
Ken out to dinner for his retirement and what nights were
we free. I don't think the party will be a success but I
felt better about their making the effort. (*Despite his
long years of service our office had till then made no
move to give him a sendoff. Because of the constant turnover, there were hardly any who'd known him long.*)

SUNDAY, JUNE 6, 1971
    After brunch we went to the Village to see THE HOUSE

OF BLUE LEAVES, a very fine play by a Yale Drama School grad who chooses not to mention Yale in his program biography. We both enjoyed it and I mentioned how we have come to take for granted the direct address to the audience which was thought horribly old-fashioned when I was learning playwriting. One would suppose it would break the illusion but it doesn't. Back to University Place to catch the bus home. The art show now spreads up there for blocks and one can hardly tell where the bus stop is. I don't think there is any art show around the Square at all any more, now that NYU practically owns everything, but it certainly has spread to side streets where one never found it in the old days. (*At the beginning and at the end of summer the outdoor art show takes place for a week or two. Originally the art was displayed on three sides of Washington Square and a few side streets immediately off it.*) We find the ride home tedious but a lot less scary than the subway. Ken has claimed to have shot nerves but I thought I was making a fast recovery. This morning, however, when I came back from getting the paper, a negro man I don't know turned in after me and even the fact that he had three children with him didn't reassure me as children are wielding knives now as much as adults. I got home with heart pounding as I expected to be mugged in the elevator. Still, Ken verbalized what I had earlier been thinking, that one cannot have the pleasant kind of afternoon we had in Benton or Augusta or, as Ken said, even Portland. We had a rich choice of theatrical fare and movies and museums today which is possible only in New York and so far this year we have averaged a theatrial event a week.

THURSDAY, JUNE 10, 1971

I pushed Ken to go over and apply at the Presbyterians today and he agreed but the prospect made him so nervous that he couldn't eat his toast at break time. All winter he talked about how he looked forward to his retirment and I was the one psychologically upset at the idea of his going. Now it is clear that he supposed he would be going right to a part-time job which he could easily obtain. He admits that the prospect of a break in his routine is shattering his nerves and even tho people are very nice to him when he applies, it is still nerve-wracking. I understand this and said we would skip all thought of job-hunting after this till he comes back for I don't want him to lose his appetite. As full-time leisure approaches, he is really feeling it and I am at a loss as to what to do. I pushed him out to hunt jobs because I thought it was easier to look for one when one already had one, but I guess it isn't

easy under any circumstances. We went downtown to shop for
vacation clothes after work and went first to eat. Ken lost
his appetite and with his went mine. I wish I could find a
way to alleviate Ken's retirement problems but I can't. I
suggested that when we come back he sign up for volunteer
work at the two hospitals without waiting for a job to come
along.

FRIDAY, JUNE 11, 1971
    Almost forgot my appointment with Dr. Fretz. When the
prostatic massage was over with (and it was quite painful
this time) I asked him about entero-vioformo for preventing
diarrhoea while in Spain. Ken cleaned out his desk in preparation for leaving and this took its emotional toll of
both of us. Bob R. asked if we had to leave right after
work tonite and said the girls would be calling us about a
party at his apartment. He didn't explain that it was a
surprise party for Jim on his retirement. As the afternoon
wore on Ken said he was feeling bad again and not at all
like a party but as before, when we got there the distraction kept us from moping about his retirement. The party
was very good for us both psychologically because the ethnic and racial mix reminded us that you can't cross the
street to avoid all negroes just because some have mugged
you. They mug their own as well. A colored girl I've often
spoken to but whose name I never knew before persuaded me
to join the dancing. Soon she was saying, "Not too loose,
dear." I love this modern dancing, detached and sexy.

SUNDAY, JUNE 12, 1971
    We cleaned house this morning then set out for Douglaston. Eric was waiting for us and also on the train were
a pianist named David Bean, his pretty wife who was a chorus girl in MY FAIR LADY and other shows and two daughters.
Joining us at their big rambling house overlooking the
Sound were Eric's nephew and wife and child, a neighbor who
attended Yale Drama School with wife and two sons, another
friend with three children. With two of Eric's children
present, we had nine or ten children and there was much
coming and going. I quite liked the Beans, who are woebegone because they are moving to Oxford, Ohio, where he has
been teaching piano for some years even as he lived in New
York and tried to make a career as a pianist here. He said,
"There's nothing terribly wrong with Ohio but there's nothing terribly good about it either." I was pleased to hear
that Eric is writing again. He and Peg took the children
out on their sailboat and in a canoe, taking them in relays.
Peg is quite deaf without her hearing aid, but such a nice

woman and she handles deftly all the coming and going in and out of the house, which eventually gets on the nerves of us staid bachelors.

MONDAY, JUNE 14, 1971
Neil met Ken in the hall and told him that Al had told him he was leaving TC. Each boss stays a shorter time than the last--Hanson 17 years, Forkner two years, Grefe one year, O'Connor six or eight months, and now Landa four or five months. At coffee break we kept our date with Bill O. up in his office. Bill gave us bon voyage cards and as he looked at it, Ken let his coffee splash. We were concerned with the resultant spots when we returned to the office and for some time didn't notice a spread that had been laid out on the work counter. Elaine, Mary, and Millie had bought sangria, sherry, cheese, and crackers, etc. for Ken to offer people who came to say goodbye to him and they plan to keep the supplies up thru tomorrow also. Lots of people did come, too. We got very little work done, indeed.

FRIDAY, JUNE 18, 1971
We had a two-hour wait in Madrid and Ken was holding on by his teeth. I got a little weary of Lulu Davis, my talkative seat companion because she never seemed to sag and keeping up with her was a chore. We had a nice quick flight to Malaga and when we got there were revived by the fresh breeze from the sea. Being at the final destination also helped our spirits. Our hotel, Maite Dos, turned out not to be in Malaga but out beyond Torremolinos. It's grandly luxurious, however, with sofa, coffee table, chairs and table inside and another set on the balcony and a little kitchen with stove and refrigerator. We hated the thought of an afternoon tour of Malaga but Jennifer had said it was today or never so after a rest we pulled ourselves together and went.

SATURDAY, JUNE 19, 1971
We both slept well and got up after nine much refreshed. Ken expressed interest in breakfast, which I was glad to hear. Again the waiter discussed the hassle between our government and the New York Times, which has been publishing secret documents showing how we got into the Vietnam War. They keep up on our affairs over here. We signed up for Monday's Granada trip but put off paying for any more till we saw if we felt as good as we did today. We took the bus to Torremolinos and wandered up and down the shopping streets. We bussed back to the hotel just as siesta was about to set in. We sat on our balcony and wrote

postcards to the sound of surf in front of us and construction behind us. Next time we come I'm sure the hills behind us will be solid with hotels.

MONDAY, JUNE 21, 1971
As our bus climbed the winding roads of the hills, it was physical effort to hold on around curves and Ken began to feel carsick. He recovered fairly quickly but we both decided to skip the trip to Ronda, which is also a matter of many curves and early rising. We were glad when the road straightened out and we enjoyed the scenery. On arrival in Granada we went directly to the Alhambra, which impressed me more on second viewing. To lunch then, where we were joined not only by the inescapable Lulu but also by a nice British lawyer with three doctor cousins in the States. When we finished dinner we headed for the men's room and were well in when we heard Lulu exclaim, "Where are you leading me?" and turned to see that she had followed us in. I got laughing so much I could hardly do what I had gone in to do.

FRIDAY, JUNE 25, 1971
Our guide was very good and explained the trees and vegetation of Mallorca. At Puerto Pollensa we all had a surprise when we boarded a boat and had a lovely ride to Formentor. The beach there was as nice as any I know because the water was clear, the sand nice, and when one tired of sun there was a grove of trees to retire to. I was sorry I had left my suit in the bus but I did go wading and found the water warm. Four of our party changed to swim suits but spent all their time standing on the beach talking and daubing on suntan lotion.

MONDAY, JUNE 28, 1971
With siesta to consider, I didn't want to get too late a start on our shopping day in Palma. Gabriel can say it's not a siesta, it's a long lunch hour, but the shops are still closed. We got lost in some of the narrow side streets which so effectively shut out both sun and cars but eventually we found our way to Calle Jaime III. After dinner Ken proposed a walk down the beach and in no time at all we came on a beautifully landscaped miniature golf course. We had a very nice close game and I enjoyed the mixture of English and German on the course, plus a little deaf and dumb language from some boys behind us, three of whom could hear and speak but who knew how to communicate with a handsome long-haired friend who couldn't. The air was heavenly soft and as we walked home we thought how

nice it was not to have to turn suspiciously when a shadow
came up behind you.

THURSDAY, JULY 1, 1971
     A tedious day, as traveling days almost always are.
Gabriel smoothed our way to leave Mallorca but we had a
long hot wait in Madrid. The three boys from Pittsburgh
decided they had been sober too long (probably twenty minutes) and started drinking again. I wouldn't mind their
drinking so much if they wouldn't brag about it. I have
never understood two things about the Irish, why they think
a hot temper is sexy and why they think getting drunk is
some kind of achievement. As our bus came into town there
was a crackerjack of a thunderstorm. I hoped Sally had put
the windows down but we got home to find she had not and
it had rained in. Mother called and was startled to hear
we were going to bed at such an early hour but we had been
up for hours.

MONDAY, JULY 5, 1971
     Decided to get things set up and sorted so Ken could
work on his scrapbook of our 1968 trip to Spain, Portugal,
and Morocco. He also has a laundry to do so that will keep
him busy. It won't get him out of the house, tho, and I'm
hoping that a desire to get out will eventually (soon, I
hope) lead him to volunteer for hospital work if he isn't
going to ask for work. We went downtown to see DEATH IN
VENICE, which Ken wanted to see more than I did. Out of
that actionless wisp of a story I didn't see how they could
get any movie at all, let alone one that ran two hours. The
answer is, they didn't. It was the slowest, most repetitive
movie one can imagine and I hated it from the first. The
boy used as Tadzio was a beauty all right but of a much
more feminine beauty than I imagined when I read the story.
There was a boy who had just a bit scene in an elevator
that we found much more sexy.

WEDNESDAY, JULY 7, 1971
     I saw Ken W. sitting with Bob R. now that Bob's boon
companion Jim is gone. I was going to join them but **shyness**
prevented. I sat alone and didn't mind it but as I got up
to go I was hit by such a wave of longing for Ken as un-
settled me emotionally for the rest of the morning. I had-
n't as many visitors asking about Spain and Ken as I had
yesterday and the boredom was excruciating. Ken called
when he got back from his shopping excursion downtown and
it was good to hear his voice. When I got home he had his
purchases all wrapped and I had my belated birthday

presents. He says he will start his volunteer work next week.

FRIDAY, JULY 9, 1971
After supper we set out for Ballet Theatre. We had just convinced ourselves that we would be brave and go by subway when we ran into Bill Ponman, who told of being mugged twice recently, once at knifepoint in the foyer of the house (the guard was watching the broken garage door) and once at gunpoint when locking his car just across the street. I decided it would be no subway for us, especially since it costs Ken no more to go by bus since he gets half fare with his Senior Citizens' card. COPPELIA got a lovely performance with Makarova and Kivitt in the leads. Much of my evening was dwelling on muggings and how to avoid them. I worry about Ken when he goes to or from his volunteer work because they mug in broad daylight now. I tried to get my mind off crime and onto the lovely ballet but it wasn't easy as at the moment I am a mass of fear.

SATURDAY, JULY 10, 1971
Ken wanted an accordion file for his papers and I remembered one I had in the dining room closet but when I got it out I found it amazingly full of manuscripts. Considering how blocked I have been in recent years, how frustrated at the lack of markets, it astonished me to realize how much I used to write. Furthermore I was impressed both by the carefulness of my typing and the quality of some of the material. I still have no idea where to send manuscripts these days as fiction is so minor a part of the contents of magazines and I am not geared to the necessary research for non-fiction but I would love to write again. I'm sure my mental health would be much better if I did.

SUNDAY, JULY 18, 1971
Between the liquor and my emotional disturbance over the party I had my first sleepless night in 3 and a half months. I thanked my stars that it has been twenty years or so since I went thru that kind of turmoil. I told myself that nobody at that party has serious designs on Ken nor he on them, which couldn't be said in the old days, but I still got upset and then of course upset because I wasn't sleeping. Neither of us felt too good when we got up but at least I got better perspective than is possible in the middle of a sleepless nite. Jim and Dick will soon be gone to Spain and that element in our life, which has been disturbing at every party we've gone to, will be

removed from our life. Jim disliked Caswell because he
stole one of his lovers and Ed was annoyed because a friend
who was visiting him had gone to a party at Caswell's tonite, tho Caswell is in a wheelchair after a nasty fall
due to drunkenness. I do wonder how these people go thru
a long life having all this emotional stress. My stomach
just won't take it. I made no mistake when I broke with
that world in 1949. I would look just as ravaged as they
do if I hadn't. One thing I missed at that party and usually do miss at their parties is any decent conversation.
My physical state deadened the anticipation I had had of
going to Pearl's, which up to yesterday I had greatly
looked forward to. It was good to have that invitation,
however, to keep from moping around the house and to provide an antidote to last nite. The hors d'oeuvres and the
dinner were both marvelous but most appreciated after last
nite was the conversation. Ken and I both even **looked** more
glowing than we did last nite. He too really belongs more
at this kind of party and likes it better.

TUESDAY, JULY 20, 1971
     Ken came by to have lunch with me after his interview
with the Director of Volunteers at St. Luke's. I went home
by way of the library and turned in books and placed three
reservations, which are now ten cents because of the increased postage. When I get home now Ken and I have so
much to talk about. We always had a lot to say but now we
almost forget to have supper because we are exchanging
news.

WEDNESDAY, JULY 21, 1971
     For the first time since 1966, I think, sleep didn't
come on the nite after a sleepless nite. At noon Eric arrived in shirtsleeves and suggested we eat at the Interchurch cafeteria. We had a nice talk, as much about movies
as any**thing else.**All his children are away. Mary and Kathi
came in to say I was going to have to store 175 cartons of
receipt forms in my office, on top of all the cabinets. I
was livid and figured out that Elaine had ordered 100,000,
or enuf to last us twenty years. I was noisy in my protest,
saying I would not work in that office for the next ten
years with cartons all over the place, that they could at
once discard 75,000 of the forms and have a nice bonfire
because Elaine and **every**body else knows we are going on
another computer in a couple of years and these forms may
not even be compatible, that a secretary who so grossly
miscalculated would be fired on the spot, that I intended
to throw out a box every nite when the janitor came with

his tub to tempty the wastebaskets, etc. I also said that either Elaine or the salesman, or both, must have had one martini too many and put the order in for 100,000 when what she should have had was more like 10,000 or two years' supply if we have a good year. I'm not thru yelling yet and have already scared them off of putting them all in my office. I think Kathi was at one and the same time appalled and happy about the implications I was making about Elaine's competence.

THURSDAY, JULY 22, 1971

After work I started to walk down to meet Ken at St. Luke's only to meet him at the corner of 120th, he having walked up to meet me. He had had a very satisfactory first day in the medical library, mostly spent tying up copies of medical journals which are being sent to the binders'. There was another 65 year old man working as a volunteer and he had coffee with him and the librarian, so his objective in getting out and meeting people was served.

FRIDAY, JULY 23, 1971

Leo's apartment has a real air. There is probably not a thing in it that I would choose but it all looks just right for him, including a rolltop desk for which he bought an old-fashioned phone to match. He has programs saved from the year God knows what and lots of books that look read. There were fourteen people present, with the novelty supplied by two neighbors, Jack and Bud, who presumably have been living together a long time like the rest of us. Jack, like Ken, retired July 1 but Bud has even longer to wait to join him than I have, being only 49. Jack is opinionated and snappish in manner but wanted to know if we were in the book as "we must get together". I had great fun playing with the cat, Tommy. His original owner had him altered and declawed then abandoned him, so Leo, who had sworn not to have another cat, rescued him. He's a biter and tackles people all the time but since I didn't pull my arm away from him, he never sank his teeth in me and was puzzled and frustrated at not being able to intimidate me as he did some others, including Larry, who more or less lives there. Jim didn't get as drunk as he does at his own parties but he was most unhappy. Dick is making him tear up and throw away so many souvenirs of his life rather than ship them to Spain, he's unhappy about giving up the cats, and I don't blame him, and I think he fears the boredom of the place when he gets there. We caught a bus almost immediately and got home at a good hour. Whereas I was upset last week with things Ken said, this time he had said very reassuring things. When we were discussing what to do about the three of us whose mates just retired, leaving us to work or in Jim's case to become dependent, Ken said, "If I win the lottery, Don can retire." And as we talked about how there was no intrigue, no attempt to play around with other people's lovers (not much temptation there for anybody, truth to tell), Ken said,"Well, as you grow older, I think you grow closer together." This is more the Ken of recent times, who mentions how long we have been together, etc. whereas last week's Ken was more the unsettling Ken of old, who tended to cast me off at parties in order to enjoy freedom. This set is generally beyond that hanky-panky, tho we have all gone thru it.

THURSDAY, JULY 29, 1971
    Ken came up this morning to see Mrs. Marsden about how much of the money paid in to his pension came from him as TIAA will then calculate for him the part which is not taxable. The visit bore fine fruit as Dorothy Marsden later called me and said she and Russell Reed had been discussing Ken as a possible solution to some of the problems they have in the TC Bookstore, and could he report tomorrow at 10:30 for an interview about a job. Russell wanted him to work full time but I didn't and Dorothy advised him as a friend to settle for his $140 a month. *(The maximum allowable without reduction of Social Security payments.)* I couldn't wait to see Ken and tell him and before 5 he came along, having finished his volunteer work early.

SATURDAY, AUGUST 7, 1971
    The morning expedition was to Maine General Hospital to see Florence's new volunteer offices and to have a tour of the new building. I'm not sure I could take hospital work for I picked up a magazine on proctology and scared myself to death as I read about rectal cancer, hemorrhoids, etc. Florence got a little defensive when Ken said she smoked too much and about other things. In the afternoon I provoked her by my indifference to the telecast of the return to earth of the astronauts. Ken is used to such statements as "See one blastoff and one splashdown and you've seen them all," but she isn't. She kept saying "God bless them" till I thought I'd throw up but I do think this extreme interest in current events which she and Ken inherit from Nellie is good for them and contributes to longevity. At six we went to the airport to greet Ross and his wife. I don't know in what terms these relations discuss Ken and me in private but they are very cordial to me in public.

SUNDAY, AUGUST 8, 1971

Ken was doubtless right last nite when he said as he came to bed, "I think we've stayed just one day too long". Florence is talked out and repeating herself on the subject of how terrible the snows were last winter, what a hard life she's had, etc. She now regrets having divorced Mike instead of overlooking his infidelities. One thing that is very different about life up here where everybody has stayed near where they were born is that they all know what happened to everybody. There is great continuity to life whereas in the city people just sort of disappear from one's life and one wonders what has happened to them. Of course what happens in Maine is often horrible, like Mrs. M's son killing himself by jumping off the roof, and Jane E's daughter dying from dope and Jane trying to keep it quiet, and Marjorie W. drinking herself to death, but one sure does know all about everybody. That would certainly be a disadvantage to the gay who tried to go on living here.

TUESDAY, AUGUST 10, 1971

It was wonderful having Ken set out with me for work again. Because his work starts at 9:30 he couldn't have break with me. He came to meet me for lunch. He was somewhat down and I wasn't sure if he was just tired from being on his feet all morning or if he was depressed because he had to work down in the stock room. I asked him at nite and he said it was both, that the work wasn't really what he wanted.

WEDNESDAY, AUGUST 18, 1971

Ken met me for lunch, then took off for home. When I got there at 5:30 he was at work cleaning out his suitcase of letters and keepsakes. Among the old things he had thrown out were three diaries from 1922, 1923, 1924, 1927, etc. I asked to have them and he let me. As diaries they are not much but to me they mean a lot. As I read of his mooning over this or that attractive male and being lovesick over Randy, I got so amused and affectionate that I was forever jumping up to kiss him. Considering his awareness, his occasional sexual activity, and the general appeal he exerts, I wonder that he had not established a relationship before he met me. I really don't get bored when Ken reads me old letters from before my time. One letter he did NOT read to me was from Jim Boothe but he threw it away with sounds of disgust so perhaps it was the one in which Jim said he felt he must put our friendship first. I have mellowed enuf about Jim to hope he finally found somebody. Ken really couldn't remember some of the people from whom he had letters, tho most brought back memories. It is astonishing how many people pass thru the ordinary life and disappear into limbo.

WEDNESDAY, SEPTEMBER 1, 1971

When Bill Rapp reported for work he was carrying his motorcycle helmet. Somehow I hadn't figured him for that type. He's manly but doesn't work at it. He was much easier on my eyes, sitting across from me, than poor Sister Gregory had been. Tho I don't care for hairy men, the hair on his arms is so golden that it doesn't put me off. I'm going to enjoy having him around and he's a good worker too. Florence wrote that she was somewhat hurt by some of the old letters Ken had sent on to her and I was appalled to find he had sent on one in which she told him of her first intimations of her husband's infidelity. Ken, so solicitous of people's feelings sometimes, can be on the other hand extremely callous, as when he recounts to me the details of his infidelities with my friends, which even after twenty years I really do not want to hear about.

FRIDAY, SEPTEMBER 3, 1971

Bill Rapp came in this morning wearing pants with exterior buttons on the fly. I wouldn't have expected him to go in for this widespread and to me erotic fashion. He seems to me, despite his lack of a wedding ring, to have that quality of a sexually satisfied man that married men often have. Perversely enuf, this kind of man excites me more than a man who seems to have sex on his mind. Ken called me to say he had had an exhausting day doing all the errands I outlined for him--getting our prescriptions filled, exchanging our tickets to LENNY for a date that didn't conflict with Forest Hills tennis, buying liquor and meat at Macy's, etc. I bussed all the way down to the Met Museum where he was waiting for me and we paid our first visit in some time. It was almost our last opportunity to see the summer loan exhibit, which ends Monday.

SATURDAY, SEPTEMBER 4, 1971

Downtown to the Ziegfeld Theatre and were astounded to find it a large theatre decorated in real old "moom picture palace" style. I rather liked it nonetheless but that kind of theatre is hard to fill these days and there were hundreds of empty seats. Of course both films were old. I had resisted 2001: A SPACE ODYSSEY because I don't care for science fiction but I made a concession because Ken wanted to see it and I liked it, tho I certainly didn't

A GAY DIARY

begin to understand the ending. Ken was probably making an equal concession in staying for THE YELLOW SUBMARINE, which I hadn't wanted to see either but whose imaginative cartooning I was astonished at and delighted with. The lobby was decorated with mementoes of Marilyn Miller, Will Rogers, Eddie Cantor, and other Ziegfeld stars, as well as Ziegfeld himself and we were fascinated by them.

SUNDAY, SEPTEMBER 5, 1971

Out for the Times but no time to read it before taking off for Trenton. It was the usual day with Mother. We had the usual dispute because she feels so superior to all the other people in the building. We saw some of the ladies sitting out on the benches provided and I think I could have some very good small talk with some of them as they looked quite nice but Mother cannot be persuaded to even go on the scheduled trip to the Amish country with them. She tells of kind acts others have done for her when she was sick and yet she seems to despise almost everybody. The only reason I argue with her and try to persuade her to participate in things there and socialize with the people is that I think her life would be pleasanter. We left in time to get home for SIX WIVES OF HENRY VIII.

THURSDAY, SEPTEMBER 16, 1971

Bill spent the day trying to straighten out his schedule and his future and came to the conclusion that he couldn't work this year. I'm not likely to get another worker I enjoy undressing mentally as I did Bill. He asked if he could leave his motorcycle helmet with us this winter but I passed up the chance to see him daily by recommending that he rent a locker now while there were plenty available and he went off to see about it.

MONDAY, SEPTEMBER 20, 1971

We stayed up late last nite watching a David Susskind program featuring four former homosexuals who had married and four who still followed the life. The so-called reformed were so self-righteous and so homely that it was sickening but it was a pleasure to see the others, mostly quite good-looking, talking about their husbands and their lovers with a good deal of humor. The strange thing was that the married ones had far more gay mannerisms than the ones still following the gay life.

SATURDAY, SEPTEMBER 25, 1971

We had lunch at Trefners's and I reveled in the

tearoom atmosphere, so quiet and genteel, and with such
good food. There are hardly any of these tea-room places
left any more for one by one the ladies who started them
in the thirties are dying off, retiring, or being replaced
by highrise buildings. At today's rents one could not start
that kind of business and charge those prices. Much talking
of the hostess with the regular customers. From there we
went to see the new hit movie SUNDAY BLOODY SUNDAY, which
sounds like a violent picture but isn't, dealing with a bisexual artist who is having simultaneous affairs with a
divorcee and a male doctor. It was a wonderful movie with
great depth of reality, since the careers of all were well
established, and their families too. It was the first picture I ever saw in which male lovers kissed squarely on the
mouth and held it, and indeed there were even scenes of
them naked in bed together. Ken and I kept bringing up
scenes in the movie, reminding each other of wonderful bits
of dialogue, delicious things that just flew by without
underlining, and I love that.

WEDNESDAY, SEPTEMBER 29, 1971
    An excruciatingly boring day at work and what is worse
I had a real bad case of nerves, leading to a loss of appetite such as I don't think I've suffered since my 1966
illness. It was all alarmingly like that and I worried myself sicker that I was going to have trouble again. Having
had so many bouts with lack of appetite, Ken was sympathetic with that, but said he couldn't see what would bring
back nerves, since all was so well with me. Last year I
attributed it all to fears of working without Ken but that
has worked out very well and I don't know what my trouble
is. The London doctor said there isn't much use looking
for causes, that one should consider an attack of nerves as
like a virus, something that one just had, but I hope this
passes quickly.

SUNDAY, OCTOBER 3, 1971
    Soon after I got to bed a band of anxiety tightened
across my chest at the fear of not sleeping but it loosen-
ed and I had a good nite's sleep with some very pleasant
dreams. Unfortunately, however, I got up deep in a sick
depression and waited all day for the miracle that happened yesterday when it went away. In the afternoon I pulled
myself together and we went to the Whitney Museum to see
the show of American quilts, which ends on the 6th, and the
Hopper Bequest. I was surprised that all of the quilts
came from the Northeast as I would have thought some might
have been made in the Middle West. I was also surprised

that the only ones which didn't date from 1850-1880 seemed
to be from the 1920's. There must have been a revival of
interest in quilts in the 20's. The patterns have most modern abstract painting beat all hollow and pre-date it by a
good deal. When we got home Ken took a nap and I again lay
down with the same inability to sleep and the same result
of increasing depression. When we got up, tho, and had our
drinks the miracle at last happened and life took on its
normal coloration, tho fears of a returning depression
hovered over my better spirits. Ken is going to see Goldstone on Tuesday about his leg and I will go about my
frayed nerves. I don't expect much help because I didn't
it in '66 when the serpasil began to get to me, and I didn't get it last winter when I complained of anxiety.

SATURDAY, OCTOBER 16, 1971
    A few guests were already on hand at Leo's and they
kept coming till there were about 18, all male. I moved
around the room and talked to almost everybody. There was
just one negative bitch that I disliked; all the rest were
fine. A visiting couple from Cleveland, together for almost thirty years, told of being burglarized three times
out there by sons of white middle-class neighbors. I felt
perfectly marvelous all evening and wished devoutly that
I could be permanently in as good health. The meal was
wonderful and I was astounded to hear that Leo and Larry
had been to a matinee of THE INCOMPARABLE MAX for there
must have been lots of work and I wouldn't dare be so insouciant as to go to the theatre on the afternoon of a
6:30 party. One of the Cleveland men asked which one I was
paired with so I pointed out Ken across the room. When I
said we had been together 25 years he said, "You must have
been a child when you met." I laughed and told him I had
been 28 and he said he wouldn't have thought I was over
40. Like my mother before me I lap this kind of nonsense
up and convince myself they meant it.

FRIDAY, OCTOBER 29, 1971
    I didn't have much of a wait for Dr. McHugh and he
was just as patient and understanding as I remembered him.
McHugh went even further than Dr. Yohalem in stating that
he thought reserpine was the cause of both the anxiety and
the depression and the insomnia and that he thought it and
I should part company forever as it is bad medicine for
me. The dangers in using just chlorthiazide to control my
pressure is that it too has a side effect, it gives one
bursitis such as Ken has just had. He said that the effect
of the reserpine lingers two or three weeks after one

comes off it, which would tie in with my experience in 1966. He thinks that I should take the elavil as prescribed by Yohalem whether it is anxiety or depression that I feel since they now know more about reserpine than they did in '66 and know that anxiety is also produced by it and is itself a form of depression. Tranquilizers and sleeping pills compound the problem, he said.

FRIDAY, NOVEMBER 12, 1971
   Had the usual morning troubles at the office and after meeting Ken for break I called the Psychiatric Advisory Board. At that number somebody told me to call another number and this turned out to be the Mental Health Foundation. He said what they do is refer you to a diagnostic therapist for a diagnostic interview then one of their case workers looks it over and calls around to find a therapist who has some time available and treats that sort of case. He gave me the name of a Dr. Arthur Perlman to call for a diagnostic interview and said I was to pay him $20 at the time.

SATURDAY, NOVEMBER 13, 1971
   To the Eugene O'Neill to see THE PRISONER OF SECOND AVENUE. Tho a comedy, it dealt with a 47-year-old man who loses his job, can't find another tho his wife gets work, and has a nervous breakdown. Tho the audience roared, I was a bit sobered when they mentioned his going to an analyst five days a week at $40 an hour with no end in sight for the treatment. I certainly can't get into that sort of thing. I will just have to suffer until the grace of God releases me as it has in the past. Today, for instance, was a nice respite. Some evenings lately I have been too immersed in self to relate properly to Ken but today I could. Even with a play striking so close to home I was in better shape than when I saw THE LAST PICTURE SHOW, which really had nothing to do with my life but depressed me painfully. We spent the evening reading and while I was feeling good I decided to work on the party menu. Oh, if only this normal feeling would last.

TUESDAY, NOVEMBER 16, 1971
   I took off for my appt. with the diagnostic therapist. He turned out to be as young as he sounded. My well-rehearsed history of depression while on reserpine didn't satisfy him. He wanted me to go back to my childhood and he wanted to know about Mother. He dragged out of me a lot of periods of friendless unhappiness that I had never thought of serving up to him and a lot of stuff about

Mother that I have long since forgiven. I made it plain that I didn't have the money for extensive analysis and he gave me some pamphlets on group therapy to take home and read. That is supposed to be less expensive and I almost think I would like it better because I didn't much like how much he pulled out of me and I really don't see that it has anything to do with my hatred of the job. Now that Mother and I are at peace, I don't want to revive old antagonisms. When I got home Ken showed me a letter from Alice, who had had a rugged week since her daughter-in-law had been thrown from a horse and fractured her skull and Toni, her daughter, had had a miscarriage. She still wanted the party, tho. I just sat down to read when the phone rang and it turned out to be that neighbor of Leo's who once said at a party that we must get together. He wants us to come to dinner with a few friends next Tuesday so our social calendar is getting filled up. Later Mother called. When I got the usual question, "Do you love me?" I decided not to be as evasive as usual and said I did. I felt guilty at having told the analyst about how we moved from Mt. Holly to Moorestown in pursuit of one of Mother's lady loves and then to Bloomsburg in pursuit of another, etc., and then left places because of debts and bill collectors. He said I seemed to have a problem with separation and as I thought back over the things he got out of me, like having our best friends the Leonards move away, and how upset I had been when leaving New York for California, leaving New York to go abroad, etc., and last year worrying about Ken leaving, it did seem a pattern tho I fail to see how it accounts for my aversion to the job, especially last year, when Ken was still there.

WEDNESDAY, NOVEMBER 17, 1971

Good nite's sleep but soon after arriving at work, one of my worst foggy spells, which really frightened me. It closed right in on me and disoriented me. Ken hung around after lunch as his dentist's appointment wasn't till four. When I walked down to 110th he was waiting for me and flashed his new tooth. When we went in the house I had that reaction of reluctance and aversion. What the hell is going on in my psyche? For hundreds of nights I have been happy to come home with Ken and have a good time reading, watching tv, etc. and we now have almost more social life on the docket than we can handle (Ruth called today to ask us out Saturday, when we are going to Alice's) so what the hell is the matter? In fear of the pain of losing him am I rejecting him or some damned thing like that? My dislike of the job I accept, tho I better learn to live with it, but this other reaction I furiously refuse to accept for Ken is by long odds the best companion anyone ever had. Furthermore, I wouldn't be the least bit surprised if he outlives me.

SUNDAY, NOVEMBER 21, 1971
  In spite of the stimulus of the party I went to sleep quickly and went on thru the nite. I had interesting dreams but I couldn't have described them in group therapy if my life had depended upon it. The book on neurosis says that that psychiatrist has found it helpful to get depressives, especially middle-aged depressives, to make a five year plan. That sounded like a good idea to me as otherwise my life till retirement seemed just like seven years of diminishing returns. For one thing I set a goal of seven new acquaintances a year for the next five years plus a replacement for every one lost, all this so that I can have some friendly supportiveness in case I lose Ken, a prospect which horrifies me. For another, I would like to write at least one piece--story, article, play or novel per year. Ideally I would like to get another job but I doubt if I have the faith or self-confidence.

TUESDAY, NOVEMBER 23, 1971
  Late in the afternoon I had an anxious period at thought of the party and then dreadful chest pains. As soon as I got out of work they cleared up. Tho I had met the hosts only once and knew none of the guests save Leo, who came last, I was utterly poised and at my absolute best. It was all male couples of long standing and no messing around, no camping. Quite a few lived in New Jersey, which I guess is why it was a mid-week party. Jack, of course, is retired and I was aghast when he asked Ken if he was available to go to Wednesday matinées with him and then I could come down for supper afterward. I don't know if Bud dislikes the theatre and he supposes I do too or what but Ken said, "I wouldn't go without Donald," which was gratifying. My only gaffe of the evening was in taking one man's Thai lover for a Japanese. As at all parties these days, we had tales of mugging and robbery. Whereas last time I got the impression that there was no trouble in that building, tonite I heard that a burglar came in one apartment while the man living with the Thai was asleep and took only cash, that the doorman had been stabbed. The party broke up early since so many had to go home to New Jersey and we left too. Two of them, by the way, do needlepoint and recommended to Ken that he try bargello work.

FRIDAY, NOVEMBER 26, 1971
   Larry called to say he couldn't come to the party as his sister was going out and he would have to stay with his mother. We then decided to invite Jack and Bud and luckily we found them free to come. Earlier in the day I had called Dr. Hurvich, the psychotherapist recommended by the Mental Health Foundation. He sounded young, softly considerate and when I said I had been indoctrinated with the idea of group therapy and had been a bit surprised when individual treatment was thereafter recommended, but he said we'd see and gave me an appointment. Leo arrived half an hour early. Tho he is an easy person, his early arrival intensified my nervousness and it continued as the guests arrived but eventually I settled down. Jack and Bud made an excellent addition, tho Jack was a bit more campy this time and his outspokenness pulls me up short now and then.

TUESDAY, NOVEMBER 30, 1971
   Had soup at school and then went to see Dr. Hurwich. His office is more lived-in than Dr. Perlman's but has the same kind of black chairs, tufted plastic that swivels, with a footstool for the doctor. There is also a couch there but I was a chair customer. Tho he is supposed to have received my papers from Dr. Perlman, I might as well never have had that diagnostic interview for all he said about it. Whereas Dr. Perlman probed and guided when I stopped talking, Dr. Hurwich just maintained silence until the thought of what I was paying got me started again. He wasn't sure I would do well in group therapy since I expressed distaste for expressing hostility or having others express theirs toward me (that shows I'm off form but I never in my healthy life minded how much hostility people expressed toward me if they weren't people I cared deeply for and I never withheld my own expressions of hostility). He said that normally he might wait for things to come out but to expedite matters he might ask me to take some psychological tests, some of which I could do at home. I was not inspired with much confidence at this session, feeling I had just gone over the same material I had gone over with Perlman and learned even less.

WEDNESDAY, DECEMBER 1, 1971
   When I got home Ken presented me with a note from Leota Donaldson saying she was visiting a friend on 22nd St. this weekend and would we be free to come to dinner Saturday. It will be nice to see her again as she was our very favorite person on the Russia tour. I also had a letter from Pearl Eppy enclosing the article her boss had

written on what magnesium deficiency could do to people, which included making them agitated and depressed. One thing that causes such deficiency is diuretic pills, which of course I'm taking. Diet is the best corrective. We watched Julia Child make soup and then the last half hour of the Carol Burnett show, which repeated a hilarious sketch by popular demand. It was one we had missed, about a nervous dentist treating his first patient, and I was roaring with laughter as the dentist got the novocaine in his own hand and went numb. He finally bashed the patient in the face with a light and this knocked the tooth out, whereupon he said, "That'll be $20." The patient then spit out another tooth and he said, "$40." I was really sore from laughing, which I haven't been in a long time.

SUNDAY, DECEMBER 5, 1971
If liking yourself is the core of recovery from neurosis as so many theories seem to say, I was in good shape today. As we started out yesterday I decided I was looking quite handsome and that my new haircut was the best in a long time. I also knew damned well I had lived up to the reputation Leota had given me for wit last night for I was in rare form. I had also beaten Ken to the punch on appreciation of the cooking and had absolutely nothing to feel guilty about. I could perfectly well see why Leota had contacted us and had all the self-confidence I have recently been lacking. While in the library yesterday I had come across one of the books Eleanor Klein recommended, THE PRIMAL SCREAM, and had browsed in it. He seems to think that all neurosis comes from not having had enuf loving contact with fathers in particular and the therapy he believes in is to have the members of his groups lie on their backs on the floor and cry out "Mommy! Daddy!" till they scream with the pain of remembrance of their primal deprivation. Well, I am not about to do it and can't imagine many people with New England blood doing it either. Certainly I wish I had had a warm and loving and demonstrative father but I don't really think many people do and I honestly don't remember to what degree Mother was affectionate, but I suspect her demonstrativeness was adequate. We resumed work on our Christmas cards and have only about a dozen left to do, none of them calling for notes such as we wrote tonite.

TUESDAY, DECEMBER 7, 1971
Judy had no sooner arrived at the office than she said, "Mr. Vining, I don't think I can stick the morning out. It's so insufferably hot in here." I said, "What

about me? I have to stay all day for years." "I don't know how you do it." Susan said it was a waste to take her shower before work, that she should wait till afterward. Tho horribly uncomfortable, with a permanently bedewed brow, I at least had no fog to contend with. Ken had bought stamps for the Christmas cards so while we watched the Julie Andrews-Carol Burnett special I put them on the envelopes. The paper had said the two comedy numbers were funny but I didn't find them so. A takeoff on Martha Graham and her troupe had really nothing to say about Martha Graham except that recently she has been tottery and even that statement was soon abandoned in favor of horsing around. As a matter of fact, Martha Graham herself does a funnier statement about herself than Carol did.

WEDNESDAY, DECEMBER 8, 1971

Left early to keep my appointment with Dr. Hurvich. I told him I was virtually my old self and I thought at first he was just going to sit there impassively but eventually he did throw in a few things like, "Well, what else has improved this week?", the answer to which was, "Everything!" or "Why do you think all these people are rallying to help you?" or "So your self-esteem has improved?" to which I said,"Yes, I know perfectly well why I get invitations to parties. Because I'm entertaining when I get there." He said he thought it was fine that I was doing so many things to help myself and in the end he gave me sixteen pictures which I am to turn over one by one and write a one or two page story about, telling what is going on, what led up to it, what the people are thinking and feeling, and what happens. I went home and Ken said Miriam had called to say they are back from Israel but are going to Washington this weekend to see Barbara but she wants us out in January. I decided to get at my homework for the therapist. As I feared, the first picture didn't stir my imagination at all. A very blurry picture of what appears to be a man leaning against a lamp-post in the snow, it gave me no sense of drama at all. In the end the therapist may have got what he wanted for my story turned out to be about my father.

THURSDAY, DECEMBER 9, 1971

While I wrote stories to go with two more pictures, Ken addressed the rest of our Christmas cards, which I later signed. The two pictures I worked on tonite were clearer and more readily suggested stories. I had to rush the second one and as often happened in my writing days, the rush seemed to help for from a writing standpoint it is much the best, even including a good concluding line. I don't see that either story tells much about me, however.

FRIDAY, DECEMBER 10, 1971
    Quite a good day for health. I burst out laughing when Judy and I were alone in the office today and she said, "Mr. Vining, do you ever get the feeling in this heat that your head is fogging up, your ears clogging, and everything closing in on you?" "Yes,"I said,"it's been costing me quite a bit of money to find out what's causing it." She said she felt sure she couldn't stand a whole day in that office and that when she leaves she has to go for a walk in the air. We had a light supper then I got at the stories for Dr. Hurvich. The pictures I had tonite had no connection with my life, as far as I could see, and all the stories are going to prove is my facility in writing. Of course little sketches like this are not salable but, by God, for first drafts and improvisations these are damned good and restore my faith in my talent.

MONDAY, DECEMBER 13, 1971
    I started on my little stories for the psychologist and really could not take the first one seriously. It showed a little old white-haired lady with a lace fichu. Nobody has seen a little old lady like that in my lifetime except on trademarks so I really horsed around with it and kidded the pants off the whole thing. Really, some of these pictures are so ridiculously dated. I don't think Dr. Hurvich is going to appreciate my comic efforts but I couldn't resist. I watched an absolutely stunning two hour television performance of TALES OF HOFFMANN. I really never get tired of HOFFMANN, CARMEN, MANON, DON GIOVANNI, MARRIAGE OF FIGARO, or LA BOHEME. I can't think of any other operas of which I can say this.

FRIDAY, DECEMBER 17, 1971
    Got out the apothecary jar and filled it with the filled hard candies I bought for the office. Left the champagne in the main office as it would have boiled and popped its cork in our office, even tho this was far from our hottest day. From the office to Dr. Hurvich's. I told him I thought the pictures were rather tacky and dated and he said they would probably have been changed by now except that they had been so thoroly tested. When I said I had nothing to complain about this week, he asked about my dreams and I had to say that I couldn't remember them even at breakfast. Then he said there was a second part to the picture business so he turned them over one by one and I

was to say which of the stories I based on them were drawn
from my own life. The best I could do is say that a couple
of elements from my own life were in two. I asked him if
that was a low level of identification and he said it was,
but not infrequently encountered. He then asked me to draw
the most horrible thing I could think of. First I couldn't
think what that was and then, as I thought of a long terminal illness, I didn't know how to draw it. He said if I
couldn't draw it, I could tell him what it was so I said
it was between cancer and severe mental illness. Later I
realized I shouldn't have zeroed in on cancer but should
have said any long terminal illness. Then he wanted to
know what I would want if I had three wishes. I had no
trouble with the first and quickly said, "Fame as a writer
after death". Later I thought that I should have said,
"Fame as a writer which lasts after death". My next two
choices weren't well put either. I said, "I'd like to die
nearly simultaneously with my roommate" and "I'd like a
quick and nearly painless death." Later I wished I had said
"For both of us". He made the next appointment for two
weeks from now and I don't think I will continue too long
after that. These games might be fun if the significance
was explained to me but since it isn't, it's an expensive
pastime.

WEDNESDAY, DECEMBER 22, 1971
    I took the Broadway bus down to the Yale Club. Eric
was waiting for me in the lobby and before we even got in
the elevator he said he could stay only half an hour,
which shocked me. (The Yale Drama School Alumni were having their annual Christmas party.) The only ones there from
our era were Ollie Flemish and Jackie Soans from the class
ahead of us and Gil Williams from the class after us. Not
at all the people one would wish to see. Ollie left with
me and suggested we have supper together. There I heard
about his trials in the last years of his mother's life and
of his two weeks in the psychiatric ward after her death,
etc. I don't mind this as much as Ken does and made a date
with Ollie to go to the Holy Apostles Church for one of
the gay services on January 9.

TUESDAY, DECEMBER 28, 1971
    The evening was given over to reading the new Opera
News and the new LIFE, generally devoted to 1971 in pictures but with 12 pages devoted to the Gay Liberation Movement. I must say it grieves me that neither the militant
homosexuals nor the militant lesbians seem to number any
attractive people in their groups.

THURSDAY, DECEMBER 30, 1971
   Ken had asked me to save any criticisms I had of NICHOLAS AND ALEXANDRA till after the show and I agreed. Actually I didn't have as many as I expected. Rasputin's clothes were much too clean (likewise hair) but there was no attempt to whitewash Nicholas and Alexandra as I had feared. He was shown as an incompetent weakling and she as a strong-willed incompetent. The murder of Rasputin wasn't well done and incomprehensibly they did not shove him thru the ice. I walked Ken up to 57th St. and sent him on his way while I kept my appointment with Dr. Hurvich. Despite the night of insomnia, he agreed with me that I seemed recovered and that we could consider the therapy at an end, always leaving open the possibility that if my symptoms return I could continue with him and the background work would be done. When I got home Ken and I had supper and then I spent most of the evening looking at the travel material, working up a very nice appetite for the trip.

FRIDAY, DECEMBER 31, 1971
   We had a hard time figuring out which of the several highly praised movies we should go see. The most satisfactory time schedule was that for A CLOCKWORK ORANGE. The audience was 99 per cent under 30. The whole subject of the film was the psychological retraining of a hoodlum and his ultra-violence in the beginning had me writhing and turning away from the screen. At one point I thought it was going to send me right back into depression and then when the hoodlums broke into a place where there were lots of pet cats I was so afraid we were going to see them beat the cats to death that I was nearly sick on the spot. I said to Ken when we came out of the theatre that the most appalling part of the afternoon to me had been the passivity with which most of the audience had stared at the awful events depicted in this film while Ken and I were writhing and I was refusing to look.

1972

SATURDAY, JANUARY 1, 1972
   TWIGS was four one-act plays about three daughters and a mother, all played wonderfully well by Sada Thompson. It's minor theatre from any literary sense but often funny and a real tour de force for the actress. We went

to Joe Allen's (*a restaurant with theatrical patronage*) to eat. Not only was the food superb but the eavesdropping was marvelous. Five musicals were to close tonite and ON THE TOWN was probably going to so there was much depression and some brave joking. At the table next to us were the harpist from the orchestra of PROMISES, PROMISES, who said he had no sentimental feelings about the closing and two girls from ON THE TOWN who were very depressed. At one point the boy said, "This may be The Last Supper. It's the last day of work." At another table was a chorus boy from APPLAUSE (*which had a scene set in Joe Allen's*) talking across the aisle to an attractive boy who for this week only is playing the male lead in COMPANY so that the regular lead can visit his family in California before going to London to play the part there. We couldn't have been in Joe Allen's at a more dramatic time than when so many shows are closing.

TUESDAY, JANUARY 4, 1972
    Skimmed the new Writer's Digest and saw an ad about a contest for 20 minute radio plays. Truth to tell, I completely forgot all my radio technique and couldn't remember script format, how to get from scene to another, how long a page of dialogue would play on the average. I'm going to call Eric and tell him about it in case it serves as a spur to him. Got out YALE RADIO PLAYS and looked at our old scripts to see how it was done.

WEDNESDAY, JANUARY 5, 1972
    Really did give some thought to radio plays today and made a list of ideas. I think I was in a fair way to go off on the wrong track when Caroline inadvertently put me on the right road with the question, "Mr. Vining, did you ever write comedy?" "Usually," I said. "Because I think you're very funny. I mean, the way you express things." So I made a note on my list of ideas "Stick to comedy." The wit and humor that ripples thru my conversation has never found its way into my writing. I need the particular situation and can't set it up as a play. Nor have I ever attempted to be witty in my diary. It has just never occurred to me, so bent am I on an accurate record (tho it is far from being that and I can't imagine how any human being could make it so). As I think of it, I don't see why it would be inappropriate to try to keep a witty diary but I still have no intention of trying. Somehow all the diarists I know tend to be sober in their journals, whatever they may be at a dinner table. Never thought of this before in my life, for all the thought I give to diaries.

THURSDAY, JANUARY 6, 1972

Downtown in time for the travelog on Switzerland at Town Hall. Ken met me in the lobby. It was a marvelous travelog, exactly to our taste--no coy jokes, no lingering shots of babies or flowers, and lots of information. It resulted in some changes in our itinerary. I had lots of magazines, etc. to read waiting at home but we had made up our minds to take down the tree tonite. Titus, who has loved lying under it breathing in the odor, looked a bit blue and we missed it ourselves. We'll miss hearing the cats ring the bells as they chase each other back and forth. As the tree dropped more, the bell got lower and this morning they rang it five times.

SUNDAY, JANUARY 9, 1972

Oliver called to cancel the meeting at the New Yorker for coffee and Danish, saying he would meet us in the vestibule of the church. Ken was a little stiff about the whole adventure. Then when we got there we saw some bearded and very informally dressed people hanging around the entrance and Ken got stiffer yet. Eventually Oliver arrived with Wes, who seemed stoned. The Church, officially the Church of the Holy Apostles, tho for the homosexual services it is called Church of the Beloved Disciple, is quite attractive inside , tho in need of some paint and repair, which it is getting. A large congregation, male and female gathered tho the priest said attendance was way down because of the flu that is going around. We were handed a copy of the mass, which went on for pages, and I didn't see how they could get thru it in an hour and a half but they did. The incense made me a little sick and religious ritual is not my dish but I decided not to hold myself as aloof as Ken was doing (a reversal of roles from those we often play) and I sang the hymns and entered as much into the spirit of it as I ever could with high church rigmarole. The sermon, tho a bit repetitious, was good from a psychological standpoint. Rev. Clements, who has had a male lover of his own for twelve years, said that the text was from Paul, who was an undoubted Saint but a fallible man who perhaps erred in asking for observance of the letter of the law rather than the spirit when he said man must not lie with man. Clements said we must start by loving ourselves, accepting our nature, then extend this love first to our gay brothers and sisters and then further, to the rest of the world. They have something they call "the kiss of peace" which they demonstrated with the hope that we would all take part. It is rather like the kiss of French generals and their men, touching cheeks and saying "The

Lord be with you" then shifting to the other cheek and giving the response "And with thy spirit". The priest first kisses the acolytes, or whatever they are, this way and then they come down to the end of each pew and pass it on to the end person in the pew, who passes it on to the person next to him, etc . Wes had departed for the Parish House long before this so Oliver took the kiss of the colored acolyte and passed it on to me, cheating by trying to make it a regular kiss. Ken received my kiss as stuffily as tho we were strangers and was lucky that a pillar was to the other side of him for many passed the kiss across the barrier to the next set of pews and lots of blacks were over there who would have given Ken pause. Ollie is enuf to give me pause ordinarily but I decided to rise to the occasion. If I ever go again, however, I will be very careful where I sit.

TUESDAY, JANUARY 18, 1972
    Called and reserved tickets for the Equity Library Theatre's revival of the cream of the three Nancy Hamilton revues, ONE FOR THE MONEY, TWO FOR THE SHOW, THREE TO GET READY. Tho the performances are free, a donation of $2 was suggested and we gladly paid. As we stood in the lobby waiting for the doors to open Ken was rather hidden behind a partition and I saw a somewhat wild character eyeing me. Eventually he worked his way over and even tho he discovered I was with Ken, he butted into our conversation. I didn't particularly mind. As we waited for the curtain I noticed Nancy Hamilton come in to sit in the back row and since I know she lives with Katharine Cornell (*probably America's premiere stage actress of the 1930's and 1940's, but never really active in lasting media like films so not known to many in her old age*) I looked a little further along the row and there, sure enuf, was Cornell. Side to she looked rather good but full face her eyes popped out in a sort of pug-dog way that was weird. The show wasn't bad but I see why none of the revues were ever really a success and also why the revue form has gone out. One sees better sketches on television.

TUESDAY, JANUARY 25, 1972
    At noon when I joined the cafeteria line a young plain girl in front of me turned right around and asked if I worked there, what my name was, etc., and introduced herself. She then asked, since I had said I'd worked there since about the time she was born, if the food had ever been good. I defended it as I always do. I could see after she got her order that she was waiting for me but while

she got salad I flew out, paid my bill, and found a table
far at the rear. No matter, she found me and asked if she
might join me. I said she might but warned that I would be
leaving soon to go read my paper. She pumped me and flirt-
ed outrageously, just as tho I were her age and not that
of her father. I haven't had this kind of nonsense in
years and years, perhaps because Ken was always with me,
but this is the second instance this year. The other woman
is at least nearer my age but so ridiculously coy when she
comes in to report how the slip of plant I gave her is doing that everybody rolls their eyes when she is gone. In
the afternoon Personnel sent me a potential worker, a boy
from Israel. They warned me that his English wasn't too
good so I said I'd hire him for research down in the transcript room and am I glad I put it that way for he smells
to high heaven, just as Mike did. I had to get out the cologne after he left. I don't want anybody to tell me that
negroes smell. These two white boys even the score for a
couple of hundred negroes. Did further planning on THE
BEES today, getting my five characters set (that was what
we were requested to have in the 30 minute radio plays so
it is certainly all a fifteen to twenty minute play can
handle).

SATURDAY, JANUARY 29, 1972
        Early in the afternoon I ran down to the ACA Gallery
to see the Rex Clawson show. I was so glad I did for a
number of reasons. In the first place I was enthusiastic
about at least a dozen of his paintings. I wanted to buy
one and was going to inquire about prices when I heard the
gallery personnel, who had been chatting, say, "Maestro"
as someone came in the door. It was, of course, Clawson
himself but I didn't want to cut into his conversation with
the gallery people about which ones had sold so I went on
home. I could only remember a few of his many wonderful
titles but the small one I asked about, less than half the
size of the one I own, sells for $450, compared to the $90
I paid (*when he exhibited at the Village Outdoor Art Show*).
I also priced a wonderful painting that was in the window
and that was $1000. The one in the window was a takeoff on
The Sanctuary, the desanctified church which has been turned into a homosexual bar. It was a wonderful architectural
rendering with all the perfection of detail that Clawson
seems increasingly good at and all over it were signs like
"10 Topless Choir Girls 10" and "10 Bottomless Altar Boys
10" and "S & D Leather Room in the Rectory" and "Orgy Room
in the Apse". When I got home I turned on the broadcast of
PELLEAS ET MELISANDE even tho I don't care for it and I

must say that I enjoyed listening to the last scenes. I guess because he suspected from the cleaning that company was coming and that he would be spending the evening under the beds, Titus was fantastically loving and love-seeking. He flew when the first guest arrived. Since we had no cat-lovers present, I made no move to coax him out but toward the end of the evening curiosity got the best of him. Victoria stayed out the whole evening, wasting her flirtation on people who ranged from indifferent to hostile. We were both a bit shocked by Ben's new wife and even more by Miriam's new husband, who is certainly nice enuf but quite heavy and unprepossessing. I heard later that the new Mrs. Rockmore said of me to Ken, "He makes STATEMENTS!" which tickled me not only because I know it's true of me but because she is nobody to talk about anybody else's opinionatedness, nor is Ben. They were at each other just like Ben and Pearl used to be.

SUNDAY, JANUARY 30, 1972
    After brunch we set out for China Institute on 65th St., which had an exhibit of gold and silver objects dating from 1500 B.C. to perhaps 1600 A.D. It was a small room and crowded, China now being so much in people's minds since we have recognized the Communist regime and the President is going there. We then walked down a block to Asia House, where they had some lovely Japanese paintings. It was lovely and nippy but beautifully clear overhead, the kind that makes last nite's speculative talk about where in Europe one would prefer to retire sillier than ever. I still like New York best.

TUESDAY, FEBRUARY 1, 1972
    Asked Bob R. if he had heard from Jim and Dick and he said that he called Marion, the woman who was visiting them, and got a very bad report. Not only is Jim not physically well but he is sunk in apathy and in a very bad mental state. Bob says there is a married man who has loved Jim for thirty years (I find this utterly incredible for I see not one lovable, interesting, or likable thing about him) and he is so distressed by the news that he wants to fly over and bring him back. Jim can't even write to him because Dick might intercept the letter (but then he doesn't write to anybody else either). I also learned that Bob has imported a Spanish fellow he fell in love with over there. He had a hard time getting him in because of the quota but finally got him a student visa and has enrolled him in the Latin-American Institute to learn English. He is going to see if this lasts for a year or so

here and then maybe they will go to Spain and start a pension just for gay people. It is interesting that Robert, who was once the little darling whom Jaime worked hard to get papers for and look after, is now the one working hard to get his own little darling into the country.

SATURDAY, FEBRUARY 5, 1972
   On the walk to the cat show in the Felt Forum the wind made our eyes water and our ears sting, which I liked and Ken hated, but then he seems to feel obliged to hate all kinds of weather--heat, rain, snow, cold--whereas all I hate is heat. The Felt Forum fills a real need in the city in offering a moderate-sized auditorium for events like this. In fact, I don't see how anyone could claim anything other than that the whole Madison Square Garden complex is a great improvement over that tacky arena where we used to have to go. Neither of us really believed that Peggy's cat was entered in the show but sure enuf she came running up to me at a point when Ken had wandered away. Her Burmese, Kubla Cahn, was a lovely cat and both the Burmese and the Abyssinian strains do appeal to me but I really don't know what sort of cat I'd buy if getting a thorobred. There were no black and white cats like Lavinius so I guess they just don't rate but I still love them.

SUNDAY, FEBRUARY 6, 1972
   We went to Hunter College for the travelog on Berlin. The lecturer was excellent but a little too eager to propagandize against East Berlin and East Germany in general. The snow had made nicely by the time we came out and was the dry, sparkling kind. Of course Ken, a foe of all weather, would have no good word to say for it but I loved it. The moment he got in the house he turned on the radio "to see what they say about the weather" as tho he couldn't trust his senses to tell him that it was snowing unless the man on the radio said so. The park looked lovely, like a Japanese painting, tho I imagine the Japanese artists would subtract a few trees and have more space.

SATURDAY, FEBRUARY 12, 1972
   Cleaned and about noon we set out on our trek to Babylon. The party eventually consisted of 17 people, four women and thirteen men. It was rather weird, as parties in that set can very well be. I had heard of Clyde and Philip at one of Jim and Dick's parties and I remember that Mac and Gene had exclaimed in horror that they were horrible people and they hoped never to see them again. I therefore expected monsters and was surprised to find them less than

that. Before the evening was over, however, I began to understand what the talk had been about. Philip, a most unprepossessing man in his sixties, came up beside me at one point and put his arm around me and hugged me as he leaned his head on my shoulder. Instead of cringing as I ordinarily might, I returned the hug but went right on talking to whoever I was talking to. Later he stood in front of me and told me that he and Clyde had been together 24 years and would probably have a 25th anniversary party and that he had had a previous love affair of ten years but after seven years the sexual element had gone out of it and he didn't like that as that made them nothing more than room-mates. He said he understood that Lee and Ruth had not had sex for ten years and he wouldn't like that, would I? When I said Ken and I didn't have anymore either, he said,"I assume then that you get it somewhere else." When I denied this he closed right in for the kill. "But you're too young to give up sex. You can't be more than 42." I said that was very flattering but--and told my right age. "That's still too young. You're terribly attractive. You wouldn't be inside my door one minute before I'd try to lay you, I'll tell you that." Fortunately Ben W. came along and broke that up. Philip later did a bit more hugging and kissing and again I kept on talking to someone else, which is probably what saved me from the usual recoil for certainly if I had been looking at him my reaction would have left something to be desired. Roberto brought his new love, just imported from Spain, and announced that nobody was to speak Spanish to Luis as he wanted him immersed in English. Of course Philip spent a lot of time practising his Spanish, which his roommate said was fluent but which certainly was not. Luis would never be my type but he had a very cute figure and a charming personality and is clearly madly in love with Roberto. He always adored everything American--music, food, clothes, everything, and is perky as a button. One couple included a grossly fat fellow named Cleve, who must have weighed 275 and a nice enuf fellow named Ronny whom he called his baby till Ronny said,"Baby! Jesus, I'm 34 years old!" Ronny did a nice job of serving the drinks and was awfully pleasant but not attractive, tho I still wonder how he can stomach sex with Cleve for ten years. In addition to being such a gross physique, Cleve was inclined to nag and upbraid Ronny. The talk was untrammeled, to say the least. Usually it is Lee who gets crocked and Ruth who has to carry on but this time Ruth got very drunk too. I understand she and Lee were fighting furiously in the kitchen but I missed that. Because there were so many of us it was buffet dinner (very late and Cleve was screaming "When are those two fucking lesbians going to serve the food?") but several sat up at the table and ate. A bit of dancing started and Ronny was dancing with Lee when someone, probably Cleve, said "I hate to see two lesbians dancing together." Bob offered us a ride in so when Cleve said he had lost one of his train tickets, I gave him mine. It was nice to be taken right to the door. Bob had his troubles en route because Luis would get affectionate while we were waiting for a light and kiss him with other cars right beside us.

TUESDAY, FEBRUARY 15, 1972
      Ken had a doctor's appointment and we were going to the Westminster Kennel Show so with the time in between he got us some theatre tickets, I having prepared the list of shows and dates for him. I met him at the Yangtze River and we had a nice dinner then bussed to Madison Square Garden. Whereas the cat show was held in the Felt Forum, the dog show is held in the main arena. There are 3000 dogs entered and going thru the benching area took quite a while. When we took seats in the arena we saw the judging of three categories. Tho a catlover and never partial to dogs, I must have fallen in love with a hundred dogs in the course of the evening. Never knew I was so fickle.

FRIDAY, FEBRUARY 18, 1972
      When I first went to the Development Office I found only Henrietta there, all the others having gone over to Horace Mann Auditorium to hear Shirley Chisholm. I decided it was too late for us to go, even tho Susan wanted to, but Susan ran over, found they had not started yet, and we went. Young black kids filled the balcony and it was an obvious source of pride for them to see a black woman who had not only got herself elected to Congress but was even running for President. On the basis of her sensible speech I would be happy to vote for her but of course the occasion is not likely to arise. I wanted also to go to the noon-time lecture on THE HOMOSEXUAL IN ART, sponsored by our new Center for Education in the Arts, but there was nobody to leave in charge of the office so I didn't. In the evening I read a while and then went on with THE BEES. I did quite well for a while and then Ken got talkative. It wasn't just talk that I could let go in one ear and out the other with an occasional "Mmm-hmm" but a steady stream of remarks that demanded answering. I stopped writing in hopes that he would soon subside but he kept on and on for a long time and when he finally quieted down my concentration was so

shattered that it took me the best part of five minutes to get pulled together again so that I could continue. I got everything done but the last scene, however, which pleased me.

TUESDAY, FEBRUARY 22, 1972

Kathi was back at work today. We had a bit of a private talk and she thinks Wintermudd's efficiency report on the Development Office may well be a first step to his becoming our next boss. Ken had left my pill bottles at Whelan's on his way to St. Luke's so called me to remind me to pick them up. I was almost there when I remembered I had left the Times in the office. I knew Ken would want to read about Nixon's visit to China so after I picked up the pills I walked back to the school for it. It was brisk and cold so I really didn't mind the extra mile of walking. We watched a creation in dance-sound-light by Alwin Nikolais, done especially for tv and full of such fancy as would have delighted Hieronymous Bosch. It had both male and female nudity so now it has reached television. And it grows steadily less shocking as we see more of it, especially since dancer's bodies are so pleasant to look at.

FRIDAY, FEBRUARY 25, 1972

Now that I am writing again I have restored to my prayers the phrase "And thank you for the talent you gave me, no matter how small, because I enjoy the possession of it." Ken gave me a French quiz tonite. It all started when he called our dinner plates "plats" and I insisted the word was "assiette". He didn't believe me and took my book to prove his point then when he lost started asking me some of the questions. We horsed around and I said "L'assiette" was a famous French saying meaning "The dog ate its dinner."

SATURDAY, FEBRUARY 26, 1972

We went to the Apollo to see SOME OF MY BEST FRIENDS ARE..., a poor man's version of BOYS IN THE BAND. It was better than I expected but the whole thing was confined to a gay bar and in the noise a lot of the lines escaped me. They made the point that the Mafia owned the place, that the police came by for their bribes, and one interesting touch was that the Italian owner could tolerate almost everything except seeing another Italian going in for the gay life. At least three sets of attractive people who were making out nicely were shown along with the closet queens, the outrageous swishes, the transvestites and the old man who was paying the bills of a rebellious man who wanted girls. When we came out Ken remarked on how sleazy it was (which it was) and got a little too righteous to suit me so I reminded him that he had gone to the Blue Parrot with Jim and to a drag place in New Jersey with Jim, and that when Jim was last heard from he was sending for his costume jewelry so he could camp around the tuberculosis sanitarium. If I had remembered it at the time I would have mentioned that Bill Snell got caught in drag in a Florida raid. But of course it's true that neither of us was ever truly campy. It must be wonderful to be gay in this permissive age, tho I have no complaints about the way I have been treated by employers or others.

WEDNESDAY, MARCH 1, 1972

Once again our electric alarm decided to go backwards and the alarm went off a little after two. At least I got a title for my second radio play out of it. COUNTERCLOCKWISE. Susan came in after a night of no sleep at all. Seems she ran into an old boyfriend yesterday and it has given her misgivings about marrying Howie. Later I had tea with Kathi and she said something is going around which causes insomnia and upset stomach, that both she and Chuck have had it. She too has her problems as she feels she is getting old and wants children but Chuck still doesn't and she thinks they may have to go to a marriage counselor. I asked if they hadn't agreed on this when they married and she said they had but said, "I have a right to change my mind." It was much like the old days when I was father confessor to people. Kathi says my personality has greatly changed since I resumed writing, that I have become a more authoritarian person. I think, and hope, that she meant to say "authoritative" rather than authoritarian. Of course she has never seen me before when I was writing and I always knew I was much happier when writing.

TUESDAY, MARCH 7, 1972

Susan came in with the latest chapter of what we all refer to as her "soap opera". Howie came to see her and offered to take her to Rome, Honolulu, anywhere for the weekend but she felt that one romantic weekend wouldn't do it and has really decided that even if she doesn't end by marrying Jack she isn't going to marry Howie so all the many wedding presents have to be returned. Ironically, Howie persuaded Susan to go see the FINZI-CONTINI movie when she felt she should study and it was there that she ran into Jack. Ken called with the suggestion that we meet downtown and walk to Lincoln Center, which we did, picking up the latest copy of AFTER DARK there. Several newsstands were sold out but eventually I got one and when I saw the

many gorgeous nearly nude male bodies illustrating new
ballets and shows I could see why the copy was scarce. The
moment one went in the lobby of the State Theatre there
was a crackling gala atmosphere. I had expected little of
MARIA STUARDA, supposing the fact that it had never been
performed in New York in the hundred years or so since its
premiere meant that it wasn't worth performing. It turned
out, however, to be a far better opera musically than ROB-
ERTO DEVEREUX. The role of Mary Stuart doesn't give Beverly Sills the dramatic opportunities she took such advantage of in DEVEREUX but she got lots to sing. Between the
acts a man came out and said that since we had all helped
the Production Fund by paying benefit prices for our seats
(which I had forgotten) we were invited to join the cast
and other members of the company in a free champagne party
after the performance. The orchestra, the cookies, and the
champagne had all been donated and to my surprise it wasn't
just one glass of champagne but as much as you wanted.
Furthermore, it wasn't even New York champagne, which is
certainly tolerable enuf, but MOET, one of the best French
brands. Eventually Beverly Sills and baritone Richard
Fredricks came out and I added their autographs to the
program. We went home in a real glow, thinking of tonite
as one of our great nights in an opera house.

THURSDAY, MARCH 9, 1972
    Dinner at the Yangtze River before going to the opera.
The audience didn't seem as apathetic as most Met audiences
and they even managed to applaud and bravo in the course of
the performance but after the charming, superbly sung and
acted performance was over there was hardly enuf applause
to get all the principals out for curtain calls. Really,
the bulk of the Met audience has all the verve of wet tissue paper. I was pleased to see DAUGHTER OF THE REGIMENT
again not only because it was the first opera I ever saw
at the Met but because it is even more tuneful than I remembered. People who think everything in the world goes
downhill get a thumb to the nose from me for this production was in every way superior to the one that opened the
Met season in 1942. Sutherland was costumed to minimize
her size and threw herself delightfully into the comedy
without overdoing it. I went prepared to resist Luciano
Pavarotti because I think a 300 pound leading man is what
gives opera a bad name but in no time he had won me over
because he is light on his feet, entered charmingly into
the comic spirit of the evening, and of course can make
light of the nine high C's in his aria. All that bulk really is absurd but whereas the tall and handsome tenor we saw

the other night strangled on high notes and looked a bit awkward in stage movement, this tub of lard sang freely and moved gracefully and playfully.

SATURDAY, MARCH 11, 1972

I knew STICKS AND BONES would not be Ken's type of play but when, at the end of the first act, I said something about how well it was written, he laced into it and said it was the worst play he had ever seen (there have been so many candidates for that title). I flared up and we had about five minutes of sullen silence then Ken decided to speak and I decided to play his game and ignore the whole incident. The whole theme of the play is how Americans choose to pretend things they don't like, like the Viet Nam war, don't exist. What I mostly thought about, tho, is how impossible it seems to be to get an audience for a serious play on Broadway these days. Even in the depths of the Depression people were not as escapist as that. Even tho STICKS AND BONES is almost certain to be a financial failure, I would like to have written it. There are all sorts of wonderful observations in it, the most striking to me being the father who wants his musical son to teach him how to play the guitar, as long as it can be done instantly. He doesn't really want to learn, he wants to be able to play at the wave of a wand, more or less the way I want to speak five languages.

SUNDAY, MARCH 12, 1972

Out for the paper and we got it read before it was time to go to Leo's dinner party. This turned out to be a sit-down dinner for ten and the only other guest we knew was Bud. He came alone because Jack is off on a cruise. There was a just-retired librarian there who was also alone, apparently having no lover at the moment, and then there were two couples, one together 26 years and the other 10. The latter pair were young and the Italian half of the duo said that tho they had known each other ten years, they had lived together only eight because when he met his Brooklyn-born Puerto Rican lover the latter was only 18 and he wasn't sure how stable he was or how long it would last and he didn't rush into sharing a place with him. We quickly got a bus home when the party broke up and we shook our heads in amazement that Leo can put together a series of gay parties without repeating many of the guests and put them together with long-standing couples, too. The gay people we used to know broke up liaisons as a rule. I made a gaffe during the evening when I mentioned my original aversion to Pavarotti because he was fat and Leo,

whom I don't think of as fat but who of course is, quietly
said,"You know, fat people fall in love too and are often
wonderfully light on their feet. Not, of course, in the
sense of dancing in ballet. And in some cultures fat is
considered attractive." "Of course, of course," I said. As
a matter of fact I consider Leo attractive myself for a
very lovely soft quality he has. I didn't get excessively
apologetic or make anything of it but I was annoyed at myself for I certainly wouldn't have wanted to wound Leo.

MONDAY, MARCH 13, 1972
    The latest chapter in Susan's lovelife. This weekend
was intensely romantic as her medical student suitor took
her up to see his cadaver. Ugh! After a light supper I
quickly read the new LIFE and the newspapers so that I
could get to work on revision and retyping COUNTERCLOCK-
WISE. Sure now that it has no chance of being used, let
alone winning a prize, I want to get it finished and dis-
patched. Which is not to say I don't revise carefully.

THURSDAY, MARCH 16, 1972
    Darryl came back from a mission to the bookstore with
something called THE LITTLE RED SCHOOLBOOK. It is a Danish
book translated into American terms about all aspects of
school life with chapters on sex that would have made me
gulp and bat my eyes if the eyes of two young people had-
n't been on me. There are no euphemisms whatever, no prejudice in favor of the missionary position, and total tolerance of homosexuality. The section on that is brief but
says something to the effect that there is nothing wrong
with being attracted to the same sex, that homosexuals
make love exactly like everybody else except that one position is impossible for them, that they often form long
stable relationships and that in time homosexual marriages
are probably going to be recognized. In today's SPECTATOR
there was another ad for gay activities at Columbia and
having had so many gay dances with apparent success they
are having their first gay movie on March 24 with $1 ad-
mission and I think we might as well go.

SATURDAY, MARCH 18, 1972
    We took drycleaning out and then went down to 86th
St. to see the new Gimbels East. I didn't expect a lot because I have seen three new department stores open in New
York--the two Korvette stores and Alexander's--and none
were really much but Gimbels East turns out to be far and
away the most beautiful department store in the city. The
decorator touch is everywhere, from the towel department

where banks of towels in the same color make it lovely, to
the currently obligatory department of chinoiserie, where
in addition to racks of vases and things, they have a little garden of stones. Prices are too high for it ever to
be my store. Two brands of cheese we constantly buy at
Macy's--Caerphilly and Double Gloucester--were 40 cents a
pound more at Gimbels East. We did all eleven floors thoroly and when we came out Ken complained of not feeling
well. I myself, after two hours in there, had some of the
same nausea I get after too long a museum visit and I was
hungry besides. He said his arm was paining him and he
didn't feel at all well. I asked if his stomach was upset
and he said no , he just didn't feel well. Then I asked
about the pain in his arm and he said it was more a numb-
ness. I said there was a difference and it was important
to describe it correctly so that the doctor could know what
the trouble was. I guess my voice rose as it can do when
people use language imprecisely and Ken said, "Don't be
impatient with me. I'm sorry if I'm annoying you." This
slapped me quickly back to 1961 when, the nite before he
went to the hospital for three weeks, I also lost my patience as he kept changing his description of his complaints until I really had no idea what was wrong with him.
Never out of sympathy with him and almost as worried as he
was, I softened immediately.

SUNDAY, MARCH 19, 1972
    Downtown to see BOYS IN THE SAND, homosexual pornog-
raphy made on Fire Island for $16,000 and cleaning up both
here and on the West Coast. I liked it ever so much better
than the type of thing one sees at the Park-Miller for several reasons--the four men involved were better-looking,
the three episodes had a suggestion of story and a bit of
humor, and in the first episode there was foreplay, love-
play during and after sex, and wonderful Debussy music on
the sound track, which took me back to the wonderful night
with Ralph C. when we had sex while the radio poured Sib-
elius' SWAN OF TUONELA all over our bodies. One fellow in
the first episode had a marvelous unself-conscious walk
and I believe I would have been content to just see him
walk. He also had one of those small edge-of-the-jaw beards
that I currently think are fantastically sexy. One thing
that was certainly new to me was that in the first episode
the blond who was in all three episodes came out of the
sea with a metal ring around his genitals and before he
started sex with the boy he found on the beach he took off
his metal-studded wrist band and wrapped it around the genitals of his partner. Whether this was supposed to push

the balls forward and make them more prominent or not, I don't know but when sex was over he removed the band, restored it to the boy's wrist, kissed him and made off. When it was over, Ken decided to rise above it. He for some reason gets grumpily sulky and moralistic. He said he didn't think he'd go to another, that he could take just so much cock-sucking. I told him it beat having a collection of old pictures and he mumbled something and subsided. He has, after all, been the collector of pornography, not I, and he apparently remains dependent on it as I, with my photographic recall and vivid imagination, never have been. Anyway, this picture did not leave me with the revulsion that the Park-Miller films do because it was shot in pleasant surroundings with beautiful people and a sense of humor animating the one behind the camera. It is really incredible that one could sit in a theatre and see explicit sex of any kind, let alone homosexual sex. If this presages the fall of the New Rome, I'm glad I was there for the decay. After supper, a nice fish and shrimp casserole, we read the paper until time for the final episode of ELIZABETH R., about Essex, naturally, but not treating him romantically or sentimentally.

TUESDAY, MARCH 21, 1972

A fair day so I took my typewriter to work with me in order to drop it off for repair on my way home. When the repair man opened the case he said, "Wow! I haven't seen one of these in a long time." The obvious inference was that it was time to buy a new machine but I said I was attached to it so he said, "Well, you know what you've got and you never know what you'll get." I'll be without it for a week and I know right now that entries will be shorter as it's too damned much work in longhand. On our way home we bought our first copy of GAY in many moons. There was an interesting interview with the producer of BOYS IN THE SAND. Lots of people, it was reported, were turned off by the "cock rings" as it seems they are called. I see nothing offensive in them tho nothing sexually exciting either. The whole world of the liberated homosexual is amazing. One of the new bath houses has as its motto, "If you come once, you'll come again," and flatly mentions cruising. But on the whole I think I was as liberated as I ever needed to be. I never dissembled as far as I can recall, from my teens on, and I don't think I was ever discriminated against except by the police. I see no reason to flaunt myself and while I often have to restrain myself from an impulse to kiss Ken in public, I don't feel horribly put upon not to be able to. It would have been nice tonite, for instance, to give Ken a connubial kiss when I found him waiting on the street for me and in the old days when he vacationed in Maine I really suffered when I couldn't kiss him goodbye but I think society has been remarkably tolerant of us and this didn't start yesterday. Did I say the entries would be short while I had to do them in longhand? Hah!

TUESDAY, MARCH 28, 1972
     Took the jelly beans and marshmallow eggs I bought last night to work and put them in the apothecary jar. Darryl and Susan went to work on them. I had a bad morning of prostatitis and called for an appointment with Fretz. When I was at my worst I reminded myself how much better it was than the depression-anxiety bit. The girls in the main office were all aflutter over the nude male centerfold in COSMOPOLITAN, their answer to years of female "playmates" in Playboy. Actually Burt Reynolds had his arm down over his crotch and no genitals showed but despite the, to me, excessive hairiness of the body, there was much joking and carrying on. On my way home at nite I stopped for my typewriter but because they had to order a part (from the Smithsonian?) it wasn't ready.

THURSDAY, MARCH 30, 1972
     Off to keep my appointment with Dr. Fretz at 10:30. The usual pleasant totally irrelevent chat before he took me in the little surgery for the prostatic massage. I had remembered that it hurt in the doing but I had forgotten how many hours it hurts afterward. As I was going thru the hall later somebody I don't know said, "Hello, I have something for you." He handed me a large manila envelope and I first thought some department was giving me changes of address but then I saw the name Patrick Lee on it and assumed he had me confused with someone else. "It's for you. You were at the movie the other nite. This is the first issue of the paper we're putting out." I thanked him and with a wink he was off. I had read that Gay People at Columbia was starting a newspaper and this was Volume One, Number One. The title they use is PRIDE OF LIONS, a nice combination of Gay Pride and the Columbia lions. Mae brought in the current COSMOPOLITAN so Caroline could see the nude male centerfold and while it was in the office I studied it. I don't know why so many colleges teach short story writing for while there must have been ten articles and twenty features, there was just ONE story and I'm sure this is typical of all the surviving magazines that used to carry six to eight an issue. But the contents also

surprised me for this is a general circulation women's magazine, the kind that used to print nothing but pablum and had a taboo on divorce in their stories. There was a long and accurate history of the Gay Liberation movement, not in the least unkind; there was an article which urged girls to sleep again and again with a man before marriage, to share large and small moments with him and not marry him unless on balance one was really happy with him; there was a poem called WHAT I WANT IN A MAN BESIDES A MOUSTACHE, in which she insisted that no men without moustaches or plans to grow one apply and then said, "I have no requirements as to your sexual equipment except that you like to use it, preferably in/on me, hopefully till we both are ninety". Clearly I must not attempt to write for any market until I study it carefully and see how it has changed since last I read it. Later in the day it occurred to me that there is material for at least a very long article in the two-generational story of Mother's lesbianism and my homosexuality. In all the literature I have read and in all the personal histories I have heard, I have not come across any other homosexual who is also the child of a homosexual. *(About eight years later this was the first of a number of articles I have sold to THE ADVOCATE.)* The only aspect of it that really scarred me, I think, was Mother's antipathy toward men, which I have always felt applied somewhat to me also. It is too bad that Mother's love life didn't turn out better but this was as much due to her character as to the times in which she lived--she was possessive, insisted on living in small towns where these relationships are hard for women and impossible for men, and like me in the beginning, insisted on involving herself with women who were only passingly lesbian. Also, I don't think I ever really saw her do anything thoughtful for anyone she loved or in any way yield up part of herself to another person. In an unintentionally hilarious letter she sent me early in my relationship with Ken she said I gave in too much to Ken, that these things should be 50-50 and if she did say so herself, no matter how much in love she had been, she had always done EXACTLY what SHE wanted to do. She defined her behavior perfectly without seeing the implications at all. On my way home I picked up my typewriter and felt I had been reunited with an old friend.

FRIDAY, MARCH 31, 1972

Caroline was complaining today that all the news was bad on television last night and I said it always was, but didn't she read the New York Times? None of those kids do

and I don't know how they live without it. I have this
week been particularly heartened by some of the positive
stories, which are usually placed on the first page of the
second section. Early in the week there was a story about
the great changes in Birmingham, Ala., so much less segre-
gated racially than it was just a few years ago and I took
great heart from the fact that at the Birmingham branch of
the University of Alabama, tho they have only 10 per cent
black students, the elected student leader is black. That
says a lot for decreasing prejudice in the young and I
was jubilant. Then I read that in the Indian state of Bang-
alore the life expectancy has in 15 years been raised from
32 to 52 and the number of doctors and nurses has been
doubled. I hugged that item to me yesterday in the face of
so much news of gloom and corruption. Today's great story
is that the U.S. is really cracking down on the states to
make them enforce an anti-billboard law and by our 1976
Bicentennial they expect that 800,000 billboards which de-
face our highways will have been taken down despite the
resistance of the industry.

SATURDAY, APRIL 1, 1972
   We did our cleaning and then set out for the Morgan
Library, where their exhibit of French illuminations was
in its last day. It was a gorgeous show and very well attended. This heartened me after a conversation I had with
Susan yesterday in the office when she said she wouldn't
ever contribute to a college after what she had paid in
tuition. I said colleges and libraries were something I
believed in supporting and she said taxes should support
libraries. I came close to impatience with her in her as-
sumption that somehow society owed us all this. I said I
thought young people in New York tended to think the world
owed them all kinds of things, up to and including a perfect husband and perfect children, just because so many
things were given them free which weren't available at
any price to a smart youngster in the Dakotas or the Tennessee mountains, for instance. She did at least agree with
me that perhaps the suggestion that New York's library
charge students an admission fee was a good one. As I
pointed out, they thought nothing of paying three dollars
to see a movie so might as well contribute to the maintenance of the library. She said to me at one point, "Don't
you think the world owes you ANYTHING?" "Not a thing," I
said.

SUNDAY, APRIL 2, 1972
   The train to Trenton was uncrowded and Mother was

waiting even tho I had told her we would walk from the station. I knew she'd be there and I hate even that short drive with her but we made it safely. When we went in her apartment it had that terrible stale tobacco smell that I sometimes notice in our place when I go out and come in. Lately I am more than ever conscious of how much of other people's smoke I am breathing in. I find myself getting irritable that Ken can't take just a few small puffs and take satisfaction from that but must take deep draughts and then blow out great billowing clouds which I can't possibly avoid breathing in. Compensating for all the many people who are giving up smoking altogether is the greater intensity with which those who do smoke are pursuing the habit. In my youth a pack of cigarettes lasted smokers quite a while, which accounted for the popularity of cigarette cases as gifts. People loaded twenty in there, offered them about, and had them for some time. Today smokers go thru two and three packs a day and it would be too much trouble for people to take them out of the package and put into a cigarette case, so the cases have gone totally out of fashion. Mother had bought just what I told her for dinner but Ken, of course, did the preparation. Last nite when Mother called and said not to bring liquor as she still had what we brought last fall I said to Ken, "Whatever problems my family has, alcoholism isn't one of them." We got the 5:55 home, reading more paper on the way. We watched the second episode of LAST OF THE MOHICANS getting goose-pimply about Indian attacks.

TUESDAY, APRIL 4, 1972
       When Susan came in this morning she again looked distressed and said, "Oh, Mr. Vining, I'm never going to be a good wife and mother!" Seems she had been playing nurse to her new boyfriend, the potential doctor, and didn't like the role. I just love waiting on Ken when he's sick, not that I often get the chance. But I suppose some people might not like it. I can't fancy Mother doing much nursing. The refrain I remember most from youthful illnesses is that totally maddening one,"If you don't care about yourself, you might think of me." I was usually infuriated right out of my illness by the implication that I had gotten sick out of sheer selfish disregard for Mother. In Susan's case I guess it is part of her rather extreme need to be loved and to be told often that she is. Since I have always preferred loving to being loved (tho I wouldn't have minded more of the latter than I ever got) I like looking after the few people I have loved, Ken, cats, or whatever. I finished up the Isherwood book, which was extremely

disappointing. I don't know where Isherwood's talent comes
from, but it certainly wasn't from his mother. Her diary
shows neither personality, place, or period. Of course she
wrote in one of those little page-a-day books and what can
one say in those? But what ever made Isherwood think it
would be of interest?

FRIDAY, APRIL 7, 1972
    Since we stayed up a bit late to watch the Dick Cavett show we thought we'd sleep a little late but the cats
didn't recognize our holiday. I kept thinking it was Saturday and that therefore we should change the bedlinen and
do our cleaning. We went downtown to the main library and
up to the Berg Collection. They had a wonderful exhibit on
1922: A VINTAGE YEAR. It included the original manuscript
of THE WASTE LAND with corrections and cuts by Pound and
by Eliot himself, first editions of ULYSSES, THE BEAUTIFUL
AND THE DAMNED, etc. It was in one sense discouraging because so many of the books are forgotten and their authors
devalued but in another sense encouraging because, after
all, there the books and manuscripts and pictures of the
authors were. I read the first page of a Van Vechten novel
I never heard of (JIMMY WHIFFLE or something like that) in
first and final versions and the superb writing made me
sick with envy, sicker to think that in spite of all that
Van Vechten has no rating today whatever nor is ever likely to have again. On our way down from the collection we
looked at more of the exhibit of menus. We had seen the
central part of the exhibit down in the foyer but the two
parts up on the landing of the great staircase we had not
seen. They had menus of a dinner given for Charles Lindbergh when he got his prize for flying the Atlantic, for
Winston Churchill, for Queen Elizabeth, etc. but to me the
most interesting was one printed for V-E Day but with the
date of the false V-E Day on it. Prices were hilarious. Up
to the Beekman Theatre, where for the first time we used
our Rugoff Theatre discount cards and got into THE SORROW
AND THE PITY for $1. It was a fascinating movie but exhausting, not only because of its nearly four hour length
(which was a real trial on the bladder) but also because
one was constantly in an emotional state. It had to do with
France under the occupation, using old French and German
newsreel clips, shots of people around Clermont-Ferrand as
they were at that time and interviews with them now. One
minute one would be empathizing with a girl who found a
German occupation soldier attractive as an individual and
them empathizing with the people who after the war shaved
her head for consorting with Germans. One was first

forgiving the Germans then being outraged by the interview with a former captain of the Wehrmacht who sat looking porcine as he said that it was pure murder when peasants put down their hoes in the field and picked up guns to murder passing German soldiers because Partisans should have some badge or hat. In the end Anthony Eden summed things up in a typical example of British civilization when he said it was not for any of us to judge these people since none of us could know what it was like to be occupied by the enemy. One interesting interview was with a British actor who served as a double agent. His chief said he was the bravest man he'd ever known, particularly since by nature he was timid and afraid of firearms. Asked why he did what he did, he at first said he didn't know and then decided that because he was homosexual he guessed he felt he had to prove he could be as brave as the next. He had a love affair with a German officer in Paris but eventually left him because he felt he was letting him down by working against his people yet knew that if he confessed the German lover might feel obliged to betray him. He inquired after him when the war was over and found he had been killed on the Eastern front. We staggered out of the movie totally exhausted, physically and emotionally. Loving the French as I do, I was much shaken by this rather convincing demonstration that the bulk of them collaborated, were anti-semitic, etc. In fact, I was given a great deal to think about by the movie.

SATURDAY, APRIL 8, 1972
     Down to the Whitney to see the Eastman Johnson show. We both like genre painting and his series on sugaring off maple syrup was wonderful. Home in time to hear the very good broadcast of OTELLO. Supper after the opera and then set out for Brooklyn Academy and the Netherlands Dance Theatre. The program was provocative (everything I've seen this week has been provocative and my brain is working on about six subjects simultaneously). MUTATIONS, the "nude ballet" of so much publicity, did indeed have nudity but it explored the whole business of clothes by having some sections danced in fairly elaborate costumes including foot-high lifts on the shoes, some sections danced by men in briefs which covered the genital area but left the rear of the body totally nude and women who wore briefs and small bras, other parts done totally in the nude, and then nude men in transparent plastic costumes. There were three films, one of a nude male solo, one of a solo danced by a clothed female and the same nude male, one of two girls and the same male very much swathed in clothes. These were

shown separately in slow motion and then three screens came down simultaneously and all were shown while there was live action in front of them. The second number, TILT, was also provocative. It used Stravinsky music which I have heard used by some other company, tho I can't think which, and several parts were repeated but with men doing what women had done or another couple doing the steps originally performed by someone else. The costumes were interesting but the men's little shorts had three tassels, one at each side and one right in front so that one thought, "Well, if you don't get the real thing dangling there, they're going to give a substitute". Tho I'm sure the very mixed crowd was partly drawn by the advertised "nudity" there wasn't a leering tone to the audience at all and one left having not the slightest feeling of sleaziness.

SATURDAY, APRIL 15, 1972

Off early to the Radio City Music Hall at Ken's suggestion. The Saturday morning price is now $2.50 whereas for years it was .99 and for a while $1.25. The last few times we went there there were a depressing number of empty seats and I began to believe the rumors that the theatre might close but today it was packed. The movie, WHAT'S UP, DOC? was a deliberate pastiche of devices from the screwball comedies of the 30's and for the majority of the audience it worked, for they howled, but it was a long time before I got a laugh out of the mechanical goings-on. They have worked wonders on the looks of the really homely Barbra Streisand since we first saw her on stage but she is still a long way from being good-looking enough to be a romantic lead. You would never believe that the same 6000 people who could raise such a commotion at the movie could be so quiet and totally unresponsive to the stage show. Neither acrobats nor jugglers nor ballet nor fashion show nor Rockettes moved them to much applause or response. I shuddered and we wondered if perhaps they are now so used to television that they are out of the habit of applause. The future of the theatre is really frightening.

SUNDAY, APRIL 16, 1972

Down to the National Academy to see the annual exhibition of the Watercolor Society of America. Wonderfully competent work but very little content. I began to make a particular search for artists who had not only the technique but the artist's fresh vision and there were mighty few. Ken had fretted before we left that we might not have time to stop off for the exhibition and still get to the concert at St. Bartholomew's on time but as it happened we

had so much time that we walked all the way down from 89th
to 50th. Fifth Avenue was cluttered with a parade of Catholics who were protesting the legalized abortion law so we
walked down Park but it isn't a very interesting street.
The concert at St. Bartholomew's was led by Leopold Stokowski, who celebrates his 90th birthday Tuesday and who had
his first American job there, 1905-1908, as organist and
choirmaster. Stokowski didn't ever turn toward the public
which gave him a standing ovation and applause afterward.
We might just as well not have been there, for all he cared,
but he waved goodbye to the choir as he left, which was a
lovely gesture. The orchestra and choir were by no means
proceeding on their own steam for his hand signals were
very clear and effective. There was some Mozart and then a
wonderful contemporary MAGNIFICAT by Alan Hovhaness, which
I loved. Stokowski may be 90 but he's keeping up with modern music. There was one hymn in the middle and I thought
I'd have to join Ken in keeping a discreet silence because
I didn't recognize the piece by name and anyway assumed my
voice would be so rusty I couldn't stand the sound of it.
As it happened, I recognized the tune and found myself in
fine voice. A man somewhere behind me had a strong high
voice and I followed him right up where I'm most comfortable if in voice at all. It felt wonderful coming up thru
my throat and I knew I could hit any high note that was apt
to come along as I was sure I had at least two good ones
above that today. How wonderful it must be to have a real
voice and real technique and feel the body responding. When
the hymn was going I was amused by the way the organist
used propulsive rhythms to keep the hymn moving forward at
a good clip when most of the congregation was trying to
drag it.

WEDNESDAY, APRIL 19, 1972
    Tho in agony from the heat, I was in a good mood and
everybody seemed especially gullible today when I went into
my put-ons. Caroline took a message for Susan from Placement Office and I said, "And she has that other message
from Jack, that if she feels that strongly about vivisection, there's no use their seeing each other any more," and
Darryl thought I was serious till Susan arrived in the afternoon and I somewhat changed my story and told her he'd
called and said it was all over between them, that any girl
who wouldn't submit to a little open-heart surgery to help
out a boyfriend who was a medical student was no candidate
to be a doctor's wife. Darryl said, "Oh, now you're making
a joke out of it. I don't know whether to believe you or
not." Kathi was just as gullible when I brought in a

package for Elaine, put it on her desk and said it must be a time bomb because it was ticking. Kathi came flying out of her cubicle to see. I must have been extra dead-pan even for me because people kept believing the most outlandish things all day. As I was going thru the source documents sent back by ISI, I came on two bundles of white slips about the size of our source documents with a tally on the front reading "Scotch 94, Whiskey 45, Beer 24", etc. Apparently they had been voting on drinks for an office party. I took the two bundles to Elaine and said, "Now I have an explanation for everything that's been going wrong with the computer."

FRIDAY, APRIL 21, 1972

Ken has returned to the point of hating to go to his bookstore job. Now it's because Mrs. Openheim is critical of him. He never could take criticism and now he doesn't have me to fight back if anybody hurts his feelings. I told him at breakfast that at his age and with his income he didn't have to stay a moment longer on that job than he felt like but that I couldn't resign for him. He fussed so much about it that I thought perhaps a physical illness was making it loom extra large to him. Thought that Ken might get worse as the day progressed so that we couldn't go to Alice's. He met me, however, at Penn Station. It was a quiet party as Abe Edel (the brother of the well-known Henry James authority) says little and says it in an almost whispering voice. Rosalind never has much to contribute, Alice isn't very forceful, and the Perls, tho normally talkative, have seen almost nothing in either movies or theatre. It was pleasant, tho, and Edel took us to the subway.

MONDAY, APRIL 24, 1972

Ken felt so sick this morning that he didn't want to go to work. Since he still thought it was nerves about the job I told him he had to go and resign and get it over with. To my surprise he decided he would. When I went to break I looked for him since he hadn't reported back to me but he didn't show up. I had been so concerned with Ken's problems that I was startled when I looked at my desk calendar and was reminded that I had an appointment to give blood at the blood drive in the rotunda of Seth Low Library. Nobody else even approximating my age was giving and I was a bit taken back by the deference and friendliness of some of the students who were giving. Only one was good-looking and I told myself again that looks weren't everything. It has been so long since I gave that I forgot much of it and things have changed, too. Before they used only plasma; now they use whole blood unless one has had certain diseases, in which case they use only a fraction of the blood. Student volunteers serve as escorts to hold on to one on the way to the refreshment table, where a terribly homely, terribly gay, no longer young volunteer was trying to be too charming and was causing the boys to exchange glances. Since our first copy of AFTER DARK arrived today I hurried to read that after supper before starting on books. They have definitely cleaned up the pictures in there but the ads still have a strong homosexual bent. Don't know whether the law clamped down or not.

TUESDAY, APRIL 25, 1972
   As I did my French this morning (I don't do it often enough nor long enough) I had some trivial idea to add to my writer's notebook. As I did so, half a dozen assorted notes fell into place as belonging together under the note I made years ago "Play about the murder of Joe Orton". Suddenly I saw something I wanted to work on and all morning my mind was racing ahead on the project. Scenes, characters, confrontations, dialogue kept coming to mind in heady profusion. As soon as Darryl went to lunch I started making notes so that I wouldn't forget all the things I had thought of. I have always fomented against books on homosexuality that ended in murder yet here I am undertaking one. I have always disliked plays about authors and stage people, yet here I go. Yet it all falls so much into place that I am going ahead anyway. Perhaps by the time I get to the last scene I will think of a way that the murder can be averted and a happier ending arrived at, tho it was Orton's murder by his lover that was the original inspiration. I know almost nothing about Orton, less about his lover-murderer, and I don't intend to do any research on the subject. I have moved the whole business to America, thrown in a bitchy little Iago, and will do the whole thing with imaginative recreation rather than biographic research. I was very excited and delighted to have my mind working in the old way.

FRIDAY, APRIL 29, 1972
   In the late afternoon the office talk turned to foul language. I made the observation that young women were indulging in it far more freely than young men and Caroline admitted that when she married Bob his language was perfectly clean and he was rather shocked at hers but that now he is slipping into it. I know how that is for words I abhor have begun to slip into my talk at home too tho they

haven't yet penetrated my public talk. In fact it was hilarious as we held a protracted discussion of the increasing use of the words "fuck" and "shit" while steadfastly avoiding the use of those words. No young man I have ever had in that office has ever used those words, whether or not girls were present, but I have now had three girls who do. Caroline asked if such words weren't common when I worked at Fort Dix and my reply was "Not among the educated." Now that I think of it I guess one reason I avoid them is that I grew up thinking of them as lower class. Without using the word I said I really didn't think the remark, "That was a shitty movie" is much in the way of criticism and this is something Caroline and Susan say a lot. When I got home Ken and I ate a light supper and then set out for City Center to see the Ailey Dancers. Ailey has a truly integrated troupe. Tho he is black, he isn't out to prove anything about the black dancer but has five or six whites and two or three Orientals in the company and gives them equal solo status. If only our white companies would be as sensible the other way around.

SATURDAY, APRIL 29, 1972
    Not much of an audience turned out for the double bill of AFTER MAGRITTE and THE REAL INSPECTOR HOUND. I found them quite amusing but was glad we had paid only $3 with our school tickets and not the $6 that our seats regularly cost. We walked over to Ed S's cocktail party. More people were present than I had expected and among them was Caswell, one of Bob Lockwood's older men whom I loathed from afar back there in 1945. After not hearing from Bob for four years, he got a long letter from him the other day. I asked if he had settled down and Caswell said he thought he had but then proceeded to say that he had maintained an apartment in both Los Angeles and San Francisco for a while but gave up the L.A. one and concentrated on S.F. till recently, when he broke up with his apartment mate and moved to Los Angeles. Sounds like the same old Bob to me. I was a bit put off because the older men there were leering, talking about cruising, and making jokes about each other's sex life as tho it were still ongoing, which I very much doubt. When we were shown the library I discovered that my taste in books is much the same as Ed's--lots of diaries and a great deal of English and French history. But Ed really is a fussy old auntie and it's hard to picture him as the public relations man for all the fanciest hotels in New York. We bussed home and decided we had had too many hors d'oeuvres to need any supper. I gave the cats my suit box to play in. Speaking of the cats, this morning when I

was lying outside the covers, I put my two feet around Victoria and lifted her high in the air. Only after I put her down a minute or two later did I realize that not many cats would be so passive when being hoisted in the air by feet. She never scratched or struggled; however I pick her up and however I hold her, she is perfectly relaxed and content.

THURSDAY, MAY 4, 1972

The heat has been turned off at school at last and we had our first comfortable day in months. After yesterday's disaster downtown when seven people were instantly scalded to death when steam pipes burst in an office building I am more than ever unhappy about working down there where the ceilings of offices and halls are a mass of pipes. I left work at 4:15 in order to get home and change so we could meet Eric and Peg at the Portofino Restaurant at 6:15. I had laid my clothes out so we were able to catch the bus on schedule. Peg and I seemed to have similar tastes as we both had daiquiris and scallopine Portofino. The conversation was interesting and I was surprised to learn that Eric hates costume drama. They go to a lot of avant-garde plays and walk out on them yet feel rather above the conventional play, which I should think they might enjoy if they didn't expect too much. When the evening ended Ken and I couldn't remember their mentioning any play they had really liked. I tried to pay for our dinners, at least, having plenty of money stored in my sock, but Eric would have none of it. He said their house was really too far out for people to come to and this was how they did their entertaining. We drove on down to the Performing Garage. One had to make one's entrance by going thru a hole which represented the rabbit hole. As for this modern version of ALICE IN WONDERLAND, it had points of interest but was not to the taste of anybody in our party. I didn't truly get any insights into ALICE nor into anything else. So the Caterpillar was played as tho smoking marijuana rather than a waterpipe and the young, who constituted almost the whole of the rest of the audience, got a few laughs out of this but otherwise it struck me as just an acting studio exercise. If one is going in for non-verbal theatre I think one might as well go the whole way and go into dance. Eric doesn't seem a whit different than he did when we were at Yale. I gave some puzzled thought as to what made him single me out as his friend at Yale. He came from such a different background and I can't quite see what it was about me that appealed to him so that he early sought me out and never did make another friend with whom he was as close. Though some people thought we were lovers, there was never a hint of that. Was it my vitality? My sense of humor (for Eric has a good one, tho he never writes comedy)? I don't know, I'm sure. I suppose I could approach it from the standpoint of what attracted me to him as a friend. Well, his early admiration of my acting did nothing to alienate me, certainly. And his sense of humor certainly. But beyond that I don't get any further going at it that way than the other way. We just clicked, that's all.

FRIDAY, MAY 5, 1972

I was interested in the fact that the flag which draped J. Edgar Hoover's coffin was given to Tolson, his lifetime buddy, just as tho he were his widow, as in a sense he may be. His (*Tolson's*) resignation as Associate Director of the FBI was promptly submitted and as promptly accepted. I took my paperback BARTLETT"S QUOTATIONS to work so that I might search for a title for the play. I don't need a final title but just something to use as a working title for I simply cannot start if I don't have a title of some kind.

SATURDAY, MAY 6, 1972

It was disgusting to see how worn the carpeting is in the Vivian Beaumont Theatre, just as it is in the Metropolitan Opera. Whoever did the buying certainly got rooked on the carpeting but there have been so many ineptitudes connected with Lincoln Center that it doesn't surprise me. Nobody ever needs to attack America. Just leave it alone for a few years and it will crumble and crack from shoddy management and shoddy workmanship.

SUNDAY, MAY 7, 1972

We allowed more time than we needed to get downtown but this enabled us to have a very leisurely dinner at Aux Steaks Minutes on 56th. The atmosphere is very French and I kept anticipating our trip to France so much and then reminding myself, "But I have this HERE, in New York." I had tongue in madeira sauce which was wonderful and Ken had a heaping plate of mussels, scallops, and shrimps. As we still had gobs of time we walked back to Fifth Avenue and saw the first part of the parade in memory of Martin Luther King. One drum and bugle corps, in particular, the Warriors, really shook the whole of Fifth Avenue with their superb playing of tunes from MAN OF LA MANCHA. Some of the Scout troops have worked out rhythm routines which were impressive and amusing and there were some black boys in the band who were really stunning. Now French restaurants

I can get in France but a negro parade I could not and I
would miss it because I find myself rooting for all the
mature men and women who have survived what they have to
survive with such dignity and for the parents of all the
cute, music-minded children who have seen to it that they
have instruments and uniforms at who knows what sacrifice.
My high appreciation of New York continued at City Center,
where we saw Les Grands Ballets Canadiens present TOMMY
and a curtain raiser called HIP AND STRAIGHT. Not only did
we seem to be the only people in the theatre over 30 but
probably the only people over 20. HIP AND STRAIGHT had the
rock musicians right on stage behind the dancers and they
were as fascinating to watch as to listen to. Several of
the male dancers were stripped to the waist, with white
tights below that, and many were quite attractive. When
they got to the scene where Tommy, the autistic boy, is
molested by his uncle they were very explicit, with the
uncle repeatedly reaching for his crotch as the boy defended it and the singers singing an unbelievable song called
DIDDLE-A-COCK.

FRIDAY, MAY 12, 1972
      A little after eleven Elaine called us all into her
office to announce that yesterday's meeting of the Board of
Trustees had appointed Wintermudd, head of the Placement
Bureau, as the new Director of Development. We were told
that President Fischer would be down to introduce Wintermudd. Again the President stared into space rather than
looking at any of us and none of my hard stares could get
him to look up. Once he started to, must have seen my direct look, and looked quickly down again. It's very strange
that a man who can't look nonentities in the eye can head
a great institution. Wintermudd seems nice and Caroline,
who has met him, says he's nice and started out in the
ministry but gave it up.

MONDAY, MAY 15, 1972
      I kept my resolve to start the play tonight. After all
my combing books for a title, I settled on CRY ON MY SHOUL-
DER, a title I had in my notebook all along. It may not be
the final one but it will do as a working title. I didn't
get to dialogue tonight but I got the set all blocked out.

WEDNESDAY, MAY 24, 1972
      Ever since Mr. Brown came up and unclogged our bathtub
drain on Monday, Ken has been saying at intervals how nice
it was to have the water flow after weeks of showers with
accumulating water up around our ankles. This morning's

shower was the first use we have made of it and when I turned the water on I said, "Uh-oh". Ken came running and pulled back the curtain. "Isn't it going down?" When he saw that I was kidding I tried to kiss him but he pulled away and did a mock mad scene. As I took my shower he kept opening the bathroom door and saying, "You know I hate practical jokes," then a minute later,"Just for that, you can make your own meat loaf," then a minute later, "And furthermore___". I laughed myself sick and was so glad I had a playmate like Ken who generally can make life very lighthearted. The whole incident made it clear to me, too, why Elaine's attempts to copy my style of kidding fell so flat yesterday. I couldn't quite figure out, yesterday, why the lies she tells normally and in all seriousness are amusing whereas her attempts to be funny with lies fell dead. Today I realized that it was because the lies she decided to tell were about things that didn't bother anybody one way or another. I knew that Ken would be upset if the water didn't run down and that it would be a still bigger joke if I never actually said it wasn't. The "uh-oh" in a very disappointed tone was all it took to bring him running. When I got home I found a letter from the hotel in Amiens which had been sent sea mail. It was in French and wanted a confirmation if I would accept a double bed rather than twin beds, so I took my courage in hand and answered in French, which should keep them amused till I get there.

SATURDAY, MAY 27, 1972

We set out for the Village, thinking we would have a look at the Outdoor Art Show before THAT CHAMPIONSHIP SEASON. There was a full house for T.C.S., mostly older people. It has been so highly praised that I was prepared to be disappointed but not to the degree or in the way in which I was. Many reviewers spoke of the fine ensemble playing but to us it had a weak link in Walter McGinn, at least at this performance, as he seriously underprojected and since he has many of the laugh lines and the lines of ultimate revelation this was a serious fault. His character was the only one not gone into in depth--he was simply an alcoholic and that is all one knew about him. The alcoholic who comes out with home truths has become just as boring a stereotype as the maid arranging the flowers while she gives the exposition used to be. After the play we walked over to the Fedora, where we had a new sexy blond waiter whose boyfriend hung around the bar till it was time to have dinner with him. They had soft shell crabs on the menu and I have never had them so decided it was about time I had a food adventure. Ken didn't know how they were eaten and I thought it quite possible I'd make a fool of myself but I didn't care. It turned out all right as I ate the whole things but like a lot of sea food it was overwhelmed by the tartar sauce so that basically what one tasted was the sauce. It isn't anything I'd have again but I was pleased to extend my experience.

SATURDAY, JUNE 3, 1972

I got down the bag of Russian scrapbook material since Ken plans to start that scrapbook this week after finishing the one for the 1970 trip. I started to sort. He can never remember what picture is where so he likes me to get everything sorted first. When I got done I was a little annoyed at myself for getting involved because I was afraid it was going to make us so late getting downtown that we couldn't see the Proust exhibit at the Grolier Club before going to JESUS CHRIST SUPERSTAR. We got down to 60th St. with plenty of time to spare for the Grolier Club and so I was able to fulfill an ambition of many years standing. They are forever having exhibits of books and manuscripts that I'd like to see but somehow I'd never gotten around to it. We walked to the Mark Hellinger Theatre and joined a predominantly young crowd for the rock show. The scenery and costumes and staging were all effective, tho an extension of the work done by the same director and designers on LENNY and some of the music was passable but there wasn't half an ounce of religious feeling in the whole thing. I emerged with a headache, probably from the decibel level of the music. All the performers used hand mikes, which the young don't mind, but which shatter theatrical illusion for me as they have to be constantly laying or reeling in wires.

MONDAY, JUNE 5, 1972

I stopped work on the play just before going to bed after doing 11 pages but Ken stayed up to finish Albert Speer's memoirs and I kept popping out of bed to make notes on further ideas for the play. In the afternoon Wintermudd came in and I asked him if he'd had a chance to consider the budget and could talk over the employee situation with me. He invited me up to his office and we had a long session that delighted me. He said perhaps we will be moving up where Placement is now, which will mean cool offices, anyway. I complained about the winter heat in our office and said it led to absenteeism and illness and general wooziness and he made a note to look into it. How glorious to have a boss like that. It was just a great session and he outlined plans for the future that sound challenging.

A GAY DIARY
WEDNESDAY, JUNE 7, 1972

Since Wintermudd is a stickler for 9-5, I didn't dare sneak out early to give myself more time to get ready for the party. I had laid my clothes out and unearthed my electric razor so that I could make the change in the fifteen minutes I had allotted myself. I had thought it a perfect day to wear my new suit because I wouldn't have time to vacillate about whether it was too mod or not but actually the quick look in the mirror which was all I had time for showed it to be as flattering as Ken said it was. He looked handsome as hell and was far and away the most attractive man at the party. All but three of the guests came from within the building. It must be a very gay building because there were three couples and a gay single there at this party and at Jack's previous party there were other gay couples from the building and besides Leo, who was not present tonite, there were still others that we met at Leo's. Two of those present tonite are on the board of the co-op and indeed one is president of it. There was none of the sleaziness that is evident at Ruth and Lee's and tho none of these people were attractive, none were as repulsive in looks or behavior as some of the guests at the Babylon party. For some reason people do not pour out their sexual memoirs to me as they do to Ken. I had a long talk with a medical doctor whose lover of 26 years died just two months ago. He told me how lost he was without him as Ira had done the cooking, decorating, handled taxes, and managed everything whereas he can't even make a cup of tea but later when he talked to Ken he told him that he'd had outside affairs and so had Ira but it meant nothing to either of them as they loved each other very much. He said he never got mad at the people Ira slept with but that Ira was jealous if he slept with mutual friends and hated the people thereafter. I certainly am with Ira there. Jack also got into sex with Ken, telling him that he and Bud still have sex three nights a week and at six the next morning on their three nights, which satisfies him so that he is not inclined to play around. Still another guest, the only campy one there and the only one who felt me up on occasion (tho discreetly avoiding the crotch) told Ken that he made his first sexual contact when he was 36 years old, having lived with his mother up to that time. Long-lived mothers were a subject of several discussions, the doctor having a still keen mother who is 92, Jack's mother having lived to be over 90, Ken's 96, Bud's 87 and still going and another man whose name I didn't catch has an ancient mother but I didn't hear her age. I wonder if there's a hormonal connection. The party broke up early and the campy

BAREFACED, DINARD, FRANCE

1972

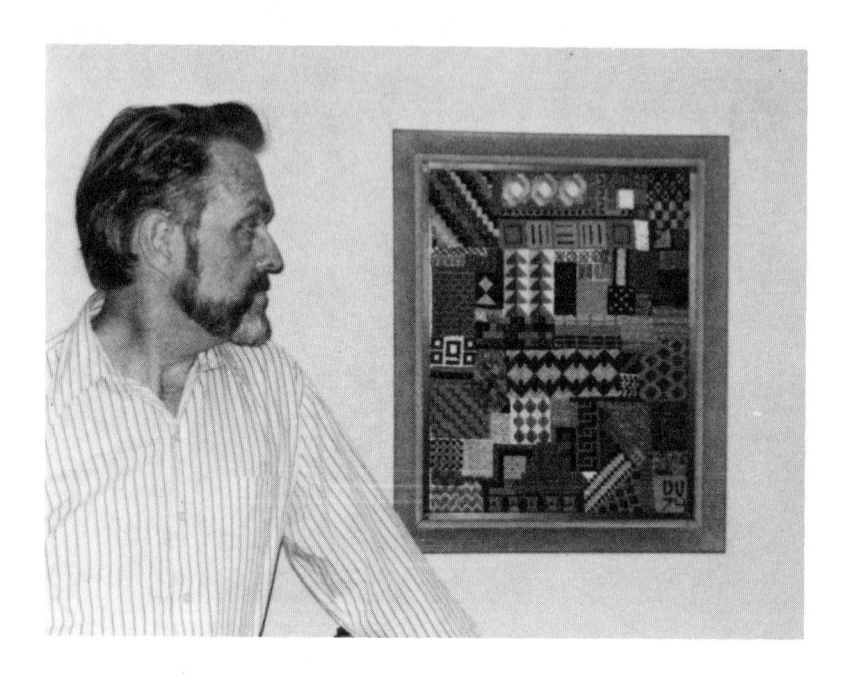

BEARDED, WITH FIRST
NEEDLEPOINT SAMPLER
1974

one at last got his chance to kiss his way around. When he arrived he was discouraged from doing this as Jack and Bud have no drapes and there were lights in the loft across the way. The doctor left with us and I was startled when, as we passed the young doorman, he said, "Good-looking doormen, too. I'll have to walk my dog around this way." The boy smiled and blushed and was clearly delighted. That approach seems to please more than it offends, as I have seen with Andy and Bob R. in the past, but I would be totally incapable of it.

THURSDAY, JUNE 8, 1972

I received a letter from something called the Committee for Decency in Literature, a dreadfully prolix thing greatly exaggerating the baleful effect of pornography. They wanted money from me but promised not to use my name so I used their return envelope to send them a blast, saying that when I gave to a cause I was proud to have my name used and I asked why people who are extreme patriots, extreme prudes, extreme rightists have such a passion for anonymity. I disagree with them but they have a right to their opinion and I will never understand why all the mail we get at the office pushing rightist causes is invariably sent anonymously. I also said there were a few things he didn't know about pornography--that it was not attended by the corruptible young, who had more immediate access to firm young flesh, that it was really not well attended at all, and that it could not continue without the connivance of the police (he claimed that police officers had told him it increased crime and violence). I seem to be on the damndest lists lately. Zipped thru the newly arrived magazines then got to work on the play.

FRIDAY, JUNE 9, 1972

When Darryl was out today Caroline told me that yesterday Abraham asked, in my absence, if I had a family and Darryl said, "No, but he likes to regard me as his son." I frowned at this and said, "He mistakes my natural didacticism for paternalism." Caroline said that what interested her was that Darryl might have said something that reflected his ideas. I said I thought it was another of the remarks right off the top of his head but she said she didn't think so. Darryl has a perfectly good mother and father and I don't think he needs substitutes any more than I need surrogate sons. The reaction of the workers is interesting for yesterday Darryl and Caroline were saying they absolutely could not imagine me losing my temper and Abraham said he could. But of course I don't, really. I don't believe in it. When I was writing on Tuesday and Ken had one of his chattery times, I came as close to it as I ever do. He was reading the paper and had something to read to me every fifteen seconds. I didn't want to send him into the sulks and I normally like his reading me items I have missed but I just couldn't make any headway at all and produced just three lines in half an hour. I would entertain the hope that now, at last, he was going to subside but before I ever got my mind back on the play he'd have something else to read and then a long comment on it. I was just about to scream when he held out a magazine picture for me to look at and I said, "I'm trying to write". Without sulks he immediately subsided and I got going at last on the play. But real losing of temper is something not natural to me and something I would discourage in myself.

SUNDAY, JUNE 11, 1972

Another gorgeous cool, sunny, breezy day. Bussed downtown to utilize the discount tickets we picked up yesterday for the Tennessee Williams play SMALL CRAFT WARNINGS. It's a very flawed play but not without interest. I really hate plays set in bars, especially if the characters are on the lower end of the scale, but except for one dreadful scene, I didn't mind this, tho some of the characters were mighty one-dimensional. The really excruciating scene, badly written and badly played, was the speech of the older homosexual who explains at much too great length how homosexuals are scarred. Sitting next to Ken was a young bearded blond who seemed to react in chorus with me to funny lines and who would shoot me a glance when we laughed. Under other circumstances, I think we could have struck up a mutually interesting acquaintance, tho whether he would be interested in sleeping with a man my age is by no means so certain. Still, I would like to have gotten to know him. It was announced that after the play Tennessee Williams himself would answer questions from the stage. His first remark was, "What are you all doing here on a lovely day like this?", which can't give his producers and backers much pleasure. Asked why he had the bartender end by inviting a girl who had repeatedly been described as filthy to stay overnite, he said, "Well, I believe anybody is better than nobody. I know some of you don't agree with me, but that's what I believe." I'm one of those who disagrees with him violently and rather pity him or anyone who can't be comfortably alone sometimes when the available sex is substandard. When my mind wandered during the Williams play it worked on my own play, a development that I enjoy considering my long fallow period of years and years.

TUESDAY, JUNE 13, 1972

When I came back in the afternoon I thought Darryl's manic attitude would drive me mad. As he was going on break I suddenly realized something and said, "Could it be that you've taken a double dose of No-Doze?" He didn't answer but Caroline's eyes opened wide and her jaw dropped. "I think you're right because when I came back from lunch he was just getting some pills from his drawer" Later Darryl admitted that he'd found caffeine pills which made him feel very happy. What a character. An interesting boy but trying, and today as he ran on and on I got a terrible feeling that Caroline may be right about the role Darryl is casting me in in his life and I grew very uncomfortable. I'm afraid his emotional involvement with me is far greater than mine with him. Only his mind interests me.

SATURDAY, JUNE 17, 1972

We left two very despondent cats, who had eschewed their usual morning gambols in favor of moping. We read the Times until I realized that the scenery along the Hudson was attractive and as novel to me as somewhere in Europe might be and it was therefore absurd of me to be reading as tho this were a journey I frequently made. The Leonards were at the station, of course, Ginny a little plumper and looking increasingly like her mother. When we got back to the house we had a lunch of open-face sandwiches, which was good preparation for our Scandinavian trip next year. We had drinks and supper and then guests began to arrive. From their various bowling teams, etc. they had rounded up all the people who painted, wrote, or had interests similar to ours. I realized that I was in alien territory when one wife made a disgusted reference to the sentence passed on the Clifford Irvings yesterday. She said, "If they'd been blacks they wouldn't have that kind of justice," and I, outraged by the leniency of the sentence, agreed only to find that she meant that had they been black they wouldn't have been punished for their forgery, conspiracy, etc. We dropped the subject because blacks are obviously the enemy to them on many counts. One the one hand they prove that blacks tend toward criminality by saying that the penitentiaries contain 80 per cent blacks (which they do not) and then they wax indignant because blacks never get sentenced, which makes one wonder if all those blacks in the prisons just walked in to use it as a motel. It was obviously pointless to discuss this sort of thing with them so I stopped. The Leonards are as bad as the rest, but then they always have been.

SUNDAY, JUNE 18, 1972

The cats were delighted to see us and were racing all over the apartment in glee. I said, "So cats don't need people, eh?" and Victoria let out a yowl of indignant protest that was so well timed we laughed ourselves sick. I was happy to be home. I guess I feel about the country as so many people up there feel about the city, that I can cope with it but I'd rather not. Since I come from the country I know one flower and tree from another but the city is my natural milieu. Perhaps if I lived on one of the streets where the only greenery I saw was a spindly tree and an occasional doorway bush I'd be more excited by the great open spaces, but I do have gobs of greenery right across the street in Central Park and a lake over there as big as some we saw on our ride. We have plenty of bigots in the city, of course, and many of them not nearly as nice otherwise as these people but still, I am comfortable in the city. A little country goes a long way with me.

THURSDAY, JUNE 22, 1972

Again went prepared for Hurricane Agnes and when I walked down to keep my appointment with Dr. Fretz I got at least some of her and arrived soaked despite boots, raincoat and umbrella. While the pain during the massage was considerable, I didn't have the lingering feeling of being internally bruised as I did last time. On the way back the rain was finer but the wind harder and like most people I had to close my umbrella or be wafted over into Harlem like Mary Poppins. When I came back from lunch I was greeted with two announcements, one that we were to go home at 3 as the school thought we should get home before the hurricane struck and another that Personnel was sending me a replacement for Abraham. It turned out to be Wintermudd's son. I would, of course, sooner not have a worker so close to the boss but hired him and it will work out all right, I'm sure. Finished the play, just five weeks after starting it. It has a great deal of work to be done on it, of course, but it is certainly the most deeply felt and least mechanical play I ever wrote. Whether that necessarily makes it the best is another question but I will enjoy rewriting it as I have enjoyed writing it. One of Ginny's guests who is working on a novel gave me the old bit about what agony it was to write, that she liked it but that it was agony. Maybe I'd be a better writer if I suffered some of that agony but personally I'm glad that I just glow when I get the right word or some good dialogue or a good piece of business.

SUNDAY, JUNE 25, 1972

Another day of much rain so we never went out. After the paper I did some work on figuring out how much money we needed to take on the trip considering that the British have just let the pound float and that the dollar is devalued further. I listed the prices of all our hotels and find they average out at $5-5.50 a day with breakfast as originally quoted and perhaps $6 when we actually get there. We stayed up late to hear the David Susskind show, which featured seven professed lesbians. I guess it was in honor of Gay Liberation Day tho they never said so but they presented a good case and lesbians often take a back seat to male homosexuals when homosexuality is talked about. I disagreed on only one point. They felt male homosexuals were less discriminated against than lesbians but Ken and I disagreed. All during my lifetime it has been socially acceptable for two teachers, two librarians, two professional women of any kind, to live together and women have always been free to kiss each other in public. If two mature men lived together anywhere except in large cities and if two men kissed each other in public there would be scandal.

TUESDAY, JUNE 27, 1972

A wearing day. As soon as Stephen Wintermudd arrived I went down to the transcript room and showed him how the work should be done, found out that I could do about five in half an hour, left them with him as models and went upstairs. At eleven fifteen he appeared in the office for no reason that I could see, said, "Oh, it isn't twelve yet, is it?" and went out on break leaving his work behind. All the cards were blank save the one he had done while I was down there and even that was not done correctly. When he came back I told him again what I wanted and asked where his work was and he shrugged. I could see that something was wrong with him but it didn't seem to be drugs. I called Personnel and asked for a replacement and then when Stephen didn't reappear at twelve, his hour of departure yesterday, I went down to the transcript room again. He was there all right but when I asked to see his work he again had nothing to show me. I took him out in the hall, apologized for not having time to give him a fairer trial, but said I just hadn't time to wait for him to get the hang of it as this was the simplest of several things I had hoped to show him how to do before I left Thursday. His response was hardly discernible but he did follow me up to the office to sign his pay slip and then silently he held out his hand to shake hands with Darryl. I put in a call to his father to explain. Dr. Wintermudd said, "No problem at this end" and then said something must have happened over the weekend as he had tried to talk to Stephen by phone a couple of times and he had seemed preoccupied. He said Stephen had had a hard time in Vietnam, his company having been nearly wiped out, and that from time to time he grew very introspective and ceased to function. Tho privately thinking I should have been told this, I was grateful that there seemed to be no hard feelings, tho both Personnel and Elaine thought I was doing the only thing I could do in putting the needs of the office first. I did feel badly that this young man should be so shattered by that damned war but neither the job nor I could have helped him., I'm afraid, for he seems totally unfocussed. I do believe his father should get him psychiatric counsel and in a hurry. Mother called, AGAIN, and I gave her the works in my tip-top style so she said, "I don't believe one word you've said." "Oh, there's a word in there somewhere that's true," I said. Then, of course, she wouldn't even believe the true things and since I never insist when people reach that state, Ken was probably right when he said, after I hung up, "It's going to take her three hours to figure out that conversation." Of course she enjoyed it. I felt so giddy with my success in confusing Mother that I conceived a marvelous scheme to confuse the office and anybody else I can think of about our trip. I remembered that at least one Mexican surplus card was in our desk and when I searched I also found some from Turkey, Greece, Maine, Florida, England, and Germany. We are going to send the office one from Turkey to start and say we were hijacked there, then one from Mexico, Greece, etc. The stamps will, of course, give the truth away but we might as well maintain the same tone we normally set in the office.

THURSDAY, JUNE 29, 1972

Off to work very conscious that it would be thirty to forty hours before I landed in bed again and therefore determined to spread my energy over the whole period and not exhaust myself early by getting excited. Caroline asked if she could go to tea with me and said it had been a wonderful year. She would like to work for me again next year but realizes I may not be able to hold the job open till she gets back from her trip. When I left she hugged me. Got home to find that Mimie had dropped by for the keys just as it was time for the cats' supper so Ken let her practice. He said even Titus greeted Mimie. I quickly shaved and changed clothes and then we got under way. We were the only two in the bus going to Kennedy and I was feeling tired

and quiet but Ken was splashing energy all over the place
as he and the driver exchanged endless banalities all the
way. The decibel level was in inverse ratio to the content,
which was nil. I held myself in check, knowing my mood the
whole day left much to be desired. The searching of our
luggage and of our person before we boarded the plane did-
n't offend us a bit as we didn't feel like being hijacked.

FRIDAY, JUNE 30, 1972
       I enjoyed the looks of several of the Greeks on board,
including a steward whose buns begged for penetration. The
French looks also appealed to me the moment we landed.
There was no trouble with customs as if you have nothing to
declare you just march out the "Nothing to Declare" gate
now. Bussed to Invalides, taxied to the hotel, small but
nice. We decided to spend the afternoon resting so Ken
started napping at once but I did diary before getting under the covers myself. We set out for a walk and were enchanted every minute for the next three hours. Whereas we
sat night after night at cafés in Madrid and looked in vain
for attractive people, here my head is swiveling every minute. I even get attracted to girls here tho only if there
isn't a ravishing man about and there usually is. When we
went back to eat dinner at our dear old Latin Cluny Self-
Service , I got the full range of beauty from a dewy, pink-
cheeked, long-haired blond busboy to a suave man in his
forties with graying hair, marvelous facial bones, and
superb grooming, and many others in between. Ken is not
too happy over my raving over this or that beauty, for
reasons I don't totally understand, but I don't let that
inhibit me. After a good dinner that cost, with wine, only
about $2, we walked some more and everywhere there was
something of interest. I constantly thought to myself how
wonderful it was that Ken and I were in full agreement on
our adoration of Paris. He could have been one of those
who liked Caribbean life or the sunny beaches of Greece or
Spain. We feel utterly alike in our ranking of favorite
cities, in our love of history (tho we part company in our
feelings about Marie Antoinette). If I weren't coming back
here for a week I couldn't bear the thought of tearing myself away from here in two days.

SATURDAY, JULY 1, 1972
       We went to the Place Maubert so I could buy some
cherries at the Saturday market and everything--radishes,
peppers, carrots, aubergines, strawberries, raspberries,
etc. was so beautiful that we took a couple of pictures.
On then to the new Memorial to the Deportees who died

between 1940 and 1945. It is one of the most stunning pieces of architecture I have ever seen. Busloads of Japanese and other tourists were pulling up in back of Notre Dame and being led into the cathedral without being told of the war memorial and they are missing a great thing but on the other hand, to have tourists by the busload there would rob the place of its marvelous solemnity. Inside the subterranean vaults the walls contain some apropos quotations including one to the effect that these deportees are equal in death to those who died in combat. There are cell-like places, none literal, and a long passage whose two sides glow with 200,000 pieces of lucite, one for each dead deportee, flanking the grave of an unknown deportee, and with a light at the far end which represents hope. A nice lunch at Le Rallye, looking down on the boulevard and noting how out-of-date are the old ideas of short Frenchmen. Nutrition improvements have led to many tall young men here, lots of them taller than I, and the fashion for tight pants with flared bottoms adds to the illusion of tallness.

MONDAY, JULY 3, 1972

As we walked about the streets it became apparent that Monday is a closed day in Amiens but among the few stores open was the Monoprix. I used to think I might miss American stores if I lived over here but the supermarket on the second floor of the Monoprix beats any store we shop in at home. Avis was open but we found that the young man in charge doesn't speak English. Ken had been insisting he would since Avis would be dealing mostly with Americans and I have been saying this Avis was for Frenchmen and asking him what American he knows has ever been to Amiens. Cornered, I plunged into French and we understood each other perfectly. So far I have encountered not one person who laughs at my French or acts obtuse as Frenchmen are supposed to do. Every Frenchman we have met has been perfectly charming and I see not one sign of this anti-Americanism which is supposed to be so rife. While Ken napped I went back for another look at the cathedral and found several things we had missed in the morning. The people who had been so industriously scrubbing the floors were still at it. Again I noticed with what intensity and speed so many Frenchmen work. Of course it was a chilly day and the cathedral was still chillier so perhaps brsk work is helpful. I sat in the park and studied my Normandy Michelin to pick the easiest route for Ken to drive tomorrow and see what sightseeing stops we wanted to make.

TUESDAY, JULY 4, 1972
    We came into Deauville right on the street where the
hotel I'd written to is located. Feeling pretty cocky about
my French these days, I dashed into the hotel and said I'd
written but had had no response. She had a room for us but
showed me a letter and a check from someone in Chester, New
York, who wanted to stay the 14th, 15th, and 16th of August and had sent a check from their local bank. Madame said
she had to take the English letters to the Syndicat d'Ini-
tiatif for translation. She said she had no rooms for them
and I volunteered to answer it for her. She was charming,
as everyone has been. She claims she doesn't speak English
but she does, better than I speak French. She gave us a
city map and we set out for the beach. The size of the
boardwalk and the looks of the males was disappointing. So
are the shops. In fact the town as a whole lacks the elegance I expected, tho it's nice in an understated way. We
found a miniature golf course that isn't too impressive
and a swimming pool that is and the attendant invited us
in to look at it (where are these anti-American Frenchmen?).
Back to our really lovely room, which costs us just $4.50
apiece with breakfast, service, and taxes.

WEDNESDAY, JULY 5, 1972
    We walked to Trouville and could see at once that that
was where the action is. For one thing, a lively market was
in progress all along the banks of the Touques (sp?). I
wasn't pleased to see rabbits there, either dressed or alive (since their fate will eventually be the same). Fish
were sold in that open-air market but they also have quite
a deluxe permanent building which is a fish market and in
which many a boy in his early teens is already learning
the business. I have wondered at the fact that tho there
are large monuments everywhere to the dead of the First
World War, there are none to those of the second. Today,
seeing the monument in Trouville, I was reminded that
France capitulated early in World War II so the heroes are
those of the resistance and those deported. Trouville added their names to the World War I monument but Bayeux has
a large monument to the deported and has named a square
in honor of the deported. Went on to Bayeux, where our hotel, the Lion d'Or, proved easy to find. We set out as
soon as settled to see the Tapestry of Queen Matilda and
the cathedral. Teleguides in English, French, and German
are available for one franc and one just puts them to one's
ear and listens to a commentary which calls attention to
all sorts of wonderful details like the picture of Turgod,
the dwarf of William, of the men wading into and out of

the water, the horses disembarking, the point at which the
lower frieze ceases to be mere decoration and becomes part
of the action as corpses litter the ground and are later
stripped by looters. They had a continuous card of the
whole tapestry for 12 francs and I paid no attention to
Ken's protestations at the price but bought it forthwith.
We rested in the lovely garden then went across the way to
the cathedral, the detail of which fascinated me, and tho
the original towers were severe they fascinated me because
they were built by Bishop Odon, who is shown on the tapestry accompanying William and wielding a mace, which as a
clergyman he should not have been doing. The price of our
tapestry ticket also gave us entree to the museum, which
had some provincial paintings not without interest because
one painter, even in the midst of the 19th C, showed women
at work in a factory. In the courtyard was a magnificent
tree called the Tree of Liberty, planted in 1797 by the
Revolutionists. We window-shopped a bit as French shop
windows are the most interesting in the world. We put on
shirts and ties for a change for supper and it felt rather
nice to dress up a bit. The dinner deserved it. The French
could cook a dog-turd and make it delicious.

THURSDAY, JULY 6, 1972
The museum of the D-Day Landing in Arromanches is superb. A huge model showed how an artificial harbor was
created by sinking first old ships and then concrete caissons on the reefs to make a breakwater. Another marvelous
model actually had moving water so that one could better
understand the difficulties of unloading trucks and supplies onto pontoon bridges. When we came out we went down
the beach to photograph some of the few remaining caissons
(meant to last only 18 months) surely bound to disappear
in another 25 years. We then decided to buy lunch material
in town and eat on the sea front. Ate and then went on to
the American cemetery at Omaha Beach, very moving and very
beautiful. As we looked over the names of those whose bodies were never found, inscribed on the walls of the rose
garden, we could see from how many national strains Americans come. Likewise in the cemetery, where stars of David mark jewish boys and crosses all others. Good white Italian marble was used for the crosses and we noted how the
Southerners often had boyish rather than manly names. From
there we went to Pointe du Hoc, where Germans commanded a
high cliff which had to be taken by methods suitable for
a beseiged castle. Here there were German gun emplacements,
lookouts, devastated barracks and weeds determined to erase
it all in time. We then headed for home with another

moving stop at the German cemetery. Here rough-hewn black stone crosses stood in groups of five interspersing flower beds in which the tiger lilies were all passé. The German crosses contain no names, as those were on plaques flat with the ground and hard to read. A bus party of Welsh arrived as we left, which made the place seem less desolate and forgotten.

FRIDAY, JULY 7, 1972

We were among the first down to breakfast and worried that we wouldn't be able to get an early start as our car was blocked by another but by the time we'd paid our bill the car had been moved. We had gorgeous sunny weather and went straight to Mt. St. Michel. The towns made Ken nervous and we fell out for a while because I couldn't always see the signs in time to tell him to turn. Once I pointed left and said "That way" and he went right then accused me of pointing every whichway. I asked how I should make it clear to him but got no answer so next time I said, "Turn right. Turn right," and he turned left. Since he habitually reverses left and right I wasn't surprised. Knowing of the reversal that goes on in his mind I sometimes, on minor matters, deliberately say "left" if I want him to go right or vice versa, but in a car I can't take the chance because the very time I say "left" to get him to go right will be the time he actually goes left and a disaster might ensue. We got to the parking lot off the causeway leading to Mt. St. Michel about 10:30. We considered beating the crowd to lunch in Mere Poularde's restaurant but decided 11 was too early to eat and proceeded up the cheaply commercialized streets to the Abbey. It was fortunate we did as we arrived just in time to get in the last English tour group before the two hour noon closing. Our guide was excellent and as always Ken and I kept close. Why some people drag along and miss so much I don't know. Our guide told us an effort had been made to lure monks back to the monastery but they couldn't stand the tourists and only one remains. Many people were gathered around Mere Poularde's when we reached it and Ken thought they were being let in just a few at a time but I decided they were just peering thru the windows to see the men beating the eggs with whisks in copper bowls and the girls cooking them in long-handled pans in the fireplace so I pushed in and sure enuf they ushered us upstairs. We ordered just the omelette but a very nice young waiter talked us into the local aperitif, "Elixir of the Monks". Ken, who had been fussing absurdly over every postcard I bought even tho I reminded him that they cost half the cost of developing a snapshot, fussed over the lunch bill too. I told him I had not come such a long expensive way to boggle over the cost of such things, that I would economize on food in Paris, Zurich, etc. We drove on to Dinard and when we saw the airport, where the car was to be left, we went over to get rid of it. We had a long wait for the bus to town but eventually it came and Ken was pleased with the room.

SUNDAY, JULY 9, 1972

Once we got on the Paris train at Rennes, Ken went to sleep. I couldn't honestly say he missed anything by not looking out the window but I did even when everybody else in the compartment was sleeping. It had looked, when we got on the train, that we wouldn't find a seat and even tho we did, Ken remained so nervous that his mouth dried up and, much as it had when we picked up the car at Amiens, virtually foamed so that he looked like a mad dog. It was raining when we came in to the nice new Montparnasse Station (it is the thing to decry the skyscraper which is violating the normal Paris skyline at Montparnassee, but be that as it may, the station part is great).

TUESDAY, JULY 11, 1972

We were at Gare de Lyon in plenty of time and saw the commuters pour into Paris. We had a direct train and when we got there two helpful boys (French stations seem to be manned by very young men) gave me a sheet of bus hours for Vaux-le-Vicomte. I had been told that today's bus went out at 10:10 but I hadn't been told that the only bus back came at 4:20. The guide was a little bit put out that there were only four of us to go around the chateau but soon gave up the wait for more. She didn't speak English but gave us an English mimeographed **text**, from which her French departed a great deal. She told us a lot more about the decorations than the text and never mentioned Moliere's presentation of a play on a platform in one room, which the text mentioned. Millions must have been spent by the Sommiers, a sugar family, to restore Le Notre's gardens, which had gone to weeds, and refurbish and refurnish the chateau, which first stood idle for years after Louis XIV arrested the owner Fouquet and had him imprisoned for misappropriating funds. Almost as soon as we finished the fascinating house tour and sat down on the steps to rest a minute before exploring the vast gardens, we heard and I felt a splatter, and some bird so high we didn't even see him had made a direct and messy hit on me. Ken wiped me off with tissues, tho we had to let some of it dry on my coat and

then we had the problem of disposing of the tissue in the
immaculate grounds. We didn't go all the way to the statue
of Hercules which ended the vista because it would have
meant walking around a canal nearly as large as the one at
Versailles, which was, after all, modeled on Vaux-le-
Vicomte and done by the same artists. We started the long
6 kilometre walk back to Melun. We got a little grumpy with
each other as Ken simply would concentrate on the great
distance ahead of us and all the other negative factors. I
was fantasizing in my mind that at the end of this trip I
would announce that it was the last trip we would ever take
together. All the time I knew, of course, that a bath, a
meal, a rest, restores the grumpiest person. I also knew
that nobody else I knew could have shared my interest in
the history and decors of Vaux-le-Vicomte as Ken does. When
we got in town the walk didn't bore either of us so much as
there was more to look at. Wheat fields tend to look alike
in very short order and both Ken and I prefer city walking.
A coke at the station brought moisture back to our parched
mouths and we began to be in much better humor. It had taken us two hours to walk it with just two brief rests.

WEDNESDAY, JULY 12, 1972

A good night's sleep for both and total recovery from
yesterday's crabbiness. I left Ken at the breakfast table
and took our clothes to the drycleaners then came back and
we went to the Carnavalet, which we thoroly enjoyed. We
bought plums and peaches in the Marais, a quiche apiece at
Place Maubert and had lunch in the room. I caught up diary
while Ken rested then we set out for the Museum of Decorative Arts to see the exhibit of English Posters 1880-1900.
We were surprised to find that tho my book had not mentioned an admission fee, there was one of 4F. Ken wasn't sure
he was that much interested but I was so suggested he see
the permanent exhibit. He then went his way and I mine. I
was crazy about the posters and got a wonderful feel for
the nineties and for the perfectly dreadful theatre of the
time. I felt a little guilty, thinking I might be keeping
Ken waiting, but as it happened I had to wait an hour for
him. I got sick with worry at one point, thinking he might
have collapsed, but I talked myself into reasonableness
and worked on my French, especially the vocabulary I might
need at the baths. Ken showed up exhausted but stimulated
and insisted I must see it and that he'd like to see it
again with me. We went to dinner at Le Menestre on Ile St.
Louis and it turned out very well except for the creme de
marrons which I had for dessert, which was nauseatingly
sweet. Ken then walked me to the Pont Marie Metro stop and

I was off to the baths. They were a smaller establishment than I expected. One took a turkish peignoir but alas they were sweaty-smelling, not clean like those in Copenhagen. The steam rooms were pitch black and I pretty much stayed out of them as I didn't want to mess with anybody I couldn't see. Aside from the sweaty peignoirs I was shocked by the way people watched while others had sex and by the way some went from sex with one to sex with another without a shower in between. To my surprise I succeeded partially with the only two men there I found attractive, one a bearded blond with whom I would have gone far beyond groping if he hadn't permitted so many people to tackle him at once and hadn't been a voyeur. The other, also a handsome blond but smaller than I have ever dallied with, returned my interest at once and we went in a cubicle together. We were hard at it when spectators gathered but when someone tried to get in the act my blond stopped them and said we wanted to be alone. The lights started flashing, the steam was turned, and the crowd was down to nothing so we thought it was closing time. My little blond said, "C'est le temps? C'est fini?" I answered "Je pense que oui," and we headed for the locker room but when we turned in our keys and he asked in French what closing time was the man said in English "We close at midnite," and the boy responded in English. I strongly suspect that my bearded one was also an American. As the dying activity at the bath had actually taken place at eleven, I had surprised Ken by my early return. I reported on my adventures.

THURSDAY, JULY 13, 1972

Somewhat before the alarm went off I realized that Ken was tucking the blankets around me where I was uncovered and I realized how much nicer that tenderness was than the sleazy goings-on last night. My one regret is that I never kissed the bearded boy as I have so long wondered what that felt like but he didn't seem to be a kisser with anyone, in contrast to the little blond, with whom I was French kissing just as tho I weren't normally averse to this. When I told Ken of my regret he said he'd go downtown and buy a moustache and beard--of horsehair. I don't know why it is that casual corporal infidelity can make the long-standing relationship better but it does. We were very affectionate today. We sat along the wall of the river and watched the gendarmes check cards of identity of all the old people lounging on the Vert Galant. Perhaps they were rounding up possible trouble-makers before tomorrow's parade. They didn't arrest anybody and saluted as they left the young people. We also watched the young and handsome

men of the fireboats, who were possibly also readying their
boats for participation in the July 14 festivities. They
were stripped to the waist and again made clear that pallor
of skin is no disgrace over here and tan not admired, which
we noted at the resorts.

FRIDAY, JULY 14, 1972
    Metroed in crowded trains to the Champs Elysees. We
got a fairly good spot to watch the parade but long before
it started I was getting dizzy from the sun and the crowd.
I must say it was impressive when it did get under way--
President Pompidou standing in an open car as he drove down
the boulevard, the Garde Republicaine with casques shining
and their horses all a chestnut color (or perhaps lighter),
planes flying overhead in close formation leaving smoke
trails in red, white, and blue, armored units including
folding bridges, medical corps, women's services, etc, and
planes, planes, planes, many absolutely beautiful in shape.
The tanks were impressive too, with men standing with arms
forward, palms down. All the equipment and all the uniforms looked as tho they came out of the factory just yesterday and generals and officers didn't ride sitting down
like fat cats but standing as much at attention as any
private. The French even do a military parade in real
style. Of course they've lost their last three wars but
they sure do put on a great parade. I began to get dizzy,
then nauseous, and think I had a touch too much sun. I
held on as long as possible then told Ken I had to get out.
I was sure I was going to faint or throw up or both but
could find no place to sit, no shade, not even anything to
lean against. I had told Ken to stay but tried to get his
attention to tell him I was going to try to make it home
but he was looking the other way. Eventually, just about
the time I thought I was going to keel over, he joined me.
We found a chair at a cafe and in time I recovered. After
dinner we walked to the Eiffel Tower and joined hundreds
in sitting on the grass for the fireworks at the Palais de
Chaillot. The fireworks were much as fireworks always are,
but no less beautiful for that.

SUNDAY, JULY 16, 1972
    When we went to bed Dijon was quiet to the point of
seeming dead but in the middle of the night, 3 o'clock to
be exact, it sounded like Athens. The laughing and the
talking on the street and the traffic was terrific. Then I
heard sounds of a fight and went to the window. The quarreling young men separated into two groups but one hurled
a cafe table at another. These seemed to be neither

Algerians nor soldiers for some of the quarrelers got in cars and drove off. Ken awoke and thought maybe a dance just got out. I went back to bed then I heard another fight and got up again. This time it was Algerians. The peacemakers prevailed and soon all the men were kissing and making up. The frank display of male emotion here is delightful. When we were leaving Dinard last week a boy accompanied by two friends saw his girl off. He kissed her as she got on the train then turned away. The next thing I knew his friend reached up and pulled his head down on his shoulder and kept his arm around him till the train pulled out and when he looked up one could see he had been crying. When we went to breakfast we were greeted by the English-speaking waitress who asked if we had slept well. She told us of going to Paris with an American girl to see, not the real 14th of July parade, but the rehearsal. I never thought of such a thing being rehearsed but it explains a great deal of the style with which it was done. Hearing that we were going to Beaune, she suggested we take the bus one way. She said we could probably get schedules at the Office of Tourism, virtually next door. Two young men were already waiting for it to open and two more came along. The second two, trying to communicate with the first two, found they were German. I was delighted to see absolutely no rancor but only a charming attempt to communicate in pantomime and pidgin language with the boys from Dusseldorf. A man came along and asked if he could help us since the office didn't open till 9:30. Here, where I expected the least English to be spoken, we have had the most. He told us the busses left from the depot but not till 10 so we took a train. Beaune looked small, dry, and uninteresting when we got off at the station but improved enormously when we got in town. En route we found a public W. C. and learned that French graffiti are much like American and highly homosexual. A tour party from Gabon had just visited the Hotel-Dieu and was having its picture taken. They gave us a mimeographed sheet in English, which was a good thing, for tho we had an excellent guide, I missed a great deal he said. One gets a little encouraged when one does well in getting rooms, tickets, food, and asking directions but as soon as rapid conversation or a lecture starts, all smugness goes and one realizes how far off real mastery of French lies. It was astonishing to realize that the Ward of the Poor was used from 1443 to 1948, 505 years in all. The court is gorgeous and the pharmacy fascinating, even tho the apothecary jars are youthful, dating from 1772 or thereabouts. The wine museum was so near to closing for lunch that the boy in charge said there wouldn't be time to go around so we decided to pass the 2 hour lunch period by eating there instead of at night in Dijon. We found an inexpensive restaurant so popular it was soon turning customers away even tho they had two floors. Restaurants do that here without apparent regret, never hurrying the customers they have, and I love it. We had beef bourguigon that was gorgeous. The wine musem was very well done, the most startling thing being a picture of three totally nude men treading grapes. The foot idea has never been appetizing but I never knew they went in nude. I don't suppose they tread them any more. We visited a Cave, where the dusty old bottles in rack after rack were fascinating and I loved a sign saying "Ne touchez pas. Respectez mon sommeil." The ride by bus wasn't all that great but did take us right thru the midst of millions of vines. I have a bit of a pang at leaving France, being so enamoured of it that I hardly look forward to the rest of our vacation at all. I like the people, who have been charming, charming, charming (and beautiful in so many instances) and the food and the landscape and the history and the music (<u>Depuis le jour</u> was on the radio) and the language.

TUESDAY, JULY 18, 1972

Switzerland, the land of hotel-keepers, so far doesn't begin to measure up to France in that respect. Service at breakfast was bad, not only for us but for adjacent tables, and when we got to Zurich the personnel of the Limmathof didn't approach the French in charm or efficiency. Neither do the Swiss compare in beauty to the French tho I did see two fantastic beauties today.

WEDNESDAY, JULY 19, 1972

The museum far surpassed my expectations. Not only does it contain fascinating things—19th C workshops of coopers, blacksmiths, comb makers, etc. toys, costumes, splendid period rooms, but it's beautifully managed with items spaced far enuf apart to let your mind breathe. I loved the elaborate pocket watches, the tile stoves, and so many things and we stayed till driven out at twelve. We have both upgraded the opinion we held of Zurich yesterday when we were hot and tired and got into an ill-chosen restaurant. Whereas yesterday I thought I had allowed too much time for it, now I don't think so. The Rhine Falls and the outdoor Schwimmbad will be a pleasant change from museums, "and churches" Ken says, tho Swiss churches are not to me tiring because there is almost no detail to study. After our naps we returned to Troika and I had the birchermuesli as planned but Ken, who is missing out on almost all the regional specialties, had a ham and cheese sandwich. We then went to the park, which at first didn't seem like cruising territory but certainly was as the night wore on. Ken stayed with me a while but finally left, taking my watch and ring with him. I saw only three or four attractive fellows cruising and they all left rather soon after seeing how dismal the prospects were.

THURSDAY, JULY 20, 1972

Dull dreams while Ken dreamed of murder for the second time (not mine so far). Before going down to the Rhine Falls we decided to eat in town. Our last two Swiss meals have seen me served hours before Ken and waiting for him. Today it was reversed. We never had such slow or lop-sided service in France. Tho raw bacon was initially as repulsive to me as to Ken I decided I could eat anything the Swiss could eat so I downed it in the interests of research and it wasn't bad. The Rhine Falls were very impressive and a high rock out in the middle had an observation tower I would have liked to go to but it was a 50 min. walk to the boat landing to get there and it also looked like a hell of a steep climb to get up there. We walked around to a spot facing the falls and took some pictures then sat on a bench. Two American ladies sat beside us. They were from Michigan and filled us in on the Democratic Convention, which apparently went much as I would like it to. For supper we had onion soup at the station buffet. It was thickened in the German way and was tasty and filling but not to be compared to French onion soup. Again the service was simply dreadful. The waitress put her tray on our table then piled the dirty dishes from an adjacent table on it right under our noses, which I have never seen done before anywhere.

SATURDAY, JULY 22, 1972

We took a trolley-bus to the Kunsthaus. Until we got to the impressionist and modern floor it was a very provincial museum but they had fine modern things--much Klee and Giacometti. Much Munch too but I have never developed a taste for Munch. We went on to the bookstore where we had seen the homosexual magazines and there the day really soured. A woman was in attendance and we lost our nerve but a handsome young man came in and quickly bought three, she pointing out a new one to him. This gave us courage but when we looked at it we more or less agreed we couldn't get it thru customs. We were debating this when the woman came over and sternly said, "You want to buy? These are not for looking." Without a word we left and Ken said,

"I don't blame her," but I was seething. It is one thing
for a native to rush in and get the latest copy of a magazine he knows well, called DON by the way, but it's unreasonable to expect foreigners to put out money for something they know nothing about. It is true, as Ken said,
that in Paris they encase them in cellophane as used to be
done in America (till so many got stung that sales must
have fallen off till they allowed browsing so one could be
sure the contents were to one's sexual tastes) but the
woman's manner encapsulated all that we have found unpleasant in the Swiss temperament. We never enter or leave the
hotel but Ken comments on the dourness and unresponsiveness of the hotel personnel and waitresses waste no charm
on customers. I think I feel about the Swiss as so many
Americans feel about the French. Some of my over-reaction
may have been the afternoon grumpiness that for a while I
was turning on Ken. Better to take it out on the Swiss. Ken
went to the park with me a while and then went home to
pack. The pickings were mighty slim. I saw only two attractive people all evening, one of whom went by when I was
busily engaged in a slow bench approach to the other. I decided to go right after what I wanted even tho it was probably unattainable and it proved to be not unattainable after all. I was reluctant to ask if he spoke English, still
more reluctant to try German phrases but eventually I was
feeling his leg. When conversation did start I found he
was a German boy from Dusseldorf who now lives here and
tomorrow he flies to Bangkok for a two-week vacation as he
has a friend who works for the airline and gets his ticket
cheap. He guarded his crotch area and when I finally attained it, I could find nothing much there. Of course the
pants fit tightly over here and I think the fashionable
young men must be very bound in. Finally he said, "I'm here
for money. Or rather--for a present." I don't think he
really was but thought that would end it, and of course it
did. After I left him, he lingered only two or three minutes and then apparently left the park alone. In fact I saw
nobody make a satisfactory contact. As no new prospects
appeared, I left at midnite.

SUNDAY, JULY 23, 1972
After breakfast we walked over to the station and
bought our tickets for Lucerne. The ticket man was jolly
and the whole day contradicted my adverse opinion of the
Swiss. We sat in the park a while (and it looks very different by day, tho I did see two men cruising, groping,
and eventually leaving together) then went for our bags.
The ride to Lucerne was pretty and almost upon arrival I

fell in love with the city. We found a boat landing where boats left for Tribschen, where Richard Wagner lived for five or six years. It was a cheap ride and a lovely one, Lake Lucerne being a far more interesting lake than the Zurich lake. The Wagner house is a nice one and in charge was a lady who in one person made up for all the lack of charm we have encountered so far. She gave each of us a catalog of the items in the house, to be returned at the end of our visit. The numbers jumped all about, but still it was a help. There was a lot of dross but also Wagner's piano, armchair, many letters, and some manuscripts. As we came downstairs Ken asked me what period Wagner lived there. I said I guessed it was when he was in trouble because Ludwig was lavishing so much money on him. The lady must have heard us and started what ended as a delightful conversation. She must get tired of the Wagnerian music which resounds thru the house but it added a great deal to the effect on the visitors. Ken kept harping on the connection with Ludwig until I explained, "He's interested in royal connections; I'm interested in creative genius."

MONDAY, JULY 24, 1972

When we went to the breakfast room we had cheery greetings not only from the hotel personnel but also from members of a British touring party. On our way to the dock I bought some more of the dark Basle cherries to take up the Rigi with us. The ride up the Rigi was beautiful, not at all scary as cablecars are. When we weren't quite up and again on top I felt a little nauseous and thought that perhaps the mountains were getting to me but it soon passed. There were small tame bullocks on top, some of whom could be hand-fed buttercups for picture purposes and who could be petted tho in all innocence as they flicked their head to get rid of flies they could bang a horn against you. We bought hot wurst and bread that a young boy was selling and ate it, along with the cherries, sitting in the meadow among the wildflowers. Ken had fussed a bit because it wasn't totally clear but I had said I probably preferred the coming and going of clouds to blazing sun. Then for a while we had pure sun and Ken came over to my side and wanted clouds back. A whole bank of them for a while obscured the cows in the slightly lower pasture and that was dramatic, too, then it drifted on by.

FRIDAY, JULY 28, 1972

As our train from Bellinzona was an express to Milan we had to get out at Lugano proper and catch a local train for the five minute ride to Lugano-Paradiso. Our room was

lovely and there was lots of English-speaking personnel.
Ken, who has some kind of compulsion about setting out his
toilet articles the minute we arrive even tho we don't
shave till the next day, started to go thru his routine tho
it was approaching two, the usual limit for the serving of
lunch. When I hurried him up he said he was sure they
would keep on serving (he always imagines things will be
arranged to suit his convenience) but when we got down
they first said the kitchen was closed then decided we
could still have the spaghetti bolognese we had ordered.
Walking down to the lake we came to the Paradiso Debarca-
dero within a few minutes of the time a boat was leaving
for the Swiss Miniature, a Swiss version of Holland's Madurodam. The boat ride was lovely and the Swiss Miniature a
marvel. It reproduced at a scale of 1/25 almost all the
major buuildings of Switzerland--Zurich's Wasserkirche,
the Chateau de Chillon, the Chateau de Thun, the Kappel-
brucke of Lucerne, plus mountain peaks, industries, etc.
Trains and boats and cablecars are functioning and because
of the ups and downs of Switzerland I really think it's
more interesting than the Madurodam.

MONDAY, JULY 31, 1972
 I never knew Ken to snore so much as he does here
where the connecting doors let the sound thru. In his
sleep at one point he said, "Jimmy, stop it! You've had
enough!" and since the neighbors don't know I'm not Jimmy
I'm not sure what they made of that. It was sunny when we
got up so there was no question of the trip even tho it
got a little gray as we waited on the terrace for the bus
to pick us up. Frau Portsch came out to talk and we had a
fascinating insight into this very erect, very chicly
dressed woman. We complimented her on her hotel in general
and on her command of languages and she said it was a result of her mother's training, that she's grateful for it
now but used to get very mad at her mother. In turn she
now can't get along with her son, who has just come home
after divorcing the Mexican he was married to, and after
spending ten years in New York as a court interpreter. "He
thinks now he wants to stay and help me run this place
but he knows nothing at all about this business and besides
he's lazy and after he's here a week we fight all the
time." She doesn't want him back and I teased by saying
"I heard him talking to someone about changing the name of
the hotel from Hotel Schmid to Hotel New York," and she
went away laughing but she had already said he's a little
mad and nothing he does astonishes her. It was a very quiet busload and our girl guide was superb, doing

everything in three languages without lopping anything off in the minority languages out of fatigue. Since the water has been affecting us I was a bit worried about one or the other of us having a sudden need for a pissoir but tho I was very happy to reach the first rest stop, there never was any crisis. This stop was in Dongo, the Italian town where Mussolini and his mistress were captured and killed while trying to escape with a fortune to Switzerland. In that twenty minute stop I saw more handsome men than I've seen in two or three nights in Lugano. In the U.S. so many of the Italians come from Naples, Sicily, etc. and we don't see too many of the Northern type, almost a different breed. These were tall, slender, not very hairy and tho their hair was mostly black, my least favored color for hair, it was clean and well-groomed, whereas the Swiss boys shock us with their unkempt and greasy hair. The brochure had said we would go to St. Moritz and return by the same route but we didn't. St Moritz itself didn't appeal to me much. The way home, tho not featuring Italian lakes or Italian men, was very dramatic scenery by way of the San Bernardino Pass whereas we had gone by the Maloja Pass. We were exhausted when they let us out at the hotel and I don't see how anybody, young or old, survives these quick European tours that would have you on another bus tomorrow. I just couldn't and wouldn't do it. One eleven-hour trip like this has just got to be alternated with one or more days of staying close to home and doing minor things.

TUESDAY, AUGUST 1, 1972
     Just before noon we went up the funicular to the top of Monte San Salvatore. We had lunch at the restaurant on top and I must say the Swiss prevent these wonderful spots from being cheaply commercialized. This country does have its troubles, however, for Ken got a Tribune and that had an article saying Lake Constance had aged 10,000 years in the last 20. Lake Lugano is already closed to swimming because of the pollution and both the floating baths in the lake and the Lido are deserted. When we went to dinner the stairway was lined with candles and the dining room was festooned with Japanese type lanterns of red with the white cross. Atop the napkins were little flags and on the tables were flowers, a ribbon, and a menu handwritten by Madame Portsch. She was in a lovely black and white Swiss national costume and the object of much photographic attention. (*It was the Swiss national holiday corresponding to July 14th in France and July 4th at home.*) Madame circulated round all the tables with ineffable charm and we learned more of her history. Her husband lost his leg before she met him,

when serving with the Red Cross in Italy in 1944. The
British and the Americans apparently didn't respect the
Red Cross in tht bombing because the Italians were smug-
gling and using the Red Cross illegitimately but she isn't
bitter and said, "That's war." It was all just wonderful
as a final evening in Switzerland and I certainly amend
the negative statements I made about the Swiss to apply
only to Zurichers. We had been told in Locarno that Lugano
had had their fireworks already but I don't know what they
could have been talking about for the half hour display
tonite beat any I have ever seen. I'll say one thing for
Lugano. It has restored our good humor with each other.
There has been no quarreling and no snapping at each other
since we arrived. The brochures say "Soothing to the nervous system" and it certainly is.

TUESDAY, AUGUST 8, 1972
    Kathi called while Elaine and I were at work and said,
"Dr. Wintermudd just called and wants you to bring your
attachments to the conference tomorrow." "I never go anywhere without my attachments," I said," but what other attachments is he referring to?" She got laughing so much
that she could hardly tell me that what he meant was the
chart of the fall's work that came with one of his memos.
I hope the vague language was hers and not his or we may
be in trouble. In a quieter part of the work day I made
some notes for revision of the play and also made myself a
revision schedule, which is the first time I have really
applied my mind to it since I finished the first draft.

THURSDAY, AUGUST 10, 1972
    In the middle of dinner I remembered seeing in the
Times that the Philharmonic was repeating its Tschaikowsky
program at the North Meadow, 102nd and Fifth, so we decided to go. I don't normally wear jeans off the block, tho
young people wear them everywhere these days, but I decided they would be fine for sitting on the ground. The crowd
was perhaps a little disappointing, certainly after the
75,000 who had jammed the Sheep Meadow to hear the program
early this week. It was a great night, tho, with the lights
of the buildings on the edge of the park very clear and
lots of stars visible above. A plane flew over with moving
lights underneath saying "Rent this billboard. Call Fly-by-
Nite" and then the number. They had a few speakers, including a black in charge of cultural something or other in
Harlem and he said it was nice to have the Philharmonic up
in Harlem where we had the Barrio with its Spanish culture,
the black community with its soul, and some of the

swingiest white folks in the city. It was a night that made one glad to live in New York. There should have been more blacks there considering that the conductor was Henry Lewis, black himself.

SATURDAY, AUGUST 12, 1972
       I went in the bedroom to tell Ken something and his eyes looked strange. "Have you been crying?" I asked and he said he was having a bad dizzy spell. Worse than that, he said he had one when Alice was here and broke out in a sweat, which I hadn't noticed. I told him he mustn't keep these things to himself, that I wanted to know about it, that if something happened and the doctor asked me if it was out of a clear sky I didn't want to say it was if there had been previous episodes. Ken said he didn't want to be always complaining and I told him to never mind but to tell me after this. He insisted on getting supper, saying he felt better, but as he didn't look too good at supper, I insisted on doing the dishes, which I like to do in any case, and he went to lie down. Titus, always a good nurse, quickly went on duty at his side but Victoria, who can't abide anybody sick, wouldn't go near the bedroom.

SUNDAY, AUGUST 13, 1972
       On my way to get the paper I saw the black lady who, with her white lady friend, was last seen leaving to spend a year in Europe. I stopped to talk to her about it and found that she had had brain surgery and that it was after that that they had decided to retire and travel. She feels fine now and we so enjoy comparing notes that she said, "I'd love to talk to you more about this," so I invited them to tea two weeks from today. I think they've been here from the beginning so it's taken us 13 years to get acquainted. We read as much of the paper as we could before going up to Mimie's for brunch. We were the only guests and Mimie was much less crabbed than she has been of late years so that we had a very pleasant time. We ate too much, of course, considering that we knew we had ahead of us one of Leo's fabulous meals. We went home and had a nap before taking off for Leo's. We weren't sure if that was going to be an intimate evening or a full-scale party, but I guess Leo doesn't bother with much less than a full-scale party, as there were ten of us. I had met all but two before but most of my evening was devoted to a new person. I tried to break away once or twice and pay more attention to Paul and Joe, the young lovers I met once before, who were rather neglected, but somehow almost all my evening was spent with Einar. Ken and I were both amused that Ray, who is

as opinionated as they come, was the one who was inclined to make an issue about MY being opinionated. It's always that type who makes a remark about it, and then spews equally firm opinions all over the room.

WEDNESDAY, AUGUST 16, 1972
    Kissed Ken goodbye for the week and went off to the sweatshop. I went down to the 55th St. Theatre to see the gay film FIRST TIME AROUND. Tho not up to BOYS IN THE SAND it was more unified than what they show at the Park-Miller and had at least a minimal theme, more or less like LA RONDE.

THURSDAY, AUGUST 17, 1972
    After breakfast I decided to start systematic revision of the play and got to page 6 but of course it will go much slower later when I get to scenes less well-written. When I got home the cats were happy to see me change into at-home clothes and I was perfectly content to stay home. I don't even turn radio and tv on, hoping to enjoy the silence but unfortunately the neighbors have their music loud enough to penetrate the walls in a dim but persistent way so I don't quite have the silence I relish. When I said something at the office about not having either radio or tv on, several were horrified, as this is unthinkable in this country.

FRIDAY, AUGUST 18, 1972
    When I had a moment to think about something besides work, I debated whether or not I would go thru with my plan to go to Beacon Baths or not. I really didn't feel sexy and could happily have gone straight home to the cats but I knew that if I didn't go in Ken's absence, I probably never would go and that fear was one thing that was deterring me. In my heart of hearts I don't yet quite believe the new era of permissiveness and thought how horrible it would be if I were caught in a raid and there was nobody to feed and look after the cats. In the end I made myself go, as I did in Paris, and it turned out even better, much better. They are located on the eleventh floor of an office building, which I knew from the directory in GAY magazine. The cost from 8-4 is $5.50 for a locker, $8.00 for a private dressing room, and they are open 24 hours a day 7 days a week. I took a locker and without my glasses had to ask the way to the steam room. It isn't so Stygian dark as the ones in Paris nor is it quite so hellish hot. One can at least make out figures and see that they are tall and slender or not and at close range one

can see one's neighbor very well tho everybody else is a
bit vague. The shower room is right outside, however, so
one can follow anybody who is attractive and freshly washed in. I specialized in beards, not only because beards
themselves attract me but because the bearded men would
have been the handsomest there even if clean-shaven. I
didn't see a single swish type there. Every one was manly
but my God, the things that went on in that steam room,
let alone in the private cubicles, which I never investigated. I can't understand how I could sit in that steam
room with at least two people watching and blithely let
the first bearded one go down on me and then turn and un-
concernedly go down on him. A veil of sorts was drawn by
my near-sightedness and another veil by the steam but I
perfectly well knew that I was being watched and I didn't
give a damn. I might very well have gone right ahead had
we been on the stage of the Radio City Music Hall for he
was a beautiful young man and a fabulous sexual technician. It's so completely out of character for a prude like
me and of course I would have preferred the privacy of a
cubicle but I really didn't have a second's qualm. If
things are done by the fat and ugly they may strike me as
obscene but when done by the beautiful, they don't bother
me at all. At one point a heavy, aggressive man cornered
me in the steam room and I was hard put to it to escape
his groping without making a scene but I did. Another time
I went in and found a huge (6'6", I imagine) bearded boy
being done from all sides. He was beautifully shaped and
every erotic zone including his nipples was being worked
on by someone and he was in a seeming transport but not so
transported that he couldn't reach out a hand to grasp me.
I almost laughed because it was so bizarre. He was beautifully proportioned and even this grotesque scene didn't
turn me off because he was such a vision. I was quite astonished at my powers of attraction, at 55, for handsome
young men in their 20's. I also gained immeasurable confidence from the comparison with my competition. I am much
more slender than most of the older men, and heavier hung
than young or old. Even the bearded giant, tho very nicely
equipped, was not in proportion to his height nor was he
my equal. It's too bad I didn't discover this long before
in the long succession of loving but sexless years with
Ken but then this whole gay revolution is a matter of the
last five years.

SATURDAY, AUGUST 19, 1972
    The subways are really defaced inside and out these
days by people writing their name (and a number, for some

strange reason) all over them with the new spray paints.
It's a poor kind of a bid for immortality or fame. Graffiti can be interesting (tho they seldom are) but this is
dull and maddening. Had a light supper consisting of one
sliced tomato before starting out for Beacon Baths. I
rather expected it would not come up to yesterday and it
certainly didn't. There were few beauties there tonite.
Eventually I did score with a beauty and I guess that's
all one really needs, when one comes down to it. This one
had no beard but a full moustache and great head of hair
on a beautiful face and body. He tried to lure me in to a
cubicle but I didn't realize it was me he wanted and I
went instead to the sauna. He followed me in and after he
made it clear that it was me he was after he said, "Come
to my room". He turned out to be a Latin, which is not my
usual dish, but he was a beauty and a very considerate
lover. He was so heavily hung that he took my championship
right away from me and while giant genitals are interesting to see and even to handle, they are very hard for me
to cope with. I think Ken and I might have had a longer
and better sex life if we had not both been more than eitheither can cope with. That such genitals can be managed by
the sexually proficient was certainly demonstrated yesterday when the young beard made it seem easy.

SUNDAY, AUGUST 20, 1972
   I got involved in reading Ken's diaries, which he
gave me when he was throwing things away. They are not very
good but still Ken comes through and I glow with love when
I read statements made so long before I knew him which are
still typical. I burst right out in uncontrollable laughter when I read, after he had been to the movies, "I would
love to possess Richard Barthelmess but Tommy Meighan is
getting old. Me for the young ones!" Strangely, I have not
minded being alone but now I am ready for Ken to return,
even tho it means having the radio and television on again.
God, the silence in the house has been marvelous. Pure
balm. I haven't even disturbed it by singing or whistling,
which I used to do when alone.

MONDAY, AUGUST 21, 1972
   Eric called and suggested lunch. He had brought along
his play for me to take home and read. I didn't understand
why I didn't get a call from Ken as I thought he intended
to turn in his bus ticket and fly home. As I was waiting
for the bus at 110th St., along he comes with his suitcase,
looking very handsome. We had a lot of jabbering to do.
Ken decided he must listen to the Republican Convention

but I thought that if I have to put up with radio and television again, I am certainly not going to start with the drivelly interviews they have at long-winded public events where so much marking of time has to take place, so I took Eric's play to the bedroom and read it. Unfortunately I can find very little good to say about it. Ken said he'd feel very embarrassed to be critical of Eric's play but I am only slightly embarrassed. I have years of experience at telling people I don't think much of what they've written and Eric can surely take it.

FRIDAY, AUGUST 25, 1972

Eric arrived promptly and we ate in the cafeteria while we discussed his play. Many of its faults were explained when he said he was under the influence of Pinter and just started to write without knowing who his characters were and without having any plot in mind. This shocked me a bit. I told him I was not a qualified critic of an exercise in Pinter style because I dislike it and have avoided most of his plays, plus those of Beckett and all other people I consider anti-dramatic. About 2:30 it started to rain and I shocked Darryl by saying, "All right, God, I give you 27 minutes to stop this." I was going to the baths anyway but as it happened it did stop. As I entered the building where Beacon Baths occupies the 11th floor there was a policeman in the lobby and a police car out front and I thought perhaps they had been raided in the wake of the scandalous bank holdup this week in which a homosexual took hostages and tried to hold up a bank and commandeer a plane to take his male "wife" abroad for a sex change operation, tho the estranged "wife" wanted nothing to do with him and preferred to remain in his mental institution. *(From this incident came eventually the movie DOG DAY AFTERNOON.)* When I got upstairs it seemed rather deserted and again I wondered but eventually the crowd built up. It was not, however, a great day there. There was an attractive bearded boy there but he was not interested in me nor, it seemed, in anybody else available. I stayed longer than usual and when I got home Ken said he had begun to wonder. As I said, "If I'd done better, I'd have been home sooner." He has been very tolerant of this whole business and fixed me some cold cuts after we'd had our drink. He'd also made a banana tapioca pudding.

SATURDAY, AUGUST 26, 1972

We delayed our departure for downtown so we could see the opening of the Olympics telecast from Munich. It was a glorious emotional binge and I was constantly fighting back tears, as Ken was on occasion. If he hadn't been here I would have gone ahead and bawled but somehow our training is against all that. Thank God men's emotions are now being tolerated. As one commentator said, "This isn't the way the world is, but the way it ought to be." I really have no patriotism at all about the games and would indeed be very upset if we won everything for I want these little nations to take home some prizes. The delirium over the Mexican who won the swimming prize four years ago was shown again and moved me as much this time as before and I loved to see him carrying their banner. Then they showed the exceedingly handsome (and very proud but pleasant-looking) Spaniard who won, in the Winter games, the only medal any Spaniard ever won in an Olympics and I melted with happiness at the sight of his beautiful smiling face. When the Israeli team got an ovation from the Germans so soon after the Germans tried to annihilate jews I found it enough to make the heart leap, and so it went all day. They explained that the young German middle-distance runner who had been chosen to carry the Olympic torch into the stadium had been chosen not because he was their greatest athlete but because he looked good and had a nice even pace of running. Others will have to judge his running but he certainly was superbly built and beautiful and his parents and loved ones must have been beside themselves with pride as he ran up the steps and stood there in all his God-given magnificence for I don't know him at all and I was nearly bursting. I was happy too when the Olympic oath was taken for all the athletes by a pretty 22-year-old German medical student, the first woman to do so. It was all just everything one could wish it to be in one's fondest dreams and I loved the whole world. We went downtown on a cloud after that.

TUESDAY, AUGUST 29, 1972

Wintermudd called and said the school architect had started to lay out his plans for the new records area but he felt that I should be there too. He brought the layout of the office and laid over it paper one could see thru and draw on and on this we played with arrangements of furniture until we eventually got one that was practical. I was very, very happy with all the arrangements and we heard that perhaps we will be moving in a week or two. There will certainly be less talking in the future than we have had in the past and we will have to keep our office neater but I can live with that in return for air conditioning and no pipes.

WEDNESDAY, AUGUST 30, 1972

Gertrude asked me if I read more of the paper at nite as well as at noon and I said, "No, I take it home to my room-mate." Darryl, ever the bigmouth, said, "Poor Mr. Jefferson. Is he just a room-mate now?" Without blinking I said, "I object to the word, too, Darryl, but we won't go into that now." Thinking about it later I decided to amplify somewhat the section of the play dealing with the best word to describe a man you live with and love. I added the line for Harold, "In the inner circle, at least, what about 'my husband' or 'my wife'?" with Ben replying, "No, for several reasons, starting with the fact that neither Philip nor I see ourselves in either of those roles." The evening—Olympics again and the play, with the play going more slowly but eventually three pages and further changes.

THURSDAY, SEPTEMBER 14, 1972

I met Frank T. waiting for the elevator. When I have seen him since his return to school I have felt a little sad because the once sparkling and sexy boy, tho still good-looking, seemed to have become a little drab. As I talked to him today about the intervening years since he worked there, the sparkle came back. I would rather bed this 44 year old man than any 10 men in their twenties that I can imagine. He asked after all the gay boys who once worked there without ever using the word or leering.

TUESDAY, SEPTEMBER 19, 1972

One of the articles in a recent New York magazine was about a marriage that couldn't be saved and one bad feature of it was the way they took each other for granted. I thought of that yesterday when I was leaving for work and Ken, who sees me to the door each morning, told me how handsome I looked. One thing neither of us does is take the other for granted. I'm always telling him how handsome he looks in this or that outfit and I really am aware at most gatherings that he is the best-looking man there by far, as well as the most genial. Today, tho, just as I was nearing the end of my coffee break (during which I was writing down for Eric my criticisms of his play and suggestions to improve it) I was joined by Frank T. Even had the boss been upstairs in his most querulous mood about over-staying coffee breaks, I could not have broken away. No man has so turned my head in years and years as Frank. It is fortunate that he is not interested in me in the way I am in him for with no trouble at all he could induce me to be unfaithful, indiscreet, and totally irresponsible. He said he had been terribly tempted to go to a movie, not

having seen one in three months or so, but made himself
come to school. I had a notion as to what sort of movie he
would have gone to but we are both keeping our hair up very
nicely. I reminded him that he had said his surfing year
had been his last play year and he said, yes, that's what
he meant and hereafter when the mood came over him perhaps
he should just go swim a few laps of the pool. I said that
if his wife hadn't gotten pregnant again he might soon have
been free of the children and could have gone skylarking
but he said that was part of the strategy, which he had
indicated the other day. "Perhaps by the time this one has
grown up I'll be stabilized, though I don't guarantee it,"
he said. The bisexual life must be very hard to handle.
For all the hurts she must have had, I don't blame his wife
for hanging on as a part of Frank is worth all of most men.
What always killed me about Frank when he was having his
most flagrant homosexual flings was that instead of being
pursued, as a youth of his charm and beauty had a right to
be, he was always in hot slavering pursuit of some (to me)
very ordinary and rather rough-cut young man. But if one
is a hunter and a wooer and takes no pleasure in being the
quarry, then that is how one is, as I should know. When I
got home the cool breeze had the cats galloping around in
joy, taking swats at ping-pong balls that lay in their
path. Ken and I were also in a very happy and mellow mood.
Even when I was fantasizing most dizzily about Frank today
I never for a moment considered doing anything that would
hurt Ken. The person doesn't walk the earth for whom I
would do that. It seems to me I love him more lately than
ever.

SATURDAY, SEPTEMBER 23, 1972
    Just as we got in bed at midnight we had one of our
nocturnal calls from the Florida Fantom, Bill Snell. He
took me for Ken and insisted we sounded alike, which is no
news, but I quickly turned him over to the genuine article,
who was talking to him nearly an hour without a stitch on.
Every time I thought of getting up and putting a blanket
on him he would tell Bill he must hang up but then the conversation would go on and on, with Ken perhaps a little
less coy than usual but sickening enough considering his
age. However, it must be six or seven years since the last
Snell call so I didn't foam at the mouth as I sometimes do.
Ken insisted he wasn't drunk this time but as far as I'm
concerned that just gives him all the less reason for calling at such a late hour. Drunk or sober, I don't think he
has ever called before midnight and I suppose we must be
grateful that it wasn't two in the morning, the hour he

used to favor so much. We decided to see how the Metropolitan Museum was for crowds on Saturday morning. It turned out to be wonderful, enough people to make you feel the place was used but not so many that they made seeing things difficult. I had seen the banners outside saying A KING'S BOOK OF KINGS but I didn't know what it meant and we happened on it merely because we went the wrong way to see the exhibit of chess sets. It was pages from the Arthur Houghton-owned SHAH NAMEH, a book of Persian history with 258 miniature illustrations started about 1524. It was beautifully displayed with little octagonal wooden benches in front of some of the pages so one could sit and study the glorious detail. I loved the way the artists, and a sultan was himself one of the best artists, varied the shape of their illustrations by having trees grow right over the border of the picture or having other elements protrude. I thought I was giving all the pictures the strictest attention but they had a 28 minute movie which told the story involved in these Persian historical myths and this drew my attention to all sorts of details I hadn't noticed. Ken had to have a smoke after those so we went out on the steps then back in to see the chess sets. The Met has apparently owned these a long time but I don't remember ever noticing them. With the match between Fischer and Spassky making chess all the rage now, they are featuring the chess sets now and they are fascinating, so many because the two sides represent two sides in a historical war, others because of their design, and some because of the differences they show between East and West (in China and India the rooks are boats rather than castles). With our last gasp of museum energy we saw the exhibit on sports clothing in the Costume Exhibit. As soon as we got home we tumbled onto our beds and slept the sleep of the dead. We decided we didn't want much supper, which was just as well since we had to leave for Lincoln Center and the controversial new production of DON GIOVANNI, which according to the paper has had many of its most boo-provoking ideas redirected. They are doing half the performances in Italian and half in English and I had chosen the English, thinking this would make it more tolerable for Ken. I didn't expect to understand the sopranos at all but hoped the men might be understandable as men's voices seem to carry better in English. As it turned out, I also understood the ladies a good deal of the time. Ken claimed he couldn't follow it any better in English but I think he was tuned out much of the time. Mozart isn't really his dish and I don't suppose I should inflict any more on him just because GIOVANNI and FIGARO are my favorites.

SATURDAY, SEPTEMBER 30, 1972
    Gathering up the mail that was to go out I saw that I could read parts of Ken's letter to Bill Snell right thru the envelope. I saw such choice morsels as "I'd like to surprise you by arriving in Jacksonville. Maybe if I win the lottery," and "I couldn't say all I wanted to on the telephone" and something that looked like "Romantic things are better said in letters." My first reaction was fury that the old fool was still playing the same coquettish game. Then I thought that it would serve them both right to have a meeting and face up to the alcoholic deterioration that must have further affected the already broken-veined face Bill presented on his visit seven years ago and the aging that has taken place in Ken's face since then. As I have seen him age day by day I still find Ken handsome (Bill never was) but Bill is probably seeing Ken in his mind's eye as he saw him twenty years ago. It is hardly anything for me to get seriously annoyed about for Ken is too cheap to spend money on a phonecall to Bill, let alone a trip down to Florida, and Bill in his turn is too lazy even to answer the letters Ken sends off after Bill's calls. I had already intended to go to Beacon Baths next Thursday or Friday but had had perfectly uncalled-for pangs of conscience. This letter has nicely removed all those.

SUNDAY, OCTOBER 1, 1972
    At the point when Mother arrived a crew of men were painting the stop lights so I didn't worry about her transit from car to house tho I went down to get her. We had a very peaceful day as I never rose to the bait about my long hair, the jeans I was wearing (I intended to wash Venetian blinds as I talked to her but the sun was so strong I never got around to it), "that fool McGovern", or anything else. I simply told her my long hair was a wig, which she at first believed, said I never discussed politics with anyone over 28 (which is true), and sloughed off everything. She had brought her camera but said she wouldn't take any pictures of me if I was going to dress like a workman. I, however, took two shots of her with her birthday cake. We got her off for home while it was still daylight and then Ken settled down to read the Times and I to go on with Altman's HOMOSEXUAL OPPRESSION AND LIBERATION. Ken and I both feel we have had a bit too much of this subject by reading three books in a row on it and last night when we got to bed we were going over our acquaintances to see if we thought there was any truth to the popular myth that gay people are unhappier than heterosexuals. We felt that George Worrell had been unhappy, that Oliver Flemish is,

that Bill Snell might be but that otherwise our gay friends seemed as happy as our straight.

THURSDAY, OCTOBER 5, 1972
From work to Beacon Baths but whether because it was a week night or because there was a threat of rain or because there was a sign saying no hot water because of boiler trouble, it was a very poor night. I hadn't even taken my clothes off when a weird character was taken with me and came to sit on a stool and watch me undress. He then proceeded to follow me everywhere and be very creepy-crawly. With most people a mere lowering of the eyelids or a slight turn of the head is taken as rejection and accepted but this character would have had to be knocked down and stamped on. There was only one beauty present and eventually he rightly concluded that there was nobody there worthy of him and he departed. I did see the orgy room in full flower tonight and it took me back to Paris. A tangle of unsightly bodies (and only unsightly bodies participate) is not for me. The Times review of TALES OF HOFFMANN was a rave, far better than I think it deserves. They said nothing about Treigle's horrible overacting or the silly way Kay Creed played Nicklausse. At one point she stood with legs apart and hands on hips, the way girls in girls' schools used to play men in 1910. Why can't they notice that men and women don't really stand so differently? The one person they had some slight criticism of was Beverly Sills and to me she was superb, avoiding all the acting excess that the intolerably conceited Treigle went in for and singing superbly.

SUNDAY, OCTOBER 8, 1972
I went out for the paper but had no time to read it as we were busy cleaning for the party. I had some prostate trouble which was increasing in intensity until by accident Ken hit me in the crotch as he turned suddenly. That made my balls sore for a while but miraculously stopped the other business so Ken said it was his form of acupuncture and he'd hit me a good one the next time my prostate bothered me. We were ready for the guests and everything went far better than we expected. Ken and I later agreed that the potroast tasted like any other potroast and that the horseradish and cranberry sauce were totally lost. So I threw the recipe out when we were washing dishes. Alice is thinking of having one of her old-time Thanksgivings and asked us if we were free. Seems she went to her daughter-in-law's a couple of times and finds she just orders the whole dinner from a caterer so that there is no mood to the whole business for Alice, who loves the

A GAY DIARY 285

preparation. I know what she means for I really did enjoy cooking the potroast even tho it didn't turn out to be so spectacular.

SATURDAY, OCTOBER 14, 1972
We got an early start for the Metropolitan Museum and the exhibit of Soviet Arts and Crafts. We were just starting to go around when the Puerto Rican we used to speak of as Junior when we first moved here came over to us. The last time we were there we didn't see him and wondered if he were still a guard. Still handsome as ever, he is getting heavier of body, alas, but what a charming young man. We shook hands and chatted a while then went on with the exhibit. Soon he came over and asked if we wouldn't like to go around with the Russian lady guide. At first we thought we'd rather go at our own pace but decided to try her a while and were so glad we did. A handsome, wonderfully knowledgeable woman, she drew our attention to so many things we wouldn't have appreciated just from the written legends. There were two large rooms of ancient things ranging from Scythian gold artifacts thru ornamental saddles of Ivan the Terrible ("The other nobles who wanted to be Tsar named him Terrible. He was really Great" she said), aniello work, icons, distaffs, carpets, religious robes thick with jewels, and then some rooms of modern things, not as good on the whole but by no means negligible either. When one went in to the exhibit they had examined ladies' handbags and asked men to open up their jackets for inspection and I thought this was strange as the things can't be any more valuable than thousands of other things in the museums but then I realized that the Jewish Defense League likes to blow up Russian things and people sympathetic to Russia and that what they are looking for is basically weapons and bombs. I don't approve of Russian oppression of jews, but neither do I approve of the tactics of the Jewish Defense League. If one had to approve the doings of a country's government before visiting it, one not only could find few places to travel but would have to move out of America. What we are doing in Viet Nam is more shameful even than the oppression of the jews even tho Americans suffer as much as anybody.

TUESDAY, OCTOBER 17, 1972
Yesterday I called and confirmed that we would try free delivery of the Times and the man said it would be here between 7 and 7:30 so at 7:15 I looked but no paper. Then as we had our breakfast I heard Victoria squeal as she does when there's somebody outside our door getting

into or out of the elevator and I realized we'll never have to bother looking for the paper if she hasn't given us the signal. Jack McNeely, with whom Ken works at the hospital, has asked him to ride with him up to their country place tomorrow and I think it's nice that Ken is going tho I worry a bit because Jack has had driving problems. I won't feel safe till Ken is back. We watched a program on Riker's Island and I learned that sentences as short as mine *(1949, see Volume Two)* are no longer served there. I doubt if there are individual cells either as they showed incredibly crowded dormitories. Ex-prisoners said that whites stayed together, Spanish stayed together, and blacks made up their own group. This is certainly a change from my time, when we were well integrated and my almost constant admirer was Jack, a Portuguese negro whose looks and degree of blackness I can't remember but whose intelligence and kindness are still vivid. Ken, of course, had no sympathy whatever for the prisoners, no matter how horrible the conditions, no matter what terrible backgrounds they had grown up in. It amused me to hear him grumbling and ranting about their deserving whatever they got, to me, who has been there. I'm sure I'd find it dreadful now but it wasn't then, tho it wasn't an experience I'd want to repeat.

SUNDAY, OCTOBER 22, 1972

When I was in the bathroom Victoria pushed the door open as she always does when we're in there and I looked out to see Titus with the last inch of a red pipe cleaner that had been lying on the floor sticking out of his mouth. I yelled to Ken but before Ken could get there Titus had taken off and swallowed the rest of the pipe cleaner. The cats have always played with pipe cleaners but never chewed on them, let alone swallowed them. Ken felt worse with worry that the wire in the pipe cleaner, which is quite sharp on the end, might damage Titus' stomach as the steel wool Alice's cat ate did his. I was upset too but as the day went on and Titus seemed in no pain or discomfort hope rose. He was so loving and lovable all day that the possibilities of the damage inside his tender organs was all the more poignant. We gave him extra food and some petromalt to help ease the wire on its way. I did a good bit of work toward the party, polished the brass and washed the kitchen and living room Venetian blinds. In the evening finished up the sixth scene of the play. One final scene to do and a new curtain for the fifth scene and then copies can be made. Truth to tell, I am now getting a little weary of living with these characters and will be glad of a change.

TUESDAY, OCTOBER 24, 1972

Ken was going to go uptown when I did and do his hospital work early but he wasn't ready and was hoping that Titus would pass the pipe cleaner so waited around. He showed up about eleven after having had a haircut and I took him up to show him the new offices. In the hall he told me he wasn't feeling well. He admitted that part of his trouble was worry over Titus. Strangely, he has this time been much more emotionally shattered than I by the threat to the cat. I decided not to get upset until Titus showed some signs of illness or distress. Of course one can vow to take this attitude and not be able to manage it. After Ken left I found myself feeling ill, but with worry over him more than over Titus, tho I must admit I began to reflect his great concern over Titus, too. Calmed down after a while.

WEDNESDAY, OCTOBER 25, 1972

Toward dawn I heard Titus go in the pan and when I went in I found he had passed the pipe cleaner at last. I didn't flush because I knew Ken would want to see the proof and I could hardly wait for him to wake up. Fortunately the alarm soon went off and he was as jubilant as I knew he'd be. It's strange to see his emotions so externalized. After supper I finished the play. It's good that the murder scene needed so little work because concentration was virtually impossible. Ken wanted to see the Carol Burnett Show, which turned out to be one of her best because of the well-written skits well played. Then he wanted to see the Julie Andrews Show. When I said, "Well, that finishes it," as I wrote the final CURTAIN, Ken said, "Diahann Carroll certainly is beautiful," so it was quite an occasion.

SUNDAY, OCTOBER 29, 1972

With so much of the cooking done, we got ready for the party at a leisurely pace. Leo and Larry were somewhat early so we had a chance to talk about their experiences in Russia. Bill and Warren arrived late but tho Ken had been braced for bitchery and snobbery from Bill, there was none of it. I talked a good bit to Warren, who was in a position to give me good advice about what to see next summer. Larry L. found that he and Ken had many similar experiences with old mothers. He told Ken that his late lover was fifteen years younger than he and that he used often to say it wouldn't work, that the day would come when he was an old man whereas the lover would still be young, and then the lover died first.

MONDAY, OCTOBER 30, 1972

When I got home I felt very rushed for AFTER DARK had come and I wanted to look at that and read the Times and get my manuscript ready to mail and eat and be ready for the Co-Op meeting at 8. Life is just a shade too full for me this week. I like a little more time for relaxation and contemplation. Ken went with me to the meeting for a change. As always, I'm so pleased at the way the races work together here. There was bitching and complaining but some things were accomplished. So many WASPS think muggings are a racial matter but they would learn differently if they heard our blacks complain of being mugged and having their cars vandalized. They are just as much victims as anybody. There is a move toward having a guard on duty in the lobby from 2-10 now, those currently being uncovered hours. Apparently some people have been mugged in the front lobby in the morning. I guess it was safer for me to go out the side door than out the front as I have been but right at this time I love going out front and seeing the park view because it has been years since the foliage in the park has had such a variety of fall colors. Temperature conditions this year must have been just right for the trees are gorgeous and one doesn't need a trip to New England to see yellows and reds of all shades. When the meeting broke up I signed up to help on the newsletter as they said they needed help.

TUESDAY, OCTOBER 31, 1972

The cats are most upset by the fact that Ken leaves the house before I do now that he's on jury duty. When Ken called he asked who I'd been writing to in Illinois as I had a letter from Victor Taylor. I said it was some fundraiser's cute way to get me to open a letter and I wasn't going to bite as I didn't know any Victor Taylor so he should throw it away. Ken can't stand the way I throw away junk mail without opening it and I got home to find he had opened it. A good thing, too, because it was from the prisoner I congratulated when he got his college degree with such a high average. It was an absolutely wonderful letter and now I am going to write and ask him what book or books I can give him or the prison library and I want to try to find out if something can't be done to get him out. That wonderful brain and character mustn't be wasted, especially in these times when the character of so many Americans is pure marshmallow.

WEDNESDAY, NOVEMBER 1, 1972

When I got to the bus stop I discovered I had left my

change purse at home and being late, I hoped I didn't have to go back for it, so I went in a luncheonette to see if they'd give me change. The proprietor claimed not to have enuf but a colored construction worker obliged me. I'm glad to see they have some colored construction workers on the two apartment towers at 5th and 110th for the unions have fought so to keep minority groups out. After supper I read THE ROMANOVS but the nineteenth century ones seem to have no redeeming qualities. We watched THAT CERTAIN SUMMER, a much-touted tv film about a 14 year old boy visiting his divorcé father and discovering that he has a homosexual marriage. I didn't feel it was by any means up to the advance raves as the dialogue was quite pedestrian. The father and his lover were sensitively played but except for one scene where the father put his arm around the shoulder of the returning lover, they were carefully kept apart. The father did say to the son, "Gary and I have a kind of marriage. We love each other very much." A watch was also shown which was inscribed on the back "To Doug with love, Gary." I kept waiting for the play to be more than it was, however. I think the adolescent's problem would have been exactly the same had his father been going with, or living with, or married to, the man-hungry divorcée who was on his trail. By changing about six lines I think the play would have been playable by another woman and then everyone would have seen how basically trite it was. The brief confrontation between former wife and lover was silly because she was made to say, "If you were a woman I'd know how to compete with you." That may seem to mean something but of course it doesn't. There must be 584,342 women in this country who didn't know how to compete with another woman and lost their man to them. Perhaps there are gay people who are jubilant to see two men depicted as in love and living together and being tender to each other but I say this play was spinach, and I say to hell with it.

THURSDAY, NOVEMBER 2, 1972

Home for a quick supper , and then off to the Garden. The Horse Show, we agreed, was a fresh experience for us and one we enjoyed this time but not one we would quickly repeat. I am not as responsive to horses as to cats but there were many beautiful animals and we did have our favorites, two of them winning first prize. The jumping was nerve-wracking because on the very first pass a horse crashed into the wall, leaving himself and his rider lame and we expected a repeat of this at any moment, especially as the height of the wall was increased to eliminate people. It never happened again, fortunately. There were a preponderance of women riders in the early events, perhaps because women have more time to ride, but the jumping was all-male tonight.

FRIDAY, NOVEMBER 3, 1972

We went down to Rae and Mae's as planned and had a lovely evening. They had nice snacks and gorgeous apples and showed us slides of their year abroad, then slides of camping trips they have taken here. They traveled for some years with a pair of young men, also a black-white combination, who have a trucking company and used to make deliveries for Rae when she had her antique shop. The young men had a camper and they stayed at camp sites, which I suppose saved both couples from any embarrassment at being turned away by hotels and motels. I couldn't believe it when Rae said they were so happy when they moved in here because up to then they had never been able to get anybody to rent them an apartment. Usually two women living together are not looked upon with as many lifted eyebrows as men are but the black and white business caused them to get many rebuffs and I suppose Carteret and Jack, the truckers, have had similar troubles. As with Rae and Mae, the black member of the twosome is the better-looking and more refined, to judge only by pictures, of course. Rae is great for addressing Mae as "Dear" or "Sweetheart" but Mae, tho not resisting it, is more reserved. She's a lovely woman and Rae is fun. I was horrified, tho, to find that she collects stones wherever she goes. When she first mentioned this and pointed to her collector's cabinet, I thought she meant geological specimens but then she showed us a huge hunk of Hadrian's Villa and some similar pieces of Greek and Roman ruins and I was aghast. I rode her all the rest of the evening about it, saying I now saw why the Colosseum and Forum had been closed for repairs.

TUESDAY, NOVEMBER 7, 1972

Up at eight and our first objective was voting. Then downtown to the Morgan Library. The exhibit was of letters of love and passion of various celebrities--Voltaire to his niece, Sarah Bernhardt to a lover, Sir Arthur Sullivan to two sisters with whom he dallied, a beautifully scripted letter written by Elizabeth Tudor to Thomas Seymour when she was 14, a letter to Walt Whitman from Peter Doyle, the streetcar conductor who was his young friend of longest standing. Downtown today we saw scores, maybe hundreds of volunteers working for McGovern, not one for Nixon and McGovern buttons are on thousands of people whereas I saw my second Nixon button just today yet the polls seem to be right that Nixon is winning. People who would be for Nixon and the Republicans don't like to flaunt it and I don't blame them for being ashamed, tho I don't understand why Republicans are ashamed to use the name of their party if they believe in its tenets. [*Many, if not most, Republicans were leaving all mention of their party affiliation off their posters and campaign literature.*]

THURSDAY, NOVEMBER 9, 1972

Ken was waiting for me in front of the Old Garden Restaurant. He looked mighty handsome for 67 and I felt very lucky to have him, lucky also to feel in good health on his birthday for the first time in three years. From there to the Felt Forum to see the Bejart Ballet in NIJINSKY, CLOWN OF GOD. The last time Bejart was here it got terrible reviews but I liked it; this time, however, I agree that it's dreadful.

SATURDAY, NOVEMBER 11, 1972

Downtown in the morning and saw the exhibit at the Museum of Contemporary Crafts on Objects for Preparing Foods. I agree with the critics that somehow it isn't as interesting as it should be and I could think of a number of things missing. They had an electric ice cream freezer but not the hand-turned kind we used in the twenties. They had a churn but a rather more primitive one than I had my turn on at the Perry farm outside of Benton. Still, the pans, cutting tools, mixing devices, grills, toasters, stoves, etc. were interesting. From the museum to the ANTA Theatre, where we had no trouble getting tickets for this afternoon's performance in the Dance Marathon series. There were many blacks at the performance as the Dance Theatre of Harlem was one of the two troupes on the bill. The other was the Paul Sanasardo Group, which I had never seen before but which I liked very much. They had a pas de deux for a black man and a white man which was the most frankly homosexual dance I have ever seen. The loving touching and resting of heads on bodies, climaxing with a covered kiss, was really quite nice since the boys were both handsome and superb dancers. The Dance Theatre of Harlem was superb. There were four men in loin cloths who danced to more primitive rhythms and finally a gorgeous man in similar red loin cloth but with derby and white spats did Harlem Rhythms. Since his body was so little covered one could see all the muscles at work and it was gorgeous. It was noticeable that Arthur Mitchell had not selected for his troupe anyone even as black as he and I wondered if he really could find no dark black ones with talent or if he was throwing a sop to the public. I hope not the latter, tho I myself find truly black skin unappealing and am delighted with the brown which his men in loin cloths all were.

SUNDAY, NOVEMBER 12, 1972

After dinner we got at the paper and just about finished when it was time for the second episode of COUSIN BETTE. Some pretty needlework patterns were advertised and tho Ken isn't far along with the one I gave him, he suggested perhaps maybe we could both work on one. I cut out the coupon to get a kit for a tulip pattern for him and an iris pattern for me. I don't know when on earth I'll fit in needlework as I want to do another play next year but even if the money is thrown away it won't be any more thrown away than the $11 I spent on the Gay Guide and the Man Power magazine.

THURSDAY, NOVEMBER 16, 1972

Met Ken at Joe Allen's restaurant. We were lucky to get a table as they were turning them away, so many tables being reserved by theatre people. I didn't feel like a visitor in the restaurant this time since I am back at playwriting. We walked up to the new Uris Theatre, stopping at the Winter Garden for tickets to MUCH ADO ABOUT NOTHING. The Uris is wonderfully well designed for the comfort of audiences as the entrance is off an arcade which shelters the entrance to the garage and gives a large covered space for people to lounge and smoke. There are escalators and gobs of lounge space and the seats are great but I'm afraid it's one of those over-sized theatres that are hard to fill in New York and that get torn down before their time. Certainly the premiere show, VIA GALACTICA, is not likely to be there long. Set in the future, it has space ships that make a certain theatrical effect, but in general the show, tho probably very expensive, looks skimpy. Some of the music is okay (by the composer of HAIR) but the book is incredibly sophomoric. I felt as tho we were seeing the Spring show at Northwest Kansas Normal College.

MONDAY, NOVEMBER 13, 1972

I was surprised yesterday when Ken mentioned with mild bitterness the fact that Bill Snell had said he'd love to have a letter but had never answered it. I wouldn't have supposed Ken would give me the satisfaction of mentioning it. I knew, of course, that no answer had come, that none is likely to come for five years, if ever, but I didn't

think he'd underline it. I went by the library to put in
reserve cards then picked up salad stuff as Ken, on his
afternoon phone call, had suggested we might have spaghetti
and salad, since we were both heavy at the Monday weigh-in.

WEDNESDAY, NOVEMBER 22, 1972
     When I went in the door I heard Ken on the phone and
he said it was for me but kept on talking. It turned out to
be Lucile Armistead, who said the Board wanted me to take
over the editorship of the 1270 News Bulletin. I went up
to Lucile's and she gave me the names of the ten people
who had volunteered to work on the paper, with warnings
that some were troublemakers and others might lack skills.
She also gave me a list of the original tenants who are
still here--88 out of the 200 apartments. I'm not sure
what her purpose was in giving me those as I am certainly
not going to close out new people from participation if I
am the editor but am in fact going to do everything I can
to lure them in, starting with Miss Ray. I am determined
to run a positive paper. Mother called, for what reason I'm
still not sure, unless it was to find out what train we're
going on, which I wouldn't tell her as I want to walk from
the station and not go crashing thru red lights in her
car.

FRIDAY, NOVEMBER 24, 1972
     We went to the Berg Collection of the 42nd St. Library
and saw an exhibit of documents forged and real. Among the
real were a long letter from George Washington and among
the forged were several purporting to be by Charlotte Bron-
te in a minuscule hand that put my smallest to shame. We
walked up to Lincoln Center for our backstage tour of the
Met. The tickets had said the tour would last an hour and
I expected it might be superficial but it really lasted
two hours and took us to the wig shop, the paint frame,
the scene model room (where the sets for the new CARMEN
looked marvelous in models), scenery-making rooms where
sets were being made for next year's TROYENS and GOETTER-
DAEMMERUNG, carpentry shops, seamstress shops where we saw
costumes for this year's ROMEO ET JULIETTE and next year's
HOFFMANN, orchestra and dance rehearsal rooms with their
springy floors to keep dancers from tiring, orchestra instrument rooms, the main stage (on which were the black
and gloomy sets for tonite's WALKURE), the orchestra pit
and the auditorium. Ken was most impressed and so was I.
Mother called this morning to ask if we got home all right.
Out of her sight I feel sympathetic to her again and feel
I should try to make her last years pleasant but when I am

in her presence it just becomes too big a chore. The narrowness of her interests, the suffocatingness of her self-absorption, the dreadful boredom are too much. Ken's mother had no education but she kept up with things in the papers and tho her comments might be superficial one could keep conversation going. There are just no signs that Mother ever went to college at all or ever had a life of the mind. How and why other people find her interesting I simply do not understand but they must bring out something in her that I don't. God knows nobody could be duller than I am when in her presence. I soon feel beaten flat by boredom if I try to relate to her. The only times when I can preserve any sparkle are when I give up on her and start horsing around and joking with Ken, which as a spectator she seems to enjoy more than our joyless relationship. Her mind was always too slow for me and I'm sure that when Ken and I take flight with our put-ons we leave her five miles down the pike, not knowing what we're really talking about or getting at but preferring at least the lightness of atmosphere even tho she may keep insisting that I stop being so silly and be serious.

THURSDAY, NOVEMBER 30, 1972

Went to the old office out of habit. So that I wouldn't get tied up in a long conversation with Lucile I asked Ken to go pick up the meeting room key. So he was the one who got caught. When I got down to the meeting room I found it in use, apparently by part of the Board. I was annoyed and had to waylay those who showed up. We ended up in the Horgan apartment and had a perfectly lovely meeting. We selected the most important stories for the first issue, listed a couple for the next issue, set the first and second Thursdays of each month as our meeting times, the middle of the month for our publication goal, and I laid down ground rules. I am pleased with our start.

MONDAY, DECEMBER 4, 1972

In the afternoon an announcement was circulated saying that on Wednesday there would be a cocktail party to entertain the carpenters, painters, and maintenance men that helped fix and move the office. I said to Wintermudd, "I suppose that at this party for the carpenters the only approved drink is a screwdriver," which he took well. I could just imagine the look of peasant blankness Dr. Hanson would have given me but then Dr. Hanson would never have made such a nice generous gesture. Eager as I was to get at I HAVE MORE FUN WITH YOU THAN ANYBODY, by the editors of GAY, I forced myself to attend to business tonight. First wrote for hotel reservations in Paris and London, then read the Times, then wrote stories for the Information Bulletin (which I find is our name, not Newsletter). I laid out the list of eleven stories in the sequence I want to run them then wrote the story on transfer of editorship.

TUESDAY, DECEMBER 12, 1972
As I had taken the morning off to keep my appointment with Dr. Smith I was able to linger over the paper longer. I was just as enthusiastic about Dr. Smith as Ken has been. He took down a full medical history then we went into the examination room. As I went over my lifetime illnesses with Smith I said, "This makes me sound as tho I'm sickly but I've missed only about a week of work in 22 years. I'm usually ambulatory with my illnesses." I decided I would not, after all, work on the news stories as planned tonite but would enjoy myself reading I HAVE MORE FUN WITH YOU THAN ANYBODY. It isn't an awfully good book but it does show that two gay lovers can have fun together over the years.

WEDNESDAY, DECEMBER 13, 1972
Toward the end of a routine day Dr. Wintermudd came out and said, "Mr. Vining, you seem to be the most relaxed person in this office. So I'm going to take you away for a while." When we got in his office he said he'd like to talk informally about my taking over the Foundation Research that Kathi has been doing, provided I thought it would interest me and that I turned out to have a knack for it (*This was part of the work Ken had done for years.*) I was afraid he was going to keep me overtime and of course we were due at Leo's at 6:30 but we settled for my trying it for about a month on a one-day-a-week basis and I took off. At one point Wintermudd said I might like to take certain papers home and study them and I said, "Not tonite. I'm going out to dinner and I don't want to risk leaving them there." But actually any studying of the work I do is going to be on office time. I have no children to send thru college, and I have inexpensive tastes, so I don't need to sacrifice my pleasure and career time to job ambitions. I wouldn't do it when young and I'm certainly not going to do it now.

SUNDAY, DECEMBER 17, 1972
We went out in the afternoon to use the tickets I gave Ken for his birthday to OH, COWARD. The little theatre was full and the show delightful. Some of the songs I knew, of course, and some I did not and the lyrics were terribly funny. With brisk pace and minimal props and gestures two

men and one woman put everything over beautifully until I felt I would sell my soul to have Noel Coward's talent. Mr. Rockefeller and Mr. Getty and Mr. Onassis may have their money--just give me Coward's talent. Light fare it may produce but I think in the end it will endure as Arthur Miller's heavy-handed plays, for instance, will not. Encountering talent can be so thrilling. Sometime this week I read a review by Benjamin De Mott of the new biography of Virginia Woolf by her nephew. I have read many reviews of that book but this review was just so superbly written, so marvelously insightful, so life-affirming that I turned back to see who wrote it, read it again, and felt like writing to the magazine. It was just a perfect short piece of writing. I felt the same way today in the presence of several of the Coward song lyrics.

WEDNESDAY, DECEMBER 20, 1972

On my way home I bought the holiday turkey as Ken was afraid the small ones might be all be gone if we waited. When I got there I found my play had at last returned from Freida Fishbein (*a prominent literary agent*). Mrs. Fishbein said that her reader had given such a negative report that she didn't feel she could handle the play but that he had emphasized that I seemed to be a playwright of professional experience and that she'd like to see something else. The reader's report was included and was devastating. He felt the love scenes between two 35 year old men would be utterly unbearable in the theatre. I was, of course, somewhat cast down by this but still retained stubborn faith in the quality of the play and remembered when Hinda Teague Hill, who read something of mine at almost every class, turned back SHOW ME THE WAY TO GO HOME (*a story with slight gay elements which I wrote in 1945*) and said she found it so unpleasant that she just couldn't face reading it again to the class and couldn't see any market for it. (*But this one script she refused to read to the class at Hollywood High Evening School was the one script I wrote for that class which DID sell, to an anthology called CROSS SECTION 1945*)

TUESDAY, DECEMBER 26, 1972

To Lord & Taylor's half-price Christmas card sale, where we quickly found three boxes we liked. Up the street to see KLM's window, which is not all Madurodam this year but has Nieuw Amsterdam then a body of water plied by a Henry Hudson type boat and Old Amsterdam on the other side. People have thrown hundreds of coins in the water after their current idiotic fashion of tossing coins into any

little body of water as tho they were all the Fountain of
Trevi or wishing wells. Down to the Felt Forum for the
Moscow Circus, which we enjoyed as much as ever. I don't
understand people who don't like circuses, especially if
they fancy themselves aesthetes. Circuses present the human
being at his physically most highly trained and coordinated
and in addition many of the performers are very
attractive. The unions would prevent such a thing in America
but I noticed that many of the performers doubled as
roustabouts when their acts were over, notably a handsome
blond youth who had been in a tumbling act. I also noted
that their roustabouts had, in many cases, long hair, as
did their performers. In fact, the long hair on the Cossack
riders added excitement to their performance just as a
horse's unplaited mane does.

WEDNESDAY, DECEMBER 27, 1972
    Rather a rushing day. I had only time to feed Lisa's
cats and check their pan, whereas what they really wanted
was love. I told Ken to go down and play with them but as
things turned out, he never got a chance. Dr. Wintermudd
asked if I could come to dinner either this holiday weekend
or the first week in January. I said I couldn't but said
the next week had openings. He then, for the first time,
asked if Ken would like to come and I said he would as I
have been a little annoyed that it wasn't mentioned before
and was determined to get across the idea that socially we
were a couple.

FRIDAY, DECEMBER 29, 1972
    Mary announced that we would go home at quarter of
four so I called Ken to announce it. He gave me a few errands
to do like buying cat food. When I got there I found
he had taken all the turkey meat off the carcass for an a
la king and was cooking the carcass for soup. He kept saying
how glad he was that I was home, which was very gratifying,
and of course I was glad to be there, too. Ken has
certainly been more demonstrative since retirement than he
had been for years. We kiss when I leave and when I come
home and especially on the days when he doesn't go to the
hospital and see people, he frequently says how glad he is
that I'm home. He was singing away as he cooked and I was
glad he was so happy. The copy of GAY that I brought home
was The Best of Gay, all repeats from the past year and
one of the articles was Is There Life After Marriage? which
I hadn't seen before. The man in that is a little bitter
that his so-called marital relationship had boiled down to
a sexless business of being merely loving room-mates, but

he admitted that they had had no common interests. It makes a big difference when one does. I always feel sorry for those with a compulsion to have sex or love with those beneath them on the social scale, or those compelled to have one-night-stands, for it cuts them out of the lovely companionship. At 8 we went down to Mae and Rae's. Rae dominated the conversation as always. I'm not an easy person to over-ride in conversation but she manages to do it with ease. She talked much of how she was in the Civil Rights vanguard for years before she met Mae, a claim I have heard before. I thought to myself that if she was really concerned about rights for negroes she might start by letting Mae say something. I have yet to get a chance to get more than two sentences out of Mae because every time she starts to say something Rae bulldozes right over the two of us. A lot of the conversation had to do with Rae's attitude toward prayer in contrast to the one I picked up from Christian Science, that is, she believes in asking for all the things she wants from God whereas I believe in asking for nothing and just being grateful for what I have. We had them come up and see our tree since it is doubtful that it will still be up on Twelfth Night, when we have asked them up.

1973

TUESDAY, JANUARY 2, 1973

To the Historical Society to see their exhibit of their complete holdings of Audubon bird paintings (they have 433 out of 435, two of blue birds being missing). We had seen an exhibit on Audubon there a few years ago but it wasn't nearly as complete. I had known he had assistants who sometimes did the backgrounds but I hadn't known that one was a mere boy of 13-15 when he worked with him. I bussed across the park with Ken but left him to go to Beacon Baths. He was less chipper about it than he sometimes is and I got some guilt feelings. He had told them he wouldn't be at the hospital these two Tuesdays as he wanted to be with me so perhaps I shouldn't have left him, tho I imagine he would have napped when we got home. As it turned out, it was one of my better times at Beacon Baths. There was considerable beauty there. I met an Italian boy from Turin who was interested in me but was too fastidious to go in the rooms because they don't change the sheets after every customer (tho God knows they are working all the time at cleaning up and changing linen). He fished around to

see if I lived in midtown and was upset to find I lived up
in Harlem and with somebody at that. When I answered his
question as to whether I had a friend by saying that I had
and that we'd been together 27 years he said I must have
been a boy. Now I damned well don't look forty but this
boy acted really stunned. He kept giving up on me and then
after some wandering circling back to me for more talk,
which was pleasant. He told me there were no such baths in
Italy, not even in Rome, but told me of those in Paris,
which he thought were cleaner. Certainly the one I went to
didn't compare to the Beacon for cleanliness. As soon as I
got home Ken and I took down the tree, much to Titus' distress. He has adored lying under that tree and only last
night I took a picture of him doing it. We took it down not
a minute too soon for it was terribly brittle. Lisa had
left a note saying she was home and would see us later so
I didn't have to go see her cats.

WEDNESDAY, JANUARY 3, 1973
When I went in the door at home the place looked
dreadfully bare without the Christmas tree. I found myself
still going at the busy-busy pace I had kept up all day
and my ears were ringing so I made myself calm down. After
supper I took a half hour nap before going to the Meeting
Room. Eleanore said she had taken a survey of people in
the building about the first issue and wanted to present
their criticisms. They consisted of such things as--we
should have used elite type instead of pica as it would
have been shorter and cost less, and we should have omitted
the line of blank space between the headings and the stories, which would also have saved space. I said, "I note
these criticisms but I reject them. I think it looks much
better with white space." Eleanore flared and said, "This
is a cooperative. I went along with your having your own
way on the first issue but we should vote on this and see
what people want." "If people have criticisms, let them
get themselves down here and work on this paper. Everybody
has great ideas on what somebody else should do but they
don't to do any of it themselves. By the way, Pat, how many
people contacted you to be on the committee to do something
for the ill." "None." "Just what I thought. And how many
people volunteered for the package room committee?" "Well,
Cathi was going to do that but she got busy and ___". I
trust I made my point with Eleanore because I kept driving
it home with great lack of subtlety all evening. Pat and
Lisa were with me on the format. I am yielding no whit of
my editorial rights to anybody. I am putting in far more
work on this paper than anybody else and I will damned

well do it as I see fit. I did not order the space between
heading and text as that was Pat's normal way of typing it
but I will back her to the hilt. Such petty considerations
of economy are ridiculous. I told Eleanore to go back to
whoever was so concerned and tell them that we saved $10
by doing the collating and stapling ourselves even tho the
Board was willing to pay for it. When I got home I found
Ken listening to some crappy tv show which was a gala put
on for the Queen at the Palladium. I took several magazines
I wanted to catch up on, including the final two issues of
LIFE (which ended publication this year after 35 years) and
went to the bedroom. The cats were infuriated that I closed
the bedroom door and Titus scratched up a storm until I
could get over and let him in. I think Ken was also offended for when the program was over, he said, "You can come
out now. It really wasn't that bad." I didn't argue but
had needed some quiet and peace after this day and was determined to have it.

THURSDAY, JANUARY 4, 1973
    Set out for City Center to see the Shenyang Acrobatic
Troupe from the People's Republic of China. It turned out
to be one of the dozen great experiences in the theatre
that I have had. The air was electric with the sense of occasion, for the troupe is here just five days and is playing in only four American cities. Gobs of Chinese were in
the audience but also lots of carriage trade and lots of
young people. All the alert people in New York, in other
words, who don't drag about getting tickets when something
good is coming to town and don't wait for critical endorse-
ment. I had expected phenomenal acrobatics but I had not
known that the decors would be so attractive. As a matter
of fact I would have been content to just listen to the
music without watching anything or content to look at the
sets without any performance in front of them, or content
to see the performers with no settings and no music but
all three together were a heavenly experience. Sometimes
they projected just the shadow of a bamboo tree on the
backdrop; at other times there might be a flowering branch
or those very peculiar Chinese mountains. Costumes could-
n't have been fresher nor could the girls have been lovelier. The men weren't much to look at but every girl was
lovely. As a matter of fact, the women did more of the
things than the men did. Their plate-spinning number was
gorgeous as they twirled six or eight pink plates on thin
green sticks and made formations. But everything was won-
derful--the comic lion dance, the nine passengers on one
bicycle, the foot dexterity number. It all ended in a

grand finale with a huge red banner which said in Chinese and English "Long live the friendship of the American and Chinese people", which led to a standing ovation (not that that means much in these days of the fad for standing ovations).

FRIDAY, JANUARY 5, 1973
     Personnel called me to say they had the job description sheets for me to fill out and perhaps I'd like to take them home to work on this weekend. When I picked them up I told them I NEVER take work home and I repeated this remark to Wintermudd, who laughed and said, "I was just about to suggest you do the same." I might as well establish this point early in the game as it's always been a cardinal rule of my life and is going to continue to be. I don't know when I would have fitted in any work on the job description anyway as I was busy this evening from the moment I got home. I was busy doing all the preliminaries for tomorrow's quiche lorraine, grating the cheese, cooking the bacon, and half-cooking the pie shell in my new quiche pan. Ed S. called to invite us for cocktails tomorrow since Ruth would be coming there after a matinee. I figured that by leaving the minute the opera broadcast was over and asking our guests if we could set the time back from 8 to 8:30 we could make it down to 57th St. and back. Ed himself has a dinner date so the party won't go on and on.

MONDAY, JANUARY 8, 1973
     After I got in bed and Ken was undressing, he somehow started a fantasy about a great success at the Continental Baths, quoting what the young men had said to him. I immediately destroyed it with a mock insulting remark and he swung his towel to hit my legs. He'd start over and I'd quote another, whereupon he'd swing his towel again. We got going until I laughed myself into a choking fit. I don't remember a word either of us said but I adored the way he went along with a gag, as he always does. Earlier in the day we had one of those episodes where he starts to talk to me when he's in the kitchen and I'm in the living room. He came to the living room just as I went the other way to the kitchen to hear better. Then he reversed and I reversed, missing each other again. That only has to happen once for one or the other of us to decide to continue the process as a joke. He falls right in with that too. It's Ken's great sense of play that makes him so delightful to live with.

SATURDAY, JANUARY 13, 1973

As the Times had a rave about the Morgan Library's new show of drawings from Christ Church, Oxford, we cancelled plans to see a movie and headed for the Morgan. Tho I admire many I don't respond strongly to them, but when I do I do. There was a Vasari <u>Procession of Pope Leo X thru the Piazza Signoria in Florence</u> that yielded new wonders every time I ran back to see it again , as I did twice. In the corridor I fell in love with something by someone whose name has already grown vague to me since I had never heard of him---Lancagno, perhaps? It was a male head with slight beard and the most gentle reflective expression. It could have been drawn yesterday instead of centuries ago and moldering as he long has been I am in love with the model.

SUNDAY, JANUARY 14, 1973

In the afternoon Ken decided he wanted to look at the highly publicized Super Bowl football game. If you give a thing enuf publicity he wants to see it even if it's far out of his normal field of interest. I retreated with the paper I still had not read to the bedroom. Tried to think why I so loathe games of that sort and decided that among other reasons I hate (1) the monotony of the single voice describing the game hour after hour (2) the ugliness of padded men, most of whom start out with what I find an unattractive bulk in the first place (3) the enervating effect of the unending excitement of the crowd (4) the very thought of team action. I might lead and I might push a group but I could never be an equal part of it and I am such an essential loner that I find the very thought of team action uncomfortable. What is more, before I fled to the bedroom there was another element visible that I had not expected, which was a lot of old-fashioned super-patriotism with recitation by some astronauts of the pledge of allegiance to the flag, some dreadful off-pitch singing by little colored girls which quickly proved that all negroes don't have musical ability, and a lot of other nationalistic rigmarole that seemed to equate football with love of country. I was perfectly happy reading in the bedroom but of course the closed door bothered the cats no end as they wanted to be with both of us.

SATURDAY, JANUARY 20, 1973

We went downtown well before theatre time as Ken wanted to see the table settings Tiffany's advertised. Before going I had decided that if we were going to Tiffany's I'd wear my nice topcoat instead of the trench coat I've been wearing so much. I almost burst out laughing when I saw the way people were dressed in the store. Tho there was an occasional elegant older person in there, trench coats, pea jackets, and some extremly casual and even scruffy garb was readily seen in there. From there we went to the Museum of Contemporary Crafts and saw a not too impressive show of modern glass, which contained nothing so amusing as some things we saw in Zurich and nothing that appealed to me much for its beauty. To the Broadhurst, one of my favorite theatres, to see Neil Simon's new play THE SUNSHINE BOYS. I think it's his best since THE ODD COUPLE and tears of laughter were streaming down my face. I can't join those who sneer at Simon. When an author can have audiences in gales of laughter as they recognize the foibles of the old, he has done as much as an author needs to do. When the men kept forgetting names or twisting them around, Ken leaned over and said, "That's like me." That may have been one reason I was laughing so much. It has nothing to do with age. Ken has always said, "Gladys Loring" when he meant "Alice Pisciotta" and "Mary Ingraham" when he meant Mary Rafferty and "Governor Roosevelt" when he means Rockefeller, etc. After shrimp soup for supper we settled down to read. I did needlework during TV but it didn't go nearly as well as it did the other night and I was inordinately depressed by this. When Ken undressed to take his bath he said his shorts had to be thrown out as they were tearing and he showed me a couple of splits. I thereupon started to tear them off him and we had a mock rape, with Ken resisting and me persisting. We got laughing so much our stomachs were sore. I finally got every shred off him and by that time we were exhausted from struggle and laughter. God knows what the neighbors thought if they could hear.

TUESDAY, JANUARY 23, 1973
Ken wasn't feeling too well at breakfast and we thought the flu might have caught up with him. I dressed for the visit to St. Luke's to see where Ken works but we weren't sure he'd be there. At one I went to St. Luke's after a hasty lunch and found Ken, very handsome in his volunteer's jacket, waiting for me inside the entrance. I got to meet Robin Carlson, the prissy part-time librarian. He fussed about the clash of colors in Ken's tie and shirt and asked if I couldn't do something about it. I told him I was so glad he was getting bold about colors that I wouldn't interfere, tho it's true that Ken does get some dreadful combinations. Ed S. had said at his party that my shirt and tie went well together but that Ken's was dreadful. They, however, are monochrome people and while it is

always safe to be a vision in blues, browns, or whatever, I think it can get pretty dull too. I certainly wouldn't want to go in a museum where the only colors an artist could use in a painting were the shades a secretary would use in matching her outfit. It is just as tasteless and just as silly, I think, to see a woman with bag, shoes, handkerchief, hat, scarf, dress and jewelry matching as to see people sometimes get an unfortunate mix. As for Robin, he was just plain drab and even badly matched colors somewhere might do him good. In the evening I read more of THE PERSIAN BOY before we started a television evening. Tho I'm still skipping a bit, I am more interested now that the boy is in love with Alexander and jealous of Hephaestion. Mary Renault writes very well of some aspects of these things, notably the fact that tho desire may have left Alexander and Hephaestion, they are still deeply in love. It was also amusing when the eunuch, used to being sent for when sex was wanted, finds himself a novice at seduction when he decides he wants to sleep with Alexander, who is making no passes at him. Tonite I read about the drunken killing of Kleitos, and it reminded me that in the essay with which I won my first money for writing, the temperance essay that won the WCTU (*Women's Christian Temperance Union*) prize when I was eleven, Alexander's killing of his friend was my great illustration of the evils of drink. When I learned of it, I don't know. Did I even then have an affinity for the homosexuals of history? The first tv show was about the migrations of snow geese, a lot prettier to look at than the wild dogs of Africa that we watched last night, and much nicer animals. This was followed by another episode of AMERICA, this time on the Civil War. I made another, this time successful, effort to improve my television hours by doing some needlework. Why I had problems the last time out, I don't know, because it went like a charm tonite. The President announced the end of the Vietnam War and I was glad tho I refused to listen to him since I knew the gist of the message. I went in the bedroom to read while Ken watched as I can't stand Nixon's face or voice. Nor do I know why this couldn't have been done years ago. The young people, tho not all war protesters are young, do deserve some credit for forcing this issue tho they may recently have felt futile in view of Nixon's general unresponsiveness to the people.

SATURDAY, JANUARY 27, 1973

On the fourth try we got a hotel in London, the Lonsdale, and the note went so far as to say they are on a nice tree-lined street, which charmed me at once. When we were in Alexander's today I got a chance to look at the much-advertised book THE JOY OF SEX and I found it a very salutary book filled with pictures of positions I never would have dreamed of but somehow not in the least obscene. What surprised me was that in virtually every drawing the man had a beard. Now this is fine for me, tho the beards were more scraggly than I like, but surely not everybody finds a beard erotic or attractive. I would have supposed they might have shown a variety of physical types. God knows beards are more wide-spread every day but they really can't be everybody's, not even every young person's, dish. Of the three males in our office I am the only clean-shaven one as both Wintermudd and Darryl have beards. The question is, when do I have time to grow one and get thru that first bad period?

TUESDAY, JANUARY 30, 1973
    Took my three girls downstairs and taught them how to research information on new grads and then rushed upstairs to a staff meeting. What a great crew they make and such clear writing and printing. Let nobody tell me that young people today can't write or print; I have one after another who does it superbly. So that Ken wouldn't get confused on what dishes we had agreed to use for what, I agreed to write them down for him. Early in the evening he said he was nervous about the party and I asked why. He said he'd like things to go well and I asked him what was the last party he could think of that hadn't. Ginny repeatedly burned on food, Miriam's gelatine salad refused to set and she served it anyway, yet we had a good time. I told him the only thing that would spoil the party would be for him to take it too seriously. I told him I hoped he wouldn't get fluttery and fussy just because it was my boss and his wife we were entertaining because they're not here as my boss but as people I like; I don't entertain bosses as such, never had the Hansons in my house in 17 years and wouldn't. The Kochers arrived before I had the salad made and Eric came and talked to me as I worked on it. Mimie arrived next and finally the Wintermudds. They all took to each other as I thought they would. Much talk of international affairs, expecially the State Dept's bringing back from disgrace those China hands who all along were against Chiang-Kai-Shek. At one point Mrs. W. said of the boss' children *(by a divorced wife)*, "Delightful children. You should meet them, Donald." "Oh, Donald knows Stephen," the boss said, "He hired him and he fired him." "What courage, to fire the boss' son," said Mimie. They told me at long last what had happened to Stephen. One of the

first names he came across in the files when doing research was the same as a boy who saved Stephen's life one day and was himself killed the next so he just stood there free-associating. Two days after I fired him he was hospitalized with a total breakdown for a month and tho better, is not fully recovered. I hoped the firing had not in any way precipitated it but the boss said I had done the right thing in letting him go and reporting to him, that his bottling up of his experiences in Viet Nam had just at that point burst out of him. Mrs. Wintermudd, who spent her childhood in Tunis, was much interested in the portrait of Ken which was drawn there in 1943 (*when he was stationed there during World War II service with the Air Force*).

SUNDAY, FEBRUARY 4, 1973
    Out to buy the Times but no time to read much before we had to leave for Staten Island. When we got to the ferry terminal at Staten Island (one now pays ten cents instead of five but pays only on the Manhattan side) we called to find out what bus to take but Ginny and Eddie came to pick us up. When we first went in the Thatchers' house it was surprisingly quiet. No children were around and even George was nowhere in evidence. Three of the boys have paper routes, from which they began to drift in. Geoffrey, once the handsomest, has lost his looks with adolescence but retains his nice personality. All seven children have that, of course, and the beauty is now Tommy. He fascinated me not only because of his beauty but because he sat at length in the company of adults, laughing now and then but never intruding into the conversation. A quiet and observant child in this country is rare and I was glad he was the one who sat beside me at dinner as he quite charmed me. They are remarkably well-brought-up children, the older ones now caught up in car ownership and reconstruction, which interested me more than I ever thought it would as they talked knowledgeably about it. The kids do much of the work too, getting the dinner ready and cleared away and the boys are in no way exempted from this just because they have a sister or two. The day en famille was in no way the horror we anticipated because these are good kids and interesting ones. As the Leonards wanted to get a start back to Albany, we didn't stay long after dinner but we lingered a while because Mrs. Butterfield, the 83-year-old negro lady who still cleans for the Thatchers and used to clean for Ginny, came to call looking lovely in a brown outfit. She's sharper than Mother and a lovely talkative type who likes city life and doesn't care for country at all. She says her phone bills are terrific, $85 a month

sometimes but that is just her way of visiting friends and relatives it would be difficult for her to visit. We got home easily, getting out at 86th and bussing from there. Getting off the bus with us was that erratic bitch, Helga Rogers, the German who married the black man, and who speaks when it's convenient and not for the next six months. As she wanted a neighbor as escort from the bus, she spoke today. Strangely enuf, when I got around to reading the Times Book Section I found that one whole page was devoted to her late husband's books, WORLD'S GREAT MEN OF COLOR. Originally published by him in 1947, I'm not sure why it's being reviewed now, tho it's called a classic. Suddenly it occurred to me that I had a hot story for the next issue of the Information Bulletin and I promptly called Mrs. Rogers up to ask if I could send a reporter around. We watched TOM BROWN'S SCHOOL DAYS, of course, and I got some more needlework done as that now regularly goes with TV.

SUNDAY, FEBRUARY 11, 1973

There were two TV programs on homosexuality, NEW YORK ILLUSTRATED, which went into the more sordid aspects and then the David Susskind program, on gay marriages. The young man who tried, and finally succeeded, to marry his lover and still got elected President of the Student Body of the University of Minnesota was among those on. They made a very good point when there was some patronizing remark about the Middle West such as I might have made. They said that in many ways the Middle West was ahead of the two coasts on these things and so it is; Illinois was probably the first state to retract anti-homosexual laws and these fellows are doing all right with their marriage in Minnesota.

MONDAY, FEBRUARY 12, 1973

A bitter cold day and the office even cold. Olga, unused to cold weather in the Caribbean, asked Jocelyn in all seriousness if, when her nose was so cold this weekend it might have broken off if someone had hit it. I said not but proceeded to tell the story of how my hands froze when I was a baby in Benton. I repeated as gospel what the ladies of the town said then, that my hands had frozen, turned black, and had to be cut off. (*The old wives were scandalized that my mother put her baby in a room of its own and believed in opening windows at night for fresh air.*) I said, "They transplanted other hands on me. You see this line right here? That's where they were joined." I was astonished when Jocelyn as well as Olga took me perfectly seriously and looked closely. (*Actually, other old wives had recommended wrapping my frozen hands in the belly of a recently butchered sheep or cow, which was successfully done.)* I still am not quite used to how convincing I can be when telling the most outlandish things with a straight face and matter-of-fact voice. Did some needlepoint during the Julia Childs program then got at my taxes. I lacked energy to do my State returns tonite, however, and wanted to get at the new copy of GAY. Helga Rogers put under my door the information I needed about her husband's book. He was 86 when he died and must have been 76 when she married him. There must have been forty years difference in their ages. Wanted to do so much more this evening but the days are just not long enuf.

TUESDAY, FEBRUARY 13, 1973

Another of the gorgeous sunshiny mornings that have succeeded each other so often this year. Kids sliding on the ice of Harlem Meer but our friends the seagulls weren't there today. I never can figure out when they'll be there and when they won't. Only when there's some ice on the lake and maybe only where there are also some unfrozen spots rather than when it's solid as today. A bad day with prostatitis so the miracle wasn't permanent Friday but maybe it'll subside and give me three perfectly comfortable months again. When Ken called I asked him if he'd contact Rae and ask her to have the minutes of the Board meeting ready for me at seven so I could get my newspaper work out of the way. She agreed and I ran down. Ken said that when he called Rae said, "Oh, we were just sitting here thinking how lucky we were to have each other to love, etc." so when I went in I said, "I hear you two have been sitting down here in a glow of love. Now, that's got to stop. The world's work doesn't get done that way. Discontent is what moves the world forward, so cut this out." As I knew I would, I got a roar of laughter from Rae, who is a hearty laugher to say the least. After I got the minutes we talked a while and when they said they subscribed to few magazines now I said I'd bring ours down when we were through. We love to have someone to give them to.

WEDNESDAY, FEBRUARY 14, 1973

On my way home from work I tried to get a Valentine's Day card for Ken but they were cleaned out of usable ones. Then I tried to get heart-shaped cookies at the bakery but they were all gone. This sentimentality was amusing in view of the fact that Ken and I had a blowup right after supper. I sat down to read the paper and he went to turn on the tv. I asked him what it was he was interested in and he

didn't answer me then on my insistence said it was the
return of the prisoners of war. As this has been done to
death, with all sorts of companies offering them all sorts
of things and of course reaping some cheap publicity for
their hotel, car, or whatnot, I retreated to the bedroom.
Ken found reception wasn't good or something and turned it
off then said sarcastically, "All right, you can come out
now." "I'm comfortable now," I said, which I was,"so I
might as well stay here and read." "Good Lord, you'd think
it would contaminate you," he said, and I blew up. "Now
look here, if I want to read in here while you watch that
it's my business." I came out when I had finished the paper and made some remark, but got no answer so we had silence till time for me to go to the staff meeting of the
Bulletin. When I returned home Ken was ironing napkins in
the kitchen and didn't talk at first but soon we were okay
again.

SUNDAY, FEBRUARY 18, 1973
    Another glorious crisp, and I really mean crisp, but
sunny day. After reading some paper we went downtown to
the 55th St. Theatre to see Casey Donovan, star of BOYS IN
THE SAND, in his latest porno movie. Tho not made by Wakefield Poole, who did the other, it was certainly made by
somebody with a sense of humor and a good mastery of film.
It wasn't just thrown together and even Ken enjoyed it. I
used to complain that these films didn't tease enuf but
just flung bodies into action but in this the tease was
dragged out until both Ken and I were amused. I must say
the point of some of the sexual devices eluded me, especially the uses to which the dildo was put. Why bother with
one of those with the real thing handy in the same dimen-
sions? I know this is a plastic age but plastic penises in
preference to the real thing? That is going too far. We
had intended to stop off at the Guggenheim Museum on our
way home and see the Hodler show but we had both gotten
rather chilled in the underheated theatre. Having read so
many accounts of the various bad effects of a chill, I decided I'd be wise to get Ken home and see the Hodler show
some other time. The sun was pouring in our living room so
much that in no time I was not only heated but over-heated.
I started ALL CREATURES GREAT AND SMALL, the memoirs of
the British veterinarian and did some needlepoint.

MONDAY, FEBRUARY 19, 1973
    As we read the paper at breakfast Ken discovered that
Bloomingdale's is having needlework classes all this week
and on Monday and Thursday nights is having them just for

men. We decided to go Thursday. The first thing I knew I was nearly late for the bus. Ken said, "We have such a good time mornings that we lose track," and I thought of all the hassles I had over the years trying to get him to come sit at the table with me instead of on the stool back to in the kitchen. Of course he was going to have a whole working day with me then and perhaps we were already seeing too much of each other. I guess in some ways we're lucky we got thru those seventeen years of constant togetherness tho on the whole I enjoyed them. We watched an absolutely superb tv program called THE MYSTERIOUS MR. ELIOT and it made me really want to read T.S. Eliot's poetry more than I have, which is to say scarcely at all. I think Ken started out intending to ignore it but he got caught up. Even in the movies' palmiest days they never offered this wonderful kind of documentary which tv does so well when it puts its mind to it. Of course the point of origin was again the BBC.

SATURDAY, FEBRUARY 24, 1973

Downtown early in order to visit the needlework departments of Macy's and Gimbel's. I bought two crewel pillow sets but found no needlepoint I liked. I was appalled at the childishness and old-fashionedness of most of the patterns. Apparently needlework, like watercolor painting, appeals to artistically backward minds. We ate at Flame Steak and then went to the Shubert for A LITTLE NIGHT MUSIC. Based on a Bergman movie that I saw but so long ago that I'd forgotten the plot, it was one of Harold Prince's beautifully stylish shows. Set at the turn of the century, it offered a chance for the women to wear lovely gowns. Two of the three stars, Glynis Johns and Hermione Gingold, have no voices whatever but they compensated for these by getting unusually good singers for the other parts. What we could hear of the lyrics were excellent but hearing was often a strain and we both complained of headaches when we got home.

WEDNESDAY, FEBRUARY 28, 1973

We got notice that we will have March 16 off and as that is Alice's birthday I thought it would be a good idea to have a party for her but later settled on a still better idea, which was to take her to lunch at Joe Allen's and then perhaps go visit some galleries with her as long as she's come in town. I called her and she was pleased. We had an invitation to dinner with the Goldbergs on the 18th so may also see Alice there but didn't go into it in case, as with the Rockmores, she was after all not invited. After supper we were off to the Forum at Lincoln Center to see a double bill at the Mini-Met. Next to us were two young men who must be hi-fi addicts like Darryl, who listens to even ordinary programs with headphones so the sound is loud and all around him. When he shushed Ken as he made a comment to me, I thought he was within his rights and when Ken offended again and the young man imperiously snapped his fingers for him to behave I was torn between annoyance and amusement, but later it got hilarious. As they played DIDO without intermission I started to consult my program at one point and he glared at me, then a man's knee cracked and he glared at that, but the topper was when I quietly scratched my leg and he flashed an indignant look. Only concern for what the poor singers might think kept me from bursting into laughter. I'm sure the young man thought he was concentrating on the opera but he was concentrating on the distractions. Tho in that small theatre no singer could have been more than 25 feet from us and were usually about 12 feet away, he was constantly cupping his ear. He could hear the smallest sigh of any neighbor and glower at them but the singers weren't as loud as they are on his hi-fi. I suppose there's a lot of this kind of thing among the young who are used to the high decibels of rock, hi-fi etc. and one wonders if they won't develop a real sort of deafness.

SATURDAY, MARCH 3, 1973

The audience for THE CHANGING ROOM wasn't as gay as I had expected. Whatever appeal the male nudity might have had was apparently nullified by the thought that the play was about a rugby team. We had looked forward to the play for a long time and at first I couldn't understand why it was such a letdown. From the nudity standpoint, I put my opera glasses away early in the proceedings because though the nudity was total, unabashed, and perfectly logical for the locker-room setting, none of the participants were attractive and after all I have seen more and more deliberately erotic nudity at the baths lately. It's amazing that the New York stage has so quickly accepted total nudity and put it in its proper place. Only a few years ago I CAN'T HEAR YOU WHEN THE WATER'S RUNNING included a whole playlet about whether an actor would or would not appear totally nude on stage, then we had the plays in which they briefly did, and now this, in which men who could easily have sat back to when nude sat full front without self-consciousness and men who could have draped a towel over their genitals didn't. How women may have felt I don't know (there were plenty present) but I found it one of the least erotic plays I ever saw. They had total courage about it and when the attendant was wiping off the athlete who had been injured and had to be helped to bathe and dress, they didn't flinch at having him briefly dry his genitals, as he really would. What really disappointed me about the play, I guess, is that I expected some insight into the minds of athletic types and didn't get any. I also expected some humor and didn't get nearly enough. The author, David Storey, has really been a member of a rugby team and if he says those men are stupid for the most part, I'll take his word that this may be so in England. Since I've started to read the sports pages of the Times this last couple of years, however, I just no longer believe that American athletes are either stupid or inarticulate. Nor do I think our lower classes are so witless and unintelligent. Working class people can be both perceptive and funny, sometimes far more so than middle or upper-class. Anyway, tho I was never bored by the play and thought it admirably done so that one almost ceased to think of the actors as actors, I did feel let down.

WEDNESDAY, MARCH 7, 1973
    Just as I stepped out of the elevator I found Lois Small about to put a note under my door, which she handed to me instead. It turned out to be addressed to me and the staff and was a little thank-you note saying, "Your Information Bulletins are just beautiful. The positive thinking of all shines on every page. I enjoy all the many things you tell of interest. Thanks again." That more than makes up for the heckling we got in the beginning and certainly justifies my insistence on reporting on neighborhood institutions.

THURSDAY, MARCH 8, 1973
    I left at five and was at the Yangtze River before Ken was. He reported that the afternoon visit he paid Lisa's cats in my stead ended with both cats in his lap, something I have never achieved. After a nice dinner at the Y.R. we walked up to Lincoln Center and joined the capacity audience for the first night of L'INCORONAZIONE DI POPPAEA. I had gone dutifully because I'd heard for so many years what a remarkable opera it was but I didn't expect to like it any better than I did JULIUS CAESAR, which nothing on earth could persuade me to see again. Actually I had one of my finest nights in the opera house. It's simply fantastic that after 301 years the scenes hold the stage so superbly--especially the scene where Seneca's friends gather when they hear that Nero has condemned him to

suicide, the scene where Nero and a friend carouse in joy at the news that Seneca is dead, and the scene where Octavia bids farewell to Rome as she goes into exile. I'm sure Nero was never as handsome as Alan Titus, who also sang superbly, and wore his costumes as tho this were his everyday garb. This is a talent few American actors possess, let alone opera singers. There is real drama in this libretto and this music and it will play as well in another three hundred years as it does now. If it isn't the hit of the operatic year, there's no justice.

SATURDAY, MARCH 10, 1973

We went to 86th St. to see the Flower Festival on the first floor of Gimbel's East. They had brought flowers from Polynesia, Majorca, Vancouver, and the Caribbean, among other places, and tho a very few were the worse for wear after a week of display, most were simply breath-taking, and displayed with gorgeous artfulness. We did the cleaning to get that out of the way before the broadcast of CARMEN began. I didn't intend to miss a note as Horne was wonderful once she got past a rather hard-sounding Habanera, and I enjoyed the spoken dialogue, never done at the Met before this season. I got a good bit of needlework done as there wasn't a lot to be done for the party. I suppose all were surprised to find it such a small party but I achieved my objective of getting to talk more to Leo and Larry. I turned Ed S. right off with some of my opinions and he went to the kitchen and told Ken he could never live with or get along with me as we didn't agree on anything. I guess what touched him off was my saying I didn't like mannered actresses, tho I knew that many people and indeed most gay ones, prefer them to those who lose themselves in the part because they feel they are more basically theatrical. Perhaps I had also offended by my statement that I was not much interested in money or in moneyed people as such for my indifference to my new raise had clearly struck everybody as the greatest heresy they had ever heard, compounded by my saying I'd have taken a similar cut in exchange for the improved working conditions. For some reason Ed, like so many other people at parties, confided his lovelife to Ken, not knowing that he considers him far more of an old fart than I do and didn't really want to have him here. He said that someone wanted to come over from London and live with him, that they adored him, but he could never live with anyone as he had to feel free to do as he wished without consulting the wishes of someone else. That is a perfectly acceptable attitude to me but I do get annoyed that people like him want the best of two ireconcilable worlds. The very first time he met me he asked if I were at Russ's with anybody and when he found I was, went on about being the only one there not with somebody and this has been repeated on later occasions, yet tho this seems to bother him more than it ought at 70 or thereabouts, he admits he couldn't live with anybody. He told Ken he'd had a lover but a good friend stole him and that the lover is now dead but he doesn't hold anything against the friend. Etc., etc. When he and Lida left he reiterated that we didn't seem to agree on anything but I didn't bother to remind him that in the past we had discovered that our reading tastes--biographies and diaries--were very much alike. He apparently feels that EVERY opinion must be alike. Ken and I disagree on many of the things considered important yet live together happily year in and year out. I think compatibility of temperament is far more important than similar opinions. I hold many strong opinions but I hold them in my head, not in my heart or gut. I don't set that much store by any one of them as there are 5003 more where the first ones come from. I think it's womanish to think that if someone is critical of something one likes it's a personal matter and a big deal.

SUNDAY, MARCH 11, 1973
    We decided to go see Visconti's new movie on LUDWIG. The Times review had been terrible but it had a full house of knowing gay people, many interested in seeing the castles as we were, and the beautiful grooms with whom Ludwig caroused. They had the courage to let him go from a fantastically handsome youth (which actor Helmut Berger is) to a corpulent, dishevelled man with rotting teeth. I didn't think it was a bad movie at all.

SUNDAY, MARCH 18, 1973
    Our trip to Jamaica wasn't bad but just as we came up from the subway our bus drove off. We had a cold wait for the next one, which Ken minded more than I did. We were the last to arrive. What was once one of the children's bedrooms has been turned into a study with a lovely view over the heights and it was there that the guests were assembled. We were introduced to a couple who said they had met us before and when the evening was nearly over I remembered the occasion but up till then I faked it, finding them nice even if I'd forgotten them. As on so many previous occasions I was treated as the very much junior guest and it got under my skin as I've always felt they were not more than three or four years my senior. Today I found out that most are about 65 and what is worse, that

Pearl, and perhaps some others, think I am 45. What bothers me about this is that it makes the apparent gap between my age and Ken's so much greater than it actually is. Just why this bothers me, I'm not sure, but it does. In a year or two my hair will surely be fully gray and perhaps everybody will accept me for my right age. One after another would say tonite, "It's slipped my mind but you're young-- what's the name of the nineteenth century man with the theory about population?" and I'd say "Malthus," then they would say "See? It makes a difference to be young," or something like that until I was really a little hot under the collar. I think they mean it to be complimentary but I find it as annoying as a black must to have constant references made to his color. Especially since I am not young.

FRIDAY, MARCH 23, 1973

We had supper and then set out for Hunter College to see the Polish Mime Ballet. The campy fellow who works in the St. Luke's library with Ken had got so excited over the near nudity on the alternate bill that he thought he might join us tonite but he didn't and we soon saw why. His joining us had depended on the report of a friend who was seeing this bill and the bare bodies were a long time coming tonight, there being much costume. At first I thought I was going to hate the program as the mime seemed so simple-minded but it built up to a marvelous number where one man was too much in love with his motorcycle and another with his guitar to notice the woman trying to make them.

SATURDAY, MARCH 24, 1973

To Hunter for the dance group. The mixed bill tonite was a delight from start to finish. I went for the wrong reasons, to see the naked male beauties, but found tonite's program in a totally different league from last nite's old-fashioned and slightly amateurish program. The costumes were marvelous and so were the non-costumes when the Grecian part of DEPARTURE OF FAUST came along. My God, those young Poles are beautiful. I also saw a beauty in the audience, a great tall bearded blond Viking wearing black turtleneck and a marvelous necklace of silver that looked just fine on him since there was nothing delicate about him.

WEDNESDAY, MARCH 28, 1973

Early in the evening I had a shocking call from Ben Taylor to tell me that Stephen Wintermudd had committed suicide by jumping out a window. Later he called again to give me more details. It seems now that it happened Sunday.

Stephen had visited his father Friday evening very wrought
up, convinced he had caused the Viet Nam war, but after a
long talk seemed more rational. The boss made a date to
play squash with him on Monday and was puzzled when he
didn't show up but the psychiatrist had said that Stephen
was 25, living on his own, and his father shouldn't act too
possessive and inquisitive so tho he had repeatedly called
him and got no answer, he had not gone round to see him.
Then he went to a faculty meeting and Dr. Reed had said
something about trouble in the TC residence buildings including the suicide of a young man they couldn't even identify. Wintermudd asked for details, saying his son lived
in that building and had anybody looked in his room. They
found a depressed note in the typewriter and his shoes under the window so they had to go to the morgue and claim
the body, which he is sure is Stephen. I don't know how I'm
going to face the boss or what I'm going to say. He has always been reluctant to talk about Steve, as tho his mental
illness embarrassed him, and I have had a suspicion from
the beginning that his attitude is wrong. I don't see any
disgrace, only a tragedy, in having mental illness in the
family.

THURSDAY, MARCH 29, 1973
    Though I was virtually certain that Wintermudd would
not be in, I didn't relish going to work today. Elaine
gathered everybody in the conference room and said the boss
had asked her to explain things to us in case we heard wild
rumors. I'd like to know if this is her phraseology or his;
if his, it makes me wonder again if he is trying to put a
little too much blame on the war and too little on himself.
Mary said (tho this may be Irish gossip) that he isn't on
speaking terms with his first wife and asked his daughter
to tell her mother about Stephen's death.

SUNDAY, APRIL 1, 1973
    In the evening we tried Masterpiece Theatre's drama-
tization of THE GOLDEN BOWL but I found it as boring as I
have always found James. It is emotion analyzed and dis-
sected by someone who never felt it. There wasn't an ounce
of warm blood in the whole hour. I nearly choked on the
dust of it all and shan't listen again. Far from finding
James' analyses illuminating I found it all sounded like
padding and at times I thought it unintentionally funny.
Even an outsider mulling over the emotional choices of a
friend or acquaintance can bring a kind of passion to his
gossiping. Ken and I certainly gossip with glee, with disapproval, with all sorts of emotions, but here people

just calmly consider things with never a quickening of reaction. Ugh!

MONDAY, APRIL 9, 1973
Went over to Low Library rotunda at 11 to keep my appointment for giving blood but their equipment hadn't arrived. It was a gorgeous Spring day so I didn't mind the extra trip. I went over again about 12:30 and by that time they were set up. Eric came in while I was waiting for a table. By the time he got thru the preliminary interview (which took a long time because he had the same dreadfully slow volunteer I had had--I guess her heart was in the right place but I don't know where her head was as she took longer to copy my name and address than a retarded child just learning to write) I was on the table. He asked if it was all right for us to talk and the nurse said it was so we had a strange conversation with me flat out and looking backwards at him. For some reason they held him up till his first blood sample was tested and he joined me at the refreshment table. This upset the volunteers there since he hadn't yet given and our badinage also disturbed their literal minds. Nowadays one is not only allowed but even encouraged to eat before giving blood but I hadn't and neither was my lunch very substantial so in the middle of the afternoon I felt very faint and rather bad. When I was walking home I met Miriam Moore and our talk made me late, so that Ken was worried. While I finished my iris needlepoint, he started the pillow he traded me. I made myself stop and do an hour's work on the play, anxious as I was to finish the needlepoint. Why I felt I had to finish, I don't know, but I did and by staying up late I polished it off.

SUNDAY, APRIL 15, 1973
I got up with signs of having caught Ken's cold. We got started for Trenton at the usual time. We walked to Mother's house. There seems to be a new development, hallucinations. She talked about blue spots on her refrigerator, which Ken humored her by saying he saw though I insisted there were no spots of any kind. Then she talked about spots that kept coming on her walls and was annoyed that I couldn't see them. Shortly before we left she asked if there was a pattern in her rug (the only pattern is the one made by the multiple cigarette burns and she wasn't near that part). I do believe she was perhaps less repetitious today than Ken was. He also seemed to think that because she was old, Mother was also deaf and he operated at a high decibel level all afternoon. Mother would

respond quietly to something I said very quietly but Ken roared right on. I was in a very passive state, working on needlework as I talked. This not only kept me awake, which I have difficulty doing in that overheated apartment, but got a whale of a lot done. I took over my finished piece but Mother wasn't interested. It is very hard to find out what she is interested in. It used to be her own advancement but since her life is now static she doesn't have that to talk about. I bring up subjects in which I think she is, or ought to be, interested but they don't last a minute. I took her a clipping about the Mystic Seaport and the ship the Charles Morgan, so we had some slight talk about her father's ship, the Robert Morgan, but that didn't get us far either. I asked if her two uncles' ships were also named something Morgan and she said they weren't and then she didn't know. I didn't really care a lot but I thought it would be something to talk about. (*All three Crossley brothers, like their father before them, had been captains of sailing vessels plying the coast out of Connecticut.*) As after every visit to or from Mother, Ken went on and on about her. He picks up every inconsistency, every pretension, every lapse, most of which I am inclined to find allowable at her present age and I get so weary, so hopeful that he will drop the subject and get on to something else. I'm just not that interested in Mother and after I have put in my day with her I want to go on to other things.

MONDAY, APRIL 16, 1973
   In the middle of the night, I woke with every muscle in my body aching. I haven't been so sore all over since I had flu a few years back. Took some medication and made up my mind that I wasn't going to work. By morning I was even worse and could scarcely speak. Ruth called to say she would be our catsitter this summer, which means the cats will have a real catlover and the house will be clean. She has to get up at quarter of five in order to catch a quarter of six train from Babylon so living here will save her a lot of wear and tear.

FRIDAY, APRIL 20, 1973
   When I got home Ken and Florence were just starting the collation and stapling of the Bulletin so I helped. When I started calling the delivery crew, however, I found that all the boys seemed to be out of town for the Easter weekend. Eventually I got hold of Chris Horgan, who came and picked up the assembled papers. Only tonite did I realize that Ken no more reads the Bulletin than he does

things I write. He is always telling me some news of the house and I say, "Yes, we had an article on that in the Bulletin a month ago," but somehow I attributed it to his forgetfulness. Today, tho, I realized I had never seen him read one and that of course he never has.

SUNDAY, APRIL 22, 1973

A glorious day, the fourth in a row since Florence came. I let them go off to St. Bartholomew's together while I stayed home to nurse my cold but when I looked out the window toward the Park I thought what a crime it was to waste such a day. Still, the view alone was gorgeous, with the little new leaves making the park look green without yet hiding the beautiful skeletons of the trees as they'll later do. When Ken returned he reported that the service was rather long and the clothes on Fifth Avenue quite freakish.

MONDAY, APRIL 23, 1973

On my way to work I stopped at the bank and got the check for the European train tickets. When Ken and Florence came up to see the office and have lunch I gave Ken the check and he picked up the tickets after showing Florence the medical library at St. Luke's. After Ken left Darryl said in all seriousness, "Every time I see Mr. Jefferson I think 'He's cute'". I made no comment. When it was time to go home it was pouring so I did the unheard of (for Ken and me) and took a taxi. When I went in the door Ken rushed toward me and said, "Shall I get a sponge to dry you off?" Cool and dry I said, "You two go to church but I'm the one that gets the miracles". He felt my coat and eventually hazarded a guess at a taxi. It hadn't cost me much and was better than a set-back on my cold, which is hard enough to shake. Florence had decided that tonight was her night to get dinner by herself and though supposedly she had done much of the cooking in the morning, it still seemed to be hours before the food was brought in. Ken is nearly going mad with all the drawn-out cooking.

TUESDAY, APRIL 24, 1973

Talked to the boss about summer workers. He asked Mary and me if we could stay just a little after five to witness something. This turned out to be his will and since the lawyer was late, we stayed almost half an hour but I had told Ken I would be late meeting them at the Met when he called to remind me to stay on the bus. The lawyer said, "All you're attesting is that it's his signature and that he's of sound mind." "Oh, well, I don't know that I want

to go that far," I said. Wintermudd takes this kind of
thing wonderfully well. Ken and Florence were waiting in
the entrance hall of the museum and we headed right for
the exhibit on GOLD. It was beautifully installed and included anything in which gold figures, from costumes for
No plays to jewelry, glass cookie jars made in New England
which get their lovely red color because gold is added to
amber glass. There was a casket from Egypt which I would
have sworn was a modern piece, so wonderfully simple was
the design, but oh, those Victorian pieces. Speaking of
Victorian things, I let Ken and Florence go on to the
Costume Institute to see the Balenciaga dresses and I
tracked down a room of Alma-Tadema paintings, displayed
as VICTORIANS IN TOGAS. For sheer technique of painting,
they are breathtaking and I don't care what anybody says,
but of course they are pretty trashy, that aside. Still,
what is the content value of so much of the abstract stuff,
particularly that done in a slapdash manner? Still had all
the time I wanted for the lavish display of Balenciaga
gowns. They ranged from hideous to lovely. When we got
home there was again great delay in getting supper. There
was a television special written and directed by Ingmar
Bergman and I offered to watch it on the bedroom set, but
Ken said he and Florence would like to see it. In one
scene the husband told somebody that except during intercourse, his wife and he never seemed to caress or even
touch each other. This is a rather fashionable complaint
now about relationships. Certainly it is not true of Ken
and me. We touch, grope, stroke, hug, put arms on should-
ers and as for the husband's complaint that he and his
wife didn't communicate, I can only say that it would be
utterly impossible for two people to communicate any more
than Ken and I do.

THURSDAY, APRIL 26, 1973
    I said goodbye to Florence when I left and I must say
this has been an easier visit than we ever had before.
Perhaps it's because she's retired and perhaps it's because
we just couldn't have any political clashes. With the Watergate scandal all over the headlines and TV it would have
been impossible for her to defend Republicans at this moment in history. I decided that I was very exercised over
it and that I would devote much of my day to writing letters and postcards hither and yon to register my outrage.
To the few Republicans I respect, like Javits and Brooks
and Weicker, I was respectful, suggesting that the Republican National Committee return all their ill-gotten and
ill-used money or give it to charity then start fresh to

accumulate clean money for future campaigns. To the people involved in all the burglary, perjury, suborning of witnesses, etc. I waxed sarcastic--urging Maurice Stans not to endanger the wives of administration men by sending them around the country with their handbags full of $100 bills such as were found on the body of Mrs. Hunt when her plane crashed. I urged him to use traveler's checks for the payoffs. To all those like Agnew who have been so loud-mouthed about the necessity to end our permissive society, I urged maximum sentences and no leniency whatever for those found guilty. I asked the American Bar Association if there would be automatic disbarment for the many lawyers involved or if proceedings had to be instituted and if an outraged citizen could do it. Got lots of spleen out of my system. When I got home the house was, as Ken had said on the phone, restored to normal. We got supper out of the way early so we could read. Ken said he never saw anybody fuss with food the way Florence did, that he thought he'd go mad when she took over half an hour to wash a head of lettuce and pat each leaf dry. "I couldn't possibly live with Florence," he said. He and I both worked at catching up on magazines.

FRIDAY, APRIL 27, 1973

Had to go to work dressed for the Crawford-Francis party, downpour or no. I didn't get too wet but by the time Ken came up to join me, the rain was worse and he wore his boots. All sorts of old-timers turned up in the Dodge room for the retirement party and many were glad to see Ken. I saw Juan Carlos, the boy from computer center who did the efficiency study of our office and I found he isn't really an efficiency expert and now teaches Spanish. As I suspected, he is gay and lives with a friend and I invited him to come to dinner on May 13 when Ruth and Lee are coming. I realized all of a sudden that a whole nest of the gay men and women had gathered in one corner but none of us gave a damn what anybody thought. Ben reminded me that a bill against discrimination against homosexuals in housing, employment, etc. was up before the City Council for the third time today, this time with some chance of passing. I went home a little the worse for wear after having agreed to meet Vi tomorrow at 2:30 at the Elgin Theatre, where there is a festival of cat films for the benefit of stray cats. Ken fixed supper, which helped counteract the alcohol, but I still developed a headache. He lay down, insisting he wasn't going to stay, but I soon had to take a blanket in and cover him. Did my diary and just about kept myself out of bed long enough to listen to the news in hopes that the Watergate scandal would sweep ever nearer Nixon.

WEDNESDAY, MAY 2, 1973
    After I got in bed Ken came out of the bathroom and said, "Now don't fail me tomorrow!" which startled me. "In what way?" He had said I might drop by on my way home and pick him up at the Nurse's Residence, where he would be getting his award for having put in 400 volunteer hours. I hadn't realized that he wanted me to be there for the ceremony. The first thing he said when I woke this morning was "Now remember the address," and, realizing that it was important for me to be there, I started teasing, saying I might have to work overtime, pretending to forget the address. Ken went along with the game, producing mock distress and tears. When he's playful like that I get irresistible urges to hug and kiss him. I had a routine day and when I got to the Nurse's Residence Ken was even waiting outside the door for me to escort me in. They had a lovely tea for the volunteers and I felt as tho I were crashing somehow so refused to have tea and sandwiches as Ken tried to persuade me to do. Ken looked very handsome and I was positively suffused with love for him as we sat there and as he went up for his awards. We shopped and went home, where I laid out the stories I wanted for the next issue of the paper.

FRIDAY, MAY 4, 1973
    After work I went to the Continental Baths, as I had told Ken last night I would. GAY magazine has always said, "Expensive but worth it" and that scared me off but lately they advertised summer rates and as it happens, for a locker it costs me just 50 cents more than the Beacon Baths, $7 for 12 hours, far longer than I would ever stay. The Continental is not to be believed and I wandered around with my mind only one fourth on the sex hunt and three fourths preoccupied with trying to observe for later description to Ken and my diary. There is a lush swimming pool surrounded by benches, sofas, hanging basket chairs, greenery, etc., several large tanks of tropical fish, a counter restaurant with tables to which food can be taken, a dance floor which I didn't see used tho a small band was playing when I arrived, a sun room where a bell rings every thirty seconds, saying that is all one should take for safety's sake. I kept my glasses on till I'd had a look around, which was wise because there are some steps that I might have missed otherwise and later nearly came to grief on because I'd forgotten them. The topper, tho, was the

steam room. The entrance was small, unmarked and unprepossessing but when I got in I nearly burst out laughing. Instead of a small rectangular room as in the Men's Residence Club and the Beacon Baths, it's a veritable catacombs of black tile, with many niches of all shapes, some which might hold two people, others designed to hold more, some almost invisible because of the black tile until you see a white body in it. The floor rises and falls and the room makes a curve and I'm sure the Romans had nothing better for the purpose. The crowd seems to be younger and better-looking but I did less well than usual, perhaps for that very reason. The young who go here aren't attracted to older men as those at the Beacon are. More blacks are here too tho not seemingly in great demand. Ironically it was a black who got a bearded blond that I and almost everyone else badly wanted. The flurry of excitement caused by the beard (the same thing happens at Beacon as I seem to be far from alone in finding beards of a certain sort erotic) clinched my decision as to whether I would try one over the long Memorial Day holiday. I don't think Ken will like it and I know Mother will have a holy fit but nevertheless my mind is made up. As not every night at the Beacon has been a sexual bonanza, I can't on the basis of this one visit conclude that I will never do as well at Continental so I'll give it a few more tries. As always after a visit to the baths, I arrived home famished and exhausted from the steam. Ken had made a wonderful bread pudding with which to top off my dinner. After I finished reporting to him on my adventures, we read. LAUGH OF THE DAY: At the baths there was one water cooler filled just with red mouthwash.

SATURDAY, MAY 19, 1973
   We could think of no errands that necessitated a trip downtown so stayed in until it was time to go to Ruth's party. Caught up in the papers, which take a deal of reading with all the Watergate investigation testimony. We were dressed and ready, watching the running of the Preakness, when Ruth called to ask if we weren't coming. I had it on my calendar at 6:30 but she said it was at 5 and it was by then past 5:30. We got there about an hour late but I couldn't see that it mattered as no hors d'oeuvres were brought out for ages after we got there and dinner wasn't served for about four hours. Ruth apologized over and over about Clyde and Phil's apartment, saying it was so filthy, and she sure makes me wonder what she will say about ours when she's staying in it. I'll clean like crazy before she gets here but she's so much more the housekeeper than we

are that I'm sure she'll find dirt to be repelled by here, too. Some of the talk involved double entendres and I was less uptight about that than I sometimes am. At the table we were talking about the period when I thought I wanted to be a brick-layer and Ken said, "Can you imagine Donald with a hod on?" and I said "I beg your pardon!" which set everybody off into more explicit rendering of the joke than was necessary. Ed S when he left said again that the conversation had been wonderful and I must come and talk at one of his parties but there was sincerity rather than bitchery in it. The last time we met he got upset at my opinions; this time he was in agreement and that made all the difference.

SUNDAY, MAY 20, 1973
   We had the Times mostly read by the time we took off for the Village to see TUBSTRIP at the Brecht Theatre of the Mercer Arts Center. I had made phone reservations yesterday which had to be picked up an hour before curtain time (a euphemism since like most Off-Broadway houses it had no curtain). As we waited in the lounge we read the very interesting historical notes about the site, which is where Jenny Lind gave all but her first New York concerts the first year, where the three Booth brothers played together in JULIUS CAESAR, where Edwin was playing when John Wilkes shot Lincoln, where Jim Fisk was shot by Stokes, etc., etc. *(The age of the building caught up with it later that year and it collapsed.)* The theatre was quite nice and the set a wonderful evocation of the Continental Baths. I was so glad I had recently been there so that the hanging basket chair, the pool table, the steam room doors, and the mattresses on the floor all had meaning. I said to Ken, "They've got everything but the swimming pool" and lo and behold two actors emerged naked and wet from some kind of tub at the front of the stage. All our disappointment in CHILDREN's MASS was made up for today as we had nine naked men, eight of them quite attractive, and lots of hilarious lines. The play would be of no interest to anyone not a homosexual but it is actually very well crafted, the several plots skilfully managed, the laughs beautifully built up to, the characters nicely differentiated, and everything highly professional. It was not without its romantic as well as its bitchy and sexually far-out elements and it knew the value of the tease. I thoroughly enjoyed myself. One of the funniest scenes had the sadist handcuffing his handsome subservient lover to the pool table. Those who didn't understand tried to come to his aid and release him and the victim who had been simulating humiliation and

saying "Don't look at me" suddenly looked up and said, "You do your thing and I'll do mine. Buzz off, trick!" But in the end, when they came to release him, they found his handcuffs weren't really locked. When they expressed surprise, he said, "Of course not. Suppose there was a fire." It was sick sex but it knew it was and was made a joke of. I wouldn't have thought there could be so much fun in sadomasochism but when the masochist opened his bag and brought out one sexual accessory after another, it got hilarious. I found the whole thing a hoot and my sentimental nature was pleased when the two romantics, disappointed in their lovers for different reasons, found each other at the end.

MONDAY, MAY 21, 1973

To Madison Square Garden to see the gymnasts of the People's Republic of China meet those of the USA. Though scores were announced, there was no strong sense of "we and they" in either the competitors or the audience, which was loaded with Chinese, of course. The lady next to us didn't seem to speak English but she kept offering us candy and it was an evening of lovely amity. The athletes of each team congratulated those who did well and at the end of the evening, when there was a mixup of recordings for the floor exercises of one of the American girls, the Chinese pianist agreed to play a piece for her and she agreed to do what she could with it. She did very well indeed, got a high score, kissed the obliging pianist, and everybody loved everybody. It was hard to tell the Chinese apart because they all have black straight hair. I remember that during the war when very little hair was allowed to show below the army caps, it was hard to tell men apart. Our men were easy to distinguish because Gary Morava, for instance, had a little monk's cap of very blond hair, Jim Culhane had wavy blond hair, Jim Ivacek had brown hair, and Marshall Avener's hair was black.

FRIDAY, MAY 25, 1973

To the moustache I set out to try I yesterday added chin whiskers and today I decided to let a fringe grow along my jaw line also. I must look awful and Mimie is the wrong kind of hostess on whom to spring a beard-in-progress but she'll just have to put up with it. It occurred to me today that this may be the wrong strategy for the baths; I may attract the wrong kind of people and be very dissatisfied with the kind of sex that is offered but we'll see. A spaghetti dinner and the evening at the Ailey Dancers. The program contained numbers in the series Ailey calls The Roots of American Dance, a revival of a Katherine Dunham number and a revival of Ted Shawn's Kinetic Molpai for men. I liked both but the Shawn got funny, and I hoped consciously but doubt it, as the men did things one is accustomed to think of the Radio City Rockettes doing. They got applause but were funny now, tho whether they were in the 30's is a question.

SATURDAY, MAY 26, 1973

To Mimie's, taking the ice as usual. We were first to arrive but were soon joined by Mr. Feng, until recently Nationalist China's Ambassador to Mexico, now settling here since Mexico has recognized the People's Republic of China, Mrs. Sia, whose husband was Ambassador to Spain, a Korean young couple who were attractive and charming, and two Americans, one a woman we had met before and a young uptight Vassar girl who works on bequests for Planned Parenthood. I talked a bit to the Americans but found them less interesting than the orientals and moved. At one point Mimie called me to the kitchen and said "You know these are Nationalist Chinese?" "Yes, of course." "But you're talking about the Chinese gymnasts and how wonderful they were." "I asked if it were permissible to mention them and they said they didn't mind." "But they do. Their son is married to Chiang-Kai-Shek's niece, T.V. Soong's daughter." I was a little annoyed at the reprimand and all the more so when Ambassador Feng himself started talking about how wonderful the Shenyang Acrobats were on television and when Mimie started making all sorts of references to the mainland Chinese and talking about the very things she had put out of bounds for me. It was particularly silly since by the time she called me to the kitchen the subject had passed far beyond any aspect of China to quite different matters. I was rather disappointed to hear that Mrs. Sia, with all her advantages, devotes several evenings a week to "cards", by which she means mah jong. I had never heard what we in America speak of as mah jong "tiles" referred to as "cards" but they said they are always called that among Chinese. The People's Republic has forbidden playing of the game, but I can see that it is more than just the Puritanism that most revolutions display for the Korean gentleman, Mr. Lee, says that endurance is part of the game as it isn't unusual to continue play through the night or for several days and Mrs. Feng says in Chinatown here games can go on for a week. I suppose the revolution can't progress very far if people are tied up in weeklong card games. Mrs. Lee and her husband had a delicious sense of humor. The three of us sat cross-legged on cushions much of the time and Mimie said, "But I have chairs and a sofa". "Too far away," said Mrs. Lee and she said she had been noticing how comfortable I looked sitting cross-legged, which she wouldn't have thought would be a natural position for me. I hadn't thought of it before because I was completely comfortable.

MONDAY, MAY 28, 1973

Another rainy day but our bus trip to Madison Square Garden exposed us to very little. From the five confusing rings of my youth (and the old Madison Square Garden, I believe) they (*Ringling Bros., Barnum & Bailey's Circus*) are down to three with the end two often showing duplicate acts as they always did. It can still give one problems as to where to look. Gunther Gebel-Williams does remarkable things with tigers and is a beauty. Between tigers and torsos I would have had my money's worth. When we saw the lions and tigers in the menagerie they were sleepy and cuddling with one another, sometimes rubbing jowls in a loving way, so I wasn't so impressed with their fierceness but still it was impressive to see tigers riding horses and elephants and changing mounts. The mounts wear pads, of course, but as I said to Ken, "I wouldn't want to put a domestic cat on the back of another animal that didn't have pads." God knows when Titus takes a sudden departure from my lap if Ken goes to the kitchen I bear the marks on my legs for days. One thing the beauteous blond Gebel-Williams does is wrap a male lion around his neck and a clown promptly appeared with a fake one around his. When we got home and Ken was in the living room I called out to ask him if he was ready for the first trick and went out with Victoria draped around my neck. One can do anything with her so without further rehearsal we went out with her standing on top of my head. Ken said, "But you're supposed to take your hands away." I decided the time was not ripe for that yet.

WEDNESDAY, MAY 30, 1973

Reaction to my beard ranged from Patty's, "I like it. I mean, I'm going to like it," thru Darryl's, "I think you're going to look wonderful with it. You have just the cheekbones for it," to a very succinct conversation with Miss Thorp when she first saw it. Miss T: "You're NOT!" DV: "I AM!" Ken didn't feel too well after a painful session with the dentist so we had a light supper and took off for the Met and the Stuttgart Ballet. It was a wonderful night of ballet with three novelties, every one good in its way. In the middle one, TRACES, they kept pulling aside curtains as they went deeper into the heroine's memories and the last scene must have been danced way over in

Hoboken. The Met was really showing off the depth of its stage in that and it may have to be modified as they tour. The audience was wonderfully responsive, not like those dodos one sits among during the opera season, afflicted with arthritis of the mind and wrist.

SATURDAY, JUNE 9, 1973
     Cleaning and I decided to do the foyer closet. It was absolutely disgusting the dirt I got out of there when I took everything out. How do people like Patty and Amanda stand working on a summer place and a winter place too? Both Ken and I can think of 134 things that are more interesting to do than housework. We went down to see the new musical version of CYRANO starring Christopher Plummer. The music is totally undistinguished and sometimes obscures the words and I felt it a cheat when the orchestra played under the death scene like some sound track of a movie. Many an actor has moved audiences to tears without the emotional crutch of incidental music and I think Plummer could have too. I have never felt he had star presence before but he gave a wonderful performance in this. We got home in time to watch Secretariat win the Belmont Stakes and the Triple Crown, by some 30 lengths. There hasn't been a Triple Crown in 25 years tho there were several in the 30's and 40's and Secretariat also broke the record. He's a beautiful horse and now too valuable to be raced any more, unfortunately. I was startled when the paper said he was still a virgin and might upset the stud plans by being impotent, sterile, or even homosexual. I didn't know horses went in for this tho dogs and bulls do.

SATURDAY, JUNE 16, 1973
     To the Village to see THE FAGGOT. The show turned out to be excellent despite what I consider a most unfortunate title. There was a funny cruising-in-the-movies scene, a funny fag-hag scene, a gay bar scene leading up to the song NEW BOY IN TOWN, a good scene with Oscar Wilde and Bosie driving each other wild but yet loving each other in different ways. Composer Al Carmines played Wilde and did it so well that I could imagine him playing the part well in an extended play. Lesbians got short shrift except for a wonderful duet for Alice B. Toklas and Gertrude Stein about how ordinary things were wonderful when shared, including making out a shopping list. Both the acting and the singing were highly competent but there was nobody attractive in the cast. Fortunately a tall slender usher with wavy blond hair was a beauty and so were quite a few members of the audience. I saw one fellow with the kind of

beard I love and am trying to emulate and he was wearing
one of the fashionable body shirts which showed his excellent torso. His lover, somewhat older and less attractive
but okay, was patting his little round bottom with pride of
possession as we filed out and I wished them well. I sometimes wonder if my life would have been better had there
been all these outspoken plays, movies, and books when I
was young, so that I took earlier action on the needs of
my body instead of just mooning about. I doubt it, really,
for I don't think there was anybody at West Chester or Yale
that I wanted and could have had. Other factors that must
be remembered about my youth are that the Depression made
the whole scene very different (*Neither I nor most youth
of the time would have been able to afford to go to gay
bars, baths, or pornographic movie houses had they existed
then nor to have shelled out for magazines and books*) and
that I really wasn't very attractive in those years. I know
that doesn't deter people much these days but I couldn't
have balanced my unattractiveness with charm and gentleness
because I'm thorny to deal with and not very gentle with
people. Thank God my looks improved even if my personality
didn't soften. I think I'm still glad I was working nights
when I met Ken because for a couple of years there my weariness softened the thorns and he was able to get closer to
me than he might have been able to had I my full normal
quota of energy. If I ever begin to envy some of these
lovely young people who feel free to love openly even tho
gay, I remind myself that one never knows the end of a life
and can't see the whole picture. Also, even among the beautiful, love isn't always that smooth and the lovers who
were fondling as they went up the aisle may have different
partners next year. I do like to see two attractive lovers
together, tho.

WEDNESDAY, JUNE 20, 1973

Both Ken and I had hot, restless nights. When I went
to breakfast, he had my presents hidden under half of the
Times. I said nothing about my birthday at the office, any
more than I had last night, but Mary remembered and gave
me a breakfast bun, a Gemini bookmark, and some silly little doodad that I haven't figured out yet. The bookmark
was amusing because it said three good fields for me were
education, finance, and show business, all three of which
I touch on. The negative characteristics, however, were
wasteful and fickle, neither of which fits. When I got home
Ken said, "We're about to have company. Neil forgot his
raincoat," so I didn't change into house clothes. Neil
stayed long enough to have a drink with us and talk a while.

He said that when they left last night Vi said I had been more open than usual, meaning about being gay, and Ken said, "Well, Don's reserved." Actually I am more open in my talk than Ken but choosy as to timing, company, and words and a little forbidding about it. Neil kissed Ken goodbye last nite, for instance, whereas he and I shook hands. Neil said he once saw Nureyev at the Continental Baths and that everyone was giving him a wide berth. Afraid of rejection, I suppose. Carlson, at St. Luke's, sent home to me two copies of THE ADVOCATE, a gay paper published in San Francisco. I knew of its existence but had assumed it would deal more with the West Coast so never bought it. There's three times as much to it as GAY, which at first seemed like an advantage, but when I saw how long it took me to get thru it, I decided I couldn't take time to read it often. No word from Mother so I guess she forgot my birthday or is sick.

THURSDAY, JUNE 21, 1973

Eric came by for lunch and we had a pleasant time. His youngest son Chris, just graduating from Princeton, is rowing in the light crew at the Henley Regatta. Unlike his two brothers--one a civil rights lawyer, the other doing tree-farming or something in Alaska, Chris doesn't yet know what he wants to do. In the evening we took the bus to Lincoln Center. The clothes worn to CARMEN were wildly various but interesting---pants suits, evening dresses, very informal dresses. The opera began very badly with a deathly slow and overly stylized first act. Tho bulky women with broad behinds appeal to men in the Spanish culture, the director and Marilyn Horne herself were too inhibited by thoughts of her size and they nearly immobilized her. This worked later when, outside the bullring in a gorgeous white dress she stood stock still for ages while Don Jose' pleaded with her but in the first act it was just impossible to get into the opera. The second act picked up when the soldiers were shown stripped to the waist. I thought, "Well, it does give an idea of the heat of Seville, but I doubt if that could happen even now in Spain and certainly not then." After all, in my thirty years in New York I have had cops whistle at me for removing my shirt when rowing in Central Park, and Jenny was upbraided by a cop for wearing a halter dress at the Freelancers picnic in the park. As a matter of fact, the Supreme Court today passed strong new laws against pornography, setting as the criterion the prevailing opinion of any community, which is going to mean chaos. Las Vegas will have tits flapping in the breeze and if the Irish Catholics in New York have their way, God knows what restrictions this city will have in time.

FRIDAY, JUNE 22, 1973
There was an absolute downpour all afternoon but despite this I went to the Beacon Baths as planned. It wasn't one of my greater days at the baths as there were no real beauties, tho two borderline cases. My beard didn't wildly attract nor did it seem to put people off. Finally a tall blond entered the steam room and as I saw all jumping to attention and getting ready for action, I got there first. By the courtesy rules of the steam room he was thereafter considered basically mine tho three others got in on the peripheral action. There was so much peripheral action, in fact, that the blond could scarcely manage to get to his knees before me, which he struggled to do. I hadn't made up my mind to do as much for him as I don't think he was circumcised.

SUNDAY, JUNE 24, 1973
We rehearsed the taking of the picture of Mother's reaction when she saw my beard but I'm not sure the snapshot we got will register her real reaction. She is somewhat slow in reaction time but she eventually registered total loathing of the beard. She wouldn't kiss me and for the first half hour wouldn't look at me. When we had some buns and coffee she turned her chair sideways so she wouldn't have to face me. She said beards were filthy, etc. etc. I laughed heartily and she said, "It's not funny. It's very sad. I may cry any minute." That is almost to a word what her mother said when she first saw her with bobbed hair. Tho this reaction was stronger and more heartfelt than I expected, my only real surprise was that as the day went on she seemed to adjust to it and actually kissed me goodbye. I had put her father's picture on the coffee table to emphasize his walrus moustache but her reaction to that was slow too and eventually she said the one thing she didn't like about her father was his moustache. She wondered how I had made off with the picture and seemed to have no recollection that she had had it made, tinted, and had given it to me one Christmas. I suggested, for the hundredth time, that she take it home and put it on her dresser since it must mean more to her. This time she happily accepted tho heretofore she got huffy because it seemed I was rejecting her father. I showed her the letter from Mystic Seaport accepting her father's logbook and the picture of his ship and she accused me of stealing those also. All in all it was quite a depressing day. The repetition

was beyond belief. She knows her memory is failing her and is very distressed about it. I do wonder how much longer she can manage her own affairs. When she first asked where we were going this summer I got out the more pictorial booklets for her to look at but she just let them lie neglected on the coffee table. She must have asked fifteen times when we were going and another fifteen times where. I gave her the answer each time as tho she had never asked before but it was a sad, sad day. She said, "You seem to have all the domestic instincts I lack." Ken tried to interest her in BETTER HOMES AND GARDENS, which featured elaborate kitchens. Sotto voce I said, "She's never been interested in that," but he said, "It can't hurt her any" and he tried to force her interest. Ken has a way of badgering people who don't share his enthusiasms instead of letting them be various. If someone like Patty doesn't want to go abroad he hammers and hammers at them whereas I am inclined to let them alone on the subject. If they like to go abroad but don't care for Paris, Ken must bedevil them endlessly on the subject. I know what Mother isn't interested in (which is virtually the whole world) and don't push it. We told her about Gay Liberation Day but despite her past feminism and lesbianism, this provokes no conversation worth mentioning. Nothing does. Mother is a prime and horrible example of what happens when an egotist grows old. There is nowhere for the person themselves to go, no further chance to realize ambitions, no chance for further praise, nothing for the ego to feed on. Mother still feels superior to the "stupid" people in her house but I'd like to bet I could find fifty in that building superior to her in intellect.

SUNDAY, JULY 1, 1973

Up and at the cleaning to be ready for the arrival of guests. We weren't sure whether or not Lee's young cousin from Sweden was coming so we didn't put the leaf in the table. He came and what a gorgeous young blond dream he was. Ruth brought some dresses to leave and Lasa brought his backpack. He will stay here with Ruth while he explores New York and vicinity then move on to see a cousin in Cleveland , then bus to Yellowstone Park. As they were on their way to the ballet, we showed Ruth where things were and I introduced both of them to Mrs. Haynes, who has our extra keys. The ride down to Leo and Larry's was hot. The other guests were Ray and Joe, Ray being less argumentative this time than usual, and Clyde and Phil, revolting as ever. Clyde and Phil turn every bit of conversation sleazily toward sex and I get sick of it. During a lull in

whatever conversation I was having with somebody I heard
Philip and Ken trading sexual history. Ken was saying something to the effect that since I went to the baths, he felt
free to have affairs with people like Walt. I thought of
the long time lag between the end of Ken's fling with Walt
(never all that much) and the start of my visits to the
baths last summer and laughed to myself but really I do
loathe this kind of confession. My past love and sex life
may be detailed herein but I never respond to that sort of
thing if it starts at parties. I think it makes one seem
so old to slaver so over past delights. I returned to the
conversation I was having at once. I understand that Philip
doesn't like facial hair, which delights me. I was amused
that Ken fed my dislike by telling me many of the disgusting things Philip said about his sex life but didn't pass
on the compliments I thought I heard him paying my looks.

WEDNESDAY, JULY 11, 1973
    All the worry that I might be questioned because I
didn't look like my beardless passport picture was for
naught. They scarcely looked at me and at our baggage not
at all. A short ride with a lady taxi driver to the Hotel
Lindbergh. No doubt it's going too far to say I feel at
home in Paris but I sure do feel instantly comfortable and
the next thing to "at home". I noticed that platform shoes
are just as much in fashion as at home. They may, in fact,
even be a bit higher here but here people walk in them with
style and panache instead of tottering along. We were very
pleased with our small but spotless room when we got settled in and there was a black cat in the courtyard outside
our window, very responsive to flirtation from above. Eventually we walked out, found our little well-remembered restaurant La Grenelle is still there and that dinner is now
between $4-5. We also found the little Rue des Beaux Arts
with the hotel in which Oscar Wilde spent his last years
and died. Then the Alsace, it is now the Beaux Arts with a
high-priced menu including a beef dish Oscar Wilde, at fifteen dollars or some such Wildean price. We walked along
the Seine with the softest, sweetest breeze soothing our
nerves and ended at the Latin-Cluny, where Ken had the tastiest cheese omelette imaginable with a heavenly smell.
Our table gave us a good view of the beautiful young people
passing by and they really are beautiful. I think France is
the country where I notice pretty girls more than anywhere
else, but beautiful males also. On Rue Bonaparte I discovered a beautiful cat in a closed gallery and we made love
with the glass between us, pressing finger to curling paw
and cheek to cheek. We walked home and at Croix Rouge,

where years ago we saw a motorcyclist injured, we saw a man in white face down in the gutter. A crowd gathered, not knowing if he was epileptic, diabetic, or cardiac but a young man broke the police alarm box, put in a call, and in no more than two minutes a police ambulance was there, a young man meanwhile having cradled the victim's head. I was thoroly impressed with the people of Paris and with the police alarm system. Ken and I just can't stop raving about the beauty of the shops on all kinds of little side streets.

SATURDAY, JULY 14, 1973

Off for Versailles right after breakfast. So much restoration has been done since we went thru the apartments 12 years ago and many pieces of furniture have been added which at least suggests how it looked. One room had velvet wall covering that was a reconstruction of winter-type walls and another silk as they had in summer. I never realized the walls were given new covering every six months. I don't remember seeing before the table on which the peace pact of 1919 was signed, ending World War I. It isn't in the Hall of Mirrors, where the treaty was signed, but in an adjacent room. We couldn't find a good restaurant open on the holiday so bought a piece of pastry apiece and went back to town. I decided to try the baths again tho between the holiday and the rain I didn't expect anybody much to be there. I was right and furthermore those who were there began to leave between 7 and 7:30. This included the only one I found attractive (bearded) who went into a room I had found empty shortly before. I assumed he'd come out again and when he didn't I investigated and found the room now housed an orgy, of which he was the center. He left soon after, satisfied six ways to Sunday I should think. It was a nice establishment and this was no doubt an off nite.

WEDNESDAY, JULY 18, 1973

We walked to the Chateau d'Angers and took a picture of the street marker which says "Place du President Kennedy" tho the Place is really just a parking lot for the chateau. The gardens down in the deep moat are lovely. Except for Carcassonne, Angers is the first fortified French castle I've been in (well, Langeais, I guess) and it was mighty impressive. A lovely formal garden is in the center and on the higher of the two levels of the wall, a riotous English type garden in which two boys were working. One was cutting all the blossoms off a hedge of lavender and it smelled wonderful. In the Monoprix we bought four bananas, a chunk of French Edam, a box of sweet biscuits, and

some grapefruit juice and took it to the lovely Jardin du
Mail to eat. We counted six gardeners at work and I even
wonder how they get all the work done. We watched men
playing boules and I thought once again how some of the
youths with long lank hair look like pictures of Jacobins.
One who certainly did despite his flairs and two-tone
shoes was really a whiz at the game and repeatedly threw
his ball directly against his opponents and sent it flying. We set out for the concert by the Philharmonic Orchestra of the Loire Valley. The Stravinsky pieces showed
us that it was a very good orchestra. When we went home I
felt we had had a simply marvelous final day in Angers,
which I think is the loveliest French city I have yet been
to.

FRIDAY, JULY 20, 1973

After breakfast we went over to wait for the bus in
front of the station. A group of young men who had been in
the hotel bar came out to get in their autos and with one
was what I had thought to be a puppy with an unearthly
howl at breakfast. Its owner had grabbed it by the nape of
the neck, taken it out to the car and thrown it in roughly
and we were furious. Seeing it again, we realized it was a
fox, which didn't necessarily make us any less indignant.
Up to the town by bus and on our rounds of the town sights
which are unfortunately mostly churches. Notre Dame was
very impressive but the cathedral, tho huge, less so and
St. Radegonde not really beautiful. Being a pilgrimage
place because she is the city's patron saint, it has hundreds of little marble slabs of thanks from donors. Many
too many, in my opinion, gave thanks for the passing of
exams, which seems a trivial thing to bother a saint with.
All the churches tended to be somewhat anti-climactic after Notre Dame and Ken began his usual grumble about being too old for sightseeing. No city could be smaller and
more compact than the old part of Poitiers but perhaps
hereafter we have to stick to major cities that have bus
tours. As I told him, this dispute about how far I'm walking him has been going on for 25 years. When he was 40 he
told me I wouldn't want to do it when I was his age, when
he was fifty he said the same and so it goes. I assured
him that my legs were tired too and my foot hurt but I
never let it stop me. "Well, I'm not going to drive myself." "No, you never have, in anything. For sufficient
reward I'm willing to make a little effort." The problem
is that Poitiers has not been that rewarding , even for
me, but I cannot guarantee wonders every day and Ken simply
will not buckle down and read the brochures and material.

I told him that in Bourges he must and if I wanted to see something he could wait in a comfortable place. I hope Bourges is compact and rewarding but who can be sure before they've been to a place?

SUNDAY, JULY 22, 1973

My new system of making Ken stay put while I investigate any street he deems dubious doesn't yet work too well. When I found Rue de l'Hotel Lallement and we couldn't see anything very palatial, I told him I'd investigate and signal to him if he was to come ahead. I foun the Hotel all right and its Renaissance features were interesting but when I turned to signal Ken he had disappeared and I had to retrace my steps. When we got to the Palace of Jacques Coeur there was a bit of a wait for the last guided tour of the morning and we bought a booklet which with some effort and not much speed I translated for Ken. The palace was full of safes and coffers, being the home of a medieval financier, but the chimneys and ceilings fascinated me most. Jacques Coeur took no chances on your not knowing whose house it was as he had hearts and coquilles St. Jacques all over the place. We were shown the privy, an amenity that, as the guide explained, was lost between Jacques Coeur's early 15th C house and Versailles of the 18th, when perfume was used to cover the odor of the lack of facilities. When we got out we felt the need of a WC and the cathedral area seemed the most likely place for one. We tried one side then the other. Finally I told Ken to sit and I'd investigate the park behind the cathedral. It turned out to contain another gorgeous garden but I found no WC. When I went back again I had trouble finding Ken. Had there been a WC in the park and I'd tried to signal, I would have got nowhere. Inronically, he was sitting not 14 ft. from public toilettes. I grant they were around a corner but how he got to the steps he was sitting on without seeing the signs, I don't know. It cost 50 centimes but for both of us it was money well spent.

TUESDAY, JULY 24, 1973

People are always talking of the forum cats in Rome (most of which were rather odd-shaped) but I never heard of the cats of Pere Lachaise. To minimize later complaints from Ken about how far I had walked him I told him to sit on a bench while I searched. I found no notable graves so asked a young man who was sweeping the street if he could direct me to the tombs of Oscar Wilde and Sarah Bernhardt. We found and photographed Oscar's rather unsuitable monument, on which two young men, presumably lovers, had

scratched their names two years ago. Probably separated by
now and serves them right for such vandalistic nonsense.
Chopin's modest grave had several fresh bouquets on it as
well as three roses and a carnation simply laid before it.
We found Moliere and La Fontaine side by side, saw Cheru-
bini's, Rossini's and Colette's together and then Ken decided to sit while I went in search of Heloise and Abelard
(a rather impressive thing with effigies). We subwayed to
Le Rallye for lunch and then I sent Ken to sit in the Tuileries while I went to see about tickets to the Folies Bergere. It was a long walk to the theatre and back to my
rendezvous with Ken in the Tuileries but I enjoyed every
foot of it. I haven't been much in that section of the
city and found much of interest. It was nice, too, to
stride along without having to think of Ken dragging along
behind me or to worry about complaints tonite and at intervals thru the winter about how I insisted on walking
even when there was nothing of interest to see. I rather
doubt that there _is_ such a thing as an area of Paris that
is without interest. Most of our acquaintances, however,
would no doubt be in agreement with Ken that what I think
of as a nice walk is enuf to kill a horse. By the time I
joined Ken, reading his Tribune, I had to admit I was
tired. Surprisingly, my legs weren't particularly tired
but the rest of me was. As the Folies curtain was at 8:30
we went home for baths and a rest before dinner. Our seats
were close to the proscenium, which meant that we missed
a few things on right stage but had a much closer view of
the performers, which to me was a very fair exchange. We
had to sit thru the corny bit of getting men from the audience to put on dresses and do the can-can but the vaudeville acts that peppered the second act were superb, the
costumes gorgeous, and the theatrical effects fascinated
me. They do wonderful things to give that shallow stage
an appearance of depth. One number was set in a prison
cell with some of the male prisoners kissing and caressing
each other. In their sleep came a vision of a naked girl
and in the following dance some of the men climbed the
bars in interesting patterns. Since one girl wasn't enuf
to go around some of the men fell to loving each other
again. I wonder what all the burgers from the American
provinces thought of that.

WEDNESDAY, JULY 25, 1973

After breakfast we headed for the Rodin Museum, carrying our raincoats as usual. I thought more of the prison
number and why I liked it so much; the caresses and kisses
of the prisoners were not just sex-starved but tender and

in need of someone to love. It's amazing that we've put off the Rodin Museum so long. Tho the Hotel Biron is lovely and some of Rodin's work impressive, I don't really think it warrants a visit the first, second, or third time in Paris. We walked to the Champs Elysees by way of the Alexandre III bridge, planning to have onion soup at the Valentin. They didn't have it on the menu but a place called The Alsace did. Ken decided he would walk down to the Place de la Concorde to have a last look, probably fancying himself riding to Marie A.'s rescue while I fantasized having helped sharpen the guillotine and rattling that empty head for the crowd (me that hates the sight of blood!).

SUNDAY, JULY 29, 1973

The Lonsdale Hotel turned out to be a credit to the Duke of Bedford, who owns it. It's immaculate and our room looks out on the garden. Never have we had such a nice cheery room in London. Two letters from Ruth and two from Florence awaited us. Ruth is really taking advantage of the city, goes to the Met Mureum at least once a week. She said Wes called shortly after I left to say that Oliver Flemish died. As with George Worrell I wonder--did unhappiness make him sick or did sickness make him unhappy? Ollie always said he couldn't afford to go abroad as he had to save for his old age--then he inherited a sizable fortune from his mother and didn't live to enjoy it. Ruth said she hoped the news didn't spoil my vacation--she doesn't know that Ollie was merely a college acquaintance, not a friend. Yet I'm very sorry about Ollie--not so much that he's dead as that he enjoyed living so little. Ken napped while I did diary and listed our options for London so that Ken could make a choice. We went to dinner at the Madras Restaurant on nearby Marchmont St. I chose the Meat Ceylon, which was described as "medium Hot" while others were "hot" and "very hot". I was soon on fire. It has been some years since I was regularly subject to hiccoughs if I ate highly spiced food but tonite I started. As Ken said, "My mouth is so numb I could have dental work without an anesthetic and never feel it". When we came out we walked. I fell madly in love with London in a way I never have before. Paris always gives my spirits a lift but I don't think London ever has but tonite I was rhapsodic. The city is getting cleaned up just as Paris did tho instead of sandblasting such as removed the grime from Paris, it is a matter of paint and reconstruction (and new structures) here. Scaffolding and fresh paint are everywhere, in this Bloomsbury area at any rate. When we got back to the hotel I studied the theatre list and was shocked at how little there was worth seeing.

MONDAY, JULY 30, 1973

To the National Portrait Gallery to see the special exhibit about Richard III. Most of the portraits were copies of copies (all with the same pose of removing a ring from his finger) but one was thought to be possibly from life. None showed deformity tho two had had deformities painted over them to make them conform to the Tudor myth. For the most part Richard was exonerated of the crimes, which gladdened our pro-Richard hearts and we didn't need the defense of Richard which a London lady started to give us. We had read so many titles and old manuscripts that I didn't think I could take the regular portrait gallery on top of it but did go to the basement to see the moderns, which included so many 20th C literary and musical masters. It was interesting to see a portrait of Augustus John in moderate youth, looking much like our present-day bearded and long-haired young men as one usually sees him in old age. When we saw Maynard Kenynes in youth one could better imagine his love affair with Duncan Grant, whose portrait of Vanessa Bell impressed me.

WEDNESDAY, AUGUST 1, 1973

When people die of heart attacks in their sleep one wonders how they can have stress in a peaceful state such as sleep. But I woke this morning after a dream in which I was going berserk with rage and a moment after that Ken was uttering long angry sentences. What did we eat that made us both so choleric? My rage was not directed at Ken. One can control, or try to control, one's emotions in waking life to prevent a cerebral accident but what can one do about one's dream life? From the Bath Spa station (they don't call it just Bath but Bath Spa) we were able to get a bus right to Dorset Villa so all Ken's weeks of worry that we'd be out of town were in vain. It proved as lovely as Frommer's book said and the proprietors just as charming. We located Pulteney Bridge, which had eluded us on previous visits, and right across the street from it in the Exhibition Hall there was an exhibit of 1000 years of embroidery, sponsored by the Embroiderer's Guild (*Bath was that year celebrating its 1000th year of existence.*). Although Ken had been fascinated by the embroidery exhibit at the Met he seemed to be taking no joy in this one even tho it showed a far greater range of work. He gave it a once-over-lightly and left so I cut short my study of the exhibits and joined him. Seems he had been preoccupied with being hot (a skylight did make it warm). His imagination did seem to be fired by an exhibition at The Octagon called 1000 Years of Monarchy, so off we went, I

hoping devoutly that his reaction was more positive than
it had been to the embroidery (which had contained a few
truly modern things such as I hope to do). The exhibit,
called SOVEREIGNS, had been put together by The Royal College of Art and was superb. There were segments devoted to
The Sovereign as Warrior, The Sovereign as Ruler, The Sovereign as Builder (giving the history of each palace and
which monarchs favored it and which didn't), The Sovereign
as Patron (not much from the 20th C, if anything), The Sovereign as Lover (a very fresh touch here in including The
Duke of Buckingham's portrait in with all the royal mistresses), The Sovereign as Individual, The Sovereign as
Mortal, All the King's Men (here the point about The Duke
of Buckingham was pressed with a squib which said James I
was besotted with him, tho in general it dealt with the
powerful ministers), The Family of Sovereigns--an almost
mathematical display of different colored fluorescent
strings indicating the lines of the various royal houses
and showing how they merged in marriage. This had to be
huge and could profitably be studied for hours by a real
history buff. One of the most impertinent sections of the
exhibit was The Sovereign as Target, which was a wall with
cartoons and graffiti, historic and imaginary, lampooning
various monarchs. We sat a while on the wall of the Circus
and had a nice talk with a lady who was walking an old and
overfed dog. We heard about the bombing and discussed the
cleaning of buildings, which is giving Bath a nice yellow
color instead of grimy black.

THURSDAY, AUGUST 2, 1973
    A good breakfast in a very cheery room with nice china
and silver started the day very well. An American woman
there with her husband was dying to carry on a dialogue
beyond our "Good morning" but I resolutely ignored the
looks and the leanings our way as I was determined not to
be a party to a reverberating American conversation in the
breakfast room. Later they went out and butted into a conversation about Watergate which was going on on the sunporch. We had no wait for the bus to town and as soon as
we got there we booked for London Sunday, for Longleat tomorrow afternoon, and for the morning tour of Bath and the
afternoon trip to Lacock Abbey and Castle Combe. Our city
tour of Bath was superb. My head was so full of facts that
I would have liked to take the rest of the day to absorb
them instead of going on another tour at two. Our afternoon tour, as it turned out, did not involve much listening
or much absorption of facts. The driver simply drove us to
Lacock Abbey, a beautiful place, told us where we'd find

tea houses when we came out, and left us to our own devices. On our walk round I had seen people down by a stream so I decided to investigate while Ken sat by the entrance. I found that BBC was shooting a film of the Restoration period by the stream. Ken and I found the tea garden in King John's Hunting Lodge (just a name, I think, not a historical site, but perhaps not) and had a "set tea". This meant scones and cakes so we almost killed our appetite for dinner. We went to a restaurant I had cased earlier and it proved to be a gem. My two trout couldn't have tasted better or looked lovelier if prepared by a Frenchman. The garnish of alternate lemon and cucumber slices with decorated tomato halves at each end was beautiful. The days of dreary brussels sprouts are certainly over in England if Ainslie's is in any way typical. As our bus-driver we drew another charmer, a handsome young man with blond moustache who is bored with his job because he says the English never speak or even respond to his greetings. He said we could sit up front and talk to him or ask questions if we liked so I did tho I think there are signs on the bus saying one shouldn't. As other passengers boarded the bus and he greeted them he got no response and his eyes would twinkle at me at each instance. "Have I made my point?" he asked after a particularly unresponsive bunch. He comes from Cornwall but says there's no large city there and tho it's pretty and he visits his parents still at intervals, he came to Bath for employment and excitement. As we got out I told him to come to New York and drive busses and he'd get excitement enuf. He'd be a lovely amusing bedmate, I think. We went down to the telly lounge. Ken paid attention to the TV but I read papers and magazines. British realism always delights me (toilets <u>everywhere</u>, even in tiny villages) but still I was startled by one magazine which, in its column of sexual advice, dealt with the problem of whether or not to swallow after having oral sex with one's husband.

SUNDAY, AUGUST 5, 1973

We got our same garden-view room when we got to the Lonsdale. After a rest we set out to have dinner at Simple Simon, a gay restaurant recommended in two gay guides. I didn't know where on Old Brompton Road it was and we got out at what turned out to be the wrong end. Ken started belly-aching about "You'd think they'd be nearer an Underground stop." "They probably are but how am I to know how they number the streets in a strange city?" When we found Simple Simon I simply could not get Ken to read the menu. He stood with his back to it and said, "I'll find something I can have." That didn't seem a sure thing with things like pigeon, lamb and chicken on the menu so I asked him if he'd forgotten his glasses. He had them but wouldn't put them on and wouldn't read the menu. The place was lovely with a purple (perhaps they think it lavender) motif, and many handsome Spanish waiters. The food was extraordinary as even Ken admitted in a downbeat voice but Ken was bearing down with all his sulky weight on what should have been the joy of the meal. I couldn't ask him what his problem was as there were people in earshot but repeated reference to the distance we had walked gave me a clue. Halfway thru the meal I wondered why I was working so damned hard to be cheerful and joyous and stopped. It was the most expensive meal we've had and one of the best in taste but also one of the least enjoyable. As the wine took effect I got more self-pitying because I'm simply at the end of my tether as to how to cope with Ken's moods. Only as we neared our womb away from home, the hotel room, did Ken display the least brightness and that wasn't 1/8 of a candlepower. If he'd come out and say what's bothering him, we might be able to make some rearrangements. No effort to get him to make decisions works yet he doesn't like mine.

TUESDAY, AUGUST 7, 1973

After breakfast to the London Museum in Kensington Palace. Somehow we missed our transfer on the Underground and had to do more walking in Kensington Gardens than I planned. I suggested we sit on a bench in the park as that museum was our only objective. It was the same old story-- in about six minutes Ken wanted to move on. As my foot was hurting I didn't ask but just plunked down on a later bench. Soon Ken said, "Well, we better get on. They might close." "Close? It's only eleven o'clock in the morning. Can't you just relax?" But on we went. First we saw the special exhibit on London in the Thirties, superbly done. Those styles hold up a good bit better than those of the twenties. I think there has been some rearrangement in the other exhibits and it's all to the good. In the section on the middle ages they have objects divided into cases devoted to "Death and Disease", "Games and Pastimes", "Trade and Finance", etc. I was interested to see that the pilgrims of the middle ages attached metal badges to their hats to show where they'd been just as people formerly put hotel stickers on their luggage and now sew cloth patches on their windbreakers. I was determined that when we came out of the museum I was going to sit down in the park and not budge for an hour but when I looked out of the window of the room in which Queen Victoria was born I saw it was pouring and I thought that killed my chances to be stubborn. When we were ready to leave, tho, the sun was shining gloriously and the rest of the day was like that, sparkling and bright. I went over by the Round Pond and dug in for a stay. Even tho it was half as long as I would have liked it to be, it was four times what Ken's restlessness would normally permit. Lots of dogs were out and running like crazy--a whippet, an Afghan, and some others who really streaked around the park in great joy. The little whippet could outrun them all but if some of the pack cut corners and got near her she ran and hid trembling between her mistresses' legs as they were bigger than she and two sheep dogs in particular were very rough and tumble. Now I could sit for two hours or more and watch things like that when I've got a stimulating museum under my belt. We went to Selfridge's when I yielded to Ken's suggestion that we move on but tho we ate in their cafeteria we bought nothing. We then walked together on New and Old Bond St. before parting, I to go to the baths. The young man at the desk asked if I'd been recommended and when I said no, said I would have to be. He asked how I'd heard of the place and when I said, "Thru the Gay Guide," he said, "You've been recommended." For one's fee one got a towel, a wraparound cloth, a sheet for one's bunk. As he pulled back the curtain to show me my bunk he interrupted two people who later got together successfully in one of the two saunas. At the Beacon the sauna is not very popular and not a scene of action but there was plenty of action here. Anyone who thinks the English are not passionate has not compared the amount of panting and gasping and soul-kissing that goes on here with what goes on in America.

WEDNESDAY, AUGUST 8, 1973

Despite my shampooing my hair doesn't get as squeaky clean here as it does at home. I've noted that relatively few Britons have the lustrous hair that young Americans have nowadays. However superior the British water may be for tea, it doesn't seem to be as good for shampoos as ours. After breakfast we headed for The Banqueting Hall of Whitehall to see the show on Inigo Jones and the Stuart Court, very beautifully done. The display rather destroyed a proper perspective on the Banqueting Hall itself but one could see that it's in a superb state of preservation. I think one of my favorite items was a Van Dyck drawing of Jones in old age tho some Jones self-portraits were also good. Despite the mortality rate, some people did reach a ripe old age in those days as Jones lived to be 79 tho Van Dyck died at 42. HABEAS CORPUS proved a fine climax to our London theatre-going, much the best play we have seen. It was something like a Feydeau farce but with much cleverer lines than I have heard in the translations of the two Feydeau farces I have seen. Alec Guiness' part is one any actor ought to be willing to pay to perform. On our way home tonite we encountered a group of morris dancers (and very good ones) dancing on the sidewalk by Russell Square. They asked for no money and apparently dance for the love of it, men young and decidedly not young.

THURSDAY, AUGUST 9, 1973

On our bus ride from terminal to airport we passed Tite St., which I had searched for in vain on my London map so I could complete the Wilde pilgrimage. *(Oscar had lived there when on trial.)* As I had no idea what section of London it was in and as it seems a short street, I never found it. On our plane was a group of blond boys I took to be a British group but which turned out to be the Trinity Soccer Team of the American International Sports something or other. One must have to be blond to belong and preferably handsome for there were some real beauties among them, one glorious and knowing every trick any girl ever knew about tossing long blond locks or letting them fall over his beautiful face. Three stewards were also absolutely gorgeous, wearing no wedding rings. American men are, after all, the most beautiful because they represent all European nationalities and combinations of same. We taxied home and found two receptive cats. Mother called, in good health and good spirits, and asked if I still had "that dreadful beard". I told her the same cock-and-bull story I'd sent to the office, that I had had to shave it off to match my passport picture. She was jubilant so I'll get to shock her again.

FRIDAY, AUGUST 10, 1973

Between heat and jet-lag I woke often in the night. Everybody in the office had believed my story that I'd had to shave off my beard and was surprised to see me with one. Distributed the lavender dolls to all the girls and the onyx paper weight to Darryl. Had a talk with Wintermudd and discovered they had decided to let Darryl go. I think it will be for his own good to make a transfer and Personnel sent him today to the typing pool. He was embarrassingly rapturous about my return, saying I was the best thing that had happened to him in a long time, etc. Mary said she hadn't heard him laugh since I went away. I

reminded him that I was the same person he used to say was
mean and later, when I razzed him about something, I said,
"Now do you remember the real me?" While Ken went up to
report to Mimie and get the parts of the Sunday Times she'd
saved for us, I called Wes to give my condolences about
Oliver. Seems he was struck by a subway and lingered for
over two weeks in a coma before he died. Wesley wants to
plant a tree in his memory, which I think is a very nice
idea. I had said to Ken just last week in England that I
could think of no better memorial than a tree.

MONDAY, AUGUST 13, 1973
    Elaine called me in to give me a preview of tomorrow's
staff meeting. Seems she (and she claims Wintermudd) feels
the divided authority over the workers creates problems
and that Mary should be in charge of that while I concentrate on research. I think that will be disastrous but I
was casual about it, merely warning that Mary tended to
get sunk in details and also tended to put off teaching
people to do things because she was concerned with some
detail of the moment. What I didn't say, but what I feel
sure is true, is that she will not get on well with students.

TUESDAY, AUGUST 14, 1973
    When the subject of supervision of workers came up,
Elaine said she had spoken to both of us and we were all
in agreement that Mary should do it all. My jaw nearly
dropped as I had not really agreed but had expressed several reservations about Mary's suitability of temperament.
I think she will have trouble holding workers of quality
but suddenly today I thought, "Oh, to hell with it. Let
them have their way," so I let Elaine's statement pass by
default. I shall miss the supervision because I enjoy it
and like the student workers but there will be other advantages. The change went into effect immediately but Mary
herself said, "I'm going to have a hard time getting myself trained not to come to you," and all the girls continued to come to me all day, tho I started referring them
to Mary. As she was busy with her damned figures, I re-
lented and made decisions on their problems.

SUNDAY, AUGUST 19, 1973
    As Alice had said she wasn't coming to the station,
we took a cab up. It was not one of my happier evenings as
Ken had one of those times when he trots out all his
grievances against me, saying I had no sympathy for his
leg troubles, dragging up the night we had to walk so far

to the restaurant, etc. I am accustomed to ignoring these as it clearly embarrasses the people from whom he is trying to enlist sympathy but at the table when he said he was going to Maine tomorrow and somebody asked if I were going he snapped, "No, I don't want him along". The real killer, tho, was when, in a medley of conversations, I heard him say, "To tell the truth, I was bored on this trip." Earlier Alice and the others had protested when he said he might have to have his leg cut off and such nonsense and had said when he said he'd asked me to go alone in the future but that I didn't want to, that there were lots of compromises to be tried first. There is no answer, however, if he is bored. There was too much theatre and music talk with Pearl and Anton for me to have time to brood about it then but by the time we got home I was slipping into deep depression. As recently as yesterday, when Ken was showing his travel snaps to Catherine, he sounded as tho he had had a good time and the snaps show none of the many wonderful museum exhibits we saw, but if his impression is that he was bored, I can't fight it. Ken got very cheery and chattery when we got home but I couldn't rise to it and when the lights were turned out, tho I didn't feel as tho I were crying, the tears started running down my cheeks. Some of Ken's remarks may have been due to his drinks but I am always puzzled by how much truth is in the remarks of people who are high. It's a dramatic convention in plays that people in their cups say what they really feel but I wonder for I know that when I'm high my viewpoint is distorted and what I'm apt to feel and say is NOT as true as what I say when I'm sober. Yet when Ken says wounding things at a party, and it's quite a specialty of his, I can never quite forget them or lose the feeling that these remarks represent his real attitudes.

MONDAY, AUGUST 20, 1973

Slept very little all night. I didn't worry about it because it wasn't like my bouts of insomnia, which have no seeming cause. I had a very definite preoccupation with trying to sort out Ken's true feelings and figuring out how to handle our life from here on to make him less unhappy. I decided that I will get no theatre tickets and make no plans for anything that Ken has not very consciously agreed to. I want him specifically to say he wants to go or I shall go alone. Being alone per se doesn't bother me but for all the differences we have, I enjoy his company tho he seems not to enjoy mine very much any more. The lack of sleep gave me a bad stomach and I got up just as depressed as I went to bed. My silence probably made Ken think I was sulking, but there was no anger in my silence, only a very deep sadness that made me feel I'd burst into tears if anybody said a wrong word to me. I decided to do my diary to see if that would pin it down and keep it all from whirring in my head but I felt just as leaden when I'd done it. I wasn't up to the bright sendoff I had wanted Ken to have nor did I embark on my ten days of freedom with the brio I had intended. I didn't feel like kissing him when I left even tho he was sitting on the hassock from which he so often sees me off in the morning. I lived deep within myself all day, with nothing transpiring outside my skin except at noon. Eric had called and suggested lunch, which we had at Interchurch Center, and for that hour I came out. As Eric is a playwright I asked his opinion of the validity of remarks made when drinking. He agreed it was a long-standing stage convention, wasn't sure how it squared with life. He said he has sometimes heard himself at parties mouthing remarks showing resentment of Peg and thought, "Is that me talking?" but felt better for getting it out of his system. What I wonder is, if Peg overheard the remarks, did SHE feel better? When I returned to the office I sank back into my deep well. Went to the 55th St. to see EROTICKUS, a homosexual film as good as the last one was terrible. It was a history of the gay film, from mere physique poses in swim suits thru increasing frankness right up to a really revolting scene of fist fucking, which had a horrible fascination despite its awfulness. Whereas no participant in that last gay film we saw was at all attractive, this picture was crawling with raving beauties. I got a bonus I didn't expect when a tall attractive man sat beside me and from kneesies quickly went on to unzipping both himself and me. We couldn't copy all the activities on the screen but we copied a few. As I walked toward the bus along 57th St. I suddenly realized I was singing so the long dark day was over.

TUESDAY, AUGUST 21, 1973

Up feeling great contrast with yesterday. I washed five shirts before breakfast. I thought much and favorably about that movie last nite. The compiler of the anthology clearly favors beards, moustaches, and long blond hair as much as I do. One pool room sequence with two gorgeous, long-haired blonds getting a desire for each other as they play pool and first fantasizing each other naked on the pool table then eventually having sex on the table, was great. Unfortunately, when this sequence returned the man next to me was going into action and while I tried hard to miss nothing on the screen, it was a little difficult to concentrate considering what was going on in our laps. Today I ended all nasty and vengeful fantasies about Ken, having reached a peaceful attitude about everything. If he goes with me on trips I will have curtailed sightseeing but the pleasure of his company; if he doesn't I'll have more expensive and extended trips and there will be compensation for his absence. I really don't care which way it turns out. With or without him I'll go to Scandinavia next year; if he goes he must pick hotels, restaurants, and choose his own sight-seeing.

FRIDAY, AUGUST 24, 1973

Mary got a card from Ken today, the one with the famous sign pointing to Denmark, China, etc., Maine. He said he didn't know why anybody bothered to go to Europe when they had it all there. Whether this was sent to rub salt in my wounds or not, I don't know, but I'll give him the benefit of the doubt, since it's a standard card and I imagine that's the standard message that 8 out of 10 people write on it. Still, it set me to brooding, which I haven't done for three days. I thought what a pity it is that Ken, with his self-confessed inability to speak his positive feelings to anybody he cares for, has no trouble whatsoever expressing his negative feelings about them, preferably before an audience. Of course he's been doing this thruout our years together (at Hugh and Ed's years ago on Christmas Eve, of all times, at Merle and Eddie's, at Hank's, at Jim and Dick's, at Leo's--now who's grievance collecting?) and I have survived when the scars healed to enjoy happy months and years with him. From work I went to the Beacon Baths. I couldn't interest the only bearded one and eventually a second choice brought me to orgasm in the steam room. I had intended to stay till seven and it was then only six but my lust deflated like a balloon and I decided to head for home. As I dressed, however, somebody else handsome was ushered in, a Latin I think, and as he undressed and I dressed he kept regretting my departure and finally groped me seductively, but it was too late. I couldn't reverse course and undress again and if he had wanted orgasm from me I simply couldn't have delivered without an hour's rest, which I don't think he was prepared to grant. I really don't like to have to dress and make a journey after sex--one ought to be able to sink back in bed, entwined in each other's arms, and let the "little death" take over. I found out that grief is certainly not making me waste away for I got on the scales at the baths and weigh 176 naked, which is scandalous. Read and did needlepoint.

A GAY DIARY

SATURDAY, AUGUST 25, 1973

I investigated the new booth up by Cohan's statue, where tickets to both Broadway and Off-Broadway shows are sold at half price on the day of performance only. No list was posted but lots of people were going to the window and we certainly shall this winter. For straight shows in particular, we shouldn't ever have to pay full price as they are seldom hits any more. I went to the David Cinema, a gay film house where DUST UNTO DUST was the feature. This had been excerpted in EROTICKUS and I knew that whatever else the bill consisted of, I would have three handsome men handled in a romantic manner. The strange thing was that everything was reversed from the way it was shown in EROTICKUS--movement toward the left became movement toward the right here and heads which had been to the right in the sex scenes were now on the left. At one point a naked man went past me down the aisle. I thought the dim light was fooling me and that he must have white shorts on but he turned and came back and sure enuf he was stark naked. There was a rather sad drama being played out in the audience for two quite attractive young men were cruising the place together--that is, I think, one was cruising and his lover was hovering nearby, a bit upset by this, I think. Perhaps he likes a pas de trois but he certainly was doing none of the cruising and I think he was rather hurt when the cruiser made a contact and was followed into the men's room. The quarry came back hurriedly, apparently not liking what deal it was they had in mind. I felt sorry for the lover, who was far more attractive than anybody his friend could have found in that grubby theatre. They're such a sober lot, those audiences. Some of the dialogue in the second film was meant to be funny, and I thought it was, but my laughter sounded as out of place as it would at a funeral and nobody else picked up the jokes.

TUESDAY, AUGUST 28, 1973

At noon I really got down to work on the new play and think I am setting up the situation much better in the new version. Eric had called to say that the movie we had settled on was no longer playing and said we could just go to dinner but in the end we decided we would just as soon see PAPER MOON. We enjoyed the movie tho I was at first surprised to find it had been filmed in black and white to increase the feeling of the 30's. Afterward we went to the Peking Restaurant almost across the street. Eric virtually took the ordering out of my hands and I went along with his adventurousness in having sharks' fins plus a more orthodox chicken and green peppers dish. He had to make a phone call to straighten out something at work and was gone a long time. I was absolutely suffused with amusement as I thought how he had steam-rollered me right into the two dishes. I'm not used to that and of course wouldn't like it for long but it tickled me, particularly in view of our domestic problems with dividing decisions. Dominant all the time I wouldn't want to be but submissive much of the time I couldn't be. The mail brought another card from Ken, of very good tone. Today I thought for the first time of something that has never occurred to me before but that I must bear in mind hereafter when I get irked at Ken's party performances. It's practically a family trait. Celia and Florence both are noted for dragging out family troubles when drunk at parties and Celia is said to have been dreadfully nasty to her husband at parties in her drinking days. Ken by no means drinks as his two sisters do nor as his brother, who was plain alcoholic, did, but alcohol doesn't make any of the four siblings happy. About Laura I have never heard but four out of five indicates some kind of trait so I must try to take it less personally hereafter, tho it isn't easy. Very funny item in the Times today about a baseball game between nine homosexuals and a team from the Village Police Precinct. 1000 attended and a gay cheerleader chanted, "Let's have a G, let's have an A, let's have a Y! GAY POWER!" The police, unfortunately, trimmed the gay team, which included some lesbians at first and second base. That's one baseball game I might have liked to see. The world we now live in leaves me gasping now and then, even as it delights me.

WEDNESDAY, AUGUST 29, 1973
    This entry completes forty years of diary-keeping without a day missed. Otherwise it wasn't a notable day. At noon I got a haircut, shorter than I like, but I guess if one is going to pay two dollars one should get something cut off. I certainly like the looks of it better long but in this hot weather it does get tiresome to have wet hair on one's head as I do all the time. Why don't other people sweat so much on the scalp as I do? And why are heat records always set while Ken is up in Maine and I am here? At noon I went in the men's room and a man who had a little colored girl in there to wash her hands whisked her out as I approached the urinal. "I want to watch," she said, "I want to watch the man pee-pee." I was so helpless with laughter, leaning my head against the wall, that I could scarcely do what I went in to do.

THURSDAY, SEPTEMBER 20, 1973

Late in the afternoon the boss came in my office and asked if I'd like to get in on the pool on tonite's tennis match between 55-year-old Bobby Riggs and Billie Jean King. I put a dollar on Billie Jean. Actually I have never liked Billie Jean but I positively hate Riggs with his male chauvinism, even if a lot of it is put on for publicity like Mohammed Ali's mouthings. Privately I thought Riggs might win but I was not about to desert women's lib and the evening's match showed that a man any age is not better than a woman. Billie Jean wiped him out in three straight sets. The telecast was abominable. The camera angle was dreadful, foreshortening the court so that it looked like a ping-pong table, cutting off the baseline toward the camera so that one couldn't see whether a ball was in or out. Besides that they kept switching during the play to shots of two boys buying soda pop or a girl wearing a Billie Jean button or some other side issue. We got the brochure about the needlepoint cruise. I let Ken make the decision without pushing it and Ken thought we might as well go.

FRIDAY, SEPTEMBER 21, 1973

Wintermudd paid off his tennis bets early. At noon I worked on the play. Toward the end of the afternoon we had a dreadful little party of farewell for Darryl, who transfers to the typing pool Monday. From work I went to the Beacon Baths and had one of my very best nights. The place was jumping and after groping quite a few I found one fresh out of a shower who was very attractive and totally willing. Putting into practice some of the lessons learned from QQ Magazine, I worked on areas I've never worked before, to our mutual satisfaction. Tho others tried to crowd in the fellow, who had a bold dark moustache, gave himself totally to me but alas, the dreadful heat and steam got the best of me before I could complete things and lest I keel over in a dead faint I had to stagger out and leave a very nice body to the vultures who had been watching. Could face no further steam so went on home, where Ken had dinner on the back burner. I made a giant leap forward in sexual technique today and wish I had had instruction earlier. What I need now is stamina or a cooler room to operate in.

FRIDAY, SEPTEMBER 28, 1973

When I called Ken (I now call him because we're going to have the new bargain phone rate and want to limit outgoing calls) I found he had walked over to Third Avenue to get some cider for the casserole. I was horrified as that's a very dangerous walk these days but the pork chop-onion-apple casserole made to a Times recipe I cut out was good. At last the materials on Sweden and Norway came. I sat back in great triumph and happiness as Ken went thru them and got the Frommer book to choose hotels. I listened to what he read and agreed but left the decision entirely to him. Never thought I'd see the day.

TUESDAY, OCTOBER 2, 1973

All of us invalids got in to work after all but we were in terrible shape. At noon I fell asleep and never wrote a word on my play. Took it home even tho I knew we were going to watch a TV mystery play that had been praised for its writing in a morning review. I thought I'd write before the show but I got steadily sicker when I got home, so achy that it hurt to walk and I had to go lie down after supper. Victoria immediately snuggled up to me tho she is not normally the nurse in the family. When I woke in a sweat she was still there but the regular nurse was also on duty for Titus had deserted Ken and come to lie with me. I hated the Hawkins episode for a lot of reasons, starting with James Stewart's corny mannerisms, a scene that stole from the Watergate hearings in shameless fashion, and a level of writing far below what we'd been led to expect. We spotted the murderer and the motivation (he was a jealous homosexual) early in the game. I think they thought they were daring to have homosexuality involved but there's not much daring involved if the man is going to talk about how awful it is to be old and unloved. If they want to be daring, let them have a scene where two homosexuals still fond of each other's company after 28 years sit watching television while one does needlepoint.

WEDNESDAY, OCTOBER 10, 1973

Ken and I met at the Yangtze River for dinner. He had called me earlier to tell me that Vice-President Agnew had resigned and admitted his guilt in tax evasion to escape charges on accepting bribes. Seldom does one have the satisfaction of seeing political leaders one has long loathed revealed to the jackasses who voted for them as even worse than one kept screaming they were. But I fear that the upshot is that unthinking people (of whom we have too many or Nixon and Agnew would never be in office) will just grow cynical about all politicians. It has been the brunt of the Nixon and Republican defense that all parties behave as they do, tho they can never give instances when pressed, and many people believe this. I decidedly do not and have

respect for many Congressmen, Senators, Governors, etc. We
both had great anticipation of ANNA BOLENA but unfortunately it wasn't one of those electric nights in the City
Opera. The confrontation scene between Jane Seymour and
Anna was good and the final aria was stunningly sung by
Beverly Sills tho for a bar or two she was slightly under
pitch. I think it's the best of the three Tudor operas but
somehow it didn't make its mark with us tonite nor with
most of the audience.

WEDNESDAY, OCTOBER 24, 1973
　　When I called Ken he said the cruise brochure had
come. Alice called and said she had pretty much decided to
go with us. She had felt she should get Thanksgiving dinner for Michael but she says he's reached a point in his
analysis where he blames everything on his mother so to
hell with him.

FRIDAY, OCTOBER 26, 1973
　　As I filed receipts today I noticed that one woman
had increased her gift from $50 to $75 but the acknowledge-
ment letter took no note of this fact. I sent Wintermudd a
memo suggesting we should have a letter that showed appreciation of the increase and he bought the idea at once as
he usually does buy my ideas. Mary protested a bit as she
thought it meant more work for her. I went to Beacon Baths
after work and since I had had perhaps my best time ever
there on the last visit, I was pretty sure this trip would
be a bomb. It wasn't, in the end, but for a long time it
looked as tho it might be. The fact that the President held
a press conference at seven didn't help any as everybody
gathered around the television set in their towels and
sneered and snickered as the President lamely excused himself and cohorts, tried feeble jokes, and lashed out at
television commentators. Then, when that was over and people resumed cruising, the steam was off in the steam room.
A dozen or more people went in and out of the steam room
in disappointment but nobody got around to complaining till
I went to one of the Japanese attendants and reported that
it wasn't working. With some difficulty he fixed it. I
found myself sitting next to a very attractive man who
seemed standoffish until the other occupants left the steam
room and then suddenly he not only made himself available
to me but made the first move. Again I didn't finish the
job, not because of physical discomfort this time but because people came in and the other guy wasn't quite unin-
hibited enough for a public performance. One of the most
attractive men there was one from whom I kept my distance

because he never took a shower and seemed to be looking for someone who finds strong body odor attractive, which lets me out. I love the smell and taste of newly washed skin but male musk has no allure for me whatsoever. It does amaze me that there is so seldom anybody delicate there. There were several at Continental Baths but here they are almost all very solid men--some much too solid. Giants abound, for some strange reason, and tho not fat and in good proportion to their height, they are not my cup of tea. Men of average height are more my dish these days. When I got home I found Ken had almost finished his eyeglass case in bargello. It's very comforting to have him to come home to and he's very nice about my nights out. I don't rub his nose in the details of my activities tho I report on sights seen and sounds heard.

SATURDAY, OCTOBER 27, 1973

To Times Square for our first visit to the Minskoff Theatre. I liked it much better than the equally new Uris for even in the last row, where we sat, one feels a connection with the doings on stage as one does not at the gigantic Uris. Tho the decors is on the austere side in the modern fashion, I found it both attractive and comfortable. As for the pseudo-revival of IRENE, it was in some parts much better than NO, NO, NANETTE and in other parts much worse. I was never bored but could never join in the slightest degree in the laughter that rocked the house and was simply appalled at Patsy Kelly. Nothing in the show bore any resemblance to human behavior and Kelly carried this grotesquerie well outside what I would consider its limits. If George Irving did a double-take, Kelly had to do an octuple take, and she had business with her feet that seemed to convulse the audience but was past my understanding as it went on and on and on and struck me as just assinine. She can never settle for making an effect but must endlessly repeat. It was nice to hear the house laugh and interesting to see them respond to every hoary device the theatre ever tried on a vaudeville stage. If Debbie Reynolds entered in a white dress they applauded, tho it is scarcely a feat to enter in a white dress and if Kelly essayed a very lousy and arthritic Irish jig they applauded even tho the chorus had done a beautifully crisp and clean version not long before. What was curious, tho not annoying like the flagrant overplaying (to which Debbie Reynolds was by no means immune) was the constant confusion of interior and exterior scenes. Very likely this is a result of the furious revision done on the pre-Broadway tour but there was a chorus of girls with parasols in a Long Island living room that must have been a garden scene, then there was a scene obviously meant originally to have been an interior scene with Patsy Kelly in a rocking chair out on 9th Avenue, and later in a garden scene there was a plush bench where obviously cast iron was called for. Despite the patching of scores, the music was not a strong factor in the end and was not well-delivered except by the chorus, a mass of singing and dancing talent. But just as I enjoyed the FOLIES BERGERE because I could see so much of the works in the wings, so I enjoyed seeing all the conventions of outmoded musical theatre trotted out and shown to be still workable with the majority of the crowd. There were thousands of old ladies and virtually no young people and I can only say that my figurative hat is off to the superior tastes of the young. It was amusing when we came home tonite because within three minutes two totally different opinions of my beard were offered. Little Mrs. Howard, the elegant policeman's widow, said, "I didn't recognize you. You've ruined yourself with that. You're too handsome for that." Then we stopped off to pick up the mail and our neighbors the Hayneses came up in the elevator with us. Mrs. Haynes said, "I've been meaning to tell you how handsome and distinguished you look with that beard. You're beautiful." A perfect example of why one has to make up his own mind about these things and why I take neither criticism nor praise too much to heart. When we were in the needlework department of Macy's today I looked at the example of the Flowers and Wheat pillow I just finished and groaned. The bullion knots and French knots were so superior to mine. Ken said mine was lovely and that nobody was ever going to put the two side by side and compare them but I said, "That's true but I know mine is dreadful by comparison. I can see what's wrong. It was a good enuf learning effort but not good." He mentioned how people at the party had praised it but I asked him what he expected guests to say and I don't care what they say. Mother laps up praise but if I don't agree with it it gives me no solace. It's nice, for instance, to have Eric, Anton, and Pearl praise my play but I knew it was damned good before they ever told me so. I also know the current play stinks.

MONDAY, OCTOBER 29, 1973

One of the tasks I left Ken with today was writing for the Scandinavian hotel reservations but somehow he got all mixed up. He had already picked one in Oslo and one in Stockholm and only Bergen remained to be selected but he looked in the Fodor book instead of the Frommer. When he said on the phone that he was all confused I told him we had marked the Frommer but he just unplugs the thinking part of his brain. He wouldn't write the letters till I had checked the dates, the hotels, etc. Decisions just don't come easy to him but with a little push he's accepting the responsibility.

THURSDAY, NOVEMBER 1, 1973
　　As I dressed this morning I told Ken that on election day I would have to leave him after a movie and not to ask me why. "Why?" he said immediately, knowing that I meant that I would be shopping for his birthday presents. "Well, this black mafia leader wants to set me up in an apartment and I have to go pick out a penthouse." He is just as good at improvisation as I am, and sometimes better, and came in looking wistful. "I hope you'll drop by to see me and the cats sometimes. We'll miss you." We went on and on for five minutes until I was overcome with laughter and affection and smothered him with kisses. Nobody, but nobody, has ever been able to keep up with me, and even best me, at these silly scenes, like Ken. I had my Bulletin meeting at nite, of course, and failed of my objective to put the paper to bed in one meeting as things were not in that good a shape. A new, lovely black lady came to make a trial visit at Pat's behest. Unfortunately she saw one of the worst meetings as Eleonore was wound up with complaints which she was loudly splattering around the room. She got so on my nerves that my ideas of resigning the editorship came to the fore again but I looked around the table at Pat, Lisa, Chris, and the new lady, Vi, and thought how nice they were to work with. Ken had enjoined me to get a catsitter, preferably Chris, but I forgot all about it till we were in the elevator and Chris was getting out. So I asked Lisa, who said it was about time she looked after my little darlings.

FRIDAY, NOVEMBER 2, 1973
　　I had expected that perhaps the four Latins would be late but none were. Rafael's George had the same sweetness of nature that Rafael has but both Ken and I were surprised at his lack of physical attractiveness considering how attractive Rafael is. The Spanish-speaking naturally clustered together but never truly became an enclave as they blended with the rest of us. Spanish is a very attractive language and though I don't know enough South Americans to know how I feel about them I do like Cubans and Mexicans so much. Rafael offered to drive us to the boat when we go on the cruise, which is typical of their generosity and willingness to make effort for friends. When I told Ken as

we did the dishes and held the party post-mortem, he was
horrified. I'm not sure whether he fears this would put
him under obligation so that he might have to make a little effort for somebody or not but he rejects this kind of
thing with a vehemence that seems to me uncalled-for. He
has been just as vehement about not having anybody see us
off tho Neil and Vi are seeing a male couple off on the
same boat the week before we go and are looking forward to
it. Ken just doesn't like to be involved in other lives,
which sometimes strikes me as too bad and likely to become
very much too bad if one of us is someday left alone. At
the start of the party Ken got a call from the St. Luke's
Director of Volunteers, asking him to come in at quarter
of seven Monday to help feed patients because there is a
strike at the hospital. I pointed out that Ruth told us
there is no cross-town bus that early and he would not only have to take a taxi but would be out on these dangerous
streets at an unGodly hour. He is so inclined to say "Yes"
when he should say "No" and vice-versa. We didn't get to
bed till after one and then Ken had to keep shutting himself up, as usual, while I chuckled. One of the nice things
about preparing for and cleaning up after a party is using
the various dishes and objects we've bought as souvenirs
in different parts of the world. Tonite, for instance, I
used only Spanish, Portuguese and Mexican tiles, Spanish
serving dishes as far as we could. All are lovely in themselves, tho we never spend much money, and resonate with
memories.

WEDNESDAY, NOVEMBER 7, 1973
    The election didn't turn out to my taste. Nobody rec-
ommended by the New York Times got in, which should show
Nixon how silly is his argument that the media are control-
ling public opinion and turning people against him. When I
called Ken he said we'd had a letter from Leisure Forum
saying that unfortunately not enough people had signed up
for the needlepoint cruise. He said we could still go on
the regular cruise and we decided we would. I had left
Ken's shoes for heeling in the morning and picked them up
on the way home. He had put in a long day at the hospital,
working on lunch this time instead of breakfast. Now the
strikers are cutting off the food supply and the hospital
isn't sure it can function if the strike continues for a
second week. Having had a taste of what is involved in
getting the trays ready for so many patients with different dietary needs, Ken says, "Those people do work hard,
believe me." Right after supper we had a call from Alice
who had, of course, got the same letter. She had never

been too sure she'd take the needlepoint lessons anyway as she didn't realize there was more than one stitch for needlepoint. She had read the play and said she intended just to start it but couldn't put it down. She could certainly put the new one down. I feel I'm making vast improvements, tho.

SUNDAY, NOVEMBER 11, 1973

Having heard that the newstand on the corner had reopened I went there for the Times today and told the man it was good to have him back. I read it fast to get as much done as possible before Mother got here. As time went on I began to fear that she'd been in an accident and I realized I didn't have the full names or phone numbers of her friends. Tho I thought it rather pointless to call her up as she was either in an accident or had had a stroke and couldn't answer the phone, I called. She was home, confused at first as to who I was and under the impression that it was Saturday and that she was to come tomorrow. She said she'd be right over but I said we couldn't wait dinner and it was too late. She began to cry and suddenly, hearing that, so did I. Ken, to whom any show of emotion is anathema, flew into a towering rage. He said, "She's just doing that to play on your sympathy. If you're going to react that way, the next five years are going to be great!" I was afraid she'd hear him as he was roaring but she was too distraught to hear him and I don't think she knew I was crying. I told her she could come over on the 25th tho we'd be just back and might have no food in the house and I told her I'd call her and remind her. I had hardly hung up after reassuring her that we forgot things too when she called back to ask "The 25th of What?". She then said that this sort of thing frightened her terribly, which I understood, and she cried again but by that time I had hold of myself. While I had her on the phone I got the numbers of Mrs. Sullivan and Mrs. Goldberg, the two friends I've heard her mention. When Ken berated me for my tears I said it was just that I don't think I ever knew her to cry about anything connected with me--over her tangled financial and emotional affairs, yes, but not in the last thirty years or so. It occurred to me, and I said so, that I didn't imagine anybody in his family had ever shed a tear and no instance was forthcoming from his memory. I did, of course, see him cry once and that was shattering to me because a remark of mine had caused it. Even as I was torn between a rush of feeling for Mother's disappointment and fear and a cringing from Ken's anger, it occurred to me (and not for the first time) that hard as it might be to grow old alone,

I think I would prefer it to doing so under Ken's scrutiny.
I dread faltering in his company or becoming in any major
way a nuisance to him for I know what that would mean. I
wrote Mother a letter that I hope was consoling but I doubt
that it was. I suggested that perhaps, despite cinders from
the railroad, she should get more fresh air into the apartment as I noticed NYU is treating those with memory problems with doses of extra oxygen.

TUESDAY, NOVEMBER 13, 1973
    Mary was a bit resentful that we hadn't been invited
to the opening of Thorndike Hall so I said she and I could
take a tour on our own. She suggested this afternoon but I
said I'd rather let Ken have his day of glory, he having
an invitation, and that we'd go some other day. Later, however, a notice came around that employees could attend
Open House between 3:15 and 4:15. Ken came up early enough
to have lunch with me and we were joined by Margaret, the
lovely Irish girl in the Controller's Office. I started
out for the Open House with Mary and Terry. We started on
the 11th floor, got our first sherry there, and worked our
way down. The delicate eggshell Venetian blinds are going
to make maintenance people curse; they may be attractive
in their fragility but the one who designed them never
washed any. They have all kinds of things for the handicapped--rest rooms accommodating wheelchairs, rails for
spastics and other cripples, mirrors thru which students
can observe methods of teaching, tv studios and audiology
equipment. On one of the lower floors they had guides to
show what they were doing and whom should I see but the
gorgeous Viking I have been smitten with in the cafeteria.
I rushed right over to hear him explain his work with emotionally disturbed boys and as he answered questions I admired his long golden hair, moustache, lashes, beard,
teeth, eyes, marvelous way of holding his 6'4", bravery in
wearing several rings and bracelet but I had noted all
this before. What was new was learning that he was intelligent, articulate, and tender. I fell madly in love. One of
his rings is a broad gold band on the ring finger of his
right hand and I hope that whether he sleeps with males,
females, or both, he never spends a night alone for I
wouldn't want him to waste that beauty of body and spirit.
I went back to the office totally moonstruck (the sherry
no doubt helping) and just couldn't concentrate on my work.
I really wouldn't want an affair with him as a young beauty
like that should sleep only with other young beauties; I
am content just to look at him and be joyous that he's in
the world.

SATURDAY, NOVEMBER 17, 1973

When we got to our cabin we found it occupied by a man with vast amounts of luggage. He was the golf pro of the ship and they'd already told him he had to move but the project was about to defeat him. They piled his bags and boxes in the corridor and we settled in. We went in search of Alice but found another woman in her room. She explained that Alice had been there but that on discovering she was sharing she had gone to transfer. We set about exploring the Rotterdam and even my legs grew exhausted from climbing stairs and walking long decks. Alice discovered us on the promenade deck as we watched the ship pull out. At 5:30 we went to the cocktail party of the Chess Forum, of which we have been made a part since the needlepoint group fell thru. There were drinks and hors d'oeuvres and the young chess masters introduced themselves and said that at ten one would play simultaneous games with all participants. Table assignment cards had been left in our cabin but Alice had none and had to stand in a long line to get one. Eventually she joined us at our round table for seven, which had as its other occupants only two North Carolina chess fans of very disparate age. They are nice enuf but of course we can't talk chess. Dinner was marvelous but I was distressed that Alice and Ken, who had been saying how famished they were, ate half or less of their entree. I simply cannot order food and not finish it.

TUESDAY, NOVEMBER 20, 1973

At nine we disembarked and got into a waiting limousine for our tour of the island. We had a nice driver and guide but a bad carload of people. One man was the type who has to show his knowledge by telling things before the guide can. I believe in listening and letting the guide talk. When we got to one of the forts I got out of my front seat and Ken, in the back, yelled at me peremptorily to open the door for the lady. As the chauffeur was on his way around to do it, I ignored Ken and when I got him alone said, "When you get your invitation to Buckingham Palace, you better learn to let servants do the work they are paid for and take pride in." He got the message and when we pulled up at the gardens where the flamingo show is held he bided his time quietly till the chauffeur got around. The obedience of the flamingo drill team was impressive. We asked to be let out in town rather than being jitneyed back to the boat and we shopped for straw bags along Bay St. Going into the dark of the stores and out into the blaze of the street intensified my headache. I really loathe the sun when it's that intense. When we went to dinner we found it was "Dutch Treat" with Dutch paper hats for the men and pretty cloth ones for the women, many of whom wore theirs for the rest of the evening. The evening entertainment was a Dutch Fair, with booths of dart games, ring the bottle, knock down the cans, etc.

THURSDAY, NOVEMBER 22, 1973

From the moment I set foot on Bermuda I liked it better than Nassau. The people are more soignée and seem far more educated. As the Bermuda laws permit only four passengers in a limousine, we enlisted as our fourth a nice woman with whom Alice had had tea. Our driver was a handsome and dignified black, Mr. Robinson. He gave us a nice running commentary as we drove around and touched down at four sights. Mr. Robinson dropped us on the main street and we split up to shop. Ken and I couldn't find much to buy and didn't feel the shopping was so great but as the overladen tourists staggered back to the tender it was clear not many agreed with us. Such comparison of purchases. At ten we went to the theatre and I continued my needlepoint as we waited for the start of the Indonesian Crew Show. Some of the ladies to whom I've talked about needlepoint asked why I wasn't at the get-together of needlepointers this afternoon. It sounds as tho it was rather a good exchange of pointers but I was too tired at that point. We had films of Indonesia before the live show. The latter was excellent except that the Javanese dance went on too long, as it always seems to do to me. The men who did it had superb hand movements, tho, as did those who in other dances played the ladies. The Indonesian Ambassador to the United States is on board and his wife took a bow because it was her birthday. Ken and I went to the buffet and were there joined by Sammy, who's an awfully friendly young man and told us how intensely he takes up everything from golf thru motorcycle racing and now chess. Like so many Southerners he at first sounds ignorant with his "ain't" and "git me" but he's been to college and has wonderful insight into himself and very definite goals. He said the Bermuda Chess Club sent the chess group a telegram inviting them to be their guests then came and took them to a member's house, where they played some matches. I rather dreaded sitting at a table with chess players but Sam and Karl have been delightful.

FRIDAY, NOVEMBER 23, 1973

After lunch we went to the theatre to see CABARET. It was neither the original play, I AM A CAMERA, nor was it the musical and the changes didn't in any way improve it. The romance with Sally Bowles was kept from the musical with the addition of a triangular affair with a Baron who slept with both Sally and the male lead. We sat in the rear of the theatre as Alice thought she might want to leave and the noise and chatter back there were terrific. Those people have lost the habit of theatre-going and think one gabbles away in theatres as one does at home while tv is on. We went up in the smoking room and both Alice and I did needlework. Deserted as usual, the smoking room was a nice quiet place till the Ritz Carlton Room opened and then people began to pass thru. A woman passing behind me said of the needlepoint, "Isn't it beautiful?" which led to a man in her party making the only snotty remark that has been made in earshot. "My daughter does that. I don't." Alice was more outraged than I, for I expected somewhat more sniggering than there has been. Soon several ladies gathered around, including the lady who coordinated the needlepoint session yesterday. The coordinator said I was already bolder and more adventurous in design and color than many of the ladies. Her husband, who brings her back designs and materials from business trips, was also very nice. Alice said, after the needlepoint leader left, "You're so much more tolerant of these people than I am. I don't see anything in her at all and don't much like her." How demanding and critical can one be of somebody who merely stops by to pass a compliment and ends by giving some usable pointers? When it comes to longer, more intimate relationships, nobody could be more demanding but casual encounters don't call for acceptance or rejection. I wouldn't want this cruise to be a day shorter or a day longer. Food would start to pall tomorrow and it was only because I could start austerity tomorrow that I could make a pig of myself again today.

TUESDAY, NOVEMBER 27, 1973
    Last evening I seemed to be recovered from my balance problems but when I got up in the night to go to the bathroom I was rocking again. From work I went downtown to the mobile discount ticket booth in Duffy Square and got myself a $6.95 ticket to THE CONTRACTOR for $3.98. They even had half price tickets to RIGOLETTO at the Met and were selling tickets to about twenty shows. A marvelous idea. THE CONTRACTOR was playing in a new Off-Broadway theatre that is very nice. It's a three-quarters round theatre, which is a form very fashionable these days but not my favorite. As for THE CONTRACTOR, it was well that Ken didn't go for I don't think he'd have liked it but I thought it the best

of the David Storey plays. I agreed with the young man next to me that it had its tediums but to me it had its fascinations too for the putting up and taking down of a tent to be used as a pavilion for the wedding of the tent contractor's daughter is quite a business. Having the actors often within a foot of you certainly shows up any phoniness among the actors but there was none tonite. The workmen looked and behaved like workmen. I didn't go out for intermission and between the second and third acts the prop people gave almost as good a show as the play as they converted a tent ready for a wedding to a tent that was an absolute mess of crumpled napkins and empty champagne bottles after the wedding. When I got home Ken had all sorts of news items saved up for me.

THURSDAY, DECEMBER 6, 1973
   As I went down the hall I saw the poster advertising the Marshall McLuhan lecture and realized I had left my ticket home. Fortunately Terry had an extra so at four I went. McLuhan's talk was dazzling and stimulating and the ideas came along so fast that one didn't have time to examine any of them. When I later did, a lot of them were more clever than true. He had said, for instance, that North Americans were the only people who went outside to be alone and inside to be with people. That doesn't hold up under examination nor do several of his other statements tho some do. I made notes during the day on stories for the December issue of the Bulletin and since only Lisa, Pat, and Vi attended we had a peaceful, productive meeting. Watched the fourth chapter of NANA, once more convinced that the girl who plays the title role is a piece of dreadful miscasting. With all the nasty things the character says and does, she should at least be voluptuous if her attraction for so many men is to be believable. Unfortunately this girl, beautiful in her way, has the wrong physiognomy and body. Her looks are as sharp as her words. Whatever the actual appearance of Mme. de Pompadour and Mme. DuBarry might have been, one could not succeed with a play about them if you put a cool, angular actress in the role of DuBarry and a soft round one in the role of Pompadour. It has to be the other way around. To a certain extent your face and body define you in life and in drama they most certainly do.

SATURDAY, DECEMBER 8, 1973
   An early start downtown, with Ken worried because I refused to wear a topcoat. As it was, with a cotton turtle neck shirt and a tweed jacket, I was nearly overcome in

the stores and busses where I spent most of my time. I admit that on the street I had to keep moving briskly but I prefer it that way. Altman's has lovely windows based on children's stories--Goldilocks, The Emperor's Nightingale, The Wizard of Oz, Raggedy Ann, The Old Woman in the Shoe, and another that escapes me. Lord and Taylor's was all the NUTCRACKER BALLET and gorgeous. Those Nutcracker windows were so lovely they took my breath away and lifted my spirits. Ken was home when I got there after a suffocating ride. I was just in time to hear L'ITALIANA IN ALGERI, which proved to be a delicious novelty and a marvelous showcase for the phenomenal talents of Marilyn Horne. Victoria usurped my lap so long today that Titus got jealous. His jealousy is never an angry, hissing one like hers. He simply keeps rubbing back and forth against me to remind me that I have a second cat. At one point such a dreadful sneeze escaped me that Victoria flew off my lap but in no time she was back. Then Titus jumped up on the arm of the chair and tho one realized that the smartest cat would not be that smart, he sneezed. Of course his little sneeze didn't make her turn a hair but it amused Ken and me. Finally she left and he quickly came up and settled for a long stay.

THURSDAY, DECEMBER 13, 1973
    Mother called, claiming not to have received my Christmas list. She said she was sure my list wouldn't amount to much as I had never been one to have many wants. That has always somehow impressed her as she mentions so often how little I ever asked for as a child. That's partly because I was a realist, knowing there was no hope and that Mother couldn't afford it, and partly because I still simply do not crave so many of the things other people seem to want. The Bulletin meeting was great. I thought a month or so ago that I was out of ideas but when we're having a meeting somebody will mention something and I'll say, "Now there's a story. Why don't you pursue it?" and their eyes light up with the realization that it is, indeed, a story. We were just talking about people who walk to work downtown from here and had chatted on for two or three minutes before I saw the obvious. Whoever brings the subject up gets the assignment even tho they didn't see it as a story when they first mentioned it.

FRIDAY, DECEMBER 14, 1973
    Went right from work to Leo's, where I met Ruth and Lee primping in the lobby. The only other guests were a couple we had not met before, Hank and Tony. Hank is

retired and never said much but Tony was talkative and pleasant. He's another who has to live with his mother. I do wonder sometimes if the chemical factors which make so many mothers of gays long-lived have also something to do with the hormonal balance in their sons. There was lots of seasonal decoration at Leo and Larry's. Leo and Larry showed slides of their trip to Portugal, Morocco and Spain and I was so entranced that I said we must return as soon as we'd been to Egypt but on the way home I found that Ken is not interested. Before closing I must mention something I'm almost embarrassed to record. This morning I had some faint hints of prostate trouble and was disappointed because it is less than two months since I went to the doctor and usually I have three good months before trouble recurs. I remembered that in THE MASSAGE BOOK, which I have been reading at bedtime while Ken listens to the news, there is a chapter on "zone therapy". I have been very scornful of this supposedly oriental belief that the parts of the body have nerve ends in the feet which, if massaged, can assuage trouble in liver, spleen, or whatever. I don't doubt that the ancient East possesses much wisdom which we in the West lack but I don't include the theory of zone therapy in it. However, I remembered that the chart of the feet showed an area just under the inside ankle and an area at the rear tendon that had to do with the prostate so I just idly massaged it. It hurt but my prostate annoyance disappeared so fast that my jaw must have dropped. I can't believe it was anything but coincidence and yet, when I thought about it, the Western treatment for chronic prostatitis is, after all, half a minute's massage of the prostate itself.

TUESDAY, DECEMBER 18, 1973

I was sorry to hear that the crystal coating that made the twigs of trees so lovely when I walked down Broadway last night was too heavy for many trees to bear and the damage to trees is dreadful all over. Though it took him four hours to get to work, Eric came over to lunch about twenty minutes after he finally arrived. We ate before getting down to my criticism of his play. He said he gave it to Peg to read this last weekend and she said, "I don't believe a word of it." I said I didn't either but tried to show him at least how to bring the missing characters on stage and how to deepen them and make them more sympathetic. I don't like the material but I didn't emphasize my distaste for it and concentrated on craft. When I got home I found our rug kits had arrived. Though I didn't promise to go far with it until I finished some of my other projects, I said I'd start tonight with Ken so we could get the directions straight. By learning rug hooking at the same time I thought we could prevent each other having unnecessary struggles and I think we did. I then went back to my cross-stitching as we had a recommended TV play to watch. The play, I HEARD THE OWL CALL MY NAME, proved as good as the reviewers said, with much good material about the Canadian Indians, among whom a priest worked and died. It cheated only in making almost all deaths quick and unmessy. Would that they were.

THURSDAY, DECEMBER 20, 1973
        Before the morning had progressed very far Roger came in to the kitchen area for coffee and Mary beckoned me out, asking me to give her five minutes alone with him. I had no work with me so went to Elaine's office to see if she had something for me to do. Before I knew it, Dr. W. came in and said, "You people have got to stop projecting. Mr. Vining, as a man of the theatre, should learn to cover his tones." He was smiling but I was downcast for a while as I do hate excessively loud people and so love being quiet in Europe. But as my voice comes from the diaphragm and does have a projecting quality, I get carried away more often than I wish. Sometimes in Horace Mann and other auditoriums (as on the Rotterdam) when I see people leaning so totally on microphones, I have a sense of power in that I know I could fill the auditorium and be easily heard without amplification (electronic, at any rate, for my chest gives amplification). But it's more my ideal to speak only as loudly as need be and I too often fall short of that ideal, partly due to habits created by the necessity of penetrating the eternal radio plus Ken's inattention and deafness. What was said to Roger I don't know but nothing that dampened our noon office party at the buffet of the Faculty Club. I asked Millie how Darryl was doing in the typing pool and asked if he was developing. "What does that mean?" said Wintermudd,"Do you mean is he maturing?" "No, that's emotional. I'm speaking of his mind and enlarging his abilities." "All I know," said Millie,"is that he wants to follow in your footsteps in everything. All he wants to be is you." "Why, you're a father image," said Dr. W. I'm not sure what kind of image I am to him but I know it's good for Darryl that he moved on. When I got home I found we had received an answer from the gay guest house in London, which gave us a choice of that or the Lonsdale. I said Ken must choose and eventually he decided that since the map showed a subway stop nearby, we might as well try the new place. The theatre was nearly deserted and when it did

fill up a bit it was clear that producer and actors had rounded up friends. Maureen Stapleton was there, among others. FIND YOUR WAY HOME has even less place on Broadway than my play. The husband torn between wife and male lover wasn't a well-written part and the actor cast in it looked like nobody so much as Adolf Hitler. Michael Moriarty, as the gay boy, however, was superb. The role is totally different from the intelligent pitcher he played in the movie BANG THE DRUM SLOWLY but in both voice and carriage he created the gayness nicely without exaggeration. Since the apex of the triangle was so personally unsexy and so shallowly written, the play couldn't make much effect. The language was forthright but it won't advance homosexuality one bit even tho it ends with the males setting up house together.

SATURDAY, DECEMBER 22, 1973
    Ruth called to invite us out on the 30th and Ken wanted me to do the dirty work of turning her down but I refused and made him continue the conversation he'd started. He said we would probably be getting back late from Alice's the night before, which is true. I like Ruth and it behooves us to be nice to a potential cat-sitter but I hate going out there and the news that Clyde and Phil are going to be there does not make the day any more attractive. I forgot to say that yesterday, when it was pouring, Elaine said, "Mr. Vining, I wish you'd do something about this weather. I have to go out at noon." I got up, went to the window, shook my finger at the sky and said,"Now you stop that before noon, do you hear?" It did and it was a running gag all day. I had done that downstairs once with good results but I don't think Elaine had seen the performance. Roger, I think, thought it was blasphemous.

MONDAY, DECEMBER 24, 1973
    We went to 57th St. well ahead of the movie so I could see the exhibit on computers, Copernicus, etc. at the IBM building. Tiffany's windows were wonderful, minus even the single jewel they usually put in their striking settings. With dolls faces made from dried apples (I believe) they had a scene in a monastery and a scene in a nunnery in their 5th Ave. windows, both full of the joy of Christmas, and on the 57th St. side they had a Christmas punch party hosted by Mr. and Mrs. Santa Claus and then the Clauses unwrapping their presents. The IBM exhibit was closed but in the corner was a display of the objects of old English Christmases before the advent of Cromwell and the Puritans. There was a wassail bowl, a plum pudding, a

huge Christmas pie, the cap and bells of the Lord of Misrule, and explanations of the derivations of these and other things, like the Boxing Day box and the Sacred Wren carried on a silken bier. All the things I like about Christmas are pagan, which is hardly a surprise at this stage of my life. We went to Bloomingdale's and bought next year's cards at half price. Our movie, DON'T LOOK NOW, was an eerie thing about second sight and it made Venice look really menacing in winter. There was a scene of marital lovemaking which was very nice and natural--as they came out of their bath and shower they talked about the flab at the husband's waist and he got weighed then sat naked to do a bit of work at the drawing board. Still naked he flung himself on the bed to read and his wife, now with a robe, lay beside him to read also. One finger stroked her hand absent-mindedly and soon she was caressing his buttocks and eventually both were aroused and made passionate love. This was constantly intercut with scenes of them dressing to go out to dinner and the praise it has won is more deserved than the censorship forced on it. It did occur to me, however, that Sarah Bernhardt and Helen Hayes had never been required to play a lovemaking scene in the buff as Julie Christie was. Acting is quite a different profession now. When I got home I was a little bothered with prostatitis and idly, well, no, not idly, purposefully but skeptically, massaged the area below the ankle that believers in zone therapy say affects that area. Once again my trouble went away. It's utterly absurd but as long as it works I'll suspend cynicism. Ken had more wrapping to do but I felt very smug at having finished and worked on my cross-stitch, which is getting more of the emphasis lately so that I can finish it.

TUESDAY, DECEMBER 25, 1973

Knowing that Mother was taking an early train, we got up and got at our presents quickly. Records, records, records, on both sides. We whisked our things away before Mother got here but she had her presents to unwrap. Both Ken and I agreed that it had been some time since we saw her in such good condition. She fretted about having had to come by train but I do believe it was relevant to her freshness and good memory for she admitted she slept on the train. As we had a bite of breakfast Ken started to reprimand her for running up her phone bill by calling so much but I said, "No lectures on Christmas." Later she said she'd like to have a canoe and remembering that she once said she dealt with my pipedreams by just letting me talk when I was a child, I let her talk on but Ken began to argue against the canoe. When I passed him in the kitchen I said, "Don't take it so seriously. It'll never come to pass." Dinner was marvelous but either we ate too much or the gravy was a bit too rich for Ken and me as we both got a little queasy. I was also tired of the smoky atmosphere for Mother smokes like a fiend and the room was almost as heavy with smoke as her own home is. I was therefore actually glad to be going out where I could get some air. There was a train to Trenton waiting to take off and seats were visible so I kissed her goodbye and sent her in alone as I thought an old lady alone would get more attention. Looking in to see if she was making out all right, I found myself just about four feet away from Jim Boothe (*at one time in the 40's my best friend until he and Ken got involved in an affair--see Volumes 1 and 2. I had severed all relations with him at that time.*) Even if he had seen me coming along with Mother I doubt if he would have recognized me, between the aging process and the beard. He looked much as he used to, still bored, still tubercularly thin, and perhaps even still tow-headed tho thru a dirty train window it was hard to tell if the hair was still blond or had turned gray. I did not, I admit, take any lingering look but hurried off wondering what on earth he is doing on a Washington train on Christmas. Seemed to be alone.

FRIDAY, DECEMBER 28, 1973

Eric called before noon to say that he had to exchange some theatre tickets and so probably wouldn't be at the Yale Christmas Party till 5:30. I was thus not as excited as I might have been when I heard that Wintermudd said we could leave at 4:15. It turned out that the party was not in Sardi's proper but on the third floor in the Belasco Room. Went on to Beacon Baths to see if some interesting out-of-towners might be there this holiday weekend. One doesn't know where they come from as there is little or no conversation but the visit was in distinct contrast to last time. There were several attractive moustachioed fellows there and at least three handsome bearded ones. In pursuit of one of those who arrived late I went into the steam room. He apparently found it embarrassingly crowded in there so quickly left and many in his wake. Before I could follow, however, I found myself face to face with another handsome bearded one, who was ready, willing, and distinctly able. He had long curly hair in which I could entwine my fingers as he gave a good demonstration of what native talent and technique can achieve even with someone my size. I would have been

happy to reciprocate but I just about managed to endure
the steam till I had my orgasm, speedy as it was, and I
couldn't stand one more second of steam. Totally satisfied,
I saw no point in sticking around even to pursue my original quarry, so I dressed and went home even as some interested parties buzzed about me. Ken hadn't eaten so we had
turkey sandwiches. Ken told me that Dina Racolin, Anton's
friend who produces plays, had called about my play and
was most laudatory. She apparently had a long talk about
it, which must have been funny since he has never read it.
I am to call her first thing tomorrow.

SATURDAY, DECEMBER 29, 1973
    Called Mrs. Racolin at the appointed time. She said
the play wasn't one they'd do but there were many things
she liked about it and since I didn't have an agent, they
thought they might turn it over to "Bobby" Lantz. She also
thought the play might do better in England and as they
produce there also, she has an agent in mind for London
too. She was very moved by the dedication, apparently having known Joe Orton, and she had thought I must too. Apparently my imagined facts tally with the actuality. We
went to the Met as soon as that conversation was ended,
chiefly to see the Costume Dept.'s exhibit on inventive
clothes of the Ten's, Twenties, and Thirties. I had never
heard of Madame Vionnet but I liked her clothes much the
best because they were more often simple. I hadn't realized
before how little color was used in the thirties. Things
were much muted then, perhaps a concession to the millions
who were living drab and impoverished lives and wouldn't
have stood for too much flamboyance. After the costume display we went up to see the Mary Cassatt exhibit. We saw
the neighborhood boy who works as a guard and I asked how
he was coming along on being a policeman but he says they
must know how to drive and he hates to drive. We mentioned
something we had seen on 110th, an improvised altar with
burning candles standing next to a white painted cross and
the name HARRY. This is where a friend of his was killed
recently and he says it's a Puerto Rican custom to mark the
spot of a death that way. He said, "They don't bother with
fist fights in our neighborhood any more. They shoot or
stab." One funny thing during the conversation with Mrs.
Racolin about agents. I said that I formerly used Chambrun
and had been told that he had been Maugham's agent. "Oh,
did your mother write too?" she said, and I was thrown for
a minute before I explained that he had been Maugham's agent, not Mom's.

1974

WEDNESDAY, JANUARY 2, 1974

Heated some of the turkey soup and took a thermos full to work since I wanted to spend my noon hour typing my part of the Bulletin. The office was cold but I loved it. Mary's radiator didn't warm her area and the boss asked if I'd get mad if they turned on mine. Mine blazed and I was glad I'd said it could be on just fifteen minutes. Dr. W. had felt the table in my office and said, "Even the furniture's cold." "It hasn't complained. Anyway, don't go touching the furniture if it's cold." Mary had come in to let me feel how cold her hand was and she remarked that mine felt warm. There was quite a contrast and it made one wonder about everybody's temperature supposedly being the same. Something is certainly different for I sit sweltering in busses and see all those people swaddled in fur and sheepskins not looking the least bit uncomfortable. This being the new year, I kept my resolution to get down to work on the third draft of the play. At the moment I am down to 11 characters (first version had 23, the second 13).

SATURDAY, JANUARY 5, 1974

When we set out for Macy's I wore, as I have been recently, just a jacket with scarf and gloves. As we passed thru the lobby Douglas, the head porter, said, "And where do you think you're going dressed like that?" "Right into a hot bus," I said. "He goes out like that all the time," Ken said, "and why he doesn't catch cold I don't know. I've had pneumonia for seven weeks because he doesn't let me turn the heat on in the apartment." My astonishment was immediately succeeded by fury and the moment we were out I lashed out at Ken. "For Christ's sake, if you really think your cold is due to our not having the heat turned on, don't go seven weeks in silence and then tell a porter about it. Tell me, and turn on the damned heat." "Oh, don't go all to pieces about it," Ken said, but looked rather pleased with himself. All of a sudden I knew how the expression "a towering fury" came about for I felt at least eleven feet tall in my anger, looking down with contempt at a three-foot Ken and ready to pour hot lead all over him. Mrs. Veenstra came running out and caught the bus with us so I had to contain myself for I don't believe, as Ken does, in embroiling outsiders in our business, but after she left I returned to a stony attitude. Then I realized that we were shopping for a party and that I had suggested we have lunch at MacDonald's because Ken has been so curious about the place, so I postponed open hostility till we got back in the apartment. By that time the sun was pouring in and making the house hot. MacDonald's proved to be the epitome of modern America. Every little thing is super-wrapped, with such a waste of paper as is disgraceful. Whole forests must have to fall just to wrap up MacDonald's junk food. The big Mac isn't bad, if hamburgers excite one, but the bun is made out of some sort of sweet sponge with only the remotest relationship to bread. When we got home Ken baked the apples to float in the wassail and the odor of cinnamon was nice. I made the banana bread for tomorrow's party. Florence wrote about her visit to Celia's deathbed and Ken wanted me to read it. Celia cried and said, "I've been so mean to you, Florence, and I love you. Why did I do it?" She's probably the only member of the family who would ever admit to her own faults, let alone apologize for them, and her condition sounds pitiful but Ken expends his pity not on the death agonies of Celia but on Florence's difficulties in visiting her. "Florence had a lot of tough breaks," he said yesterday. "Such as?" I said, impatiently. "Oh, it was hard being divorced." "That was over 40 years ago. What else?" "Oh, she had a hard time and was short of money in the thirties." "Who wasn't? And she had an accident 35 years ago. I was in a cast for 18 months at the same time and I hardly ever think of it." "But Florence was in a cast for a YEAR," he said, as tho that were longer than 18 months. That flummoxed me. When Florence comes to visit in May, I MUST NOT be drawn into discussion of any of her grievances, I MUST control my impatience with her self-pity. In the first place, I'm a host and in the second place she can't change her temperament at this late date, supposing there ever is a time one can change it. In youth one can at least try. I have always considered myself my own enemy, one whose sloth must be watched and forbidden. It is the only thing that would make me feel some validity in the birth sign, for I feel like two people, one terribly lazy, and one ambitious and energetic and not of a mind to let the other get away with inactivity. One of the many lucky things that have befallen me in life is NOT having a downbeat temperament. When I was talking to Ken about Florence's attitude toward life, her inability to forget anything bad that ever happened to her or to remember anything good, I said that my accident, my term in prison, my poverty in the Depression, had all made positive contributions to my life. It goes beyond just appreciating health, freedom, money in the bank and food in the cupboard. Other good things resulted besides. But I get too wrought up with these in-law things, partly because some of them carry over to Ken, tho fortunately in much diluted form.

SUNDAY, JANUARY 6, 1974
I really don't see how this permanent daylight saving time is supposed to save "energy" for one turns on just as many lights on a dark morning as on a dark evening. We had a very congenial day choosing dishes for the party and even the rather complicated business of making the wassail went along well. Eleonore, Vi, and Joyce all wore long dresses and I hope weren't disappointed that it was only a party of eleven. Toward the end of the evening Joyce asked if we needed help with the Bulletin and was instantly accepted onto the staff. We had a pleasant time cleaning up and putting away but oh, what a lot of leftovers we have.

WEDNESDAY, JANUARY 9, 1974
Elaine had asked me to come to work late so that I could buy some stamps for the office on the way but since several inches of snow were on the ground, I left at the usual time, figuring busses would be late. They were so late, in fact, and the assembled crowd was so large that I suggested to several who go my way that we walk. Nobody young or old was interested in that suggestion so I took off alone. I'm never fearful of mugging in snow or rain as criminal types, tough as they may be otherwise, cower before bad weather. The snow was fluffy, dry, and sparkling as I went so I was happy as a penguin. Any view of the park could have been framed and made a lovely picture. I was exhilarated by the feeling that I was not at the mercy of transportation and that my body would serve me well.

THURSDAY, JANUARY 10, 1974
Neil has a rather cozy apartment. The guests of honor were a Bob and Bill who retired in their forties (never found out how they acquired enough money to do that) and own a house in Katonah and a house in Spain, for which they're departing Sunday. The two Johns who live together were there but the very much older one left before the party got too far along (they say he gets depressed and just takes off). Absolutely no hors d'oeuvres were served, not even a pretzel or a peanut, and the drinks were strong so I had to be very careful because I know that set doesn't bring on the food for a long time. I got the feeling that Amanda felt I was stepping over the line of permissible remarks in this very particular atmosphere where

the lesbians and fag hags admit to knowing so much, make remarks of their own, and yet in ways pretend to a sort of flirting with the men. That little bit of hypocrisy I find hard to take. There is none of this nonsense at the heterosexual parties we go to and so it seems all the more absurd for these people to pretend an interest in the opposite sex which we all know they don't really have. Who's kidding whom and why?

FRIDAY, JANUARY 11, 1974

I had great plans for writing at noon but Norris asked me to join them in the cafeteria. At first we were alone and conversation was lively but then Pinkham, the old fiddlefart (to borrow a word from George Worrell's mother), joined us and Norris goes into a daze. I was dying to get away and write but there was no opportunity to leave politely and I went back to the office in great frustration. I did dash out to write on my afternoon break but by the time I had read over what I had, I added only five lines. I was also distracted by the entry into the lounge of a handsome young man I had first seen at tea break in the morning. I had plunked down where I could look at him thoroly and he held up beautfiully under scrutiny. He certainly made clear the validity of the expression "easy on the eyes". Some people truly are and unfortunately some people are also genuinely hard on my eyes. In the evening I got right to work on the play after supper. I intended to do only the regular hour but I just couldn't stop. Everything is just so smooth and wonderful that I don't want to lose momentum. Ken worked on his rug, which is coming along nicely. He's still doing a very impressive job of cutting down on smoking and I'm very proud of him. The new QQ Quarterly came and has some good articles on gay fidelity, the dangers of liver trouble to masochistic gays who let themselves be too abused, and other realistic pieces.

SUNDAY, JANUARY 13, 1974

Tested all the records I bought yesterday. As I played the DAPHNIS AND CHLOE and felt the same old urge toward orgiastic dance that I have felt since I fell in love with the piece in 1934 or so, I thought again how little my tastes have changed over the years. I show a discouraging lack of growth, I fear, for French symphonic music still appeals with its sensuous shimmer, the operas liked in my teens are the same operas I like now (L'INCORONAZIONE DI POPPAEA has to be heard again before I know it it joins GIOVANNI, FIGARO, ROSENKAVALIER, HOFFMANN, CARMEN, MANON,

BOHEME, etc.), writing is still a passion, and only in the field of art do I discern real progress. I used to hate drawings and now I like them almost better than paintings. However, let the young have their baroque music; I still want to rip off my clothes when I hear the Ravel or the Dance of the Seven Veils, and I still am moved by BOHEME and ROSENKAVALIER.

FRIDAY, JANUARY 18, 1974

From work right to Beacon Baths, where I had positively my worst night ever. There was only one attractive man there and he was making himself so readily available to all and sundry that I didn't go beyond groping for fear of what germs he might have picked up on his promiscuous way. One young bearded man who may have been a war veteran was spread out plainly displaying the fact that he had only one leg. I know that people who are maimed like that attract certain people, and I'm glad for their sake that it's so, but I'm not in that category. I didn't waste much sympathy on the blight of his sexual life for he's apt to do as well as I did and probably better.

SUNDAY, JANUARY 27, 1974

Read the paper and cleaned and then we discussed what movie to go to. I had read in today's Times further praise of THE LONG GOODBYE but Ken, who favored THE STING, said, "That sounds dreary, like that thing about emigrants." "What do you know about it that sound dreary?" He shrugged, remembering nothing about it, really. "I'll go see it myself sometime. THE STING sounds as if it's about bees, if it comes to that." Ken went off in a silent sulk but in time we resumed communication, had brunch, and set off to 86th St. to see THE STING. As the picture opened on a littered street with a breadline in the background and continued with scenes in garbage-strewn alleys, filthy toilets, brothels, gangster's garages, betting parlors, Depression rooming houses with unmade beds, and whatnot, I got more and more amused. No picture could possibly have been more dreary. What's worse, we couldn't follow and couldn't believe the gimmicky plot. Paul Newman, whose beauty, even now that he's over fifty, would light up the corridors of a coal mine, didn't have as large a part as we could wish and his character was no more characterized than any of the others. After supper I did some needlework, put in an hour on my play (worrying a lot less about characterization when I saw what the movie got away with). We watched the latest episode of UPSTAIRS, DOWNSTAIRS, in which much of the dialogue was superb and the people very real.

THURSDAY, JANUARY 31, 1974

I bought the latest PLAYGIRL. As AFTER DARK gets more conservative, PLAYGIRL gets bolder and shows more and more nude men, most quite delectable, much more appealing than the men in most homosexual magazines because they really are men, this side or that of thirty, rather than boys.

SATURDAY, FEBRUARY 9, 1974

The snow stopped early in the night but it was lovely this morning. Unfortunately Ken had had a night of stomach ache and didn't feel he could manage our planned expedition. I decided to go ahead to the Metropolitan by myself so I could get the tickets to the lecture series on English Houses. It was so lovely out and the snow so crunchy rather than slippery that I decided to walk to the Met. If I thought I was going to have the tapestry show to myself I was very wrong. Of course the walk and the buying of the tickets meant that I got to the tapestries an hour after opening but the place was crowded. Crowded with wonderful people too. A very high proportion of sleek beautiful women and good-looking men, casually but nicely dressed. I loved them all. The Apocalypse Tapestry from Angers was the oldest and to read that after the Revolution it was used to wrap orange trees against the winter cold was horrifying. It was not the prettiest. Those from the Metropolitan's regular collection hold up beautifully and can be seen in a new light because hung in a new place. Those from the Cluny are always lovely to see but there were many from all over and even though I have been in some of the chateaux and cathedrals to which they belong, I don't remember most of them. There was a wonderful educational room in which the whole process of tapestry-making was clearly explained and there was a 14 minute movie on THE HUNT OF THE UNICORN series that called my attention to so many details and explained so much symbolism that I was first suppressing tears and then sobs. It was just overwhelmingly beautiful. So was the whole exhibit. When I came out I felt so full of head and heart that I thought I needed to walk some more so walked on down to Alexander's, where I hoped to pick up some shirts at the sale where Ken got so many yesterday. I got seven at $1.99 each, which is phenomenal these days.

TUESDAY, FEBRUARY 12, 1974

Late in the afternoon Wintermudd buzzed me on the inter-com and asked if I could come in for four or five minutes. Apparently he had been brooding on my remark at the staff meeting that it would be the bloody day when I came in to work on Saturday so he wanted me to understand his understanding that professionals were not on the same 9-5 basis that clerical staff was, and that since the union would be enforcing hours more than ever for clericals, professionals might have to take up the slack. I said I understood that emergencies might come up but that I had always felt that if they were chronic something was wrong with either the system or the personnel. I also pointed out that if I resisted staying after five, I did not resist coming in early and had done it for years. I kept a polite surface but I dug my toes in. I wasn't happy with the whole thing and if administrative thinking is to use professionals to do work left undone by the unionized clericals, then I think I better be less passive about the organization work that is going on among professionals. I realize I am being rigid, perhaps immature, and perhaps unAmerican but American business has in large part been the work of men who don't want to go home. Those who do have been forced to follow the example of the personally unhappy but I like to go home and intend to do so. I had a lovely letter from Frank McMullan *(last of my professors at Yale Drama School to retire)* thanking me for giving the book to the Drama Library in his honor and saying he remembered me particularly for my tolerance of other people's opinions and for my perspicacious comments in class. I doubt if he really remembers me all this much time later and he probably thinks those things are just what anybody would like to hear. Naturally I choose to view them as true. I often disagreed with Frank but I liked and defended him even so. I don't, however, think of his directing classes as ones in which I made many comments but I suppose if there was any opportunity, I did. I have never been shy about offering opinions.

SATURDAY, FEBRUARY 16, 1974

Cleaning for the party. Rae arrived first and she brought us the paperback edition of her translation of the complete poems of Cavafy. Miriam arrived without Leo, saying his daughter was in town and they were supposed to be baby-sitting but she had come alone and by subway. The Wintermudds own Rae's book and know it well and of course Melina and Rae had a certain amount of conversation in Greek. Rae read some of their favorite poems in what I felt was a rather overdramatic way, tho Ken thought it was fine. Much conversation had to do with theology, this being Wintermudd's field of expertise, and Miriam was shocked to hear I'd never missed saying my prayers in over 30 years as she felt that wasn't the real me at all. I think it is. She feels she's not religious and that I'm not either, that I'm a humanist. I said I did think I was religious and when I said I liked to feel there were forces larger than myself at work, Dr. Wintermudd viewed that as a religious feeling. At one point when we were all yammering, he said, "The trouble with your parties, Don, is that nobody talks."

SUNDAY, FEBRUARY 17, 1974

Last night I had said how continually intense people wear me out and Bill said he thought I was terrifically intense, with which Miriam agreed. That is because she sees me only at parties, and Ken and I are always "on" at parties, tho Ken retreats from most arguments while I plow right in. But both of us need to relax when parties are over. I couldn't and wouldn't do as some people do, and go from party to party, and we're both a bit weary with the thought that we have two parties next weekend. I know what Bill and Miriam mean by my intensity but it isn't what I mean by intensity at all. I have convictions but they are not visceral, and I can project but I don't do it on and on. I think I correctly defined myself as a sprinter. Bursts of energy must be followed by a good deal of placidity. Both of us were tired today and Ken went in for a nap as soon as we'd had brunch. I tried to stay awake but nodded off so often that eventually I went in and joined him. Mimie called to ask if we were free to come save a dinner party for which illness had caused cancellations. Ken, not knowing who it was, was grumbling on his bed that he wasn't going out, that he didn't feel well, etc. but I decided to make him do the declining. When I gave him the phone he accepted instead. The Chinese firepot is perhaps not the best dish in the world to have when disease is passing around for we all had to reach into the pot with the chopsticks we were eating with and fish out bits of the meat, cabbage, onions, noodles and whatnot for our bowls of rice. I did well with my chopsticks and it was all tasty even if not my idea of the most sanitary eating. Mimie's cousin had announced, when accepting, just as we had, that he had to see UPSTAIRS, DOWNSTAIRS so we left in time. It was a very good episode dealing with the visit for dinner of King Edward Vll and Mrs. Keppel and, peripherally, with the eating habits of the Edwardians. I was happy when Alistair Cooke's final commentary pointed out that the bulk of Londoners by no means ate like that and indeed suffered from malnutrition.

SATURDAY, FEBRUARY 23, 1974
    In my mail when I got home was a letter from President Nixon's physician. When Nixon kept saying he felt fine and couldn't see why he needed a physical I wrote Tkach and asked if the President couldn't set a good example in any thing . He replied that in five years he had had eleven letters in the vain (sic) of mine and I was the first with the courage to sign my name. It was just the sort of letter one would expect from a Nixon aide, right down to the misspelling. Sickeningly pious, he said he would pray for me as I seemed to have a lot of hatred in my system whereas Nixon had none. I rocked with laughter, remembering the many Nixon sneers at the press, his entertainment of the construction workers who beat up students protesting the Viet Nam War, his "enemies list", etc. I immediately decided to take the letter to the party and to all parties I go to this year. It is part and parcel of the kind of bull Nixon and his aides give out all the time. We were joined on the bus to Patty and Amanda's by Vi and her friend Gertrude. There were eleven at the party, including Michael P. and his consort George, a teacher from another school. George seems very level-headed. Charades were inevitable with that set but as I now know the symbols and as they're not intense about them, I am no longer intimidated. I worry a little about Ken, who hates games, but he didn't seem as nervous or bothered tonight and cracked a lot of jokes so I relaxed.

TUESDAY, FEBRUARY 26, 1974
    Took the bus from Riverside Drive so I wouldn't be late to Dr. Smith's. Decided to go to the john and had a horrible shock when my urine was extremely dark. At first Smith minimized the dark urine, not realizing how dark it was, but when he saw the sample he and the nurse immediately exclaimed and rushed to test it. It contained blood and pus and he thought I might have something that sounded like "hemorrhagic cystitis" in the bladder. He said I should see Dr. Fretz as soon as possible and he gave me a prescription. On to the Met to meet Ken. Mostly women attended the lecture on English Houses, which was to be expected. We bussed home and since I'm not to have alcohol I had to have my evening Bloody Mary without vodka.

WEDNESDAY, FEBRUARY 27, 1974
    No blood in my urine and no irritation today. Ken asked me to buy vanilla ice cream on my way home as he had used up the extra apples in a deep dish apple pie. He had put molasses in it, which gave it an interestingly

dark taste. As we were going to listen to Leonard Bernstein's MASS on TV I got my stint on the play out of the way early. As for the mass, Vienna was the perfect place for the European premiere of a piece so full of schlag. I don't pretend to understand it, knowing little or nothing of the liturgy, but it struck me as trashy. I was nevertheless impressed by the sincerity and professionalism of the Yale people who staged it and performed it. Yale remains the Ivy League university most interested in the arts. Just as the mass started our phone rang and it nearly killed Ken not to answer it but when I said I absolutely would not talk to anybody and miss the mass, he hesitated long enough for them to give up. If it were anything important, the caller would call back and if it's Mother, so will she. It never bothers me to ignore the phone if I have television to watch and don't want interruption but Ken's curiosity bothers him.

THURSDAY, MARCH 7, 1974

All day there was talk of the "streaking" on the Columbia campus last night. When this latest college fad first started, "Streaking" meant such a quick naked dash across a campus that nobody could identify you. At Columbia last night, however, they stripped before gawkers, marched around naked accompanied by a band and posed for pictures which appeared in today's SPECTATOR. All I can say of the boys is that it was either a chilly night or they're underendowed on that campus. One girl even stripped and posed and I must say looked better than any of the boys.

FRIDAY, MARCH 8, 1974

We certainly must have exhausted all possible jokes on the subject of streaking now at TC. "Didn't catch cold last night when you were streaking, did you?" etc., etc. When I got home after shopping Ken was posing for me in a pair of new brown slacks with flares and wide cuffs. I've been resisting those as I prefer cuffless pants but he looks great in them and ironically they cost him only $4. His new records were quite danceable music and we shattered precedent and danced together. It happened that the piece wasn't too suitable and we didn't do too well but it was nice to have Ken in my arms and he lacked the self-consciousness he has shown if the idea came up before.

TUESDAY, MARCH 12, 1974

Finally got hold of Dr. Fretz to inquire about the

i.v.p. results and he said I should see either Dr. Smith
or him as the X-rays showed my kidneys larger than normal.
Thinking of Pearl's long dreadful years of kidney transplants and dialysis, I was a bit cast down, but was comforted by the realization that if I were told I was to die
this summer I wouldn't do a thing differently (except perhaps have a lawyer draft a proper will). There is nothing
I want to do that I have not done; all I want is more and
variations of same. Bussed to meet Ken at the Met, where
our lecture series kept to its high level. The lecturer
showed some Elizabethan houses like Burghley House and
Millerton (?) Hall that he found architecturally deplorable and made the point I've often made when looking in
antique stores, "Horribly tasteless things survive and
don't become any better thru mere survival."

FRIDAY, MARCH 15, 1974
    Because I had a holiday, Ken asked if 8 were time
enough to get up. I agreed but habit and the cats had me
up somewhat earlier. We went down to the library first, so
I could see the exhibit in the Berg Collection, currently
Other People's Letters. There were letters from about 50
Americans from Benjamin Franklin to Clifford Odets and 50
English. I noticed that the Americans in particular, but
the authors as a whole, had quite small scripts. Since Ken
was eager to be off to the Morgan to meet Alice as arranged, I hadn't a lot of time to note the contents of the
letters but one from Walt Whitman to a soldier to whom he
wanted at once to be father-image and more was, as the
captions said, pathetic. Alice was not yet at the Morgan
so we were able to go to the men's room. The current exhibit, fifty years of acquisitions, was full of choice
things, if not as many great drawings as at some other exhibits. The autograph score for PIRATES OF PENZANCE was
there and I never knew that it was the only Gilbert and
Sullivan operetta which had its premiere in America (here
in New York). We went to Patricia Murphy's for lunch. Alice wanted to shop afterward so we parted. As I had suggested our going to the Empire Cat Show before FASHION,
we went home and napped. Was very glad I had gone ahead
to the cat show. The attraction of going tonight was that
it was devoted to house pets. The female judge was good
at explaining things to the spectators so that I learned
the difference between a classic tabby and a mackerel
tabby (which I knew Titus to be) and between a calico and
a tortoiseshell. I knew it was useless to buy our cats a
toy at the stands as they'd rather have any little rattly
thing--top of a toothpaste tube, scrunched-up piece of

paper or whatever. Met Ken at the McAlpin Rooftop Theatre and we found the musical version of Mowatt's FASHION modest but stylish and amusing.

SATURDAY, MARCH 16, 1974
It was a near thing my getting home in time to hear the beginning of THE TROJANS but I made it with no more than a minute to spare. Never having heard the opera before, I was determined to pay full attention. Ken and the cats napped but I hooked my rug. When the opera finally ended after 5 hours I was totally exhausted, perhaps by the physical effort of so much hooking as well as by the concentration on the new music. I barely had enough energy left to stagger to the bedroom. Hurried to have a bath as we had ahead of us Laurence Olivier in THE MERCHANT OF VENICE on TV. Set in the 1880's, it was beautifully done. Olivier was superb in the role that must always have been complex and never more so than in the last generation when jews hate to have the play done because of its anti-semitism. Without in the least underplaying Shylock's vengeance (but cutting and underplaying the "my daughter, my ducats" speech) Olivier ended by getting sympathy because the Christians were so gloating and cruel in the trial. As soon as THE MERCHANT was over (and what lovely poetry) we had the last chapter of JACK THE RIPPER. This week has been a bit too rich in good television considering all the other things we had to do. Next week appears to be quieter and I can use it.

THURSDAY, MARCH 21, 1974
Walked down to keep my appointment with Dr. Fretz. He showed me the x-rays and indicated that the kidneys were unusually large but none of it meant anything to me since I don't know what my insides should look like. He says I appear to have cysts on my kidneys replacing tissue and wants me to go to the hospital for something called a retrograde pylogram "under anesthetic", as he kept emphasizing. Naturally this didn't make me happy. I asked what would happen if this new pylogram confirms his opinion, and he said, "We watch you". So it sounds as tho there's nothing to do if they do turn out to be cysts. Tho blue, the bad news and the rain together didn't make me feel as bad as I felt with no precise cause when I had my anxiety-depression attacks. I thought of getting a will made to assure Ken and Mother the income of my estate while preventing Mother from squandering it or Ken from hoarding it and passing it on to the family and I thought of places I want to visit while I can. I always used to say that since

I was psychologically and financially almost over-prepared for retirement, the irony of life made it almost certain I'd never reach the age. Being now equally prepared not to live that long, the irony of life may dictate that I do after all. Better to live as tho every day might be your last than as if you had all the time in the world.

FRIDAY, MARCH 29, 1974
Snow started to fall fairly early in the day and everybody came to me and jokingly asked me to use my influence to stop it, as I often have the rain. Michelle said, "Tell him to cut it out." "Him?" I said,"I never said who it was I gave my orders to. Him?" I said I myself liked the snow and didn't think one should abuse one's influence. Interestingly enuf, the only other person taking pleasure from the snow was Dilzia, our Panamanian, to whom it's a novelty. As she left for the day she leaned in my office and told me not to give orders to stop it. I went from work to the Beacon Baths, where I had a poor time. The place was more mobbed than I've ever seen it but not with beauties. There were waits to get a shower and the steam room was often so crowded one couldn't get in. At first there were other problems seldom encountered there. Two very unattractive and desperate types breached the etiquette of the place by pursuing me and pawing me despite my clear lack of interest. Usually one need only move away to nip an unwelcome pass in the bud and one certainly need do no more than push away an aggressive hand once but these two persisted as tho I were some delectable, utterly irresistible Adonis and my only escape was to leave the steam room entirely, which infuriated me. The sheer tonnage in the steam room was repulsive but when I got out on the street I realized that the sheer tonnage of the average mature American, gay or otherwise, is fantastic. What a huge bulky people we are when youth is past, and even in youth for that matter. Ken had postponed supper till I got home and then we had marvelous asparagus on toast.

FRIDAY, APRIL 5, 1974
Early in the morning I had a call from a man at Trent Center saying Mother had scarcely been out of bed this week. He's been having her neighbors go in and fix her at least one hot meal a day but she isn't eating and he thought a doctor should see her. I agreed and wrote the letter he asked me to write, giving him authority. I was shaking when I hung up but soon calmed down. What saddened me somewhat the rest of the day was that I couldn't think of much that would motivate Mother to get well. She just

never has enjoyed things with the intensity I often feel--
not books, music, food, objets d'art, or anything I can
think of. When I was a little down about my kidneys I told
Dr. Smith that I didn't think I had the courage to undergo
dialysis twice a week if I ever had to. Then we went to I
PURITANI and several times I thought, "Oh, yes, it would
be worth dialysis if one survived thru it to hear a performance like this." Several recent tv shows have given
me the same kind of intense pleasure. The program on the
Mayas was fascinating and two of the archaeologists were
very handsome men so that I was thrilled that men so attractive would be so unconcerned with their looks and
plunge intensely into a career full of tedium, danger, and
intellectual reward. Then tonite I came home to Ken's version of Mrs. Wintermudd's fish dish and it was heavenly.
We had some of the surplus mornay sauce on bread and I
nearly floated away on euphoria. What would do that for
Mother? I wish I knew. I can remember nothing that ever
did, except praise. And where is that to come from now?
Ken was deeply and happily involved with GLORIANA but I
never saw Mother read with that kind of joy. Nana did,
chuckling and cherishing Reader's Digest or mystery novels. Her musical tastes were far from profound but she did
get intense pleasure from some things. It is perhaps deplorable that Ken and I like gossip so, and commendable
that Mother doesn't, from one standpoint, but not when you
realize that in her this stems not from a virtuous decision to avoid it, but from an indifference to the frequent
fascination of other people's lives.

SATURDAY, APRIL 6, 1974
      Jack McNeely called to give us the name of the woman
lawyer who does wills, which I had asked for. Downtown in
time to buy some records and to eat lunch at the Yangtze
River before the opera. It was a delicious performance of
L'ELISIR D'AMORE, which we had never seen before and could
never see in a better performance. Again Pavarotti's mam-
moth size didn't turn me off as it might be expected to.
He bounds onto the stage and up stairs as tho he weighed
130 pounds instead of a probable 310 or more. Judith Bleg-
en, the Adina, sang like an angel and acted with grace
but her soubrette movements were of the stage and would
never be tolerated in life. Pavarotti, on the other hand,
fitted the style yet was perfectly natural. Such an economy of means in his acting! Always perfectly involved in
the role, he was absolutely charming. His puppy-like delight when he finally won Adina was delightful and his
singing was as effortless as his acting.

A GAY DIARY

SUNDAY, APRIL 7, 1974

Called Mother and found she'd been out last night to a pageant. She was about to go out today and was furious to learn Mr. Berger had called. I asked if she got the card on which I asked for her doctor's name and address and she said, "Yes, but I don't intend to give it to you." She said, "If he calls again, you tell him I'm free, white and over 21." When I said he seemed skeptical about osteopaths and I had defended them, she said, "Good for you!" She was clearly far from death's door as she had been made to seem Friday.

SATURDAY, APRIL 13, 1974

In the evening to the new Harkness Theatre to see the new Harkness Ballet (she fires her troupes and starts over about every two years). The second tier, where we sat, is steeply raked but I don't think the last seat is more than 40 feet from the stage. This type of theatre has been out of favor with architects in my lifetime but I have always preferred it to what they give us instead, theatres where banks of seats recede to a distance of a block or so from the stage till all possible involvement with stage proceedings is lost. In this kind of theatre vaudeville stars could have been heard singing in their natural voices without the amplification everybody uses today. As to the performance, it started with the best version of FIREBIRD I've ever witnessed, the only one that has put on stage the same excitement that's in the orchestra pit. Critics sneer at the choreography of the Harkness but I don't give a damn--this was a magnificent FIREBIRD and knocks the spots off the bland Balanchine version. The monsters were really menacing and what sexy little jocks Rouben Ter-Arutunian had designed. The final scene was sumptuous enuf for the Tsars. Tho the theatre has a seating capacity less than our other dance houses, it wasn't sold out. Negative reviews play their part, I guess, but if it were called the Royal Luxembourg Ballet, the place would have been full of snobs no matter what the reviews. The empty seat next to me was filled for the second ballet by a young dancer from the Harkness junior troupe who started chattering to me about having danced in CINDERELLA today in Allentown, Pa. The talkativeness I understood but not the kneesies he went in for during the ballet. He'd had a good look at me when talking to me and I must be nearly old enough to be his grandfather so I found his placing of his warm leg over against mine incomprehensible if gratifying and pleasurable. The thing with many men, especially gay ones, was to wear a fitted shirt unbuttoned half way down so that hairy chest was well exposed (undershirts are very out!). This was fine on young and attractive men but not so good on some who refused to face their lack of natural endowments or their age.

SUNDAY, APRIL 14, 1974
   Ken and I bussed to the Village to see BAD HABITS. The bus had to detour at 57th St. because Fifth Avenue had been closed to traffic to make it a mall for the Easter "parade". I was appalled at what people were wearing at what started as a parade of new clothes worn to church on Easter. We saw hundreds of people, only two of whom seemed to have on new clothes. Other people had thrown on windbreakers and wrinkled pants to go see what other people were wearing, which turned out to be windbreakers and wrinkled pants.

MONDAY, APRIL 15, 1974
   Eric called to make a lunch date and had his criticisms ready on my play. He thought it charming, the most commercial thing of mine he'd ever seen, well-constructed, but caught my ambivalence about Sorrow and ended by hating him. As he talked, I saw the ways to fix the flaws and tho I had told myself I wouldn't start revision till I came out of the hospital, I will.

THURSDAY, APRIL 18, 1974
   Ken came up to the school to join me for the trip to the lawyer's. The woman lawyer works in her apartment on 66th St., having fallen out with the office where she apparently formerly had desk space. With a yellow pad she outlined the living relatives, which is where I fell into trouble. She said I must find out the names of my female cousins so they could be notified of probate. Ken arranged to leave everything to Florence but if she were dead to divide it between Lu, Linda, and me, the first time he has mentioned me at all. The lady said my plan to have my estate go in trust with interest to go to Mother and Ken was impractical because the estate was too small for a bank to bother with. She didn't seem to think the arrangements for giving my body to a teaching hospital thru the Living Bank was practical unless they had a local branch (one is supposed to telegraph them) and she said I could be cremated as she planned to be and have the ashes thrown in the East River. I'm virtually certain that can't be done as rivers would be intolerably polluted if it could be and I'm skeptical about some of her other advice.

FRIDAY, APRIL 19, 1974
    At noon I wrote to Yale to see if I could arrange to leave them everything on condition they pay income to Mother and Ken during their lifetimes. I also wrote to Aunt Gertrude (*the only survivor of my father's four sisters*) to learn the names and addresses of my cousins, tho I still don't see why they have to be involved, even to be notified of probate. I was startled, to say the least, when Elaine told me of how funny Ben Webber was last nite, the drunker he got the funnier, and of their walking home together. "I hope Stella wasn't keeping supper for him." I thought about that in silence for a while then said, "You're talking about Ben Webber?" "Yes, didn't you know he got married? I think she's from Venezuela and he has a 16 year old stepson." To myself I thought that I hoped he managed to remember it was the mother's bed he was supposed to get into, not the stepson's. Gossip that I am, I could hardly wait to get home to tell Ken, gossip that he is.

SATURDAY, APRIL 20, 1974
    Up a bit annoyed because Ken hadn't set the alarm, hoping to sleep late. To see the exhibit on Byron in the lobby of the 42nd St. library. Ken said his legs hurt and I theorized that walking thru crowds was more tiring than the walking we do most Saturdays, when we beat the crowds downtown. We sat on the library steps to rest before going in and as we watched people I said, "I'm going to do a lot of this this summer but you'll get restless." "No, I won't,"Ken said. "Last summer you were too tired to walk, too restless to stay put and relax." "I won't get restless." After not more than 2 minutes 8 seconds he said, "Well, I guess we'd better go in." The only reason I didn't guffaw was that I had a chill of premonition and no idea how to deal with the situation. The Byron exhibit was marvelous with perhaps the most exciting single item a letter from Byron admitting that up to that moment he had been hoping Shelley's boat had survived "the recent Gale of Wind." In the evening to the Billy Rose Theatre for a preview of JUMPERS. I loved the verbal-and-thought play and there was plenty to look at besides. Because of the departures from realism I feared Ken might hate it but he was amused and I could feel guilt-free as far as having dragged him to something not to his taste.

THURSDAY, APRIL 25, 1974
    Slept well and not as nervous during the morning as I might have expected. Bathing and packing took some time,

of course, and so did reading the Times and visiting Lisa's cats. Finally the moment came to kiss Ken goodbye and get the bus to St. Luke's. It was at least a bright and pleasant day. All the others coming in, with one exception, seemed to be male and all seemed to be from New Jersey. Two or three looked as tho they'd be pleasant room-mates but the one I got, nice enuf, is here for open heart surgery and chit-chat didn't seem in order. From the window I have a nice view and can see our house. Sunset reflected in the windows of the two new towers on 110th was quite spectacular. All the personnel seem very nice and many admired my needlepoint when I turned to it after tiring of reading MAXIMILIAN AND CARLOTA. Things started off with a blood test and a chest X-ray today. En route to the X-ray dept. I reencountered the lady I'd seen in the waiting room. Turned out her brother had done a book on needlepoint which is coming out in the fall.

FRIDAY, APRIL 26, 1974

I was whisked downstairs for an i.v.p. This time a whole bottle of dye was put in my veins and at one point a weight was put on my stomach and strapped down hard. I suspect this was to push the gas out of the photographic area but don't know. Dr. Fretz joined the young doctor as he showed me the negatives and both agreed that my kidneys were about twice normal size because of cysts. I asked if there was anything I did about it and they said, "Live with it." Back to the room but before long another trip, this time for an EKG, which seemed a bit like an electrocardiogram. That trip, like last evening's, I made on foot tho the morning trip had been in a wheelchair. To the room and then, just before noon, another trip and this time on a stretcher. This was for the cystoscopy, which I guess Dr. Fretz did. The anesthesia was injected in the back of my hand and quickly put me out. When I came to in the recovery room I seemed to feel just as bad as I ever did coming out of ether or gas--I loathe the feeling of trying to get myself coordinated and failing. I knew, and I guess the nurses did too, that I was recovering when a nurse said of a man who was full of complaints, "Get him out of here. He's a pain in the ass," and I started laughing. The other nurses got laughing at my laughter and the original one said, "It's not funny when you work here all day." Back to the room once more, with the promise that now I could eat and drink. As it was past lunchtime they had to heat the food up and before that was accomplished my room-mate had a heart attack. His wife and the doctor were with him at the time and it was very impressive to see how nurses and doctors rallied and worked as a team. By the time they took him off with a very nice consideration for his quietly weeping wife, I had lost my appetite. Even after my long fast I had to force my food down. I was in a bad sag of weariness when Ken called the first time. Not knowing if more was on my schedule, tho it seemed I had no energy for anything more, I didn't start any needlework but alternated rest and naps with the reading of MAXIMILIAN AND CARLOTA. Urinating is terribly painful and sometimes produces blood but Dr. Fretz dropped in and said no growths were found on my prostate or in my bladder, tho the latter is somewhat inflamed. Because the new i.v.p. was so clear he had decided against a retrograde pylogram, which was what I thought I mostly came in for. He said I could go home tomorrow. After supper I had another wave of great weariness. The pill lady said it was the effect of anesthesia. All the hospital personnel, with one minor exception, have been wonderful. People can grouse all they want about Manhattan becoming increasingly black but I don't know how they'd ever man the hospitals without blacks, Puerto Ricans, and foreign doctors. More power to them! Their personalities generally seem very well suited to the work, too, and there's lots of cheer and charm but this is also true of the whites. If one has to be in a hospital, and I hope I never do again, St. Luke's must be tops. In the evening a new room-mate was brought in, a man I fear far gone in terminal cancer, tho that is only supposition on my part. A friend and wife had brought him and he's been here previously. The friend was solicitous and kind, though a crude working type. He came over to me and said that when the man was here before he had as room-mate a black man who smoked cigars, which bothers him. Sotto voce he said, "These blacks, they got nothing up here (tapping his head). Know what I mean?" It didn't seem the time nor place to argue this point tho I was dying to tell him that if blacks were all that stupid his friend's goose would be cooked as black nurses and attendants have his life in their hands. The wife broke down tho she'd pull herself together when her husband called. It has been a revelation to see the bravery and grief of these two wives. I grew up convinced that women hated men because Mother did and because she reported the failings of her friends' husbands in a way that made me feel the wives despised them (though Aunt Letty later set me straight on that). I have to be constantly taught that even when a woman is not financially dependent on a man (this man's wife works) they still grieve for a dying husband, even if he's unprepossessing to an outsider.

SATURDAY, APRIL 27, 1974
        All I had to pay as I left was a 69 cent phone bill, tho bills from Fretz, an anesthetist and for tests will no doubt arrive in time. The day was glorious but as I walked the short distance to the bus stop I realized I didn't feel too good. I was nauseous and dizzy but I got home all right. The new rug looked wonderful and it was good to be home. I wasn't sure I had the energy to go out but the day was too beautiful to waste and Ken had been housebound for two days so I thought I'd chance it. Opened my mail and found that Yale has a sort of mutual fund to which my estate could be willed and pay income to my heirs. Aunt Gertrude also sent me the names of my cousins. To see the new version of THREE MUSKETEERS. The audience, alas, is used to seeing films on television and talking incessantly with just offhanded attention to what is going on on the screen. Ken fretted about it until he was adding almost as much to the distraction as the others, as I reminded him. Later I decided that the audience was not entirely to blame for not getting engrossed in the movie. It was of completely incompatible styles, mixing much realistic detail about the ruggedness of life in those days (muddy barnyards, steamy laundries, slop buckets emptied into smelly streets, cruel street fair games, cruel hunts by royalty with falcons or beaters) with comedy which was pulled down by this heavy preoccupation with social comment. As comedy it debunked the old swashbuckling films by having those who leaped upon horses from a distance miss and fall into the mud, or having swords break from the hilt. This kind of thing was amusing for perhaps the first 32 times but not for 132, when it became such a pattern that one expected nothing to work and was seldom fooled. Almost total miscasting completed the disaster that kept one from viewing the film as either comedy or adventure and from caring for the characters one way or another. As Cardinal Richelieu, Charlton Heston not only lacked the force to rule France but made one doubt that he could control the Bingo Committee of Our Lady of Angels in Prairie du Chien, Wisconsin.

MONDAY, APRIL 29, 1974
        Just before I went in the office I removed my left arm from the sleeve of my jacket and tucked it behind me. When Mary asked what happened to my arm I said they amputated it but of course I hardly expected credence. I hated the mess accumulated on my desk in my absence but I got most of it cleared off. Nancy Panella was on the bus I took home and discussed my hospital stay. When I got off I had an interesting experience. Sitting next to me had been a

negro youth I had barely seen peripherally but he got out at my stop. I was carrying groceries and he said, "I couldn't help overhearing what you were saying. My ancestors believed that food had a great deal to do with health and seeing what you've bought there, I think that will be very good for your health. I hope so." I had celery, lettuce, raisins and a box of bran cereal visible. The boy's hair and beard were a bit wild but looking at his face I saw it was really beautiful and lit from within by sweetness as well as intelligence. The short exchange before we parted got my evening off to a very nice start. I did needlepoint while the President talked to the nation about his innocence in all Watergate matters. Being so highly prejudiced, I naturally found him totally unconvincing. Wrote to tell him so.

WEDNESDAY, MAY 1, 1974
I sent more cards to Washington but decided that it behooved me to use my pen on behalf of a more local issue, the Homosexual Rights Bill which was to have been considered yesterday but was postponed. Expected to pass two weeks ago, seven or eight other cities having passed similar measures, it suddenly got opposition from the Archdiocese and from the firemen's and policemen's unions. I addressed what I think was a marvelous letter to Councilwoman Aileen Ryan, who has wavered and then voted against it in the past. Several times defeated, the measure is bound to pass within a few years if not this time for several councilmen are very persistent in reintroducing it.

THURSDAY, MAY 2, 1974
I wrote two more cards to City Councilmen, this time to two who have steadfastly supported the Homosexual Rights Bill. This political writing is getting in the way of my creative writing but is important. On my way home at night I had minor shopping to do and as a joke I bought two large cakes of Palmolive Soap to give Ken as a present for the 28th Anniversary of our meeting in the steam room. It made it all the funnier that the price stamped on it was 2 for 69.

SATURDAY, MAY 18, 1974
Changed my bed and took the electric blanket off for the summer. OVER HERE was a smooth if corny show of war days and at first rather depressed me because the period clothes and period dances seemed so inexpressibly ugly. I was determined not to comment and spoil Ken and Florence's time but when Florence went to the ladies' room Ken said,

"It's certainly not a pretty show!" The audience was lapping the show up and greeting the elderly and portly Andrews Sisters as tho they were still in their prime but what delighted me about the show was some of the bitter scenes that dealt with realities. The black market scene should have made people bleed with its picture of what their patriotism really amounted to in a pinch, and one scene dealt with the fact that blacks were not then integrated in the services. Another scene dealt with the ill temper bred by shortages, etc. I was surprised by these astringent scenes and they made the show for me. All the songs were clever pastiches of the 40's songs. Neither about them nor about any other aspect of the 40's am I nostalgic. After the show we went to Joe Allen's, where every bite I ate was delicious. At the table next to us was Brian Bedford, star of JUMPERS, looking a bit glum with good reason since that marvelous show closes tonite. I don't think Florence saw the young man come in and kiss Bedford. Only today did it sink into my consciousness that all the posters in Joe Allen's are for shows that failed.

THURSDAY, MAY 23, 1974
After work picked up Eric at his office and we subwayed to the Village. The triangular block where once the Sheridan movie theatre stood has now been turned into a lovely garden, chock full of iris right now. I almost think I like iris even better than lilacs, which I generally think of as my favorite flower. I even like their odor, not generally that much admired. We ate at the Casa da Pre where both Eric and I had delicious sweetbreads. We then walked along Bank to the Berghof Playhouse, where we picked up our tickets. Hivnor was not about, which disappointed us as Eric had said he would have to leave at intermission. Not only was he up late last nite at a political meeting where Peg was nominated for State Assembly but he has a commuting problem. He has seen the first half of more shows than anybody I know. Many prominent actors took part in the staged reading of THE ASSAULT ON CHARLES SUMNER. The cast was gigantic and the merits of the play more literary than dramatic so that a reading suited it fine. The Village on a mild night was marvelous as I walked to University Place. The houses and the people were equally attractive and as I reached Fifth Avenue a glorious vision passed before me. Wearing what appeared to be a gaucho hat and pants with a bolero of Indian design was a gloriously handsome young man with golden hair in a large braid down to his waist. He walked with not a soupcon too much or too little confidence and would have made my evening even if

it had been disastrous up to that point, which it was far
from being. As the bus came up Madison Avenue I saw hoards
of policemen around St. Patrick's and decided that Intro
2, the homosexual civil rights bill, had been defeated in
City Council today and that the dear antediluvian Cardinal
Cooke who, with police and fire unions, had fought it so,
was being protected from gay militants. It looked like an
awful lot of burly force was thought necessary to protect
Cooke from those who had been described as too limp-wristed
to fight fires. It is mortifying to think that ten other
cities have given gays civil rights before New York has
and that the tone in sophistication and justice of this
city I love should be set by firemen and policemen. It is
only one segment of the Catholic church that has been on
the attack for two of the three most fervent supporters of
the bill are Catholic, one a priest. Florence could not be
persuaded to stay over the holidays and packed tonight.
Later she realized her ticket was at the bottom of the
bag.

MONDAY, MAY 27, 1974
    After lunch downtown to see MY FAT FRIEND. On the one
joke of a fat girl's dieting to catch a lover and then
finding he really likes fat women many changes were worked
out. Her campy gay lodger who ridiculed and prodded her
into reducing proved a great part for George Rose. The audience loved his often cruel wit. That type of gay person
they'll accept as long as he's unattached. It was a shock
to me to read that many City Councilmen voted against Intro 2 because they reacted against the Gay Activist's
stress in their publicity on gay marriages. In my propaganda cards and letters I had stressed the longevity of
many relationships, hoping this would counteract the campy
cruising images in the public mind. According to the papers this caused a backlash as apparently the unattached
cruiser is more acceptable. It has certainly been that way
in the plays. Unhappy, lonely, frustrated homosexuals have
been repeatedly shown but there have been few gay relationships such as I used in CRY ON MY SHOULDER and the current
play. I'm determined to keep on slipping lastingly coupled
gays into my plays but in future propaganda sent Council
members I'll change tactics.

THURSDAY, JUNE 6, 1974
    Washed a reversible sleeveless sweater, one I'd had
at the office, so I can take it on the trip in case it's
cold in Scandinavia. I really enjoy washing clothes to an
absurd degree. Thought last night as I washed shirts what

strange pleasure it gave me. If only I liked other cleaning chores that much. Mrs. Sizemore's bill came today and was an amazingly low $50. I'll get the check tomorrow and also a contribution for the National Gay Task Force. They ran a full-page ad in the Times today seeking money and volunteers in their fight for civil rights for homosexuals. I'm sending only $25 but I also marked a willingness to volunteer. I don't suppose Ken will but maybe he can be drawn into it slowly.

FRIDAY, JUNE 7, 1974

Today was the first Friday on which summer early closing took effect. Went right to Beacon Baths. Going early like that gets one the early-bird rate but not many are there at that hour. Eventually, however, I had my finest day by far. I keep wondering at what age it will prove futile for me to visit the baths but never in my palmiest days did I do better than I did today. I was showering when I saw someone highly to my taste go in the steamroom. I rushed in and nearly got trampled by the other admirers who quickly came in. He sampled the wares available and settled on me. The others took whatever corner of him was available and tried to slide between us or drive me off with unwelcome attentions to idle parts of my anatomy but he and I clung to each other. Eventually we left the steamroom and in the shower he was complimentary. He then surveyed the cubicles, all his admirers in his wake, and when he found one empty led me in. I snapped the bolt on the door and shut out those who would have observed or interfered again. In the cooler, less hectic atmosphere of the private cubicle we made love for a long time. Both my beard and my genitals excited him and he was everything I like in a lover--handsome, moustachioed, beautifully built with a body nearly hairless except in strategic places, superb technician, and kind. He brought me to orgasm twice and even then was not inclined to rush off. Only toward the end did I notice his wedding ring. Once I would have recoiled in primness but 30 years after all my friends I have adopted the attitude, "Oh, what the hell." I knew I wouldn't top or even equal that experience so showered and headed for home. He came to the locker next to mine to get his cigarettes and looked just as good when I had my glasses on as he had when I had them off. He continued the compliments. Just can't understand it. I know I'm lucky enuf not to be bald, and careful enough not to be fat, and vain enough to keep my gut pulled in instead of letting it sag and yet--this dark beauty can't have been much this side of thirty if he was that and we were making love as equals, with no role-playing, no nonsense and absolute rapture on his part.

SATURDAY, JUNE 8, 1974

In the afternoon we went up to the Museum of the American Indian to see the beadwork exhibit. The display techniques are excellent and so is the titling in the cases--nice and large and legible. Lots of the beadwork was beautiful but I especially liked a less crowded piece where delicate sprays of blue flowers were worked on a dark suede pouch. The museum was very busy, tho few people I know ever speak of going, and many were foreigners to whom the Indians are glamorous. They're somewhat glamorous to me, too, after today because so much more sophisticated artistically and so much more various than I ever realized. Thinking of yesterday, I couldn't remember any sexual experience I ever had that was quite so mutual. I've generally been more interested in what I was doing than in what was being done to me but what that young man did with his moustache gave me new ideas of how to use my beard (I have to be taught these things, as I have no natural flair). By the same token, tho few people seem to be as interested as I in mouthing balls, this fellow was beside himself as I did it, in no way minding the temporary neglect of his gorgeous penis. (One can talk and write this explicitly now that several magazines with circulations in the millions do). After a supper of London broil I got busy on the play, first retyping the two bad pages and then proceeding to the end. Was glad to be done after a year and a half. Now I can buckle down to reading about Scandinavia. Already Sidney Clark's chapter on Sweden's history has made a lot clear to me.

SUNDAY, JUNE 9, 1974

Paper in the morning and then a highly reluctant facing up to the painting of the front hall. Between missing places where paint should be and getting it where it shouldn't be, it was a mess. Victoria somehow walked in the droppings and left a pale green trail across the top of the credenza and I had paint in my ear and in my beard. We threw the roller and pan out, vowing never to do our own painting again. Some people claim to enjoy it and say it's easy. Well, the writing that makes doctoral students sweat in some cases might be easy for me but painting isn't. I was exhausted and after my bath collapsed on the bed. When I headed for bed I suddenly saw myself in the mirror, glowing. If I looked like that Friday I understand the attraction but I think it's more likely I looked like that because of Friday, and such subsequent events as finishing the play and having a full, rewarding weekend.

MONDAY, JUNE 17, 1974
A girl called about being catsitter, which gave us someone to fall back on in case we didn't accept the fellow we were interviewing tonite and I knew that would make The Great Worrier happy. Lowenthal called to ask if he could come earlier than the appointed time and the phone had no sooner rung than Ken was assuming he was cancelling. He turned out to be a heavy boy from the Bronx, just back from three years study of acting in London. Titus hid out thruout his visit tho he peeked around the foot of the bed at him. He had surprised us earlier when Pat Robins brought me the June Bulletin for proofing & Titus came right out. She hasn't been here that much but he seemed to feel he knew her and felt safe coming out. Our TV programs were an hour-long one on THE FORGOTTEN WAR, which dealt with the disastrous Allied intervention in the Russian Revolution and a shorter one on Renoir. The latter must have been magnificent in color but was surprisingly effective in black and white.

TUESDAY, JUNE 18, 1974
Neil called to say he couldn't make the party and informed me that the older of the two Johns we met at his party had died in May. They had been together 25 years and the survivor is understandably lost. I considered inviting him to the party tho his mood may not be partyish. Ken didn't react at all to the idea.

WEDNESDAY, JUNE 19, 1974
Spoke to Patty and she thought John D. would appreciate being invited to the party. She told Vi, who came and sat with me at tea break. She told me about the death of John C.. Set out for the bank and died on the street. This reinforced my decision not to postpone a trip to Egypt more than a year. The decision was further reinforced in the evening when I went to the bathroom after we finished the dishes and found my urine dark with blood. I grew faint with fright but pulled myself together shortly. Each trip to the bathroom was filled with suspense and, eventually, disappointment. The hemorrhaging didn't stop and I guess I'd better try to get an appointment with Dr. Fretz tomorrow if only to get a new prescription for gantrisin. Well, at least I've made 57 even if I don't make 58.

THURSDAY, JUNE 20, 1974

My first and in some ways best birthday present was clear urine after the bad evening. Fortunately it remained that way all day so I made no doctor's appointment. As we had our breakfast I unwrapped my birthday presents--all practical things. An adaptor that will permit me to take my electric razor and hair dryer abroad, film, a sleep mask to keep out the midnight sun, etc. Ken suggested we have dinner in Yorkville so after drinks at home we went down and decided to try the Bavarian Inn. I had liver dumpling soup with dumplings the size of Hermann Goering.

MONDAY, JUNE 24, 1974

The party went very well until somebody commented that Ken wasn't eating. I was furious, went to the kitchen and told him that nobody else we knew felt it necessary to put off their own eating. I took command then and there, wouldn't let him help with the dessert, so he ate. After supper charades were suggested, as they always are with that crowd. To our great surprise Titus emerged from the bedroom early in the party and freely came and went thru the evening. Even the outbursts of raucous laughter didn't seem to frighten him too much. I had not finished my rug on purpose so that Ken could have full glory for his and the first thing I knew I saw him putting mine back in the closet after having shown it to Amanda. I also heard him later telling people the contents of my will, probably inaccurately. Honestly, one has no secrets if he's around.

TUESDAY, JUNE 25, 1974

Left early to go see Dr. Smith. At last I was able to settle all the questions in my mind and got a feeling that I was not at the mercy of my kidneys. There are things I can do. Drinking much liquid, far from putting a strain on my kidneys, would help them keep down the accumulation of urea and should be done. If I hemorrhage or have any sign of urinary infection, I'm to take gantrisin right away as my kidneys aren't in shape to cope with infection. Clearly it is a serious business but having things I can do about it is more to my taste than just waiting helplessly for the end. From Dr. Smith's I took a bus down Second Ave. to visit Alice at the New York Infirmary. Alice looked much better and I stayed about an hour.

THURSDAY, JUNE 27, 1974

Set out for the East Side Airlines Terminal by bus. The terminal is a ghost town now. The various airlines have closed their booths and I think the restaurant has closed too. There was a long, slow-moving line for the airport busses so there was more fuming from Ken. We arrived more than half an hour before the time on our tickets but we were told we were too late, that our plane was fully loaded. Ken really went to pieces then and there were recriminations about our not having started early enough, vows not to make more trips as this kind of thing spoiled the whole trip and made it not worthwhile, declarations that he was literally sick about it. Attempts to calm or reassure him simply led to an explosion. Ken's nerves are harder to cope with than the crises which precipitate his outbursts. When the supervisor explained that they had been sent a plane with 50 fewer seats than they expected and it became clear that many others had been bumped from their flights, Ken calmed down but by that time I had a headache. A couple of hotdogs helped and so did his return to being a good companion when the supervisor booked us on a 9 o'clock flight with a transfer in Copenhagen. Our seats were by the kitchen, which gave us a fascinating chance to watch the space-saving methods used in serving meals aloft.

FRIDAY, JUNE 28, 1974

Stockholm was ablaze with sun and I was glad I'd brought the white jacket I almost left home. We changed money, took the bus in to town, and found our hotel very near the Central Station, which is why Ken had picked it. It's in an old building which has different hotels on different floors, much like Madrid, and Ken was rather put off by this. I'm glad it had been he who picked it. When the receptionist proved charming and the room bright (probably 22 hours a day), clean, and sufficiently roomy, Ken was content. Stockholm promises to be interesting and a city Ken and I can handle without undue physical effort for him. Ken was first awake and anxious to go out. We had a highly successful evening. We wandered, going to the island on which the parliament building sits, then to the park at Karl XII's Torg. Men were playing chess with large wooden pieces about two feet high. Flowers were gorgeous there. Ken said, "And you told me Stockholm wasn't much." "I certainly take it all back," I said, delighted with the place. It's a mass of aesthetic treats from the jewelry, ceramics and glass in the store windows to the beautiful young men with their long legs and white pants tight over their little round rear ends.

SATURDAY, JUNE 29, 1974

Thanks to my sleeping mask the light didn't disturb my rest. Set out for the City Hall in lovely sunshine. For

our tour we had a tall wryly humorous guide who made the
history and present government of Sweden remarkably clear,
making unobtrusive comparisons of the Hanseatic League with
today's Common Market and the Vietnam War with the Thirty
Years' War. We headed for the NK department store to get
us kaopectate and Lasse's mother a gift. Since we were
short of time and short of ideas for gifts I suggested we
wait and send a hostess present after the visit. Ken blew
up, said that was ridiculous. I said I'd heard of it being
done and couldn't we discuss it reasonably but Ken said,
"It's the same old story. We can't agree and it spoils the
whole trip. It's just impossible, etc., etc." I decided I
wouldn't have his short perspective and think that two minutes' difference of opinion could wipe out a glorious morning nor the day to follow. I told him to do as he liked
about the gift, that I had no ideas, but after a fruitless
quick browse in the gift dept. Ken gave up. When we returned to the hotel the man at the desk said we'd had a call
just after we left from Lasse's mother, who wanted us to
have lunch. Ken, having been unable to finish the lunch
he'd picked out, said he just couldn't but I thought we
couldn't refuse. When Lasse jumped out of the car I recognized him even though he's wearing his hair longer. His
parents, Gunnar and Ethel, are very attractive and charming. They drove us to Skansen, which I had not planned to
visit because the walking it involved would have led to
another outburst from Ken. He could say nothing to the
Svennerstens so he got to see the old historic Swedish
buildings after all. First they took us to a lovely restaurant where we had smorgasbord. There must have been
herring in ten different ways and tho I have always avoided it, I tried it five ways and liked them all. On the
second round I also tried reindeer meat, which I don't need
again. Their business, it turns out, is running a photo
laboratory with 25 employees. After some sightseeing of
the city, they took us to the lab for a tour of that, also
fascinating. Ulf, a good-looking friend of Lasse's from
the marine laboratory on the West Coast, was waiting for
him at the photo laboratory and they left us there. Ethel
and Gunnar said none of their three children were interested in carrying on the business. We thought we had by
now taken enough of their time but they proposed further
driving around, ending at their lovely home in the sub-
urbs. Here we re-encountered Lasse and Ulf, changed into
informal clothes. There were drinks on the terrace, slides
of last summer's fishing trip to Finland (Lasse absent in
America but son John and daughter Marie along) then a
marvelous light salad. It was interesting when seeing the

slides to see one totally unself-conscious scene in which
the teenage daughter and the 17 year old son John were totally naked while Ethel and the friend wore bathing suits
as dinner was prepared or eaten on the vacation boat. The
body was accepted so naturally. At a very late hour they
drove us in to the hotel. It had been a wonderful day
(Ethel and I had talked much opera) but so stimulating that
Ken and I agreed we wanted a quiet day tomorrow. He had
scarcely seen their home when he realized how unsuitable
any gift we had bought would have been. Flowers abound
from their own garden, ceramics made by Lasse in their home
kiln are all over the house and lovely candles (which Ken
had tentatively proposed) were, as he quietly pointed out
to me, all over. Though there was, of course, no retraction
of the stormy noontime ranting, I think Ken realized how
close he had come to a dreadful mistake. We can send something back from America. I can't imagine what but it will
surely be better for time taken to think about it now that
we know house and people.

TUESDAY, JULY 2, 1974
   Only 7 were on our tour to Uppsala and Sigtuna. The
Swedish landscape still is a bit too much like our Northeast to be interesting but the stops were nice. Long before
we returned to the hotel I saw my 5,134th handsome Swedish
man. So often a man who would turn heads in New York looks
like just another member of the chorus here, with the same
marvelous features, hair, skin, tall figure, and nowadays
the same blue denims tight to his crotch and rump. But
neither Ken nor I have seen a single one we think is gay.
I guess they're just amply supplied with beautiful young
women and I can't blame them for being attracted for big
breasts, big buttocks, and thick thighs are as uncommon on
the girls as on the boys and the faces are lovely. When a
couple passes it's sometimes hard to decide whether the
young man or young woman is prettier.

WEDNESDAY, JULY 3, 1974
   Our friend the sea gull reappeared on our roofledge
this morning and fared better than before as Ken gave him
(or her) some of his toast. As today was to be devoted to
the old city we marked pages in a book we had on it as to
the buildings we wanted to see. The Palace didn't open till
10. Eventually we had a nice tour with a guide of marvelous
beauty. His sense of humor and intelligence made him enormously appealing to both of us. We went home a different way
and by accident discovered the street where all the sex
shops are. They have something for every taste but mine---

picture books for those who love fat, who like little girls or little boys, women with giant boobs, or whatever, including sado-masochism, but in the windows at least nothing for men who like men in their prime. An awfully strong indication of pedophilia and quite aside from the non-appeal of children to me, those in the pictures weren't even good-looking children. From my standpoint it was all very unerotic, from black condoms to candles in the shape of a penis; any ten minutes on a bench brings sights more erotic than the sex shop windows as handsome young men in tight blue pants go by. I decided that Stockholm is my favorite European city after Paris. There is not the interesting sightseeing to be done as out of London and evenings would eventually pall without theatre but the charm and humor of the people (not to mention their beauty), the light delicious food in great ethnic variety (Italian restaurants are all over), the high level of design, the many places to sit, all make an awfully enjoyable city, as does its compactness. Window-shopping after dinner is a pleasure.

THURSDAY, JULY 4, 1974

We dropped into a bank to cash enough traveler's checks to pay for our hotel room and we found that here in Sweden even banking is an aesthetic experience. Not only were the young men and women behind the counter beautiful but so were the appointments of the bank. We walked the short distance to the Nordiska Museet. Frommer had said it was a mixed bag, but what a glorious bag! The historical part had armor belonging to Gustavus Vasa and Gustavus Adolphus, the costumes worn to the fatal masked ball by Gustav II and his assassin Anckerstrom, gorgeously embroidered horse caparisons belonging to Queen Christina, some of her fancy guns, coronation robes, etc. There was also a wonderful section on 100 years of clothing, the highlight of which may have been the display of the great number of undergarments once worn by men and especially women compared with the thin little briefs they now wear.

FRIDAY, JULY 5, 1974

Even with the extra bag of food and bag of purchases it wasn't much trouble getting to the station since we were so near. We ate half our provender as breakfast, the other half about eleven. The cookies were delicious tho I bought them chiefly because they are called "pricks" and we had ribald nonsense about the pricks being awfully soft, etc. Ken and I looked carefully at every farm and town for a cat but saw none till we were so near Oslo that we weren't sure whether it was our only Swedish cat or our first Norwegian cat. No cats and no gay boys in Sweden? "We may have seen someone gay without knowing it," Ken said, "But we certainly know a cat when we see one."

SUNDAY, JULY 7, 1974
      Another huge breakfast downstairs with more prosperous adults stealing food (*from a meat-and-cheese-laden buffet table*) to stash in their handbags. It was particularly interesting to hear an American lady at an adjacent table arguing against her own conscience and her husband's disapproval as she made sandwiches and hid them away and then saying, "After we go to church, we'll go see___". We had decided to devote the day's sightseeing to the Museum of the Resistance and the Akershus nearby. I studied the ways in which underground newspapers were made and distributed and radios hidden after the Nazis made Norwegians turn in all radio sets, just in case Nixon ever tries a coup. The exhibit was realistic about disagreement among resistance groups, about informers, about differences of opinion between the military and the resistance groups themselves as to what they should do and about the toll in hostage deaths as a result of some of their deeds. Also about failures and futilities. When we finished the museum we needed a rest for legs and eyes before seeing the interior of the Akershus so we sat on the high promenade and had a perfectly wonderful view of the harbor, more variously active than Stockholm's seemed to be. Home to nap then in to watch news in the television lounge. As they did last night, they went into serious matters in more depth than American tv and had no trivia, no playing up of the newscaster's personalities. Even tho in Norwegian, it gave me more nourishment than our overly cute news at home, with its excessive emphasis on crime. Last night there were sections on the Japanese and Canadian elections, which I've never seen U.S. tv give more than glancing mention to. Americans seem determined to be trivial.

THURSDAY, JULY 11, 1974
      The ride to Bergen was the most beautiful and interesting I ever had. The landscape was so varied, from lovely farming valleys up to spectacular glaciers then down below timberline again and eventually to marvelous fjords. The amount of snow took me completely by surprise. At some points great banks of it were leaning against the snow sheds thru which the train passed. Melting snow made wonderful racing streams and waterfalls and in my book Norway surpasses Switzerland for scenic beauty. It was wonderful

to see Ken enjoying himself so and being very playful.
Since the explosion in Stockholm our first Saturday all has
been amiable but today we were especially compatible. Bergen capped the day by exceeding our expectations, as did
the Hotel Bristol. For $11 apiece we have the best room
yet. I don't think I ever had a more wonderful day of traveling, interesting, comfortable, beautiful.

SATURDAY, JULY 13, 1974
   Walked to the aquarium. The walk along the heights of
the town was lovely, giving wonderful vistas down to the
water either way. The aquarium turned out to be the best
and most instructive I've ever seen. The fish were arranged
according to their preferred habitat--under wharves, on
sand, at 200 meters deptth, etc. In the window showing the
underpinnings of a wharf they had gone so far as to include
bottles, cans, and other debris such as one might find on
the seabottom there. The design of the whole place was
lovely. So was a tall blond father carrying a child that
we saw by the seal pool. Ken thought we'd have to go a long
way to top his beauty but at night I saw a taxi driver that
I thought at least as well-formed and handsome. We rested
at a vista point on the other side, from which we could see
the Leda, the ship on which we go to Newcastle. We had only to step to the corner to get our bus for the tour and
we had a wonderful guide, more mature but still beautiful
in a fortyish way. Warning was given before we started that
10 minutes walk was required at the Grieg house and 5 minutes steep climb at the Fantoft Stave Church but nobody
withdrew. The Grieg house was furnished just as he left it
at his death in 1907, I think, so was very Victorian but
cozy and beautifully situated on a promontory. One had to
go downhill to see his grave set in the cliff at the water's edge, then up and down again to see his little red
studio. The warning about the climb to the Stavkirch was
no idle one. It was a fierce ascent. Ken was too proud to
rest but I wasn't. The church, a magnificent example 800
years old, was originally somewhere on the Sognefjord but
in 1893 was sold and moved. Many, unvalued by parishioners,
were apparently sold for firewood and of 800 or so in the
middle ages only about 30 remain. On the ride back to town
the guide was very instructive about Bergen, describing
the varied industry, and Ken kept ribbing me about my prediction that it would be provincial and peasanty. Never
have I been more wrong.

TUESDAY, JULY 16, 1974
   We taxied to the Bergen Line pier and found the Leda,

not impressive from the outside, a very lovely ship inside. In fact we needn't have gone first class as tourist looked very nice. Our cabin was very nice but we spent very little time in it as the public rooms were so attractive and uncrowded, especially a "garden veranda" where the big windows looking out over the stern were lined with flowerboxes full of plants and flowers much like the windowsills of Bergen. There was rain and fog most of the day, which some deplored but which I liked because it showed us the wilder side of Norwegian weather, which we've hitherto missed. We got in conversation with a nice young Englishman with wife and 20-month old son. After we got out of Stavanger the bar was allowed to sell liquor and we were joined there by the nice English couple. Ken got sleepy so even tho I loved the sound of the rain against the lounge window I joined him in lurching toward the cabin. Paper buckets had been placed in the corridors at intervals and Ken took seasick pills, lent the Englishman one, but I seemed to feel okay. I love the feel of the sea, which I never got on the Rotterdam.

WEDNESDAY, JULY 17, 1974

Ken was rather bothered by the pitching and rolling of the ship in the night but I loved it. Now and then my feet would go above my head and then we'd go the other way and I'd be propping myself against the footboard. When I started to shave there was a sudden explosion and the lights went out. Why the converter didn't work I don't know for the voltages seemed to be what they should be. I had to finish shaving in the men's room next door, using Ken's razor and shaving cream, which meant a messy lot of shaving cream in my beard. Dressing and packing in the dark stateroom presented problems. Though I felt fine in all the roughness and thought my seafaring ancestry was showing itself, when we headed for the cafeteria, well down, I began to be a little queasy. When we got to the food line I told Ken not to sit near anybody who had eggs. Considering that reaction I decided I'd be wise to take one of his seasick pills. Landing went smoothly, as did the bus transfer to the customs shed and the bus to Newcastle Station. It was a good thing we had reserved seats as at the various stops, not many, the train filled and people were standing in the vestibules. I was in quite a euphoric state for we had two handsome young Norwegians beside us and more across the aisle and the sunshine made the English landscape in Yorkshire look very nice. But then the train stopped dead for an hour and the blazing sunshine made me both hot and sleepy. Somehow our engine had broken down and they had to send for another. We pulled in to King's Cross an hour late, quickly got a nice roomy taxi and were off to Dennis Welsh's hotel. He greeted us with bare torso and undisguised gay manner, which was okay, and showed us to a marvelous huge room where a letter from Florence was waiting for Ken. Once settled in we went out to explore the neighborhood, which we found being upgraded with gallons of paint and lots of remodeling.

THURSDAY, JULY 18, 1974
We took a No. 9 bus from Kensington Gardens down Piccadilly. We rapidly did a great deal of business--confirming our flight home at Pan Am, cashing traveler's checks at a bank, getting information from the Egyptian Tourist Office, booking the Chartwell-Hever Castle tour for Sunday at the Hall Porter desk in the Regent Palace, copying off plays we might see and their theatres from the list by the ticket agency in the lobby of the R.P. then going and getting tickets to CHEZ NOUS for tonight and BLOOMSBURY for tomorrow.

FRIDAY, JULY 19, 1974
Our objective today was the Churchill Centenary Exhibit in The Fine Rooms of Somerset House. I never knew S.H. had exhibition rooms before and as it turns out this is the first time in the 150 years of their existence that they've been open to the public. I tried to pay attention to the lovely rooms as well as to the exhibit they contained. Starting with a room of mementoes appertaining to the first Duke of Marlborough and Sarah, the exhibit continued to be very inclusive right through the years of World War II though not much beyond. Churchill's painting was certainly extremely variable in quality. He appears to have had no imagination at all, painting just what he saw and not seeing drama or tension anywhere. We walked to St. James Park and watched people feeding the land and water birds but a few drops of rain fell and that gave Ken his excuse to go home to bed. I pointed out that people weren't even moving from benches or grass and were taking no notice of the sprinkle but he said he didn't care what they did but he wasn't going to get wet. While he napped I did diary. Also did some needlepoint, finishing the fifth (*Christmas*) tree decoration, the octagon. I don't think I've ever been to the Phoenix Theatre before. As for the play, BLOOMSBURY, I loved it. How much of the marvelous dialogue is Peter Luke's and how much is taken directly from Virginia Woolf, Strachey, etc. I don't know but I

loved the free form. At the intermission I said, "It's marvelously well written." Ken's silence warned me to desist, that he didn't care for it. Literary lives do not, of course, interest Ken at all. In fact, lives of achievement in any field aren't apt to interest him. Inherited money, not earned, is what interests him, titles and power inherited rather than seized or earned, is what interests him. By the end of the play he had been somewhat won over, perhaps, but mostly by the campy lines involving Strachey's homosexuality. Daniel Massey did a fine job as Strachey but maintaining that high-pitched voice must be a little difficult. When we got home we went over the possibilities for tomorrow and settled on Windsor Castle, which we haven't seen in some years. I then went in to shower and encountered the first beauty I've seen here. With long wavy blond hair and small beard, he was testing the water while wearing bathing trunks. With his beautiful figure I hoped he wasn't a neurotic afraid to bare his loins out of embarrassment for his small equipment or something. I needn't have worried for he soon slipped his trunks off and revealed beautiful genitals that matched the rest of him. I think we were making slow progress toward each other when a third person came in and that spoiled it. Went to bed fancying a follow-thru with the young beauty.

SATURDAY, JULY 20, 1974

It was a gray day so we decided against Windsor and referred to our Quick Guide to London for substitutes. As the Theatre Museum is in this area we decided to start with that and then see whether the weather suggested the Victoria and Albert or Windsor. The Theatre Museum is celebrating its 10th anniversary and is due to move next year to larger quarters. Small as it is it contained a lot of fascinating things--Sarah Siddons' dressing table, a script for SCHOOL FOR SCANDAL prepared by a scribe at the time of the first production, David Garrick's repertoire for 174 nights in I forget what year with receipts for each performance, Irving's more complex account books with repertoire, receipts, disbursements, etc., lots of letters from Shaw, Barrie, Bernhardt (one asking Irving how he got the wonderful thunder effect in FAUST, which she wanted to use in her forthcoming CLEOPATRA). The lady in charge was charming, apologizing ever so much because she was required to inspect all handbags and packages for bombs. To the Victoria and Albert. There we started with the embroidery dept., which we had never seen before. This led us to the discovery of the jewelry rooms. Ken, who had groaned with fatigue when, after a rest outside the museum,

snapped out of it when he saw Fabergé Easter Eggs from
1897 in which the surprise was a model of Nicholas and Alexandra's coronation coach or a brooch given Queen Elizabeth I to comemorate the defeat of tht Armada, a miniature
portrait on the back and a goldwork portrait on front. Now
to the evening--we ate nearby where I had a steak and kidney pie that was mostly kidneys but fine with me. Then to
the Westminster Theatre and OH, KAY. This my third samp-
ling of the musicals of the twenties and definitely the
last. Not only I but the entire audience sat silent as
about 100 would-be laugh lines or gestures went by in the
first act. When television gives us such mechanical trash
these days, as it often does, it has a recorded laugh
track to provide the laughs and the poor actors might have
been grateful for one. There were more and louder laughs
in any one scene of BLOOMSBURY than in this whole show and
the laughs, like those in CHEZ NOUS, were at recognizable
characters and human foibles. When theatre's only object
is to amuse and it signally fails to do that one is left
with nothing.

MONDAY, JULY 22, 1974
 Walking along Cheyne Walk we saw where Rossetti and
Swinburne lived and where George Eliot died. We were waiting for a 39 bus to take us to Piccadilly Circus when I
consulted my map to see if any other number would do. My
eye lit on Tite St. and seeing it was almost the next
block, we went to see where Oscar Wilde lived at the
height of his fame and fortune. There is no plaque and
if it's the original building it's certainly been much
made over but at least it's called Oscar Court. We cashed
checks then I called the agent to whom my play had been
sent. He was most cordial, said they'd written me July 3
to call as soon as I arrived. I said I thought I'd sent
my London address and when he looked up my letter he said,
"Oh, you're with Dennis Welsh." There were other indications that he knew him, which tickled me. If he's considering me as meat in addition to talent he's in for a shock
when he sees my age. He said they liked my play tho it
presented obvious difficulties and would like to talk to
me. The weather and the sights we'd seen already had me
light of foot but I was in even more of a dancing mood
after that.

TUESDAY, JULY 23, 1974
 Mr. Fisher proved a handsome, florid man of great
charm. Mr. Bliss, who's really in charge of the play dept.
came in and joined us for a discussion of the play and its

possibilities. They like it, want only minor revisions
really, and will handle it tho they feel it falls between
the two schools--the art play and the commercial play.
They suggest that my curtains are weak but said it's tre-
mendously actable and many actors would be anxious to play
Ben. When they started discussing the weak ending of one
scene I said, "May I make the embarrassing confession that
I don't remember it?" They were pleased that I didn't consider the play as now written holy writ and would consider
their suggestions. Mr. Bliss said, "What disappointed me
a bit and what surprises me now that I've talked to you
for five minutes is that the humor dropped off." After we
had agreed I would work on it and supply new pages, which
I'd either send or give to Mr. Fisher when he comes to the
states toward the beginning of October, Mr. Bliss left us
and Fisher and I went on talking. He told me certain facts
and prejudices of British audiences and critics that will
be useful in future writing. I have a feeling that Fisher
is himself gay and that when he comes to New York and
calls me, as he said he would, hair will come down further. They were awfully complimentary. Ken was very happy
for me. He had gone down to watch guests arriving at the
Queen's Garden Party. We turned around almost immediately
to go downtown. We had only a short way to go to the Criterion and our play ABSURD PERSON SINGULAR. It was terribly funny, the middle act being perhaps the funniest single
act I ever saw as a wife tried repeatedly to commit suicide by various means only to be thwarted by party guests
who mistook her purpose and proceeded to help. When she
put her head in the oven she was discovered by a friend
with a cleaning compulsion who thought she was cleaning
the oven for Christmas and proceeded to do it for her. I
was weak with laughter before that suicide act was over as
the successive suicide notes were used by friends to make
lists on the back.

THURSDAY, JULY 25, 1974
      Sunny again for a nice final view of London. We took
our leave, or Ken did, of Mr. Welsh, who hasn't been notable for charm tho he certainly has for a spotless effic-
ient hotel. Bob and José, who dreamed of a gay hostelry in
Spain, would have drowned one in charm and forgotten to
wash the sheets or order milk for breakfast. On the whole
I'll take the efficiency. As we bussed thru London and I
saw all the painting and construction going on with workers stripped to the waist, I wondered what dear old Victoria would have thought of that. Tho New York has had hellish heat, it was comfortable when we landed and I didn't

have as difficult an adjustment as I sometimes do. We found the house in a bit of disarray and Peter explained that he was a little bit behind in his timetable. We waited for him to take his leave but he didn't so I proceeded to unpack. A copy of my play had been returned and eventually I found out another reason Peter hung around. He'd read the play, was fascinated by it, is gay himself, etc. I ignored him at frequent intervals, continuing to unpack. When his call finally reached the woman I heard him say,"Well, I'm not going to just dash out the door. Give me half an hour." As he had already stayed two hours or so, I wouldn't have called it dashing out the door. When Peter finally left, Ken, tired after the long day, said, "I thought you'd never let him go. You kept him talking." I, equally tired, also lost my temper and said,"I was out of the room unpacking for half an hour at a time. If you had a magic method for getting rid of him, you should have used it." "What could I do?" "Well, you seem to think I could have got rid of him." Ken drew in his horns, warmed up some soup, and went to bed. Peter said the cats never slept with him but they've staked out their places on our beds tonight.

SUNDAY, JULY 28, 1974
      After some reading of the paper we set out downtown to see A VERY NATURAL THING, a sort of soap opera with males instead of heterosexuals. Thought certainly not art, it maintained a level of intelligence in its dialogue that I really didn't expect, and also was realistic in its depiction of male love affairs. One lead was romantic and first fell for a Yalie who didn't want to say "I love you", just wanted sex. Eventually they were playing house as intensely as anyone but then the restiveness set in. Much of the dialogue has come out of my mouth or Ken's, but what interested me was that sometimes one character would be saying things I've said, then the other. After the breakup, the lead met a real beauty at a gay liberation march but the movie ended with him still fearful of accepting the other's proposal to live together, so the ending wasn't soupy. There was no hard-core pornography in it, which may be why the acting was so much better than it usually is in these things. Genuine actors would be willing to play love scenes in the nude if no action but kissing and caressing was required and genitals were not displayed until a final slow motion run along the beach. We finished the paper when we got home and then I got supper as I wanted to try the shrimp-mushroom-tomato-thin lemon slices salad that Ethel had served us in Stockholm. I lacked dill to complete her marvelous dressing of mayonnaise-whipping cream-chili

sauce but it was delicious and I was happy to see Ken keep going back for more. Read much of THE BEST LITTLE BOY IN THE WORLD, an excerpt of which I read in NEW YORK magazine and liked, and the whole of which is very funny.

TUESDAY, JULY 30, 1974
Ken went back to his volunteer work at St. Luke's today. He also mailed my new play to the Register of Copyrights and the O'Neill Foundation. I had every intention of working on the play for London but Lisa came to get a report on the trip and by the time she left I didn't feel like it so devoted myself to finishing THE BEST LITTLE BOY IN THE WORLD, which proved a very astute look at the homosexual world from one who was almost as gauche and naive when they entered it as I was. It gave me a lot of laughs and I recommended it highly to Ken, who seems to be standing a little aloof from it.

SUNDAY, AUGUST 4, 1974
Paper. Cleaning. I was absolutely soaked when I got thru and not too upset when I stepped into the shower and found there was no hot water. Normally I don't have the guts for a cold shower but today it was no hardship at all. I got the pictures ready to take to Leo's, culling quite a few to Ken's distress. We didn't have the luck to get an air-conditioned bus (that's a lottery which I win only on rare occasions) and the trip down was torture. Whenever Ken touched me, and I never knew him to touch me so much, it made my clothes stick to my body. I hated to say anything, and I didn't, but I even hated to rest my own hand on my knee as it was hot. Leo and Larry's apartment is air-conditioned, fortunately, and a gin drink helped. Both Leo and Larry were wearing caftans bought in Morocco and a surprising amount of jewelry. It's a cool-looking garment and I may buy one for house wear. Al, the friend from Cincinnati, tho about 65 and not now showing any signs of ever having been attractive, regaled us with tales of males and females wildly smitten with him, from World War II on. Such devotion and passion I never inspired and I can't see how on earth he does but I guess if Russ can, anybody can. Much furniture has been changed around to accommodate Larry's things when he moved in and I like the new arrangement.

TUESDAY, AUGUST 20, 1974
My parting from Ken this morning was in considerable contrast to last year's, when I was so put out with him, so sure our relationship was falling apart, that I didn't

even kiss him goodbye. We've been quite amiable with each other lately and it amazes me that I was foolish enough last year to take so seriously something he said at a party and in his cups. I called him about noon today to say goodbye, as my usual hour for calling would have been too late. At noon I typed more of my play and on my afternoon break I read the first act of Eric's play. I thought for a moment or two that it represented a great leap forward but before long it fell into the same old grooves. The cats were startled to see me come home and for a while couldn't pull themselves out of the funk Ken's departure with suitcase had left them in. When it finally sank in that they weren't to be deserted by both of us, they were happy beasts.

FRIDAY, AUGUST 23, 1974
At noon I finished up the typing on the first scene of GAY REQUIEM. To the baths, where I had a very active time if by no means as satisfactory as the visit before last. At one point three of us with beards were entangled in a triangle of unrequited desire. I liked a tall bearded blond, who really wasn't interested in me but in a black-bearded fellow wearing the first cock ring I've encountered at the baths. The latter, however, was more interested in me so we were all tolerating the one we weren't interested in as a lure for the one we were. An excess of steam finally broke it all up. As always after the baths I was famished and probably wiped out all losses from dieting in the one meal.

SUNDAY, AUGUST 25, 1974
Mother's house smelled as smoky as usual so I set about opening a window. "Oh, lots of dirt will come in," said Mother,"I'll turn the air-conditioning on instead." "That won't do it," I insisted and put one window way up. As soon as I got the food unpacked I whisked her out to the benches in the yard, again emphasizing what oxygen would do for the failing memory she worries so much about. Eventually the sun got hot and we went up to the apartment to have dinner. When she opened her refrigerator the odor of rotting food was overwhelming and it was jammed. She said she'd bought a lot of stuff she'd thought she was going to eat and then had eaten out. That's nothing new, nothing related to age. She always bought on whim and let stuff spoil. I hated working in her kitchen. She said two tiny glasses such as cheese spread comes in were the only glasses she had. I refused to believe it, knowing one cupboard contained nothing but glasses. In front of that she had a collection of a dozen or so juice and soda bottles. "They don't give

refunds on those and I don't know what to do with them."
"Throw them out. That's what you do with them." I took them
to the trash room then found lots of glasses in the un-
blocked cupboard, including the nice ones I gave her. When
I threw out the bottles she said, "See, I need you to come
live with me and look after me." When I snorted she said,
"No, I guess that wouldn't be good for either of us." But
on other occasions when I got authoritative, she said,
"Who died and left you boss?" Surreptitiously I kept looking at my watch and thinking the day would never pass.
When I got back to New York I was more fatigued by the afternoon in Trenton than I would be by 2 1/2 weeks work on
the job. When I got home I had the first drink I've had
since Ken left.

SUNDAY, SEPTEMBER 1, 1974
    Couldn't finish cleaning before it was time for us to
go to the State Theatre to see THE MIKADO. It was a lovely,
amusing, and beautifully sung performance and I so envied
Gilbert and Sullivan their fantastic talent. I envy and
covet all talent but given a choice I think I'd prefer to
have the light and graceful talents of Mozart, Gilbert and
Sullivan, Jane Austen, Cole Porter, Paul Klee, Emily Dickinson than the weightier talents of Wagner, Balzac, Michelangelo, George Eliot, Rembrandt. It's not that I admire
George Bernard Shaw more than Ibsen or Noel Coward more
than Eugene O'Neill (oh, that was a bad choice for I dislike O'Neill though one has to respect his aims even if
not his achievement) but I would just rather possess the
airier talents. I'd rather have written ALICE IN WONDER-
LAND than MOBY DICK, the piano music of Chopin than the
symphonies of Schumann.

SUNDAY, SEPTEMBER 8, 1974
    A DAY OF INFAMY. President Ford gave a total pardon
to Richard Nixon for anything he might have done while in
the presidency. The top of my head came right off when I
heard of it and I sat down and wrote furious postcards to
Ford, Atty. Genl. Saxbe, the two New York Senators and
the Governor, as well as the new Chairman of the Republican party. To abort everything this way is just to continue
to cover up the Nixon and Republican crimes. To justify
the pardon on the grounds that Nixon's loved ones have
suffered enough is a weird new principle of law on which
any prisoner in the land might justifiably pounce. They
all have loved ones, most of whom have suffered far more
than the Nixons. They have risen far above the financial
position their talents might have brought them and if they

are somewhat shamed, they have fat bank accounts and two
mansions to wallow in. I stopped writing cards only because
I ran out but I am absolutely going to assail members of
Congress. We went down to the Museum of the City of New
York to see the Eugene O'Neill exhibit. His manuscripts
were done in a script smaller than my finest but a very
nice hand.

MONDAY, SEPTEMBER 9, 1974

After supper, as I worked on my crewel, I was surprised by a call from the National Gay Task Force, saying I had volunteered to work and now my time had come. I had given up all idea of ever hearing from them. They have a mailing to get out and I agreed to go from work tomorrow night and help. The fellow sounded surprised when I agreed so perhaps quite a few people had been giving excuses.

TUESDAY, SEPTEMBER 10, 1974

Subwayed to 14th St. and reported to the Gay Task Force office. There was nobody in the reception office, nobody in the mail room, nobody in another office but I pursued the sound of voices and finally came on Bruce Voeller, the bearded blond head of the thing and a few of his staff. He's been much publicized because he used to be a doctor at Rockefeller Institute and had two children from a marriage he broke up to move in with a male lover, but his manner is modest and business-like. As the coordinator of volunteers hadn't yet arrived, he had Natalie Rockhill, a well-publicized lesbian, give me a list from which I was to address envelopes. Voeller and the regular staff went home, saying goodbye nicely, and eventually an older volunteer arrived. The older man began to complain bitterly about youth chauvinism in the gay world, saying the cruelty to the older ones was terrible. The ensuing conversation reminded me of some I'd had with George Worrell and Oliver Flemish. To assure the man that not everybody was hung up on the young I said I'd rather go to bed with Paul Newman, in his fifties, than any ten young people. "Yes," he said,"with Paul Newman, but how about Sidney Greenstreet?" Aside from being dead, Greenstreet in his prime weighed nearly 300, which seemed another problem from being old and I said I wouldn't have been interested in him even when young but that we all knew from ads in the gay papers that chubby chasers existed. 'Yes," sneered the man,"but not many." I then asked him if I understood then that he himself didn't particularly care for the young. "Yes, I like them, too." Vic mentioned a couple of bars that catered to older men and the other man sneered again,

"Yes, but have you seen them? Miserable, unhappy, alcoholic." In other words, he wanted young people forced to see his attraction tho he's not young but he's not interested in starting by seeing the attractions of an older man himself. Nothing any of us suggested was the answer. When he complained of being lonely I said I could conceive of sharing a home with another man in a non-sexual relationship, which would answer the problem of loneliness. But that didn't interest him either. Vic suggested the West Side Discussion Group, which does have an interesting series of lectures on homosexuality with social hours afterward, but that didn't interest. He's just exactly like Oliver and George. One couldn't advise them either because they wanted a gloriously beautiful young man wildly in love with them and totally uncritical and with absolute subservience. The trouble with all of them is that they're really not very nice people. They never give people a chance to fall in love with them slowly by being nice to them so that preconceptions against age or looks are lost as one comes to love the whole person.

TUESDAY, SEPTEMBER 17, 1974
    Bob R. brought me a copy of today's SPECTATOR in which one wantad sought a houseboy for two desperate students, 19 and 20, who would reward with bed and other pleasures, satisfaction guaranteed. I took it with me when I went to do my volunteer work at Natl. Gay Task Force. Victor said that volunteers generally show up once then never again. He's efficient and his manner with disturbed gay people who call for advice is admirably understanding but his charm, like mine sometimes, is more dutiful and calculated than spontaneous. Bruce Voeller, on the other hand, and his lover Bill, both of whom worked with us on the mailing, are naturally and easily charming. A fellow worked a while with us, a lesbian pre-med longer, but mostly it was Victor, Bruce, Bill, and me. I recognized a lot of big names in the arts as members but didn't even pass them on to Ken when I got home. I intend to stick with it even tho I end the long day very tired as I think the gay political movement is being handled very well by Bruce and cohorts. Both he and Bill, who is in charge of the mail room for Colt studios (high-class physique and porny pictures) wear their hair in a pigtail. Bruce, formerly married and still an active father, is the softer and more feminine of the two. Ken fixed soup when I got home.

WEDNESDAY, SEPTEMBER 18, 1974

Ken had the Bulletin collated and ready for delivery when I got home so I called the delivery boys. We ate hastily then were off to the State Theatre. There was the usual electric first-nite City Opera crowd and we got a perfectly marvelous performance of DIE FLEDERMAUS, which I have often heard but never seen. Only unforeseen catastrophe could keep Johanna Meier, the Rosalinda, and Ruth Welting, the Adele, from becoming major stars. Were it not for the longueurs of the third act I could see it again. At least the Frosch was funny and got guffaws but there would be diminishing returns the second time.

SATURDAY, SEPT. 2, 1974

I suggested we go to the half-priced ticket booth in Duffy Square and see if they had tickets to Peter Nichols' THE NATIONAL HEALTH. On our way to the booth we discovered a new and stunning garden behind the Exxon Bldg. on Sixth Ave. There's another garden in the block to the north which has a waterfall like the one in Paley Park. That alone would have made my day but it continued great. NATIONAL HEALTH, like the author's JOE EGG, is a terribly funny play even tho three of the men in the hospital ward die in the course of the play and another is virtually lobotomized by a second motorbike accident after he got out from the first. The actors hardly seemed like actors. I admired the play so much I wanted to go home and tear mine to bits. Of all the many things I laughed at I think what struck me funniest was the overworked woman doctor who had been on duty 29 hours and kept falling asleep. Finally she leaned over to listen to a patient's chest and never came up because she fell asleep right there.

SUNDAY, SEPT. 22, 1974

In late afternoon by train to Alice's, last to arrive. I took a quiz book with me to read on the train and was mortified to find how ignorant I was. I did the ones in fields I never studied and got so demoralized that I switched to fields I supposedly knew something about but was haunted by my ignorance. Strangely, when we arrived at Roslyn I found my memory in an atypical lapse and forgot so many things that I suddenly understood Mother's panic and shared a bit of it. Of course Mother's memory was never much because of lack of interest but I have a reputation for phenomenal memory and it was a second disturbing experience perhaps not unrelated to my doing badly on the quizzes. Everybody was quite delighted, as people generally are when I seem fallible or weakened. It was a pleasant but strange evening as somehow at the table everybody began to confess to thievery of one sort or another. I admitted to childhood shoplifting but that came to an end when I was 9 or 10 whereas Pearl talked of taking blankets from a spa quite recently and Rosamund talked of gambits by which she escaped paying for meals she and her daughters had in good restaurants. Joseph, Rosamund's new husband, was seriously shocked. All the males seemed moralistic, the women all lacking in guilt, but I found it hilarious for middle-class women to be outdoing each other in confessing their crimes. I pretended to be fixing hidden microphones behind pictures and under the table. It was a very silly but pleasant evening.

SATURDAY, SEPTEMBER 28, 1974

As Ken's cold had taken a turn for the worse he started mumbling, "I'm not sure I want to spend $5 to see Jack the Stripper," and I jumped right in and said that if he had any doubts I didn't want him to go. It started to rain and he said he probably shouldn't go out anyway. I agreed it was wise not to but went ahead by myself. Had a look at the mobile ticket booth but it was nearly matinée time and they had nothing much to offer so I went ahead to the Male Burlesk Show. It was in progress as I arrived and Rob Roy was just removing the last g-string to reveal that he had very little under it, but his figure was nice. Two more strips led up to the star turn of Jack the Stripper and all figures were good but the show was terrible. Jack did some stunts with burning torches and rings of fire and I quickly checked the exits for if anything had gone wrong that place would have been a firetrap. Upstairs there was burlesque for heterosexuals with girls no doubt doing more or less what the four men were doing for us and every now and then it struck me funny. To fill the time between stage shows (five a day, just like old-time vaudeville) there were movies and I think the total budget for the one we saw must have been $5.38. It was in parts so terrible it was funny. I didn't stay for the whole thing, having seen what I came to see. I don't need to repeat that either as I can see beautiful bodies at the Beacon Baths and do more about them.

FRIDAY, OCTOBER 4, 1974

I left work at 12:30, taking half a day's vacation to help get ready for entertaining John Fisher and friend. As I suspected, the "chum" was the man John has lived with since 1947, a very nice Irishman with a strong cross in one eye. I thought John's hair would come down tonite

and it sure did. He admitted they'd gone to the baths in
San Francisco (New York is their last American stop, not
their first as I supposed) and eventually we were showing
them our collection of the best centerfolds from Playgirl.
John, tho born in New York, went to live in Los Angeles in
1919, his stepfather being one of the early film directors.
He originally acted in England before going into the talent business and we learned of many distinguished clients
in the course of the evening so my play really is in the
hands of a major agency. Furthermore, John wasn't just here
to dish gay gossip for he asked me to make sure we didn't
forget to see that he had what I'd revised of my play before he left. We seemed to be in almost total agreement,
as in London, on our feelings about theatre. He and Pat,
too, are very anxious to go to Egypt. They may look around
for a good mid-winter trip and we may all go together. I
said we'd each take one side of a pyramid and see which of
us reached the top first, the prize to be two free weeks
in the intensive care ward.

SATURDAY, OCTOBER 5, 1974
It was a glorious sparkling day and we were so happy
for John and Pat that they'd have a splendid final impression of our city. They said last nite that the media had
led them to believe New Yorkers were all cowering behind
their doors and litter was piled in the streets but they
found it vibrant and Times Square far less squalid than
Piccadilly Circus. We had lunch at the James, where the
counterman ordered Ken to take his pipe off the counter.
My seeing some reasonableness in the request since fruit
salad and other food were up there got me included in Ken's
general fury at the criticism and I got the silent treatment. Ken said we'd never go there again and I didn't repeat my error of commenting as I don't care. Peace was reestablished before we got to the Plaza Theatre, where we
saw AMARCORD, a perfectly marvelous Fellini movie. It was
hilarious, moving, and thought-provoking. In one or two
episodes it was also gloriously romantic as when a great
snowfall hit an Italian city and when the citizenry went
out to sea in small boats and waited to see the great liner Rex pass, all lit up on its maiden voyage. Fellini's
genius includes one of the greatest talents for casting
that I ever saw. He uses grotesque size and shape for the
ultimate effectiveness--a midget nun who successfully orders an insane man down out of a tree after all family
efforts to get him down fail, a huge-breasted tobacconist
who presses her great breast in the mouth of an adolescent
boy who's been intrigued and tells him, "Suck, don't blow."

All the rest of the day Ken and I were reminding each other of great bits. Mother called as we sat down to eat, still didn't know what train she'd take so I suggested 10 and told her I'd meet her at eleven. "Are you going to be mean to me?" she asked. "Oh, I may beat you about three times and put thumb screws on you, but aside from that__." "I was just kidding. You've never been mean to me, dear." Which is as big a lie as Mother ever told but not one I argue with as I do with some. About ten the phone rang again and I said, "Oh, dear, she's spoiling it." But it was John calling from the airport to say what a wonderful day they'd had and a wonderful evening. They went to Lincoln Center and John said nobody had ever told him how good the theatre library was and as a Londoner he was envious. Which shames me into going there more often, something I've been meaning to do.

TUESDAY, OCTOBER 8, 1974

Another enjoyable day at work, researching trustee prospects, which makes one feel one's work is having considerable impact, or could. At noon I had another good work session, adding more humor to the play. When I called Ken I got a report on his visit to Columbia Travel. The cheapest staterooms were already all booked for the Caribbean cruise on the Maxim Gorki but there were others more toward the bow for only $40 more. I told him it was completely up to him then he told me he'd already booked us for February 4 subject to my approval. I was delighted and immediately put in a memo asking for the vacation time.

SATURDAY, OCTOBER 12, 1974

Slept better than I meant to as I meant to keep watch over Ken's covers and prevent him from being uncovered after his tossing. He slept well into the morning and I decided not to vacuum today lest I disturb him. When he woke I fixed him tea and while he was in the bathroom I quickly made his bed up fresh, for which he was appreciative. He clearly couldn't go to the party in Babylon but I was afraid if neither of us went we'd just get asked soon again so when I determined that he wanted no food and would be all right here alone, I decided to go. It wasn't as bad a time as Ken anticipated and I can roll with the punches more. Lee's mother, using a walker as she recovers from a broken hip, was pleasant and unobtrusive and quickly spotted the Swedish writing on the wrappings of the wooden bowl from Stockholm that I took. Dinner was good tho Ruth picked mercilessly at Lee all evening. They had all seen each other just last night at Clyde and Phil's. It seems so stupid to me the way they arrange two parties for the same set of people on the same weekend so that inevitably you get boredom when people hear Clyde telling me what he had told the others just last nite. Going in to dinner Philip came close to me and said, "Twenty years ago you must have been quite a dish," but after dinner he fell asleep for an hour or two so age and liquor saved me from more than a surreptitious grope of my posterior. Lee told me that her mother, to whom I showed our snapshots of her relatives in Sweden, had taken a great fancy to me and had told Lee in Swedish that she hoped things developed between her and me. "I don't rub her nose in the facts of life," said Lee. Since I couldn't see the slightest effort being made by Clyde and Phil to moderate their outspoken talk in front of Lee's mother, including pantomimed masturbation at one point, I don't know why she doesn't catch on. Clyde and Phil really are terrible people, just as Mac and Gene said they were when I first heard them discussed. Everybody had been solicitous about Ken and Ruth asked if I'd like to call and see how he was but I had phoned him just before I got on the train and didn't think another call was necessary. They gave me some cake and pot roast for him and tho I knew it likely that all food would still be repulsive to him, I took it.

TUESDAY, OCTOBER 22, 1974

I went down to National Gay Task Force after work and there we had quite a decent turnout for volunteer work. We worked on a mailing and I'll be lame tomorrow from collating and creasing four pages for mailing. In the early part of the evening one fellow was holding forth on his first night as a hustler, when he claimed he made $90 servicing three customers. He's a very naive boy (21) from Cleveland who just found out what "clap" is and the conversation was hilarious to Victor and me. At 21 the boy is well on his way to turning bald, is thick through and has no good features except teeth so I hope those who call his agency are not too shocked at what they're getting for their $40. He says he really tries to please his customers but nothing he could do would ever please me. Only one of the nine tonite could interest me in the slightest but I stick strictly to business there, being so much older than they are. The Task Force, pressed for money, is moving at the end of the month to smaller offices on the 5th floor. I worked till nine.

FRIDAY, OCTOBER 25, 1974

Good work on the play at noon. After work I went to Beacon Baths and had one of my better visits. None of my three reciprocated but all were nicely complaisant. Having done so well I went home early and Ken joined me in a drink then fixed supper for me. He'd made a pumpkin pie which he surprised me with. It certainly is having the best of all worlds to have a good night at the baths and then go home to Ken.

MONDAY, OCTOBER 28, 1974

The Plymouth was packed with a very literate audience and part of the set was a ring of seats on the stage. EQUUS is a marvelous play, a marvelous defense of passion, and I admire it no end. The nudity in the crucial scene leading to the blinding of the horses wasn't interesting because Peter Furth is not my type--too pale, too slight, uncircumcised (tho I discovered Friday that isn't bad if the person is just out of the shower). What an actor Furth is, however, and as for attractive men, at least two of those who played the five horses up on hoof lifts and with masks, were gorgeous of face and body. EQUUS was only the second play without music I've ever heard "Bravo"ed and the other was GHOSTS, 35 or so years ago. I joined then but not tonite, any more than I joined the abortive attempt to start a standing ovation, but I certainly didn't resent the "bravos" as I do this damned nonsense of giving almost anybody and anything a standing ovation. The script has a fluidity I envy, the horses' costumes are simple but illusion-creating, the acting was magnificent, the audience intelligent and responsive--a really great night in the theatre. Some of its appeal to Americans comes, alas, from the nudity and the violence but if that gets people into the theatre I shan't quibble. I just hope they take to heart the author's bias toward passion and don't confuse it with the violence or think that's a necessary outgrowth.

TUESDAY, OCTOBER 29, 1974

Haunted by the play all night. It was one of the most erotic I've ever seen (not the nude scene but the embracing and riding of the horses) which seemed strange in view of the fact that horses have never been my thing as cats are. Then, as I took my shower, it struck me that both the author's verbal rapture and my reaction were probably based on the fact that the horses were depicted by magnificent-looking men. Would it have been the same had they been played by women? I think not. Shaffer did a very good, non-chauvinist thing in making all the women working or professional women--the woman judge provided vocal variety but he needn't have made the psychiatrist's unseen wife a dentist, the girl's unseen mother a shopkeeper, the boy's mother a former teacher, and I'm glad he did. The day started off well with a call from Mother to say that she forgot to mention in the letter she'd sent me that the Mobile Meals have been coming for two weeks and are fine. Worked on the play at noon. Ken had picked up library reserves including THE FRONT RUNNER, a homosexual love story about coach and runner and written, surprisingly, by a woman. Of course Mary Renault writes the most established books on homosexual love but it's usually excessively idealized whereas Patricia Warren knows the whole current scene and slang, including a bit that was news to me, which is that masculine-appearing gays who prefer other manly gays are called "macho gays".

SATURDAY, NOVEMBER 9, 1974

Brought out Ken's birthday presents as we had breakfast, very annoyed at myself for having forgotten to get him birthday cards. I didn't like those at the one place I looked and never thought of it again. We went downtown just in time for the matinee of ABSURD PERSON SINGULAR. The first and second acts of the play seemed less effective than in England but I think the last act was much better done here, bringing out not only more humor but more bitter content. There seemed in general an attempt to make the characters more real, less caricatured, and while this sacrificed some laughs, it perhaps paid off in the end. When we came out Dr. and Mrs. Wintermudd were waiting for us out in front of the theatre where they'd seen EQUUS and we proceeded to Joe Allen's. Wintermudd insisted on paying for the drinks and we toasted Ken on his birthday. Rather than have coffee there, Wintermudd suggested we taxi up to their place with them and have espresso and brandy. Conversation had been reasonably general at the restaurant but at home Melina again couldn't get a word in edgewise as Wintermudd took stage center and held it. He is so terribly hung up on family and his childhood memories, many of which we've heard before, and about which there is little that is fascinating. Ken and I left about 9:30, both very irritated at not getting an opportunity to probe Melina more, for we find her charming and interesting. I had other reasons for deciding not to entertain Dr. W. in the future but they are reinforced by my realization that he must, absolutely <u>must</u>, be the star. I think this accounts for his putting me down any time Melina compliments me. She said, for instance, that she imagined I was good with and sympathetic to employees, whereupon Bill quickly said, "Oh, no, he's very caustic." Now this is simply not true. The only employee I have ever ridden was Darryl, with whom

it is a joke. Bill just cannot stand having Melina say
anything good about my understanding, empathy, or things
like that and once before bluntly said, "Oh, no, I'm more
so than Don." It amuses me, of course, because it shows his
vulnerability, as does his tendency to be pompous about
the wine, a scene Ken and I chose to ignore in the restaurant, seizing the opportunity to get a word with Melina.
However, Ken and I agreed it was nice to have them join us.
Had we left it at that, I think it would have been better
but we didn't, and our visit to their house was certainly
not unpleasant, despite the size of Dr. W's ego.

SATURDAY, NOVEMBER 23, 1974

We got up early and were at the Met soon after it opened, trying to beat the crowds into the new exhibit of
romantic costumes from the movies. Even that early plenty
of people were there. Some of the costumes were copies,
others had had their fur parts restored, but most were originals. The earliest were those of Lillian Gish for ROMOLA (lovely) and WAY DOWN EAST (awful). 3 or 4 of Mary
Pickford's (designers for two were unknown and I suspect
they were bought off the racks and messed up for her ragamuffin roles), one of Irene Castle's and several of Mae
Murray's for MERRY WIDOW. Perhaps the loveliest were those
for Garbo (almost anything but those for MATA HARI, which
I always hated), for Norma Shearer as Marie Antoinette. A
lot of dresses from Marilyn Monroe's personal wardrobe
were shown and the costumes from GONE WITH THE WIND will
thrill many. Some costumes were made with the expected
theatrical cutting of corners but still photos from the
movies showed how sumptuous they looked in the film. Others were sumptuous, unnecessarily so, even to the close
eye.

FRIDAY, NOVEMBER 29, 1974

We got a late start downtown, which put me rather out
of patience with Ken, but I had a highly successful Christmas shopping day and that restored good disposition. We
laughed about several things yesterday, especially when a
mother was shown bathing a child in a bathtub on some tv
ad and Ken said, "There you are, bathing Donnie." "No," I
said,"we didn't have a bathtub in Benton." "Who said so,"
Mother said, bridling. "I said so. There was no running
water in the Benton house. We had a privy at the foot of
the garden, a pump on the back porch, two buckets of water
in the kitchen, and we took our baths in a washtub in the
middle of the kitchen floor." Mother thought a while then
said, "You're right." I don't think I even saw a bathtub

till I was five or six. Which is okay, but privies are not okay. I loathed everything about them--odor, temperature, public progress to and fro. I was also amused when, after I had shown Mother I was holding her return ticket and cut short her fortieth attempt to search her bag for it, she said, "You're more like my father than my son."

SATURDAY, NOVEMBER 30, 1974
We passed some time in the Times Square Marboro book store. The browsing cost me money as I bought Van Vechten's THE TIGER IN THE HOUSE, which for all my aelurophilia I have never read, and a book called SEXUAL HERETICS, an anthology of English homosexual literature 1850-1900. A full house was at the Majestic to see the next-to-last performance of MACK AND MABEL and when the Majestic is full you've one helluva crowd for the place is huge. All during the first act I thought the mild-to-bad reviews were too carping for I quite enjoyed it, especially Robert Preston's outsize star presence and wonderfully rhythmic way with a song. The second act, however, made the show's untimely demise perfectly understandable. After an act with slapstick numbers it is hard to have an act in which William Desmond Taylor is shot, Mabel dies of drugs and tb, and Mack Sennett goes bankrupt and loses his studio. There is just no way to make that material jolly. I didn't mind the liberties taken with the facts (Mabel apparently never loved or slept with Sennett as they have her doing here, almost certainly never acquired the dope habit from Taylor, whose murder may well have resulted from his attempt to break up the dope business that was preying on stars) but somehow the only way to have kept the show from getting depressing would have been to stop a lot earlier in the story. After supper, as I took a shower, I suddenly decided to resign the editorship of the 1270 Information Bulletin as of the January issue instead of next June's. I wrote a letter of resignation, suggesting either a black editor for a change or just the issuance of Eileen's minutes with items that should be kept in camera blue-pencilled before it was retyped. I think that will satisfy the cooperators as I don't really think there's any demand for a newsy paper. I feel very relieved that two more issues will be it. I think I have exhausted my ideas for making the paper effective and that fresh ideas are called for. I enjoyed doing it and gained tremendous confidence from it as I think I did a superb job, but no use in repeating myself. Delivered the resignation to Eileen when I returned to her the four sets of minutes that were digested for the last issue.

SATURDAY, DECEMBER 7, 1974

Off to an early start downtown. We got off at Lord & Taylor's and looked at their very interesting windows based on Thomas Nast's drawings, as their interior decorations are also based on Nast. Then to Altman's, where we were a bit disappointed to find them repeating windows they had last year. I hope the recession isn't going to lead stores to declare these things an instant tradition and throw more artists out of work. Radio City is also repeating and of course Saks always looks the same inside. Ken and I parted at Altman's. I walked all the way home up Madison and enjoyed every foot of the way tho eventually my left foot and ankle were painful. I went in lots of little stores I'd never been in and bought minor things along the way. American shopkeepers, either because of high overhead or pressure to sell, or lack of quite the French elegance, somewhat overload both their windows and their stores. There isn't the restful space between items. As a result one is weary not so much because one has walked between 80 and 90 blocks (which after all is under 5 miles) as because one has been assaulted by so many sense impressions.

TUESDAY, DECEMBER 10, 1974

As I felt absolutely top-drawer, there was none of last week's hesitation about going to the volunteer night at Gay Task Force. As Victor is down with the flu, Bob H. was again in charge of the volunteers. I started by doing the usual pasting on of address labels but the latter part of the evening Bob and I went into Bruce's office to proof the mailing list, which is being put on Cheshire labels. I noticed a big calendar on the wall on which Bruce plots the activities of the six members of the staff, a different color for each and what they must have done by what date. Tho the office is messy, they are more organized than they look and I'm all for what they're doing. I'd rather put in time there than on the 1270 Bulletin. Two other volunteers were brought in to proof the new list too and unfortunately they were both chain smokers. The smoke was like needles in my eyes. It gave Bob a headache so at 8:30 he decided we'd quit. I was half way home on the bus before I stopped tasting smoke in my lungs.

FRIDAY, DECEMBER 13, 1974

There were just two other couples at Leo's--Joe and Richard, whom we have met a couple of times before there and Jack and Tony, whom we have not. Leo and Larry had the usual overwhelming amount of decoration for Christmas.

Never was a house so overfurnished and yet attractive to me. From India they brought back about three tons more of statues and all sorts of things. They asked if we wanted to see some of the slides before dinner and some after and since there were 600, we allowed as how that would be fine. Even Ken, who says "Ugh" at the very mention of India, had to admit that the palaces, hotels, gardens, temples, etc., were beautiful and that the sculpture, erotic or otherwise, was fascinating. 119 degrees heat isn't appealing, however, no matter how much reassurance they gave us that it was a different, less objectionable kind of heat and sometimes even Leo and Larry would admit, "Now THERE it was really hot."

SATURDAY, DECEMBER 21, 1974
   I had the plum pudding made by the time the opera broadcast started. I liked JENUFA as a novelty tho Astrid Varnay who sang (?) Kostelnicka, is so far over the hill vocally that it was an embarrassment and no service to Janacek. It was too bad, in a way, that after listening to opera all afternoon we had to go out to the opera at night but there was no helping it. L'ITALIANA turned out to be very easy to take, even after an afternoon of JENUFA. The sets and costumes were lovely. Horne, of course, is an absolute phenomenon of a singer and a natural comedian. Costumed to minimize her bulk, she carried it well and how she did sing!

THURSDAY, DECEMBER 26, 1974
   I thought of several funny things that happened during Mother's visit yesterday. At the table, as the plum pudding was being praised, Mimie said, "You taught him well, Mrs. Vining," and Mother all but got up to take a bow while I tried to suppress laughter. Later, on the bus to the station, she saw an ad placard about a restaurant featuring pecan pie. Somehow I mentioned I'd made one and she said, "Send me the recipe. I'd like to make one." I laughed and said,"You never made a pie in your life so why start now?" She insisted she had so made a pie and I asked, "When? 1911?" "Well, sometime. I've certainly made one." At least when I make fun of her she **can** laugh.

FRIDAY, DECEMBER 27, 1974
   At noon I worked on ARIADNE and the ideas just flowed. From work to Beacon Baths, where the best-looking person I saw all evening was just starting to leave as I arrived. He hesitated before putting on his shorts, gave me a good look at a beautiful body, and I think if I had smiled and

given encouragement he would have stayed. Had I known that
poundage was going to be more common than pulchritude, I
surely would have taken action. Left earlier than usual
because the pickings were slim. No, slim they weren't,
come to think of it.

SUNDAY, DECEMBER 29, 1974
    Ken wasn't quite sure he wanted to go see the gay
revue LOVERS, recommended to me at Gay Task Force. In the
end he decided we might as well go. There was a cute ad
today announcing a New Year's Gala and saying "Laugh over
what you cried over last year". There has been no official
opening as yet (lots of shows are trying that these days)
and that may account for the sparse crowd. There is, of
course, no nudity in its consideration of gay relationships but there is a great deal of wit and truth in the
lyrics, some melody in the songs, and very professional
acting, singing, direction. Two boys were Latin types,
two were tall leather types (much the handsomest and much
the best singers) and two were conservative suit types,
representing a couple that had been together twenty years.
There was a realistic attitude rather than either cynicism or sentimentality and it all struck the right note
for me. There was a good number on "Fights" which showed
the three couples each having a different kind of squab-
ble but my favorite, I think, was the lusty number set at
the trucks, where the tallest fellow did a marvelous song
about lust as opposed to love and minced no words in the
lyrics about the kinds of sex available at the trucks.
There was a good song about the kind of fidelity that
matters as opposed to the fidelity of the body and another excellent number about role-playing and not ever forgetting that it's a man you're living with. Mother called
and at first sounded quite sensible but then got addled.
Then she couldn't remember when I was coming over and
didn't seem to have written it down yesterday after all
we went thru on the phone so later she called back to say
she'd found her calendar book. I gave her the date, reiterated that it was a checkup visit, and she read back,
"Jan. 27. Donald coming over. Beware!" Now what can you
do with someone like that? It just infuriates Ken that I
get more amused than exasperated the way he does. But that
"Beware!" tickled me no end.

1975

THURSDAY, JANUARY 2, 1975
    Did a bit of needlepoint while watching A FAMILY AT WAR but never got around to any reading till I went to bed. Tho I have three books by my bed, I've been concentrating on SEXUAL HERETICS. Of course much of it involves pedophilia, which I still struggle to understand without avail. There is, for instance, a poet called John Nicholson, I think, whose picture was taken with one of his boy muses. The boy is a decent-looking boy but the older man is really very attractive and he's the one who would attract me. The thought that he wouldn't have been interested in anybody past boyhood is depressing. Mooning about over a boy seems like such pastel passion. The minds of young boys could be interesting and challenging to try to mold, but their bodies? Tho sado-masochism doesn't interest me--I hate to be hurt and withdraw on moral grounds from inflicting hurt--but I can project myself into the psychology of the S-M people up to a point. I cannot project myself into the mind and psyche of a pedophile, however.

SATURDAY, JANUARY 4, 1975
    To the David, thinking that if PRISON FOR LIFE had run six weeks, it must be superior to the run of pornographic films we've been getting. It wasn't. The scenarist had a good notion of the proper fantasies but they didn't have the performers who could embody them nor the technicians who could film it well. The whole fantasy of the guard who forces the prisoner to have sex with him then falls in love with him was ruined from the outset because they didn't have a man who personified tough masculinity but a man more diminutive than the prisoners and softer, whose uniform was so ill-fitting that he clearly felt as absurd as he looked. Beat Ken home by less than five minutes, which was his good luck because he'd forgotten his keys. I heard the last act of L'ITALIANA and the tribute to Milton Cross, who died yesterday after announcing all but two of the opera broadcasts since 1931. He was woven into the fabric of my life but the last two or three years he's sounded old and fumbling and I really thought he should be replaced, sentiment or no sentiment. Worked on my needlepoint while we watched an excellent TV version of ANTONY AND CLEOPATRA based on the Royal Shakespeare Company production. Janet Suzman was a mature and mercurial queen, Richard Johnson a believable leader of men,

and tho I never learned who played Octavius, one could see him ruling the empire and growing into Augustus. It was tiring and for once I was rather glad for commercial breaks. But TV, for all the crap it puts on to fill the empty hours, is truly providing treats these days at frequent intervals, and this wasn't on the educational station but regular commercial TV.

SATURDAY, JANUARY 11, 1975

Did our cleaning since we didn't want to be downtown till the opening of the discount ticket booth at noon. The one I was interested in was THE RITZ, now previewing. When tried out at Yale it was called THE TUBS but because TUBS-TRIP has since played here, a title change was obviously needed. I would say that Terence McNally was as untouched by inspiration when he picked the new title as I was when I retitled CRY ON MY SHOULDER. The play, however, is a fount of inspiration. As I looked at the gathering audience for THE RITZ I could see almost nobody I thought belonged at a play set in a men's bath but as it turned out, none of the main characters are gay and the humor of the play largely derives from their being out of their element. When the play got under way the scenery and lighting got in a tangle and the curtain had to be rung down. There was consternation on the part of the production crew and I think the small attractive blond I saw holding his head was McNally but eventually they started over and all went well. The play is immaculately crafted, very funny, and once again I admired the talent of McNally inordinately. Gay Task Force will probably hate his caricatures of a chubby chaser and a screaming queen but in this case I'm not inclined to be supersensitive. The two bath employees were presented as lovers who had remained so for three years but otherwise all was pretty gross, tho a couple of good-looking types were wandering in towels from room to room. Ken, somewhat impatient at the mixups and delay in starting, eventually found the farce irresistible and was reminding me of funny lines in the evening.

FRIDAY, JANUARY 17, 1975

Peggy had redone her apartment and it looked splendid. Ken and I had good cards and our study paid off as we realized what each other's bids meant. At one point Pat and Peg said they knew the years were flying by but they didn't feel a bit older. Ken and I said we did. When Pat said she felt just the same inside and Peg agreed I let it pass but thought what a lot of nonsense it was. I most certainly do feel the passage of time in both good and bad ways. I may

be wrong in thinking I'm wiser and more mature but that's
the way I feel. I also know that I can't walk as far as
vigorously, stay up late as many nights, dance and fool
around, or do a lot of things I once did. Perhaps Peg and
Pat never really were vigorous and thus don't see much
difference but I make a lot of concessions to myself and
with the years will make more. The cruises are a concession not just to Ken's age but to my own. I think older
people who say they feel exactly the same are lying to
somebody, either to others or to themselves. Lots of things
are better rather than worse but they certainly are not the
same.

WEDNESDAY, JANUARY 22, 1975
   Ken's news today was that Leo called to say that Mac
died suddenly of meningitis after four days' illness. He
went stone deaf four days before he died. He and Gene both
certainly went fast. Mac was only 54. He wanted to be buried in Ct. with Gene but his sister is going to bury him
in the Bronx. Nobody would dream of separating a married
couple but with the bodies of male lovers families do what
they damned please.

TUESDAY, FEBRUARY 4, 1975
   Manhattan's new ship terminal, opened in November, is
very nice indeed and so was the Maxim Gorki. Our room is
larger by far than the one we had on the Rotterdam and we
have a bathtub as we didn't last year. Room stewards and
some dining room personnel are female but the waiters in
the Rossia lounge, where we had tea while waiting for our
delayed departure, are male and attractive. Dinner was superb and our tablemates are a nice quiet couple from Mass-
achusetts and a nice quiet couple from Kingston, Ont. The
way of serving meals is nice as they bring the food around
to show you and ask if you'd like some, rather than having
you order sight unseen from the menu. I like that and
tried some things that turned out very interesting. I do
like Russians so much.

WEDNESDAY, FEBRUARY 5, 1975
   In the night things crashed about in our closet and
on our dresser but I felt all right. Perhaps as a result
of all the water I drank on my bathroom visits, however, I
felt far from all right in the morning. The stewardesses
were sick too so many rooms, including ours, never got
made up. We tried to get some bracing air but because of
the pitching and the slippery decks, we were locked in. We
took refuge in the Zhulagi Lounge, where recumbent bodies

were everywhere. I did needlepoint to distract myself. Ken wasn't badly off and went down to get me a second Bonine tablet. Whether it eventually worked or the seas improved I don't know but I was able to pick my way thru quite a good lunch. In mid-afternoon we had our first Russian lesson (but the teacher is an American from the mid-west), working from mimeographed sheets. Even with so many down sick, there was a full lounge for the lesson. The captain's reception, like life boat drill in the morning, was put off till tomorrow. Joyless Julia, the lady who with poker face kept getting jackpots in the early evening yesterday, wasn't in the casino so much because her winning streak seems to have ended. Many of us thought she was a shill but apparently she belongs to the group of travel agents who are guests on the trip. Win or lose, her face has no expression as she feeds coins in endlessly. I counted and fifteen dollars in five minutes is the norm for demon gamblers.

THURSDAY, FEBRUARY 6, 1975

Everybody is hale and hearty again. The sea was smooth, the sun blazed, and appetites were hearty. At eleven there was a talk on San Juan (where we are having our stay shortened from 32 hours to 21 because of a new law forced thru by the owners of half empty hotels, which permits cruise ships to come in for only 24 hrs). We also heard about St. Thomas and what stores had agreed to stay open for our Sunday visit. Since I didn't come to shop, I don't mind but many ladies are distressed that shopping will be limited and in the case of Martinique, out altogether because of carnival. After lunch we sat a while on deck till time for our Russian lesson. Attendance was almost double yesterday's and we reviewed then went on to food and how to greet the captain at his reception. Dinner was fantastic. Ken went all to pieces when he saw the red caviar on the table. As the rest of us weren't much interested, I not at all, Ken ate the whole thing. An excess of vodka plus natural greed led to him making a spectacle of himself. Any elegance inherent in caviar went overboard as he was less the Grand Duke than the first peasant to loot the Winter Palace, the way it went down.

SATURDAY, FEBRUARY 8, 1975

Up a little after five to go up to the Lido deck and watch the ship come in past El Morro. Unfortunately it wasn't really light enough to see anything except a sentry box silhouetted against the sky. After breakfast we were off on the tour to the rain forest. The trip gave us a look at the countryside, which gave me now an impression of poverty, now of bankruptcy because of the many condominium apartments unsold due to inflation. I'm not sure that the empty condominiums weren't the more depressing. The rain forest was rather a disappointment as we never left the highway. On the way to the beautiful Luquillo Beach we stopped at a restaurant. By heading straight for the "caballeros" we missed the demonstration of a cock fight, and glad I was, too. Back to the boat for lunch and when we talked of the '39 New York Fair, Chris Graham said I must have been very young then. He was surprised to find I was exactly his age and I was annoyed inwardly that even with a graying beard some people assume I'm younger than I am. One man asked Ken if I was his son, which is really outrageous. In the afternoon we set out with our little maps to walk around San Juan. Back to the ship lame and weary and we both had long soaks in the tub.

MONDAY, FEBRUARY 10, 1975

The Russian class was in the morning today so after some needlepoint on deck, we reported to it. Questions rather off the subject of numbers and describing ills to the doctor nevertheless brought interesting answers from Susie. She said the young waiters and waitresses, stewardesses, etc., had to put in a year of national service after high school to repay the nation for their education and that was what they were doing on the ship. They have a choice of type of work and have elected this. At 11 a talk was given on the three remaining islands we're seeing. Nothing could be promised for Martinique because of carnival but I went to Janine and asked if she thought we could make a private deal with a taxi driver. She doubted it but I asked what the regular tarriff would be so I'd have a base for paying a little more to anybody who'd take us to St. Pierre despite the holiday. She said the cruise office charged $14 a person when able to offer the tour. Took the tender to the pier. Taxi drivers approached us and the first one quoted $20 a person, which Ken didn't want to pay. Other drivers approached saying, "Want a tour of the island?" and Ken, from that habit we share of saying "no" to almost anything, kept saying it. "Now stop that," I said, "A tour of the island is exactly what I want and you close out all negotiation." We found the shopping street as dead as we'd been told it would be but soon the first driver was running after us saying he'd found two more passengers. The driver's English was good, he stopped whenever he thought we might like to take a picture, and he waited while we went in the museum at St. Pierre devoted to the catastrophic eruption of 1902. He drove us back in time for the start of the carnival. We had already seen some boys wearing masks at St. Pierre but in Fort-de-France groups of boys ran around in drag burlesquing a wedding party. The book that told us all costumes must be black and white was totally wrong for the men in drag wore any color dress they could lay hands on. The Martiniquais, if that is the word for the natives, are just about the handsomest group of blacks I've ever seen. The old public lavatories seem to have been taken out of commission before the newly built ones were ready for use so we had coke at a bar in hopes they'd have a rest room. They didn't and we decided to go back to the ship and then return to the Savannah when the day was cooler and the carnival had got up a head of steam. As it turned out, once we got to the boat and went to the john, we got involved in the arrival of the new crew and the departure of some of the old. If I ever had the idea that the Russians were unemotional, today would have dispelled it. The return of certain beloved officers or friends led to kissing regardless of sex and great whooping joy on the part of stewardesses. (*New crew and those returning from vacations at home were on board a ship anchored nearby, which was to take those who had completed their year of national service and those career people who had vacation-time coming, back home.*) The departure brought tears from some left behind and much kissing again. The men usually kissed each other full on the mouth and with apparent feeling, not the routine stylized kissing of the French. So many of the arriving and departing young people were attractive, a wonderful antidote to a surfeit of grandparents aboard. I spotted three really sensational blonds, including an officer. Ken attributed the tailored shirts and nice clothes of the departing to purchasing while abroad. But the new people off the Rossia also had tapered shirts and modern clothes. We found the new crew far from settled in at dinner and there was such chaos that the platinum-haired woman who presides over the Crimea Dining Room pitched in to serve the venison and at one point looked distressed enough to cry. People who hired cabs today were all comparing prices and we paid more than most but I refused to join Ken in fretting about it. Nobody, no matter what they paid, saw the Beauharnais house (*where the Empress Josephine was born*) and nobody but us seemed to care. We sat on the deck a while, waiting for Martinique to disappear in the distance the way the Rossia had, but it's a big island (my favorite so far) and we gave up.

TUESDAY, FEBRUARY 11, 1975

When we went on deck to see what Antigua looked like Ken asked me if I'd heard the band on the adjacent boat. It was I who was later able to bring him the delicious news that the adjacent boat was Queen Elizabeth's yacht Britannia. The "boat" immediately became for him "beautiful", whereas to me it could easily be an extremely well-kept ferry doing the Maine-Nova Scotia run. It has royal purple ropes tying it to the docks but its lines have the dowdiness of everything the House of Windsor wears, says, or owns. I was glad Ken had the excitement, however. The Queen is not here nor is she coming here but the yacht's to pick her up in Nassau and take her to Mexico on a state visit. For our taxi tour of Antigua, as with our Martinique tour, I sat up with the driver and I thought Ken and the couple in the back would never stop talking of past trips and pay attention to what they were supposed to be seeing today. Ken later decided it was the lushest and loveliest island yet. I don't quite agree but I don't strongly disagree either. Nelson's dockyard, a restoration project starting with more remnants than Williamsburg, was interesting and beautiful. After lunch we went over to a nearby shopping center which several people said had nothing to offer. To us it offered beautiful Antiguan cotton shirts. I ended up buying 3, Ken 2, and we got Lisa a dress. Later I heard a steel band over there and went over. Ken didn't want to go and missed some marvelous playing by a group calling themselves the All Saints Symphony, All Saints being the second largest village on the island. There were pelicans on the rocks nearby and all told Antigua, in which I had little advance interest, was very interesting. After supper we walked off as Ken wanted to see the Royal Yacht lit up. Natives were looking in the portholes and giggling for several of the crew were in their quarters dressed in no more than their underpants. Unfortunately we saw no attractive ones and none of the crew compares with the Russians in beauty.

WEDNESDAY, FEBRUARY 12, 1975

Right after breakfast we went up to sign on for the St. Maarten tour. No signs of poverty as at Antigua and if less lush in growth, it had much nicer houses and incomparably better stores. The people are almost as handsome as those on Martinique and when we bought cologne and perfume on Philipsburg's Front St. we were waited on by a gentle and charming very very black, very very beautiful young man. Once again we failed to locate a men's room and decided that since our sightseeing and shopping were done, we'd taxi back to the boat. Sudden rain led others to join us and what a crabby pair they were. These people bitched about the awful food. "You don't like the soups?" I asked, and they agreed they were fine, as was the ice cream and the bread and the crab meat appetizers. Everything I mentioned was fine but they still condemned the food. They thought the waiters and waitresses were sober and charmless and couldn't speak English, which had me aghast. Then madame started on the Russian doctors, who, because they don't know English, she suspected of not knowing how to do x-rays on her injured knee. "Look," I said, "the Russians have just brought back cosmonauts from 30 days in space so I think they can manage x-rays." Ken said the driver was quite beside himself with joy when I said that. Next madame, sitting right next to a native, started in on St. Maarten, saying it disappointed her as she expected it to be as clean as Holland and it wasn't and nobody could quote her a price on her Royal Doulton or her Hummel figurines. I got back to the ship absolutely seething at the sheer rudeness of talking this way about a person's country. We New Yorkers are used to having our city run down and too many inhabitants do it themselves but— there goes my blood pressure again. I took my camera to dinner to take our table companions and Vasha, behind me, said "Say cheese!" So the dining room personnel don't know English and are sober! Jesus, such nonsense. But some of these crabs would sober a laughing hyena.

SATURDAY, FEBRUARY 15, 1975
Ken skipped the final Russian lesson in favor of picking up the pictures from the photographer's shop. It wasn't much of a lesson anyway as we sang <u>Ochi Chornye</u> and <u>Moscow Nights</u> then got talking about the no-tipping policy and how to reward our beloved Russian kids within the letter of the law. At 11 there was a talk on landing procedures and here, as thruout the day, we were joined by Ethel and Bob Banks, the Staten Island mother and son who find us so terribly amusing. Over and over they courted a visit from us which over and over we slid over. At dinner we had so much laughter that later on deck Bob and Ethel asked Ken what on earth I'd said that made Naydine laugh so much she couldn't eat. They spent much of the evening with us up in the Rossia lounge, listening to the really excellent Russian orchestra. Suzie had told us that the singer, my lovely Rasputin-with-clean-hair, was really a lawyer and didn't know how to sing till he met his wife while doing cruise work and was taught by her. As we listened to the Russian orchestra we watched the dancers and noted that the worst

of all was Frederic, the flamboyant and loud but handsome
gay fellow who's been traveling with his lover. I think
perhaps he might have danced better if it had been his
lover or some other man in his arms. At one point Frederic
did a can-can and THAT he did well. The other gay couple,
two French-speaking Canadians, kept to themselves, tho especially
amiable when passing us, recognizing us as brothers
or sisters or whatever.

SUNDAY, FEBRUARY 16, 1975
   We quickly got thru customs and a chatty taxi driver
got us quickly home. The cats were beside themselves with
joy and I thought they'd never stop frolicking. Interesting
mail from Gay Task Force about upcoming legislation
for gay rights and urging all gay groups to use the phrase
"Affectional preference" when pushing legislation to make
it clear that we want rights not only to sleep with our
own sex but to openly love and pair off with them in more
lasting ways. It has been used in Minnesota's already passed
laws and strikes me as a very good choice of words.

FRIDAY, FEBRUARY 21, 1975
   At three we had an envelope stuffing session with even
the boss joining us in the conference room. He wasn't
too happy about the poor planning that had necessitated
the hand operation. I was larking about as usual and nobody
was a better audience than Dr. W. "We should have a
tape recorder here, with Mr. Vining in this rare mood."
"Rare nothing. He's like this all the time," Mary said.
"I bet your plays aren't as funny as you are today," the
boss said. "Certainly not." I have thought before and I
thought again today why the things I say that crack people
up are never usable in plays. One reason is that stage humor
of today comes from foibles of character, whereas my
personal humor is verbal and fantastic. Besides, characters
would never say the things which in life give me my
openings. From work to Beacon Baths. It seemed to be an
evening for people with size and erection problems. I'm
not a size queen but with people who have problems I tend
to feel they are homosexual out of fear of ridicule from
women, not because they have a genuine interest in other
men. There is that feeling that homosexuals are desperate
enough to settle for anything, tho it can't take them long
in the baths to find out how totally wrong a concept that
is.

MONDAY, FEBRUARY 24, 1975
   Walked into a bank with no line and whizzed thru my

business with the teller then went over to cash in my bond. There I met up with a woman who must just have entered the work force after years in the kitchen. She should go back to the kitchen, preferably into the oven, for she was the slowest thinker I've met up with in years. If one asked her her name I doubt if she could tell you in less than eleven minutes and 45 seconds. Her head seemed to be full of corn meal mush and old oil sludge. Her bovine stupidity put me in a terrible temper to start the day because I wouldn't have been late for work if it hadn't been for her. Not that several people weren't later. At noon I read over my play, correcting the errors in the casino scene that became clear the moment I actually observed people in the casino on the Maxim Gorky. At 8 we went to Vi's for the needlework group. We had a good and profitable time. I recruited Vi for the Social Committee.

TUESDAY, FEBRUARY 25, 1975

Left about ten notes asking people to join the Social Committee so I might get two or three favorable responses at least. Called Eric and he joined me for lunch. He's been living in town so he could investigate Off-Off-Broadway groups and get someone to put on his play. He feels I should be more aggressive in peddling mine, too, but I want to write, not be an agent. On the way home I went to the library to get HORSEMAN RIDING BY for Ken and picked up more books for myself. As tho that were not enough reading matter, Carl had given Ken several copies of THE ADVOCATE, which always takes a lot of time to read. It does report well on the advance of homosexual rights and one needn't read all the kinky wantads as we do, but if they're time-consuming, they're sometimes fun. Came across two new kinks tonight, a man who is turned on by formal clothes--tuxedos, tails, etc. and one turned on by cigars. But there are as many who want deathless love and idealized relationships as there are who want enemas and scatology, but some are as extreme in girlish romanticism as the others are in whorehouse lust.

SUNDAY, MARCH 2, 1975

The Times, the rest of my cleaning left over from yesterday, then at five down to Leo's. Ray and Joe, Joe and Richard were there again, and a Charles who is vaguely familiar but who hasn't been encountered recently. He's an unimpressive lawyer who admits he's still in the closet, the only one of us who is. Ray asked Richard, the Italian, if he and Joe entertained his family (yes) and if there were any problems (no). He said, "Well, we've never had with our families either. I hear about these people who do but Joe and I got together years ago and we've always entertained our families who've been perfectly fine about everything."

WEDNESDAY, MARCH 12, 1975
     Druth joined me on break and I found out that she does the lighting for Les Ballets Trocadero de Monte Carlo, the drag ballet company. I love the name one of the male ballerinas has taken, Mme. Tchickaboumskaya. I asked if a whole evening of ballet satire wasn't a bit boring eventually but Druth said they did very different things including a takeoff of Loie Fuller by a man over 6 ft. tall who calls himself Lottie Flutter. As I said to Druth, it seems a little late in the day to be satirizing Loie Fuller, whom scarcely anybody alive has seen and whom Druth had never heard of till she read the program notes. I told her they ought to be satirizing Martha Graham (whose company has been revived tho she no longer dances) and Alvin Ailey and perhaps Harkness but so many people pull the teeth of their satire by satirizing things out of the past. Carol Burnett was always satirizing movies of the thirties and forties instead of those of today. Satire ought to have as its aim a correction of absurdities but if you apply it to the dead past it's too late to correct anything.

SUNDAY, MARCH 16, 1975
     Forgot to say that two days ago I was reading the Yale Alumni Magazine and found myself quoted twice in an article on "The Student Playwright--An Endangered Species". It was an outgrowth of that questionnaire I filled out so long ago. After supper we bussed down to City Center and got tickets for the Joffrey Ballet for $2.00, only a little more than half of what a first-run movie costs. I certainly saw why critics said THE RELATIVITY OF ICARUS seemed more about a homosexual relationship than about Icarus for the poses struck by Daedalus and Icarus must surely have been inspired by a wonderful night of very athletic sex. The dance was more related to modern dance than to ballet but was all the better for it and the two beautifully built boys could not possibly have worn smaller straps. Years ago we were bored by Balanchine's version of JEU DE CARTES but this new one by John Cranko gave me more laughs than WHERE'S CHARLEY. In the top balcony, at least, the Joffrey audience is very young but perhaps that's because not many of us old duffers can make those damned stairs.

TUESDAY, MARCH 18, 1975

As we were dressing this morning Ken said, as he so often does, "What would you like for supper tonight?" but instead of saying "I don't care" I surprised him and immediately said, "Cottage cheese and fruit salad". He then said, "What about tomorrow?" and I did it again. "Sausages, little boiled potatoes, and apple sauce," whereupon he did a mock faint on the bed. When he got up I said, "And Thursday a souffle' and Friday stuffed peppers. As for next week___", whereupon he fainted again. Since he was so funny about it, I waited till he got up again and said, "Now in April___" but that time he ran to write down what I said. It was a good way to start the day and as long as I recorded our Friday disagreement at such length I felt I should record what is much more typical of life with Ken. As tho I hadn't books enough lots of magazines arrived and Carl sent another copy of THE ADVOCATE home with Ken. Reading the sex ads takes up such a damned lot of time. QQ also arrived and now has an insert of personal ads. Unlike Advocate advertisers, many of these admit to being 40 or over. When they say 40 I read 50 and if they say 50 I read 60.

WEDNESDAY, APRIL 3, 1975

To Lincoln Center for the first night of DIE TOTE STADT. Maria Jeritza, who made her Met debut in 1921 in the opera, the first German opera done at the Met after World War I (*during which all German opera was dropped from the repertoire, a fate that befell only MADAMA BUTTERFLY during World War II*) was present and looking lovely in pink and long gold gloves. She was generous in her applause and Carol Neblett and John Alexander certainly deserved it but the opera is a Germanic bore.

THURSDAY, APRIL 4, 1975

It's very nice when I come home to have Ken say, "I'm glad to see you." He said it last night as we settled into the restaurant booth and I thought that since he says it so often and with such apparent sincerity, it really isn't so awful that he's never been able to bring himself to say "I love you." After supper we went downtown to the Golden to join a very gay crowd at the preview of P.S., YOUR CAT IS DEAD. Too much of the humor depended on scatological language, which I really deplore as a cheap way of getting laughs, but there was some wit, too. I enjoyed it but still don't think it will be a success. As we came home gusts of wind swept thru Shubert Alley and we could hear the screams as the wind hit different groups of people.

SUNDAY, APRIL 6, 1975

Ray and Joe have a lovely apartment filled with beautifully displayed mementoes of their travels (Ray spent two years in China in the late 30's). The Jefferson Party Syndrome made its appearance before Ken had had more than a sip of his drink and therefore before alcohol could take much of the blame. The parade of our differences of opinion started, to the embarrassment of almost everybody, and if I protested that I was being misquoted Ken would say, "Oh, don't let's argue," as tho we never did anything else. Since Joe and Richard have been together 13 years (they look too young for that), Leo and Larry 14 or 15 years and Ray and Joe well over 20, I'm sure they've all had many and serious disagreements but being sensible and civilized people they don't trot them all out in hope of belated support from the assembled company. Eventually Ray sat down at the piano and played, as he did at Leo's, but I was too depressed by that time to sing along as I did before. Dinner restored my good spirits and the evening was generally pleasant because I like everybody there so much. On our way home, however, Ken began to burble and said, "I think we looked very nice. You looked very nice." By that time a compliment in private was not only not able to restore the buoyancy I had had beaten out of me in the first half hour of the party but it even brought back my depression as I tried to figure out which Ken was the real one, which attitude the really felt one. I don't think Ken is even conscious of his compulsion to put me down in public and he would be incapable of reform but it certainly cuts down my anticipation of pleasure at parties and the actuality of pleasure.

MONDAY, APRIL 7, 1975

Got up as depressed as I went to bed but know it's silly for Ken's party behavior, after all, has been exactly the same since the forties and if I've lived with it this long, I can live with it longer. After supper to Madison Square Garden, where we were part of a not very large audience for the Tour of Champions figure-skating exhibition. It was marvelous and as I watched those beautiful bodies doing fantastic things with such grace I thought, "Who can worry about rough spots in human relationships with such marvels to occupy one's mind." I was also mindful of the fact that though nobody else we've talked to was even aware of the figure-skating tour nor interested when we mentioned it, Ken was. So if our interests frequently diverge, they also converge at many more points than some couples.

FRIDAY, APRIL 11, 1975

I spent so much time talking to Maurice at noon that I got nothing done on PILLORY GREEN except to name a few more characters. From work to Beacon Baths, where in very short order I made an advance off a long-standing plateau. For the first time in my life I did a black. He was really brown and beautiful and bearded and I had seen him nearly soap his skin off in the shower but even so it's rather surprising that with very little hesitation I suddenly dropped my long-standing prejudices about color and weight (he was huge and husky and quite possibly 190-200 pounds). It shouldn't have surprised me that it was in no way different from whites, but I fear it did.

SATURDAY, APRIL 12, 1975

Down to the Morgan Library to see the show on Sir Arthur Sullivan, very extensive and wonderful. The black guard who became so fascinated with my remarks last time wasn't there today. Perhaps he became fascinated with one too many customers, but I must say that the doorman there is perfectly chosen for the job. He's very polite and thanks one for coming when one leaves, as tho it hadn't been a great treat we should be grateful for. Home and I thought I'd hear just the last act of VESPRI SICILIANI but we ran into David Haworth. Ken asked him how he was coming along in getting his apartment furnished and he said to come back with him and see. David is free with show business gossip and has known almost everybody. We gulped at some of his revelations. Now I don't always believe all that a gay says about others in this world as they like to push the borders of our world back till they include almost everybody, but there's no denying that time spent with David is spicy time.

FRIDAY, APRIL 18, 1975

By arrangement met Ken downtown so we could go see the porny movie BEHIND THE GREEK DOOR (the title is a takeoff on the heterosexual porny hit BEHIND THE GREEN DOOR). I had called Ken and suggested that he go early and try for tickets to SAME TIME, NEXT YEAR so he presented me with the tickets for my birthday. The short subjects at the Adonis were terrible this time and both Ken and I closed our eyes in boredom. I was startled when he lunged toward me. A very well-dressed but very black man had sat two seats from him on the other side and had reached out and taken his hand. He had quickly indicated that he was with me and leaned my way. I was amused and delighted that it had happened to him for I think he gets the feeling

that he is past attracting anybody but me and now he knows
better. We had gone to the men's room and found it very
lush with nice wall paper depicting a scene in a Japanese
steam bath. There it was I who was startled to find the
man at the next urinal losing an eye looking at me as tho
I were a beautiful twenty. The movie lived up to the coming attractions. There were six of the nine men involved
that I would quite willingly bed, tho I would balk at several of the things they did in the film. Ken, having less
aversion to huskiness or avoirdupois than I have, might
have included two more on his fantasy list but we didn't
discuss it.

TUESDAY, APRIL 22, 1975
    Eric called to ask if I had anything to say about his
play after seeing it, in addition to what I'd said after
reading it. I thought not but we made a luncheon date anyway and it turned out I did have some suggestions he found
useful. I don't really think he should bother further with
that play but it's always valuable to think how a script
could be made better even if one doesn't intend to do it.
From work to meet Ken for dinner at the Yangtze River before the premiere of the Bolshoi Ballet. Across the street
from Lincoln Center protesters stood with banners and passed out leaflets. Naively they asked that we boycott the
performance. Now nobody who had a ticket was going to give
it up. I don't approve of oppression in the Soviet Union
or anywhere else but I don't approve of Tsars either but
would have gone to the ballet if it had come from Tsarist
Russia just as readily as I went tonite. SPARTACUS is in-
termittently, perhaps largely, a trashy ballet but I was-
n't inclined to worry overmuch about that when in the center of the pinchbeck and rhinestones a veritable Kohinoor
diamond was to be seen. Vladimir Vasiliev as Spartacus was
a technically fabulous dancer, a marvelous actor, and an
absolutely gorgeous man. Nureyev is a marvelous dancer but
never appealed to me physically. I would walk the entire
tracks of the Trans-Siberian railroad, even with my game
leg, if at the end I was sure I'd find Vasiliev waiting
for me with open arms. Blond, tall, bearded--a vision. And
what star presence! Alone on the vast stage he could fill
it with his aura and the enormous auditorium too. In fact,
if they'd removed the walls of the opera house I'm sure he
could have turned up the candlepower till it radiated to
the outer edges of the whole Lincoln Center complex. But
he wasn't specifically selling himself. Every muscle large
and small, every brain cell, and all his viscera were every second fully devoted to his role. He provided quite

some contrast to Bill Washburn, who got in our elevator, spotted us before we spotted him and turned back to. His rear view is, if anything, worse than the front and at any angle poor snobbish Bill looks like someone conceived with the last inadequate dribble of semen an aged father was ever able to produce.

SUNDAY, APRIL 27, 1975
      Was tickled by a story in the Times about a rash of homosexual marriages taking place in Boulder, Colo., where a woman city clerk sees no reason not to issue licenses and an assistant district attorney says, "Who does it hurt?" An indignant cowboy, thinking to make the whole business absurd, marched into city hall and demanded a license to marry his horse but was turned down because the horse, only 8 years old, was under age.

TUESDAY, APRIL 29, 1975
      Went right from work to the Met Museum, where Ken was waiting for me so we could see the Scythian gold. Never has a Tuesday night when I've gone been so crowded but God knows it must be better than on weekends. And one could see the pieces very well, with a little patience sometimes. Ken and I thought we were perhaps most impressed with a gorgeous comb in which there was exquisite detail right down to the beards and shield decorations of the miniature gold warriors atop the comb. We saw the guard who used to live across the street from us. He's certainly out of the stage we witnessed when his boyfriend from upstairs lay on him as they looked out the window and was clearly smitten with him for some months: tonite he was ogling a girl in tight red slacks.

WEDNESDAY, APRIL 30, 1975
      At two minutes of five the boss said he wanted to meet with me and Elaine for five or ten minutes. Into his office and discovered that I was, in a sense, on the carpet, tho the talk with me was the first of a series to be held with each worker individually. All built around the bad morale in the office, the talk with me indicated that perhaps my levity didn't set the right tone of professional authority to give the workers a model. But we got into the whole picture and I went on the attack. I went into the various things that I thought were responsible for the indifference and the turnover, from the failure to introduce workers or take any personal interest in them to the coldness of the computer cards compared with our old cards, which told so much about a graduate that they came alive. Wintermudd said

I was giving him the kind of feedback he wanted from me
and he made notes but I don't think Elaine was happy with
the feedback at all. I don't for one minute believe that
my lightness of mood leads people to take their jobs less
seriously than they should but it's a tenet of American
life today that one cannot be light-hearted and serious at
the same time so for the necessary pre-retirement period
I shall confine my humor to the non-working hours. Must
mention that last Mon. night, sitting at the far end of
the long table where we were doing needlework, I heard Ken
telling Joyce at the other end that one reason he wasn't
going with me this summer was that I was going to do some
mountain climbing. (*Ken had decided to skip the summer
trip to Europe but to go with me the winter of 1976 to
Egypt.*) I've heard him tell other people that and considering that in my prime I could hardly bear a stepladder
top and that now even a modest gradient may throw my foot
out, it's utterly absurd. I don't know why he keeps saying
it when he knows it's not true and that I turn five shades
of purple even in a cable car.

FRIDAY, MAY 2, 1975
    The lake and the hills behind it were misty when I
came out to go to work and as the flowering trees in the
area are not quite fully out, everything looked muted and
lovely. That lake is an everlasting joy. Recently, on a
windy day, Ken called me to the dining room window to see
how a brilliant sunset reflected on all the little choppy
waves and made the lake look to be on fire. Whether it's
autumn and the colors of trees are as lovely as they were
last autumn, or winter and the seagulls are on the ice
floes, it always starts my day out well to see it as I
start out. I nearly slipped and cracked a couple of jokes
today but generally kept myself under wraps.

SATURDAY, MAY 3, 1975
    There being no shows or movies we wanted particularly
to see, it seemed a good time to go to the Library of the
Performing Arts and look up the 1920's PHOTOPLAY. It's ridiculous that we haven't been there more often for their
collections on dance, music, theatre, etc., are marvelous.
We each took a bound volume covering six months of 1925
and exchanged them when through. I remembered that PHOTO-
PLAY didn't just puff movies that bought ads but even I
had forgotten how they laced into the majority. Ken often
says, when I get critical of old movies, "We thought they
were great at the time" and my standard reply is "Not all
of us did." PHOTOPLAY proved my point with bells on for

they said over and over of a star that they'd had a run of mediocre movies and even criticized Gloria Swanson for falling out of character when she played an old lady in one movie. While waiting for Ken to finish his volume I explored the contents of the shelves and found many books I want to look into further, including one on the theatres of New York and another on Ziegfeld which reproduces in color many of the gorgeous Urban sets. The latter also listed the number of performances for the various editions of the FOLLIES and considering their fame the runs were astonishingly short--60 performances, 88 performances, etc. In Marboro bookshop I bought a book I saw them advertise for $1 last Sunday, FRIENDS; A TRUE STORY OF MALE LOVE. Very forthright and good as far as I've gone.

MONDAY, MAY 5, 1975

Glum in the office, even for a gray Monday. It certainly isn't easy for me to cover my natural cheerfulness. When I called Ken he informed me that Florence was, after all, coming for a visit. I must watch myself for as Ken and I did dishes he made some mildly sarcastic remark about Florence's supposed sacrifices for their mother and I jumped right in and said, "Whatever she did she did dutifully and completely without love or charm, just as I do with Mother. The only difference between us is that I realize how badly I do it and somewhat regret it, whereas Florence wants medals." All of which is true but needn't be spoken. I must, must, must be a good host. To the Bolshoi Ballet. Stunning performance of IVAN THE TERRIBLE, a better ballet than SPARTACUS tho it gave Vasiliev less chance to be beautiful. Tonite, instead of blond hair and beard, he had black. He perhaps had less stunning things to dance, too, but what an acting performance. I was perfectly convinced that he could walk off that stage and rule all of Russia right this very minute. In SPARTACUS there was a glorious stage effect when the soldiers of Crassus impaled Spartacus on their spears and lifted his body aloft. Here the final picture of Ivan was of his body raised aloft tangled in the six bell ropes which had been used throughout the ballet. I must do much reading in the encyclopedia.

WEDNESDAY, MAY 14, 1975

An early call from Mother to ask if I could meet her in New York and get her to the train to Poughkeepsie *(for an alumni reunion at Vassar)*. This being Commencement Day at Columbia, it was hardly convenient but I agreed since I was happy that at least she had decided against driving.

I heard another woman's voice in her apartment, trying to
get her started. Ken and Florence said they'd meet her at
Penn Station and take her to Grand Central. I gave Ken $40
in case Mother had not found her purse and hadn't gone to
the bank. It was, of course, a busy day at school with the
boss and Elaine out most of the time at the convocation,
Alumni Council dinner, commencement, and then the reception
in the court. Only box lunches were sold in the cafeteria
so I walked down to Chock Full O Nuts to eat. As I went by
the Barnard campus their convocation was in progress and I
think it may have been Lillian Hellman who was speaking. I
listened some but became aware of nearby noise and turned to see a policeman filled with hate for educated girls
telling one, "Don't get smart, girl, or I'll drag your ass
to the police station and don't think I won't just because
you're a woman." The girl's boy friend put his arm out to
defend her from the policeman and the girl took refuge behind the boy while she called the policeman a fink and I
thought how this little scene wrapped so much of the confusion of women's position all up in one package--the resent-
ful chauvinist, the protective male, the girl being aggressive to a point but hiding behind the protective male.
Home and heard some distressing things about Mother.
Though the coat she was wearing Sunday was all right, today she was wearing one minus two buttons and with cigarette burns. Her luggage consisted of a box in which she
said she had another dress which she'd washed and which
wasn't dry. And again she was carrying a load of bills.
Every time she's come over she's been well-dressed , more
so than in her prime, and I guess this trip just flustered
her too much. She told Ken she was going abroad again and
wondered if there was any chance she could get on the same
plane with me. I had evaded her questions as to whether I
was even going and though Ken has now let the cat out of
the bag, Mother won't remember and I can deny it. I have-
n't decided what would be easier on her, to spare her the
panic she gets when she thinks of my being away, to tell
her only at the last moment, to tell her that Ken will be
here and run the risk of his being pestered, or what.

FRIDAY, MAY 16, 1975
    Not too long after I got home I had a call from one
of Mother's classmates, who said Mother had been very confused yesterday at the luncheon and she had worried about
her going home so had invited her to stay with her. Apparently while she was out, Mother had taken off by taxi to
go home and she was worried she wouldn't make it. She
sounded in a much better mental state than Mother and was

very nice. There were just eleven at this mini-reunion and I should say it would be Mother's last. She recommended that for other people's sake I should have the Motor Vehicle Bureau take Mother's license away. She'll have one unholy fit but I think I may make the move at last, tho I think she'll go on driving without it. As Mrs. Cleary said Mother spoke of coming to the house by taxi, we expected her momentarily. When we hadn't heard from her by nine I called and found her quite calm and collected. There was no sign of the confusion the strain brought out in her at Vassar. That comes and goes and every time I think it's come to stay, it goes away again. I told her not to tell me about the reunion, that she's always complaining she has nothing to put in a letter and now she has.

SATURDAY, MAY 17, 1975

As Florence and Ken were going to see the Hollywood costume exhibit at the Met, I went on ahead downtown and said I'd meet them at the theatre. I went to the Adonis to see the new porny film. Jack Deveau, the lead producer, seems to have quite a sense of humor and would to God people in the audience did for they sit in stony silence and make my laughter seem like desecration of the temple. Some of the humor may be disgustingly bizarre, as when by fakery it is made to seem that a huge black dildo being thrust into a rectum is coming out the person's mouth, but it's humor of a sort appropriate to pornography, at least. What I really loathe, and hate to see becoming a part of almost every porno movie, is the fist-fucking. I had time after the film to drop in Sam Goody's bargain store. All records on sale were a fantastic 39 cents. I bought a record of HAIR done by the Tokyo company and a record of selections from NO, NO, NANETTE. Ken and Florence showed up at the Helen Hayes Theatre soon after I got there and we enjoyed RODGERS AND HART from the time the overture struck up till the curtain came down. Played the HAIR record but that rock music isn't congenial to Florence so I tried NO, NO, NANETTE but tho she liked it better she'd rather talk than listen so I didn't finish it. Tonight she and Ken were going over his war experiences, Ken insisting that one must obey every order or get shot, I making but not bothering to stress the old point that there is no situation in which some degree of rebellion is impossible to a rebellious personality. But of course Ken is not that and I am. Rebellion would be as completely impossible for him as obsequiousness and unthinking obedience is for me. Each type of personality is needed in the world; neither can do the other's work.

TUESDAY, MAY 27, 1975
      Did needlepoint in the evening and then we watched the tv version of A MOON FOR THE MISBEGOTTEN with the cast from last year's hit Broadway production. I was glad I never spent money to see it for even as a free offering it bored me into a headache. Colleen Dewhurst is a marvelous, powerful actress but Jason Robards is my idea of a routine actor, no more. I was feeding the cats when he did his big soliloquy and the vocal monotony as heard from the kitchen was dreadful. O'Neill, whose wave length I have never been on, must bear much of the blame for the boringness for he can never say anything less than five times and he maintains a very wavering line in his plays, circling back to things already mentioned too often. I finally went to bed before the ending, unable to take any more of this play, which has substance enough for a one-act play but insists on going on like the Ring Cycle.

MONDAY, JUNE 2, 1975
      Kept my lunch date with Eric and Bob Hivnor. I pretty much kept out of the discussion of Eric's play and Bob's main advice seemed to be to move on to other material. That Eric seems reluctant to do and he said, "I think I must have been raped as a child, to be so fascinated with the idea." When Bob suggested shelving it, I mentioned that I had shelved one revised and two incomplete plays. Though superficially very different, my plays do deal with divorce or separation too much and I'm determined that this shall be no part of the next one. It's relatively incidental in SORROW but very central to DIFFERENCE, ARIADNE ABANDONED and PILLORY GREEN. I want to take it out of the latter. Our evening highlight was an hour by Lord Clark called IN THE BEGINNING, about Egyptian civilization. I learned a great deal and we had our enthusiasm for next winter's trip heightened.

WEDNESDAY, JUNE 4, 1975
      At noon I walked over to Riverside Drive to work on my German and the wind was terrific. After supper we went down to Lincoln Center to see the Stuttgart Ballet. BROUILLARDS had humorous passages that made us laugh aloud, not too common in dance except with the Paul Taylor Company. ARENA was a stunning number for men, more modern dance than ballet, about a contest for power. When Marcia Haydée did some stunning leaps and turns in VOLUNTARIES there were those who hushed all attempts at applause, the organ apparently making them feel they were in church and that applause was sacrilegious.

SUNDAY, JUNE 8, 1975

Because we didn't want to get tangled in the Puerto Rican parade we took the subway to Astor Place and the Public Theatre. The man who talked to Ken when both were in line for tickets to A CHORUS LINE sat next to us and he and his wife were very pleasant. I was afraid that the good reviews might have built me up to a letdown but I loved A CHORUS LINE from the first moment to the last. The music isn't strong but it's serviceable and the book and dancing are excellent. I think it's spare and timeless enough to be successfully revived after a generation or two and that can't be said of all shows.

TUESDAY, JUNE 10, 1975

At noon I broke away from Maurice in time to get in a German lesson over in Riverside Park. I decided that since there was a tv program I wanted to see next week on Tuesday I'd better go do volunteer duty at Gay Task Force tonite. I wanted to find out what the plans were for the Gay Pride Parade on June 29. The volunteers, with one exception were people I'd seen there before. There, as elsewhere, a few people do all the work. T/Sgt. Matlovich, the man who is fighting a dishonorable discharge from the Army since he admitted his sexual orientation, is now a member of Gay Task Force and is to be the guest at the two pre-parade dances as well as the Gay Pride Parade.

THURSDAY, JUNE 12, 1975

Reading the text, I noticed that the new contract has a paragraph guaranteeing acceptance by the union and the college of workers without regard to "sex, religion, marital status, sexual preference, or union activity". As the Gay Task Force is making a study of company policy on discrimination against gays I thought they'd be interested in that and sent it to them. As we finished supper Ken went to the kitchen and the moment I saw candlelight I knew what he had done. He came in with cupcakes with candles in them to celebrate my 25 years at TC. God, it's no wonder I love the man.

SATURDAY, JUNE 14, 1975

SATURDAY NIGHT AT THE BATHS, set in and co-produced by the owner of the Continental Baths, had surprised me by getting a good review in New York Magazine for the sensitivity of its exploration of bisexuality. It deserved the review, however, for it was both written and acted well. I would have liked the man the straight pianist in the baths eventually slept with to have been a good deal better

looking but it was very nicely done. The two sex scenes
weren't pornographic as genital organs were only briefly
shown but I didn't mind that at all. I was so grateful for
a literate script and one scene in which a team from the
gay baths played football against a straight team in the
park had been hilarious. What went on in the scrimmages
was just about what one would expect and the pileups were
very funny too.

TUESDAY, JUNE 17, 1975

Waiting for me was a reservation for what, from the
brochure, looks like a very nice hotel indeed in Vienna.
Ken said Carl Oakes still wanted me to go see BOYS, BOYS,
BOYS with him and sent his phone number so I called him.
We don't agree on what is or is not good pornography (I
like the tease and he wants immediate action; he likes
youth and I like more maturity, etc.) but I'll try not to
throw up when he points out someone he thinks is attractive.

FRIDAY, JUNE 20, 1975

We got up at 6:30 and a good thing too for as I ate
breakfast Ken brought in a great pile of birthday presents
which took quite a while to unwrap. As I learned from the
paper that BOYS, BOYS, BOYS gives their Saturday show at
10 I had to call Carl and change our plans to meet at 6:15.
He suggested I make the reservation in a fake name, saying
he always did for things like that. I laughed and said he
was still living in another world, that of course I'd use
my own name. Carl is so prissy and stuffy that I can't
resist wearing my new necklace when I meet him. Dinner at
Joe Allen's. Prices have gone up there and it's beginning
to get out of our range. There was a greater mix of ages
in the audience for SAME TIME, NEXT YEAR than I had expected
and there was also more fun to be had out of it than I
expected. The author's years in television show for each
of the six scenes is basically a tv skit with somewhat
more sex than tv would allow. Mechanical and old gags are
mixed in with some acute observations to produce a play
totally without literary quality which nevertheless entertains.

SATURDAY, JUNE 21, 1975

At nine fifteen I met Carl Oakes and we were off to
BOYS, BOYS, BOYS, the male burlesque show. It was all it
had been described as being and more. I thought my head
would burst trying to remember all the details so I could
tell Ken. They let anybody in free who'll walk into the

theatre naked and half a dozen did, carrying their clothes
in shopping bags. They then invited anybody who didn't
know this standing offer to take theirs off now and get a
free pass for a future show, at which point half a dozen
more did. One man about forty, both good-looking and well-
built, not only entered naked and allowed almost any willing member of the audience to suck his cock but kept walking back and forth to either get more of the free wine at
the bar or to get rid of it in the lavatory. Carl said,
"He's too old for me," but I said, "It isn't his age I object to, it's his exhibitionism." The first act surprised
me by being a great deal more professional than I expected. The boys clearly had dance talent and dance training
and had been properly choreographed and rehearsed. The
costumes were also very good, much more impressive than
the genitalia they eventually revealed. Some of the jokes
were funny if dirty and I was thinking that sometime Ken
should come. After an intermission during which there was
quite public coupling going on in the lobby, the second
act ruined the impression. I couldn't get excited about
another strip tease which in the end was going to reveal a
body I'd already seen emerge from another costume, the numbers were clearly less well rehearsed and they just didn't
know where to stop. I got a headache from the loud noise
of the taped music, my eyes hurt from the accumulated smoke,
I lost interest in seeing a pudgy old and a pudgy young
person sitting across from me naked and playing with each
other, and I got just horrendously bored. Some reasonably
attractive people were there and some were even naked but
the one I liked best, a tall bearded young man who sat the
other side of Carl, never came back after intermission. He
thus proved that he had the intelligence to quit while he
was ahead. I would have left but felt I'd be safer going
to the subway at one in the morning if I left when the
crowd did. As it turned out, the crowd didn't leave, for
when they took their bows the homely but hard-working master of ceremonies announced that they were going to turn
out the lights and let the audience get acquainted with one
another. Anything I might have been interested in would by
then have been entirely too shopworn and I just wanted to
get out. During the early part of the evening I had been
able to meet Carl half way even tho he is attracted to
blacks and tiny boyish bodies but in the second act he was
laughing uproariously at acts I considered way out of control and inexpressibly vulgar while I was getting stuffier
and more like a Calvinist in Messalina's Rome all the time.
Was rather relieved to find Ken asleep so that I didn't
have to spend another hour or so making a report, for the

last thing he'd said when I left was "Don't miss a dirty detail." Carl said to let him know when I wanted to go again and I said, "Not in less than two or three years" but as I left him I said, "Well, it's been an experience," and it sure as hell was.

SUNDAY, JUNE 22, 1975

Mother had forgotten I wrote I was coming but was delighted to have me there. She had also forgotten my birthday. As soon as I put the dinner in the refrigerator I got to work. Somehow Mother has lost her upper plate. The story of how and where varies but generally it is that it went down the toilet. This meant that she couldn't eat the shrimp cocktail I took even when the shrimp were cut up. Whereas last time she screamed and cried when I tried to throw out moldy bread and empty bottles, this time she was quite agreeable to my throwing out anything I wanted to except letters and cards from me (of which she has a formidable collection). She has kept every piece of junk mail going back God knows how many years. Having cleared the desk top I opened the drawers to put stuff away and found them full of more junk mail. One drawer was almost entirely my letters so I couldn't make room there. On the next trip I'll have a go at the drawers tho Mother may not be in so amenable a mood then. Today she said, "I'm so lucky to have you" and "I hope you have somebody to do this when you get old." Mother wasn't so reluctant to have me go today and what a blessed relief to get out of there. Ken was watching some open golf tournament when I got home so I rested a while in the bedroom. I was both horrified and tickled when, after I told of Mother's saving butter, salt and pepper, he said, "And you threw out all that salt and pepper! You could have brought it home!" I realized then that he's always pocketing it on planes and putting it in kitchen cabinets in much the same way. I also throw that out when I get tired of seeing it around for months. There seems to be no hint of the hoarder in my nature but more than a hint of the vandal for I just love throwing things out. I can't abide piles of miscellany lying about and am always asking Ken if he's thru with the postcard that came two weeks ago, or the program of the show we saw ten days ago, or the latest offer of Reader's Digest, or the clippings Florence sent. Whatever my failings in old age may turn out to be, I don't think I am threatened by a life among useless accumulations.

THURSDAY, JUNE 26, 1975

Waiting for me was a lovely concerned letter from the

woman who runs Mobile Meals in Trenton. She visited Mother
last Thursday (which Mother never mentioned)after a volunteer reported that the teeth were gone. They had already
switched to a soft diet but found that Mother wasn't even
eating the mashed potatoes nor bothering to cut the soft
meat and the volunteer threw out the old sandwiches Mother
was accumulating so she wouldn't eat bad food. I guess
Mother's long indifference to food is compounded by depression but I don't know how to improve that situation.
I wrote a rather stern letter about seeing a dentist. I
find myself getting shorter of patience than I perhaps
should with an 85-year old but I know perfectly well that
Mother's desk was just about as big a mess in 1941 as it
was the other day, that she never knew how to buy or use
up food. She never had sense about time, sense about money
or a sense of order and I'm tempted to say she never had
much sense. Her life has been a disorderly mess ever since
I can remember it. She can get out to get herself a carton
of cigarettes so she ought to be able to arrange for new
teeth. She's shrewd enough to lie about her age on her
driver's license, shrewd enough to get men in the house to
take her car for inspection so no official gets a look at
her, but I may have to go over there and get her dental
appointments myself. How I'll see to it that she keeps
them I don't know. Her disconnected telephone is nothing
new either. In New Haven, if not well before, she ran up
huge phone bills despite my nagging her to write instead
of calling and of course the phone came out. She was then
50 and age had nothing whatever to do with it. I wrote a
note of appreciation to Mrs. Wright, who must be a lovely
lady and perfect for the job.

SUNDAY, JUNE 29, 1975
    Had brunch with Ken and then set out by bus to join
the Gay Pride Parade. I decided not to go to Christopher
St. and march the whole way as the 6th Ave. route goes so
many blocks where there is no habitation, only closed business places on Sunday, and it seemed pointless. I got out
at 50th, thinking the parade might have reached that point
by then but it hadn't so I walked down to Bryant Park and
waited. Police were in readiness all along the route. I
was afraid the Gay Task Force group would come along early
and that I wouldn't get to see much of the parade if I
joined them but the groups from out of town were right
after the Parents of Gay Children group and the Task Force
group was in the last quarter of the twenty-or-so block-
long parade. I quite agree with someone who said, "Well,
it's the prettiest parade in New York" for there were some

stunning men in it, many in shorts. There were a few floats but not many. What I loved most was a handsome, muscular man carrying a sign which said, "I'm healthy and happy to be in love with another man," while his equally handsome male lover walked laughing beside him with his hand resting on his shoulder. If all the couples looked like that, it would be lovely. Contemplating those two making love is very pleasant, which I can't always say. As the first several blocks of parade went by I noted that almost everyone was young and wondered if I really belonged in the parade at all but when the National Gay Task Force banner appeared I ran across the street and joined them. Looking about me I discovered a number with graying hair and also decided that we had the best mix of sex and race as well as age. I heard derogatory remarks from only one man at a crossing. Much of the sparse crowd seemed to be gay itself and there were laughing taunts from the marchers of "Chicken!" but I think many on the sidelines were simply more interested in seeing the parade than in being in it. They certainly weren't hiding their homosexuality. As we passed Radio City Music Hall somebody in our group yelled "Free Art Deco!" and another yelled "Free the Rockette 40", lampooning protest groups and their chants. When we got up to the bandshell in Central Park we found a mob of vendors as well as participants. I ran into Roberto and Jose-Luis, who told me that Bruce Voeller is one of the 8 owners of The Ballroom restaurant. Bruce, by the way, has removed his beard and so has his lover. They marched sometimes with arm on shoulder, sometimes hand in hand, and make a nice couple. When the program started Bruce introduced Leonard Matlovich, the sergeant who is fighting army discharge following his open declaration of homosexuality and to whom I sent a card of encouragement when it came out in the Times. Suddenly I realized with a start that he was the one I had been marching behind or beside thru much of the march. He's a cheerful rather than a grim sort and thanked everybody for their support. It's noticeable that more mothers than fathers support their gay children publicly. A terrific thunderclap seemed to me a clue to head home as several people have lately been struck by lightning so I took my leave of Roberto and Jose-Luis. Got home before the rain was heavy. Tho I normally go to bed when Ken turns on the eleven o'clock news, setting no store by tv news whatever, I decided to see what coverage they gave the parade. I'm not sure it accomplished much except to give a feeling of solidarity. Tho there were transvestites and camps in the parade, the general deportment was nothing to be ashamed of and even the more outre marchers didn't bother me as once they would have. One quite fat and homely boy fell in with our group and turned out to have a bottle of champagne and some paper cups in his knapsack, offering drinks to all takers. I took none because I thought those who had walked all the way deserved it more.

SATURDAY, JULY 5, 1975
    Ken and I went quietly downstairs before our hosts were up. They had coffee ready down there so we had some and I did needlepoint till they appeared. After breakfast the prospective purchasers of their house phoned to say they were in the vicinity. Only the wife had seen the place and wanted husband and son to see it. We sat on the back lawn to be out of the way. First the son and then the husband and wife came out to talk with us and later Ginny said we'd found out more about them than they had. Coast Guard people, they're being transferred to Albany from Maine. She has been teaching ceramics to a class of 60. What I liked was that the teen-age boy, who has to be here by the start of the school year so that he can go out for football, sat down at the piano and could hardly be pried loose to move on. When the buyers had left in great satisfaction we took off to see Saratoga Springs. It turned out to be a rather sad sight, filled now not with grand hotels but scads of motels and quick food concessions. Only two hotels with porches and columns remain and one of those is closed and clearly doomed to soon be a pizza parlor or Hamburger Heaven. Ken treated us to a Planters Punch at the Gideon Putnam, a large old hotel catering principally to people held together with scotch tape and bailing wire. We then went to visit the battlefield and before we'd finished walking to the ten places on the historic tour I thought Ken might need a bit of tape and wire himself. Ginny had fixed a picnic so we ate that in a grove set up for the purpose. Hearing so much about the financial arrangements of early retirement certainly has me toying with the idea. One loses 20 per cent of one's Social Security and perhaps a similar amount of one's pension but I certainly intend to consider it.

TUESDAY, JULY 8, 1975
    Terry hand-delivered a note from Wintermudd congratulating me on the 25 years and the bonus. *(Three months' vacation was granted as a bonus for completing 25 years of service.)* He somewhat spoiled the effect by a last paragraph saying he hoped I'd discuss any plans to use the time so we could check how it fitted into the office schedule. Later Mary, who had had lunch with Elaine for the

first time in weeks, said they were all in an uproar about
my bonus vacation because I had to take it this year in
addition to my regular vacation and that would be terribly
inconvenient. The memo said nothing about taking it this
year and had a whole lot of spaces to write in time taken
so it was silly to get so excited. I checked with Personnel
and got the logical answer "If we'd intended to limit it,
we'd have said so." Mary said, "Let them stew a while."

THURSDAY, JULY 10, 1975
    Waiting at home were the books on Bales Tours and a
slip saying they had made us a provisional reservation on
a tour of January 29 (*for Egypt*). After an appropriate
supper of borscht we were off to the Bolshoi Opera. I did-
n't wear a jacket because of the humidity and found myself,
in the balcony at least, with a great deal of company. Met
lots of people we know. The strongly adverse notices WAR
AND PEACE had received struck me as unwarranted tho the
second act is something of a bore. All notices have reiterated the notion that Russian women singers all have
strident, metallic voices. Well, either my ear is not as
delicately tuned as that or we were lucky for I found nothing unpleasant in the voices of the only two women with
sizable parts. The first act went on so long that my bladder was sorely tried and I told Ken that if they didn't
provide an intermission soon they'd have to rename the opera WAR AND PEE.

SATURDAY, JULY 20, 1975
    Struggled to work out a shopping route that would put
the least strain on Ken's legs but the places were too
widely separated. So we arranged to meet at Lincoln Center
and Ken stayed home to wash shirts while I shopped. When I
met Ken he said I had just missed seeing the whole Bolshoi
Opera troupe having their picture taken in front of the
Met and then taking pictures of each other. EUGENE ONEGIN
turned out to be a quite marvelous opera. The production I
saw years ago by the then modest City Opera proved to have
been just a sketch of the possibilities but this was a lavish rendition. We had a cast that couldn't be faulted.
Galina Kalinina did a fine Tatiana without a trace of metal in her voice and Nesterenko, who hadn't impressed me
much as Kotuzov, did a ripe plummy interpretation of the
very lovely Prince Gremin aria and deservedly stopped the
show. On the whole, one of my more memorable times in the
opera house.

SATURDAY, JULY 26, 1975

    We went to the Met to see the exhibit of French painting of the revolutionary period to 1830. I expected to see, and didn't mind seeing again, paintings I had seen at the Louvre. Instead they had gathered paintings from many museums it's unlikely I'd ever visit, with some from Toulouse, St. Omer, Lille, Aix-en-Provence, Rouen, and quite a few from Montpelier. From so many angles it was fascinating and one thing that piqued my curiosity terribly was the number of women painters, including Marguerite Gerard, pupil and sister-in-law of Fragonard, who did marvelous small-scale work, and a rival of Mme. Vigée-Lebrun that I'd never heard of, Adelaide _____-Guiard, and whose name already escapes me. While Vigee-Lebrun liked to paint royalty and royalists, her rival sided with the revolution and did a quite benign portait of Robespierre, among others. I liked a battle painting by a Baron Lejeune who was a general, a painter of battle scenes, and a quite marvelous technician. In a painting depicting a scene from his life where he was stripped by guerillas he had marvelous detail and one of the men who had been stripped and run through was a marvelously beautiful man. One got a real sense of war, with a guerilla listening to a watch he had just taken as loot, another looting the saddle of a fallen horse, still another putting powder in his gun and another about to bash a fallen soldier with the butt of his rifle, and the horses were superb. I'd like to know more about Baron Lejeune, too. He makes generals who paint like Eisenhower look sick. We staggered out of the museum drunk on David, Ingres, Gericault, and lots of lesser known painters who in at least one painting had hit impressive heights. After resting we went to Yorkville, ate at a Chinese restaurant then went home. No sooner had we arrived than a fierce storm blew up between us. We were talking about a man who lived in the Men's Residence Club when we did and starved to death. Ken assumed it was lack of money, I said one couldn't be sure, that people living alone often don't feed themselves properly, and said I'd worried a bit about how many cans of tomato soup he'd eat while I was away. I only meant that he always seems to have that when I'm not home for supper and as a steady diet for three weeks I don't think it's adequate. He took it wrong and snapped, "Criticism all the time gets tiresome." "That wasn't criticism. That was concern. Sorry I mentioned it." He went on in nasty vein and I said I didn't care if he drank iodine every night while I was away. The last time we had separate vacations he lived at the club and ate in restaurants regularly. Shall say no more about it, however.

SUNDAY, JULY 27, 1975

Mother was amiable enough when I got there and I guess has no reason not to be since I found no letter from the Motor Vehicle Bureau rescinding her license. I quickly got at the business of her desk, which she had already quite littered again. She asked me several times where her car was, could tell me nothing of the nature of the accident, but had the court case on her calendar. Going thru the papers I found summonses for another accident in February and later, going thru her checks at home, I found she'd paid off a couple of people after accidents. She ate the food I'd brought over with no difficulty and was so delighted to be waited on that she kept hugging me and finally suggested I move over and take care of her. Ken was watching tennis when I got home and I stayed in the bedroom after changing. One thing I hate about tennis on tv is that the commentators won't shut up. I guess ours is going to be a home like all those in which wives are driven mad by husbands who can't be pried from the tv in football or baseball season. But they still do have seasons whereas tennis is now all year round and at the moment both Saturday and Sunday. I just can't take it and shall arrange to go out if Ken's addiction continues.

MONDAY, JULY 28, 1975

In the evening we had needlepoint group with a turnout of eight. Marion was there and told of hitting herself in the face with a hammer while putting up a shelf in her New Hampshire summer place. That wasn't funny but she went on to say, "Gentleness isn't my style. My father used to say I shook the house when I just brushed my teeth." That was such a superb capsule description that I laughed myself into tears. My uncontrollable laughter in itself struck Joyce and Evelyn so funny that they were laughing at that but I don't think Miss I-Travel-A-Lot was too amused by my laughter. To a degree that repays her for the time her ungainly joshing offended Ken but at any rate I couldn't help it and when I got upstairs and was packing I started laughing all over again at the thought of it. We were friends when she left, though, for I asked her if I could get a good scarab ring in Egypt or if it was all junk and she, who is often in Egypt, said she'd tell me right where to go. As I packed I found myself getting a bit blue about leaving Ken. It's the poignance I always feel when leaving the cats magnified by leaving Ken also.

WEDNESDAY, JULY 30, 1975

An early morning refueling stop in Shannon and a

glorious Irish morning it was! The airport is new since we were there and the free port is now huge. Frankfurt airport is gigantic and it took some wandering to find the exchange office but otherwise all was simple. They had a train right from airport to Hauptbahnhof. Near the terminal I found the Hotel Terminus, where I got a spotless, adequate room for $10. Ken wouldn't be a bit upset with it if he were here. After washing up, doing diary, and studying my itinerary, I set out to have a look at the town which I am leaving so early tomorrow. If it looks interesting I can come back from Vienna a day early. Tho I was sleepy on the plane I am stimulated now by the foreign atmosphere (tho American airbases keep Frankfurt from being as foreign as some places I'll be later). I loved Frankfurt right from the start because it was a genuine city with marvelous shop windows to look in, ranging from a store selling the most modern, most imaginative jewelry I ever saw gathered in one place thru pastry shops, clothing shops, and very frank sex shops where homosexuals get their window display along with bust lovers. The city was bustling with beautiful people yet it was also full of cafés in which people were taking their leisure. Ken would have enjoyed so many things I saw today but he certainly wouldn't have enjoyed the walk it took to see them. I got exhausted and kept falling asleep when I sat down to rest. In my hotel room by 7:30 despite the presence on the street of so many good-looking men.

THURSDAY, JULY 31, 1975

On the Munchner Strasse where my hotel is located I found a supermarket and for a little over $2 I got 10 peaches, two luscious tomatoes, a pack of about 8 slices of dark gutsy bread, a package of cheese spread with ham in it and a hazelnut chocolate bar. Armed with these provisions for the journey I paid my hotel bill, reserved a room for my return and went over to the station. Never full, our train was virtually empty after Munich. I saw everything all day thru Ken's eyes as well as my own. Whereas yesterday would have been a day of great contention about walking, today would have been a day of great content. Without effort one could sit and see lovely scenery and when I got to Innsbruck I quickly found a room for under $10, near the station. I hadn't remembered Innsbruck as so charming or I'd have had Ken here before now. After some admiring of the decorated and flower-boxed houses I went back to the room and had a bowl bath of great thoroness then washed shirt, socks, and underclothes. Headed for a restaurant whose menu I liked. About $3 got me a delicious but mouth-blistering soup, a pork steak with pommes frites and lots of salad. Dessert was half a canned peach, a bit of a come-down after ten whole fresh peaches but the dinner was a real bargain. On my way to cruise the garden I thought might be the one the Gay Guide says is good for outdoor cruising, I heard a band. Seeing the gleam of brass and the bob of feathers I went down to the Goldener Dachl, where a folk program was just beginning. Gorgeous men abounded and when I finally tore myself away to go cruising I found nobody there. I hustled back to where the beauties were but after just so many folk dances and folk songs I decided to go back to the hotel. After doing diary I did some needlepoint. Am happy to see I still have the inner resources to travel alone.

FRIDAY, AUGUST 1, 1975

After going thru 3 floors of folk museum all I can say is that simplicity of design has never rated high in the South Tyrol. The carving is wonderful on beds, cupboards, ceilings, cookie and butter molds, etc. At breakfast, even without being cornered, I used my German with success. Again in the afternoon I used it, in buying postcards by number. Went to the Hofgarten to rest. It began to sprinkle so I headed for the hotel. I got there rather in the grip of the blues and missing Ken. I find myself talking to myself about what I must do, what I must pack, etc. I did see someone who'd been on my plane and we waved cheerily but they were going up the Hafelekar as I was going down. My mood, I'm sure, is also affected by exhaustion. Ken may sometimes hobble my actions but I guess his complaints may also keep my physical activity down to a less exhausting level.

SUNDAY, AUGUST 3, 1975   (Bolzano-Bozen, Italy)

The breakfast room was lovely, with stunning furniture and decors and everybody said "Guten Morgen" as they entered so it was cheery. Got to the station almost an hour ahead of time and started dialogue on ON THE PORCH. When it came time for my train I couldn't understand why a train going North should be on my track. Then my eye caught the station clock and I must have blanched as I discovered I was an hour behind and had missed my train. Where the time zone changed I don't know because I've been okay on other trains. I could see Ken's reaction at being left behind but had he been with me, we'd probably have corrected watches before this. At any rate there was a Verona train scheduled 40 minutes from the time I corrected my watch so I sat down and did more work on the play. The Verona train, when it came, was virtually empty.

Several Alpine soldiers with jaunty feathers in their hats were apparently going home on leave. Each had taken a whole compartment so they could sleep but were waking and getting out at Trento, Rovereto, etc. I was left alone at Trento but at Ala a tall Italian in skin-tight white pants got on. What's more he chose my compartment and before we were fairly under way was rubbing his basket. I couldn't quite believe it but he left no room for doubt and since he was handsome I was quickly involved, when we hit a tunnel thoroly involved. An Italian man in heat is not the most suave of lovers, tho he may have been conscious of the shortness of the journey. He turned out to be married with two boys 9 and 10 but his wife isn't enough for him. He spent some time in London years ago but German is his first tongue and he said he used English mainly for sex with Americans. His difficulties with English led to some misunderstandings as when he told me of his two boys I thought he meant he had slept with two nine or ten and said "That's too young for me". He said his was an American cock because it was so big but I assured him all Americans weren't so phenomenal. He was certainly too big for what he proposed doing to me on the train to Venice, or even right on that train as we pulled into Verona, and besides, we had run risks enough even though he kept watch out of the compartment. At Verona he had to make a phone call and I contrived to lose him, fearing his impetuosity and sexual appetite, but the Venice train was so crowded that even he wouldn't have been that bold. When I got to Venice I tried first the Hotel Terminus, since I'm in a rut of Hotel Terminus, Hotel Station, etc. but they were full and I continued to the Principe, where Ken and I stayed. They had only a bathless room and seemed rather surprised that I happily took it. Washed up a bit as heat and sex had left me sweaty, then set out on foot for St. Mark's, casing restaurants. On the way I saw that there's an exhibit of Diaghilev designs so that's what I shall see instead of the Accademia. I found out that tho I admire the looks of many a dark Italian, it is still blonds that really turn me on, especially bearded ones. There was an impeccably dressed one on the vaporetto, with a little chin beard and moustache and I adored everything about him. Wouldn't find him flinging himself at someone in a train compartment. My beard seemed a definite plus today as my wild lover fondled and petted it in his rough and ready fashion but I'm still thinking of reducing mine to the chin.

MONDAY, AUGUST 4, 1975
    The Diaghilev design exhibit was of particular

interest to me since my second play was about Nijinsky and
Diaghilev. I so wished Ken could see the posters, sketches
and costumes, even if he showed more interest in the sumptuous palace housing it. Our ballet companies now certainly
don't seek out such leading artists for their design. I
tried to get in the little restaurant with the 1500 lire
tourist menu, again they weren't interested in a single
person and made excuses. I continued to the square where I
ate last night and there found a very good menu for 1900--
spaghetti, liver Veneziana, salad, and ice cream. I also
learned at long last what some men see in boys. There was
one named Paolo, about 14 or 15, who may have been the
proprietor's son or may have been an apprentice waiter or
both. He wasn't trying to be boyish but to grow into a man
as fast as possible. Nature wasn't obliging him much with
his moustache but his tight pants showed it was doing all
right otherwise. If he heard tourists say something while
they studied the menu he'd run and ask another waiter what
it meant then he'd rehearse it. The San Gregorio area where
the Guggenheim Foundation is located is another lovely one
I haven't visited before. Young people thronged the museum
whose Pollocks struck me as unimpressive but which had some
good things by many modern artists. I thought I was seeing
Klee when I saw the works of Victor Brauner, a good imita-
tor with nothing of his own to add, but real Klees came
later.

THURSDAY, AUGUST 7, 1975
    By six I had had enough sleep so did needlepoint. Graz
looked even better today. The inner city is laid out like
Vienna with an Opernring, Burgring, etc. but I'm sure it
has even more benches than Vienna. Headed up the Schloss-
berg, right in the middle of town. It was a hard hot climb
and I decided I'd do it just this once but make my visit
thoro. Was right by the Glockenturm when it struck noon,
quite an experience. Came down and ate at a self-service
place and tho tempted by my beloved gulaschsuppe, I passed
it up in order to try Serbian bean soup, which was marvelous. I must say that Graz has all its old buildings well
marked. I decided to go to the folk art museum, which opened at three, then home to rest and back for an organ
concert in the church.

FRIDAY, AUGUST 8, 1975
    To the tourist information to find out where the ar-
senal was and what the hours were for the Eggenberg Palace
before I went way out there and found them closed. The
arsenal turned out to be on the Herrengasse and I had

passed the entrance several times. It has 4 or 5 floors of 16th C and 17th C armaments, which Graz used to pass out when the Turks made any of their numerous raids. Visited the Stadtpark, where one allée was planted in 1787 and it was lovely but about that time I was attacked by the lonesome blues. Except for the people on the train, the seducer (seducer? practically a rapist) and the people between Villach and Leoben, I haven't had extended conversation with anybody for ten days. Snapped out of it when I took the trolley to Eggenburg Castle. Like the arsenal, the Eggenburg Castle was more interesting than I bargained for. While waiting for the guided tour of the show rooms I went thru the hunting museum they have there, and hated it. Among other things they have the hunting records by type of animal or bird of such people as Franz Josef, who killed a total of 50,520 animals or birds and Kaiser Wilhelm, who killed 78,330. Add that to the many other reasons I have for hating those two. Of course both were responsible for many times that many human deaths. As for the Marquis of Ripon, he shot 500,520 things including 222,976 pheasants. I hope estate taxes forced all his family to take jobs that give them no time for slaughter and that the dear Marquis is in hell having his gizzard pecked by pheasants.

SUNDAY, AUGUST 9, 1975

It was no reflection on Graz that I got up today with great anticipation of the trip to Vienna. Ken and I were always relieved when we came into a great city after touring the provinces. We always did the provinces first as they'd be too anti-climactic afterward. The scenery was beautiful till we approached Vienna. Had a good-looking cab driver to the Hotel Schweiger, where my room proved smaller than those I've had so far but spotless. A letter from Ken was waiting for me and the first line, "First--we miss you," made me burst into tears. I didn't think he'd say it even if he felt it and I certainly missed him. Got a list of theatre and music events in Vienna and then headed for the Rathaus to see the Johann Strauss exhibit, done in the same way and in the same place as the Beethoven exhibit Ken and I saw last time. Programs, letters, pictures, his own musical instruments, furniture of his, scores, pictures of the stars of his operettas, and in the last room 40 chairs with adjacent earphones to listen to five programs of his music. I listened to Program 4, which ended with the music of EIN NACHT IN VENEDIG because that is playing now and I don't know it so wanted to know if I should go. I should. The women tended to listen not nearly as long as young men--just as they don't pursue hobbies with the same passion. In search of a place to eat before seeing if I could get tickets to MERRY WIDOW I discovered that the Kartnerstrasse has been turned into a pedestrian mall. Not even streetcars are allowed on this one as in Graz and there are metal banquettes surrounding trees. I saw a Winerwald and seeing that they had the same menu the one in Graz had I sat at an outdoor table and had virtually the same meal I had the first night in Graz. As I ate I realized I was on the street with the gay bar, gay hotel and gay baths. Had no time for those tonite as I was heading for the Theatre an der Wien. I was able to get a ticket for tonight for a little over $3 so took my camera back to my room and while there did some diary. I don't know what got into me in Vienna with German. In Graz I cowered if people spoke to me in German and I muttered my phrases so low no errors could be heard but neither could my words. I told myself I wouldn't need it in Vienna, that all business people speak English. Yet at restaurant and theatre I didn't even find out if they spoke English, I just struck out loud and clear in German with great success. I even heard myself counting my money in German and counting is the last thing I do in a foreign language. No, learning verbs and grammar is the last thing but counting is next. I seem to have reached a new plateau, tho it's still the lowest one in the foothills. When I got to the theatre (Ken would have loved how near it is--three or four blocks) I saw that all the men had jackets on but fortunately an American school party was up in the third ring with me and they were in shirtsleeves. Nobody my age, tho, and I won't make that mistake again. I don't know if *this* Theatre an der Wien is the original one in which LUSTIGE WITWE made its 1905 debut and in which FIDELIO was first given but it's lovely. As for the production, it was a model of how to make these old operettas viable. Marilyn Tschau, the widow, showed how it could and should be sung. A mezzo rather than a soprano, she was lovely. It was all acted in a modern low key instead of the exaggerated style so often seen in revivals of period pieces. The result was that even the usually stilted emotional scenes had a reality. I wanted so much for Ken to be there. They probably cut the text for it didn't seem to run on as operetta books can and even the comedy, so often outrageously overdone and unfunny, was deftly done and I laughed. The production was lovely to look at and what a gorgeous score. Lots of Hungarian-type names in the cast and one really saw the conglomerate nature of Vienna's population. After the show I went to the Kartnerstrasse and watched people a while. I must say the Austrians obey traffic lights, not crossing till they get the pedestrian signal even if no car is in sight. I have quickly given up my New York ways and wait also.

SUNDAY, AUGUST 10, 1975

Walked over to the Belvedere and after all these years of frustration was at last able to get in. No international conferences, no repairs. It's now the gallery of 19th and 20th C Austrian art. Certain rooms and the stairway are still as sumptuous as in Prince Eugene's day but many have been made plain to hold art. The work of Gustav Klimt is very weird but I like Egon Schiele and there are some good Kokoschkas. Bought lots of postcards and promptly found a shady bench in the park in front of the palace and wrote Ken a card in my smallest script. A little oriental man, part of one of the many parties being rushed from bus to garden and back again without seeing the inside of the palace, ran around taking hurried pictures. It made me so glad I have time to do things in a more relaxed way. I went to see the Alpengarten, a rambling place with every Alpine plant labeled and some absolutely fascinating in shape and texture. The botanical garden was right next to it so I wandered in there a while, thinking I could see the Museum of the City of Vienna some other time if need be. As it turned out, I had an hour and a half there too and was pleased at the prominence they gave writers and performers, so seldom considered a part of history at home. I just finished going round the four floors covering the gamut from Roman settlement thru Turkish seige to World War II when it was time for them to close at 1. After that there was nothing to do but wander and that was fun. Decided that if I were going to try for a ticket to EINE NACHT IN VENEDIG tonite I'd better go back to the room a while, rest, shower, and especially, have some water. It's hot here tho sitting in the shade can be comfortable. The Theatre Raimund wasn't as attractive as the Theatre an der Wien but I gather it's old too. Neither did NIGHT IN VENICE compare with MERRY WIDOW except in the quality of the score. Walked over to see if Gay Guide was right in saying the Rathaus Park was cruising ground still. In a meager sort of way it is but not worth another visit. Soon walked on home as those fountains, tho lovely, attract mosquitoes. Tho Vienna has been far from dull this weekend, I look forward to seeing it go about its business tomorrow.

MONDAY, AUGUST 11, 1975

After doing some needlepoint, down to breakfast, and

then to the Opernpassage to arrange for the Budapest trip. Had to get two photos for the Hungarian visa, which they arrange for. The photomat machine was in the Stefl department store and many people were using it. The Hungarians will be sure I'm a spy when they see those photos. That all attended to, went to the Albertina, where the exhibit of graphic masterworks wasn't large but certainly choice. One room of Albrecht Durer's drawings and watercolors would alone have been worth the trip to Vienna. A youngish man with hair in pigtail was sitting in front of them as tho he might acquire genius by proximity. If he worshipped Durer I can't blame him. A self-portrait at 16 showed he always had it and there were some exquisite, vibrantly living watercolors--the wing of a bird, done in 1512, a view of Innsbruck in, I think, 1520, a little tiny sketch of a bouquet of violets. Also worth the trip to Vienna was the Spanish Riding School. Because the horses don't perform in summer I guess I thought one couldn't get in but for 10S they let one visit the horses in the stables and then visit the Fischer v. Erlach room and hear a historical and descriptive recording. The young horses seem to be dark; I think I heard they get white as they get older. They have marble basins for oats and water and they certainly deserve no less. I think the riding school room may be the single most beautiful room I ever saw tho God knows it's got competition right here in Vienna. I walked home by way of the Stadtpark and as I passed the Johann Strauss statue a tv or film unit was photographing it. Lots of Americans going to the opera at Schonbrunn, as when Ken and I went. There was a bearded violinist in the orchestra who quite took my eye and had the performance been weak I could have enjoyed the evening looking at him. But the performance was by no means weak. The overture, which contains all the lovely melodies later sung, was so well-played that I thought the singers' recapitulation might be a let-down but not a bit of it. It was one of the pleasantest, most enjoyable evenings of opera I've ever had. I've always loved DON PASQUALE, a fine workable libretto and a string of melodies, and I certainly saw it get its due. Hearing an Italian opera done in German gave me little pause and I wasn't long put off by having a Japanese sing Ernesto. He is the third good tenor I've heard in as many days and the best of the lot. The director contrived to keep everybody believable and natural instead of going in for excessive horseplay. Overheard some people on American Express tour who've just had today here. God almighty!

TUESDAY, AUGUST 12, 1975

Planning my day, I kept finding more museums and exhibits of interest right in Vienna so decided to skip the trip to Eisenstadt. On some future visit, with Ken I hope, Eisenstadt can be made an outing for us. I'll also save the Abbey of Melk, Brno, etc. Vienna itself more than satisfies me now. Had a look inside St. Stephen's then went to the Mozart Figaro-Haus. Some things there are facsimiles which I remember to be the case at Schubert's birthplace, but some were original including a program from the first MAGIC FLUTE. From there to the Roman ruins under the Hohmarkt, which I just discovered yesterday, when they were closed. One could hear the clipclop of the fiacre horses' hoofs overhead as one looked at the remains of staff officers' headquarters dating from 100 B.C. to 4 or 5 hundred A.D. Started for the Schottenkirche concert in time to eat in the Opernpassage. The Univ. of Connecticut Concert Choir drew an overflow crowd and covered themselves with glory. Some numbers they sang from the front of the church, some from high up in the organloft but everywhere they sounded quite marvelous. Of the whole batch I think only two girls were pretty and the only handsome man was a light negro soloist (another good tenor!). Walked to Kartnerstrasse to sit as concert had started at seven and it was quite early. I had hardly more than arrived when my eyes met those of a tall good-looking cruiser. I expected just mutual inspection but he stopped in his tracks then reversed directions. When I sat on a bench he sat beside me without coyness and launched conversation. I suspected him of being a hustler after money and the fact that he never mentioned it up to the time he gave up on me doesn't necessarily prove he wouldn't have in time. When he discovered I couldn't take anybody to my hotel he said he had a room, lived alone, and we could go there. I asked if we could walk and he said it was too far but a 5 minute taxi ride would do it. Taxis going there would no doubt be easy but taxis back? If he had lived in the vicinity I'd probably have gone with him and if he'd been more completely to my taste I might have anyway but tho his face was handsome, his manner pleasant and seductive, his basket plainly adequate, he was a bit tall and thin for me. Thin was what he was with clothes on; skinny is what I think he'd be without them. Eventually he gave up and moved on and not long afterward I went back to the hotel.

WEDNESDAY, AUGUST 13, 1975

On my way to the Museum of Applied Art I sat a while in the Stadtpark. Nearby was the sorriest-looking pigeon I

ever saw in my life and I've seen some pretty sorry ones.
"Bist du krank oder alt?" I asked it then decided that was
stupid. It makes sense to talk to a cat or dog in its own
language but you'll never convince me that anything so stupid as a pigeon could ever master German no matter how long
it lived here so it might as well be talked to in English
it doesn't understand as   German it doesn't understand.
So stupid that he didn't even sense the low esteem in which
I hold pigeons, the poor ugly thing tottered over and stood
about one inch from my foot, as tho I had taken him under
my wing, so to speak. Hating ugliness and stupidity as
much as I do, I must say I nevertheless felt sorry for it.
An old gentleman on his way to a bench to read his paper
pointed to the bird and said "Krank" then a lady came along
with crumbs apparently saved especially for him. Unfortunately, before he could make up his mind to bend over and
eat them, some sparrows flew in from a distance, probably
Lapland, and got at least half. But that happens even with
well pigeons. They're not exactly fast thinkers. Just realized I'm maligning the great deliverers of messages (tho
not in the last three wars) but they must surely be a different breed from those in public places. I know I went to
the Museum of Applied Art on my 1952 visit but not, I
think, on either of my two visits with Ken. That's a crying shame because it has so much he loves--glass, porcelain, furniture, medallions. I was very taken with little
disks containing portraits, perhaps in ivory, by Hans
Kels, 15th or 16th C. After lunch I went to the Kunsthistorisches and there I ran into Kels again. There was a
simply amazing backgammon board he had carved and more
disks, which are the playing pieces. Those of the set had
the most exquisitely done scenes in each instead of portraits. What a master! How untalented it makes one feel.
Decided this was the day to have pastry and coffee at Demel's, as Ken might not let me back in the apt. if he
thought I never went. I chose a piece of cake with little
strawberries on it and that and "kaffee mit schlag" cost
me $3, more than my lunch or dinner. So once is enuf for
that. Truthfully, like much fancy-looking pastry, it
doesn't taste all that good. Home and delighted to find
another letter from Ken. He suggested perhaps I could find
a retirement present for Ruth here, a thought that had already occurred to me. Even 4000 miles apart our minds run
in the same channels.

THURSDAY, AUGUST 14, 1975
        Was at the Kunsthistorisches before it opened at ten.
En route I had seen in a store window a jigsaw puzzle of

the Lipizzaners in the Redoutensaal and resolved to take
that to Ken along with a Sacher torte. I had a dizzying
hour and a half on the painting floor of the Kunsthistorisches, trying to make sure I missed none of the little
side rooms which so casually contained nine or so Velas-
quez portraits or half a dozen things by Durer. What rich
holdings they have! Rested a while in the park to clear
my head then went on to the Theatre Museum. In sharp contrast to the Kunsthistorisches, which is so elaborate that
few palaces can rival it, the Theatre Museum has plain
white walls except for one of the ten rooms, which has a
chandelier and some plaster work on the ceiling. This
plays up the exhibits as a museum should, and very interesting they were as they traced Viennese theatre from Baroque to the present. When I looked at the pictures of the
original women in MERRY WIDOW I thought--why should anyone object to updating the book or orchestration of the
show? We wouldn't dream of casting the girls at Maxim's
with buxom girls such as they favored then but always cast
with the style of beauty currently in fashion. Set out on
my trip to the Wienerwald by trolley No. 43 as instructed
by the article in the N.Y. Times. I went by way of the Au-
ersperg Palace, where Gluck and Mozart conducted, and by
one of Beethoven's many Viennese houses, this the one
where he composed the MISSA SOLEMNIS. The trolley ride out
to Neuwaldegg wasn't attractive nor was the town itself.
After nearly giving up as I walked thru the long little
suburb, I finally came to the woods. Walked in them about
half an hour but the uneven terrain hurt my bad foot so
after taking a couple of pictures of sun filtering thru
trees, which probably won't come out, I got the trolley
back to the center. Instantly I felt better going toward
the center. I hung around for the 5 o'clock Strauss concert outside the Rathaus. It drew an overflow crowd but
was a very mild concert. The greeny woods of the Wienerwald may be fine for some people but I think the trees in
the parks are lovelier for the space around them allows
them to take proper shape and develop individuality. When
the Strauss concert got a bit boring I looked at those in
the Rathaus Park and trees just couldn't be lovelier.

FRIDAY, AUGUST 15, 1975
    Busloads of tourists were descending on Schonbrunn.
This city is crawling with French, which hurts no city as
far as I'm concerned. By a mistake I could have rectified
if I'd had a mind to, I got in with a group that was being shown around the showrooms in German and French. This
made a good double language lesson for me and in the

limited vocabulary of furniture, French and Austrian history, and parts of rooms, I now do just as well in German as in French. I must have known that the walls of the million room were hidden in the Salzburg salt mines during World War II and that it took 2 yrs. to restore them but I'd forgotten that. Went out in the garden after the tour and again ran into a tv film crew, possibly doing other scenes of a life of Strauss for the scene involved a band playing the Rakoczy March on the Schloss steps. From there to the Volksgarten to see the roses. Like some of us people, some roses turned out to have looked better in the twilight. Many can bear the full light of day, tho, and I took a few flower photos, something I never do. All these odd marks on the page are where I kept falling asleep as I wrote.

SATURDAY, AUGUST 16, 1975

Our hotel in Budapest was the Beke, with a certain old-fashioned air about it--high ceilings and great high double doors to the rooms, Shakespearean murals in the restaurant. It turned out that I had been booked into a double room with an English chap in the insurance business in Vienna. So, tho the Floridians invited me to join them and an Australian for lunch, I stuck to my room-mate. Lunch was nice and during it our pretty guide Katharina passed out small maps of the city and told us the program. This afternoon was at leisure. I had found out from Katharina that the art museum stayed open till 6 and was free today so that's where I headed. I suppose any museum is bound to be a letdown after the Kunsthistorisches but even so Budapest's is the kind that gave art museums a bad name. Perhaps Vienna over-restores, overcleans, but here a brown pall is on everything and it's like looking at pictures in twilight. Vibrancy of color is nowhere, hardly even in their impressionists. Had just about enough strength to walk back to the hotel for a rest in my room. The boulevards of Budapest are broad and tree-lined, the transportation excellent and the people attractive but it hasn't won me yet. Being seen on a wet weekend is a double handicap to any city. Dinner was in the cellar with a "gypsy" orchestra that played Lehar, Liszt, etc. more than gypsy music tho later they went from table to table with a basket for tips and got into "echt Hungarisch". A boy 10 or 11 played with them, flashing the most joyful smiles from time to time and I wondered how long it would take the little beauty to develop the somewhat bored manner of the other musicians. He and the handsomest musician were the ones who went from table to table (they know what they're doing) and the kid was being exploited but charming birds off trees. He isn't in that orchestra just for his youth and looks, however. He earns his place with first-class fiddling and real brio. It got hot in the cellar so I decided to go for a walk to the Danube. It changed my attitude toward Budapest completely. We're staying in Pest so I walked across to Buda and back. I looked in the record stores and find they have western, non-Communist records. At the theatre they're doing Shaw's SAINT JOAN and MRS. WARREN'S PROFESSION, Shakespeare's RICHARD II and MERRY WIVES and Edward Bond's BINGO, which puts them one ahead of New York since we've not seen that. Saw some handsome youths and the goods in the stores are very nice.

SUNDAY, AUGUST 17, 1975

One of the Floridians with us was repelled by tongue at any time and by pickles at breakfast so I happily ate hers as well as mine. Our tour of the city started at nine. The cultural life all seems to take place in Pest but the vistas are from the Buda hills. A new Hilton hotel is being built cheek by jowl with St. Matthews' (?) church. After a meal we were off on the long, hot, tedious ride back to Vienna. Many slept for quite a while but since I don't expect ever to return to Budapest or Hungary I tried to look at it. I had gone out for a walk before breakfast to see what Budapest looked like on a Sunday morning and I found it looked like the most bustling town I'd ever seen on a Sunday. At 7:30 lots of people were going somewhere. Flower sellers were setting up their stands, food markets were open and busy. I thought perhaps this meant they were less religious than some but the churches were full and Katharina, our guide, later explained that the state somewhat supports the church financially. Communist domination has apparently not changed that and they are paying for the rebuilding of historic churches destroyed in war or revolution. In today's bright sunshine Budapest looked very attractive with its great wide Danube on which flotillas of motorboats were racing at one point. We left Vienna in a sprinkle and we returned in a downpour. Was glad to be back with my needlepoint, glad to be back in Vienna. Good to be alone again in a room, too.

TUESDAY, AUGUST 19, 1975

It was hot in Frankfurt when I arrived. Feel the trip has been very reassuring as to my being able to be alone. Definitely felt no loneliness in Vienna. Which is not to say I didn't often want Ken along to see something marvelous with me.

SATURDAY, AUGUST 23, 1975

At five we set out for Leo and Larry's. Ruth's note of invitation to her retirement party had said that the woman major she worked for was straight and therefore we'd have to be careful. Since I never get very drunk and am not much given to camping, we were never the threat. We did, of course, have to forego the arrival kisses that Leo and Larry would normally get. I was a bit puzzled that Lee was not there but Major Thorwaldsen had taken Ruth to the theatre this afternoon and Lee came along later with a lesbian friend who, I later learned, had once been a Ziegfeld Follies girl, tho you'd never guess it now. Far from finding the presence of Major Thorwaldsen inhibiting, I hit it off with her right from the start. Lee, who got drunk fairly quickly, made remarks which I hoped the major didn't ever hear across the rather compact room, about how she could have been a general if the Italian half of her didn't come out her mouth, about how she claimed to hate queers but was almost certainly one herself, etc. Leo and Larry had been out to a matinee of the Alvin Ailey dancers and still got home in time to receive guests at six. They are out in the kitchen a great deal during the party and yet one doesn't get a sense of never seeing the hosts. They really are masterful at party-giving. Ed S. was there and at one point I heard him whispering to someone about some new romance and saying it was flattering and made him feel young but he spared me these confessions. Somehow I feel this sort of thing just emphasizes age, as did Dick's stories of having had offers during the Depression from people who would have kept him on Park Avenue at the $10,000 a year level and having answered that he already lived on Park Avenue and 10,000 wouldn't keep him in silk underwear. I suppose, since he's still a presentable man, that as a youth he might have been a raving Swedish beauty but he seems even then to have been a snot. He goes in for much self-advertising about the friends he makes on his many long cruises and how they say he's the most charming man on board but I seem impervious to his charm. Our preoccupations about people are, of course, very different. People's money interests him but to me is irrelevant. Anyway, I liked the major and the former Follies girl, who seemed very level-headed. She persisted in trying to get me to dance when the dancing started but I refused, not only for the reason that I don't do it well (tho I could do as well as any of those tipsy people) but with all the lurching going on I could see weight suddenly thrown on my bad foot. After a couple toppled onto my lap I retreated out of range.

MONDAY, AUGUST 25, 1975

Kissed Ken goodbye for ten days and before he even left he was saying he wished he hadn't arranged so long a stay. I read the paper so he could take it with him and read it on the bus. Did some surgery on my office plants today as they were all leggy but just have no more room for the cuttings that have rooted. To Needlework Group and five came.

FRIDAY, AUGUST 29, 1975

From our last three o'clock summer closing I went straight to Beacon Baths. For a couple of hours there was nothing but rather uninteresting groping. Lots of people were there but no beauties. Then suddenly I saw a blond bearded beauty going to the showers. I quickly followed and on into the steam room. Made my move quickly and had his acquiescence before anybody else had quite pulled themselves together. For the first time I was able to complete the job in the steam room. The steam went into one of its periods of decline so it was more bearable. This meant we became quite visible and had a circle of spectators but I never care when it's a beauty I'm involved with and that he certainly was. I felt I had vastly improved my technique and to a certain extent I have but it was relevant that among the blond's virtues was the fact that he was of a size I could conveniently handle. I'm afraid I still couldn't manage somebody Ken's or my size with the same ease. Another nice thing was that he didn't rush away after orgasm but let himself relax competely and stayed to be petted a while. His legs were hairier than I usually like but it was blond, blond hair and that's okay. I decided I'd not equal him for a long time and was going home then saw that he had settled in front of the tv and that there was a seat beside him. Since just sitting beside him with the hairs of our arms touching was a sexier experience than sleeping with any fourteen others at the baths I was quite happy till I realized he was repeatedly dozing off. I went home totally satisfied even tho there had been no reciprocation, feeling it had been my second best encounter of all time at the baths and very high on the list of my lifetime experiences. I fondled his trim beard and moustache much as the Italian man on the train fondled mine.

FRIDAY, SEPTEMBER 5, 1975

Only yesterday Darryl wrote me one of his notes asking for philosophic guidance and said, "You seem to me to have an amazingly peaceful soul". I told him in my banal and hasty reply that he must remember I was in the calm harbor of age but had mended a lot of torn sail and held hard to the rudder in stormier days but the implication was that that was all behind me. He should have had a look into my soul today and he wouldn't have found it so peaceful. I was a mass of spiteful fantasy all morning (*because I had waited home in vain for Ken's arrival and had had no word as to why he hadn't shown up*), knowing full well that I was only raising my blood pressure to no purpose, that my devastating dialogue would never be spoken, and that it was all silly beyond words. The boss asked me when Ken was due back and I said, "Two days ago." He said that he asked because if I were still alone, Melina had thought of having me over Monday but that if Ken was coming back, later would be better. "If we're speaking," I said. Well, when I got home after shopping Ken had arrived just one minute before and I would estimate that by ten o'clock 182,345 words had cascaded from our lips. Mostly his, as he was so wound up that an "Oh?" or "Uh-huh" was sufficient from me but I was in no way inclined to be sulky. He claimed he had told me he wouldn't be back till today but we weren't disposed to argue over that. I was glad to have him back and all my vindictive and cold fantasy of the morning was simply my way of dealing with what the psychiatrist said I had trouble dealing with, separation.

FRIDAY, SEPTEMBER 12, 1975

The new PLAYGIRL had an article on Loving an Older Man, followed by a test. I took it and answered "No" to all questions but one, not feeling that older men had any of the things to offer that the questions said. It turned out that this was good as 0-1 Yesses meant one loved the older person only for qualities one had in common and was not specifically turned on by his age. Well, that's certainly true as far as my love for Ken goes. His age is not only no part of his attraction but I fell when distinctly prejudiced against age.

SATURDAY, SEPTEMBER 13, 1975

We got an early enough start downtown to make the first show at the Radio City Music Hall. They are reviving SOUND OF MUSIC, which we avoided when it first came out because we were so sick of the then over-played music. The best part of it is still the Austrian scenery. The audience was pitifully small and all thru the stage show, a very good one, the pall of death was on everything, for the Music Hall is a terminal patient which may have remissions like some cancer victims but is as surely doomed. When you've known it in the days when people lined up to get in and when there was electricity and excitement in the audience, it's sad to go there now and see all those empty seats. I still think it's physically beautiful with all the art deco but it's just a question of time. I never really grieved for the ugly old Metropolitan Opera House despite the good times I'd had there because the same activities were continuing at another site, but huge movie palaces like the Music Hall are not adequately replaced by today's intimate theatres.

FRIDAY, SEPTEMBER 19, 1975

Darryl resumed correspondence (*he was as near as the typing pool in the basement, to which he had transferred when Wintermudd insisted he be let go, but he had spells of bombarding me with notes and letters signed V.F.T.B. for "Voice from the Basement" to which I replied when I had the time with notes signed O.M. for "Ol' Massa", a reference I initially had to explain to him.*) with a further request for my reflections on life and reality, saying he believed the opinions of those in their 30's, 40's and 50's could hasten his maturity. I replied that I could not recall ever getting any good advice from an older person, couldn't recall asking for any, and felt that it would probably be useless as they lived in different times, different places, with different talents, different bodies, different family situations, etc. Can an only child advise a member of a large family or vice versa; can a homely person advise someone with personal beauty or charm; can a gregarious person advise a loner? I just don't see how. All I can keep harping on with Darryl is "Get out and live!" I told him to count any month lost in which he hadn't tried something new and to be wary if he weren't sometimes scared as it probably meant he wasn't taking enough risks. But is even that advice really valid? When I took my risks in youth were they as risky as his would be? Times were more propitious for risk-taking and I had more external advantages of looks and glibness so that it was perhaps less risky. I do wish he would get another job instead of settling in at TC for life.

SATURDAY, SEPTEMBER 20, 1975

Downtown to get tickets for ICE FOLLIES at the Music Hall for the day of Mother's visit. Then the Morgan Library. Tho I knew there was an exhibit there of illustrated children's books I really went to see the Jane Austen bicentennary exhibit. I hadn't thought myself interested in children's books, for some reason. In the entrance lobby as I looked at Lewis Carroll's copy of ALICE with Tenniel's original pencil sketches a young woman wheeling a baby (never saw that there before) exclaimed, "Isn't it exciting? I just can't believe it." She maintained that glow as she went round the exhibits and I thought again what a restorative oasis the Morgan always is for me, and the people who go are part of it. I didn't really know Kate Greenaway's work and was most impressed by it but there were many choice items. Ken seemed interested enuf in all that but didn't get up and follow me back to the library after we rested. I was gone so long looking at Jane Austen's writing desk, the lock of her hair, her letters and her manuscripts, that eventually he showed up but he didn't take the same interest in it that I did. Authors don't cut much ice with him, even tho he enjoys reading. Just as when he enjoys a play or movie he seems to think the actors made it up, so he seems not to realize or care that his reading pleasure is provided by an author. He's impressed that Beverly Sills can sing Bellini's and Rossini's music but not much impressed that Bellini and Rossini could write it. This is a little unfair to Ken, perhaps, but not as egregiously so as I could wish.

WEDNESDAY, SEPTEMBER 24, 1975
    In the afternoon I had a most welcome visit from Jocelyn Black. She has completed a masters in business administration at Stanford, concluded that she doesn't care for California and that the East Coast is more stimulating, has a job already with National City Bank as a statistical analyst. She's still a stunning girl with marvelous bone structure and a quick mind and I was flattered that she came to see me. Apparently Anselmo had not known that I used to be in charge out there in the records room until he heard Ed ask if that had been one of my former employees. I heard him say to Ed, "Mr. Vining used to be in charge out here?" get an affirmative answer and then say, "I could listen to him all day." I was stunned, thinking I had perhaps been talking too much, then remembered how much I had really drawn out of Jocelyn and decided that Anselmo must have been sincere. If I don't look out I'll have another disciple, a la Darryl. I keep telling them all that one can't really give advice because we all live such different lives (*Jocelyn, for instance, was black and female and gifted in mathematics, in which I am virtually retarded and Anselmo was Latin and an athlete.*) but of course I do, in the end, give it.
It seems probable that my great affinity for intelligent young people comes from the fact that I am myself immature but my acolytes seem to think I have great wisdom and

and maturity. The more I insist that I don't myself believe older people have much wisdom, the more they contradict. Did I EVER really feel like confiding in an older person or take advice from them? I can't remember ever doing so or wanting to do so. I don't think I really tell them so much as ask them a lot, which clarifies their thinking.

THURSDAY, SEPTEMBER 25, 1975

On my break I wrote cards to Senators Tunney and Muskie thanking them for their efforts on behalf of Sgt. Matlovich's fight to stay in the army despite declared homosexuality. I'm also going to write to the other Senators and Representatives who helped out when Bruce and the Task Force group asked them to. I feel more and more loyal to the Gay Task Force as I see that Bruce and the others really work on the political action that counts. With the new higher fares I'm probably not going to go down and seal envelopes even as often as I did before but I'm going to use my pen in the fight even more than I did. So few people get around to writing political figures that those of us who do have a force beyond our numbers. After supper I went down to the Social Committee meeting, taking my needlepoint so that the time wouldn't be lost. It was a rather effective meeting. We decided to buy tables, hang what drapes we could, hold a coffee to unveil it all, have a pot luck supper later in the year, arrange for more film showings by Debby, have the usual White Elephant Sale and start the exercise classes again.

SATURDAY, SEPTEMBER 27, 1975

To the Metropolitan Museum. They have no special shows at present but I hadn't seen the Lehmann wing (Ken saw it while I was away). The addition is nice but the collection doesn't thrill me. Even where some of the names are big, it doesn't seem the examples are great. His kind of collecting doesn't excite me and I rather offended the easily offended Ken when I said I like people like Gertrude Stein and Peggy Guggenheim who went out on a limb, gambled on their own taste, and collected living artists of their own time rather than someone like Lehmann who collected chiefly long-endorsed names. In the evening we had the first in the series of Classic Theatre tv shows, MACBETH. It was superbly done with Janet Suzman doing just as good a Lady Macbeth as she did a Cleopatra, unmannered and modern, suited to the intimacy of the tv camera as it all was, without forgetting that it was poetic drama. I look forward to the whole series.

SATURDAY, OCTOBER 4, 1975
    We went downtown, had our passport and visa photo taken, then went up to the Passport Office and filled out the form while waiting. With a lunch stopoff we went to the Garden Clubs Flower Show in the tent in Bryant Park and found it a bit different from last time but no less fascinating. I had forgotten that needlework on flower themes was one contest area and I could hardly wait till I got home to call or leave notes for all the members of the needlework group who might not know of this horribly under-publicized show. I'm certainly walking Mother around it tomorrow even tho she's never been one for shows, fairs, or anything like that. I had intended to go home with Ken and clean house but he said he might turn the baseball game on so I decided to stay downtown. Went to the Adonis, where a well-reviewed porno movie was in its last days. I knew it would move on to one of the numerous other theatres but the Adonis is the only one that's a really clean and well-appointed, even lush, theatre. When they played "Kiss Me Again" during a rimming scene it struck me funny. Victor Herbert's reaction were he alive to see that, would be choice.

SUNDAY, OCTOBER 5, 1975
    On tv was a program on the Roaring Twenties which managed to come up with some fresh material from the archives. I hadn't realized, for instance, that Calvin Coolidge was recorded on talking films or that talking newsreels existed when Coolidge welcomed Lindbergh back from France. Later there was the first episode of a six-part series on the fight for women's rights in England, a really wonderful episode on the Pankhurst family. Again I was convinced that one firebrand is worth about 8 million apathetic ordinary citizens. The individual really can do so much, both for good and ill, that one gets a great sense of power if convinced of this. I don't happen to feel that gay civil rights matter nearly as much as women's rights but the latter fight isn't really yet won for on Nov. 4 New York State votes on the Equal Rights Amendment.

THURSDAY, OCTOBER 16, 1975
    Ken told me when I called that Jack MacNealy was annoyed that Ken hadn't understood I was included in the invitation to their country house Saturday, that they expected me. Ken hadn't been sure I was invited and knew I'd rather not go so told him I had tickets to the Joffrey Ballet, whereupon Jack said I could turn them in, that of course they wanted me to come. I had had quite a wonderful

and jam-packed day planned for myself--the movie DOG DAY AFTERNOON, the exhibit of Imperial Japanese Art at the Japan Society, followed by the Beacon Baths, but Ken's lie had been so lame that I felt I had to go. I wish I could ever teach him not to give specifics when he lies, then the other person can't find flaws in the story, can't catch you off base later, doesn't know what arguments to put up. But I do appreciate the fact that the MacNealys consider us so much a couple that Jack couldn't understand why Ken would even imagine they didn't mean the invitation for both of us. There is a lot more tolerance in the world than some gay literature would lead you to believe.

FRIDAY, OCTOBER 24, 1975

At noon Eric delivered his latest play for criticism and then we went to Riverside Church for an abominable lunch but good talk. By arrangement I met Ken at the Japan Society to see the art works from the imperial collection, here in connection with Emperor Hirohito's recent visit. The building itself is lovely. The exhibit was not large but I particularly loved several scrolls, one showing several roosters, others from a series devoted to the months. One room had paintings by the present empress, all very competent and a screen really very lovely. We walked up Third Avenue to a supermarket to make what should be our final purchases for the party. As we walked up we saw some of the handsomest hustlers I've ever seen, not crude types unable to make a living any other way but of a beauty and tone I've never seen working the streets, clearly $50-$100 a night types. As I write this, tho, I marvel that we were both so sure they were in it for the money. They might well be good-looking young men cruising the streets to make a connection for their own pleasure. Yet we did both instantly feel that they were a new breed of hustler and agreed they would be worth whatever they charged if one's lust could survive the exchange of money at all, as mine could not.

SUNDAY, OCTOBER 26, 1975

When I went out for the Times I hoped to get some bread for the party but the store wasn't open. When I started to read the Times I found out why. We were supposed to set our clocks back last nite and return to standard time so it was only 6:30. This meant a long delay before I felt free to vacuum or even run the sweeper. However, there were quieter things to do to get ready, like polishing the brass candlesticks. Bob R. called to say they had a visitor from Mexico and could they bring him along. The visitor, with the unMexican name of Eric, turned out to be a charmer. He works for an airline, travels all over and speaks English, Portuguese, Spanish, Italian and French. "Well, why not German," I said, "Are you a slow learner or something?" Maurice was last to arrive, the Latins having been surprisingly prompt, and Maurice was wearing a stunning jacket he'd made himself. I had told Ken not to put any liquor in my drink as I thought I would then pay more attention to my duties as a host. As a matter of fact this time it was Ken who got talking and didn't even turn the oven on for the casserole. I grew afraid that people would eat so many hors d'oeuvres that they'd be too full for dinner so I got things started. Since Maurice and José were drinking screwdrivers and we hadn't much orange juice, I went out to the store and got more unobtrusively, and on the whole did a much better job of carrying my share of the load. Neither Ken nor I were upset over the dinner's shortcomings even tho José is chef of what is currently considered THE restaurant in SoHo. José has six other cooks. He wants to fire one because he's macho "and the rest of us are queens so that's no good."

THURSDAY, OCTOBER 28, 1975
When I came out of a staff meeting, Ken had called to say he'd had success in getting tickets to the TRAVESTIES preview and would meet me at Donnell Library. A wonderful audience gathered and it was nice sitting in the orchestra for the price one will soon pay for the last row in the balcony. The play was too surrealist-absurd for Ken's taste but I loved it and doubt if I'm going to see anything as good in years. No doubt many of the jokes involving James Joyce went over my head since I haven't read Joyce but I had a great advantage in having played in IMPORTANCE OF BEING EARNEST for several scenes are takeoffs of scenes in that. Stoppard is just marvelously imaginative and writes superbly for actors. There were an astonishing number of gorgeous men in attendance. So nice to know so many beautiful males have brains enough in their heads to go to a play that literate. John Wood did an absolute tour de force in the lead, which many a future amateur will mangle in colleges from coast to coast. I do think Stoppard is probably the best playwright now writing in English.

FRIDAY, OCTOBER 31, 1975
At noon lunch with Eric to discuss his play, on which I could give a much more favorable report than usual, since his local color and plot were good, his confrontation immediate and his action on stage for a change. But it's

only half long enough. Did a little work on my own play on
afternoon break and think I'll take it home next week and
work on it there an hour a night. From work to Beacon
Baths. Not many attractive ones there but what most attracted me I got. About 6'3" (that's height I'm speaking
of), bearded, slender, and good-looking, he instantly returned my interest and with backward glances led me toward
the orgy room. I seldom go there because it's so dark you
can't see who you're involved with but in this case I knew
and we were soon in each other's arms. Others began to
gather round so I suggested we find a cubicle and we did,
locking the door. I surprised Ken by getting home early
(no use hanging around when you've had the best).

THURSDAY, NOVEMBER 6, 1975
    In mid-morning I had a call from Carl, who told me,
in his prissiest PHD manner, "Sunday is Kendall's 70th
birthday." "NO!" I said, rather sarcastically. He told me
that they were having Open House in the library in Ken's
honor from 1:30 to 3 and that I was welcome and so were
any of the people who worked with him and knew him at TC.
Vi Denison said she'd love to go and she met me by the
arch. I had wondered how such a party could be held in
the doctor's library without disturbing the doctors but it
turned out to be in Nancy Panella's office. She had baked
and beautifully decorated a three-tier cake which dominated
a table all set up with candles of graduated heights, and
there was a lovely coffee urn. Tho I started in a chair
beside Ken, who looked very handsome in his blue volunteer's jacket, as ladies arrived I went over and sat on the
steps to the library. Carl joined me and started gossiping
like a little girl allowed to stay up late on party night.
I could see that Vi was a bit out of things so drew her
into it. We went back after an hour. The party went on long
after the scheduled hour and my 4:30 call to Ken found him
still not home. Sixty people showed up and he was certainly
pleased.

SUNDAY, NOVEMBER 9, 1975
    We had beautiful weather for Ken's 70th birthday. The
cats enjoyed the unwrapping of presents and the cord from
the lasagna pan was more fun for them to play with than any
toy I could get them. They won't play at the same time but
patiently wait and take turns. Since our theatre and restaurant outing was to Greenwich Village, I decided not to
wear a jacket in this hot weather. It was nearly 80 yesterday and I have a feeling it topped that today. In the end,
because Ken was wearing a jacket I wore one too so we both

appeared ridiculously overdressed in the Village. Didn't see a single other jacket till intermission of the play when I noted some of the elderly men had them on. BOY MEETS BOY was a very cute takeoff of 30's musicals with the love interest another man instead of a girl. The hero was handsome and the beloved, tho not, was an excellent actor whose sincerity gave him a certain appeal, tho not to me a physical one. Perhaps the highlights were a Rogers-Astaire dance done by the two men and a takeoff of the Folies Bergere with men as the strippers instead of women. The production had good pace (it ran seven months Off-Off-Broadway before becoming Off-Broadway) and Ken was thoroly pleased with it.

THURSDAY, NOVEMBER 11, 1975
PRIVATE CHRONICLES is quite thought-provoking in its theorizing on diaries, particularly as it challenges the opinions of Ponsonby, which so influenced me years ago. Fothergill quite scoffs at Ponsonby's standards of sincerity and spontaneity, pointing out that Pepys' famous passage on the great fire was in fact written up later and he actually did first drafts so that in the diary he finally had bound, all is a fair copy. Fothergill thinks a highly self-conscious diary like Barbellion's and Anais Nin's is the true twentieth century breakthrough, whereas both have always set my teeth on edge. He feels all the greatest diarists have a certain amount of deliberate art in their diary. Not to put myself in that class, I do admit to drafting a certain amount of wordage in my mind in the course of a day and admit that Fothergill is right in saying diarists actually do things because they think they will make good diary entries. Conversely, a series of routine entries spurs one to shake up one's life, and that is for the life's sake, not the diary's. Fothergill is right, as far as I am concerned at any rate, in saying that after a diary has gone on for a certain time it invariably occurs to the diarist that there just may be a book in it and that one tries to shape it somewhat. Most of my attempts to catch the true flow of life have failed. When I thought the diary misrepresented life by being too somber I tried the LAUGH OF THE DAY and it was several years before I gave that up because the clear strain of remembering something distorted just as much in its way. Then I thought the HEADLINE OF THE DAY would give a larger perspective and abandoned that after several years because it was just as false. And there are innumerable other distortions. It isn't really true that the busiest day provides the shortest entry but a day's entry can be in so

many ways unrepresentative of the day. One is too tired
or too sick to deal properly with major events or forgets
to put things in. Ken frequently reminds me that I said I
must put something in my diary, usually something funny or
ironic or outrageous, and frequently I have already gone
past that point & forgotten it. And things get taken for
granted and are left unmentioned but play a larger part in
one's life than one supposes. I don't think my diary represents me any better than snapshots do. In snapshots,
espe ally if I have just removed my glasses, I look passive and dreamy and sober far too often whereas in actuality I am animated, aggressive, or at least abrasive, and
full of more jests than vapours. But I suppose my diary is
as fair a record as any, as truthful as most autobiograph-
ies, and certainly as close as I can get to the truth. I'm
sure I'll get much more to reflect on as I continue with
PRIVATE CHRONICLES but I swear Fothergill is never going
to sell me Anais Nin or Barbellion. It is perhaps their
utter humorlessness that turns me off. And since two husbands are never so much as mentioned in the Nin diary, how
truthful is that? I don't really like the tendency to
sneer at Ponsonby as I think his books were exceedingly
valuable to me in learning to diarize effectively. In the
sense that I came across those books early (ENGLISH DIAR-
IES and MORE ENGLISH DIARIES by Arthur Ponsonby), thought
about them a good deal, and altered my diarizing accord-
ingly toward the frank and specific, I have not been an
unself-conscious or untaught diarist since my teens. But I
do believe a diary loses a lot of what I value in them as
both reader and writer if it is not for some years a private thing. When Nin writes up a party and then shows the
masterpiece around to all and sundry for praise of her
writing or whatever reason, I feel she is going into another kind of writing altogether.

THURSDAY, NOVEMBER 13, 1975
    On the way to Trenton I finished PRIVATE CHRONICLES.
Fothergill perhaps convinced me that the Nin diary is a
work of art but he didn't make me like it. The quotations
were clearly superb writing but while I wish I wrote much
better I don't really think fine writing is the point of
a diary. Good reporting matters more to me. Nin is good
at that only on one level. One would never know she ate,
went to the bathroom, had sexual relations, looked after
a home, or delighted in picking out clothes. There is
little that is concrete in her diary. One may make faces
when Pepys mentions food more often than one salivates
but one knows he is a body whereas she is all quivering

sensibility. Fothergill points out Barbellion's pretentiousness but he overlooks Nin's, which I find as bad or worse at times. When I got to Trent Center I found that Mother didn't know I was coming. Sat right down to clear off the desk so Mother could find the important papers among all the clutter of junk advertising mail. I found letters addressed to minor creditors and checks made out to them and not mailed but when I found the bank statement I was astonished to find her with a balance of over $1000, more than she ever had in her life. This shows what happens when you get rid of the draining expense of a car. The ladies brought Mother's meal and collected for the week's meals but neither they nor I had much success in getting her to eat it. She's bored with the meals and her legs are swollen (she probably hasn't taken her pills) but she's not badly off. I wanted to call the bank about getting Mother's checks sent directly there but Mother had a fit because it would look as tho she couldn't run her affairs. Will write. As I walked to the station I found myself singing with relief at being out of there. After supper the Social Committee meeting. All plans were completed for Sunday's coffee, with a good distribution of chores.

IN CONCLUSION

This seems as good a place as any to stop both this particular volume and A GAY DIARY as a whole. After the passage of a few years it is possible that I may bring out an additional volume but perspective and distancing from events are necessary before that happens and one is never sure that the years needed to acquire those will be given one.

The diary is still kept to this day and as of August 29, 1983 will have been kept for half a century without a day's break.

So that no reader who has come this far will feel he has been left with loose ends, I can tie a few of them up in summary.

On our return from Egypt in February 1976 I found my mother had been removed to a hospital following a cigarette-caused fire considerably more serious than the several which had preceded it. At the insistence of her justifiably frightened neighbors, she was not allowed to return to her apartment and, disoriented from poor nutrition and improper dosages of medicine, she had to be placed in a nursing home. Here she lived for five largely cantankerous years, getting admirable care, and dying suddenly at lunch one day in August 1980, just two months short of her 91st birthday.

On the work scene, I found Wintermudd's philosophies of employee relations increasingly more suitable to the East India Company c. 1892 than to modern times, with the result that the atmosphere of unhappy workers and constant turnover led me to take early retirement in December 1979. Before doing so I utilized my 3 month vacation bonus to take Tuesday and Thursday mornings off for many months while I prepared the first volume of A GAY DIARY for publication.

Running into the attitude in regular publishing channels that they'd love to publish a gay diary if it weren't such a happy one and more accurately reflected the anguish and misery which they felt sure were the lot of the homosexual, I decided to publish it myself.

Establishing my own small press, I named it after the most famous of all diarists, Samuel Pepys, and became an entrepreneur as well as a writer. In addition to the four volumes of A GAY DIARY The Pepys Press published, in 1982, an anthology of 24 diaries brought out under the title AMERICAN DIARIES OF WORLD WAR II, well-received by critics and selling well. Between books I turned out stories and articles for a market which had not existed in my younger days—such gay periodicals as ADVOCATE (where my pieces appear most frequently), BLUE BOY, GAY COMMUNITY NEWS, IN TOUCH FOR MEN, MANDATE, etc. Having, at least for the time being, completed publication of A GAY DIARY, I plan to do even more free-lance writing for these and similar markets.

To my activism with the National Gay Task Force has been added an even more active participation in the many-faceted activities of SAGE (Senior Action in a Gay Environment), a New York intergenerational group concerned with making older gay males and lesbians less isolated from the gay community, more a part of an extended family of gays. Currently I work with their Group Activities Committee, which stages various events including a monthly social attended by an average of nearly two hundred gay males and lesbians of all ages; I also work with their Oral History Project. This, my continuing work with NGTF, and my writing and publishing of gay material, has immersed me more thoroly in the gay world than ever before. It is, I find, a society much more to my taste than it was in my youth. Evolution and revolution have made gays far less campy, precious, bitchy, and self-concerned than once they were, and far less neurotic. If less feverishly amusing, they are much nicer people.

Travel continues, sometimes with Ken (Egypt, another Caribbean cruise on a Soviet boat, by bus to the Southern States where Ken did his stateside service during World War II, France) and sometimes alone (Sicily with a gay group, London, a Mediterranean cruise, China).

Though some friends have died they have not been the closest ones and younger replacements seem to make the friendship network grow ever larger.

I find, in fact, that my seventh decade is perhaps the happiest of my life. This is partly due to the late flowering of my writing career but in addition I find no diminution of my love for Ken, for New York City, for male beauty, nor for any of the other things which gave me pleasure in earlier decades. I persist in thinking that the keeping of a diary has contributed to my appreciation and enjoyment of life and so the diary will continue as long as life does, or at least as long as rationality persists.

None of the things I feared about age has come to pass. I have not turned into a stuffy conservative (or even a non-stuffy conservative) in my political and social thinking; sex has not become just a memory (Hallelujah!); I have become jaded only, perhaps, about opera, a rather static art compared to all others; I have not lost relish in writing and feel I am at the peak of my form; I do not find the world any more alarming or depressing now than at any other point of history and so far I don't think I'm any more of a crab than I ever was (at no age would I have ever won the Sweetness and Light Award). As yet I am not clicking my tongue in disapproval of the doings of the young, though now and then I let fly some less than complimentary things about their elders.

May the lot of all my readers be as satisfying to them as mine is to me!

BEARDLESS AGAIN
THE ENTIRE EDITORIAL, ADVERTISING, BOOK-KEEPING AND
SHIPPING STAFF OF THE PEPYS PRESS INSPECTS THE FIRST
PRINTING OF A GAY DIARY, VOLUME ONE, 1979

POOLSIDE, 1982
NATIONAL GAY TASK FORCE VOLUNTEERS PARTY

INDEX

Absurd Person Singular,408, 421
Adrianna Lecouvreur, 61
Advocate, The,330,436,438
After Dark,103,228,243,288, 376
After Magritte,244
Agnew Spiro,321,352
Albee, Edward,62
Alcobaca,49
Alexander the Great,304
Algeciras,54
Alice,2,15,23,24,26,41,49,78, 86,127,134,152,211,242, 274,284,286,303,310,345, 346,353,357,360-362,367, 381,397,415
Alice in Wonderland,245,412, 474
Alice Tully Hall,102
Alkmaar,68,137
All Creatures Great and Small,309
All Over,176
Alma-Tadema, Lawrence,320
Alvin Ailey Dancers,244,325, 437,471
Amanda,29,36,124,171,174,193, 328,373,379,397
Amarcord,417
American Dream,62,71
Amiens,248,258,262
Amsterdam,137,138
And Puppy Dog's Tails,101, 103,161
Andrews, Julie,215,287
Andrews Sisters,392
Angers,334,335,376
Anna Bolena,353
Antigua,433
Antony and Cleopatra,427
Arromanches,260
Austen, Jane,412,474,475

Bad Godesberg,125
Bad Habits,386
Bad Ischl,146,148
Ballets Trocadero de Monte Carlo, Les,437
Bamberg,125,151
Barthelmess, Richard,277
Batalha,50
Bath Spa,339,340
Beacon Baths,275,278,283-285, 298,299,322,323,331,343, 348,351,353,369,375,383, 394,416,419,425,435,440, 472,478,480
Beaune,266
Bedford, Brian,392
Bejart Ballet,172,291
Benton, Pa.,154,155
Berchtesgaden,148
Bergen,355,402-404
Berg Collection,238,293,381
Berger, Helmut,314
Bergman, Ingmar,320
Beriosova, Svetlana,40
Berlin,137-139,143
Bermuda,361
Bernhardt, Sarah,290,336,368, 406
Bernstein, Leonard,103,380
Best Little Boy in the World, The,410
Black, Jocelyn,475
Blegen, Judith,384
Bloomsbury,405,407
Bob R.,30,38,78,109,110,122, 129,131,176,191,197,200, 223-226,251,408,414,453, 478
Boheme, La,26
Bolshoi Ballet,441,444
Bolshoi Opera,455
Bolzano-Bozen,459
Booth, John Wilkes,324

INDEX

Boothe, Jim, 22, 41, 69, 205, 228, 369
Borstal Boy, 130
Boulder, Co., 442
Bourges, 336
Boy Meets Boy, 481
Boys, Boys, Boys, 449
Boys in the Band, The, 36, 41, 42, 44, 56, 80, 101, 227
Boys in the Sand, 232, 233, 275, 309
Brauner, Victor, 461
Brewster, Kingman, 17
British Museum, 182
Brooklyn Museum, 175
Buckingham, Duke of, 340
Bud, 203, 212, 213, 230, 250, 251
Budapest, 465, 469, 470
Bullitt, 66
Burial of the Count of Orgaz, The, 53
Burnett, Carol, 159, 214, 215, 287, 437
Burton, Richard, 107
Butch Cassidy and the Sundance Kid, 117
Byron, Lord, 387

Cabaret, 361
Camp Curry, 4
Canterbury Tales, 78
Capri, 93, 94
Carlsbad, 141
Carmel Mission, 5
Carmen, 293, 313
Carmines, Al, 328
Carroll, Lewis, 474
Carter, Lynne, 170
Casbah, 54
Cavafy, Constantine, 377
Cavalleria Rusticana, 132
Cavell, Edith, 138
Cavett, Dick, 160, 238
Chanel, 116
Changing Room, The, 311
Charlottenburg Palace, 140
Checkpoint Charlie, 138
Chez Nous, 405, 407
Child, Julia, 119, 159, 169, 214, 308
Chisholm, Shirley, 226
Chopin, 337, 412
Chorus Line, A, 448
Christie, Julie, 368
Churchill, Winston, 405
Circle in the Water, 130
Civilian Conservation Corps, 155
Civilization, 158, 164
Clark, Kenneth, 159
Clockwork Orange, A, 218
Closely Watched Trains, 25
Clyde, 224, 323, 332, 367, 418, 419
Cockerell, 40, 41
Coco, 108, 114, 116
Coeur, Jacques, 336
Colette, 159
Colt, Zebedy, 117
Columbia Spectator, 34, 37, 41, 191, 231, 380, 414
Columbia University, 1, 22, 35, 37-39, 64, 106, 380, 444
Comden, Betty, 103
Come of Age, 104
Company, 126, 178
Continental Baths, 322, 324, 330, 354, 448
Contractor, The, 362
Cooke, Alistair, 378
Cooke, Cardinal, 393
Coolidge, Calvin, 477
Coppelia, 201
Corelli, Franco, 133
Cosi Fan Tutte, 112
Cousin Bette, 292
Coward, Noel, 296, 412
Cranko, John, 437
Cross, Milton, 427
Csarkoe Selo, 187
Cuvillies Theatre, 150
Cyrano, 328
Czechoslovakia, 141, 143

INDEX

Damned, The, 124
Dance Theatre of Harlem, 291
Danny La Rue at the Palace, 179
Dante, 91
Daphnis and Chloe, 374
D'Arcy, Roy, 102
Darryl, 192, 193, 231, 233, 241, 243, 251, 253, 255, 278, 280, 305, 311, 319, 327, 344, 351, 366, 422, 472, 474, 475
Daughter of the Regiment, The, 229
Dave J., 20, 21, 41, 44, 66, 70, 74, 76, 79, 97, 102-105, 107-109 117, 121, 123, 144, 145, 167, 174, 175, 178, 191, 192
Davies, Marion, 6
Davis, Bette, 170
Death in Venice, 200
Death of Bessie Smith, The, 62
Deauville, 259
De Carlo, Yvonne, 178
De Pompadour, Mme., 363
De Mott, Benjamin, 296
Dempsey, Mark, 87, 123
Deveau, Jack, 446
Dewhurst, Colleen, 447
Diaghilev, Serge, 460, 461
Dick, 109, 110, 114, 131, 132, 163, 193, 201, 203, 223, 224
Dickens, Charles, 182
Dickinson, Emily, 412
Dido and Aeneas, 311
Dijon, 265, 267
Diller, Phyllis, 170
Dinard, 262, 266
Dirtiest Show in Town, The, 133, 161
Disneyland, 6
Dog Day Afternoon, 478
Domingo, Placido, 61, 122, 160
Don Giovanni, 142, 282
Don Pasquale, 465
Don Quixote, 171, 184
Dongo, 272
Donn, Jorge, 172

Donovan, Casey, 309
Don't Look Now, 368
Doyle, Peter, 290
Drawn from Life, 11
Du Barry, Mme., 363
Dunham, Katherine, 325
Durer, Albrecht, 465, 468
Dust Unto Dust, 349

Eakins, Thomas, 159
Early Churchills, The, 176
East Berlin, 224
Ed S., 202, 244, 301, 313, 324, 471
Eden, Anthony, 239
Edith, 189
Eggenberg Palace, 461, 462
Egypt, 417, 443, 455, 457, 483
Eliot, George, 407, 412
Eliot, T.S., 310
Elizabeth I, 160, 407
Elizabeth R., 233
Elisir d'Amore, 384
Empire Cat Show, 381
Englander, Henry, 78, 86
Englander, Miriam (later Goldberg), 24, 78, 79, 86, 127, 162, 164, 215, 223, 305, 310, 377, 378
English Diaries, 482
Equal Rights Amendment, 477
Equus, 420, 421
Erlach, Fischer v., 465
Erotickus, 347, 349
Estoril, 48
Eugene Onegin, 455
Expo 67, 11-14

Faggot, The, 328
Family at War, A, 427
Fashion, 381, 382
Fatima, 50
Fedora, 169, 248
Fellini Satyricon, 125
Femme Infidele, La, 123
Fidelio, 463
Find Your Way Home, 367

INDEX

Finney, Albert, 29
Firebird, 385
Fireman's Ball, The, 65
Fishbein, Frieda, 296
Fisher, John, 407, 408, 416, 418
Fledermaus, Die, 415
Flemish, Oliver, 217, 220, 221, 283, 338, 345, 413, 414
Florence (Jefferson), 34, 45, 56, 69, 70, 107, 115, 116, 160, 164, 170, 204-206, 318-321, 338, 350, 372, 386, 391-393, 405, 444-446, 451
Folies Bergere, 337
Follies, 177, 194
Fonteyn, Margot, 40
Foreplay, 165
Fortune and Men's Eyes, 36
Forty Carats, 71
Fountain of Trevi, 297
Forest Hills, 60, 99
Franco, Francisco, 52
Frankfurt, 458, 470
Frank, Anne, 138
Franz Ferdinand, 145
Franz Josef, 145, 146, 462
Freedomland, 6
Fretz, Alfred, Dr., 162, 164, 167, 197, 233, 254, 379, 382, 388-390, 396
Friends, 444
Front Runner, The, 421
Fuller, Loie, 89, 437
Furth, Peter, 420

Gagarin, Yuri, 14
Gallagher, Helen, 172
Garbo, 70, 175, 422
Garrick, David, 406
Gay Magazine, 108, 124, 134, 175, 233, 275, 297, 308, 322, 330
Gay Deceivers, The, 111
Gay Guide to Cruising, 191
Gay Liberation, 235
Gay People at Columbia, 234
Gay Power, 123
Gay Pride Parade, 448, 452
Gay Pride Week, 135
Gay World, The, 110
Gebel-Williams, Gunther, 327
Geese, 75-79
Gene, 132, 152-154, 169, 170, 177, 429
Gentle Bonaparte, The, 56
Gerard, Marguerite, 456
Gettysburg, 156
Gielgud, John, 163
Gilbert and Sullivan, 412
Gingerbread Lady, The, 165, 167
Gingold, Hermione, 310
Gish, Lillian, 422
Goethe, 141
Golden Bowl, The, 316
Gone With the Wind, 422
Gosausee, 147
Goya, 51
Graham, Martha, 43, 44, 215, 437
Granada, 198, 199
Grands Ballets Canadiens, 247
Grant, Duncan, 339
Graz, 461-463
Great American Dream Machine, The, 170
Great White Hope, The, 60
Greenaway, Kate, 475
Greenstreet, Sidney, 413
Grefe, Ed, 96, 101, 102, 104-106, 111, 113, 114, 120
Grieg, Edvard, 403
Grimes, Tammy, 118
Grolier Club, 249
Guggenheim Foundation, 461
Guddenheim, Peggy, 476
Guinness, Alec, 344

Habeas Corpus, 344
Hair, 25, 36, 190, 446
Hallstatt, 147
Hamilton, Nancy, 221
Harkness Ballet, 71, 385
Harlem Meer, 1, 308
Harris, Julie, 71

INDEX

Haydee, Marcia, 447
Hayes, Helen, 71, 80
He Who Gets Slapped, 103
Hearst Castle, 5
Hellman, Lillian, 445
Heloise and Abelard, 181, 336
Hemingway, Ernest, 158
Hepburn, Katherine, 108, 116
Hephaestion, 304
Herbert, Victor, 477
Hermitage, The, 186, 187
Hershey, Pa., 155, 157
Heston, Charlton, 390
Hill, Hinda Teague, 296
Holy Apostles Church, 217, 220
Home, 163
Homosexual Oppression and Liberation, 283
Hoover, J. Edgar, 246
Horne, Marilyn, 330, 364, 425
Horse Fair, The, 104
House of Atreus, The, 68, 71
House of Blue Leaves, The, 195, 196
Hovhaness, Alan, 241
Huntington Gallery, 9
Hurvich, Martin, Dr., 213, 215, 216, 218

I Can't Hear You When the Water's Running, 311
I Have More Fun With You Than Anybody, 294-295
I Heard The Owl Call My Name, 366
If It's Tuesday, This Must Be Belgium, , 80
Importance of Being Earnest, The, 479
Incoronazione di Poppaea, L', 312, 374
Innsbruck, 458
Iphigenia in Aulis, 37
Irene, 354
Irving, Clifford, 253
Irving, George, 354
Isherwood, Christopher, 237

Italiana in Algeri, L', 364, 425, 427
Ivan the Terrible, 285
Ivan the Terrible, 444

Jack, 203, 212, 213, 230, 250, 251
Jack The Ripper, 382
Jack The Stripper, 416
James I, 344
Japan Society, 478
Jenufa, 425
Jeritza, Maria, 438
Jesus Christ Superstar, 249
Jewish Defense League, 285
Jim D., 75, 78, 109, 110, 114, 131, 132, 170, 176, 193, 197, 200-204, 223, 224
Joe Allen's Restaurant, 219, 292, 392, 421, 449
Joe Egg, 29, 415
Joffrey Ballet, 124, 437
John S., 11, 20, 41, 44, 56, 66, 70, 74, 76, 79, 83, 97, 102-104, 107, 108, 117, 118, 121, 122, 136, 174, 175, 178, 191, 192
John, Augustus, 339
Johns, Glynis, 310
Johnson, Eastman, 239
Johnson, Lyndon, Pres., 23, 33
Johnson, Richard, 427
Jones, Inigo, 343, 344
Jones, James Earl, 60
Jones, T.C., 170
Joy of Sex, The, 305
Joyce, James, 479
Julius Caesar, 312
Jumpers, 387, 392

Kafka, Franz, 142
Kaiser Wilhelm, 139, 462
Kathi, 113, 165, 195, 202, 203, 227, 228, 241, 273, 295
Keeler, Ruby, 172
Kelly, Patsy, 354-355
Kels, Hans, 467
Kennedy, Robert, 44
Kensignton Palace, 342

INDEX

Kent State University, 129-130
Keynes, Maynard, 339
Khovanschina, 186
King Edward VII, 378
King, Billie Jean, 351
King, Martin Luther, Jr., 33-34, 246
Klee, Paul, 412, 461
Klimt, Gustav, 464
Kocher, Eric, 107, 118, 127, 197, 202, 217, 219, 245, 246, 277, 278, 280, 305, 317, 330, 347, 349, 355, 365, 369, 386, 392, 411, 436, 441, 447, 478, 479
Kremlin, 183, 184

Lacock Abbey, 340
Laguna Beach, 8
Lake Garda, 91
Landman, Doris, 119
Lantz, Robert, 370
Larry, 177, 203, 209, 213, 287, 313, 332, 365, 410, 424, 425, 439, 471
Lasse, 332, 399, 400
Last of the Mohicans, The, 237
Last Picture Show, The, 210
Lavinius, 1, 2, 18, 21, 25, 29, 36, 43, 55, 56, 65, 67, 70, 71, 81, 82-84, 86-90, 93-97, 152, 178, 224
Langdon, Harry, 191
Lee, 132, 163, 193, 225, 250, 332, 364, 418, 419, 471
Lejeune, Baron, 456
Lemmon, Jack, 8
Lenin, 186, 190
Leningrad, 158, 185, 188, 189, 193
Leo, 109, 131, 132, 177, 203, 209, 211-213, 230, 250, 274, 287, 295, 313, 332, 364, 365, 410, 424, 425, 429, 436, 439, 471
Leonards, Eddie and Ginny, 2, 34, 36, 61, 75, 76, 80, 81, 83, 84, 86, 89, 97, 98, 108, 114, 154-158, 160, 164, 165, 193

Leonards (cont'd) 211, 253, 305, 306, 454
Lewis, Henry, 274
Library of the Performing Arts, 443
Life Magazine, 217, 300
Lincoln Center, 40, 102, 228, 246, 282, 293, 311, 312, 441, 447, 455
Lind, Jenny, 324
Lindbergh, Charles, 238
Lindsay, Howard, 29
Lisbon, 47, 50, 51
Little Night Music, A, 310
Lockwood, Bob, 41, 72, 244
Lohengrin, 29
London, 27, 179, 181-183, 189, 190, 295, 304, 338-340, 401, 408
London Museum, 342
London Philharmonic, 128
London Theatre Museum, 406
Long Goodbye, The, 375
Loot, 33
Los Angeles, 2, 9, 244
Louis XIV, 262
Lovers, 426
Lowenthal, Peter, 396, 409
Lucerne, 269, 271
Ludwig, 314
Lugano, 270, 272, 273
Luke, Peter, 405

McGinn, Walter, 248
McGovern, George, Sen., 129, 130, 283, 290
McLuhan, Marshall, 363
McMullan, Frank, 377
McNally, Terence, 428
McNeely, Jack, 286, 389, 477-478

Mac, 131, 132, 152-154, 169, 170, 177, 224, 419, 429
Macbeth, 476
Mack and Mabel, 423
Macy's, Gimbels, and Me, 27
Madison Square Garden, 16, 224, 289, 325, 327, 439

INDEX

Madrid,31,49,51,53,198,200
Mae,290,298
Magic Flute, The,466
Makarova,Natalia,168,201
Malaga,198
Mallorca,199,200
Manon,31,32
Maria Stuarda,229
Marie Antoinette,258,338,422
Marken,137
Martinique,430-433
Massage Book, The,365
Massey, Daniel,181,406
Matlovich, Leonard,448,453,
  476
Maxim Gorki (ship),418,429,
  436
Mayerling,73
Mefistofele,102
Meier, Johanna,415
Meighan, Thomas,277
Mercer Arts Center,324
Merchant of Venice,The,382
Merman, Ethel,178
Merry Widow, The,102,147,422,
  463-464,468
Metropolitan Museum,104,206,
  282,285,319,320,370,376,
  381,442,456,476
Mikado, The,412
Milan,90
Miles, Sarah,180
Miller, Arthur,296
Mimie,68,89,95,121,127,159,
  162,256,274,305,325,326
  345,370,425
Minskoff Theatre,354
Mitchell, Arthur,291
Moliere,175,337
Monterey,5
Monroe,Marilyn,422
Monument to a Dead Boy,20
Moon for the Misbegotten, A
  447
More English Diaries,482
Morgan Library,66,236,290,
  302,381,440,474,475

Moriarty, Michael,367
Moscow,158,182
Moscow Circus,16,297
Mother (Marjorie Vining),30,34
  62,85,125,160,161,164,173
  177,191,192,200,207,210,
  211,214,235-237,256,283,
  293,317,323,330,331,332,
  344,358,359,364,368,369,
  380,382,383,385-387,411,
  415,418,421,422,425,426,
  444-446,451,452,457,474,
  477,483
Mozart,282,466,468
Mt. St. Michel,77,261
Much Ado About Nothing,292
Munch, Edvard,268
Munich,149,150,181
Murphy, Rosemary,62
Murray, Mae,102,422
Museum of Decorative Arts,263
Museum of Modern Art,23,168
Museum of Natural History,28
Museum of the Resistance,402
Mussolini, Benito,272
My Fat Friend,393
My Father and Myself,111-112

Nadelman, Gabe,120-121
Naples,92,93,132
Nast,Thomas,424
National Academy,240
National Gay Task Force,394,
  413,414,419,424,426,428,
  435,448,452,453,476,484
National Health,The,415
National Portrait Gallery,339
Nazare,49-50
Neblett, Carol,102,438
Neil,329,330,373,396
Netherlands Dance Theatre,239
New Haven,63,65
New York Diary,18
New York Historical Society,
  15
Newman, Paul,117,375,413

INDEX

Nicholas and Alexandra, 56, 57, 218, 407
Nichols, Peter, 415
Nicholson, John, 427
Nijinsky, 461
Nijinsky, Clown of God, 291
Nikolais, Alwin, Dancers, 110, 227
Nin, Anais, 10, 481-483
Nixon, Richard, Pres., 65, 129, 227, 290, 291, 304, 321, 352, 357, 379, 391, 402, 412
No Laughing Matter, 32
No, No, Nanette, 172, 174, 177, 446
Nordiska Museet, 401
Norman, Is That You?, 121
Norway, 352, 402
Nozze di Figaro, Le, 23
Nureyev, Rudolf, 40, 171, 330, 441

Oakes, Carl, 449-451, 480
Oh, Calcutta, 87, 123
Oh, Coward, 295
Oh, Kay, 407
Oh, What a Lovely War, 123
O'Keeffe, Georgia, 159
Olewiler, Bill, 82, 191, 198
Olivier, Laurence, 382
Omaha Beach, 260
O'Neill, Eugene, 412, 413, 447
On The Town, 219
Orton, Joe, 33, 243, 370
Oslo, 355, 401
Ostia Antica, 94
Otello, 239
Over Here, 391

Pageant of the Masters, 9
Pagliacci, I, 132-133
Palma, 199
Panella, Nancy, 370, 480
Paper Moon, 349
Paris, 27, 188-190, 262, 266, 269, 295, 333-334, 338, 401
Pat, 17, 22, 38, 42, 75, 76, 80, 96, 97, 128, 161, 177, 428-429

Patty, 29, 30, 36, 124, 174, 193, 327-328, 332, 379, 396
Patriot For Me, A, 107
Pavarotti, Luciano, 229, 230, 384
Paul Taylor Dancers, 111
Pearl Fishers, The, 176
Peggy, 17, 38, 42, 75, 80, 128, 177, 224, 428, 429
Pepys, Samuel, 481, 484
Pere Lachaise Cemetery, 336
Perlman, Arthur, Dr., 210, 213
Pershing Square, 9
Persian Boy, The, 304
Peter and Paul Fortress, 187
Peter the Great, 187
Philip, 224, 225, 331, 332, 418, 419
Photoplay Magazine, 443
Pickford, Mary, 422
Pinter, Harold, 16
Pirates of Penzance, The, 381
Places and Pleasures of New York, 169
Playgirl Magazine, 376, 416, 473
Plummer, Christopher, 328
Poitiers, 335
Polish Mime Ballet, 315
Pompeii, 93-94
Pompidou, President, 265
Ponsonby, Arthur, 482
Poole, Wakefield, 309
Porter, Cole, 412
Portugal, 46, 48, 53
Potsdam, 140
Prado Museum, 51
Prague, 141, 145-146
Preston, Robert, 423
Primal Scream, The, 214
Prince, Harold, 310
Prince Igor, 77
Prisoner of Second Avenue, The, 210
Private Chronicles, 481-482
Private Lives, 118
Promenade, 83

INDEX

Psychology Today, 110
P.S., Your Cat Is Dead, 438
Puritani, I, 384

QQ Quarterly, 374, 438
Queen Christina, 70
Queer Kind of Death, A, 12

Radio City Music Hall, 66, 73, 80, 89, 240, 276, 453, 473, 474
Rae, 290, 298, 308
Rafferty, Mary, 87, 96, 113, 165, 173, 198, 202, 303, 316, 329, 344, 345, 348, 353, 359, 366, 371, 435, 454, 455
Rasputin, 218
Rasputin and the Empress, 70
Ravenna, 91
Ray, 274, 332, 436, 439
Ray, Lisa, 294, 297, 299, 312, 356, 363, 388, 410, 433
Real Inspector Hound, The, 244
Redford, Robert, 117
Redgrave, Vanessa, 180
Redl, Alfred, 107
Regensburg, 125, 151
Rembrandt, 412
Renault, Francis, 170
Renault, Mary, 304, 421
Residenz Museum, 150
Reynolds, Burt, 234
Reynolds, Debbie, 354
Rheingold, Das, 75
Rhine Falls, 267-268
Richard III, 339
Richardson, Ralph, 163
Riggs, Bobby, 351
Riker's Island, 286
Rise and Fall of the Third Reich, The, 31
Ritz, The, 428
Riva, 91
Robards, Jason, 447
Roberto Devereux, 160, 229
Rockhill, Natalie, 413
Rockmore, Ben, 2, 162, 223, 310

Rockmore, Pearl, 2, 23, 78, 152
Rodin Museum, 337-338
Rogers, Helga, 307-308
Romanovs, The, 289
Rome, 91-93
Romeo et Juliette, 293
Rorem, Ned, 18-19
Rose, George, 393
Rosenkrantz and Guildenstern Are Dead, 18-19
Rotterdam, ship, 360, 366, 404, 429
Rudd, Mark, 40, 66
Ruth, 131, 132, 163, 193, 211, 225, 250, 318, 321, 323, 332, 338, 364, 367, 418-419, 467, 471

SAGE (Senior Action in a Gay Environment), 487
St. Bartholomew's, 319
St. Isaac's, 187
St. John the Divine, 22
St. Luke's Hospital, 202, 203, 227, 303, 319, 330, 357, 388, 389, 410
St. Maarten, 433-434
St. Moritz, 272
St. Peter's, 92
St. Pierre, 431-432
St. Thomas, 430
Same Time, Next Year, 440, 449
Sanasardo, Paul, Group, 291
San Francisco, 244
San Juan, 430, 431
San Marino, 9
San Simeon, 5
Sans Souci, 140
Santa Catalina, 7
Saratoga Springs, 454
Saturday Night at the Baths, 448
Schiele, Egon, 144, 146, 465, 468
School for Scandal, The, 406
School for Wives, The, 175
Score, 161
Screw, The Sex Review, 76
Secretariat, 328

INDEX

Segovia, 52, 53
Sennett, Mack, 423
Seville, 53, 55
Sexual Heretics, 423, 427
Shadow Theatre of Malaysia, 189
Shaw, George Bernard, 412
Shawn, Ted, 326
Shearer, Norma, 422
Shenyang Acrobatic Troupe, 300, 326
Shepard, Ernest, 11
Show Me The Way To Go Home, 296
Siddons, Sarah, 406
Sills, Beverly, 31, 32, 229, 284, 353, 475
Simon, Neil, 167, 303
Sintra, 48
Six Wives of Henry VIII, 207
Small Craft Warnings, 252
Smith, Craig, Dr., 379, 384, 397
Snell, Bill, 69, 228, 281, 283, 292
Soane, John, Museum, 180
Some of My Best Friends Are, 227
Sondheim, Stephen, 103
Sorrow and the Pity, The, 238
Sound of Music, The, 473
Spain, 193, 197, 200
Spanish Riding School, 465
Spartacus, 441, 444
Speer, Albert, 249
Spitting Image, 74
Staircase, 27
Stans, Maurice, 321
Stapleton, Maureen, 71, 367
Starry Night, 23
Staten Island, 34, 81, 194
Steber, Eleanor, 112
Stein, Gertrude, 168, 189, 328, 476
Stewart, James, 352
Sticks and Bones, 230
Sting, The, 375

Stockholm, 355, 398, 401-403, 409, 418
Stokowski, Leopold, 158, 241
Stoppard, Tom, 479
Storey, David, 312, 362
Strachey, Lytton, 66, 67, 405, 406
Strauss, Johann, 462, 465, 468, 469
Streisand, Barbra, 240
Student Homophile League, 35
Stuttgart Ballet, 85, 327, 447
Sullivan, Arthur, 290, 440
Sunday, Bloody Sunday, 208
Sunshine Boys, The, 303
Susskind, David, 207, 255, 307
Sutherland, Joan, 229
Suzman, Janet, 427, 476
Swan of Tuonela, The, 232
Swanson, Gloria, 446
Sweden, 352, 395, 399, 401, 402, 419
Swiss Miniature, 271
Switzerland, 220

Tales of Hoffmann, The, 284
Tangier, 54
Taste of Honey, A, 167
Taylor, Elizabeth, 107
Taylor, Paul, 447
Taylor, Victor, 288
Taylor, William Desmond, 423
Ter-Arutunian, Rouben, 385
That Certain Summer, 289
That Championship Season, 248
Thatcher, George and Rita, 81, 193-195, 306
Thompson, Sada, 218
Thompson, J. Walter, 22
Three-Cornered Hat, The, 124
Three Musketeers, The, 390
Tiffany's, 302
Tiger in the House, The, 423
Titus, 99, 100, 102, 109, 113, 114, 119, 120, 123, 127, 128, 136, 152, 153, 158, 162, 166, 220, 223, 256, 274, 286, 287, 299

INDEX

Titus (cont'd), 327, 352, 364, 396, 397
Titus, Alan, 313
Toklas, Alice B., 328
Tolson, Clyde, 246
Tom Brown's School Days, 307
Tomasson, Helgi, 71
Tommy, 247
Torremolinos, 198
Tosca, 32
Tote Stadt, Die, 438
Travesties, 479
Traviata, 40
Trefner's, 207-208
Treigle, Norman, 102, 284
Trelawny of the "Wells", 169
Tretyakov Gallery, 185
Tristan und Isolde, 122
Trojans, The, 382
Trouville, 259
True Grit, 89
Tubstrip, 324, 428
Tunis, 306
Turandot, 122
Twelfth Night, 35
Twigs, 218
2001: A Space Odyssey, 206
Tschau, Marilyn, 463

Ulysses, 238
University of Alabama, 236
University of Ghana, 162
Unknown Soldier and His Wife, The, 19
Upstairs, Downstairs, 375, 378
Uris Theatre, 292

Valeria, 10, 45
Van Dyck, Anthony, 343-344
Van Gogh, Vincent, 13, 23, 175, 176
Van Vechten, Carl, 238
Varnay, Astrid, 425
Vasiliev, Vladimir, 441, 444
Vassar, 444, 446
Vatican Museum, 92
Vaux-le-Vicomte, 262, 263

Venice, 368, 460
Verona, 91, 94, 460
Versailles, 26, 27, 334, 336
Very Natural Thing, A, 409
Vespri Siciliani, I, 440
Victoria, 96-100, 102, 120, 127, 128, 136, 152, 153, 223, 245, 254, 285, 286, 327, 352, 364, 395
Victoria and Albert Museum, 406
Victoria, Queen, 343, 405
Vienna, 71, 144. 145, 380, 461-466 469, 470
Vietnam, 25, 37, 105, 198, 230, 256 285, 304, 306, 316, 379, 399
Vigee-Lebrun, Mme., 456
Vilella, Edward, 77
Vivat! Vivat Regina!, 179, 180
Voeller, Bruce, 413, 414, 424, 453, 476

Wagner, Richard, 270, 412
Wallingford, 153
War Games, 79
War and Peace, 455
Warren, 40, 57, 58
Warren, Patricia, 421
Washburn, Bill, 39, 40, 42, 57, 58, 442
Washington, George, 293
Washington Square, 21, 196
Waste Land, The, 238
Watergate, 319, 321, 323, 340, 391
Waterston, Sam, 74
Watts, Alan, 42
Welsh, Dennis, 405, 407-408
Welting, Ruth, 415
West Side Discussion Group, 414
What's Up, Doc?, 240
Where's Charley?, 437
Whitman, Walt, 290
Wienerwald, 468
Wilde, Oscar, 328, 333, 336, 344, 407

INDEX

William the Bastard, 21
Williams, Herschel, 65
Williams, Tennessee, 252
Winslow Boy, The, 179
Wintermudd, Dr., 227, 247, 249,
     250, 254, 256, 273, 279, 294,
     295, 297, 301, 305, 316, 320,
     344, 345, 351, 353, 366, 369,
     371, 376-378, 421, 422, 435,
     442, 454, 474, 484
Wintermudd, Stephen, 255, 256,
     305, 315
Wolff, Beverly, 160
Woolf, Virginia, 296, 405
World's Great Men of Color, The
     307
World Trade Center, 81
Worrell, George, 69, 118, 283,
     338, 374, 413, 414
Wurzburg, 164

Yale, 35, 63-65, 387, 390, 428, 437
Yale Club, 16
Yale Drama School, 196, 197, 217,
377 377
Yale Radio Plays, 219
Yalesville, 152
Yellow Submarine, The, 207
York, 156
Yosemite Park, 4
Your Own Thing, 35

Zeffirelli, Franco, 133
Zelda, 158
Zorba, 70
Zurich, 267, 270, 271, 273